# PRAISE FOR *THE LAST TSAR*

'The capstone to a brilliant career, Tsuyoshi Hasegawa's *The Last Tsar* is certain to become the definitive work on the chaotic, earth-shattering demise of the Romanov destiny. No historian before has dissected these tumultuous days with such clarity, precision, and insight'

Douglas Smith, author of *Rasputin*

'*The Last Tsar* is a terrific account of the February 1917 Revolution in Russia that knocks down many of the pillars of our usual interpretations. Elegantly written and magisterially researched'

Robert Service, author of *A History of Modern Russia*

'Hasegawa's masterful book is like a slow-motion picture of Russia approaching the edge. Yet only the weakness, inaction, and stupidity of the last Tsar, as well as the stunning recklessness of the Russian elites, pushed the empire into the breach. A chilling lesson on how the ineptness of one man, and the opportunism of many, can pull down not only an outdated regime, but the entire temple of state, law, and civil society'

Vladislav Zubok, author of *Collapse*

'Hasegawa, whose previous works enriched our knowledge of what happened on the streets and in the corridors of power during that fateful year of 1917, has produced here an intimate and highly absorbing account of Russia's last hereditary autocrat. It is likely to be the definitive one for many years to come. From the cult surrounding Rasputin to the tense minute-by-minute plotting of the generals, Duma politicians, aristocrats, and the tsar himself, *The Last Tsar* brilliantly conveys the messy reality of imperial power coming apart at the seams'

Lewis Siegelbaum, emeritus professor, Michigan State University

## ALSO BY TSUYOSHI HASEGAWA

*The February Revolution, Petrograd, 1917:*
*The End of the Tsarist Regime and the Birth of Dual Power*

*Crime and Punishment in the Russian Revolution:*
*Mob Justice and Police in Petrograd*

(As editor) *The Cold War in East Asia, 1945–1991*

(As coeditor) *East Asia's Haunted Present: Historical*
*Memories and the Resurgence of Nationalism*

(As editor) *The End of the Pacific War: Reappraisals*

*Racing the Enemy: Stalin, Truman, and the Surrender of Japan*

*The Northern Territories Dispute and Russo-Japanese Relations,*
*Volume 1: Between War and Peace, Volume 2: Neither War nor Peace*

(As coeditor) *Russia and Japan: An Unresolved*
*Dilemma Between Distant Neighbors*

(As coeditor) *Japan and the United States: Troubled Partners in a Changing World*

(As coeditor) *Perestroika: Soviet Domestic and Foreign Policies*

(As editor) *The Soviet Union Faces Asia: Perceptions and Policies*

*The February Revolution: Petrograd, 1917*

# THE

# LAST

# TSAR

## THE ABDICATION OF
## NICHOLAS II AND THE FALL
## OF THE ROMANOVS

### TSUYOSHI HASEGAWA

BASIC
BOOKS

LONDON

First published in Great Britain in 2024 by Basic Books UK
An imprint of John Murray Press

2

Copyright © Tsuyoshi Hasegawa 2024

Text design by Sheryl Kober

Genealogical chart and maps by Patti Isaacs

A CIP catalogue record for this title is available from the British Library

Hardback ISBN 9781399819831
Trade Paperback ISBN 9781399819848
ebook ISBN 9781399819862

Printed and bound in Great Britain by Clays Ltd, Elcograf S.p.A.

John Murray Press policy is to use papers that are natural, renewable
and recyclable products and made from wood grown in sustainable
forests. The logging and manufacturing processes are expected to
conform to the environmental regulations of the country of origin.

Carmelite House
50 Victoria Embankment
London EC4Y 0DZ

www.basicbooks.uk

John Murray Press, part of Hodder & Stoughton Limited
An Hachette UK company

The authorised representative in the EEA is Hachette Ireland, 8 Castlecourt
Centre, Dublin 15, D15 XTP3, Ireland (email: info@hbgi.ie)

*To my wife, Debbie Steinhoff*

# CONTENTS

# CONTENTS

# NOTE ON DATES AND NAMES

The dates in the book are according to the Julian calendar, used in tsarist Russia. In the nineteenth century it was twelve days behind the Gregorian calendar, and in the twentieth century it was thirteen days behind. As for personal and geographical names, I followed the Library of Congress transliteration system with some modifications. The names of the tsars and tsarinas are rendered Anglicized. Therefore, I used Nicholas and Alexandra rather than Nikolai and Aleksandra, but I retain the Russian original names for all others, with some exceptions; thus, Aleksei, Mikhail, Ksenia, Pavel, Aleksandr, and Pyotr rather than Alexis, Michael, Xenia, Paul, Alexander, and Peter. Soft signs are either omitted or rendered as *i*, and the ending *ii* is rendered *y*: hence, Vasilievsky rather than Vasil'evskii. The Cyrillic letters я and ю are often rendered as *ya* and *yu*, but not consistently; I use Rodzyanko and Milyukov rather than Rodzianko and Miliukov, but Maria, Tatiana, and Anastasia rather than Mariya, Tatiyana, and Anastasya. The letter *ë* is often rendered as *yo*, but in other cases I rendered it as *e*; thus Pyotr Stolypin, rather than Petr or Peter Stolypin, but Mogilev and Tikhmenev rather than Mogilyov and Tikhmenyov. For the bibliography, however, I maintained the strict Library of Congress transliteration system. I ask the indulgence of the readers for inconsistencies.

# Preface

The 1917 abdication of Tsar Nicholas II marked the end of three hundred years of Romanov rule in the Russian Empire. This event would eventually lead to the Bolshevik coup in October, the Russian civil war, and Soviet rule. Yet despite its epoch-making significance, the process by which Nicholas II abdicated and the monarchy ended has never been examined closely.

No crumbling autocracy has captured the public imagination as much as that of the Romanovs—bumbling Tsar Nicholas II; his wife, the spiteful Alexandra; and their tragic devotion to Rasputin as a miracle worker for their hemophiliac son. What most of us know is that the tsar fell, the Russian Revolution intensified, and Lenin and then Stalin arose, and with them decades of world-changing Soviet history. Most of us presume this chain of events was practically inevitable. Most of us are wrong.

When World War I broke out, the Russian monarchy could have taken advantage of the upsurge of patriotic feeling to sustain itself. Nicholas II did nothing of the sort. Clinging to archaic notions of autocracy and egged on by his wife, he squandered an opportunity to create a government of national unity that integrated all layers of society. Nicholas's intransigent refusal to rid himself of the pernicious influence of the empress and Rasputin alienated potential supporters in the society at large and even within his own family. The prestige of Nicholas's autocratic power fell to its nadir—and then came the February Revolution.

In February 1917, while the war continued along Russia's western front and mass uprisings shook the Russian capital, another fight broke out among Russia's elite (aristocratic, military, and political leaders) over the empire's political future. This fight has received insufficient attention. Existing accounts have treated the end of the Romanov dynasty as either a foregone conclusion, preordained by the structure of the tsarist state, or a simple betrayal of Tsar Nicholas II by aristocrats, liberal politicians, and generals. Neither perspective fits with the facts. Nicholas II faced repeated opportunities to pursue and encourage paths that would have diminished but preserved the Romanov dynasty. But the tsar proved unequal to the task of seeing past selfish, antiquated reasons as rapidly unfolding events increasingly constricted his choices.

The abdication saga has been glossed over in both popular and scholarly histories of the Romanovs and the Russian Revolution, which present a version of the story that is simple but misleading: Against the backdrop of discontent among the liberal elite and a widespread popular revolt, Tsar Nicholas II was pressured to compromise his hold on power, then relinquish it entirely. He attempted to pass the throne to his brother Mikhail, violating the succession laws in the process, further weakening the Romanov position. Isolated and under pressure himself, Mikhail refused the throne, thereby ending three centuries of Romanov rule.

The broad strokes of this account miss a story full of choices, roads not taken, and ill-fated decisions. Incorporating new archival material and synthesizing the extant scholarship, I present the argument that the end of the monarchy was *not* a preordained, inevitable conclusion, dictated by the structure of the Russian state and society, but rather a contingent process, where major actors in the drama played crucial roles and where, had alternative options been taken, events would have followed a different trajectory.

Before and during the revolution, Nicholas II could have renegotiated Romanov power; this highlights how contingent the situation remained up until his greatest blunder, his abdication on behalf of his hemophiliac son. Along the way, a great many schemes, lies, misunderstandings, mistakes, and coincidences gave shape to the story of the dissolution of the monarchy. Generals, bureaucrats, revolutionaries, legislators, royals, and retainers sought to outmaneuver one another while Petrograd burned and military units mutinied, slaughtering officers. The actions of the various key players were, by and large, uncoordinated, with each acting in response to the immediate situation as it developed.

Two elite groups played the most crucial role in the abdication saga: the Duma liberals and the military high command. Each group had internal divisions, and these divisions and conflict within each group had important consequences for the outcome. Mikhail Rodzyanko, the head of the Duma liberals, and Adjutant General Mikhail Alekseev, the chief of staff, each acting independently, navigated through the divisions and conflicts within their own group and attempted to steer the course by presenting a series of recommendations to the tsar. These recommendations, like the first toppling domino, led to Nicholas's abdication and eventually the end of the monarchy. It was these two monarchists who played the most decisive role in slaying the monarchical system.

The book is divided into two parts. The first chapter provides the background, introducing Tsar Nicholas II, his wife, Empress Alexandra, and their relatives. It examines Nicholas's concept of autocracy and introduces the characters who played major roles in the abdication drama during the February Revolution. The rest of Part I examines how Nicholas II failed to create a government to unite the country during World War I and managed to alienate all segments of society against his rule.

Part II examines in detail the process by which, between February 27 and March 3, 1917, Nicholas's relatives, the Duma leaders led by Rodzyanko, and the high command, led by General Alekseev, presented a variety of options to change the nature of the Russian autocracy and address the crisis at hand. The first option they presented was to form what they called a "ministry of confidence"—essentially, the continuation of the existing governmental structure, with the inclusion of liberal representatives in the government. The second was to form a constitutional monarchy—which in this context was called a "responsible ministry," where the tsar and the government were to be "responsible" to the parliament. The third and last was to demand his abdication. Nicholas II eventually decided to abdicate, but in violation of the succession law, he abdicated not only for himself but also for his son, seeking to transfer the throne to his brother Grand Duke Mikhail. But under the pressure of the Duma liberals and the Provisional Government, Mikhail decided not to accept the throne, thus ending the monarchy. Each for his own reasons chose to throw the monarchy aside and reap the whirlwind.

The last tsar, Nicholas II, is a highly controversial subject. An enormous volume of sources—archival, primary, and secondary—is now available, and I cannot claim that I have examined all of this material. Surprisingly, important sources are still missing that might provide a clue to crucial issues, and available sources are often contradictory. In this book, I have avoided detailed historiographical analyses and source criticisms in order to tell a coherent story out of the thick forest of sources. Where sources are not available or contradictory, I have chosen the interpretation I consider the most reasonable. Other interpretations are possible, and I hope that others will continue to seek answers to the mysteries surrounding the tragic end of the last tsar.

While I was writing this book, the world plunged into crisis after crisis. With multiple wars raging, democracy all over the world is being challenged by the rising tide of autocracy. Recent events have sparked a global desire to better understand autocracy: how it rises, how it operates, and how it collapses. In the story of the fall of Nicholas II, we can perhaps begin to untangle the relationship between autocrats and the wars that either empower or destroy them. Some autocrats feed off the passions of war, rallying both the people and the elite to the cause. Others respond to war by planting the seeds of their destruction. For a time, Nicholas II could have taken either path. Contrary to Karl Marx's words, history never repeats itself, as a tragedy or otherwise. But as Mark Twain allegedly said, it often rhymes. I hope the reader finds many rhymes in the story I tell in this book.

# PART I

# ROAD TO DESTRUCTION

In the hereditary states accustomed to the reigning family the difficulty of maintaining them is far less than new monarchies; for it is sufficient not to exceed ancestral usages, and to accommodate one's self to accidental circumstances; in this way such a prince, if of ordinary ability, will always be able to maintain his position, unless some very exceptional and excessive force deprives him of it. . . . In as much as the legitimate prince has less cause and less necessity to give offence, it is only natural that he should be more loved; and, if no extraordinary vices make him hated, it is only reasonable for his subjects to be naturally attached to him.

—NICCOLO MACHIAVELLI, *THE PRINCE*

# CHAPTER 1

# Nicholas II

## *Autocracy, Family, Religion*

A fter almost three centuries under the rule of the Romanov dynasty, the Russian Empire entered the twentieth century at once blessed and cursed. Modernity penetrated all aspects of life. Streetcars and automobiles ran alongside horse-drawn cabs and hand-pushed carts in the streets of its capital city, St. Petersburg. Sumptuous palaces constructed in the eighteenth century and even middle-class apartment buildings were refurbished with modern doorbells, elevators, telephones, and flush toilets. Banks, the stock exchange, department stores, and luxurious shops bustled; cafes, restaurants, and nightclubs flourished. People flocked to see movies, and newspapers were sold in kiosks all over the city. Industrialization was taking hold, financial and banking institutions mushroomed, and a vibrant civil society, independent of the state, was emerging, with an increasingly self-assertive middle class clamoring for participation in the affairs of the state.

To rule over this vast, complex, diverse, and dynamically changing empire, state, and society would have been a challenging task for any ruler. European ideas of liberty and equality, unleashed by the French Revolution, had penetrated Russia, capturing many layers of society. The new urban poor, migrating from the villages to the cities in search of employment, looked at privileged society with envy and hostility. Peasants in the countryside, though finally emancipated from serfdom, still thirsted for land they felt they were entitled to. In the borderlands, there were rumblings of minority nationalities clamoring for national autonomy. Demand was mounting for the kinds of political participation granted to citizens in other European countries. Fate did not smile on Russia when at the turn of the century it fell to Tsar Nicholas II, the most ill-equipped and inadequate ruler in all of Europe, to implement the necessary policies in response to the changing times. As American historian Richard Pipes puts it, "Russia had the worst of both worlds: a tsar who lacked the intelligence and character to rule yet insisted on playing the autocrat."[1]

Nicholas was born on May 6, 1868, the first son of Emperor Alexander III and his wife, Empress Maria Fyodorovna, formerly Princess Dagmar of Denmark. That day was the Feast of St. Job, considered to be an ill omen. Nicholas took this omen seriously. Deeply superstitious, Nicholas time and again repeated that he had been born under ill stars; he carried this fatalism throughout his life, accepting as God's will every catastrophe that befell his empire and his family.

Nicholas II's grandfather Alexander II (r. 1855–1881) had won glory for embarking on the Great Reforms: emancipating the serfs, creating a system of local self-government (the zemstvos) and municipal government, initiating modern legal systems, and implementing military reforms. Nevertheless, the "Tsar Liberator" failed to "crown the edifice" by granting the constitution that the educated elite had asked of him. The Great Reforms ended when the Tsar Liberator was assassinated by bombs thrown by terrorists in 1881, on the day he intended to grant a limited consultative representative institution.[2]

Nicholas's father, Alexander III (r. 1881–1894), interpreted this tragedy as a signal that the Great Reforms had been a mistake. He was determined to restore autocracy and carried out a series of counterreforms. He harked back to the ideas of Muscovy in the seventeenth century, before Peter the Great embarked on Westernization, and he sought to restore traditional Russian values, deeply rooted in Russian Orthodoxy. He reimposed Nicholas I's (r. 1825–1855) slogan, "Autocracy, Orthodoxy, and Nationality," and envisioned an empire united by Orthodoxy and ruled by autocracy unencumbered by any other forces. Six feet six inches tall and possessing an imposing physique, a charismatic character, and abrupt, often boorish manners, he ruled over Russia as a true autocrat.[3]

Alexander III could not turn history's clock back completely, for fear that Russia's status as a great power might slip. Aided by an able adviser, Sergei Yulievich Witte, he encouraged industrialization and the professionalization of the bureaucracy. Modern times and the autocratic tradition began to diverge.

As the tsar's eldest son, Nicholas received a good education from first-rate scholars. He was a fair student with a good memory, but he lacked intellectual curiosity and the ability to think critically, and he did not excel. His education was more akin to catechism with emphasis on rote memorization. The only subject that truly had a lasting influence on him was religion, taught by Konstantin Petrovich Pobedonostsev, the archconservative procurator of the Holy Synod. Pobedonostsev drummed into Nicholas's brain the incompatibility between a constitution and parliamentary principles on one hand, and the sanctity of autocracy on the other. "Constitution" became the word Nicholas hated most.

Secluded in the palace with his tutors, he developed a fondness for the company of military officers to compensate for his lack of association with other young men. He came to love inspections in the parade ground but confused the superficial exactitude of military parades with military discipline. He was given the ceremonial rank of colonel but never possessed any professional knowledge of military affairs nor combat experience.[4]

Though he feared his father, he adored his mother. The empress doted on him, giving him detailed instructions on how he should behave and talk when dealing with adults. Her instructions were always concerned with external appearances, formality and etiquette, manners, and behavior, but never with the substance of statecraft. "She kept her son," historians Greg King and Penny Wilson write, "in an oppressive cocoon where he remained emotionally dependent."[5]

Nicholas was constantly afraid that he could not measure up to their expectations. His rather miserable physique—he was only five feet nine inches tall—along with his immaturity, intellectual limitations, feminine character, and shyness were constant disappointments for Alexander III. His father would snap at him in front of others, "You are a little girl!"[6] Perhaps because of his worry about Nicholas's femininity, Alexander encouraged his liaison with a ballerina, Matilda Feliksovna Kshesinskaya, with whom Nicholas had a passionate love affair before his marriage.[7]

To familiarize the tsarevich with affairs of state, Alexander III placed Nicholas on the State Council. Once, settling down to a late breakfast at Alexander III's regular residence, Anichkov Palace, after attending a State Council session, the tsarevich proudly began narrating his contributions to the discussion of a government project. Alexander III rudely cut him off, reprimanding his son not only for getting involved in a project he knew little about but also for openly talking about political matters at breakfast. Nicholas was humiliated. This was a lasting lesson for the young tsarevich on how an autocrat should behave.[8]

Alexander III thought he would have more time to shape the tsarevich, but he was struck down by nephritis at the relatively young age of forty-nine in 1894, and the throne was thrust on twenty-six-year-old Nicholas without warning. He spoke of his fears to his boyhood friend

Grand Duke Aleksandr Mikhailovich (who had married Nicholas's sister Ksenia and was known familiarly as Sandro), blurting out, "Sandro, what am I going to do? What is going to happen to me, to you, to Ksenia, to Alix [his soon-to-be wife], to mother, to all of Russia? I am not prepared to be a Czar. I never wanted to become one. I know nothing of the business of ruling. I have no idea of even how to talk to the ministers."[9] Being tsar was not the role he chose but rather an unwanted burden, "a heavy cross."[10] As historian Bernard Pares commented, "The tradition that a system of autocracy should produce a succession of autocrats is entirely fallacious."[11]

Had Nicholas relinquished the duty of governing the state, leaving it to his capable advisers and busying himself with hobbies, Russia would have been much better off. He could have been a good constitutional monarch. Unfortunately for Russia, Nicholas had a stubborn sense of duty. He was possessed with a sense of mission to maintain the autocracy he had inherited from his father and bequeath it to his son. But he did not have his father's charisma, willpower, strength, or towering figure, and he knew it. Unfortunately for the Romanov dynasty and the Russian Empire, the more aware Nicholas became of his own inadequacy, the more stubbornly he clung to his duty.

When Nicholas was young, he always bowed to the wishes of his domineering parents, with one exception: his romantic pursuit of Alix of Hesse-Darmstadt.

Princess Alix was a granddaughter of Queen Victoria of England. Her mother was Princess Alice, Queen Victoria's second daughter, who was married to the grand duke of Hesse-Darmstadt. Born on May 25, 1872, from an early age she was surrounded by death. When Alix was two years old, her brother Friedrich (Frittie), who suffered from hemophilia, fell from a window and died of a brain hemorrhage. Grand Duchess Alice never got over Frittie's death. Five years later, Alice's children were stricken with diphtheria, and the illness claimed the life of Alix's older sister. Soon the disease spread to Alice herself, and she died. Alix was six years old. She carried the grief all her life.[12]

Alix was Queen Victoria's favorite granddaughter, and she spent many holidays and Christmases in England. Her native principality, Hesse-Darmstadt, was German, but it fought against Prussia in the Prussian-Austrian War, and she had no interest in Germany otherwise. What most distinguished her was her deep immersion in religion. Perhaps because of the many deaths that surrounded her, she sought the meaning of life in the Lutheran faith. This religious faith became, according to her biographer, "a protected fortress that no invader could penetrate."[13]

Her relationship with Russia began when her older sister Elizabeth, or Ella as she was known in the family, married an uncle of Nicholas's, Grand Duke Sergei Aleksandrovich, and she traveled to Russia for Ella's wedding. There in St. Petersburg, Nicholas and Alix met for the first time. He was sixteen years old and she was only twelve. She was nicknamed "Sunny," for her brilliant eyes and shining smile, but she was extremely shy. "When a fit of it [shyness] came on her," one of her biographers, E. M. Almedingen, notes, "it expressed itself in chilly manner, hooded eyes and a buttoned-up mouth."[14] The sixteen-year-old boy and the twelve-year-old girl fell in love—though they could not have known what lay ahead for them.

Marriages within royal families in Europe were always connected with state interests, and Nicholas's parents saw no particular value in a marriage connecting Russia to an insignificant principality such as Hesse-Darmstadt. But in 1891, Nicholas told his father that he would not marry anyone except Princess Alix. Alexander III and Maria Fyodorovna suggested a marriage with a princess in Prussia or France. But Nicholas would have none of it. It is not hard to see why. Alix was a beautiful girl, well educated, serious, and highly religious. But Alix's infatuation with Nicholas is hard to explain. His education was not distinguished, and he was not dazzlingly handsome, although he had beautiful, captivating blue eyes. But he was kind when she was lonely, and that seemed to matter a great deal. Queen Victoria was not keen on the possibility of the marriage of the two, either. But Alix, too, confessed that she would not marry anyone except "Nicky."

Alexander III made some private inquiries about Alix in Darmstadt and England. Two of her qualities came to light: she was very intelligent but rather stubborn. In retrospect, the investigation was not thorough and did not mention anything about Alix's being a possible carrier of hemophilia, despite the fact that there was abundant evidence that Queen Victoria's offspring carried the disease.

In 1894, Alix's older brother Ernest married his cousin in Coburg, Bavaria. Alix was there for the wedding when Nicholas arrived unexpectedly and proposed; Alix accepted. Princess Marie Louise, Alix's cousin, was sitting in her room when Alix flew in, threw her arms around her cousin's neck, and said, "I am going to marry Nicky!"[15]

Nicholas's parents finally consented to the engagement, but an obstacle still remained. Conversion to Orthodoxy was a prerequisite to marrying the future Russian tsar. Alix was a deeply devout Lutheran and for a long time resisted the prospect of converting. Her sister Ella, who had converted to Orthodoxy when she married Grand Duke Sergei, attempted to persuade her, but Alix still resisted. When Tsar Alexander was dying, Alix came to visit her future father-in-law on his deathbed. Just before the tsar took his last breath, Alix finally consented to convert, removing the final obstacle to the marriage.

While she was happy with the preparations for the wedding, she was outraged by the sight of her future husband's relatives treating her fiancé with contempt and indifference. She admonished her weak husband: "Be firm. . . . See that you are always the first to know . . . don't let others be put first and you left out. You are your father's son and must be told all and be asked about everything. Show your own mind and don't let others forget who you are."[16] From that time on she took on the role of a domineering coach on the sidelines, encouraging and chastising her weak-willed husband to be strong and firm and to act like a true autocrat.

The wedding was scheduled to take place in St. Petersburg one week after Alexander III's funeral. It was in the funeral procession that the new empress was introduced to the public for the first time. Alexandra rode alone in a coach, behind the rest of the family. As she passed, the silent crowd strained to see the future empress. Old women crossed themselves and murmured: "She has come to us behind a coffin."[17]

One week later, the wedding took place. Since the country was still in mourning, there was no reception after the wedding, and no honeymoon. The wedding was arranged so suddenly that not even their living quarters were prepared for the newlyweds, and the couple had to make do with six cramped rooms of the dowager empress's Anichkov Palace. Alexandra had to sit between her husband and her mother-in-law for every dinner and breakfast.[18] Nevertheless, on their wedding night, Alexandra wrote in her husband's diary: "At last united, bound for life, and when this life is ended, we meet again in the other world and remain together for eternity."[19] These words would prove prophetic.

Alix was shy, awkward, and too serious, so it did not take long for the new empress to be alienated from St. Petersburg high society, which approached the newcomer with disdain, contempt, and resentment. At one ball Alexandra spotted a young woman whose decolletage she considered too low. She dispatched a lady-in-waiting to tell the young woman, "In Hesse-Darmstadt, we don't wear our dresses that way." The young woman replied: "Pray tell Her Majesty that in Russia we do wear our dresses this way."[20]

Ballet was performed on Sundays and Wednesdays at the Mariinsky Theater, where aristocratic patrons flocked to see the performance and socialize during the intermission. Alexandra rarely came to the theater, but on one of the rare occasions she attended, "not once did a smile break the immobile somberness of her expression," and she left before the intermission. Meriel Buchanan, the British ambassador's daughter, who witnessed the scene, wrote: "A little wave of resentment rippled over the theatre. Women glanced at each other and raised their shoulders expressively, men muttered despairingly below their breath."[21]

Eschewing St. Petersburg society, Nicholas and Alexandra made the Alexander Palace in Tsarskoe Selo, twenty-six kilometers south of St. Petersburg, their permanent home. When they retreated to Tsarskoe Selo, the dinners, receptions, and balls sponsored by the imperial couple ceased.

Alienated from aristocratic society, Alexandra had only a few friends with whom she established close friendships. One exception was Anna Aleksandrovna Vyrubova, a daughter of the court chamberlain. Their relationship began when the empress took pity on the sick sixteen-year-old girl, "heavily built, with a round head, fleshy lips, limpid eyes devoid of expression ... very devout but unintelligent."[22] Anna became fanatically devoted to the empress, serving as her confidant.[23]

Although Alexandra was unpopular among Nicholas's relatives and the aristocratic circles, she would remain mostly unknown to the public until World War I.[24] Unlike Nicholas, Alexandra was rarely the object of satirical caricatures during the revolution of 1905–1907, and even when Rasputin's name came to figure prominently, the empress was not a major target of attacks but was merely criticized as his protector. It was only during World War I that Alexandra would become the target of vicious attacks from all quarters of society.

Nicholas's coronation took place in Moscow in May 1896. After swearing an oath as emperor and autocrat of all the Russians, he crowned himself, then placed a crown on Alexandra's head. Walking out, they greeted the thunderous crowd from the Red Stairway in the Kremlin.[25] To Nicholas, the coronation was not merely a ceremony; it was a profoundly meaningful spiritual and religious experience. Autocracy was to him a sacred mission, and he had been anointed by God. To Alexandra, the coronation was the moment confirming that she had left behind Darmstadt and England and truly become a Russian empress, *matushka* (mother) of the Russian people.[26]

Their happy moment did not last long. After the coronation, thousands of common people came to Khodynka Field, on the outskirts of Moscow, where enameled cups with the imperial seal were to be given out as souvenirs and free beer was to be provided. A series of inept security measures adopted by the governor-general of Moscow, Nicholas's uncle Grand Duke Sergei, resulted in a stampede in which thousands were trampled to death. Though Nicholas and Alexandra were shocked to hear the news of the tragedy, they allowed themselves to be persuaded by Uncles Sergei and Vladimir to attend a ball thrown by the French ambassador. The callousness of the imperial couple dancing while thousands lay dead in ditches shocked the public. Nicholas earned the nickname "Nicholas the Bloody."[27]

One of the duties expected of Alexandra was to produce a son, a tsarevich, so that Nicholas could bequeath the throne he had inherited from his father to their son. Alexandra gave birth to children almost every two years after their marriage. The first daughter, Olga, was born in November 1895, followed by Tatiana in June 1897, Maria in May 1899, and Anastasia in June 1901, but, alas, no boy. Though each birth was a joy, the joy was intermingled with disappointment, as well as some jealousy of Nicholas's sister Ksenia, who had six sons. This may explain how Alix became vulnerable to the influence of religious charlatans and mystics.

Alix was profoundly religious before she married Nicholas. Her religiosity was colored by the mysticism that was in vogue in Europe then. She espoused Orthodoxy with the fervent enthusiasm of the newly converted and carried the mysticism still further.[28] Nicholas's uncle Grand Duke Sergei, who was responsible for the Khodynka tragedy, and his wife, Elizabeth (Ella), Alexandra's older sister from Hesse, had great influence on the imperial couple. Through Sergei and Ella, Nicholas and Alexandra became fully immersed in the cult of saints, divine images, and miracles.[29] Their unfulfilled wish to have a son also accelerated this penchant. According to Alexandra's confidant Anna Vyrubova: "They believed that prophecy, in the Biblical sense of the word, still existed in certain highly gifted and spiritually minded persons. They believed that it was possible outside the church and without the aid of regularly ordained bishops and priests to hold communion with God and His spirit."[30]

Alexandra's mysticism first led her to Philippe Nazier-Vachot of Lyon, a fraudulent occultist who claimed healing and other powers, including the ability to predict the sex of a fetus.[31] He entered the empress's orbit thanks to the two sisters of the reigning king of Montenegro, Princesses Militsa and Stana, known as the "Black Princesses," who were deeply immersed in the occult, seances, and magic.[32]

The Black Princesses introduced Philippe of Lyon to the imperial couple in 1901, and Nicholas and Alexandra were immediately enraptured by the exotic charlatan. From March to July 1901, they met almost daily, calling Philippe "our friend." Alongside seances and prayers, the occultist began to offer political advice that Nicholas and Alexandra were eager to hear. Philippe advised them to "resist any political reforms that would weaken the tsar's autocratic power and told their majesties that a constitution would mean the ruin of both Russia and Nicholas himself."[33] He mistakenly predicted Alexandra's pregnancy with a boy, with the warning that the news of her pregnancy should be kept secret, even from doctors.

Philippe's meddling in the imperial family became a concern with the couple's relatives and influential advisers. The dowager empress and Alexandra's sister Ella warned about the danger of such an imposter frequenting the palace and giving illicit advice. Prince Vladimir Petrovich Meshchersky, an archconservative monarchist and the editor of the right-wing newspaper *Grazhdanin* [*Citizen*], warned Alexandra of the danger of associating with the French occultist. Alexandra replied: "I do not give anyone the right to talk about this, no one dares to touch on my private life." Meshchersky reminded the empress that her spiritual world was not merely her private matter. Any association with this fraud would surely inflict damage to the prestige of the autocracy.[34]

Under pressure, Nicholas reluctantly agreed to banish Philippe of Lyon from Russia. Before he left, Philippe gave Alexandra dried flowers that he claimed had been touched by the hand of Christ, an icon, and a bell that would ring when anyone who was not her friend approached her. As he left, he told Alexandra: "Be calm, Your Majesty. Another friend will come and he will protect you when I am no longer here."[35]

The couple's interest in mysticism next led them to take an interest in Seraphim of Sarov (1754–1833), an ascetic monk who spent more than twenty years in a log cabin. He was famous for having spiritual visions, healing power, and the gift of prophecy. His fame spread widely, and pilgrims flocked to his grave. Nicholas and Alexandra campaigned for the canonization of Seraphim over the objections of the procurator of the Synod, Nicholas's former tutor, Konstantin Pobedonostsev, who jealously guarded the organized church's prerogatives and was reluctant to recognize someone outside the church as a saint. Alexandra interjected: "The Sovereign can do anything."[36] Nicholas and Alexandra made a pilgrimage to Sarov and actively participated in the canonization ceremony.

When Alexandra finally gave birth to her son, Aleksei, in July 1904, she firmly believed that it was due to the intercession of Seraphim.[37] But this joyous moment gave way to a nightmare when the imperial couple discovered that the boy had inherited hemophilia.[38] Fearing that the incurable disease would exclude their son from the succession, the imperial couple decided to keep it a secret.[39] Unable to find a cure in medical science, Alexandra began to seek one in prayers and divine intervention, as she deepened her retreat into a private life with her children.

The family was close-knit. The four daughters called themselves "OTMA," a team whose name was derived from the first letters of their names.[40] Aside from the privileges and ceremonial functions they would have been obligated to perform, their life was ordinary, perhaps more ordinary than that of any other aristocratic family of the era. They dressed themselves and slept on hard camp beds. Olga and Tatiana shared a room, and Maria and Anastasia another.

Aleksei, the heir, was the center of the family. All the family members' attention and care were focused on Aleksei. He was a spoiled and rambunctious kid, fond of doing daredevil stunts. To prevent accidents, two sailors from the imperial yacht *Standard*, Andrei Derevenko and Klimenty Nagornyi, served as his personal attendants and bodyguards.

According to his Swiss tutor, Pierre Gilliard, who had the most intimate opportunity to observe the boy beginning when he was nine and a half, Aleksei lacked discipline. The tutor found that his pupil displayed a "mute hostility, which at times reached a stage of open defiance." Disagreeing with the boy's personal physician, who advocated close supervision to avoid accidents that might lead to uncontrolled bleeding, Gilliard advised the imperial couple that the tsarevich should be free from constant supervision and thereby learn self-discipline. Surprisingly, Nicholas and even Alexandra agreed with this advice. Things went well for a while, but one day Aleksei was standing on a chair in the classroom when he slipped and bruised his knee. The boy could not walk the next day, and in the following days the swelling spread from the knee to the rest of the leg, causing excruciating pain. Nicholas and Alexandra uttered no word of reproach; on the contrary, they attempted to prevent the tutor from falling into self-recrimination and despair.[41]

Gilliard describes Alexandra's tender loving care for Aleksei after this accident. She sat at his bedside day and night. The boy rested on his mother's arm, groaning with pain and murmuring "Mommy." Gilliard observed:

His mother kissed him on the hair, forehead, and eyes, as if the touch of her lips could have relieved his pain and restored some of the life which was leaving him. Think of the tortures of that mother, an impotent witness of her son's martyrdom in those hours of mortal anguish—a mother who knew that she herself was the cause of the sufferings, that she had transmitted to him the terrible disease against which human science was powerless! Now I understand the secret tragedy of her life! How easy it was to reconstruct the stages of that long Calvary![42]

No one whose child has teetered on the brink of death could avoid being moved by this scene. Like any parent in that situation, Alexandra must have longed to change places with her son and bear the child's pain herself. And Alexandra knew that modern science had no cure for Aleksei's hemophilia. Who could blame her for seeking salvation in prayers and miracles?

The problem was that Alexandra was not an ordinary mother. She was the empress and Nicholas the emperor of one of the great powers in the world. Aleksei's health was not merely a family matter but a concern of the state and the empire as a whole. Hemophilia in European royal families was not necessarily a closely kept secret, but it was "a highly delicate matter rarely discussed in royal circles."[43] Queen Victoria was a carrier of the gene for hemophilia and passed on the trait to several of her children. Victoria's son Leopold died of this disease. As noted earlier, Alix's own brother Frittie died of complications of hemophilia at the age of three. King Alfonso XIII of Spain, who married another of Queen Victoria's granddaughters, Victoria Eugenie of Battenberg, had four sons, two of whom were born with hemophilia. The king blamed the queen for transmitting the disease and rejected her in bitterness and revulsion.[44] In contrast, Aleksei's illness drew Nicholas and Alexandra even closer together.[45] Love sometimes works in a diabolical way.

Nicholas and Alexandra had a happy family life with their loving children, centered around their religion, outdoor sports, walking in the woods, and taking photographs. But Nicholas was the head of the Romanov dynasty. Unlike Alexander III, who managed the household as an autocrat, Nicholas often wavered when it came to his relatives' morganatic marriages, inviting resentment, resistance, and contempt from his relatives.

None of Nicholas's siblings had a happy marriage. His younger sister Ksenia Aleksandrovna had seven children with her husband, Sandro, but both husband and wife had extramarital affairs, although they never divorced.[46] Nicholas's youngest sister, Olga Aleksandrovna, married Prince Peter, duke of Oldenburg, who was fourteen years older than she. For the fifteen years of their marriage Olga remained a virgin, since Prince Peter was uninterested in sex with women and refused to consummate the marriage. The unhappy woman fell in love with an artillery officer, Nikolai Aleksandrovich Kulikovsky. After her marriage to Peter was annulled she married him, although he was not a member of a royal family.[47]

Alexander III's second son, Georgy, died in 1899. His third son, Mikhail, became the heir apparent after Nicholas's assumption of the throne. Ten years apart in age, Nicholas and Mikhail were never close. When Empress Alexandra gave birth to Aleksei, Mikhail was designated regent in case Aleksei became tsar while still a child. Freed from the onerous burden of being the heir to the throne, Nicholas's younger brother immersed himself in a series of love affairs with women whom both the church and Nicholas, as head of the household, would never permit him to marry. Nicholas twice rejected Mikhail's requests to marry a woman he chose—initially his first cousin, Princess Beatrice of Saxe-Coburg-Gotha, and soon after, his sister Olga's lady-in-waiting Aleksandra Kossikovskaya. These liaisons further strained the relationship between the two brothers.[48]

In 1907, the young Grand Duke Mikhail met the woman who would change his life, Natalia (Natasha) Wulfert. She was the daughter of a successful lawyer in Moscow, Sergei Sheremetievsky. After a divorce from her first husband, she had married Captain Vladimir Wulfert in Mikhail's cuirassier regiment, stationed in Gatchina. Soon Mikhail and Natasha

# Genealogy of the Romanovs

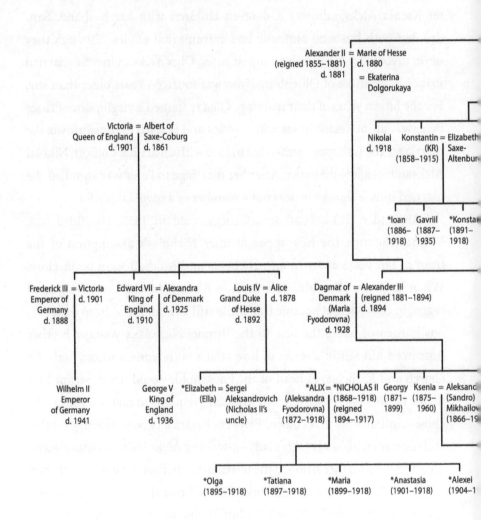

Alexander II = Marie of Hesse
(reigned 1855–1881)   d. 1880
d. 1881   = Ekaterina
Dolgorukaya

Victoria = Albert of
Queen of England | Saxe-Coburg
d. 1901 | d. 1861

Nikolai   Konstantin = Elizabeth
d. 1918   (KR)   Saxe-
(1858–1915)   Altenbur

*Ioan   Gavriil   *Konsta
(1886–   (1887–   (1891–
1918)   1935)   1918)

Frederick III = Victoria   Edward VII = Alexandra   Louis IV = Alice   Dagmar of = Alexander III
Emperor of | d. 1901   King of | of Denmark   Grand Duke | d. 1878   Denmark | (reigned 1881–1894)
Germany   England | d. 1925   of Hesse   (Maria | d. 1894
d. 1888   d. 1910   d. 1892   Fyodorovna)
d. 1928

Wilhelm II   George V   *Elizabeth = Sergei   *ALIX = *NICHOLAS II   Georgy   Ksenia = Aleksand
Emperor   King of   (Ella)   Aleksandrovich   (Aleksandra | (1868–1918)   (1871–   (1875–   (Sandro)
of Germany   England   (Nicholas II's   Fyodorovna) | (reigned   1899)   1960)   Mikhailov
d. 1941   d. 1936   uncle)   (1872–1918) | 1894–1917)   (1866–19

*Olga   *Tatiana   *Maria   *Anastasia   *Alexei
(1895–1918)   (1897–1918)   (1899–1918)   (1901–1918)   (1904–1

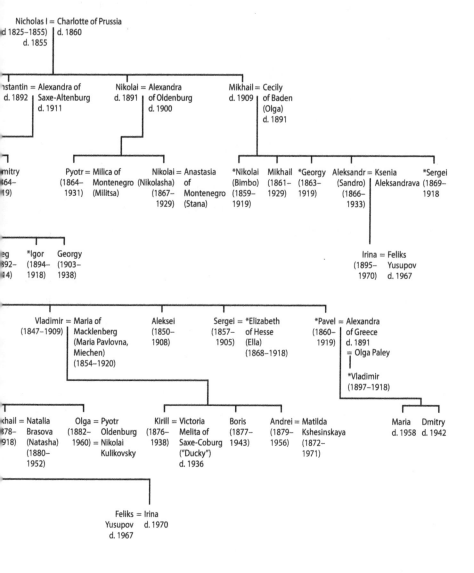

Nicholas I = Charlotte of Prussia
d 1825–1855) | d. 1860
d. 1855

Constantin = Alexandra of          Nikolai = Alexandra          Mikhail = Cecily
d. 1892 | Saxe-Altenburg      d. 1891 | of Oldenburg        d. 1909 | of Baden
         d. 1911                        d. 1900                      (Olga)
                                                                     d. 1891

Dmitry          Pyotr = Milica of      Nikolai = Anastasia    *Nikolai  Mikhail  *Georgy  Aleksandr = Ksenia         *Sergei
1864–           (1864–  Montenegro  (Nikolasha)  of          (Bimbo)   (1861–   (1863–   (Sandro)  | Aleksandrava (1869–
19)             1931)   (Militsa)    (1867–    Montenegro    (1859–    1929)    1919)    (1866–                    1918
                                     1929)     (Stana)       1919)                       1933)

eg      *Igor    Georgy                                                           Irina = Feliks
892–    (1894–   (1903–                                                           (1895–  Yusupov
44)     1918)    1938)                                                            1970)   d. 1967

        Vladimir = Maria of         Aleksei       Sergei = *Elizabeth    *Pavel = Alexandra
        (1847–1909) Macklenberg     (1850–        (1857–   of Hesse      (1860– | of Greece
                    (Maria Pavlovna, 1908)         1905)    (Ella)        1919)  | d. 1891
                    Miechen)                                (1868–1918)          = Olga Paley
                    (1854–1920)
                                                                                *Vladimir
                                                                                (1897–1918)

khail = Natalia      Olga = Pyotr       Kirill = Victoria    Boris    Andrei = Matilda              Maria     Dmitry
878–    Brasova      (1882– Oldenburg   (1876–   Melita of   (1877–   (1879–   Kshesinskaya         d. 1958   d. 1942
918)    (Natasha)    1960) = Nikolai    1938)    Saxe-Coburg 1943)    1956)    (1872–
        (1880–               Kulikovsky          ("Ducky")                     1971)
        1952)                                    d. 1936

                     Feliks = Irina
                     Yusupov  d. 1970
                     d. 1967

* Denotes those executed during the Bolshevik revolution

became lovers. Angered by his wife's infidelity, Wulfert challenged Mikhail to a duel. This became a huge scandal, embarrassing the Romanov family. Nicholas had to bribe Wulfert to agree to divorce Natasha, but the tsar adamantly refused to grant Mikhail permission to marry a twice-divorced woman with no royal title. Natasha gave birth to Mikhail's son before her divorce, adding another embarrassing element to the scandal.[49]

In October 1912, Aleksei had an accident in the hunting village of Spala in Poland and nearly died. When he learned about Aleksei's brush with death, Mikhail feared that if something happened to Aleksei and he became the heir, he would never have the chance to marry Natasha. Eluding the secret police ordered by Nicholas to watch their every move, they managed to marry in the Serbian Orthodox Church in Vienna in November 1912. Angered by Mikhail going behind his back, Nicholas demanded that Mikhail immediately divorce his wife and sign a document renouncing his right to succeed to the throne. When Mikhail rejected both demands, the tsar banished the couple and ordered them never to return to Russia. The angry older brother then issued a decree, ratified by the Governing Senate, to confiscate all of Mikhail's property and turn it into a trusteeship. This was followed by a "manifesto" revoking Mikhail's position as regent-in-waiting.[50]

One wonders why, if Mikhail did not wish to become tsar, he refused Nicholas's demand to renounce his right to succession. It would not have been possible for Nicholas to strip Mikhail of his right to succession simply because of his morganatic marriage with a divorced woman; the year before, an investigation had concluded that Nicholas's cousin Kirill Vladimirovich could not be deprived of his right to succession on the basis of such a marriage, and Nicholas accepted that decision. While the tsar was endowed with the right to appoint anyone as regent, and thus could revoke any such appointment if he wished, the Law of Succession was rigidly prescribed. Nicholas and Alexandra believed that Mikhail's decision not to renounce the right to the throne was the result of Natasha's influence.[51]

When World War I began, Mikhail begged his brother to let him return to Russia to serve in the army. Nicholas relented and allowed the couple to return home, and Natasha was allowed to assume the surname Brasova but was not given the title of countess (though she was often referred to as Countess Brasova). Still, Natasha remained persona non grata at the court. Nicholas and Alexandra never met her, although many imperial family members visited her.[52]

Whether or not Nicholas ever rescinded his earlier decision to deprive Mikhail of the right to become regent is an open question. As we will see, the ambiguity surrounding Mikhail's status in terms of the succession was to have important implications later, during the February Revolution.

The tsar had four uncles on his father's side. Grand Duke Vladimir Aleksandrovich occupied the post of commander of the Imperial Guard Corps, responsible for protecting the imperial family in the Alexander Palace. Before Alexander's death, Vladimir was rough and crude in dealing with the young grand dukes, and he treated the future tsar with contempt.[53] After his father's death, Nicholas appointed Vladimir, the most senior grand duke, as the military governor of St. Petersburg. But Vladimir's incompetence led to the 1905 massacre of demonstrating workers known as Bloody Sunday (discussed later in this chapter). Vladimir's eldest son, Kirill Vladimirovich, was a naval officer. He barely survived when his battleship, *Petrpavlovsk*, was blown up by a Japanese mine in Port Arthur in April 1904, during the Russo-Japanese War. After the war, in October 1905, Kirill infuriated Nicholas by marrying against the tsar's wishes. The impropriety was heightened by the match's dazzling complexity, since Kirill married his cousin Victoria Melita of Saxe-Coburg and Gotha, who was divorced from her first husband, Prince Ernest Louis of Hesse, Alix's older brother. Nicholas was outraged, stripped Kirill of his title, and banished him from Russia. Vladimir protested in anger, shouting at his nephew, pounding his fist on the desk, and ripping off all his military decorations with the words "Now as you have degraded my son, I no longer wish to serve you."

The scandal led to a household investigation, which, as we have seen, concluded with the judgment that Kirill's morganatic marriage was not sufficient cause to revoke his right to succession.[54]

Vladimir died in 1909 of a brain hemorrhage. After his death, Nicholas relented about his harsh treatment of Vladimir's son and allowed Kirill to return to Russia, with his wife (who was known as Ducky) receiving the title of Grand Duchess Viktoria Fyodorovna. Kirill became third in the line of succession, after Aleksei and Mikhail. During the war, Kirill served as the commander of the Marine Equipage at Tsarskoe Selo, tasked with protecting the imperial family and the palace.[55] Still, there was no love lost between Vladimir's family and the imperial family. Vladimir's widow, Grand Duchess Maria Pavlovna the Elder (known as Miechen), a strong-willed woman, harbored the ambition of elevating her sons to be closer to the throne.[56] Her ambition and her enmity for Alexandra colored the intrigues of the Romanov relatives against the imperial couple. Kirill and his marital entanglement would also cast a shadow on the abdication drama during the February Revolution.

Grand Duke Aleksei Aleksandrovich, the third son of Alexander II, pursued a naval career and gained the title of grand admiral of the Russian navy, but he loved women more than ships. "Not interested in anything that did not pertain to love-making, food, and liquor," he resisted any naval reforms, pocketing precious state funds for his personal use. The failure of the naval reform led to the humiliating defeat of the Baltic Fleet in the Battle of Tsushima in 1904 in the Russo-Japanese War.[57]

Another uncle, Grand Duke Sergei Aleksandrovich, married Princess Elizabeth (Ella) of Hesse-Darmstadt, Alexandra's elder sister, in 1884, as we have seen. They were childless. There was conjecture that Sergei was a homosexual. Perhaps because of his struggle with his sexuality, the grand duke became fervently Orthodox. Ella converted to Orthodoxy and, as a new convert, dedicated herself to her newfound religion with fanatic devotion. Religion was what bound the couple. Recall that it was the influence of Sergei and Ella that led Nicholas and Alexandra to become interested in Seraphim and make the pilgrimage to his canonization ceremony.

Sergei served as military governor of Moscow province, and it was he who was responsible for the tragedy on Khodynka Field at Nicholas II's coronation in 1894. It was also Sergei, together with Vladimir, who advised Nicholas and Alexandra to attend the ball at the French embassy despite this tragedy. Grand Duke Sergei completely shared with his brother Alexander III a devotion to the principles of autocracy and other reactionary ideas. The first thing he did as military governor was to expel twenty thousand Jews from the city of Moscow and repress a student movement. This policy earned the enmity of the revolutionaries. In February 1905, he was blown to pieces inside the walls of the Kremlin by a bomb thrown by a member of the Socialist Revolutionary Party's terrorist organization. Ella had to collect the bits of her husband's body strewn all over the snow. From that day on, Ella completely immersed herself in religion, and she founded the Orthodox convent of Martha and Mary. Later Ella became critical of how her sister Alexandra allowed herself to be influenced by Rasputin. This criticism angered the empress, who broke off her relationship with her sister.

Nicholas's uncles Vladimir, Aleksei, and Sergei exerted a powerful influence on the young, inexperienced tsar at the beginning of his reign. A vexed Alexandra, watching from the sidelines as her husband was bullied by his uncles, repeatedly urged Nicholas to be firm and act like an autocrat.

The only one of his paternal uncles who did not bully Nicholas was Alexander III's youngest son, Grand Duke Pavel Aleksandrovich. Pavel married a Greek princess, Alexandra, and had a daughter, Maria Pavlovna (known as the Younger). But immediately after Alexandra gave birth to her son, Dmitry, in 1891, she died of complications of childbirth. The young widower soon began a relationship with Olga Karnovich, a married woman with three children. After Olga divorced her husband, Pavel married her in 1902 in defiance of his family and Tsar Nicholas's prohibition. The grand duke was banished from Russia. His two children, Maria and Dmitry, were raised by Sergei and Ella. Just before World War I began, however, Nicholas pardoned him. Pavel and his wife, who was given the title of Princess Paley, built a house in Tsarskoe Selo in May 1914.

Vladimir's family formed a closely knit group, known as the Vladimirovich clan, led by Vladimir's widow, Miechen, and including her sons, Kirill, Boris, and Andrei. The sons of Grand Duke Mikhail Nikolaevich (Nicholas I's son and Alexander III's uncle) formed the nucleus of another closely knit group, the Mikhailovich clan. Nikolai (known as Bimbo), an established historian, had definite liberal leanings. His brother Aleksandr, Nicholas's boyhood friend, was marred to Nicholas's sister Ksenia, and another brother, Sergei, became the inspector of artillery, close to General Mikhail Vasilievich Alekseev; Sergei was also Nicholas's boyhood friend. When Nicholas ended his relationship with Matilda Kshesinskaya, he asked Sergei to take care of her. The ballerina wound up in a triangular relationship with Sergei Mikhailovich and Andrei Vladimirovich, eventually choosing the latter as her husband. Perhaps, because of Sergei's role in protecting Nicholas's former lover, Alexandra considered Sergei to be her personal enemy.

Another relative worth mentioning was Nicholas II's distant cousin, Grand Duke Nikolai Nikolaevich, known as Nikolasha among the family. He was the first of the Romanov family to have graduated from the Nikolaevsky Academy of the General Staff. He served in the Russo-Turkish War, receiving the St. George's Cross for bravery. He chaired the Council of Defense and supported the young officers advocating military modernization after Russia's defeat in the Russo-Japanese War. He was serving as the commander of the St. Petersburg Military District when the 1905 revolution took place. Together with Sergei Witte, he recommended that Tsar Nicholas issue the October Manifesto (discussed later) to save the dynasty from being overthrown by the revolution—advice for which Empress Alexandra never forgave the grand duke.[58]

Tall, at six feet six inches, and slender, with broad shoulders, a stern, determined face, graying hair, a goatee, and an English-style mustache, Nikolai Nikolaevich possessed charisma as a military leader, *vozhd*—a quality that Nicholas II did not possess. Little wonder that Nicholas felt jealous of his cousin, and that Alexandra treated Nikolasha as her husband's rival, plotting to usurp the throne. Nikolasha's marriage to Stana, one of the Montenegro Black Princesses, did not help his relationship with the imperial couple.

Stories of Grigorii Efimovich Rasputin, a Siberian peasant who rose to near the very top of the power structure in the Russian Empire, are legion. A majority of these stories dwell on his miraculous healing power, with which he saved Tsarevich Aleksei from death. Abandoned by modern science, Nicholas and Alexandra found in the miracles performed by Rasputin the only hope to save the life of their son and the autocracy.[59]

The questions of how Rasputin rose from the small village of Pokrovskoe in Siberia, how he influenced Nicholas and Alexandra, and what role he played in the erosion and eventual destruction of the monarchy are more complex than the mere story of Rasputin as a miracle healer.

Who was Rasputin? He was not an ordained priest, nor a monk. He was not associated with the organized Orthodox Church. He was not a *starets*, an ascetic who practiced religious awakening and meditation through prayers in isolation. He was not a horse thief, as is often said, nor was his youth wild and dissolute. He engaged in pilgrimage, going from one holy place to another, acquiring the ability to relate to all kinds of people and to read deeply into their psychology.

The Orthodox Church, with its priests and rituals, stood at the center of village life, but "pagan spirits, sorcerers and hobgoblins lurked around its boundaries."[60] People often sought healing and miracles from wandering pilgrims and *starets*. They represented authentic Russian popular Christianity, though often outside the organized church. Rasputin mastered the scriptures and acquired the ability to preach in simple language, citing appropriate passages. This talent caught the attention of some in the Orthodox Church hierarchy, and he took advantage of that to enter established society.

One thing this holy man could not abandon was his sexual drive. His genuine religious convictions were merged with sexual appetite, and he elevated these two into a convenient theology: "You have to sin to repent, and you have to repent to be saved." He was a consummate psychologist, able to spot the sources of people's anxieties, frustrations, and pains and soothe them with appropriate passages from the scriptures, often accompanied with gentle touch. Everyone who met Rasputin was mesmerized by his piercing gray-blue eyes, which seemed to penetrate the depths of the soul. Admirers began to congregate, worshipping Rasputin's words as the words of God, and from this Rasputin created a cult-like following.

Rasputin was a crafty manipulator. At each stage of climbing the social ladder, he took advantage of those who supported him, but as soon as their utility to him was exhausted or as soon as they began criticizing his behaviors as contrary to Christian preaching, he had no qualms about declaring them enemies who needed to be destroyed. Early supporters within the Orthodox Church, such as Archimandrite Feofan, the hieromonk Iliodor, and Archbishop Germogen, who introduced Rasputin to St. Petersburg high society, became Rasputin's archenemies. Militsa and Stana, the Black Princesses, were the ones who first brought Rasputin to the imperial palace to introduce him to Nicholas and Alexandra, but eventually they would become estranged from him as well.

It should not be surprising that this filthy Siberian *muzhik* (peasant), even in a loose blouse and baggy trousers with a goat-like smell, could transfix elegant, high-class salons; think of other cults in history, such as those around Charles Manson, Jim Jones, and Shoko Asahara (Aum Shinrikyo in Japan), conspiracy theories such as QAnon, and Donald Trump's MAGA movement in America, all of which attracted many devoted followers. At a time when Russia was going through rapid modernization and traditional values became loosened, confused people, having lost the traditional ballast and certainty of their moral compass, searched for something to alleviate anxiety, emptiness, and the feeling of a spiritual void. Some members of the elite, even the educated, were attracted to spiritualism, occultism, and seances, while others found themselves drawn toward the Freemasons. Rasputin's cult represented this *Zeitgeist*. Had Rasputin not been accorded access to the pinnacle of power, the cult around him would have been but an obscure footnote to Russian history.

It was Militsa who first brought Rasputin to Tsarskoe Selo on November 1, 1905. Nicholas wrote in his diary: "We have got to know a man of God, Gregory, from Tobolsk Province." Rasputin's manners were perfectly calculated to the tastes of the imperial couple. "He was respectful but never fawning; he felt free to laugh loudly and to criticize freely, although he larded his language heavily with biblical quotes and old Russian proverbs." Instead of addressing the tsar and the tsarina as "Your Majesty" or "Your Imperial Majesty," he called Nicholas *batiushka* (papa) and Alexandra *matushka* (mother).[61] "He is just a good, religious, simple-minded Russian," Nicholas commented about Rasputin. "When in trouble or assailed by doubts," he confided, "I like to have a talk with him, and invariably feel at peace with myself afterward." Alexandra went further, "believing that Rasputin was a personal emissary from God to her, to her husband and to Russia." Robert K. Massie, a popular biographer of Nicholas and Alexandra, aptly describes the significance of the meeting of Rasputin with the imperial couple: "He had all the trappings: he was a peasant, devoted to the Tsar and Orthodox faith; he represented the historic triumvirate: Tsar-Church-People."[62]

Many eyewitness accounts attest to the miraculous disappearance of Aleksei's hemophiliac pains in Rasputin's presence, after his intervention, or even after a telegram from him. Following the Spala accident, after all the doctors had given up and the tsarevitch's death bulletin had been prepared, a telegram from Rasputin arrived, saying, "God has seen your tears and heard your prayers. Do not grieve. The Little One will not die. Do not allow the doctors to bother him too much." In another case, doctors had once again given up hope when Alexandra asked Anna Vyrubova to summon Rasputin. He came, looked at the boy, and said: "Don't be alarmed. Nothing will happen." He then walked away. The boy fell asleep, and by the next day Aleksei had recovered.

Skeptics argue that these were mere coincidence. Rasputin timed his appearances, whether in person or by telegram, for the opportune time: after the doctors had already administered all possible treatments to stop the bleeding. Others add that in the imperial court, Rasputin had his agents, notably Vyrubova, who knew what was happening and helped him time his appearances for the best effect. Still others point out Rasputin's shifty words, which always left him an escape. For instance, after a railway accident that almost killed Vyrubova in January 1915, Rasputin rushed to the scene and said: "God will give her back to you if she is needed by you and the country. If her influence is harmful, on the other hand, He will take her away. I cannot claim to know His impenetrable designs."[63] It was a clever way of not committing to the outcome one way or the other.[64]

It is important to stress that Rasputin did not heal Aleksei's hemophilia. Despite Rasputin's intervention, Aleksei continued to have the disease. At best, all Rasputin might have done was to stop the child's bleeding on any given occasion. One plausible explanation is that there is an unknown connection between the mind and illness. Alexandra sought salvation in prayers, and Rasputin offered those prayers, along with hope, which eased the mother's anxiety; Aleksei was totally dependent on his mother, and the mother's confidence that he would recover reduced the boy's anxiety. Rasputin's biographer, Douglas Smith, writes:

> What matters was that Ale[ks]ei did not die while Rasputin was alive, and this was enough for the anxious mother. (Although Ale[ks]ei did not die from his illness after Rasputin's death either, it deserves noting.) Alexandra was convinced that it was faith—both hers and Rasputin's—that safeguarded her son's life. And it was through the lens of faith that Rasputin's acts took on the aura of miracles.[65]

Not long into Nicholas's rule, change began to shake the autocratic, unchanging Russia the tsar had attempted to freeze in place. Cracks began to show after Russia suffered a series of humiliating defeats during the 1904–1905 Russo-Japanese War: it surrendered Port Arthur, it suffered a defeat at Mukden, and its Baltic Fleet was annihilated at the Battle of Tsushima. Then, on Sunday, January 9, 1905, thousands of workers led by Father Georgy Apollonovich Gapon marched toward the Winter Palace, singing "God Save the Tsar," to present a petition to the tsar, requesting universal suffrage and improvement of their working lives. Troops fired on the demonstrators, killing or wounding more than a thousand. This event, known as Bloody Sunday, marked the beginning of the 1905 revolution, in which not only disgruntled workers but also members of educated society revolted against autocracy, with peasants rising up against landlords as well. The historian Richard Wortman has summed up the depth of the crisis: "The 1905 Revolution seemingly belied the fundamental premise of the National myth—the Russian people's unswerving devotion to the tsar, which had spared Russia the upheavals of the West."[66]

Yet, this time at least, the tsarist regime managed to prolong its life by promising concessions. Urged by Sergei Witte and Grand Duke Nikolai

Nikolaevich, Nicholas II issued the October Manifesto on October 17, 1905, in which he guaranteed basic civil liberties—freedom of religion, speech, assembly, and association—and promised to establish a national legislative body known as the State Duma. This amounted to a fundamental change in the state structure. To Nicholas, however, this was merely a temporary retreat; as the founder of the new system, he "clearly felt himself entitled to change it when he saw fit."[67] He soon regretted having gone along with the manifesto, and never forgave Witte and Nikolai Nikolaevich for pressuring him to accept it.[68]

What followed after the October Manifesto was a series of political reverses that culminated in the Fundamental Laws issued on April 23, 1906.[69] The Fundamental Laws defined the monarch's power as "autocratic." Nicholas wanted to define it as "autocratic and unlimited," but when he met with objections, he relented and dropped "unlimited"—a change that he justified not because he accepted the limitation of his power but rather because he believed "autocratic" was synonymous with "unlimited" and therefore redundant.[70] He remained convinced that "he retained the primary legislative authority that allowed him to issue the October Manifesto, that he was the creator of the new institutions, and that he alone could change them."[71]

To the disappointment of the liberals, the new legislative body was to be bicameral. Together with the State Duma, the State Council was created, with half of its members directly appointed by the tsar. The Duma was encumbered by all kinds of restrictions. One of the glaring examples of the Duma's powerlessness was Article 87 of the Fundamental Laws, which gave the government emergency power to enact a law while the legislative chambers were not in session. The Duma had no power over appointments and dismissals of ministers, which remained the exclusive prerogative of the tsar. The Council of Ministers was not responsible to the parliament. The Duma had no legal power to check the conduct of the tsar and his bureaucracy. In other words, the new system was not a genuine parliamentary system, where the executive power was answerable to the legislative power. Nonetheless, the state structure was significantly modified with the introduction of the legislative chambers. It was no longer a complete autocracy, but it was not a genuine parliamentary system.[72]

There was no question that Nicholas would have rescinded the October Manifesto and abolished the Duma altogether if he felt he could. But the political reality after 1906, characterized by the emergence of party politics and a vibrant press, dictated that he had to learn to live with the new institution, albeit reluctantly. The question is whether Nicholas had a chance to develop the new reality into something akin to *Rechtsstaat*, in which he agreed to limit his autocratic power. Had he listened to Witte's advice, he could have moved Russia in that direction, but his stubborn notion of autocracy prevented this option.[73]

Nicholas II rejected not only the Duma but also the state bureaucracy. Despite its inefficiency and legendary corruption, Russian bureaucracy had developed since Alexander I's administrative reform, producing such eminent statesmen as Witte, Mikhail Mikhailovich Speransky, Pavel Dmitrievich Kiselev, Dmitry Alekseievich Milyutin, and Pyotr Arkadievich Stolypin. As historian Dominic Lieven has argued, by 1905 "the focus of most civil servants' loyalties had shifted from the dynasty to the state and the nation."[74] But Nicholas considered ministers to be irritating intruders who came between the tsar and the people. He abhorred the ministerial intervention. He disliked Witte and Stolypin, whose strong personalities and leadership might overshadow him. He played one minister against another, enhancing his own prestige. There was no mechanism to coordinate the policies of various ministries, resulting in rivalries, conflict, and intrigues among them. As Bruce Menning points out, this amounted to "divide and misrule."[75]

Nicholas II did not have a secretariat or a personal secretary (comparable to an American president's chief of staff) to serve as a clearinghouse for information emanating from ministries and departments of the executive branch. Each minister presented his report to the emperor without coordination with others. In most cases, Nicholas simply rubber-stamped reports presented from ministries he was not much interested in or had little knowledge of, but he jealously guarded his prerogative to appoint and dismiss ministers.[76]

Countering Nicholas's desire for the continuation of unchanging autocratic rule, a set of liberal groups vied for reform. The liberals were mainly divided into two groups. The more moderate of the groups, the Octobrists, were led by Aleksandr Ivanovich Guchkov and Mikhail Vladimirovich Rodzyanko, who took the position that a modus vivendi was possible between the Duma and the emperor's government. Rodzyanko, a heavyset man nicknamed "The Bear," held monarchist ideas, but he cherished the Duma as the legislative body that could check the excesses of the executive branch. Guchkov was a staunch monarchist also, but over time he became critical not only of the empress and her association with Rasputin but also of the tsar himself. While Rodzyanko was committed to peaceful means to achieve reconciliation between the government and the liberal opposition—at least until the February Revolution—Guchkov eventually became convinced that the only way to save the monarchical system was a palace coup to remove Nicholas and Alexandra.[77]

The other group, led by Moscow University history professor Pavel Nikolaevich Milyukov, was the Constitutional Democratic Party (known as the Kadets, from the abbreviation of the Russian name), who insisted on a genuine parliamentary system. Brilliant, dogmatic, and arrogant, Milyukov exerted dominant leadership over the party, maintaining a precarious unity threatened by the struggle between the party's right wing, represented by Vasily Alekseevich Maklakov, brother of the reactionary minister of internal affairs, Nikolai Alekseevich Maklakov, and its left wing, led by Nikolai Vissarionovich Nekrasov. The party perceived itself as transcending all narrow class interests and aiming for the welfare and freedom of all people.[78] Situated left of the Kadets was the Progressive Party, organized by Moscow industrialists led by the brothers Pavel and Vasily Pavlovich Ryabushinsky and by Aleksandr Ivanovich Konovalov.

Another opposition leader was the socialist Aleksandr Fyodorovich Kerensky, who advocated a revolutionary path to overthrowing the tsarist government. Earning prominence as a lawyer representing the oppressed masses, he was elected to be a deputy of the Fourth Duma. His fiery speeches against the government and appealing to his liberal colleagues to join the revolution were often censored, but they elevated his stature as a leader who could link the masses with the liberal opposition. He headed a Masonic organization through which he cobbled together a wide network of activists.[79]

One important peculiarity of the Russian Empire was the degree to which the system's prestige rose and fell with the personality of the autocrat. And under Nicholas II its prestige vastly declined. As historian Boris Kolonitskii has argued, the prestige of the system fell as people perceived Nicholas as a weak and incompetent military leader who did not measure up to their expectations of a *vozhd*, or supreme leader.[80]

More than anything else, the Rasputin affair contributed to the catastrophic erosion of the autocracy's prestige. As Rasputin's fame spread, stories both true and false swirled regarding his wild sexual escapades and debauchery. This alarmed government officials and Nicholas's relatives.

One of the first influential politicians who advised Nicholas on the Rasputin affair was Pyotr Stolypin. In 1908 Stolypin warned Nicholas of the danger of associating with Rasputin, armed with information gathered by the chief of the Okhrana (secret police), who concluded that this "crude and debauched fiend" should not be allowed "within cannon fire" of the imperial court. But Nicholas flatly refused to accept his warning.

"This is my personal business and has absolutely nothing to do with politics," Nicholas answered. "Are we, my wife and I, not permitted to have our own personal acquaintances?" Stolypin admonished Nicholas that the sovereign's responsibility extended to his personal life as well, and that his continuing association with Rasputin would seriously damage the moral authority of the throne. This advice fell on deaf ears, and Nicholas's confidence in Stolypin waned.[81]

As the media busily printed new rumors about Rasputin, the Duma took up the issue.[82] Guchkov delivered a sensational speech at the Duma on March 9, 1912, declaring that the church and the state were in danger. He condemned Rasputin as a debauched reprobate who had insinuated himself in the "alcove" of power and wielded malicious influence. A resolution of inquiry was passed, and the chairman of the Duma, Rodzyanko, took it upon himself to collect the data needed for the inquiry. He compiled a file on Rasputin full of incriminating information. Rodzyanko had two meetings with Nicholas and presented him with the information, but the tsar was unmoved. Breaking his promise to keep the documents secret, Rodzyanko freely shared them with his colleagues. Nicholas and Alexandra thereafter considered Rodzyanko and Guchkov personal enemies.[83]

All the while, Nicholas's relatives grew increasingly apprehensive about the pernicious influence of Rasputin. The tsar's own mother, the dowager empress, expressed her frustrations to former prime minister Vladimir Nikolaevich Kokovtsov: "My poor daughter-in-law does not perceive that she is ruining both the Dynasty and herself. She sincerely believes in the holiness of an adventurer and we are powerless to ward off the misfortune which is sure to come."[84] Nicholas's relatives were gingerly getting closer to an alliance with the Duma liberals against Rasputin and the empress.

To counter the growing criticism, Nicholas staged a series of historical celebrations to stress the unbroken bond between the autocracy and the people: the two hundredth anniversary of the Battle of Poltava in 1909 (a battle against Sweden during the Northern War), the one hundreth anniversary of the Battle of Borodino in 1912 (a battle against Napoleon), and the tercentenary of the Romanov dynasty in 1913.[85] The last featured a series of elaborate commemorations, even as the country was becoming more and more critical of the autocracy. The liberals were becoming more strident in their criticism (especially after the celebrated Beilis case in 1913, as we will see later), while the workers' strike movement gained momentum and reached its crescendo with a general strike in St. Petersburg in July 1914.

As the country became more divided, Russia also faced a crisis in international relations. In the first decade of the twentieth century, the great powers in Europe were starkly divided into the Triple Alliance (Germany, Austria, and Italy) and the Triple Entente (Russia, Britain, and France). Russia needed peace to rebuild its military strength and restore its international reputation after the humiliation of the Russo-Japanese War. But treaty obligations and military agreements by the members of the Alliance and Entente had created a volatile situation where a small crisis might trigger a war that could engulf the world. The new era ushered in by the 1905 revolution further complicated Russia's foreign policy. The tsar and his government could no longer ignore public opinion, which was decisively moving against Germany and Austria.[86]

In 1907 Austria decided to annex Bosnia-Herzegovina, which it had occupied since 1878, provoking a nationalist outcry from the Serbians. Although claiming to be the champion of the Balkan Slavs, Russia did not possess any military means to protect the Serbs against Austria's decision. Foreign minister Aleksandr Petrovich Izvolsky negotiated with Austrian foreign minister Alois von Aehrenthal and made a deal to recognize the annexation in return for Austria's consent to open the Turkish Straits—the sea passage from the Black Sea to the Mediterranean—to Russia. Aehrenthal, however, betrayed Izvolsky before Izvolsky betrayed the Serbs. In March

1909 Vienna demanded that Russia and Serbia formally recognize the annexation, threatening to invade Serbia if they did not. The German government fully supported Austria, demanding that Russia accede: "We expect a precise answer, yes or no. Any vague, complicated or ambiguous reply will be regarded as a refusal." Given its military and political weakness, Russia had no choice but to retreat. It had to accept the annexation, and it did not get access to the Turkish Straits.[87] The Bosnian crisis of 1908–1909 greatly contributed to anti-German and anti-Austrian sentiments on the part of the tsar, the government, and the broader public. As Dominic Lieven writes, "The Bosnian crisis was a vital turning point in Russia's road to 1914."[88]

As German-Russian relations cratered, Pyotr Nikolaevich Durnovo, former minister of internal affairs and a conservative monarchist, wrote a memorandum to Nicholas in February 1914. He warned that given the conflict between Britain and Germany, a European war would be a possibility, but if war came, it would be a protracted struggle that would test the overall strength of a country—not only its military but also its financial resources, transportation network, and political strength. Russia was ill-equipped for such a war. Russian armaments were inferior, and any such war would necessitate expenditures beyond Russia's limited financial means. Any defeat on the battlefield would result in a surge of opposition to the government, but the opposition would not be limited only to politics; it also inevitably would lead to a social revolution, since the masses, both workers or peasants, favored the principles of socialism. Liberal opposition was merely limited to an intellectual movement. There was a profound gulf between the masses and the intellectuals, and the Duma liberals, lacking real authority in the eyes of the people, would be powerless to stem the popular tide. Russia, therefore, should at all costs avoid such a war. It was a stunningly prescient memo, and Nicholas's failure to take it to heart would cost him.[89]

On June 15, 1914, the Austrian heir apparent, Archduke Franz Ferdinand, and his wife, Sophie Chotek, were assassinated in Sarajevo, Bosnia, by the young Serbian assassin Gavrilo Princip, a member of the Serbian secret organization the Black Hand. This assassination provoked a chain of events that eventually led to the outbreak of the First World War.

Despite the dark clouds gathering in European capitals, the imperial family took their annual summer short cruise along the Baltic coast on the *Standard*. As they were boarding the imperial yacht, Aleksei caught his foot on a ladder and twisted his ankle. This resulted in a hemorrhage that caused the boy excruciating pain.[90] During the same cruise, the imperial couple received more bad news. Rasputin had been stabbed and seriously wounded in Pokrovskoe by Khiyona Kuzminichna Guseva, a deranged devotee of Rasputin's archenemy Iliodor.[91] One can easily imagine that the imperial couple were more preoccupied with Aleksei's condition and the fate of Rasputin than with the events that followed the assassination of the Austrian archduke in Sarajevo.

As a crisis mounted after the assassination in Sarajevo, Durnovo was not alone in opposing Russia's war against Germany. He had unexpected allies in different quarters: Sergei Witte and Rasputin. Witte told his old friends that to fight for Russia's prestige was "a romantic, old-fashioned chimera."[92] As for Rasputin, because he was close to the peasants, he sensed what war would cost in peasants' blood and livelihoods. Still recovering in bed from the wounds inflicted by the deranged woman, he sent a telegram to Nicholas: "Let Papa not plan war, for with the war will come the end of Russia and yourselves and you will lose to the last man."[93]

On July 10, the Austrian government handed an ultimatum to Serbia, which included a provision forcing the Serbian government to accept the result of the Austrian investigation of the assassination. It also demanded an answer within forty-eight hours. The next day, when the text of the Austrian ultimatum reached foreign minister Sergei Dmitrievich Sazonov, he exclaimed, "This means war in Europe!"[94] From then on, events moved rapidly from bad to worse.

Clearly Nicholas did not desire war. On the day he received the news of the Austrian ultimatum, he remarked, "None of them [the leaders] would wish to let war loose in Europe to protect the interests of a Balkan state. War would be disastrous for the world and once it has broken out it will be difficult to stop."[95] At the Council of Ministers meeting held on this day, however, he was forced to accept partial mobilization in four military districts along the border with Austria. On July 15, rejecting Serbia's conciliatory response to the ultimatum, Austria declared war against Serbia. On the following day, the tsar reluctantly accepted a general mobilization proposed by Sazonov and other ministers. But upon receiving a telegram from Kaiser Wilhelm (who was Nicholas's cousin), indicating that Russian preparations for war would endanger Wilhelm's attempt to mediate between Austria and Serbia, Nicholas rescinded the general mobilization, reverting to the partial mobilization. On July 17, Sazonov and agriculture minister Aleksandr Vasilievich Krivoshein, convinced that the war was imminent, put strong pressure on Nicholas to adopt a general mobilization. Nicholas became deathly pale and replied in a choked voice: "Just think of the responsibility you're advising me to assume! Remember it's a question of sending thousands and thousands of men to their death!"[96] But in the end, the emperor gave in. Between 6 and 7 p.m. on this day, the tsar issued the order for a general mobilization.[97]

Nevertheless, he still clung to the hope that war could be avoided through the kaiser's intervention. He decided to send an emissary to Berlin to appeal to his cousin's goodwill, though he knew that the general mobilization would diminish his hope. But all the ministers who assembled in Petergof on July 18 took it for granted that the war was inevitable. Nicholas was willing to withdraw the order for a general mobilization if that would ensure peace, but his ministers opposed such a move. Nicholas was too weak to overrule his ministers, and too weak to oppose Kaiser Wilhelm. Two days later, Germany declared war against Russia.

Nicholas did not want war, but neither did he intervene forcefully to avoid war. The tsar's diary for these crucial nine days from July 11 to July

20 shows that he was curiously detached from the events that would lead to the catastrophic war.[98]

It was the ministers, especially Krivoshein and Sazonov, who pushed the tsar to accept war. They were convinced that Austria was taking a bellicose position with Germany's backing. Furthermore, they said, Russia's honor and prestige were at stake, and the Russian public would not tolerate their country backing down again.[99] The ministers were determined not to repeat the humiliation that Russia had suffered as a result of the Bosnian crisis. They had to take a strong stand, they argued, so that Germany would not bully Russia again. They were all swept up by what Witte called "the romantic, old-fashioned chimera."

Nicholas hoped his cousin Kaiser Wilhelm, whom he called Willy, would be able to avoid war. Finance Minister Pyotr Lvovich Bark recalled that on the day he learned of the Austrian ultimatum, Nicholas said that he found it "hard to believe that the man who had sat in the neighboring room twenty years before when Nicholas and Alexandra became engaged could now deliberately be starting a war which would engulf all Europe."[100] The Willy-Nicky correspondence during these crucial days reveals that while Nicholas was sincere in trusting Wilhelm's putative attempt at mediation, Willy took advantage of Nicky's naivete. On the day he rescinded the initial decision to institute a general mobilization, Nicholas sent a conciliatory telegram to Wilhelm, insisting: "We are far from wishing war. As long as the negotiations with Austria on Serbia's account are taking place my troops shall not make any provocative action. I give you my solemn word for this." He signed it "Your affectionate Nicky." The tsar still clung to the illusion that war could be avoided. But later that day he received a telegram from Wilhelm brazenly asking that Nicholas suspend even the partial mobilization against Austria, arguing that any Russian mobilization would endanger Wilhelm's role as a mediator between Austria and Serbia. With this assertion Wilhelm was setting the stage for all the blame to fall on his Russian cousin if war did indeed break out.[101]

The picture that emerges from these crucial ten days is a tsar pushed around by his ministers as well as his cousin Willy, and forced into a fateful war that he did not want. This is hardly the picture of a powerful autocratic ruler, grabbing the bull by the horns and dictating the course of events rather than being buffeted about by them.

At the 11 a.m. meeting of the Council of Ministers on July 18 Nicholas spoke, informing those assembled that he intended to serve as supreme commander if war came. The ministers were aghast. Everyone knew that the emperor was not a military strategist; he would be blamed for errors and defeats in battles, and his assumption of the supreme commandership would necessitate his presence at the military's general headquarters, the Stavka, not only disrupting the functioning of the government but, through Nicholas's absence from the capital, also opening up the possibility of meddling by the empress and Rasputin in governmental affairs. The opposition to Nicholas's plan was unanimous. Even the usually docile prime minister, Ivan Logginovich Goremykin, spoke against the tsar's intention. Nicholas kept silent, clearly bristling at his inability to impose his will on his ministers. The next morning, he appointed his cousin Nikolasha as the supreme commander.[102] At 7 p.m. on July 19, Germany declared war against Russia.

Nicholas would not learn of the German declaration of war until he went to his study before dinner at the Alexandria Cottage in Petergof. When Nicholas reappeared, he looked pale. He told the family that war had been declared. Alexandra began to weep and the daughters burst into tears.[103]

After midnight, Nicholas was having tea with Alexandra in her room when he received a telegram from Wilhelm that had been sent before Germany's declaration of war: "Until I have received this answer, alas, I am unable to discuss the subject of your telegram. As a matter of fact, I must request you to immediately order your troops on no account to commit the slightest act of trespassing over our frontiers."[104]

Nicholas read and reread it, unable to understand what his cousin meant. He read it to Alexandra. She asked: "You're not going to answer it, are you?" "Certainly not!" was his response. Finally, Wilhelm's insincerity and betrayal struck him. Nicholas felt that "all was over forever between him and Wilhelm."[105] He would never forgive the kaiser, whom he had trusted to avoid war.

On the following day, July 20, Russia declared war against Germany and Austria. A world war had begun.

CHAPTER 2

# Russia Enters the War

In 1914 not a drop of rain fell between Easter and the summer in most of European Russia. Crops died, dust from dry fields yellowed the city streets, and the smell of burning grass hung in the air. Anna Akhmatova captured the superstitious, fearful mood in her poem "July 1914":

*The sun has become a sign of God's disfavor;*
*Since Easter no rain has sprinkled the fields.*
*A one-legged passer-by came and,*
*Alone in the courtyard, said:*
*"Terrible times are drawing near.*
*Soon the earth will be packed with fresh graves.*
*You must expect famine, earthquakes, pestilence,*
*And the eclipse of the heavenly bodies."*[1]

Yet in spite of the gloom, patriotism surged in St. Petersburg as war broke out. Around 1 p.m. on July 20, 1914, Emperor Nicholas II and Empress Alexandra, accompanied by their daughters, sailed from their summer residence in Petergof to St. Petersburg on the imperial yacht *Alexandria*. They left behind Aleksei, sick in bed with internal bleeding. At the mouth of the Neva River, they were greeted with a gun salute from the newest and most powerful ships of the Russian Imperial Navy, *Gangut* and *Sevastopol*. On the English Embankment, the imperial family changed to a steamboat. When they reached the Winter Palace, the crowd who had been waiting for their arrival since early morning welcomed them with a loud hurrah. Spontaneously they erupted in the hymn "God Save the Tsar." The guns of the Peter and Paul Fortress, across the Neva, thundered to mark the arrival of the emperor.[2]

In the Malachite Room of the Winter Palace, the emperor signed the manifesto declaring war. The manifesto appealed to the entire society to unite around the throne. It declared: "In this hour of trial, let us forget our internal discords. Let us strengthen closer unity of the Tsar with His people and let Russia, standing up like one man, expel the insolent offensive of the enemy."

After signing the manifesto, Nicholas and his family went into Nikolaevsky Hall, so massive that it could comfortably contain three thousand people. It was filled with members of the Romanov family, court officials, high government officials, generals, admirals, officers of the guard regiments, high-ranking officers of the St. Petersburg Military District, and foreign diplomats. Conspicuously missing were the members of the Duma. The tsar read the manifesto to the assembled dignitaries, and Father Aleksandr Petrovich Vasiliev, religious adviser to the imperial family, read the prayer of supplication for Russia's victory over the enemy. After the prayer, the emperor swore to the assembled guests, "I hereby solemnly declare that I will not conclude any peace until the last soldier of the enemy leaves Our land," the identical oath that Alexander I had pledged when he entered the Napoleonic Wars in 1812. The speech was met with thunderous cheers, and many knelt and cried.[3]

The imperial couple's next stop was the red-draped Middle Balcony, which faced Palace Square, filled with people holding portraits of Nicholas and Alexandra and Russian flags. When the imperial couple emerged onto the balcony, thousands in the square knelt, crossed themselves, and sang "God Save the Tsar."[4] Princess Cantacuzene saw many tearful eyes as Nicholas II swore Alexander I's oath once again. As she described the scene:

> A hardened old military man said gently, "See how devoted and serious they are; and how they pity their Emperor, and wish to help him!" "The Emperor holds trump cards in the great game he must play," said another. "His people have brought him their gift of loyalty today; and his proud aristocracy, as well as his peasants, are of one piece in this!"[5]

The imperial couple left the balcony reassured that the people and the tsar were united, that the people worshiped the tsar, and that they needed him. There was a thunderstorm in St. Petersburg later that day, but crowds lingered long after the couple had withdrawn from view. Even torrential rain could not chase the people away from Palace Square.[6]

Almost as an afterthought, Nicholas invited the members of the Duma and the State Council to the Winter Palace—belatedly, on July 26, the day the legislative chambers were convened. There the emperor implored the members of the parliament to do their duty to the end. Mikhail Rodzyanko, chairman of the Duma, replied, "With a firm belief in the grace of God, we will grudge no sacrifices until the foe is vanquished and Russia's honor vindicated." Tears in his eyes, Nicholas made the sign of the cross. The "sacred union," it appeared, still encompassed both the tsar and his liberal opposition.

After the invited deputies trekked back to the Tauride Palace, the entire membership of both chambers, with the exception of a small number of socialist deputies, solemnly pledged their support of the government. The Central Committee of the Kadet party, the center of the liberal opposition, voted almost unanimously for unconditional support of the government and suspension of criticism. Only Fyodor Izmailovich Rodichev, a Jewish member of the Kadets' Central Committee, raised an objection: "Do you really think that those fools could bring us a victory?" Despite his skepticism, the Kadets' statement, written by its leader, Pavel Milyukov, proclaimed: "We are united in this struggle; we set no conditions and we demand nothing. On the scales of war, we simply place our firm will for victory."

But concealed behind this seeming unity were fundamental divisions. While Nicholas was pleased to accept the liberals' pledge to suspend criticisms in support of the government, the liberals hoped that the government would respond to this conciliatory gesture by asking them to join in the common struggle against the enemy.[7] But the government remained the same, with the subservient Ivan Goremykin as its head. No war cabinet was formed with the participation of liberal opposition leaders. Nicholas failed to take this opportunity to form a government of "national salvation."

Outwardly Russia seemed a country united. The workers' strike movement, which had gained momentum after the massacre of protesting workers by a brigade of soldiers at the Lena gold mine in 1912, had reached its peak on the eve of the war, and at the beginning of July 1914 a general strike had been declared in St. Petersburg, with barricades in the streets. After the declaration of war, however, the strikes quickly dissipated.[8] Patriotic sentiment appeared so widespread among workers that the Bolshevik activists admitted that it was physically dangerous even to speak against the war.[9]

But behind the euphoria of national unity, Anna Akhmatova predicted the coming of a holocaust:

*A sweet smell of juniper*
*Comes floating from the burning woods.*
*The soldiers' wives bend over their children and moan,*
*The weeping of widows echoes through the village.*

*Not in vain were the prayers offered;*
*The earth yearned for rain.*
*The trampled fields were sprinkled*
*With warm and red moisture.*
*The empty sky is low, so low*
*And the voice of the one who prays sounds soft:*
*"They are wounding Your most holy body,*
*And casting lots for Your garments."*[10]

A darkness undergirded the spontaneous patriotic demonstrations. On July 20, a huge anti-German demonstration in front of the German embassy near St. Isaac's Cathedral turned into a rampage. Mobs occupied the embassy building, threw papers and furniture from the windows, built a huge bonfire in the square, and finally, amid the enthusiastic cheers of the crowd, knocked down the massive Dioskouroi sculpture atop the building. The fact that these outbursts were technically supportive of the government was hardly reassuring to city leadership—one embassy employee had been killed in the melee. The city governor of the newly renamed Petrograd (formerly St. Petersburg), Prince Aleksandr Sergeevich Obolensky, banned further demonstrations.[11]

Despite Nicholas's abiding faith that the common folk supported the tsar, Russia, and the war effort, evidence to the contrary was swift to emerge. Few peasants willingly responded to the government's call for mobilization, and some rioted within weeks of the war's declaration. In July and August, at many assembly points in the empire, mobilized and reserve soldiers joined with their families and villagers to attack police and loot liquor and food stores. Already unhappy to be sent to war in the name of "national honor," an abstract concept that they hardly understood, they were particularly incensed that the government was breaking with tradition and carrying out the mobilization without liquor. One of the largest riots took place in Barnaul, in Tomsk province, where several thousand garrison soldiers attacked government buildings, including the prison and police station. They ransacked the state-run wine warehouse, set fire to buildings along three streets, and took complete control of the city for a full day. Residents fled. Only imperial army units brought from outside were able to restore order. Altogether, 112 men were killed and 160 rioters arrested. Similar riots took place across forty-three provinces, resulting in the deaths or injuries of more than five hundred rioters and one hundred law enforcement agents, all of it kept secret from the public.[12]

Under the euphoria of patriotism, violence bubbled, ready to erupt. The masses at the lowest rung of society were ready to deploy it against whatever enemy was convenient, whether Germans, those with German-sounding names, Jews, or government officials suspected of treason.

The First World War revealed a schism between the new century into which the world was plunging and the old era it was leaving. It was the first modern war for which countries' entire industrial resources were mobilized and national economies were restructured. It was fought with armaments produced by the most advanced technology available at that time. Tanks, airplanes, poison gas, and submarines made their first appearance in warfare, and the advent of new technology made traditional military strategy obsolete. With infantry rifles capable of firing up to fifteen rounds a minute at a range of three kilometers, cavalry was rendered useless. Yet tanks were not yet fast or well-armored enough to become a dominant weapon of war, so armies were forced to rely on horses for mobile attacks in spite of their severe limitations.[13]

Even more vital was the scale of changes to society that the war demanded. The wartime economy had to be organized for armament production. "It was a war," as American historian Laura Engelstein writes, "that affected society from top to bottom and demanded its full engagement, under a regime used to seeing civil initiative as a threat rather than a resource."[14] Eventually Russia would be knocked out of the war, not because its military technology was inferior to that of its enemies but rather because its sociopolitical system could not withstand the strain of protracted modern warfare. To paraphrase British historian Norman Stone, Russia's defeat was caused by the conflict between a twentieth-century war and a nineteenth-century body politic.

The war exposed numerous weaknesses of Russia's political-military system. The theater of war was extended roughly from the Baltic Sea in the west to Minsk in the east, and from St. Petersburg in the north to the Black Sea in the south. Organizational chaos resulting from a hastily adopted Statute on the Field Administration of Troops on Wartime conferred plenipotential military and civil power on the supreme commander over the entire zone of active operations. Coordination between the high command and the civilian government became difficult, since the jurisdiction of the Council of Ministers could not extend to the zone of military operations. Though theoretically the tsar was to preside over both military and civilian administrations, Nicholas neither embraced this task nor created a war council to coordinate it in his stead.[15]

The army's military leadership was hopelessly divided between entrenched traditionalists, who insisted on the importance of fortresses and cavalry commanded by aristocratic officers, and modernizers, who emphasized the role of infantry and artillery. The army was further divided between front commanders and the War Ministry, and between the northwestern front and the southwestern front. Grand Duke Nikolai Nikolaevich, the tsar's cousin once removed, who had been appointed supreme commander, established the general headquarters, called the Stavka, at Baranovichi in Belorussia (now Belarus), some three hundred kilometers behind the extended front line. Despite his reputation as a *vozhd*, or great military leader, Nikolai Nikolaevich was not a decisive commander. Although he was not entirely a figurehead, he left operational decisions to two generals under him who could not get along. The avidly xenophobic chief of staff, General Nikolai Nikolaevich Yanushkevich, was in charge of administration, while his rival, Quartermaster General Yury Nikolaevich Danilov, took charge of operational decisions.[16]

Nicholas II played no part in resolving conflicts within the military, likely because he did not comprehend the issues that divided them. Though his favorites won their appointments by skillfully currying his favor, many of them were militarily incompetent. The notable exception was the appointment of Mikhail Alekseev as the chief of staff of the Stavka in 1915.[17] He was given the title of adjutant general (imperial aide-de-camp), which granted the recipient the privilege of gaining access to the emperor without an intermediary.

At the war's outset, Russia loomed large in the calculations of both friends and foes. Germany's Schlieffen Plan sought to avoid a two-front war by knocking France out first, before Russia completed its general mobilization, and only then attacking Russia. The French General Staff hoped to counter this by adopting Plan XVII, which depended on Russia attacking Germany as soon as Germany mobilized. Though the Russian General Staff planned to attack Austria-Hungary first, under French pressure they relented; the disappointing result would set the tone of the war effort to come.

As Plan XVII demanded, the Russians attacked East Prussia on August 2, before the Russian general mobilization was complete. The commanding officer of the northeastern front was General Yakov Grigorievich Zhilinsky, a traditionalist sixty-one-year-old cavalry officer of Polish descent.[18] Zhilinsky sought to employ a pincer movement, with the Russian First Army, commanded by General Pavel Karlovich von Rennenkampf, a sixty-year-old Baltic German nobleman, attacking from the north, and the Second Army, commanded by General Aleksandr Vasilievich Samsonov, marching from the south, in hopes of destroying Germany's Eighth

Army, commanded by General Maximilian von Prittwitz, and pushing the Germans out of East Prussia.

Russia's East Prussian operations were marred by "poor leadership, failure of communications, inadequate transportation, and severe shortages of supplies, guns, and ammunition."[19] The Russians' First Army scored an initial victory at Cumbinnen, but instead of pursuing Prittwitz's numerically inferior army in coordination with Samsonov's Second Army from the south, Rennenkampf foolishly decided to attack the fortress of Königsberg. The German chief of staff, General Helmut von Moltke, dismissed Prittwitz, appointed General Paul von Hindenburg and his chief of staff, Major General Erich Ludendorff, to head the Eighth Army, and deviated from the Schlieffen Plan by sending reinforcements from the west.

Prospects for a German victory were remote when Hindenburg and Ludendorff took charge. But Ludendorff learned from intercepted wireless transmissions, carelessly sent uncoded, that Rennenkampf had failed to pursue the retreating Eighth Army. Seizing on this blunder, Hindenburg and Ludendorff decided to gamble. Leaving only a skeletal force to defend the north, they sent the bulk of the Eighth Army south toward Samsonov's position.[20]

Samsonov's Second Army was exhausted before the battle even started. They had marched through the rugged Polish terrain with little food for the troops or fodder for the horses. Rennenkampf had insisted that the German army was retreating and that Samsonov's Second Army needed only to cut off the escape route for the retreating army. Zhilinsky agreed, and wrote to Samsonov: "The enemy evidently has left only an insignificant force at your front." Little did he know that the German army was headed his way, equipped with massive artillery and overwhelming infantry. Misled by his commander, Samsonov sent his forces to pursue what appeared to be a retreating unit, but they walked into a trap near Tannenberg. Entrapped, surrounded, and bombarded by artillery fire, Samsonov's army was completely annihilated. More than ninety thousand soldiers surrendered, and Samsonov himself committed suicide.[21]

With Samsonov's Second Army utterly destroyed, Hindenburg and Ludendorff turned to Rennenkampf's First Army. After a decisive battle at the Masurian Lakes on August 27, Rennenkampf beat a hasty retreat. In military circles, von Rennenkampf was bitterly renamed "Rennen von Kampf," meaning "flight from the battlefield."

The East Prussian campaign was a devastating failure for Russia. Altogether more than a quarter of a million men were lost during the first thirty days of fighting in East Prussia.[22] Nikolai Nikolaevich dismissed Zhilinsky and appointed General Nikolai Vladimirovich Ruzsky as the new commander of the northeastern front, but Rennenkampf stayed on for a little longer as the commander of the First Army.

Several weeks later at the Galician front, the Russians faced a less capable enemy. Under the command of Adjutant General Nikolai Iudovich Ivanov, with Alekseev as chief of staff, the armies of the southwestern front were tasked with making up for the defeat in East Prussia. General Ivanov was assisted by capable officers: General Ruzsky commanded the Third Army (until he was appointed as the commander of the northwestern front to replace Zhilinsky), General Aleksei Ermolaevich Evert the Fourth Army, and General Aleksei Alekseevich Brusilov the Eighth Army. Ivanov, Alekseev, Ruzsky, Brusilov, and Evert, all of them adjutant generals, would go on to play major roles in determining Nicholas II's future during the February Revolution.

Ivanov's efforts began with promise, as his forces scored victories in the Battle of Zlota Lipa and the Battle of Gnita Lipa, capturing the key city of Lvov from Austria. But once again initial success was marred by confusion. Ivanov planned to pursue the Austrian army north. To do so, however, he would need the aid of the northwestern army, and Ruzsky, newly appointed as its commander in place of Zhilinsky, opposed this offensive.

Two weeks passed without a resolution of the conflict between commanders, and the Austrian army slipped away.

Alarmed by the impending collapse of the Austrian army, Hindenburg and Ludendorff decided to take charge. The German Ninth Army traveled three hundred kilometers south through forests and marshes, as there were no railroads in that area. Though the Russians were apparently in an advantageous position, Hindenburg decided to break through the Russian line and seize the strategic city of Lodz. Though outnumbered, Hindenburg had the advantage of knowing exactly the whereabouts of the Russian forces and their strategic plan thanks to Russian wireless communications.

The German attack began as Ruzsky was poised to lead the northwestern army in an attack on Silesia. The Stavka ordered Ruzsky to delay, but he was defiant once again. By the time he realized that a major German offensive had been launched and recalled his army, it was too late. The Stavka attempted to bolster the defense of Lodz with fourteen thousand reinforcements, but incredibly, all these reinforcements were sent without rifles. Upon the arrival of fresh German reinforcements from the west, the Russian defense collapsed, and Lodz was in German hands before Christmas.[23]


Russia's first year at war was devastating in virtually every respect. The Russian army suffered a tremendous, avoidable defeat at Tannenberg and the Masurian Lakes, and lost control of Lodz. A temporary victory in Galicia could not compensate for these defeats. Before the end of the year, Russian losses in killed, wounded, and those taken prisoner exceeded a million and a half men, a number equal to about three-quarters of Russia's peacetime army.[24]

There were many reasons for Russia's poor performance on the battlefield, but the scarcity of ammunition was a key factor. Minister of war Vladimir Aleksandrovich Sukhomlinov and the Main Artillery Administration had grossly underestimated the demand for shells and rifles, partly because the Franco-Russian General Staff consultations prior to the war had assumed that the war would be over within six weeks. Not only were they wrong about the length of the war, but they failed to grasp how many shells and rifles modern warfare would demand. Based on the expenditures of the Russo-Japanese War, the Main Artillery Administration expected a reserve of seven million shells to last the entire war. As it turned out, that was not enough to keep the guns firing for ten days. Sukhomlinov and the Main Artillery Administration had made no preparations for mobilizing Russian industries to cope with the great demand, relying on the absurdly low production capacity of existing factories. The most that the existing munitions factories could provide in 1914 was only nine thousand shells a month. This resulted in an acute shell shortage. As for rifles, the army required each month 100,000 to 150,000 new rifles, but Russian weapons factories could provide only 27,000. As a result, in the first year of the war, many soldiers were left without rifles, and had to wait for their comrades to fall to pick up their rifles.[25]

Yet the shell and weapon shortage was just the beginning of the Russian army's problems. The number of officers killed, wounded, or captured during the first year of fighting exceeded the initial size of Russia's entire 1914 officer corps by more than 50 percent.[26] There were not enough personnel to train new recruits, who arrived at the front ignorant and undisciplined. Officers complained incessantly of the poor quality of the soldiers, "who held rifles like peasants with a rake." As a result, unnecessarily harsh measures were imposed on the soldiers. But the officers, fresh from a few weeks of rushed training, were themselves often incompetent, and the soldiers responded with insolence, inertia, and passive resistance. A chasm was widening between the officers and common soldiers, and it would only grow wider in the years to follow.

Russia's manpower was considered its most formidable strength. Its standing army of 1.4 million men before the mobilization was the largest in the world, exceeding the combined peacetime forces of Germany and Austria-Hungary. Fully mobilized, it could expand to five million soldiers. Nevertheless, closer scrutiny would reveal the weakness of the legendary Russian military.

> The procedures adopted by the infantry called for three years of active duty beginning at the age of twenty-one, followed by seven years of reserve status in the so-called First Levy and eight more in the Second Levy. After this, [the reservists] . . . spent five years in the National Militia (Opolchenie). In the first six months of the war, Russia would field 6.5 million men: 1.4 million on active duty, 4.4 million trained reservists of the First Levy, and 700,000 fresh recruits. Between January and September 1915, the army would induct another 1.4 million reservists of the First Levy.

By September 1915, the army had exhausted almost all of its trained reservists. What was available was just 350,000 reservists in the First Levy, the Second Levy, the militia, and untrained masses of new recruits. Russia's supposedly impressive manpower had already been used up before the war was halfway over.[27]

The soldiers themselves struggled with the demands of war. Where other modern nations used the military as the vehicle to instill a sense of nationalism and integrate the masses of recruits into a cohesive "nation," Russian army life was more reminiscent of life under serfdom. "Russia" remained a remote, abstract concept for many peasant-soldiers, whose first commitments were to their native communities.[28] Officers addressed privates using the pronoun *ty* (thou), as masters addressed serfs under serfdom, and the soldiers were required to address their officers as "Your Highness" (*vashe prevoskhoditelstvo*). Soldiers (as well as officers) took an oath to the tsar, not to the motherland. And if the tsar's authority eroded, the army faced the risk of total collapse. As the poet Zinaida Gippius wrote in her diary: "The dark masses go to war on orders from above, by inertia of blind obedience . . . but the *narod* [people] know absolutely nothing about the war. . . . And when the *muzhik* [peasant] ceases to be meek, he becomes terrifying." Would they remain meek or turn ferocious? Gippius asked: "Could there be a revolution in the midst of war?"[29]

Although a surge of patriotism at the outbreak of war had hypnotized Russian society, which appeared to have been united behind the tsar, the humiliation of defeat seemed to have broken the spell. The liberals renewed their criticism of the government. The workers awoke from their somnolence. Russia now faced pressure not only on its borders but from within.

After the fall of Lodz, Hindenburg and Ludendorff were determined to pursue the Russian army. After a short lull over Christmas, their Eighth and Tenth Armies attacked Lyck, encircling Fortress Augustovo. Though the traditionalists had emphasized fortress defense, this strategy proved futile when the fortress fell. This German victory, however, was offset by an Austrian defeat. Przemysl, the heavily fortified site of the Austrian General Headquarters, which had withstood a six-month siege, finally capitulated to General Ivanov.[30] Though General Ivanov advocated further pressure on the Austrian army, his old feud with Ruzsky flared up once again, and Ruzsky insisted on attacking the Germans instead. The Stavka took Ivanov's side, sending reserve units to the southwestern front for a continuation of Ivanov's Carpathian campaign.

Ruzsky resigned in protest, but even this was not enough to resolve the conflict. Though the Stavka appointed General Alekseev, Ivanov's former chief of staff, to command on the northwestern front, Alekseev immediately echoed Ruzsky's position, demanding massive reinforcements. Worsening the confusion, the Stavka then accepted this request, reversing itself and diverting Ivanov's reinforcements. Ivanov's forces still managed to seize Tarnov in mid-March, but Alekseev adamantly refused to reinforce the southwestern front, bringing Ivanov's Carpathian campaign to a screeching halt.[31] The animosity among these military commanders would do much to determine the future of the Russian Empire.

Ivanov's deep thrust into the Carpathian Mountains forced a change in German strategy. Where Hindenburg and Ludendorff had employed pincer tactics against the Russian flanks, the chief of the German General Staff, General Erich von Falkenhayn, had a more direct approach in mind: he planned to aim his forces at the heavily fortified Russian lines and break straight through. The new strategy Germany adopted was August von Mackensen's "steamroller." General Nikolai Nikolaevich Golovin characterized it as "a gigantic beast dragging its tail of heavy artillery behind it, battering the defenseless Russians, who lacked the equipment and ammunition to respond."[32]

Mackensen's "steamroller" was first tested in battle in the narrow span (about thirty-five kilometers) between Gorlice and Tarnov. Mackensen's Eleventh Army amassed the heaviest artillery concentration seen in the Great War. His forces encompassed more than a third of a million troops against 219,000 men of Russia's Third Army, commanded by General Radko-Dmitriev. The huge difference was the number of heavy artillery pieces: Mackensen was equipped with 334 pieces against Dmitriev's 4 heavy guns, which turned out to be defective.

Beginning at 9 a.m. on April 18, Mackensen rained nearly three-quarters of a million rounds with Teutonic precision on the poorly prepared Russian Third Army for twelve hours. Russian trenches were totally obliterated. When Mackensen's infantry attacked the next morning, they met no resistance. "All the Russians," one German recalled, "who were not killed and wounded were stunned or contusioned."[33] Only 40,000 of the total 200,000 men retreated to the San River, and the Germans took more than 140,000 prisoners.[34] Falkenhayn's strategy was successful, and as Mackensen's army thrust into the east, it repeated the smashing victory of the Tarnov-Gorlice gap over and over: positioning heavy artillery out of range of Russian guns, then showering shells on the Russian trenches until they were completely pulverized, leaving the infantry to mop up what remained. Mackensen's forces recaptured Przemysl on May 19, and Lvov in mid-June.[35]

On June 19, at the German Supreme Headquarters, Falkenhayn decided to drive the Russians out of Poland entirely, in the hopes of knocking Russia out of the war in the process. Mackensen's army, coming from the south, and General Max von Gallwitz's army, coming from the north, thrust into Poland. On July 22 Warsaw fell. The Russians themselves destroyed Fortress Ivangorod before it could be captured. As for the coveted fortress of Novo-Georgievsk, more than 100,000 men with 1,600 guns and 1 million shells were wiped out on August 5. On August 13, Mackensen's forces broke through to Brest-Litovsk, and no Russians remained in Poland. Once the Germans crossed into Russian land, however, the economic backwardness they encountered slowed down and eventually halted their advance. Not strategy, not manpower, but the lack of railways and roads was responsible for saving the Russian army from complete disintegration.

Over the summer months of 1915, the Russian army lost 1.4 million casualties and another 1 million taken prisoner, while surrendering a huge swath of territory including Poland, Galicia, the Baltic provinces, Belorussia, and Volynia.[36]

As the Russian army retreated, the Stavka adopted the ill-advised "scorched earth" policy that the legendary hero General Mikhail Kutuzov had used during the Napoleonic Wars. Everything that could be exploited by the occupying Germans and Austrians was put to the torch. Civilians were also expelled from the war zone: Poles, Jews, Ukrainians,

Lithuanians, Belorussians, Latvians, and Russians left their homes and fled to unknown destinations in the Russian interior. Only one-fifth voluntarily chose to leave their homes; the rest were forced to migrate.[37] Especially violent was the expulsion of the Jews. General Yanushkevich, the chief of staff, considered Jews to be spies for the enemy and made their expulsion from the western borderlands an official policy. "Having escaped the onslaught of rape, pillage, and murder committed by the Russian troops passing through their villages," Laura Engelstein writes, "the dispossessed were often set upon by the local inhabitants, who pelted them with stones and accused them of stealing."[38] By the end of 1915, a million Jews had been uprooted, and tens of thousands perished.[39] Agriculture minister Aleksandr Krivoshein remarked, "It is impossible to conduct war simultaneously against the Germans and against the Jews."[40]

Refugees flocked into urban centers. By December 1915, Petrograd was filled with eighty-four thousand refugees, a number that increased to a hundred thousand by March 1916. Refugees suddenly constituted one-quarter of the population in Nizhny-Novgorod and Ekaterinoslav, one-fifth in Kharkov, and three-tenths in Samara.[41] Krivoshein called the refugee issue "the most unexpected, the most menacing, and the most irremediable" of all the wartime crises.[42]

War had brought catastrophe upon catastrophe of unforeseen ferocity to Russia. The dimensions of these crises had been unforeseen, and no one could adequately cope with them.[43] But the tsar and his government made a bad situation far worse.

Nicholas II was by and large a bystander to the war, taking no initiative in leading it. In his diary entries from August 2 and September 23, when the East Prussian campaign was conducted, Nicholas mentioned little about the fortunes of war. On August 10, he noted that he had received good news about the Russian offensive against the Germans from Nikolasha; on August 18 he acknowledged the "sad news" about the defeat of the Second Army commanded by Samsonov. On August 21, he once again welcomed the good news of the seizure of Lvov and Galicia, and on September 9 he mentioned the Russian advance in Galicia. His diary during the period was otherwise devoted to mundane matters: weather, having breakfast and tea with his relatives, taking a walk, and rowing a boat with his daughters. He expressed no grief upon hearing of the Russian defeat in East Prussia.[44]

Though he did not comprehend the depth of the problems that the wartime nation was facing, he recognized that his leadership was under fire. As the war in East Prussia raged, Nicholas visited the Stavka and made appearances near the front to signal the emperor's interest in the war. Being seen among the soldiers and people was a way of upholding the monarchical-patriotic message that the tsar was united with the people.

A photograph taken during a September 22 visit to the Stavka at Baranovichi shows Nicholas with Nikolai Nikolaevich, Yanushkevich, and Danilov, looking at a map on a table. Though the photo implied that the tsar was in charge of military operations, in reality he played no role whatsoever in making any war plans. In a letter to his wife, he commented on this scene: "We lay on top of big maps," he explains, "full of blue & red lines, numbers, dates, etc."[45] Nevertheless, this photograph was printed on postcards and widely circulated.[46]

At the Stavka, Nicholas broached the idea of visiting Fortress Osovets, on the river Biebrza in the northeast of Poland, fifty kilometers from the border with East Prussia. The German Eighth Army had approached the fortress on September 13 and bombarded it with heavy artillery, but the fortress withstood the assault, and the Germans retreated. Nicholas's visit to a location on the front where battle was being waged would boost his prestige and buttress the image of a tsar willing to risk his life to support the army. Nikolai Nikolaevich opposed his visit, fearing the disruption to military operations, not to mention the risk to the tsar's life so close to an active battleground. Suspecting that Nikolai Nikolaevich was undermining the tsar's authority, Alexandra, supported by Rasputin, urged Nicholas to visit Osovets.[47]

On September 24, Nicholas went to Fortress Osovets unannounced. The commandant, General Karil-August Shulman, hurriedly assembled the soldiers and accompanied the tsar to a church service, even as others were digging forward positions at the fortress.[48] Although the tsar's visit to Osovets was hailed as demonstrating his leadership among the soldiers, it is difficult to gauge the soldiers' actual reactions. Most likely General Shulman and the soldiers were irritated by the disruption of urgent preparations for the impending German attack on the fortress. No ceremony was performed, no medals of bravery were handed out to the soldiers, and no shouts of "hurrah" were sounded.

Many other carefully prepared and staged visits to cities and fortresses followed. On March 9, 1915, the tsar received news that the Austrian fortress of Przemysl had finally fallen into the hands of the Russians. Nicholas considered it appropriate to take a trip to the newly conquered regions of Galicia to earn the allegiance of the Galicians, over the objections of Nikolai Nikolaevich. In April, Nicholas visited Lvov, the capital of Galicia, and from there he went to Przemysl.[49] But in May, as we have seen, Mackensen's formidable war machine broke through the Tarnov-Gorlice gap, advanced deeply into Russian-occupied Galicia, and recaptured Przemysl, inflicting profound humiliation on the Russians.

Despite the propaganda efforts to publicize the tsar's visits to the front, what emerges most sharply from the historical record is the public's criticism of Nicholas at this time. Russian historian Boris Kolonitskii cites one characteristic comment from a lower-class commoner: "Wilhelm is winning because his sons are in the army, and he himself is with his soldiers, where he is winning over our stupid [durak] Tsar. He is sitting in Tsarskoe Selo."[50] Another Stavropol peasant commented on Nicholas's visit to Ekaterinodar: "He did not visit the wounded, and spent [the] entire two hours in the women's college. He is such a fool [*durak*] as Lukashka Sixfinger. His head is as small as my fist, and his brain does not work." In Tiflis, a resident blurted out: "Here is a fool [*durak*] coming to Tiflis to stroll, but Wilhelm is not strolling. He is doing his business, seizing Russian cities, will take Warsaw and other cities."[51] Striking are their references to the tsar as a "fool" and the comparison with Kaiser Wilhelm, who was doing a better job as the sovereign of his country. Ironically, the more officials tried to perpetuate the myth that the tsar and the *narod* were one, the wider the gap between them became.

As the German advance pushed the Russians out of Poland, criticism was increasingly directed at Nicholas himself. Kolonitskii quotes a sixty-two-year-old unskilled worker from Perm province who blamed the tsar for giving up Warsaw, suggesting that he might as well be replaced by the drunken toilet cleaner in his factory. A Don Cossack soldier made this comment: "Our Sovereign must be shot for not preparing shells. When our enemy is making shells, our Sovereign is chasing gophers."[52] Even elites and officers began to speak of their dissatisfaction.[53] Prince Nikolai Borisovich Shcherbatov, minister of internal affairs, stated at the Council of Ministers meeting in August: "In my reports I . . . presented letters obtained through military censorship, from people of various social classes, including some closest to the Court. In these letters one can vividly see the dissatisfaction with the government, with the regulations, with the confusion in the rear, with the military defeats, and so on. Moreover, the Emperor himself is held responsible for much of this."[54] The unflattering remarks revealed that the myth of unity between the tsar and the people was crumbling with every battlefield humiliation.

While Nicholas was away from Tsarskoe Selo conducting inspections and photo opportunities, Empress Alexandra wrote her husband almost daily. Those letters, written in English, paint a rambling portrait of her work as a nurse in the military hospital in the Catherine Palace in Tsarskoe Selo, their two older daughters' work as nurses, Aleksei's health, and other family matters.

Empress Alexandra plunged herself immediately into voluntary work for the war efforts. She mobilized women of all walks of life to sew necessities for soldiers on the front, oversaw the conversion of palaces into field hospitals and warehouses for war matériel, and even became a certified nurse in her own right. Her two older daughters, Olga and Tatiana, also became certified nurses. Nicholas's sister Olga established a field hospital in Rovno, and later one in Kiev. Grand Duchess Maria Pavlovna the Younger, daughter of Grand Duke Pavel Aleksandrovich, volunteered as a Red Cross nurse at the dangerous East Prussian front, and as the army evacuated, she became the head nurse in Pskov, the site of the headquarters for the northern front.

Alexandra and her daughters dedicated themselves to caring for the wounded, changing clothes, bandages, and bedsheets, taking temperatures and pulses, washing the patients, administering medicine, talking with patients, and often assisting with surgeries. On September 19, 1914, daughter Olga wrote in her diary: "There was an operation on Korzhenevsky of the 102nd Vyatka Regiment. Tatiana removed the infected bone from his left hand."[55] On October 21, 1914, Alexandra proudly wrote to Nicholas: "For the first time I shaved the leg of the soldier by the wound. Today I worked all the time alone without a sister or a doctor."[56]

Alexandra's work as a nurse was never a publicity stunt. She felt the pain of the wounded and did her best to assist them. She took pride in the work, as did Olga and Tatiana. The girls established a good rapport with their head nurse, Valentina Chebotareva. In addition to their regular work in the morning, they willingly, without anyone asking them, returned to the hospital to sanitize the instruments, and signed their letters to Chebotareva as Nurse Romanova I (Olga) and Nurse Romanova II (Tatiana). Olga developed a secret, unrequited affection for one of the patients, though Chebotareva and Tatiana knew about it; Olga shed tears when he left the hospital to return to the front.

Alexandra's letters to Nicholas reveal how Rasputin was working his way into the imperial family. Rasputin rarely appeared in the palace, and Alexandra went to the house of her close confidant Anna Vyrubova to meet him. In her correspondence she repeatedly refers to Nicholas's distant cousin Grand Duke Nikolai Nikolaevich. The empress remembered all too well that Nicholas had initially flirted with the idea of assuming supreme command of the war effort before handing the position to his cousin. Nikolai Nikolaevich and his brother Pyotr Nikolaevich happened to be married to the Black Princesses, Stana and Militsa, who had once been close to the empress. But by now that relationship had soured, and soon Alexandra and Rasputin turned on Nikolasha as well.

Nikolai Nikolaevich's appointment as the supreme commander had profoundly disappointed the empress and Rasputin. Alexandra, urged by Rasputin, had been strenuously and incessantly campaigning against Nikolai Nikolaevich for months. As early as September 20, 1914, Alexandra had written to Nicholas that Nikolasha was plotting to take the throne with the aid of the Black Princesses.[57] Then on January 29, 1915, the empress complained about Nikolasha making all kinds of decisions on his own, trying to play the part of the tsar. She insisted that this "ought to be put a stop to—one has no right before God & man to usurp your rights as he does . . . Me it hurts very much."[58] On March 5, she advised the tsar: "Don't tell N. [Nikolai Nikolaevich] & go off where it suits you & where nobody can expect you." In her mind, Nikolasha was intentionally keeping the tsar from visiting the front, to prevent the tsar's prestige from being enhanced among the soldiers.[59] On April 4, 1915, she wrote to Nicholas: "Though N. [Nikolai Nikolaevich] is so highly placed, yet you are above him. The same thing shocked our Friend [Rasputin], as me too, that N. words his telegrams, answers to governors, etc. in your style—his ought to be more simple & humble & other things." Afraid that Nicholas might think that she was meddling in affairs she should not be involved in, she reminded the tsar: "A woman feels & sees things sometimes clearer than my too humble sweetheart," and admonished her weak husband: "A Sovereign needs to show his will more often. Be more sure of yourself and go ahead—never fear."[60]

Nicholas's planned visit to recently captured Przemysl did not please Rasputin, who said: "God will help; but it is (too early) to go now." Nonetheless, Nicholas's visit was settled. Rasputin suggested that if the tsar was determined to go, he should go there alone, without the supreme commander. Alexandra fully agreed with this suggestion.[61] Nicholas responded with uncharacteristic force: "Darling mine, I am not of your opinion that N. ought to remain here when I go to Galicia. On the contrary, just because it is a conquered province, the Commander in Chief must accompany me." He had no intention of usurping the glory of the Russian military victory, in which he himself had no role whatever to play.[62] The campaign against Nikolasha had not yet succeeded in turning Nicholas against his cousin. When only two months later Przemysl was retaken by the German-Austrian forces, making a mockery out of Nicholas's celebration of victory, Alexandra saw Rasputin's warning as a message from God. She redoubled her efforts to convince Nicholas to fire Nikolai Nikolaevich, repeatedly returning to the warning from "our Friend" that her husband had ignored.

Rasputin was beginning to insinuate himself into political matters through Alexandra's influence. In a letter to the tsar on June 10, Alexandra advised Nicholas to oppose the Stavka's plans to call up new recruits, leaning heavily on Rasputin's counsel. She argued, "N. [Nikolai Nikolaevich] has only the army to think of & success—you carry the internal responsibilities on for years. . . . No, hearken unto our Friend, believe Him. He has yr. interest & Russia's at heart—it is not for nothing God sent Him to us."[63] Displeased, Nicholas responded tersely.[64] On the following day, she once again reminded her husband of Rasputin's advice not to go to Przemysl, and not to enter the war, all of which her husband had ignored, pleading: "Please listen to His [Rasputin's] advi[c]e when spoken so gravely & wh. gave Him sleepless nights!—one fault & we shall all have to pay for it."[65]

Her campaign against Nikolai Nikolaevich was relentless while Nicholas was away, and we can safely assume that her campaign only grew stronger when Nicholas returned to Tsarskoe Selo on June 27, though we lack the letters to document its course from there.

Nicholas's government at the outbreak of war was headed by the tsar's faithful servant Goremykin, who had replaced Vladimir Kokovtsov in January 1914 as the chairman of the Council of Ministers. But Goremykin was overshadowed by two powerful men in the cabinet: the reactionary minister of internal affairs, Nikolai Maklakov, and the progressive minister of agriculture, Krivoshein.

After the outbreak of war, Nikolai Maklakov strongly argued in favor of the dissolution of the Duma altogether. But Krivoshein favored cooperation with the Duma, and proposed to reconvene the Duma not later than February 1, 1915. In the end the Council of Ministers adopted a compromise, accepting Krivoshein's proposal with a possibility of further postponement. Nicholas approved this decision. So long as the Duma supported the "sacred union" and did not protest being prorogued after its one-day session in July, there was no reason to adopt Maklakov's policy and risk arousing a sleeping dog.[66] At the same time Nicholas allowed Maklakov to pursue a repressive policy against the liberal opposition. Censorship was introduced the day that Russia declared war; the Ministry of Internal Affairs harassed voluntary organizations; and two moderate liberals, Vasily Maklakov (Nikolai Maklakov's brother) and Pyotr Berngardovich Struve, were imprisoned for their work defending a Russian Jew named Menahem Beilis, who was put on trial for "ritual murder" in 1913. But the Duma accepted its dissolution without protest. In Raymond Pearson's words, in late 1914 the government achieved what it had failed to do in peacetime—it reduced the Duma in practice from a legislative assembly to a consultative one.[67]

As military defeats accumulated, however, the Duma increasingly became the center of the liberal opposition to the government.[68] The Octobrists, who constituted the majority of the Duma, were weakened by internal division, and quickly lost influence over the liberal groups outside the Duma. They were confronted with the question of how to divorce their monarchist principles from the monarch, who seemed to follow uncritically the unwise advice of the empress and Rasputin.

The conservative opposition to the government found its leader in Rodzyanko. While elevating the prestige of the Duma as the voice of the entire population, he privileged the influence of aristocratic circles. But as the Octobrists' influence waned, the Kadet party began to assert unmistakable intellectual leadership within the Russian liberal movement. Under Milyukov, the passionately nationalist Kadets were enthusiastic supporters of the war, maintaining that all citizens of Russia, regardless of class and nationality, should exert themselves to the utmost to ensure victory. Their criticism of the government stemmed from a lack of confidence that Nicholas and his ministers would be able to mobilize the whole of Russian society to prevail on the battlefield.

Outside the Duma, liberals used voluntary organizations to express their views. On July 30, 1914, a congress of zemstvo representatives created the All-Russian Union of Zemstvos for the relief of the sick and the wounded. A little later the municipal self-governments followed suit by forming the All-Russian Union of Towns. These two voluntary organizations were headed, respectively, by Prince Georgy Evgenievich Lvov and Mikhail Vasilievich Chelnokov, both Progressists. They began organizing relief for the wounded and the sick, supplying sanitary trains and hospitals, aiding evacuees, combating epidemics, and getting food to the populace.

Despite the practical tasks they set for themselves, patriotism was not the only motive behind the zemstvos' and municipal self-government activists' participation in war efforts. Émigré historian George Katkov's criticism of the voluntary organizations as a Trojan horse through which the liberals attempted to take over the entire state machinery may be an exaggeration, but he has a valid point: some activists in the Union of Zemstvos and the Union of Towns sought to make them instruments of political reform. It is precisely for this reason that the minister of internal affairs, Nikolai Maklakov, opposed the creation of the voluntary organizations and after their establishment attempted to curtail their activities. When Rodzyanko requested permission to hold a meeting of the zemstvo representatives to discuss the supply of boots for the army, Maklakov refused on the grounds that the zemstvos would, under this guise, demand a constitution.[69] Despite Maklakov's objections and obstructions, however, the Union of Zemstvos and the Union of Towns became deeply involved in the war effort. From the government's point of view, the activities of the voluntary organizations became such an integral part of the war effort that it could no longer ignore them. This mutual dependence, at a time when polarization between state and society was progressing to what would eventually become an irrevocable point, became the unique characteristic of the relationship between the liberals and the government during the war.

The dissatisfaction of the liberals with the government in the spring of 1915 led to the expression of three demands: to allow increased participation in the war effort by representatives of society, to reopen the Duma, and to dismiss unpopular ministers. Faced with a series of humiliating military defeats, Nicholas would eventually be forced to make these concessions.

The retreat of the Russian army wounded the pride of patriotic Russians, who believed the shell shortage to be the cause of the defeat. In the spring and summer of 1915, the shortage was at its most critical point;

furthermore, the reserves were exhausted, and new orders failed to arrive from the War Ministry. In early May, Rodzyanko and a number of Petrograd financial and industrial magnates petitioned the tsar, urging the creation of a council to improve the supply of armaments. Nicholas accepted their petition and on May 14 the Special Council for Improvement of Artillery Supplies for the Active Army, composed of a chairman, three representatives of the Duma (all Octobrists), representatives from the War Ministry, and two Petrograd financial magnates representing private industry, had its first meeting.[70] This concession by Nicholas was the beginning of a period of reconciliation.

The Kadets refused to participate in the special council on the grounds that minister of war Vladimir Sukhomlinov, a major culprit in creating the shell shortage, headed it.[71] Instead they prepared a legislative bill for the creation of a centralized body to deal with all war supply matters—a body that was to be under the tighter control of the Duma. In responding to these criticisms, the government countered with an attempt to reorganize the special council. It created four special councils under four different ministries: the Special Council for Defense under the war minister, the Special Council for Transportation under the minister of transport, the Special Council for Food Supply under the minister of agriculture, and the Special Council for Fuel under the minister of trade and industry. The government made concessions to the liberals by extending membership on these councils to representatives of the Duma, industry, the Union of Zemstvos, and the Union of Towns. Nevertheless, the government firmly maintained bureaucratic control over the councils, chaired by the respective ministers, who had veto power.

The Moscow industrialists and other smaller provincial industrialists had resented being excluded from the special council created in May, which at its establishment included only representatives from the Petrograd oligarchs. This frustration led them to establish the War Industries Committees to mobilize smaller industrialists in the war effort. The

Moscow industrialists, who championed the opposition to the Petrograd magnates, succeeded in taking over the leadership of the War Industries Committees, and elected Aleksandr Ivanovich Guchkov chairman of the Central War Industries Committee, and industrialist and politician Aleksandr Ivanovich Konovalov vice chairman.[72]

With the creation of the special councils and the War Industries Committees, the government opened the door to include representatives of Russian civil society in the mobilization of resources for the war. But the liberals were not satisfied—they also needed scapegoats.

In mid-May, during an audience with the tsar, Rodzyanko recommended the dismissal of four ministers. He suggested dismissing Nikolai Maklakov (minister of internal affairs), Sukhomlinov (minister of war), Ivan Grigorievich Shcheglovitov (minister of justice), and Vladimir Karlovich Sabler (procurator of the Holy Synod). At the same time, the liberals demanded the reopening of the Duma, which had been suspended since the outbreak of the war except for a three-day session to pass the budget in January 1915. The liberal campaign for the convocation of the Duma and the dismissal of unpopular ministers found sympathetic ears even in the government. Seven ministers, led by agriculture minister Krivoshein, meeting at the apartment of foreign minister Sazonov, decided that the Duma should convene as quickly as possible and that, to encourage cooperation with the Duma, the four ministers should be dismissed. Even Goremykin supported this opinion.[73]

Alexandra and Rasputin opposed the reopening of the Duma, as well as the dismissal of these unpopular ministers. Facing mounting criticisms about the military defeats, however, Nicholas ignored their advice, and on June 5 he agreed to dismiss Nikolai Maklakov.

Next the liberals directed their attention toward Sukhomlinov. They held this conservative war minister responsible for the catastrophic shell shortage in 1915. They wanted a pound of flesh from the government for the humiliating defeat, and no one was better suited to be that scapegoat than Sukhomlinov, a favorite of the tsar and tsarina. The liberals' demand was supported by anti-Sukhomlinovites in the army.

In February Sukhomlinov's slipping prestige was dealt a heavy blow by the arrest of his protégé Colonel Sergei Nikolaevich Myasoedov. Suspected of being a German spy, Myasoedov was tried by a military tribunal and executed, although there was actually no evidence to substantiate the charge against him. The affair was a "judicial murder" carried out by Sukhomlinov's enemies, including the man who would become his successor, General Aleksei Andreevich Polivanov. It marked the beginning of a vicious whispering campaign that contributed, with its innuendos and inflated, unsubstantiated charges appealing to the popular imagination, to Sukhomlinov's downfall and eventually to the imperial government's loss of prestige.[74]

In the face of mounting pressure from the liberals, the army generals, and now a majority of his government, Nicholas regretfully parted with Sukhomlinov. "It is for him much better to avoid a scandal," Alexandra advised her husband.[75] On June 11, unable to tell Sukhomlinov the bad news personally, Nicholas had a letter of dismissal delivered to his home. The following day, Sabler, a staunch supporter of Rasputin, and Shcheglovitov, one of the forces behind the notorious prosecution of Menahem Beilis, were fired, despite Alexandra's strenuous objections.[76] Sukhomlinov's personal enemy, Polivanov, against whom the empress attempted to influence her husband's decision, was appointed the new minister of war.[77] The only reactionary minister left in the cabinet was its chairman, Goremykin.

Having lost the campaign to retain the unpopular ministers, Alexandra soon found another of her priorities scuttled when Nicholas acquiesced to liberal demands to reconvene the Duma on July 19.

After a series of victories, the liberals were now divided on the tactics to be employed at the new sessions. Progressist Ivan Nikolaevich Efremov attacked Milyukov and advocated pressure to force Goremykin out.[78] The split between left and right had become more serious within the Kadet party. The left-wing Kadets criticized Milyukov's leadership and his inaction in the face of the mounting crisis in the country. They insisted on reviving the Kadets' legislative plans, which included a demand for the establishment of a "responsible ministry"—namely, a government responsible to the parliament.

Milyukov strongly opposed such a demand. In his opinion, it would be impossible to pursue the war without the cooperation of the government, and the war should be the foremost priority of the Kadets, one to which all other demands should be subordinated. He countered their demand with one for the establishment of a "ministry of confidence." The difference was not merely semantic. The term "ministry of confidence" referred to liberals' acceptance of the bureaucracy after a change in personnel. It would not involve any changes in the Fundamental Laws. This demand also implied the inclusion of the representatives of society into the government, creating a genuine "sacred union of national defense." In contrast, the demand for a "responsible ministry" was tantamount to the demand for a constitutional monarchy, where the government was to be responsible and answerable to the parliament. A "ministry of confidence" would be a coalition of the liberals and the bureaucracy, while the liberals would take the leadership in a "responsible ministry." Vasily Maklakov, Nikolai Maklakov's liberal brother, representing the Kadets' right wing, stated: "The slogan of a responsible ministry is at this moment revolutionary" and was to be rejected.[79] Milyukov and Maklakov feared that stepping up political demands would contribute to the revival of a mass movement. Indeed, as early as July 1915, there was a sharp increase in strikes. According to Milyukov, "not to support the government now would mean to play with fire."[80]

Just as the Duma session was opening, the military situation grew even worse. As the Germans pushed through Poland, on July 16 the new war minister, General Polivanov, declared that the nation was in danger. This brought two reactions from the liberals. One group, represented by

Milyukov, urged reformers to proceed with caution, while more radical liberals, such as Nikolai Nekrasov, concluded that it was now time to attack the government even more aggressively. Nekrasov suggested to his Kadet colleagues that it was time to be prepared to "take all power and all responsibility into our hands." Milyukov, on the other hand, appealed to the government: "Remove the road block, give the public organizations a way, give the nation internal peace." Despite the Progressists' insistence on the establishment of a responsible ministry, a majority of the Duma liberals accepted Milyukov's moderate demand: the formation of a ministry of confidence.[81]

In June 1915 Grand Duke Konstantin Konstantinovich, known as a poet under the pen name K.R., died.[82] Though he was buried in the Romanov family vault at Sts. Peter and Paul Cathedral, the ceremony was unusual. The customary procession from the Marble Palace to the Fortress did not take place. No members of the public were allowed to attend. No one knew if the emperor and the empress would attend the funeral at all, and when they arrived, it was by a devious route and with a doubled escort. In contrast to the enthusiastic reception of Nicholas and Alexandra on the balcony of the Winter Palace at the outbreak of the war less than a year earlier, the imperial couple had to sneak into the funeral like a hunted man and woman.[83]

Fissures in the "sacred union" came to surface. In her letters to Nicholas, Alexandra, under the advisement of Rasputin, campaigned for the tsar to hold on to his autocratic prerogatives, but Nicholas appeared set on a reconciliation with liberal opposition. And then the crisis of the summer of 1915 erupted.

# CHAPTER 3

# Parting Ways

The period of reconciliation suddenly came to a screeching halt in the summer of 1915 when Nicholas decided to assume supreme command of the Russian military and to prorogue the Duma.

Nicholas's decision to take over the supreme commandership was prompted by his concept of the duties of the sovereign in time of war, by the need to solve the problem of having dual civilian and military administrations, by his intention to boost the morale of the army in the wake of catastrophic military defeats, and by the empress's jealousy of Grand Duke Nikolai Nikolaevich.[1] Despite all of the military setbacks of the previous year, Nikolai Nikolaevich remained popular among the public, and he was perceived as a real military leader (*vozhd*) in contrast to the "incompetent" Tsar Nicholas. Nikolai Shcherbatov, minister of internal affairs, who was in a position to know public opinion, noted: "Grand Duke Nikolai Nikolaevich, despite all that has happened at the front, has not lost his popularity, and hope for the future is connected with his name not only in the army but also within the wider circles of society."[2] Adjutant General Aleksei Brusilov stated: "The entire army, yes all of Russia unconditionally believed in Nikolai Nikolaevich."[3] Illustrated images of Nikolai Nikolaevich appeared in the press often, both together with Nicholas and sometimes without the emperor, elevating the grand duke right next to the emperor in importance among the Romanovs. Empress Alexandra had watched the upsurge of the grand duke's popularity with jealousy and resentment, believing that the grand duke harbored ambitions to conspire with Duma liberals to replace the emperor.[4]

Nicholas's decision to assume the role of supreme commander carried grave consequences. As soon as he took over, any subsequent military defeat would taint the prestige of the emperor. More importantly, the new task would require Nicholas to stay at the Stavka (which had been moved from Baranovichi to Mogilev on August 8, 1915, as the Germans continued their offensive), giving the empress and Rasputin free rein to meddle in government policies in the capital.

When the news of Nicholas's decision was announced on August 6 at the meeting of the Council of Ministers, a majority of the ministers were aghast. During the cabinet meetings in the days that followed, from August 9 to 11, various ministers expressed their concerns about the emperor's decision to assume the supreme commandership. Shcherbatov remarked: "The government is hanging in the air, having no support from either below or above." Agriculture minister Aleksandr Krivoshein, the most outspoken opponent in the council of the tsar's decision, came to the conclusion that the only way out of this political crisis would be to reach a compromise with the Duma.[5]

On July 17 the Duma was reconvened. On August 11 and 12 the representatives of the Duma and the State Council met and decided to form the Progressive Bloc. This constituted two-thirds of the Duma, excluding only those from the extreme right and the extreme left. The central focus of the Progressive Bloc's program was its demand for the formation of a ministry of confidence (essentially, replacing personnel in the government and reaching out to the liberals in the government while retaining the same structure of government), rejecting a more radical demand for the formation of a responsible ministry (a de facto move toward a constitutional monarchy, which would require changes in the Fundamental Laws). Politically, the Progressive Bloc was characterized more by a willingness to reach a compromise with the government than by hostility toward it. In the words of Pavel Milyukov, its foremost leader, the formation of the Progressive Bloc was a "safety-valve of the drowning monarchy," and "the last measure to find a peaceful way out of the situation, which was from day to day growing more and more threatening."[6]

In the middle of August, anticipating the reorganization of the government, liberal circles were busy formulating lists of cabinet members acceptable for a ministry of confidence. Contrary to Alexandra's suspicions, the liberals had no intention of taking power. Milyukov stated bluntly, "We do not seek power now. . . . It is now only necessary to change the head of the government with a wise bureaucrat." Vasily Maklakov, a moderate liberal, added that a government simply could not be formed by the liberals alone, "because we don't know anything about administrative matters. We don't know the techniques. And we don't have time to learn now."[7] In the background of the political crisis was the specter of a rapidly growing workers' movement in Petrograd.[8]

The majority of the cabinet members wanted to petition Nicholas not to assume the supreme command. But Council of Ministers chairman Ivan Goremykin emphatically rejected the majority opinion, declaring that he would rather resign than join such a mutiny. Finally, the majority went ahead without Goremykin and composed a joint statement to the tsar. Only two members of the cabinet, Goremykin and minister of justice Aleksandr Alekseevich Khvostov, opposed the joint statement. The collective letter recommended Goremykin's dismissal and concluded: "We venture once more to tell you that to the best of our judgment your decision threatens with serious consequences [for] Russia, your dynasty, and your person."[9]

They also favored a compromise with the Progressive Bloc. Nicholas's assumption of the supreme command and his rejection of compromise with the Progressive Bloc, they feared, would drive the liberals to the side of revolution against the government.

Nicholas believed autocracy should not bend even under mounting pressure, whether it came from the workers' strike movement or from the Progressive Bloc in the Duma. Alexandra had been whipping up her husband to be a true autocrat and never to allow a constitutional government in Russia.

Goremykin immediately left for the Stavka, not to inform the tsar of the majority opinion of the Council of Ministers but to privately recommend immediate prorogation of the Duma and dismissal of the disloyal ministers. As Goremykin said to the ministers: "I am old, I have not much longer to live, but whilst I am alive I shall fight to preserve the Emperor's powers. Russia's strength lies in the monarchy."[10]

When Nicholas had reluctantly dismissed Nikolai Maklakov on June 5, the latter had warned him that the slightest concession to the liberals would open the floodgates to further demands. This warning now seemed to be borne out. The tsar had agreed to let the representatives of public organizations participate in the special councils; he had dismissed, though grudgingly, the unpopular ministers; and he had opened the Duma. Despite all these concessions, it appeared that the liberals' voice against the government was growing louder. Even worse, his own ministers were now raising criticisms. On August 22, in the opening ceremony of the special councils in the Winter Palace, Nicholas stated: "I needed the Duma for securing defense. Now all the programs have been accomplished. The rest will be done by Article 87."[11] Article 87 of the Fundamental Laws allowed the government to make laws without the approval of the legislative chambers while they were not in session.

This was the day when the ministers dispatched their collective petition to the tsar. Precisely on this day, defying their desperate plea not to do so, Nicholas left for Mogilev to assume the supreme commandership. It was a momentous decision, and it arguably sealed the fate of the monarchy and the fate of his family.

It followed Alexandra's tireless campaign against Nikolai Nikolaevich and for a hard-line stance for autocracy. Over the course of a month and a half in Tsarskoe Selo, she had finally managed to convince her husband to assume the supreme commandership. Nevertheless, after he left for Mogilev, she was seized with apprehension that her weak husband might change his mind. On August 22, she fired off a letter:

> You have fought this great fight for your country & throne—alone & with bravery & decision. Never have not fear for what remains behind—one must be severe & stop all at once. Lovy, I am here, don't laugh at silly old wify, but she has "trousers" on unseen, & I can get the old man [Goremykin] to come & keep him up to be energetic . . . I too well know yr. marvelously gentle character—& you had to shake it off this time, had to win your fight alone against all . . . You remain firm as a rock, for that you will be blessed. God anointed you at your coronation, he placed you where you stand . . . Our Friend's [Rasputin's] prayers arise night & day for you to Heaven & God will hear them . . . Only get Nikolasha's nomination quicker done—no dawdling, it's bad for the cause & for Alekseev too—& a settled thing quieten[s] minds even if against their wish, sooner than that waiting & uncertainty.[12]

Nicholas responded from Vitebsk on the way to Mogilev: "Feel strong and decided. Shall telegraph this evening when all is over."[13]

For his part, Nicholas had grown tired of compromising with the liberal opposition. The Russian army's great retreat was over, and the German advance had finally stalled. Under the able leadership of war minister Aleksei Polivanov, the supply of shells and artillery was increasing. As the military situation improved, Nicholas grew less concerned about internal criticism. A backlash from the right wing had struck a chord in him. On August 20 and 22 at a meeting of the Council of the United Nobility, Aleksandr Nikolaevich Naumov, future minister of agriculture, expressed his dissatisfaction with the government's permissiveness in allowing the liberal elements to influence policy. The council's chairman, Anany Petrovich Strukov, wrote a letter to Goremykin on August 23 warning that concessions to liberal demands would endanger the existing state order.[14]

Most influential was Alexandra's persistent campaign to dismiss Nikolasha, which had finally borne fruit. "All is for the good," she rejoiced.[15] But she followed this victory lap with careful advice: "Go straight to bed without taking tea with the rest & [having to] see their long faces." To make sure Nicholas would not change his mind, she reminded him of the icon, blessed by Rasputin, that she had sent him.[16] Even after Nicholas dismissed his cousin, Alexandra was anxious to dispatch Nikolasha to the Caucasus as soon as possible. "Lovy order him south quicker . . . Be firm in that too, please."[17]

Nicholas's meeting with the grand duke was not recorded, but Nikolai Nikolaevich apparently accepted his dismissal without protest. On August 23, Nikolai Nikolaevich issued his last order as the supreme commander: "I firmly believe that, knowing that the Tsar himself, to whom you pledged allegiance, will lead you, and you will show new, unprecedented deeds, and that the Lord from this day forward will show anointed, all-powerful assistance to give the victory."[18] The grand duke was ordered to leave for the Caucasus immediately. Nicholas did not allow him to go through Petrograd.[19] Alexandra had won. His wife "in trousers" was in command.[20]

Following Nicholas's decision, Grand Duke Andrei overheard a conversation between Alexandra and Nicholas's sister Ksenia. To Ksenia's question why Nicholas had decided to replace the popular Nikolasha, Alexandra answered: "Again about Nikolasha. Everyone is now talking about him. I am sick and tired of hearing this. Nicki is more popular than he."[21]

The ministers were traveling to Mogilev to petition the tsar to change his mind, and Alexandra worried that at the last moment Nicholas might succumb. She wrote to him in advance: "Remember to comb your hair before all difficult talks & decisions the little comb [Rasputin had given you] will bring its help."[22] Rasputin's comb must have strengthened Nicholas's resolve not to listen to the ministers.

On September 2 Goremykin informed his colleagues in Petrograd of the tsar's latest decision: to prorogue the Duma immediately for an indefinite time, and to refuse the collective resignation of the ministers.

The ministers exploded. Polivanov warned that the prorogation of the Duma would be the beginning of a general strike. Foreign minister Sergei Sazonov shouted: "Tomorrow blood will flow in the streets and Russia will plunge into an abyss." To this, Goremykin replied: "The Duma will be prorogued on the appointed date, and no blood will flow anywhere."[23]

No blood flowed immediately, but there was shock among Nicholas's relatives. The dowager empress was stunned by her son's decision to replace Nikolai Nikolaevich. Breaking her custom not to interfere in politics, she remonstrated with her son to keep Nikolai Nikolaevich. Among the court officials, Count Vladimir Borisovich Fredericks, the minister of the court and a faithful servant to the tsars for more than fifty years, risked disgrace to enter a protest of his own. But when Fredericks sought to warn the tsar of the danger of Rasputin, Nicholas cut him off, saying: "I know what you are going to say. Let's continue to be friends, but don't talk about this anymore."[24] Prince Vladimir Nikolaevich Orlov, who had served as the emperor's secretary in the chancellery, remained an outspoken critic of Rasputin, and warned the tsar about Rasputin's negative influence on the emperor's prestige. He earned the enmity of the empress for this, and was banished to the Caucasus to join the grand duke. The emperor lost a valuable servant who had given him honest counsel.[25] The only relatives who supported Nicholas's decision were Grand Duke Vladimir's sons Kirill, Boris, and Andrei, and their position stemmed from clan rivalry against Nikolai Nikolaevich.[26]

Those who hailed the tsar's decision did so partly because they considered that the tsar's taking the command would eliminate the fundamental structural weakness stemming from the duality between the military and civilian authorities, and partly because they took comfort in the thought that since he would be away from the capital, the tsar would be freed of the influence of Rasputin. Meanwhile, critics saw Rasputin's influence behind the tsar's decision; furthermore, they suspected the tsar's decision was the first step toward a separate peace, and that the German party at the court was conspiring to achieve this. It is, of course, difficult to gauge accurately the public's reaction when public opinion polls did not exist, but, examining the wide range of opinions, historian Boris Kolonitskii concludes that the reaction was overwhelmingly negative. The opinions of the masses that the censors caught were uniformly critical of Nicholas's decision.[27] Lev Aleksandrovich Tikhomirov, a former revolutionary who turned into a staunch monarchist, wrote in his diary on October 5, 1915, "I don't know how the war will end, but after this, revolution seems completely inevitable. Things are moving so fast that only those who have personal interest will remain faithful to the Dynasty, but these people who are sold out, of course, will be the first traitors when the threatening hour approaches."[28]

The chance for reconciliation between the government and the liberals was lost. Milyukov's biographer Thomas Riha concludes: "The monarchy's last chance for survival had been missed in 1915, when discussion was still possible. Once the people began to make their demands in the streets, it was too late to rely on the Bloc, which had been the tool of evolution, not of revolution."[29]

If Goremykin's opponents in the cabinet proved to be right in the long run, in the immediate aftermath the strategy pursued by Nicholas and Goremykin was successful. The liberals swallowed the humiliation of the prorogation of the Duma in silence. Behind their inaction was fear of a mass movement. The liberals wished to avoid any action that might ignite a fire among the masses. The moderate Kadet Vasily Maklakov stated: "If

Russia went on strike, the government would perhaps yield, but I would not want such a victory." The Duma spent the last day of its session on September 3 in a businesslike manner without a murmur of protest.[30] Mikhail Rodzyanko and the representatives of the zemstvos separately requested an audience with the tsar. He flatly rejected their requests, remarking: "I, of course, will not receive such self-proclaimed plenipotentiaries."[31]

After the political crisis in the summer of 1915, the relationship between the government and the liberals grew to resemble a bad marriage. Reconciliation was no longer possible, mutual distrust was only growing, but neither side wanted to make a clean break. The government continued to ignore the liberals' demands, but it stopped short of declaring total war on them. The liberals were outraged, but they were unwilling to raise a hand against the government. However sour and rancorous their relationship had become, the war and the fear of a revolution from below kept their marriage together.

After the summer of 1915, this relationship can be conveniently divided into three successive periods by the tenures of three ministers of internal affairs: Aleksei Nikolaevich Khvostov (September 26, 1915–March 3, 1916), Boris Vladimirovich Stürmer (March 3–July 9, 1916), and Aleksandr Dmitrievich Protopopov (September 16, 1916–February 27, 1917).[32] Each period was marked by the progressive deterioration of the integrity and cohesion of the government and the increased influence of the court camarilla represented by Alexandra and Rasputin. In a remarkable display of what would later be called "ministerial leapfrog," Russia burned through four prime ministers, five ministers of internal affairs, three ministers of foreign affairs, three ministers of war, three ministers of transport, and four ministers of agriculture between September 1915 and February 1917.

The court camarilla took vengeance on the "rebel" ministers who had dared to show sympathy with the liberals in the summer of 1915.

Krivoshein, the leader of the "rebel" ministers, was dismissed in October 1915. In March 1916, Polivanov fell victim to a vicious campaign spear-headed by Alexandra. And one morning in July 1916, Sazonov opened the newspaper and read a rescript of the emperor dismissing him as foreign minister.[33]

After the failure of the Progressive Bloc to reach a compromise with the government, the liberals splintered. As the Progressive Bloc pursued a cautious, even timid, policy of moderation under Milyukov's leadership, refraining from sharply attacking the government, the left openly sought ways to influence the masses. By creating a Workers' Group under the War Industries Committees, in an attempt to organize the labor movement under the moderate wing of socialists, the left wing of the bloc succeeded only in alienating the industrialists from the liberals. It would take until the autumn of 1916, when the supply of food reached a serious situation and labor unrest had recovered its prewar vitality, for the liberals to begin raising their voices against the government.

In the meantime, they sat motionless, like a passenger riding in a car driven by a mad chauffeur on a dangerous mountain road, frozen in fear that any move on their part might cause the car to plunge off a cliff.[34] When the climactic moment came, they told themselves, they would move fast to take the wheel. But not yet.

The first to take Nikolai Maklakov's place as minister of internal affairs was Aleksei Nikolaevich Khvostov ("Fat Khvostov"). Unlike his conservative but forthright uncle, minister of justice Aleksandr Aleksee-vich Khvostov, who had opposed his nephew's appointment, Fat Khvostov was a scoundrel. His elevation to the new post had come only through the intercession of Rasputin, Anna Vyrubova, and the empress.[35] Hostile to the liberals, Khvostov engineered the postponement of the Duma session scheduled for November and banned congresses of the Union of Zemstvos and the Union of Towns (which had formed a loose confeder-ation, the Zemgor, headed by Georgy Lvov).[36] He made preparations for the election of the Fifth Duma, and wrote what came to be known as the Khvostov Memorandum, which was designed to exclude all parties left of the Zemstvo-Octobrists from the next election.[37] The liberals, under Milyukov's leadership, barely reacted.[38]

As noted earlier, due to the German offensive, the location of the Stavka had been moved from Baranovichi to the historic city of Mogilev on August 8, 1915. At the same time, the northwestern front was divided into the northern front and the western front. The northern front was commanded by Adjutant General Nikolai Vladimirovich Ruzsky (save for a brief period under the command of General Aleksei Nikolaevich Kuropatkin), and the western front was commanded by Adjutant General Aleksei Evert.

Unlike when it was in Baranovichi, where staff officers, including Nikolai Nikolaevich, slept in special railway cars, the Stavka in Mogilev was installed in the government buildings at the very center of the city. Two buildings stood facing the semicircular governor's square in front, the Dnieper River behind, the governor's mansion on the left, and the governor's administrative building on the right. The governor's mansion was used as Nicholas's office and residence. This was a typical provincial governor's mansion, far from palatial. When one entered the mansion and walked up the stairs to the second floor, one would be in an entrance hall, with a portrait of Nicholas II hung between huge mirrors. One side of the hall led to the dining room, and the other side of the hall led to Nicholas's office, where he received ministers and other guests. The emperor's office was connected with the bedroom, where there were two simple iron beds, one for Nicholas and the other for his son, Aleksei. Other parts of the sleeping quarters were occupied by Count Fredericks and General Vladimir Nikolaevich Voeikov.[39]

The governor's house and the headquarters of the Stavka were separated by a small garden, which was guarded by sentinels from the St.

George Battalion, the most elite of the elite units (composed of recipients of the St. George's Cross for valor), as well as the palace police under the command of the palace commandant.[40]

After Nicholas became the supreme commander in the summer of 1915, Nicholas and Alexandra decided to send Aleksei to the Stavka to live with his father. This was the first time that the boy lived separately from his mother. They thought it was important for Aleksei to experience military life and learn a thing or two about administering the government, an experience that Nicholas himself had not had the chance to have before acceding to the throne. But there was little that a ten-year-old boy could learn and absorb. Other than his daily lessons of academic subjects and foreign languages, he mostly sat at the breakfast and dinner table, often disrupting conversations. The father doted on him, taking him along on his daily walk. The only military things Aleksei participated in were reviews of military ceremonies and parades, the same kind of "military" affairs that his father had learned in his youth.

The most important decision-maker at the Stavka was not Nicholas but the chief of staff, Adjutant General Mikhail Alekseev, who lived in a small room next to the quartermaster's office in the governor's administrative building. This building, where Alekseev and his quartermaster general, Mikhail Savvich Pustovoitenko (and later General Aleksandr Sergeevich Lukomsky), resided and had their offices, was the nerve center of the Stavka.[41] This was where the telegraphic office was located and the Hughes apparatus (a type-printing telegraph apparatus, akin to a teletype) was installed.

Every morning at ten o'clock, the emperor left the governor's mansion, walked to the next building, escorted by the palace commandant and the duty officer of the tsar's convoy, and ascended the stairs to the quartermaster's office on the second floor, where he received the reports given by his chief of staff and the quartermaster general, while his escorts waited outside. It was, however, a breach of military tradition for the supreme commander to come to the chief of staff's office rather than the other way around. The departure from this tradition contributed to the debasement of the emperor's prestige in the eyes of the officers at the Stavka.[42]

Alekseev, who had risen from humble origins, had the reputation of being one of the best military leaders, as he not only understood the complexities of military strategy and tactics in this unprecedented world war but also had extensive knowledge of logistics, armaments, and mobilization. Since Nicholas was merely a figurehead, not at all involved in any operational plans and executions, General Alekseev virtually served as the supreme commander. He had served as the chief of staff under Adjutant General Nikolai Iudovich Ivanov at the southwestern front and then as the commander of the northwestern front before he was appointed chief of staff at the Stavka. As Bruce Menning writes, Alekseev "owed his career not to favoritism and protection, but to hard work and mastery of his profession . . . He had little time for the niceties of court etiquette and the necessity to cultivate favor."[43] His weakness was his proclivity to make decisions, however minor, on his own, without delegating to his subordinates.

Two experiences had a lasting influence on Alekseev's thinking. The first was the defeat at Mukden in the Russo-Japanese War, where, as the quartermaster general of the Manchurian Third Army, he experienced a total annihilation of his army. The second was Bloody Sunday of 1905, when his wife, Anna, witnessed the massacre of demonstrators by loyal troops from her apartment window. Alekseev's commitment to preserving the army's will to fight and his horror of pitting troops against the Russian people would play important roles in the decisions ahead.[44]

Alekseev had a rather reticent manner, which did not help create a good rapport with the tsar's entourage, who kept their distance from the chief of staff. Many witnesses observed that he established good working relations with the tsar, that he remained loyal to the tsar, that he loved the tsar, and that Nicholas liked his chief of staff.[45] But behind his outward respect and deferential attitude, Alekseev nursed a profound contempt for his superior. On one rare occasion, he confided to Father Georgy Ivanovich Shavelsky, the protopresbyter of the army and navy and a member of the Holy Synod. "What can be done with such a child? A crazy woman governs the state, and she is surrounded by a gaggle of the same suit."[46]

Nicholas was surrounded by his entourage and protected by army units specially designated to guard the emperor. The soldiers of those units had an insignia with the letter "N" on their shoulders, to signify their prestige and special proximity to the emperor. Among the entourage, the two most important were Count Fredericks and General Voeikov.

Fredericks, a Baltic German nobleman, was already seventy-seven years old in 1915 and his memory and hearing had faded, but he had impeccable knowledge of court etiquette and customs. Nicholas and Alexandra, fully aware of his frailty, liked the old man and did not have the stomach to fire him.

Voeikov, a forty-nine-year-old major general with a handlebar mustache, had an impeccable pedigree: he had the lineage of the famous Dolgoruky family on his mother's side and had graduated from the exclusively aristocratic Corps of Pages. He had served in His Majesty's Life Guard Hussar Regiment, attached to the imperial court. He had the honor of being Tsarevich Aleksei's godfather and was allowed to build a summer house near the imperial palace in Tsarskoe Selo. Voeikov was Nicholas's closest adviser and the unquestionable leader of his suite. Nonetheless, he did not have the respect of the other members of the tsar's entourage. According to Major General Dmitry Nikolaevich Dubensky, a court historian, he was a careerist, distinguished only by his superficiality and by the lack of depth that was required for the role assigned to him.[47] According to Rear Admiral Aleksandr Dmitrievich Bubnov, who served under the chief of Naval Staff, Admiral Aleksandr Ivanovich Rusin, at the Stavka, he was "a repulsive sybarite-cynic, with limited intellectual capacity and a narrow worldview of the Hussar officers, possessing an arrogant self-importance, loudly mouthing retrograde, Black-Hundred opinions, impressed the sovereign with these ideas, and had ill-fated influence on him."[48]

The era of internal affairs minister Aleksei Nikolaevich Khvostov came to a quick end, not because of liberal criticism but because of the power struggle within the ruling circles. Khvostov had dreamed of replacing Goremykin as chairman of the Council of Ministers, as Goremykin's high-handed opposition to the Duma began to worry the tsar.[49] But Rasputin, who at one point had been Khvostov's benefactor, was in the way of his ambition. To get rid of this obstacle, Khvostov engineered a seamy intrigue that involved his hired agent in a plot to assassinate the "holy man." Rasputin became suspicious of Khvostov, and the Rasputin clique both at the court and within the cabinet turned against him. When Nicholas finally dismissed Goremykin in February 1916, it was not Khvostov but his rival, Stürmer, who took over the vacant post. The new head of the cabinet was closely associated with Rasputin and strongly supported by Alexandra. The police chief Stefan Beletsky, a key figure in Khvostov's assassination plot, betrayed his master, and the entire plot became known to the Rasputin clique and eventually to the public. Khvostov was dismissed in disgrace, and Stürmer took over the Ministry of Internal Affairs as well, as recommended by Rasputin. The sordid scandal further contributed to the erosion of the authority of the tsarist government.[50]

Stürmer's appointment as chairman of the Council of Ministers on the eve of the opening of the Duma was meant to appease the liberal opposition. Nicholas feared that the retention of Goremykin, who had proposed postponing the scheduled Duma session, might provoke a stormy protest from the liberals. Rasputin and Alexandra were in favor of this tactical maneuver to pacify the liberals. On February 9, 1916, when the Duma opened, to the pleasant surprise of the liberals, Nicholas made an extraordinary gesture of goodwill by appearing personally at the Duma, accompanied by Grand Duke Mikhail. A few meaningless words uttered by the emperor were enough to soften the tone of the speeches by the Duma liberals and to raise hopes that this conciliatory gesture would be followed by further concessions on the tsar's part.[51]

But Stürmer's declaration immediately dampened these hopes, for it was a repetition of the government's refusal to make internal reforms as long as the war continued.[52] During the relatively long session, which lasted from February 9 to June 20, 1916, the Duma accomplished little. The military situation improved, as the next section will discuss. And whenever internal reforms came up for discussion, irreconcilable differences divided the Progressive Bloc. Milyukov was absent in the latter part of the Duma session, since he elected to join the Duma deputation to Western Europe.

The only bright spot for Russia during the spring and summer of 1916 was on the battlefield. Only one general appeared to have learned from the bitter experience of defeat the previous year, coming up with a unique strategy to counter Mackensen's "steamroller." That was General Brusilov, appointed commander in chief of the southwestern front in March 1915 as a replacement for General Ivanov. Where other military leaders attempted in vain to counter Mackensen's offensive by amassing large numbers of troops and artillery, Brusilov advocated a strategy of building numerous entrenchments along the front, assembling combined forces of infantry, cavalry, and artillery, and attacking at the same time at various points along the long front. By the time Brusilov took command of the southwestern front, the manpower situation and the supplies of rifles, bullets, and shells had vastly improved, thanks to the energetic policy of the war minister, Polivanov. Brusilov recruited special fortification engineers and vigorously trained artillery, cavalry, and infantry officers and men.

In April 1916, Brusilov proposed a daring offensive against the Austrian army. Alekseev approved the plan. This effort would become Russia's most stunning victory in the war.

The Brusilov Offensive began on May 22, 1916, with simultaneous, incessant bombardment along the entire front against the entrenched Austrian army. Russia's Eighth Army captured Lutsk, while the Eleventh, Seventh, and Ninth Armies moved from the south toward Lvov. The onslaught brought the Austrian army to the verge of surrender.

But two things intervened to prevent a total victory. First, German headquarters sent the German army under Hindenburg to take over the operation. Second, Evert (on the western front) and Kuropatkin (on the northern front) at first refused outright to send reinforcements to assist Brusilov, and then agreed but delayed sending those troops. As a consequence, Brusilov's forces exhausted the available manpower and artillery and were forced to suspend the operation in August. Brusilov was furious at Evert and Kuropatkin. He resented even Alekseev for his reluctance to force Evert and Kuropatkin to send reinforcements.[53] Brusilov's hostility would endure and inform the climactic struggles over the future of the tsar.

Nicholas played no part in the Brusilov Offensive. While the Russian army was engaged in a deadly battle, the supreme commander spent most of his time reading a soppy English tale, "Little Boy Blue." When he did intervene, it resulted in disaster. At the last stage of the offensive, when Brusilov desperately needed reinforcements, Alekseev decided to send some of the elite imperial guards that he had reserved for special operations. Nicholas chose his favorite commander, General Vladimir Mikhailovich Bezobrazov. In the words of historian Bruce Lincoln, Bezobrazov was "notorious for his bad judgment" and "had repeatedly been relieved of lesser commands for incompetence and outright insubordination." One of Bezobrazov's two deputies was Grand Duke Pavel, Nicholas's uncle, "who knew nothing about military affairs." Their incompetence resulted in a wholesale slaughter of the best soldiers and officers of the elite imperial guards.[54] Whenever Nicholas intervened in military matters, things got worse.

The military leaders, who hitherto had stayed out of domestic politics, were becoming increasingly concerned with the internal political situation, which was beginning to affect the morale of the soldiers in the trenches and the barracks. On June 15, General Alekseev recommended to Nicholas the establishment of a dictatorship to resolve the nation's economic woes and the perennial problem of the lack of coordination between military authority and civilian authority. This recommendation reflected the military's growing concern with the procurement of military supplies and the deterioration of the food supply system, which was worsening problems in the cities and was also beginning to affect the provision of the army.[55]

It appears that Alekseev was interested in elevating Grand Duke Sergei, the inspector of artillery at the Stavka, to the dictatorial position, in an effort to cut the Gordian knot of the dual administrations of the supreme command and the civilian government in Petrograd. The secret recommendation was leaked to Rodzyanko, who opposed the appointment of the grand duke to the post when he met with Alekseev at the Stavka.[56] Alekseev was not happy that his memorandum had been leaked to Rodzyanko; after meeting with him, Alekseev commented about the chairman of the Duma with disgust: "That chattering turkey!"[57] Alekseev's view of Rodzyanko at this meeting was to have an influence on the relationship between the two men in the subsequent drama during the February Revolution.

Neither the Council of Ministers nor Nicholas accepted Alekseev's recommendation of the grand duke for this position. At a meeting presided over by the tsar on June 28, the Council of Ministers decided to give Stürmer dictatorial power.[58] Stürmer took over the foreign ministry, conceding the ministry of internal affairs to Aleksandr Alekseevich Khvostov (not to be confused with his scandalous nephew, Aleksei Nikolaevich Khvostov).[59]

Alekseev had not expected this outcome. Deeply offended, he swore that he would never cooperate with Stürmer, and exclaimed: "Now I would not be surprised if tomorrow [the tsar] appointed Stürmer in my place as chief of staff."[60] This turn of events also reinforced his critical view of Alexandra and Rasputin. When the empress handed Alekseev an icon from Rasputin and requested permission for him to visit the Stavka, Alekseev replied: "The day of Rasputin's arrival at Stavka will be the day of my retirement."[61] The fiasco of his recommendation to put in place a dictator was an important turning point in Alekseev's attitude toward the imperial couple. As Menning argues, General Alekseev and other officers of the high command were shifting over time to a position of "passive opposition."[62] Alekseev's sympathy with moderate liberals deepened to the extent that he would become willing to give a hearing even to plotters of a palace coup, as we will see.

The government's official journals and popular magazines printed a series of photographs showing Nicholas and his son reviewing military units in various places they visited, the tsar in a simple officer's uniform and Aleksei in Cossack uniform or an infantry private's uniform. These images were also distributed in the form of postcards in mass circulation and in documentary films. But the government's efforts to spread patriotic imagery of Nicholas inspecting troops and receiving military honors seemed only to worsen the public's view of the tsar.

At one point the tsar awarded the St. George's Cross to a noncommissioned officer. The excited officer grasped the sovereign's hand, despite the protocol being not to touch the sovereign. Nicholas immediately wiped his hand with a handkerchief, in full view of his soldiers witnessing the ceremony. With this act, the abiding faith in the unity of the tsar and the *narod* was thrown to the winds.[63] When a documentary film of Nicholas being given the St. George's Cross was shown, someone in the darkness of the movie theater shouted: "The Tsar is with Georgy, but the tsaritsa is with Grigory [Rasputin]."[64] The tsar was no longer immune to criticism, and as the war dragged on, that criticism grew more strident—and more violent.

During the war Nicholas was often accused of being "weak" and "incompetent." But he was now also called a "fool" (*durak*), which replaced an earlier epithet, "bloodsucker" (*krovopiitsa*).[65] The use of *durak* conveys a degree of contempt many times worse than "bloodsucker." Several people were arrested and brought to the court for spreading the following satirical ditty: "From Petersburg to Altai / There is no autocrat more stupid than Nikolai."[66]

Denunciations of the tsar were becoming more frequent, and explicitly referring to violence. In 1916, a forty-eight-year-old peasant in Kazan province by the name of P. Yakovlev was sentenced to nine months' imprisonment for "insulting" the tsar and the members of the royal family. Being a literate peasant, he had been asked by the villagers about what newspapers were reporting about the war. In July he was said to have remarked: "We must put a bullet to the Tsar and Nikolai Nikolaevich, only then the war will be over and people's blood will stop flowing." Later when he was asked about peace, his answer was more violent: "What is peace to you? There will soon be an all-Russian conference, they will come down on the Sovereign Emperor and the Heir, and then they will finish them off and they will burn down the government. As they crucified Jesus Christ, they will crucify the Sovereign Emperor and the Heir. After that it will be easier to live."[67] An illiterate peasant in Vyatka province declared: "We must shoot our Sovereign in the mouth so that the bullet will not get out of his ass."[68] In May 1915, a peasant in Perm province stated, "Our Tsar is more treasonous than anyone because all leaders are Germans. We must expel all of them and kill the Tsar."[69]

Nicholas and Alexandra lived in blissful ignorance of such widespread discontent among simple folks who they mistakenly believed supported them enthusiastically.

Though Alexandra continued working as a nurse, tending to wounded soldiers and officers, she was not a healthy woman. She had constant backaches, pains in her hands, chronic kidney disease, a weak heart, gout, and constant toothaches. She smoked to ease her pain and took all kinds of medicine: "I take a mass of iron, arsenic, heart medications." She had trouble walking and sometimes relied on a wheelchair. Since she had trouble walking, she had to install an elevator between the first and second floors in the Alexander Palace. Her health conditions, however, remained secret from the public.[70]

In spite of her selfless volunteer work, Empress Alexandra proved to be an easy target for criticism. What better scapegoat for defeat in a war with Germany than the "German woman," who could not even speak proper Russian? A series of baseless rumors spread and came to be believed not only among the common folk but also among the elite. Alexandra was at first portrayed as a German sympathizer who cheered when Russians suffered defeats and wept at German defeats. This accusation soon developed into more vicious rumors of her treasonous acts—betraying Russian state secrets via telegrams and letters, and even communicating with the Germans via a secret wireless station in Tsarskoe Selo.[71]

After Nicholas's assumption of the supreme commandership, these rumors grew ever wilder. While Nicholas was at Mogilev, it was Alexandra in Tsarskoe Selo, the rumors held, who actually governed Russia, together with Rasputin. Some rumors contended that Alexandra was plotting with Rasputin to overthrow or even kill Nicholas to take his place as tsar, as Catherine the Great (r. 1762–1791) had killed her husband, Tsar Peter III (r. 1761–1762). Other rumors insinuated that the empress and Rasputin had sexual relations or that the empress and her confidant Anna Vyrubova were lesbian lovers. There was a rumor that Nicholas was going to divorce the empress and send her to a nunnery. None of these salacious rumors had any foundation, but their volume was growing, smearing the prestige of the imperial couple and setting the stage for open discussions of a palace coup.[72]

As the war's impact on the Russian economy led to a food crisis in the autumn of 1916, the workers' strike movement picked up momentum, and liberals finally raised their voices against the government. The liberal newspapers demanded the opening of the Duma. The Progressive Bloc entrusted Rodzyanko with the task of seeking an audience with the tsar to press this demand, but Nicholas refused to receive him.

Both Alexandra and Rasputin became concerned with the food supply problem, but their solution was to transfer the matter to the Ministry of Internal Affairs, and to blame the city governor of Petrograd, Prince Aleksandr Obolensky. To address the food supply question, Alexandra proposed the solution put forth by Rasputin: "that goods, flour, butter, bread, sugar should all be weighed out beforehand in the shops & then each buyer can get his parcel much quicker & there won't be such endless tails."[73] Alexandra, of course, did not realize that this "brilliant" idea not only would have solved nothing but also would have made matters worse. Nicholas too was aware of the seriousness of the food supply problem, but he had no idea how to handle it. He confessed to Alexandra: "I have never been a merchant & simply do not understand those questions about provisions & stores!"[74]

As Petrograd began to show signs of restlessness, the moral decay of the government became more manifest. Stürmer's private secretary, Ivan F. Manasevich-Manuilov, a journalist connected with the Rasputin clique, was arrested for bribery and extortion, on the order of minister of internal affairs Aleksandr Alekseevich Khvostov (again, not to be confused with his scoundrel nephew). In this incident Rasputin's name surfaced again. Stürmer's "dictatorship" was dealt a heavy blow, and Nicholas lost his enthusiasm for the "dictator." After Manasevich-Manuilov's arrest, Stürmer's intrigue against the elder Khvostov intensified. The upright minister of internal affairs had already incurred the disfavor of the tsarina for having former war minister Vladimir Sukhomlinov brought to trial despite her repeated entreaties to release him from prison. On September 16, Aleksandr Alekseevich Khvostov was dismissed, but Protopopov, instead of Stürmer, was named acting minister of internal affairs.


Simbirsk, a small, poor province along the middle Volga, is said to have given the Russian Revolution three gifts: Lenin, Kerensky, and Protopopov. Protopopov, a landowner in Simbirsk, a member of the Octobrist party, and vice chairman of the Duma, was the first representative of civil society (as opposed to a bureaucrat) to head the Ministry of Internal Affairs. Chairman of the newly formed Council of Metal Factory Owners as well as of the Congress of Bankers, he was closely associated with the conservative Petrograd financial and industrial magnates. He harbored a secret desire to assume a governmental post, and to achieve that purpose he did not hesitate to use the influence of the court camarilla. Starting in 1903 he had maintained a secret association with Pyotr Aleksandrovich Badmaev, a Buryati doctor specializing in Tibetan medicine, whose circle Rasputin and other court dignitaries also frequented. Syphilis contracted as a guard cadet initially brought Protopopov to Badmaev. Through this dubious doctor, Protopopov was acquainted with Rasputin. Alexandra actively campaigned for Protopopov's appointment to the position of minister of internal affairs.[75] Unaware of this maneuver, Rodzyanko recommended that Nicholas appoint Protopopov minister of trade and industry. As it became obvious to Nicholas and the court camarilla that Stürmer's "dictatorship" would not resolve the food supply crisis, Protopopov's proposal to mobilize the help of the business community in solving the problem caught their attention. Nicholas was at first hesitant to appoint Protopopov. After all, he was an Octobrist, from the party of Rodzyanko. Referring to Rasputin's advice, he cautioned his wife, "Our Friend's ideas about men are sometimes strange, as you know--so one must be careful especially in nominations of high people."[76] But Alexandra persisted: "Protopopov is a suitable man, Gr[igory] says--had to tell you."[77] Faced with Alexandra's relentless campaign, Nicholas caved and appointed Protopopov acting minister of internal affairs. Protopopov met with Alexandra many times before he had a two-hour audience with the tsar on September 28. Before the meeting the empress had sent Nicholas a list of questions that he should ask Protopopov, reminding her husband to keep the paper in front of him during the audience.[78] Nicholas had completely capitulated to Alexandra, who advised that he should not consider anybody else but Protopopov for the position.[79]

The liberals' initial reaction to Protopopov's appointment was overwhelmingly favorable. But their enthusiasm soon turned into anger as he began to behave more like a representative of Rasputin than a representative of civil society. To the consternation of his liberal colleagues in the Duma, the former vice chairman of the Duma tactlessly appeared before the Duma's Budget Commission in the uniform of the chief of the gendarmerie—a symbol of tsarist oppression. Attempting to recover the confidence of his former colleagues, Protopopov asked Rodzyanko to arrange a meeting with the liberal leaders. To his surprise, he was greeted with sharp rebukes and denunciations at the meeting. Milyukov declared that the liberals could not be friendly with "the person who serves with Stürmer, [the person] who sets Sukhomlinov free, the person who persecutes the liberal press."[80]

Deeply offended, Protopopov never again tried to reach a compromise with the liberals but rather took vengeance through such repressive measures as banning all public gatherings without the presence of police. The liberals could not forgive the defector who had crossed over to the enemy camp, and the Octobrist party formally stripped him of his membership.

With the food supply increasingly in crisis, the chairman of the Special Council for Food Supply sought to extend participation by local self-governments in grain procurement. In response, at the Council of Ministers meeting on October 15 Protopopov attempted to concentrate all food supply matters in the hands of the Ministry of Internal Affairs. Despite objections from the majority of the ministers, Protopopov appealed to Nicholas, who approved Protopopov's proposal to remove liberals from the food supply mechanism. As soon as Protopopov's proposal reached the ears of the liberals, their reaction was quick and unanimous: on October 18 the Budget Commission unanimously adopted a resolution denouncing the proposed policy. The prospect of a liberal offensive on the eve of the opening of the Duma session led Protopopov to waver at the last moment. His assistant, General Pavel Grigorievich Kurlov, director of the Police Department, warned him that if he adjourned the Duma in response to its criticism of his policy, it might provoke a large-scale disturbance. To the disappointment of Rasputin and Alexandra, Protopopov had to withdraw the proposal.[81]

The food crisis, the awakening of the strike movement, and Protopopov's provocation stirred the liberals to action just as a new session of the Duma loomed on November 1. The radical wing of the liberals criticized Milyukov's policy of moderation, demanding the adoption of a slogan that called for the establishment of a responsible ministry and advocating an ultimatum to the government from the Progressive Bloc on the Duma's opening day. Against these radical opponents, Vasily Maklakov argued that the Duma was not capable of creating a responsible ministry, given the fundamental differences on basic issues among the various parties within the Progressive Bloc. "If we want to go all the way, we must talk about more than a responsible ministry," he said, "but we will not talk about that." "Fight we must; the government is rotten," said Vasily Vitalievich Shulgin, the nationalist party head and a monarchist. "But since we are not going to the barricades, we cannot egg others on. The Duma must be a safety valve, letting off steam, not creating it." The only matter they agreed on was their opposition to Stürmer and Protopopov. On this basis, Milyukov and Shulgin set out to prepare a draft declaration, from which any demand for a responsible ministry was conspicuously dropped. This timidity disgusted the Progressists, who withdrew in protest from the Progressive Bloc. The left-wing Kadets threatened to follow. It was necessary for Milyukov to do something to prevent the collapse of the Progressive Bloc by keeping the Kadets within the bloc.[82] The liberals felt the earth was moving underneath their feet; they were sensing the coming of revolution. Later Milyukov admitted: "I thought at that moment, it seems, that revolution was inevitable, and if so it would be necessary to take it in our hands."[83]

On the first of November, Milyukov dropped a bombshell. In a speech he attacked Stürmer, insinuated his rumored intrigue for a separate peace, and ended each paragraph with the rhetorical question: "Is this stupidity or treason?"[84]

The speech caused an immediate sensation, even though Milyukov had no factual evidence to support an accusation of treason. Stürmer himself and the minister of the court, Count Fredericks, requested the stenographic record of Milyukov's speech, but, fearing a libel suit, Rodzyanko removed his entire speech from the official stenographic record.[85] However, the speech was printed clandestinely and widely circulated among the urban population as well as among the soldiers at the front. At a time when scandal was clouding the government, Milyukov's speech fed the population with what they wanted to believe: that the government was treasonous. With this speech, as Russian historian Igor Arkhipov states, the liberals burned the bridge behind them. No constructive dialogue with the tsar's government would be possible after this.[86]

Stürmer suffered the humiliation of having to sit through Milyukov's tirade. Afterward the prime minister, pale with anger, read the government's declaration and then immediately walked out of the hall. Later that day, at a cabinet meeting, Stürmer angrily declared that either the Duma or he had to go. All the ministers except three, however, thought that if one or the other had to go, it should not be the Duma. By this time Nicholas himself was inclined to agree with the majority in the cabinet.

Nicholas hesitated to take strong measures against the Duma in November, despite Milyukov's speech, for two reasons: pressure from military leaders and pressure from his own relatives. After the failure of the "dictatorship" that Alekseev had recommended, Alekseev and his commanding staff at the Stavka sympathized with the Progressive Bloc's demand for a ministry of confidence. Alekseev strongly advised Nicholas against measures to repress the Duma because such measures would lower the morale of the soldiers. It is interesting to note that in November Alekseev allegedly agreed to take part in a plot engineered by Prince Lvov to deport the tsarina to the Crimea.[87] Presumably at Alekseev's urging, minister of war Dmitry Savelievich Shuvaev and navy minister Ivan Konstantinovich Grigorovich appeared at the Duma, imploring the Duma liberals to get down to the practical tasks of national defense.

Nicholas's relatives were greatly disturbed by the meddling of Rasputin and Alexandra in internal politics, which reached its apogee in the autumn of 1916. Because of this, the relationship between the dowager empress and Alexandra became further strained. Standing between two empresses, Nicholas always took the side of his wife.[88] At that time, the dowager empress lived in Kiev. Nicholas's mother had sworn that she would never set foot in Petrograd as long as Alexandra was there. Her son-in-law Grand Duke Aleksandr Mikhailovich (Sandro) was the inspector of the newly created aviation units and lived in Kiev, while his wife, Ksenia, Nicholas's sister, lived with her children in Petrograd. Nicholas's sister Olga managed a hospital in Kiev. The dowager empress, Sandro, and Olga could often be found in the dowager empress's boudoir, discussing the disturbing political situation. They loved Nicky but hated Alix.[89] The dowager empress told former minister of agriculture Aleksandr Krivoshein: "He cannot govern Russia without the support of exceptional men and in opposition to public opinion."[90]

At the end of October Nicholas took a trip to Kiev, where he was confronted by a number of relatives including the dowager empress, Sandro, Grand Duke Pavel, and Grand Duchess Maria Pavlovna the Elder (Miechen). Everyone who saw him in Kiev was struck by the change in his outlook and demeanor. His face had become gaunt, with new wrinkles, and there were dark bags under his eyes. During his talk with his mother, he did not speak much, and when he did, he shifted aimlessly from one topic to another. Aleksei's tutor Pierre Gilliard noticed that the father, who was usually patient with Aleksei, snapped at his son a couple of times.[91] This was the last time the dowager empress saw her son and grandson while Nicholas was the emperor and Aleksei the heir.

After Nicholas returned to Mogilev, Grand Duke Nikolai Mikhailovich (Sandro's older brother, known as Bimbo), an accomplished historian with close connections to the moderate liberals, visited the tsar and handed him a letter advising him, in the strongest terms, to rid himself of Rasputin's influence and to be cautious of his wife's advice.[92] But Nicholas's loyalty to his wife was unbending. He immediately sent this confidential letter to Alexandra. After reading the letter, she told Nicholas to ship this "shady character and a grandson of a Jew" to Siberia. She wrote:

He is the incarnation of all that's evil, all devoted people loath[e] him . . . He & Nikolasha are my greatest enemies in the family, not counting the black women [Militsa and Stana] & Sergei [Sergei Mikhailovich]. He simply could not bear Ania & me. . . . I don't care personal nastiness, but as your chosen wife—they dare not Sweety mine, you must back me up, for your & Baby's [Aleksei's] sake. Had we not got Him [Rasputin]—all would long have been finished, of that I am utterly convinced.[93]

On November 5, 1916, Grand Duke Nikolai Nikolaevich, former commander in chief, visited the tsar at the Stavka and strongly recommended the establishment of a ministry of confidence. During the conversation the emperor did not utter a single word, and at the end he shrugged and ushered his cousin out of the room. The grand duke sensed that the fate of the monarchy was sealed.[94] Two days later, in a conversation with Father Shavelsky, the grand duke declared: "The thing is not about Stürmer, not Protopopov and even not about Rasputin, but about her [the empress], and only about her. Remove her, send her to a nunnery, and the Sovereign will become different, and everything will change. Until then all other measures will be helpless!"[95]

The family persuaded Alexandra's sister Ella, who lived in a convent in Moscow, to come to Tsarskoe Selo to see her sister. Ella told Alix candidly about the mood in Moscow and about the danger posed by Rasputin. Angered by her sister, Alexandra asked Ella to leave the palace immediately. Ella's servants, who were in the middle of unpacking her baggage, were told to repack and carry the baggage back to the carriage. Ella left for Moscow, and the sisters never met again.[96]

Sandro was gravely concerned for his boyhood friend, whom he saw as hopelessly mesmerized by Alix. He took five trips to the Stavka to attempt to talk sense into Nicholas, but whenever they talked about politics, an icy look appeared on the tsar's face. He told Sandro, "I trust no one except my wife." Sandro talked to his brothers Sergei and Bimbo. Sergei was more pessimistic than Sandro; he had completely given up any hope of changing Nicholas's mind.[97]

On November 11, Nicholas's brother Grand Duke Mikhail wrote a letter to Nicholas in an attempt to help him "open his eyes" to the "serious danger not only for you and for the fate of our family, but also for the integrity of the state structure." He went on, "I have come to the conviction, we are standing on a volcano and that a smallest spark, the smallest mistaken step could provoke a catastrophe for you, for us all and for Russia." Though he professed that he had no intention of criticizing anyone, he ventured an opinion: "By removing the most hated persons in whom not only the society but all Russia had clearly no confidence, [replace them] with clean persons, you will find a sure way out of the current situation in which we find ourselves, and you will receive the support for such a decision from the Council of State and from the Duma."[98] He would receive no reply from Nicholas. The tsar did not intend to entertain any advice from his brother, who was, in his view, under the influence of his conniving wife, Natasha Brasova.

Under pressure on multiple fronts, however, Nicholas consented to dismiss Stürmer. On this Alexandra agreed. She wrote to Nicholas: "Since Stürmer plays the role of a red flag in this madhouse, it is better to force him to resign."[99] At this time Nicholas made a rare attempt to free himself of the influence of his domineering wife. He resented receiving a list of candidates from Alexandra and Rasputin, and wrote back: "Only I ask you. Don't let Our Friend [Rasputin] interfere. I assume the responsibility, and therefore, I wish to be free in the selection."[100] On November 9 he dismissed Stürmer and, over the objections of his wife, appointed Aleksandr Fyodorovich Trepov as his successor. Alexandra later told Viktoria Fyodorovna (Ducky), Kirill's wife: "The Sovereign is weak-willed. Everyone puts pressure on him. I now take upon myself governing in my hands."[101]

The Progressive Bloc greeted Stürmer's downfall as a victory. Milyukov's tactics had worked. Without making any constitutional demands, as the Progressists and the radical Kadets had insisted, Milyukov restored the prestige of the Progressive Bloc as a leading center of the opposition to the government. After his speech on November 1, Milyukov's popularity reached its zenith. Moisei Sergeevich Adzhemov, a member of the Kadets, noted, "I am convinced that by the new year of 1917, there will be a triumphant funeral of autocracy." But there were voices of caution and apprehension. An Octobrist, Colonel Boris Aleksandrovich Engelgardt, warned that Milyukov's speech had added fuel to the fire, inciting the masses to revolution.[102]

Trepov, who had been minister of transport prior to his appointment to the premiership, was a conservative but honest bureaucrat, not connected with the Rasputin clique. Unlike his predecessors, Trepov saw the necessity of cooperating with the Duma and was interested in establishing in the Duma a new right-wing majority willing to work with the government. He attempted to lure the conservative elements of the Progressive Bloc into this majority, thus crippling the strength of the liberal opposition. To achieve this, he was prepared to sacrifice Protopopov, who by this time had become a bête noir for the liberals. Trepov succeeded in gaining the tsar's approval of Protopopov's dismissal. He also made an unsuccessful attempt to bribe Rasputin to leave the capital.[103]

The liberals heaped verbal scorn on Protopopov, but they were careful not to criticize Trepov and his government. The most sensational attack on the government, however, came from totally unexpected quarters. On November 19, the right-wing deputy Vladimir Mitrofanovich Purishkevich, a founder of the reactionary Union of the Russian People and a staunch monarchist, delivered an impassioned speech in the Duma before a hushed audience in which he attacked the "dark forces," led by "Grisha Rasputin," that had infiltrated the court and the government and that promoted the interests of the enemy, and he termed the perennial appointments and dismissals of the ministers "ministerial leapfrog." The liberals welcomed this speech enthusiastically. "Better late than never," commented Milyukov.

"Purishkevich opened his eyes, admittedly belatedly, but nonetheless he opened his eyes."[104]

Purishkevich's speech represented the opinion of the conservative element of the country, which, because of its firm belief in the monarchy, was all the more disturbed by Rasputin's influence and Alexandra's meddling. On November 26, the State Council, the usually conservative upper house, known as "the gravedigger" for its tendency to bury the Duma's legislative initiatives, passed a resolution urging Nicholas to remove the "dark forces" from the government. The Council of the United Nobility, which held its congress from November 27 through December 1, 1916, also passed a resolution attacking the "dark forces" and calling for the establishment of a government that could cooperate with the legislative chambers.[105] This was a stunning change of opinion among the conservatives, considering that little more than a year earlier the Council of the United Nobility had expressed its dissatisfaction with the government's flirtation with the Duma.[106]

At the end of November, a family gathering took place in Grand Duke Andrei's house. Grand Duke Pavel, as doyen of the family, was entrusted with the task of persuading the tsar to change his policy. Nicholas received Pavel on December 3, but Pavel's plea to give the nation a constitution, or at least a ministry of confidence, fell on deaf ears. "What you ask is impossible," Nicholas declared. "The day of my coronation I took my oath to the Absolute Power. I must leave this oath intact to my son."[107]

Although Nicholas had occasionally showed flickers of independence from his wife, once Alexandra began her relentless letter-writing campaigns, he easily gave in. Alexandra furiously fought to keep Protopopov, telling Nicholas to honor her wish "for Baby's sake." "Darling, remember that it does not lie in the man, Protopopov, or x.y.z.," she continued, "but it's the question of monarchy & your prestige now, which must not be shattered ... [by] the Duma."[108] She invoked God's authority: "The Holy Virgin guards you & Gr[igory] prays for you & we do all so hard."[109] Then on the following day, she bombarded her husband with admonitions: "Be the master, listen to your staunch Wify & our Friend believe us. Look at Kalinin [Protopopov] & Trepov's face—clearly one sees the difference—black & white, let your soul read rightly." And four days later: "Lovy, look at their faces—Trepov & Protopopov—can one clearly see the latter's cleaner, honester & more true. You *know* you are right, keep up your head, order Trepov to work with him—he dare not be against your order—bang on the table. Lovy, do you want me to come for a day to give you courage and firmness? Be the *Master*."[110] As for Rasputin's influence, Alexandra wrote:

> Oh, my dear, I pray to God so passionately to convince you that in Him [Rasputin] lies our salvation. If He weren't here, I don't know what would become of us. He is saving us with His prayers and His wise advice. . . . He [Rasputin] lives for you and for Russia. We must hand to the Baby [Aleksei] a strong country and cannot be weak for his sake; otherwise, it will be much more difficult for him to reign.

She encouraged her wavering husband: "Be like Peter the Great, Ivan the Terrible, and Emperor Paul," giving examples of monarchs who used cruel punishments on their subjects. She expressed intense anger against the enemies of autocracy, suggesting that the tsar should exile opponents such as Milyukov, Lvov, Guchkov, and Polivanov to Siberia and hang Trepov for compromising with the Duma.[111] These outbursts were enough to make the weak-willed sovereign capitulate. Though it was clear that the empress was unhinged, the tsar went along with her. Faced with his wife's furious bombardments, Nicholas decided to keep Protopopov.

To Trepov's credit, he had the courage to confront Nicholas. He requested that the tsar dismiss Protopopov, and he made this an indispensable condition of serving as the chairman of the Council of Ministers.

Met with the emperor's rejection of his request, he asked the tsar to accept his resignation. Nicholas replied in an imperious tone: "Aleksandr Fyodorovich, I order you to carry out your duties with the colleagues I have thought fit to give you." Trepov left in anger, but he did not resign.[112]

Those who dared to tell the tsar to remove Rasputin were one by one exiled. Sofia Nikolaevna Vasilchkova, wife of a state councilor, Boris Aleksandrovich Vasilchkov, was banished after she wrote the empress about the pernicious influence of Rasputin. Aleksandr Arkadievich Kaufman, in charge of the Red Cross at the Stavka, was dismissed and exiled from the Stavka. Father Shavelsky, the protopresbyter who earned the ire of the empress for repeatedly expressing his views on Rasputin, almost resigned. He was dissuaded only by the tsar's physician, Dr. Sergei Petrovich Fyodorov.[113]

In the middle of November, after finishing his report to the emperor, Father Shavelsky was coming down the stairs in the Stavka headquarters. Grand Duke Dmitry Pavlovich encountered him on a landing. Shavelsky told him about his talk with the tsar on the subject of Rasputin, concluding by saying, "As you see, Your Highness, I did my duty, now it is your turn." "Listen," Dmitry mysteriously answered. "Perhaps, I will fulfill my duty."[114]

Faced with mounting criticism, Protopopov attempted to muzzle the liberals by closing down all the proposed meetings of the Union of Towns and the Union of Zemstvos. He also banned the meetings planned by civic organizations, such as associations of pediatricians, the polytechnical society, dental school assistants, and the historical circle of Shanyavsky People's University.[115] This was tantamount to a declaration of war against all segments of society. On December 16, the last day of the Duma session before Christmas recess, Milyukov stated:

> Our goal has not been fulfilled, and this must loudly be admitted. To the same degree that the faith in the popular representation is being lost, other forces, gentlemen, are entering into action. We

are now experiencing a terrible moment. Before our very eyes, the liberal struggle is getting beyond the framework of strict legality and like in 1905 illegal forces are again emerging. The atmosphere is full of electricity. One can feel in the air the approach of thunder. No one knows, gentlemen, where and when lightning will strike.[116]

Sure enough, several hours after this speech, lightning struck at last.

CHAPTER 4

# The Bullet That Killed Rasputin

A t the end of the night on December 16–17, at Yusupov Palace on the Moika River in Petrograd, Rasputin lay dead. That was the prelude to revolution.

Prince Feliks Feliksovich Yusupov and a right-wing Duma deputy, Vladimir Purishkevich, had led the conspiracy to murder Rasputin. Yusupov was the husband of Nicholas's niece Irina, and Purishkevich was the head of a monarchist party, the Union of the Russian People. They were joined by Grand Duke Dmitry, Nicholas's first cousin. All believed that Rasputin's pernicious influence on the imperial couple was endangering the monarchy. As noted in Chapter 3, Purishkevich had delivered a speech at the Fourth Duma on November 19 denouncing the "dark forces" led by Rasputin, who he claimed was working for German interests. On that same day, Yusupov visited Purishkevich, and the plot to assassinate Rasputin was hatched, with Lieutenant Sergei Mikhailovich Sukhotin, an officer of the Preobrazhensky Regiment, and a Polish doctor, Dr. Stanislav Lazovert, eventually joining the conspiracy.[1]

The details of Rasputin's assassination continue to fascinate and intrigue many. The most often told story is the following: Yusupov invited

Rasputin to Yusupov Palace on the excuse that his wife wanted to see him. In the cellar, while upstairs a gramophone was playing "Yankee Doodle Dandy," which Yusupov falsely claimed was for the entertainment of his wife's guests, Yusupov offered Rasputin some poisoned cakes and wine, which, surprisingly, had no effect. Getting nervous, he made an excuse to go upstairs to consult his fellow conspirators. Yusupov then took Dmitry's revolver and went downstairs, and while Rasputin was praying in front of an icon, he shot him in the back. Rasputin fell on the bearskin rug, with blood spreading on the rug. Dr. Lazovert examined the body and declared him dead. The conspirators went upstairs and congratulated themselves for the patriotic action they had performed. But when Yusupov went downstairs to check on the corpse, Rasputin opened his eyes, leapt up, and attacked Yusupov with a wild roar. Yusupov managed to free himself and called for help. Purishkevich rushed downstairs to see the wounded Rasputin crawling out the door into the snow-covered courtyard, leaving a trail of blood behind him. Purishkevich caught up and fired two shots, killing him. The conspirators wrapped the dead body with linen, shoved it into an automobile, drove to Petrovsky Bridge, and threw the body into the icy Little Nevka River.[2]

This is the story told by Feliks Yusupov. But this story has been disputed by others, and much ink has been spilled over questions surrounding the assassination. Why didn't the poison work? Who shot Rasputin and where? Was he still alive when he was thrown into the river? What role did an English intelligence officer play in the assassination? According to Rasputin's biographer Douglas Smith, "What really happened at the Yusupov home on 17 December will never be known. All that can be said is that Rasputin was killed by three bullet shots, one delivered directly into his forehead at extremely close range."[3]

Far more important than the details of the assassination is its impact. The assassination of Rasputin was a desperate attempt by the monarchists to save the dying monarchy, but as poet Aleksandr Blok wrote: "The bullet that killed

Rasputin fell on the very heart of the reigning dynasty." As an astute contemporary witness, Crimean police chief Aleksandr Ivanovich Spiridovich, further observed, that bullet not only was the fatal shot that killed the tsar, his family, and many members of the dynasty but also dealt the coup de grâce to the entire political and social structure of Imperial Russia.[4]

On December 17, Tsar Nicholas II was at Mogilev. He attended an important conference to discuss the military operations in the forthcoming spring 1917 offensive. The conference was presided over by the acting chief of staff, General Vasily Iosifovich Gurko, in place of General Mikhail Alekseev, who had fallen ill with uremia and taken a leave of absence to treat his illness in Sevastopol, in the Crimea. After breakfast with the front commanders Aleksei Brusilov, Aleksei Evert, and Nikolai Ruzsky and war minister Mikhail Alekseevich Belyaev, the tsar took his usual drive and walk, following which he returned for tea. It was then that he received the disturbing news from his wife. "We are sitting together—can imagine our feelings—thoughts—our Friend has disappeared." She recounted that Rasputin had been invited by Feliks Yusupov to meet his wife, Irina. "This night big scandal at Yusupov's house—big meeting, Dmitri, Purishkevitch etc. All drunk, the Police heard shots, Purishkevitch ran out screaming to the Police that our Friend was killed." She begged Nicholas to come home quickly, asking to have the palace commandant, General Vladimir Voeikov, arrange the train immediately.[5]

Yet Nicholas did not appear to be in a hurry to return to Tsarskoe Selo to comfort his wife in her distress. Nicholas's diary for December 17 reveals no information regarding Rasputin's disappearance, simply noting, "After tea a meeting on military matters took place at the staff until dinner and then from 9 to 12½ hours."[6] After learning during that meeting that no train was available that day, Nicholas sent a telegram to the empress after eight o'clock that evening: "Voeikov could not arrange a train today. Ask Kalinin [Protopopov] to help."[7] This curt response was almost tantamount to saying: *I can't help you. If you need help, ask Protopopov.*

News of Rasputin's assassination had already reached a wide circle of the officers at the Stavka. The commander of the gendarme corps in Tsarskoe Selo, Count Dmitry Nikolaevich Tatishchev, traveled to Mogilev on December 18 to report to the tsar about the assassination.[8] The officers at the Stavka greeted the news with delight, and some celebrated with champagne. Even among the tsar's entourage, no one grieved the disappearance of Rasputin, though everyone wondered about the consequences of this event.[9]

In Tsarskoe Selo, the distraught empress had a prayer service in the palace that night. Anna Vyrubova and her friend Lili Dehn rushed to the palace and sat until midnight with the empress and her oldest daughter, Olga. All slept together in one room that night, awaiting the telephone call from Protopopov.[10]

On the following day, the emperor went about business at hand. He received the report of General Aleksandr Lukomsky, the new quartermaster, who had taken over the position vacated by his predecessor, General Mikhail Pustovoitenko. Then, after taking a meeting with General Gurko, he cut the military conference short to head back to Tsarskoe Selo. Before his 4:30 p.m. departure, he walked with Gurko on the train platform, talking of military matters, but the emperor did not discuss Rasputin's murder. As the train passed through Orsha, Nicholas received the empress's telegram informing him that Yusupov and Grand Duke Dmitry were now detained in the capital. Only then did he send this telegram to the empress: "Anguished and horrified. Prayers [and] thoughts together. Arrive tomorrow at 5."[11] Then he added: "Great frost. Sitting ended at 4."

It is difficult to know how Nicholas really reacted to Rasputin's death. In his diary on December 18 Nicholas merely wrote, "The day was sunny with 17 degrees below zero. I read all the time in the wagon," and noted, "I slept well." The contemporary reader can't help but react with surprise: he slept well? After the news of the disappearance of the holy man he and his wife had depended on? Would a man "anguished and horrified" add immediately a comment on frost and what time a meeting had ended?

Yet sure enough, throughout the railway journey he maintained his usual calm, without showing any emotions. Voeikov, the only person whom the tsar talked to about Rasputin's death, had the impression that Nicholas was actually relieved by the disappearance of Rasputin from his life.[12]

Before Nicholas's arrival at the palace, the empress still had no information about Rasputin's whereabouts and clung to the hope that he might still have survived. Fearing for the life of Vyrubova, she ordered her confidant to move into the palace, giving Vyrubova's house over to Dehn.[13] Dehn was not superstitious, nor a devotee of Rasputin, but when she slept in Anna's bedroom, Rasputin's icon fell with a thud. She dreamed of thousands of feet marching toward the palace, only to find upon waking that the place was quiet, with a tight police presence.[14]

On December 19, Rasputin's body was finally found in the icy river.[15] The news was sent to the palace. At 1:50 p.m. Alexandra cabled Nicholas: "They found [Rasputin's body] in the water."[16] The finality of the tragedy now dawned on Alexandra. She, Vyrubova, Dehn, and the daughters wept.[17]

The emperor's train finally pulled into Tsarskoe Selo station at 6 p.m. on December 19. The empress and the couple's daughters had been waiting for his arrival.[18]

Now that Rasputin's corpse had been found, the question arose: where should the body of the controversial holy man be buried? The palace commandant, Voeikov, strongly argued that Rasputin's body should be buried in his native village, Pokrovskoe. To bury him in Tsarskoe Selo would lead to a scandal, he feared, and his grave would surely be defaced. The farther from the imperial palace Rasputin's body could be laid to rest, the better. Protopopov initially agreed with Voeikov, but when Voeikov brought this suggestion to Vyrubova, the empress's confidant vehemently objected. He had to be buried in Tsarskoe Selo. Protopopov correctly guessed that Vyrubova's and Alexandra's wishes were in alignment, and he conveniently changed his mind. He warned the empress only that if they transported Rasputin's body via the railway, the train would encounter demonstrations on the way.[19]

After midnight, the empress summoned Voeikov to debate the matter further. In his audience with the empress, Voeikov recommended that Rasputin be buried in his native village, as this had been his wish. This was an impromptu lie, and the empress knew that "our Friend" had wished for nothing of the sort. When Voeikov expressed his fear that Rasputin's grave in Tsarskoe Selo would become a magnet for anti-Rasputin crowds, Alexandra became angry, saying that vandalizing Rasputin's grave would be sacrilege.[20] After Voeikov left, the empress decided that Rasputin should be buried in Tsarskoe Selo on December 21, not inside the imperial compound, but just outside, in the village of Aleksandrovka, where Vyrubova was building a church. Even Alexandra did not dare bury him inside the park that belonged to the imperial household. Rasputin's family was not consulted about the burial, and Nicholas did not interfere. Once he learned about the burial arrangements, Voeikov pleaded with Nicholas not to attend the burial. Nicholas remained silent.[21] As usual, this was a sign that he disagreed. Of course, Alexandra took it for granted that Nicholas would attend the burial, and Nicholas did not dare to defy her wishes.

On December 21, a plain coffin with a simple cross without any inscription was laid in the grave at 8 a.m.[22] According to Anna Vyrubova, an icon from Novgorod with the signatures of Alexandra, Vyrubova, and the grand duchesses was laid on the chest of the deceased, but it may be that Vyrubova fabricated the story.[23] Vyrubova and Dehn arrived first, and at 9 a.m., two motorcars carrying the imperial family arrived (except Aleksei, who stayed behind in the palace). Nicholas, Alexandra, and their four daughters came to the grave. Alexandra was carrying a bouquet of white flowers. She was pale but composed until she saw the coffin, and then tears began to fall. Father Aleksandr Vasiliev of the imperial court chapel read a brief sermon, blessing the soul of the deceased.[24] The empress and the daughters each tossed flowers into the grave. Then Nicholas and Alexandra tossed a handful of earth into the grave. No one from Nicholas's entourage joined the ceremony. Rasputin's family was not invited. The ceremony was over within an hour.[25]



The assassination of Rasputin did not eradicate the ills of the Russian government. In Vasily Shulgin's words, "What was the sense of killing the snake after it had stung?"[26]

Although the authorities forbade newspapers from printing any mention of the assassination, the news spread quickly and widely. People kissed each other in the streets and burned candles in Kazan Cathedral to celebrate the death of the "holy devil." People queuing for bakeries and butcher shops rejoiced, saying, "A dog's death for a dog!"[27] Officers and soldiers embraced each other, like an Easter celebration. A soldier at the front, who later became a Bolshevik, reminisced that the soldiers greeted Rasputin's murder with great joy, and that Purishkevich, his murderer, became a hero.[28] Professor Yury Vladimirovich Lomonosov, who was traveling on assignment for the Ministry of Transport, reported that soldiers and officers who came across Purishkevich in the train greeted him with shouts of "hurrah" and thanked him for the assassination.[29] This sentiment was not universal, however. Aleksei's tutor, Pierre Gilliard, noted: "The untutored masses cared nothing about him. . . . Many considered his death an act of vengeance on the part of the courtiers who were jealous of their privileges. 'The first time that one of ourselves gets to the Czar, he is killed by the courtiers,' they said."[30]

The tsar and tsarina now barricaded themselves within their small world and increasingly became more suspicious of and hostile to the outside world.[31] After Rasputin's murder, Nicholas seemed tired both physically and mentally, while the grieving empress was clearly unwell. Her visits to the Znamenie chapel became more frequent, and she spent many hours praying. The empress stopped visiting the hospital that previously had been so important to her. Olga and Tatiana continued to go to the infirmary, dutifully performing ordinary nurses' chores in spite of their grief.[32] Olga confessed to their head nurse, Valentina Chebotareva: "Perhaps, he had to be killed, but not that horribly. But this is a family matter and I should not talk about it. It is a shame to recognize that the relatives . . ." It is not clear whether Olga felt shame that a relative was involved in the murder or felt shame because of how the relatives were reacting to the murder.[33] Olga complained that she could no longer talk freely on the phone, since it was tapped. Censorship had now expanded to the children of the imperial family.[34] As for the empress, despite her grief, Rasputin's murder hardened her resolve to stand firm against her detractors. "I have suffered enough," she confided to Chebotareva. "I cannot stand any more. I have to grab the bull by the horn."[35]

Among the imperial family's entourage the mood grew dire. Count Fredericks confessed that he might as well finish his life by taking a dose of poison. Admiral Konstantin Dmitrievich Nilov had already lost faith in the fate of the monarchy, repeating within his close circles in his usual drunken stupor, "There will be a revolution, and they will hang us all, and I don't care which lamp post I will be hanged on." Nilov warned Nicholas about plots for a palace coup, but Nicholas did not pay any attention to those rumors.[36] The admiral even suggested that the tsar should send the empress away. Nicholas rejected this recommendation, saying that the empress had no one to protect her except him and he would never abandon her under any circumstances.[37] Only the palace commandant, Voeikov, remained unperturbed, placing total confidence in Protopopov's assurance that all precautions were being taken to prevent disturbances.[38]

The reaction of Nicholas's relatives to the assassination was mixed. Many rejoiced. The tsar's sister Ksenia wrote: "Thank God that he's been killed." Grand Duke Dmitry's sister Maria Pavlovna the Younger felt pride in the brave action of her brother. Ella, Alexandra's sister, sent a telegram to Yusupov's mother, blessing her son's action. She wrote to Maria Pavlovna the Younger that she was thrilled with Rasputin's murder, and that "Providence had deigned to select her brother and Feliks." Grand Duke Nikolai Mikhailovich, in whom Yusupov confided and with whom he corresponded after he was banished, wrote that he was sorry that they did not complete the extermination operation they had started.[39] Nicholas's mother, the dowager empress, thanked the Lord for removing Rasputin, but she was upset that a member of the imperial family was involved in the murder. Nicholas's sister Olga wrote in her memoirs: "It was a vile conspiracy. There was just nothing heroic about Rasputin's murder." Grand Duke Aleksandr (Sandro) was concerned that his son-in-law and his cousin were involved in the murder, and immediately left Kiev for Petrograd.[40] On the whole, the relatives became apprehensive that Rasputin's violent death would be a prelude to something more catastrophic. Fearing that Nicholas's stubborn refusal to adopt reforms would bring the entire dynasty to its doom, they intensified their efforts to change his mind. But the more they talked about reform, the wider the gulf became separating the imperial couple from Nicholas's relatives.

The involvement of Grand Duke Dmitry in the assassination drew the rest of the imperial family together. Dmitry's father, Grand Duke Pavel, asked his son point-blank if he was involved in the murder. Dmitry swore on the name of his dead mother and the icon that he had no blood on his hands. That may technically have been true: Dmitry did not pull the trigger. But his presence at the assassination scene and his participation in the plot were beyond doubt. Although Purishkevich, taking advantage of immunity as a Duma member, escaped to the front and Yusupov retired to his private estate, Grand Duke Dmitry was placed under house arrest on December 18 at the tsarina's command. Many of the grand dukes and grand duchesses considered this action illegal, since she had no authority to issue such an order. Only the tsar could order the arrest of a member of the imperial family. On the following day, Grand Duke Pavel sought an audience with Nicholas and asked what authority Alexandra had to arrest his son. Nicholas lamely supported his wife and answered that it had been his order. He rejected his uncle's plea to free Dmitry while the preliminary investigation was under way.[41]

On December 21, the day Rasputin was buried, a number of relatives met at the home of Grand Duke Andrei. Miechen, Pavel, Kirill, Boris, and Sandro attended. They decided to send Sandro to Nicholas with a request to release Dmitry. When he had his audience with the emperor, Sandro pleaded with him to treat Yusupov and Dmitry with leniency and to consider them as misguided youths. Nicholas responded: "A nice speech, Sandro. But are you aware that nobody has the right to kill, be it a grand duke or a peasant?"[42]

Adamantly rejecting the pleas of his relatives, Nicholas on December 23 ordered that Dmitry be deported to Persia to serve in the army. The grand duke was to leave immediately on that day on a special train, and no one, not even his father and sister, was to be allowed to see him off at the station. Miechen, Kirill, Ducky (Kirill's wife), and Sandro got together at Andrei's house to discuss how to head off Dmitry's exile. They contacted Mikhail Rodzyanko, but the chairman of the Duma remained powerless. Finally, they reluctantly concluded that there was nothing they could do.

It did not take long for Nicholas and Alexandra to be reminded of Rasputin's special power over their family. On December 28, Aleksei bruised his hand while playing. He was in excruciating pain and nothing could stop his bleeding. Alexandra brought Rasputin's blue shirt and laid it under Aleksei's pillow, asking the suffering boy to think of the deceased holy man before he fell asleep. When Aleksei awoke in the morning, he felt much better. The empress, of course, attributed this to the influence of her "Friend."[43] Rasputin's hold over Alexandra continued even after his death.

On December 29, Grand Duke Nikolai Mikhailovich (Bimbo) confided to Shulgin and Mikhail Ivanovich Tereshchenko (vice chairman of the Central War Industries Committee) about his wish to "finish off

Aleksandra Fyodorovna and Protopopov. The idea of murdering them had not yet taken a definite form, but it was a logical necessity; otherwise, things would become worse than they are."[44] According to Princess Cantacuzene, a close observer of aristocratic circles, some were openly hoping that Vyrubova, Protopopov, and the empress herself would be assassinated as well; otherwise a bloody revolution would be inevitable.[45] The life of the empress was threatened not by bomb-throwing terrorists but by relatives of her husband.

Nicholas's isolation from his family deepened as they protested his punishment of Dmitry. The relatives gathered at Vladimir Palace (Miechen's palace) on December 29 and presented a joint petition to the emperor, signed by sixteen members of the family, requesting his permission to transfer Dmitry to a place with a better climate given his bad health.[46] In the eyes of Nicholas's relatives, the imperial couple were acting out of vengeance. Dmitry's motives were "pure" and "patriotic," but he was deported "brutally" against the wishes of most of his relatives. On December 31, Nicholas rejected this petition: "No one is given the right to be involved in a murder. . . . I am surprised that you addressed such a petition to me."[47] This was a slap in the face, and it further solidified the relatives' hostility toward Alexandra and their disappointment with Nicholas, who was under the thumb of his vengeful wife.

On the last day of 1916, Nicholas and the daughters went to an evening prayer service. Olga wrote in her diary: "Lord, save us and have mercy on us in 1917, the new year."[48] Nicholas wrote in his diary: "I prayed fervently that the Lord may have mercy on Russia."[49]

Those family members who dared to criticize the tsar and tsarina, even privately, were now exiled from Petrograd. Grand Duchess Maria Pavlovna the Younger, a sister of Dmitry and a daughter of Pavel, was put under house arrest because she had dared to bid her brother farewell at the station. On December 31, Bimbo was punished by expulsion from the capital for speaking out against the tsarina privately at a yacht club.[50] At the beginning of January, Kirill was banished from the capital to Murmansk. Colonel Aleksandr Nikolaevich Linevich, a close friend of Grand Duke Andrei, was summoned by the tsar and asked about the "antigovernment activities" of his friend. Nicholas stated: "It is a pity that he talks too much and speaks ill of me. . . . What on earth does he have against me? It seems that I have paid sufficient attention to him."[51] In a few days Andrei left for Kislovodsk. The tsar's relatives saw in these acts the intrigue of the tsarina—the "Hesse woman," as Nikolai Mikhailovich called her, a foreigner and an intruder. "The emperor's orders," writes Nikolai Mikhailovich, "remind me of the vulgar Florentine nobles in the epoch of the Borgias and the Medicis."[52]

On January 2, Sandro wrote a letter to his brother Bimbo. He said that Nicholas wanted to banish him from Kiev. The only hope was the intervention of the tsar's mother.[53] Dowager Empress Maria Fyodorova wrote in her diary: "Very painful situation in the capital. Only God can open the eyes of poor Niki so that he will no longer follow her advice. If that does not happen, all this will bring us to unhappiness."[54] Nevertheless, the members of the Vladimirovich clan were exiled. As noted earlier, Kirill was sent to Murmansk, Andrei to Kislovodsk; their brother Boris was sent to the Caucasus, and their mother, Miechen, left the capital.[55]

Yet in spite of this stern reaction toward his family, Nicholas's passivity in dealing with the assassins revealed the hollowness of his autocratic power. After the murder, Aleksei asked his father, "Papa, surely you will give them a good punishing? The man who killed Stolypin was hanged for what he did!" Nicholas did not reply. Purishkevich left for the front, Yusupov was exiled to his estate, and Dmitry was sent to the army in Persia, but the investigation was suspended. No one was found guilty, and none of the murderers was punished. As Rasputin's biographer puts it, "Rasputin's killers had gotten away with murder. The lesson was easy for every Russian to draw: the state did not dare touch the perpetrators."[56] Politically, it would have been impossible for Nicholas to complete the investigations and try the murderers in open court. That would have exposed the poison that penetrated deeply into the dynasty, irrevocably damaging the emperor and the empress.

The failure to talk sense into the tsar led some of the grand dukes to rest their hopes on the moderate wing of the liberal movement. After Rasputin's assassination, the grand dukes frequently met with Rodzyanko. Nicholas's relatives were radicalized enough to see that a compromise with the Duma and the establishment of a ministry of confidence was the only way to fend off the approaching storm. Some even discussed the possibility of a palace coup. According to Maurice Paléologue, the French ambassador to Russia, at a party given by the industrialist Aleksandr Nikolaevich Bogdanov on December 22, Grand Duke Gavriil Konstantinovich promised the other industrialists present that he would talk with his relatives about the possibility of removing Nicholas and establishing a regency. Presumably, Grand Dukes Kirill, Boris, and Andrei wanted to establish a regency under Grand Duke Nikolai Nikolaevich.[57] Miechen suggested to Rodzyanko that the tsarina should be forcibly removed. As the historian Valentin Dyakin notes, the grand dukes' "conspiracy" is more indicative of their despair than of a serious plan.[58] "They want the Duma to put the match to the powder," commented a moderate Kadet, Vasily Maklakov. "In other words, they are expecting of us what we are expecting of them."[59] Clearly, the majority of Nicholas's relatives had already deserted him before the revolution, although they themselves did not have the courage to remove the emperor and the empress.

Fears of revolution were rife. On January 3, 1917, Rodzyanko was unexpectedly visited by Grand Duke Mikhail. That followed a visit the grand duke had made to Miechen and her two sons, Grand Dukes Andrei and Boris, before the latter two were exiled, so it is not difficult to guess that they may have encouraged Mikhail to make contact.[60] The grand duke asked Rodzyanko if there would be a revolution. The Duma chairman responded that people would not start a revolution as long as the war continued, but the danger came from the empress and the court camarilla, who were allegedly plotting a separate peace. "Should such rumors be confirmed," Rodzyanko explained, "a most terrible revolution will break out, and will sweep away the Throne, the dynasty, all of you and us too." The only way to avoid this catastrophe would be, first, to replace the current government with a ministry of confidence—that is, maintain the structure of the government as it was, but change many of the personnel. Second, the empress must go. Mikhail asked Rodzyanko if a responsible ministry—in essence, a constitutional monarchy, involving changes to the Fundamental Laws—would be necessary. Not yet, the Duma chairman answered, only a ministry of confidence, headed by someone who enjoyed the confidence of the nation. Mikhail asked the Duma chairman if he would head such a government. Rodzyanko said that he would, on the condition that the empress should be removed from all state affairs. Rodzyanko asked the grand duke to seek an audience with the tsar and urge him to make political concessions and to stop the empress's interference in politics.[61]

On January 10, Grand Duke Pavel invited the French ambassador, Paléologue, to his home at Tsarskoe Selo. The grand duke told the ambassador about the desperate situation of the tsar, wholly under the influence of the empress and totally rejecting any advice from his relatives. On the train journey back to Petrograd, the ambassador discussed with a "Madam P." the conversation he had had with the grand duke. Madam P. told him: "The tragedy now on its way will be not only a dynastic crisis but a terrible revolution: we can't escape it." Paléologue reminded Madam P. about the blindness of Louis XVI and Marie Antoinette, and quoted Mirabeau's prophecy in September 1789: "All is lost. The King and Queen will perish. The people will batter their corpses!"[62]

On February 6, Grand Duke Mikhail had a meeting with General Aleksei Brusilov. Mikhail had been serving as commander of the Guards Cavalry Corps under Brusilov, but in January he was appointed inspector general of cavalry, and he came to see Brusilov to bid him farewell.[63]

Brusilov lamented the dire situation in Russia, which desperately called for political reform. The general asked the grand duke to convey this view to the tsar. Mikhail expressed his complete agreement with the general about the need for domestic reform, and promised to convey his view to his brother, but he confessed that he had no influence whatever on the tsar, since "he [the tsar] finds himself under such influence and pressure that no one is in a position to overcome it."[64]

Sandro returned to Petrograd following a long talk with the dowager empress, and after meeting with Mikhail, Sandro agreed to deliver a plea for reform to Nicholas directly. On February 4, Sandro wrote a letter to Nicholas stating: "Russia without the tsar cannot exist, but you must understand that the tsar alone cannot administer such a state as Russia." It would be necessary to have a government that enjoyed the confidence of the Duma. He did not advocate a responsible ministry, but he did recommend a ministry of confidence.[65]

On February 10, Nicholas invited Sandro to breakfast with his children, but the empress refused to join them until the emperor brought Sandro to the empress's mauve bedroom. The grand duke found Alexandra lying on her bed in a white lace peignoir. Nicholas sat at the end of the bed. Alexandra's face was serious and hostile, as if she were waiting for an attack. The grand duke told them that although he himself was an enemy of the parliamentary system, he could see no other alternative than the formation of a ministry acceptable to the Duma to relieve the tension in the country. The empress, smirking cynically, interjected: "What you are talking about makes me laugh! Nicky is an autocrat! How could he share his God-given right with anyone else?" Sandro responded: "Your husband ceased to be the autocrat on October 17, 1905," referring to Nicholas's issuance of the October Manifesto. "You should have thought then about his 'God-given right.' It is, alas, now too late. Perhaps, in two months everything would be overturned and there might be nothing left that would remind us of the autocrats sitting on the throne of our ancestors." Nicholas said nothing, simply sitting at the end of the bed and smoking. In desperation, Sandro raised his voice at Alexandra: "I see you are ready to perish with your husband. But don't forget us. Must we all suffer from your blind foolishness? You don't have the right to bring your relatives along to the abyss." The grand duke stood up and kissed her hand, but she did not reciprocate, and the grand duke left the room. The next day Sandro and Mikhail tried again to sway Nicholas in a meeting together, but it was a waste of time.[66] Sandro wrote a letter to his brother Bimbo: "Nothing good will come from Tsarskoe Selo. The question is this: either to sit on hands and wait for the ruin and shame of Russia, or to save Russia, taking heroic measures."[67] What Sandro meant by "heroic measures" is not clear, but the Mikhailovich clan was clearly ready to take drastic action to save the dynasty.

On February 14, when the Duma resumed its session, Feliks Yusupov wrote a letter to Bimbo from the estate to which he had been banished: "How could they not understand that if what has to be done cannot come from the top, then it will come from below, which will surely spill so much innocent blood." He suggested that "if it is not too late," a resolute measure should be taken: while the emperor was traveling to the Stavka, Bimbo should, with the help of General Alekseev or General Gurko, arrest Protopopov and Ivan Shcheglovitov, and banish the empress and Anna Vyrubova to Livadia. "Only such a measure," the murderer of Rasputin wrote, "could save the situation."[68] It should be kept in mind that Yusupov mentioned Alekseev and Gurko as possible participants in the conspiracy, although it is unlikely that Yusupov, in exile, could have been in contact with the generals. And he had no idea that Prince Georgy Lvov and Aleksandr Guchkov were seriously engaged in a conspiracy of their own, as we shall see.

On February 17, the dowager empress wrote a letter to Nicholas and sent it to the Stavka in Mogilev, not to Tsarskoe Selo, so that the letter could not be intercepted by Alexandra via Protopopov. She implored

Nicholas, as the other relatives did, to "lighten Dmitry's lot, not letting him go to Persia." She lamented: "This is not like you with your good heart to behave like this. This has pained me so much."[69] We do not know if Nicholas responded to his mother's letter, but it is likely that he ignored it.

If Nicholas was relieved by the disappearance of Rasputin, his relatives' interference on behalf of the murderer and their outcry seemed only to drive the imperial couple even closer together. Shutting out the world, Nicholas and Alexandra secluded themselves in their private retreat, frightened by a mystical premonition that they were doomed, but unable and unwilling to do anything to escape this fate.

While Nicholas and Alexandra retreated into their cocoon in Tsarskoe Selo, pornographic caricatures of Alexandra's alleged dalliance with Rasputin were circulating widely, creating a lucrative underground market, reminiscent of the spread of pornographic literature and illustrations about Marie Antoinette on the eve of the French Revolution. Those underground pornographic leaflets may have been more damaging to the tsarist regime than all the revolutionary underground literature. Coincidentally, on the wall of Alexandra's mauve boudoir, where Sandro had pleaded with the couple to change course, hung a portrait of Marie Antoinette.

The removal of Rasputin did not end the influence of the court camarilla. On December 20, Protopopov was promoted from acting minister of internal affairs to full-fledged minister. Nicholas's government now moved further to the right, elevating the few individuals he and Alexandra perceived to be loyal and expelling reformers. Then, on December 26, Aleksandr Trepov, the chairman of the Council of Ministers, who had striven to achieve some compromise with the Duma liberals and who had offered Rasputin money to leave the capital, was dismissed. Prince Nikolai Dmitrievich Golitsyn, a sixty-six-year-old bureaucrat with connections to the tsarina through the Red Cross, but not through Rasputin, was named chairman in his place. The old man, who had considered himself retired from active duty, was dumbfounded and initially declined to accept the offer on the pretext of illness, but finally had to surrender to the will of the sovereign.[70]

On January 1, 1917, with a single stroke of the pen, the tsar purged the appointed members of the Progressive Bloc in the State Council and replaced them with members who had right-wing credentials. Reflecting the right-wing swing of the State Council, it elected as chairman the former minister of justice, Ivan Shcheglovitov, notorious for his role in the anti-Semitic Beilis case in 1913.

Yet the right wing was divided. Enlightened members of the bureaucracy feared that the nation was headed blindly toward catastrophe and believed that the way out would require a compromise with Duma liberals. During the Christmas vacation, Aleksandr Krivoshein, Aleksei Polivanov, Count Aleksei Aleksandrovich Bobrinsky, and Aleksandr Sergeevich Taneev (Anna Vyrubova's father) were involved in a series of meetings with the Duma liberals. Regarding themselves as prime candidates to head a government, they were receptive to the idea of the formation of a ministry of confidence.[71] At the same time, an even more reactionary element around the former minister of internal affairs, Nikolai Maklakov, and Aleksandr Aleksandrovich Rimsky-Korsakov, a leader of the Union of the Russian People, encouraged the tsar to take a firmer stand against the Duma by dissolving it altogether and ordering a new election to purge the liberals. Rimsky-Korsakov's memorandum, which was handed to Protopopov on January 15, proposed to change the laws governing the Duma in such a way as to increase the right-wing element, purge undesirable elements from the state apparatus, and hand the State Council over to the right wing.[72] Nicholas, however, did not adopt such radical recommendations. All he did was to postpone the opening of the Duma until February 14, as Protopopov advocated, overruling Golitsyn's proposal to resume the Duma session on January 13.[73]

Rasputin's murderers and those who rejoiced at the death of the "holy devil" expected that his disappearance would lead to the improvement of the political situation. Their expectations were immediately betrayed, since Rasputin's place was simply taken by Protopopov, who managed to insinuate his way further into the imperial couple's circle through Anna Vyrubova.

Vyrubova had previously acted as a conduit between Alexandra and Rasputin, but after his assassination, she became more influential, serving as an important link between the empress and Protopopov. Through Vyrubova, Protopopov had intimate knowledge of the empress's mood and feelings. He did not hesitate to invoke the memory of Rasputin, pretending to be the faithful successor of the deceased, although Rasputin had been keenly aware of Protopopov's scheming character. As Rasputin had once said, "He [Protopopov] has a sense of honor that is like a garter belt. He can stretch it whenever he wants it."[74]

It was a measure of the colossal decline of autocracy under Nicholas II that the fate of the empire rested on an ambitious man known to be mentally unbalanced. Suffering from "evil illness," a euphemism for venereal disease, Protopopov was a patient of the dubious Buryati doctor Pyotr Badmaev and a psychiatrist named Vladimir Mikhailovich Bekhterev. He was also under the influence of a shady psychiatrist and occultist, Karl Perren, who claimed to have the power to predict the future, and a master of necromancy, Prince Aleksandr Borisovich Kurakin, who claimed to resurrect Rasputin's ghost in secret seances.[75] The tsar's cabinet was now controlled by a man in thrall to Rasputin's ghost.

Unable to command respect even from his colleagues in the cabinet, Protopopov became a symbol of the regime's corruption and intransigence as well as the focus of public hatred for the government after Rasputin's death. He was also a key figure in the structure tasked with keeping Petrograd secure, and his incompetence only worsened the tsar and tsarina's growing problems.

The tsarist government was by no means blind to the rapidly growing public furor against the regime. Anticipating major disturbances, the government began to take precautionary measures in late 1916. The men in the civilian branch of the government who were in charge of the security of Petrograd were Protopopov, the minister of internal affairs; the director of the police department, Aleksei Tikhonovich Vasiliev; and the Petrograd city governor (*gradonachalnik*), Major General Aleksandr Pavlovich Balk. But because Petrograd was designated as part of the theater of war, civilian authorities were relegated to a secondary role there, and it was the military branch of government that was primarily responsible for maintaining the security of the city. At the end of January 1917, the supreme command separated Petrograd and its vicinity from the front and formed an independent Petrograd Military District under Major General Sergei Semyonovich Khabalov. A lack of coordination between the civilian and military authorities hindered effective enforcement of security measures. The difficulty was further compounded by the ambiguous division of jurisdiction between two military authorities, the commander of the Petrograd Military District and the war minister, Belyaev.

Protopopov's choices of Vasiliev and Balk only made matters worse. Protopopov had dismissed the deputy minister of internal affairs, Pavel Kurlov, who was an expert on police matters, and replaced him with the inexperienced Vasiliev, who was known to be a heavy drinker and who made sycophantic compliments to please his boss. The new police chief was the person to whom the chief of the Okhrana (secret police), Konstantin Ivanovich Globachev, sent daily reports meticulously assembled from his agents, who infiltrated into every corner of society and organizations. Vasiliev found Globachev's reports too pessimistic and altered the reports to say what his boss wanted to hear.[76] As a consequence, Protopopov dismissed the possibility of a spontaneous mass uprising exploding in the future, as Globachev warned time and again in his reports.

And Balk had been Protopopov's choice to replace Prince Aleksandr Obolensky as Petrograd's city governor in November 1916. Protopopov was able to dismiss Obolensky because Alexandra was outraged by remarks made by Obolensky's sister attacking her close relationship with Rasputin.[77] Balk, the former assistant to the chief of police in Warsaw, was well aware that he was not qualified to fill this important position, but the offer was too good to refuse.

Protopopov stacked the civilian leadership of Petrograd with incompetent loyalists, but what mattered most was the incompetence of Petrograd's military leaders. The man in direct command of troops was Khabalov, who had spent his entire career administering military schools without ever commanding troops on a battlefield. He graduated from the Mikhailovsky Artillery School in 1878, served in the Russo-Turkish War, attended the Nikolaevsky Academy of the General Staff, and became the head of various military schools before receiving the appointment as commander of the Petrograd Military District in November 1916. According to Balk, Khabalov was "incapable of leading his own subordinates and, above all, of commanding troops."[78] General Ruzsky, commander of the northern front, whose jurisdiction included Petrograd then, conducted an inspection tour in November 1916, when the city was hit by workers' strikes, and Khabalov sent one of his officers to accompany the general. Ruzsky was stunned by the ignorance of this officer about the situation. Ruzsky had to turn to General Aleksei Alekseevich Manikovsky, head of the Main Artillery Administration, for necessary information.[79]

Equally unimpressive was Belyaev, whom Nicholas once described as "an extremely weak man who always gives way in everything and works slowly." Like Khabalov, he had spent his entire military career behind a desk. He was a military bureaucrat rather than a battle commander. After serving as the General Staff's representative to the Rumanian front, he was appointed war minister on January 3, 1917, replacing General Dmitry Shuvaev, who had irritated the tsarina with his outspoken opposition to Rasputin. In this unusually quick promotion Belyaev undoubtedly took advantage of his connections to the court camarilla.[80] His narrow bureaucratic mind obviously could not compensate for Khabalov's inexperience. Aleksandr Ivanovich Verkhovsky, future minister of war in the Provisional Government, was even more uncharitable: "Cold careerism and military illiteracy were combined in him with a supreme contempt for people and the willingness to sacrifice thousands of lives, if it was necessary for his personal success."[81]

Had Khabalov obtained assistance from capable officers, his inexperience might not have been catastrophic. When it came to formulating security measures, it was assumed that Lieutenant General Aleksandr Nesterovich Chebykin, who enjoyed the confidence of other officers, would take actual command of the troops in Petrograd. Chebykin, however, fell ill in early January, necessitating Khabalov's hasty appointment of Colonel Vladimir Ivanovich Pavlenkov of the Preobrazhensky Regiment as a temporary replacement. This was a poor choice, since Pavlenkov, who had arrived in Petrograd from the front only at the beginning of February, "was not familiar even with the topography of the capital and did not know at all the sentiments of the army units."[82] Moreover, Pavlenkov suffered a mild heart attack shortly before the outbreak of the February Revolution and had to conduct most business from bed. Khabalov thus found himself commanding troops without the help of more experienced field officers.

The men in positions of major responsibility were mediocre, ailing, unimaginative, lethargic, incompetent, or some combination of those. But the weakness of the security structure went deeper than the personalities of its leaders. It was essential that good communication exist between Petrograd and the high command at the front, for obviously if any disturbances in the city went beyond the ability of the Petrograd authorities to handle alone, reinforcements would have to be brought in. But the relationship between Petrograd and the military leaders at the front was marred by hostility and distrust. One can trace this mutual animosity to the way the Petrograd Military District had been detached from the northern front.

It was inevitable that a conflict of interest would arise between the commander of the northern front, General Ruzsky, and the men in charge in Petrograd, Khabalov and Belyaev. As the front commander, Ruzsky regarded the transfer of necessary supplies and provisions from the industrial regions of the Petrograd Military District to the front as the highest priority. On the other hand, Khabalov and Belyaev were concerned with provisions not only for the garrison units stationed in the city but also for the workers in war industries and the civilian population in the capital. As the supply of goods, particularly foodstuffs and fuel, fell sharply during the first months of 1917, the two men in Petrograd began to complain bitterly that Ruzsky was endangering the security of Petrograd by giving the front unduly favorable treatment.[83] This was a matter of priorities that any country engaged in total war encountered, and an efficient government would have made a rational readjustment of priorities without impairing the integrity of the government as a whole. Not so in Russia. Khabalov and Belyaev chose intrigue, employing the political influence of Protopopov and the tsarina, a modus operandi that was prevalent in the tsarist government.

Relations between Protopopov and Ruzsky had been strained since November, when Ruzsky objected to Protopopov's food supply policy. This objection had coincided with the liberals' outcry against Protopopov's policy and had increased the suspicion the minister of internal affairs felt toward the "liberal" commander of the northern front. It seemed more important to place the Petrograd Military District under Protopopov's direct control, not subject to the military intelligence network. Ruzsky, on the other hand, reacted with irritation to Protopopov's meddling in military censorship. Declaring that military intelligence had different goals and purposes, he refused to downgrade it to a tool of the political police.

As for the allocation of provisions, Ruzsky considered the Petrograd Military District a "burden" to the northern front, and in principle he did not object to its detachment from his jurisdiction. What he did object to was the way it was detached.[84]

Three weeks before the outbreak of the February Revolution, Protopopov relayed the complaints of Khabalov and Belyaev to the tsarina, and engaged in a vicious attack on Ruzsky's character, while insisting to the tsar that for security reasons the Petrograd Military District should be separated from the northern front.[85] Whether it was because of Alexandra's bedroom propaganda or Protopopov's argument as an expert on the security of Petrograd, Nicholas decided to detach the Petrograd Military District from the northern front. It was the dubious manner in which this decision was made, more than the decision itself, that angered army leaders, especially Ruzsky. If this incident reinforced their contempt for Protopopov and the tsarina, they were also embittered by the disgraceful conduct of Khabalov and Belyaev. The separation of the Petrograd Military District from the northern front also made the boundary between the two ambiguous. Ruzsky unilaterally drew a narrow line, placing Luga and Finland under his jurisdiction. Luga and Finland were to play an important role in the February Revolution.

The security forces consisted of the police and the reserve soldiers. In Petrograd there were 3,500 policemen assigned to sixteen precincts. Since the police alone would not be able to cope with large-scale labor unrest, in such a circumstance the security authorities hoped to rely on the reserve soldiers stationed in Petrograd. Although we do not have wholly accurate figures, there were said to be between 160,000 and 271,000 troops in Petrograd. If we add the number of garrison troops in the vicinity of Petrograd (Tsarskoe Selo, Petergof, Gatchina, and others), the government could count on 322,000 to 466,000 soldiers to protect the capital from insurgency.[86] The enormous concentration of reserve soldiers in Petrograd warrants this statement: "The whole city had been turned into a military camp."[87] This large number of soldiers apparently gave the authorities the illusion that Petrograd was invulnerable to any internal threat.

However, the composition of the Petrograd garrison troops had changed over time. The guard regiments and the Cossacks could no longer be relied upon to prop up the regime, as they had done in the 1905 revolution. According to Colonel Boris Engelgardt, an Octobrist deputy of the Duma:

It was no longer the army in peacetime, united in strict discipline under the commanding officers, whose interests were closely connected with the existing system. —No, it was armed mobs capable at any moment of exercising their own will and their demands. . . . [The reserve battalions] were not military units, but rather hordes of armed people. Not united in discipline under commanding personnel, they were more reserves of flammable material than a prop of the regime.[88]

Protopopov held a misconception common among the reactionary politicians of the time: that a revolution would be possible only at the instigation of a group of subversive elements. His main method of combating the revolutionary movement was thus to emphasize police repression of underground revolutionary organizations.

At the end of December 1916 and the beginning of January 1917, Protopopov's police raided Bolshevik underground organizations and decimated their Petersburg Committee. Next on Protopopov's list was the Workers' Group of the Central War Industries Committee, considered to be a moderate wing of the revolutionary organizations. On January 27, Protopopov made a decisive move by having his police arrest the members of the Workers' Group in Petrograd.[89] He was apprehensive that such drastic measures might trigger a large-scale strike movement among the workers. When that did not happen, he became more convinced that he had successfully eradicated the potential troublemakers and thus had also eliminated the possibility of the immediate outbreak of revolution. He paid little attention to the more disturbing signs, often signaled by his own Okhrana agents, that the despair and frustration of the workers might impel them to take spontaneous action on their own, and that the discontent had spread to the garrison soldiers.

Immediately after the arrest of the Workers' Group, Nicholas entrusted the reactionary former minister of internal affairs, Nikolai Maklakov, with the job of composing a draft manifesto for the dissolution of the Duma and preparations for a new election. Maklakov willingly carried out this task.[90] According to this plan, the tsar was to order the dissolution of the Duma and set a new election for December 1, 1917.[91]

Protopopov, however, did not agree with Maklakov on the timing of the dissolution of the Duma. As a former Octobrist, he was more aware of the volatility of the liberal opposition, within which rumors of a palace coup were widely circulating. An ill-timed dissolution of the Duma might push them to action. He engineered instead the postponement of the Duma opening until February 14.[92]

Protopopov's policy did not satisfy the reactionaries. Maklakov and Shcheglovitov criticized him as "too soft" on the liberals, while those in the bureaucracy who accepted the liberals' demand for the establishment of a ministry of confidence believed that Protopopov was leading the government into a headlong collision with the opposition. The net result was further disarray in the right wing and the government. In fact, the government all but ceased to exist in the last two months of the tsarist regime. Relying more and more on his unofficial but more effective channel of political influence through Vyrubova and the tsarina, Protopopov stopped attending the meetings of the Council of Ministers. Golitsyn could not stomach Protopopov, who had made him look like a fool on the matter of the postponement of the Duma session, and unsuccessfully attempted to dismiss him by petitioning the tsar. But under the tsarina's protection, Protopopov remained untouchable.

The "ministerial leapfrog" continued. Top-level bureaucrats in the ministries of education, justice, finance, foreign affairs, and trade and industry stopped working on major policy proposals because they had no idea how long their ministers would be in office. The high officials of the ministry of internal affairs did not know where to send their reports since Protopopov refused to accept them. Two of Protopopov's deputy ministers finally gave up and walked out on him. The post of deputy minister remained unfilled in the ministries of foreign affairs, justice, internal affairs, transport, and education.[93] Thus, while the tsar was helping to wipe away the tears of his grief-stricken wife, his government stopped functioning, becoming leaderless and demoralized.

The erosion of the government's authority caused concerns among the diplomats representing the Allied nations. British ambassador George Buchanan and French ambassador Maurice Paléologue were in constant communication with the Duma liberals as well as the grand dukes. On December 31, 1916, Buchanan had his last audience with the emperor, and made an unusual recommendation to change the way the emperor was conducting his business, at the risk of meddling in another country's internal affairs. He suggested that the emperor rid himself of his wife's pernicious influence, fire Protopopov, and appoint a ministry of confidence to restore the confidence of his people. To this, Nicholas replied: "Do you mean that I am to regain the confidence of my people or that they are to regain my confidence?" Buchanan's desperate pleas fell on deaf ears.[94]

On January 7, 1917, Rodzyanko had an audience with the tsar. He reported that the public's criticism of the empress was growing, as they suspected that she was supporting Germany, but Nicholas was in no mood to listen to him and accused the Duma of being busily engaged in insidious propaganda against his wife. "Give me the facts," he said, pressing the Duma chairman for evidence. Rodzyanko justified his remarks by saying that since the sovereign was surrounded by dishonest and unreliable men, such rumors would naturally spread on fertile ground. Nicholas said that he had tried his best to reign over Russia for twenty-two years, and asked Rodzyanko: "For twenty-two years it was all a mistake?" Rodzyanko took a deep breath and answered: "Yes, Your Majesty, for twenty-two years you followed the wrong course." With such a brutally candid but insulting answer, it is no wonder that Nicholas rejected Rodzyanko's plea to make political concessions.[95]

Sometime in January—we don't know exactly when—Lieutenant General Aleksandr Mikhailovich Krymov came from the front to visit Rodzyanko and asked him to arrange a meeting with the Duma and other liberal leaders. At that meeting Krymov gave them the grim picture at the front. "The spirit is such," Krymov was quoted as saying, "that the news of a coup d'état would be welcomed with joy. A revolution is imminent, and we at the front feel it to be so. If you decide on such an extreme step, we will support you." There was an ominous silence. Then Andrei Ivanovich Shingarev, one of the Kadet leaders, said: "The General is right. A coup d'état is urgent. But who will have the courage to undertake it?" The Octobrist Sergei Iliodorovich Shidlovsky said fiercely: "No need to pity or spare him, when he is driving Russia to ruin." Heated arguments ensued. Someone quoted Brusilov's words: "If I had to choose between the Emperor and Russia, I would choose Russia."[96]

This account reveals several important elements. First, such a conspiratorial meeting did take place in January, and General Krymov did serve as a conduit between the army and the liberals. Second, it reveals that both the army and the liberals were ready for a palace coup, but that each side wanted the other to take the initiative. Third, the question of "abdication" (*otrechenie*) or "overthrow" (*nizlozhenie*) was presented. Shidlovsky argued that violent overthrow of the tsar should be contemplated. It will be important to remember the different views of Shidlovsky and Rodzyanko on a palace coup to remove the tsar in the context of the abdication drama during the February Revolution. Fourth, although neither Aleksandr Guchkov nor Nikolai Nekrasov was present, Mikhail Tereshchenko, who was an important member of Guchkov's plot for a palace coup (discussed below), was present and offered the most radical option. Finally, someone said that if a coup was to take place, Brusilov would support it. When we examine the high command's actions during the abdication drama that lay ahead, these words about Brusilov must be kept in mind.

Besides the army and the liberals, there was another group that wanted a palace coup without wishing to lift a finger to start it. That was the relatives of the emperor. Sometime in early January, Miechen called Rodzyanko to her apartment, where the Duma chairman found her sons Grand Dukes Kirill and Boris. Maria Pavlovna openly supported a coup and advocated that the empress be "annihilated." Rodzyanko claimed to have stopped the conversation and told her that he would pretend no such conversation had ever taken place.[97]

On February 10, Rodzyanko again sought an audience with the tsar. In what turned out to be his last audience, the Duma chairman begged Nicholas not to dissolve the Duma. In his opinion that was the only possible way to prevent the outbreak of a revolution, since the Duma alone had a restraining influence on the people's passions. But Nicholas proved to be more combative this time than at the previous audience. While Rodzyanko expressed fear of an impending revolution, the tsar responded: "My information indicates a completely different picture. As far as the mood of the Duma is concerned, if the Duma allows itself to make such sharp attacks as the last time, then it will be dissolved." Rodzyanko left with the depressing feeling that nothing would change Nicholas's mind, and he soon became convinced that forcible removal of the emperor was required to carry out reforms.[98]

In later years, Rodzyanko would portray himself as the opponent of a palace coup to remove the tsar, trying to exonerate himself of the accusation that he was the slayer of the monarchy. In an interview given in May

1917, however, Rodzyanko revealed his true position: "A political coup was the only way out. For a palace coup to be successful, one has to have firm and courageous people, and not the kind of slush which the tsarist family represents."[99] How the chairman of the Duma implemented his idea during the fast-developing events that took place in the February Revolution will be our focus in the following chapters.

On the eve of the February Revolution, rumors of a palace coup were circulating widely in Petrograd. Most of the talk was nothing but gossip, wishful thinking, or rumors. But two groups of conspirators went a little beyond salon talks.

The first group centered around Prince Georgy Lvov, the head of the Union of Zemstvos and a leading figure in the liberal voluntary organizations. He became directly involved in the conspiracy for a palace coup in November 1916, when he proposed to General Alekseev a joint action to remove the pernicious influence of the empress, especially after his June recommendation to establish a dictatorship was rejected. Although Nicholas and Alexandra trusted the chief of staff, General Alekseev had become concerned about the growing influence of the tsarina and Rasputin in internal politics. Empress Alexandra had once suggested to Alekseev that Rasputin be invited to the Stavka, but Alekseev had indignantly vetoed the idea, declaring that if Rasputin set foot in the Stavka, he would resign his post. In November 1916, there was a rumor that the empress was planning to come to live with the tsar at the Stavka to exert a stronger influence on him. The general instructed his subordinates not to convey any confidential information about troops to the tsar while the empress was at the Stavka. He had become extremely concerned with domestic politics since Stürmer's appointment, and it was rumored that he sent a memo in red ink to the tsar urging the dismissal of Stürmer.[100] According to émigré historian Sergei Melgunov, this finally led Alekseev to support the plot.

Lvov's plan was to arrest the empress in the train on her way from Tsarskoe Selo to Mogilev, deport her to the Crimea, and force the tsar to form a ministry of confidence headed by Lvov. This plan was to be executed on November 30. But before that date, Alekseev fell ill with uremia and took a leave from the Stavka to convalesce in Sevastopol. When Lvov came to Sevastopol to confer with Alekseev, Alekseev rejected Lvov's proposal for a palace coup. According to Melgunov, this was because any proposal that might include the forcible removal of the tsar himself went further than Alekseev could tolerate.[101] According to Lvov's niece Nikitina Polusadova, who was an active member of the Union of Zemstvos and accompanied Lvov to Sevastopol, Alekseev shouted at Lvov: "Leave me alone to focus on the recovery of my health, and don't get me involved in politics."[102] Significantly, Alekseev did not report his conversation with the plotter to his superior officer—in this case, Nicholas himself—as his oath required.

On December 9, 1916, a small group of conspirators headed by Lvov gathered in his apartment in Moscow to discuss another plot. At this meeting, attended by Nikolai Mikhailovich Kishkin (a member of the Kadets and vice chairman of the Union of Towns), Mikhail Mikhailovich Fyodorov (a Progressist and the leader of the Zemgor), and Aleksandr Ivanovich Khatisov (mayor of Tiflis and chairman of the Caucasian branch of the Union of Towns), Lvov revealed a new plan that would remove Nicholas and install Grand Duke Nikolai Nikolaevich in his place. The conspirators were to use a small guard unit sympathetic to the grand duke to arrest the tsar and deport him abroad, and they were to incarcerate Alexandra in a monastery. Lvov revealed to those present that the army's support for this plan had been confirmed by General Aleksei Manikovsky, head of the Main Artillery Administration and a member of the Masonic organization.[103] The conspirators accepted Lvov's plan and entrusted Khatisov with the delicate task of recruiting Grand Duke Nikolai Nikolaevich into the conspiracy.

Nicholas's cousin did not reject the idea outright, but he raised two questions. He asked how people with deep monarchist sentiments would react to the forcible removal of the tsar, and he wondered about the possible reaction of the army to such an act. The grand duke asked for two days to think it over. When Khatisov returned two days later, Nikolai Nikolaevich answered that he had decided not to join the plot, since his chief of staff, General Nikolai Yanushkevich, believed that the soldiers would not understand such an action. The plot collapsed.[104] The conspirators gave up on the idea of Grand Duke Nikolai Nikolaevich taking over the throne, and opted instead to have Nicholas abdicate in favor of his son under the regency of Grand Duke Mikhail.[105]

As historian Boris Kolonitskii points out, it is interesting that Nikolai Nikolaevich did not cite his allegiance to the tsar as the reason for the refusal.[106] Nor did he report this alleged plot to the tsar, who was his commander in chief, or to Nicholas's chief of staff, Alekseev. Both Alekseev and Nikolai Nikolaevich had already violated their oaths before the revolution even started.

Another, more serious conspiracy regarding a palace coup was floated among the Duma liberals early in October. At a meeting of the leaders of the Progressive Bloc that included Pavel Milyukov, Vasily Maklakov, Andrei Shingarev, Aleksandr Konovalov, Mikhail Tereshchenko, and Nikolai Nekrasov, Guchkov presented his idea for a palace coup. It was initially shot down by the Kadets, led by Milyukov. According to Guchkov, Milyukov opposed the plan, fearing that a palace coup would touch off a mass revolt from below. Guchkov retorted that a palace coup would be the only means of avoiding such a revolt. The participants settled on a policy of seeking Nicholas's abdication in favor of his son, Aleksei, under Mikhail's regency. It should be noted that at this time no one, including the Kadet members, believed that the monarchical system should end.[107]

After the meeting, Nekrasov and Tereshchenko came to see Guchkov, and expressed their agreement with Guchkov that a palace coup should be attempted. They formed a committee of three, and would later be joined by Prince Dmitry Leonidovich Vyazemsky, an officer of the Life Guard Cavalry Regiment. An aristocrat, Prince Vyazemsky feared that his class would be the first to be eliminated by an anarchic mass revolt. Therefore, before such a mass revolt occurred, it would be necessary to carry out a surgical operation at the very top of the political power structure; the idea was to save the existing political system by cutting off the part affected by gangrene, and this surgery had to be performed by the leaders of the elite, who knew how to manage governmental affairs. Prince Vyazemsky's participation was a godsend for the plotters, since because of his privilege and his lack of involvement in liberal causes, he was not under police surveillance, and so was free to contact like-minded junior officers. He recruited Captain Dmitry Vladimirovich Kossikovsky of the First Cavalry Division, stationed in Novgorod province. Incidentally, Captain Kossikovsky was a brother of Aleksandra Kossikovskaya, a lady-in-waiting for Nicholas's sister Olga; it was Aleksandra Kossikovskaya with whom Grand Duke Mikhail, the tsar's youngest brother, had fallen in love in 1906 and whom he asked Nicholas for permission to marry, a request that the tsar rejected. Captain Kossikovsky had served as an adjutant to Grand Duke Nikolai Mikhailovich.[108] It is not clear, however, whether Kossikovsky had kept in touch with Mikhail Aleksandrovich.

The involvement of the two officers made Guchkov's plot far more serious than Lvov's. The conspirators considered three options. The first was to seize Nicholas at Tsarskoe Selo, but this option was immediately discarded, since they would encounter stiff resistance from the troops protecting the imperial family. The second option was to seize the tsar at the Stavka, but to implement this, the conspirators would have to have the prior consent of the high command. Although the conspirators had a good idea that Alekseev was favorably disposed to the coup, they were not sure about the rest of the officers, especially the middle-rank officers, who might remain faithful to their oath of allegiance. This option also had the danger of provoking an internal war between units led by officers loyal to the tsar and units that might support Nicholas's abdication. Moreover, they did not wish to involve the generals, who would become implicated if the plot ended up in failure.

They finally agreed to implement a third option: they would seize the imperial train along the railway line between Tsarskoe Selo and Mogilev (possibly near a village in Novgorod province formerly owned by Alexander I's notorious adviser Aleksei Andreevich Arakcheev) when the tsar traveled between the imperial palace and the Stavka. This was precisely where Captain Kossikovsky's 1st Cavalry Division was stationed. According to this plot, after the imperial train was seized, Nicholas would be forced to sign a manifesto, prepared by the plotters, under which he would abdicate in favor of his son under the regency of his brother. Then a new government would be formed under the new child tsar, mainly composed of former popular government officials such as Krivoshein and Sazonov. Guchkov did not believe that a government solely composed of liberal leaders would be advisable.

What would the plotters do if Nicholas refused to agree to abdicate? In his interview with diplomat Nikolai Aleksandrovich Bazili, Guchkov stated that there was no affirmative plan for violence: "The idea of terror against the holder of the supreme power was not discussed, but it was considered unacceptable in the given occasion. Since the emperor's son, the heir, was elevated to the throne, with his brother in the capacity of the regent in the duration of his minor age, we considered it unacceptable to force the son and the brother to swear [to the positions] through a pool of blood."[109] Nevertheless, the conspirators did not exclude the possibility of regicide in the extreme case.[110] The conspirators were convinced that the country's sympathies would rally around the innocent twelve-year-old new tsar. Guchkov could not identify any other suitable candidates from the House of Romanov. "Mikhail is a good and honorable man, but he has no willpower and he is under some kind of influence," he said, clearly referring to the influence of Mikhail's wife. And when Bazili asked about Grand Duke Nikolai Nikolaevich, Guchkov answered: "Our relationship toward Nikolai Nikolaevich was strained on a series of critical points."[111]

On January 27, the day when Protopopov arrested the members of the Workers' Group of the Central War Industries Committee, a meeting of "public figures" took place, although we do not know exactly who attended. Presumably, a palace coup was discussed, but not all the participants were committed to Guchkov's plan, although it is important to note that "they declared it impossible to remain neutral in the event of a coup d'état."[112] After this meeting, according to historian Oleg Airapetov, Guchkov and other Duma members took a trip to Sevastopol to visit the recuperating General Alekseev. According to Voeikov, who heard from Gurko that Guchkov had confided his plot for a palace coup to Alekseev, Alekseev allegedly responded: "I will not join the coup, but I will do nothing to block it." Guchkov later told Bazili that "he [Alekseev] was informed so much that he was virtually an indirect participant."[113] In fact, Alekseev did not participate in the plot, but his knowledge of Guchkov's plot and his acquiescence to it should be kept in mind when we examine the abdication drama in the February Revolution.

It is important to note that whether or not they were actually involved in a plot for a palace coup, most liberals knew about the plot and were ready to take over the government once the revolution broke out, though Milyukov and the mainstream Kadet members were not involved in Guchkov's plot, fearing that such a coup might touch off a revolution from below. On February 3, Engelgardt talked about the possibility of a coup with Shingarev and Milyukov. They sifted through suitable names to head a palace coup, and the names of Lvov, Guchkov, Milyukov, Polivanov, and Shingarev came up. Shingarev excused himself from the plot, but Engelgardt was in favor. "It was decided to force the 'boy' [Aleksei] to sign a document prepared in advance," Engelgardt testified, "to form a [ruling] council around him made up of Rodzyanko and Polivanov as well as the ministers Prince Lvov . . . Milyukov, and Guchkov."[114]

Two other meetings of "public figures" regarding a coup took place, one at a restaurant, Medved, on February 20, and the other at a secret apartment rented by Guchkov on Troitskaya Street on February 21. Milyukov and Shidlovsky argued that they should not take an active role in any coup until the dust settled. But those who advocated a palace coup insisted that they should go ahead and initiate it, since nothing would be gained if it was carried out by others. "A bear's killer does not permit others to share the hide," they argued. The conspirators mapped out a concrete plan: since Nicholas had left for Mogilev on February 22, the day of the operation was set for early March.[115] The conspirators knew exactly when the tsar planned to leave Mogilev for Tsarskoe Selo and which railway route he was going to take, though we do not know where they obtained this information.

Previously, at the beginning of February, Tereshchenko had approached Sandro and sounded out his cooperation with a palace coup to remove Nicholas. The grand duke flatly refused to cooperate, citing the inviolability of his oath of allegiance to the emperor. Nevertheless, he became aware of the plot at that time.[116]

Military leaders were increasingly aware that a plot of some kind was imminent. As we have seen, Alekseev received Guchkov in Sevastopol and thus became familiar with the palace coup, though, as mentioned above, Alekseev told Guchkov, "I will not cooperate with the coup, but I will not act against it."[117] Another account of what is presumably the same meeting was provided by Anton Ivanovich Denikin, who fought later with the White Movement under Alekseev. "Some Duma representatives," he wrote, went to see Alekseev when he was recuperating, and revealed a plan for a palace coup. Alekseev categorically opposed such a move during a time of war, and attempted to talk them out of this in the name of maintaining cohesion of the army. Later, that group also went to see Ruzsky and Brusilov, who approved the idea of the coup. The details were kept secret, but the main idea corresponded to Guchkov's plot.[118] Ruzsky allegedly said after the revolution that had he known of such a plot, he would have joined it. And, as we have seen, Brusilov also is said to have declared: "If I had to choose between the Emperor and Russia, I would choose Russia." Admiral Adrian Nepenin of the Baltic Fleet was said to have thought over the possibility of a palace coup on many sleepless nights.[119]

Even Grand Duke Nikolai Nikolaevich took two days to think about the possibility of joining Lvov's plot, although he rejected it in the end. It seems clear that the high command was vaguely aware of a plot and sympathized with it, but refused to join the conspirators. One must remember that the highest echelons of the high command had already shifted their allegiance to the motherland rather than to the tsar, and they were psychologically prepared to jettison the emperor to whom they had pledged allegiance "at the cost of their lives."

Interestingly, the existence of the conspiracies, though not the details, was known to the police and the government. Major General Konstantin Globachev, director of the Okhrana, reported to Khabalov on January 19 that "our domestic Yuan Shih-k'ai"—the group of Guchkov, Konovalov, and Lvov—intended to take advantage of unexpected events for their personal ambitions. A week later Globachev wrote a more specific warning that a group led by Guchkov, Lvov, Sergei Nikolaevich Tretyakov (a Moscow industrialist and member of the Progressive Party), Konovalov, and Mikhail Fyodorov

regard as unachievable their dream of seizing power under the pressure of the demonstration of the masses of the population, and all the more rest their hopes exclusively on the conviction of the inevitability in the near future of a palace coup, supported at least by one of the two army units sympathetic with this group.[120]

Nicholas entertained the notion of arresting Guchkov, the central figure of the conspiracies, but Protopopov, who believed that his arrest might provoke a more dangerous reaction than the conspiracy, talked him out of it.[121] Knowing of the existence of conspiracies and yet being unable to move against the conspirators revealed the dysfunctional quality of the security authorities.

Also significant was the extent to which a wide segment of society, even those who supported monarchical principles, accepted as a lesser evil the possibility of a palace coup. As mentioned above, Miechen suggested to Rodzyanko the notion of the forcible removal of the tsarina. Grand Dukes Nikolai Mikhailovich and Aleksandr Mikhailovich also suggested the possibility of a palace coup to none other than the prosecutor of the Petrograd Circuit Court, Sergei Vladislavovich Zavadsky, who in turn did not conceal his sympathy for the idea.[122]

At the center of all these collective pressures from aristocratic circles was Rodzyanko. The conservative elements of society, sensing the impending storm, came to regard the moderation of the Duma's chairman as the last and only hope. Rodzyanko, in turn, solidified his strength with the aristocracy to counterbalance his slipping popularity among the liberals. Grand Duke Mikhail provided him with a vital link to the rest of the grand dukes.

On the morning of February 14, Rodzyanko hurried to see the acting chief of staff, General Gurko, who happened to be in Petrograd, and informed him that he had reliable information that a palace coup was being planned and would be carried out. Gurko immediately took a train to Tsarskoe Selo and requested an audience with the tsar. One of the court officials, Z. V. Arapov, was sitting in the next room. He heard nothing for the first fifteen minutes, then suddenly he heard Gurko's thundering voice: "Your Imperial Majesty, you are willfully preparing yourself for the gallows. Do not forget that the mobs will not stand on ceremony. You are ruining yourself and your family." Nicholas's answer was inaudible, but a few seconds later Gurko stormed out of the room, pale and trembling, and muttered: "We are done with."[123]

Everyone who approached the tsar with suggestions for how he might avoid the possibility of a coup was struck by both the inflexibility and the calm with which Nicholas refused their recommendations. Many felt that an invisible wall separated them from the sovereign, who did not seem to comprehend what they were saying. In a way, their impression was correct: after Rasputin's assassination, Nicholas was living in a world far removed from reality. There was something intensely personal in his understanding of the responsibility of a sovereign. To Nicholas, politics could not be separated from his own personal morality and religion. While his critics presented a compromise with the Duma as a political alternative, to Nicholas there could be no such alternative, since it would strike at the heart of his moral and religious convictions. He could not accept it without breaking his sacred obligations to God. In this conviction, Nicholas and Alexandra were united.

All attention now focused on the opening of the Duma on February 14. The moderate wings of the revolutionary parties, organized by the Central War Industries Committee under Guchkov, Tereshchenko, and Konovalov, became so radicalized that they called for a demonstration on this day in the hope of collaborating with liberal forces to topple the government. But the radical revolutionaries, including the Bolsheviks, distrusted the liberals, so they did not support this call and instead suggested a demonstration on a different day. Protopopov was so alarmed that he took precautionary measures to prevent the demonstration by arresting the leaders of the moderate socialists. Milyukov, similarly sensing the impending revolution, published in the Kadet newspaper, *Rech* [*Speech*], an appeal to workers not to participate in the demonstration; it ran side by side with Khabalov's warning that any demonstration would be severely punished. The disunity of the revolutionary parties, Protopopov's precautionary security measures, and Khabalov's appeal dampened the enthusiasm of the workers, and the expected demonstration in front of the Tauride Palace on February 14 did not take place. Protopopov and Milyukov breathed a sigh of relief.

When February 14 passed without incident, it seemed to Nicholas that all these panic-stricken conservatives had fallen victim to alarmism. He was impressed with Protopopov for his sound advice and superb job of keeping Petrograd secure. He was confident that despite the increasingly strident criticism against him, the Duma would not join the revolution in the midst of war, and that the army was solidly behind him.[124]

On February 19, the emperor decided to leave Tsarskoe Selo for the Stavka to resume his duty as the supreme commander. Brushing aside the palace commandant's misgivings about departing the capital with political unrest reaching a boiling point, Nicholas expressed his confidence in Protopopov, who assured him that nothing would happen and that all necessary measures had been taken to deal with any disturbances.

On February 20, the emperor received Golitsyn and made sure that the chairman of the Council of Ministers had in his possession the imperial decree to prorogue the Duma with the date left blank so that Golitsyn could issue it when he found it appropriate.[125] On the day before his departure, Nicholas received Protopopov again, who guaranteed complete calm in the capital and wished the emperor a pleasant journey. According to E. M. Almedingen, "there was no apparent necessity for the Emperor to leave for Mogilev at the end of February 1917. Everything was quiet at the front and the plans for the spring offensive had already been made."[126] Perhaps General Alekseev had urged him to return to Mogilev, the intention being to separate the emperor from the empress. Or perhaps Nicholas was tired of his wife's relentless campaign to have him stand firm, and he needed a rest from all the nuisances of government affairs and above all the constant haranguing from his wife to assert himself as a true autocrat.[127]

On February 22, a sunny, nippy, frosty day, Nicholas left Tsarskoe Selo, having spent two months there. Nicholas and Alexandra had breakfast with his brother Mikhail. This was the last time the two brothers would meet before his abdication. When the emperor and empress left the palace, the soldiers of His Majesty's Convoy, His Majesty's Regiment, and the palace police stood at the gate and shouted in union, "Greetings to Your Imperial Majesty!" On the way to the railway station, Nicholas and Alexandra stopped by the Znamenie chapel to kiss the icon of the Virgin Mary. Upon arrival at the station, Alexandra kissed her husband. This was the last time Alexandra saw Nicholas as the emperor. Behind the pavilion stood the golden cupola of Fyodorovsky Cathedral, glittering in the sun, and the church bells were ringing after the service.[128]

After a tearful embrace, Alexandra stopped again at the Znamenie chapel to pray before she returned to the palace. She prayed for a long time and wept with unexplainable premonition.[129] That night she wrote a letter to Nicholas: "My very Own precious one, With anguish & deep pain I let you go—alone, without sweet Baby's tender, warming, sunny companionship! . . . I can do nothing but pray & pray & Our dear Friend does so in yonder world for you—there he is yet nearer to us—Tho' one longs to hear his voice of comfort and encouragement." Then she returned to the litany of his need to stand firm, to show the whip and make everyone fear him.[130]

Nicholas knew full well that her sugary expressions of love concealed sharp fangs of rebuke and admonition. And long after "the holy man" had been assassinated, the couple had to live under the shadow of Rasputin. Nicholas did not have the courage to reject all this. All he wanted to do was to escape into what was ostensibly his duty but that actually was a sinecure, a role in which he would not be bothered by ministers' visits and reports, his wife's constant nagging, and the long shadow of Rasputin.

On the way to the Stavka, Nicholas dispatched a telegram to his wife: "Am traveling well. In thoughts am with all of you. Feel lonely and sad. Am grateful for letters. Embrace all. Good night. Niki."[131] He wrote in his diary: "Read, bored, rested. Did not go out because of coughs."[132] On the following day, February 23, he woke up at Smolensk, read in French a book about Julius Caesar, and arrived at Mogilev at 3 p.m.[133] By the time his telegram reached Tsarskoe Selo, the workers in Vyborg district were out in the streets, demanding bread. The February Revolution had begun.

# PART II

# ABDICATIONS

It is never possible for the tyrant to trust that he is loved
. . . and plots against tyrants spring from none more than
from those who pretend to love them most.

—Xenophon, *Hiero*

If there be any in this assembly, any dear friend of Caesar's, to him I say that Brutus' love to Caesar was no less
than his. If then that friend demand why Brutus rose
against Caesar, this is my answer--not that I loved Caesar less, but that I loved Rome more.

—Shakespeare, *Julius Caesar*

CHAPTER 5

# Revolution Erupts in Petrograd

T he tsar arrived at Mogilev station at 3 p.m. on February 23 and went
to meet Adjutant General Mikhail Alekseev at headquarters for half
an hour before he retired to his residence in the governor's house, where
he received a letter from Alexandra and learned that Olga and Aleksei
had become sick with measles. He missed his son, looking at "all his tiny
things, photos, and toys," and almost felt that Aleksei was asleep in the
bedroom there, but reminded himself that he should not fall into this sen-
timentalism, and convinced himself that it was better that Aleksei had not
come to the Stavka with him.[1]

Alexandra had written out of worry that without her at the Stavka,
her weak-willed husband, whom she had kept on a short leash at Tsarskoe
Selo, might cave under the pressure for political reforms.[2] He responded
to his wife's admonishments to remain firm: "What you write about
being firm—the master—is perfectly true. I do not forget it—be sure of
that, but I need not bellow at the people right & left every moment. A
quiet sharp remark or answer is enough very often to put the one or the
other into his place."[3]

His life in the Stavka proceeded uneventfully, as he followed his typical routine, methodically dividing his time between ceremonial teas and suppers, audiences to hear formal reports, daily outings, and games of dominos. One member of his entourage, Colonel Anatoly Aleksandrovich Mordvinov, noted: "One day after another passed like two drops of water."[4] This gave a semblance of stability at the Stavka.[5]

The capital, however, was hardly serene and far from stable. On the day Nicholas arrived at the Stavka, women workers in Petrograd's working-class Vyborg district walked off the job, demanding bread. Women's strikes engulfed other factories in this industrial section of the capital, involving close to 60,000 workers and 32 large plants.[6] By the next day the strikes were spreading to other parts of the city, swelling the number of strikers to 158,000 from 131 factories.[7] The liberals in the Duma angrily denounced the government for bread shortages, while the socialist deputies summoned their liberal colleagues to join the "revolution" that had already begun.

On February 24, Prince Nikolai Golitsyn, chairman of the Council of Ministers, sent a telegram to Nicholas, informing him that in order to resolve the "disturbances in the streets," he intended to convene a joint meeting, inviting four ministers, the chairman of the Duma, and the city governor to discuss mechanisms for solving food supply issues.[8] Aleksandr Protopopov was pointedly excluded from this meeting. It was the first telegram to mention the "disturbances," but initially no one in the Stavka appeared to pay much mind to this news.[9] If anything, Nicholas was distracted by the spread of the measles among his children, and likely irritated by Golitsyn's flirtation with the Duma liberals and the exclusion of his trusted adviser, Protopopov.

The empress was preoccupied with her sick children, but through her conversations with Lili Dehn and court officials, she learned about the unrest. She wrote in her letter to Nicholas on February 24, "Yesterday there were rows on V.[asilievsky] ostrov [Island] and Nevsky, because poor people stormed the bread shops—they stormed Filipov['s bakery] completely & the Cossacks were called out against them. All this I know unofficially." This meant that she had not received an official report. Alexandra urged Nicholas to "expel Kedrensky [Kerensky] from the Duma because of his dreadful speech—this is necessary (military law in wartime) and will set an example."[10] Still, the empress had complete faith that Protopopov would put down the disturbances.

On February 25, the unrest in the capital reached a critical stage. A general strike began that day, encompassing more than 200,000 factory workers and 173 factories. Students and people from the middle-class joined the movement. Massive demonstrations surged through Nevsky, with protesters carrying banners saying "Down with Autocracy!" and "Down with the War!" The Cossacks deployed to suppress the unrest appeared passive, and often openly showed their sympathy with the demonstrators. On Znamenskaya Square, where demonstrators congregated in front of the Nikolaevsky railway station, a police chief was killed. The security authorities, headed by General Sergei Khabalov, responded to the demonstrators with utmost sluggishness. The use of arms was strictly forbidden.[11]

On that day, Pavel Milyukov, Andrei Shingarev, and other Kadet leaders met at breakfast. They discussed whether the movement in the streets was a revolution or simple street disturbances. Fyodor Rodichev predicted: "If this is a revolution, the tsar's head will roll."[12] In the Duma session, liberals pursued their strident attack on the government for the food shortage without expanding their criticisms to urge overthrow of the government. But socialist deputies' speeches calling for a revolution were so inflammatory that the chairman, Mikhail Rodzyanko, found it necessary to order Kerensky to stop speaking. Fearing that the street disturbances would push the Duma to take a more radical stand against the government, Rodzyanko hurriedly adjourned the Duma session until Tuesday, February 28. It would be the last official session of the Fourth Duma.[13]

On that morning, the empress's utmost concern was the condition of her sick children. She was especially concerned with Aleksei, who was running a temperature of 38.5 degrees C.[14] But the information that reached the Alexander Palace in Tsarskoe Selo that day began to worry Alexandra. She telephoned Protopopov and inquired about the situation in Petrograd. The minister of internal affairs reassured her that since Khabalov was taking energetic measures, there was nothing to worry about.[15]

She wrote a letter to Nicholas:

> It's a hooligan movement, young boys & girls running about & screaming that they have no bread, only to excite—& then the workmen preventing others fr. [from] work—if it were very cold they wld. [would] probably stay in doors. But this will pass & quieten down—if the Duma wld. only behave itself—one does not print the worse speeches but I find that anti-dynastic ones ought to be at once very severely punished as it[']s time of war, yet more so.[16]

On that day, Count Pyotr Nikolaevich Apraksin, marshal of the court, made a report on the disorder in Petrograd, and volunteered his negative views of some of the cabinet ministers, presumably criticizing Protopopov. Alexandra became angry, throwing a chair at him. Count Apraksin went home and told his wife that he could no longer continue to serve the empress.[17] The innermost circle of the imperial palace was growing tired of the empress.

Alexandra also received the new governor of Tauride province, General Vladimir Vasilievich Boisman, with whom she discussed the disorder in the capital. Boisman suggested that to deal with the shortage of bread, Khabalov should start baking bread in military facilities. She agreed and asked Boisman to bring the idea to Protopopov. It is clear that as far as the empress was concerned, Protopopov was in charge, not Golitsyn or agriculture minister Aleksandr Aleksandrovich Rittikh. During the conversation, however, Alexandra opposed repressive measures. She spoke against shooting, repeating, "Shooting is not necessary. Only order must be restored."[18] She used the same words in her letter to Nicholas on February 25.[19] Khabalov had been following the game plan that prohibited shooting, but order had not been restored.

Additional information about the situation in Petrograd arrived at the Stavka through two channels. One was via telegram to General Vladimir Voeikov from Protopopov. The minister of internal affairs reported that although precinct police chief A. E. Krylov had been killed on Znamenskaya Square, the movement as a whole appeared unorganized and spontaneous, and that Khabalov was taking energetic measures to end further disturbances.[20] The second channel was a report from the capital security authorities to the Stavka. The war minister, Mikhail Belyaev, sent two telegrams to Alekseev, in which he assured the general that the "disorder" showed nothing serious and would be dealt with by the next day.[21] More important was the report sent by Khabalov himself. This was the first time that the chief of security authorities in Petrograd informed the Stavka of the unrest in Petrograd that had begun two days before. He reported that on February 23 and 24 many factories had gone on strike "due to the shortage of bread." Demonstrators had pushed onto Nevsky Prospect, stopping streetcars and breaking some store windows. But "troops did not use firearms" and "four policemen received minor injuries." Khabalov further reported:

Today, on February 25, the workers' attempts to penetrate onto Nevsky were successfully paralyzed. A part [of the demonstrators], who managed to reach Nevsky, were chased away by the Cossacks. In the morning, the police chief of the Vyborg District had his hand broken and suffered an injury to the head struck by a dull object. Around three in the afternoon the police chief Krylov was killed on Znamenskaya Square while he was dispersing the crowd. The crowds were driven away.[22]

The report was filled with misrepresentations and distortions. Besides giving the impression that the security authorities had the situation under control, the report did not mention the paralysis of the capital from the general strike, nor that waves of demonstrators were occupying the whole of Nevsky. The killing of the police chief itself should have indicated the seriousness of the situation, but Khabalov omitted the alarming fact that it was the Cossacks, deployed to disperse the crowds, not the demonstators, who had killed the police chief. At the end of the report Khabalov added:

> In order to end the disturbances, the Petrograd Garrison troops were joined by five Squadrons of the 9th Reserve Cavalry Regiment from Krasnoe Selo, and a company of Life-Guard Combined Cossack Regiment from Pavlovsk, and five squadrons of Guard Reserve Cavalry Regiment were ordered to be deployed in Petrograd.[23]

Upon receiving the report, Nicholas should have wondered: if the situation was under control, why would Khabalov bring in reinforcements? But he did not raise such questions. Alekseev clearly did not yet take the situation in Petrograd seriously either, since the Stavka had received Khabalov's telegram at 6 p.m. on February 25, but Alekseev did not show it to the emperor until February 26.[24]

Exactly what happened next remains hazy. According to Khabalov, on February 25 he received the following order from Nicholas: "We command that tomorrow you put an end to the disorders in the capital, inadmissible at the grave time of war with Germany and Austria."[25]

Nicholas's letters, telegrams, and diary do not explain the thinking behind this order. In his diary entry for February 25, there was no mention of the disturbances, nor of any order to Khabalov to put down the disturbances. Khabalov's February 25 report on the disturbances was not given to Nicholas until the following day; therefore, that telegram did not play any part in the tsar's decision. Historians have not been able to locate Nicholas's original order in the archives. The account of this order comes from the later testimony of Khabalov before the Provisional Government's Investigating Commission. The chairman of the Investigating Commission asked Khabalov where this order was presently located. Khabalov answered that he had handed the order to "the head of the staff," who did not give it back to him.[26] According to Khabalov, the order was received via Hughes apparatus at the General Staff and delivered to him from the General Staff. Precisely whom he had in mind by referring to "the head of the staff" is not clear. Khabalov interpreted Nicholas's order as instructing him to switch strategies, and he claims that it prompted him to deploy troops and issue the command to shoot demonstrators.

This raises the question: did Nicholas really issue this order? Since no copy of this order has been found, there is a possibility that this putative order might be Khabalov's fabrication to justify his order to shoot demonstrators. Even if we suppose that the tsar did indeed issue this order, it did not say specifically that Khabalov should use firearms to suppress the demonstrators. Considering the extent of the general strike, and the fact that it almost paralyzed the city, the order to "tomorrow put an end to the disturbances," as Nicholas allegedly commanded, would have given Khabalov no choice but to resort to shooting demonstrators. In any case, if he did issue such an order, Nicholas did not realize that it would trigger a chain of events destined to lead to more serious consequences. On that night, Protopopov and police chief Aleksei Vasiliev sent the police to arrest more than one hundred activists. Perhaps, they, too, followed Nicholas's lost order to "put an end to the disturbances."[27]

The general strike on February 25 created a crack in the government. At midnight, Golitsyn convened a Council of Ministers meeting at his apartment. Foreign minister Nikolai Nikolaevich Pokrovsky suggested that it was time for the Council of Ministers to resign and form a new ministry by negotiating with the Duma. Despite the strong opposition from Protopopov, the majority of ministers favored Pokrovsky's suggestion, and decided to send Pokrovsky and agriculture minister Rittikh to the Duma for negotiations.[28]

In Mogilev, according to Dmitry Dubensky, a court historian, some of the entourage became concerned with the lack of active intervention to suppress the disturbances. Dubensky, Dr. Sergei Fyodorov, Admiral Konstantin Nilov, and Rudolf von Stackelberg discussed the situation. They were leaning toward the necessity of political compromise. Dubensky's statement that he, Nilov, Stackelberg, Vasily Aleksandrovich Dolgorukov, and Count Vladimir Fredericks favored a responsible ministry—essentially, a constitutional monarchy—should be taken with a grain of salt, however. They must have been aware of Nicholas's adamant opposition to introducing a constitutional system. But it is possible that they favored a ministry of confidence, which would essentially involve keeping the existing governmental structure, but bringing in new personnel who were more acceptable to the liberals. The entourage closest to the emperor was now moving in the direction of political concessions.[29]

How the high command reacted to the disorder in the capital is not known. According to Colonel Boris Nikolaevich Sergeevsky, the head of communications under Quartermaster General Aleksandr Lukomsky, the Stavka was preoccupied with the preparations for spring operations and not paying much attention to the disturbances in the capital.[30] It appears that military leaders did not yet take the situation seriously, since they remained in the dark due to Khabalov's and Belyaev's misleading information exaggerating the strength of the security forces. Adjutant General Nikolai Ruzsky, of the northern front, later stated in an interview with Grand Duke Andrei that although rumors of disturbances reached him, no official reports arrived at the northern front until much later.[31]

Considering the ill feelings that Khabalov, Belyaev, and Protopopov harbored against Ruzsky, it was likely that these three, responsible for the security of the capital, wished to deal with the crisis on their own without the intervention of the northern front commander; the result was that the high command was kept in the dark.

Unlike the generals at the Stavka, Grand Duke Mikhail took the "disturbances" in the capital seriously. On this day, the grand duke and his wife, Natasha Brasova, came to Petrograd to attend a concert at the invitation of French ambassador Maurice Paléologue. Arriving in Petrograd, he went to the house of his administrative assistant, Aleksei Sergeevich Matveev, for breakfast. From there he and his wife were invited to a dinner hosted by Count Ippolit Ippolitovich Kapnist and his wife. There he met Aleksei Klopov, an official of the Ministry of Finance, who had close connections with Prince Georgy Lvov. The host of the dinner, Kapnist, was an Octobrist member of the Fourth Duma, close to Rodzyanko. Clearly, Mikhail had maintained contact with Lvov and Rodzyanko. The dinner conversation revolved around what was happening in the city. Matveev's report on the situation disturbed Mikhail so much that he decided not to attend the concert, and went to Matveev's apartment instead to compose letters, including a letter addressed to General Brusilov. He stayed at Matveev's until midnight, after which he returned to Gatchina with his wife and his secretary, Nikolai Nikolaevich Johnson.[32]

On February 26, Nicholas attended Sunday mass at the church, accompanied by the commanding officers at the Stavka, including General Alekseev.[33] During the service, the tsar felt an excruciating pain in his chest that lasted for a quarter of an hour. He could hardly stand and his forehead was covered with sweat. He later recounted to his wife that he did not feel his heart beating for a while, but his heartbeat came back when he knelt before the Virgin Mother's image.[34] After the church service, the tsar went to the Stavka headquarters to receive Alekseev's report, which did not take long. Then, around noon, Nicholas had his usual Sunday breakfast, inviting many guests, including foreign military representatives and their aides. After breakfast, there was the customary "circle," where he conversed with the guests. Externally, it looked like a typical Sunday.

While the church bells were ringing in Mogilev, however, bloody scenes were unfolding in Petrograd. Prompted by Nicholas's putative order, the security authorities began their offensive against the demonstrators. Troops systematically fired on demonstrators in the center of the city. No fewer than 170–200 demonstrators were killed, making this event the second "Bloody Sunday" of Nicholas's reign.[35]

While shootings were taking place in Petrograd, stillness and silence enveloped Tsarskoe Selo, which was covered by a veil of freshly fallen snow. But inside the Alexander Palace, the empress was busy taking care of her sick children and her confidant Anna Vyrubova, who also was stricken with measles. The children's conditions became more worrying as fevers spiked above 39 degrees Celsius. Aleksei's condition was especially concerning, as his fever had risen to 39.5 degrees, and his entire body had broken out in a rash. Tatiana had an uncontrollable cough, and Olga had huge blotches of rash across her whole body. The two younger daughters, Maria and Anastasia, were assisting their mother in watching over their sick siblings. While frantically caring for her children and Anna, the empress received a letter from Protopopov, who assured her that with the arrests of the ringleaders, "by tomorrow everything will be calmed."[36] Buoyed by the good news, Alexandra sent a letter to Nicholas, relaying the information she received from Protopopov that the government had taken "rigorous measures," including the arrest of the ringleaders of the movement, and she predicted that everything would return to normal by the next day. She recommended the introduction of a ration system, insisting that this was not like the 1905 revolution, since this time it was only a matter of bread. She also informed her husband that she and Maria had gone to Znamenie, their family chapel, to light a candle. They then visited Rasputin's grave and picked up a piece of wood from it. "He died to save us," she wrote.[37]

After she sent the letter to Nicholas, without changing out of her nursing uniform, she hastily went to receive Nikolai Fyodorovich Burdukov, editor of the right-wing newspaper *Grazhdanin* [*Citizen*]. He gave the empress a very pessimistic prognosis regarding the government's handling of the crisis. The journalist strongly urged that the empress and the children should leave Tsarskoe Selo immediately. Since this information contradicted what Alexandra had heard from Protopopov, she calmly responded to Burdukov that she was waiting for a report from Count Pavel Konstantinovich Benckendorff, grand marshal of the imperial court, and ended the meeting abruptly by saying: "I believe in the Russian people. I believe in their sense, in their love and devotion to the Sovereign. Everything will pass and everything will be all right."[38]

In the meantime, the Stavka and Nicholas continued to receive optimistic appraisals of the situation in Petrograd from Protopopov and Khabalov. The minister of internal affairs reported that the crowds who gathered on Nevsky near the City Duma, Ligovsky Prospect, and Znamenskaya Square had been fired upon and dispersed. By five o'clock Nevsky was completely cleared of demonstrators. The Okhrana arrested the leaders of the underground revolutionary parties, including thirty participants who attended a meeting at the Central War Industries Committee. Protopopov reported that the 4th Company of the Pavlovsky Regiment had attempted a revolt, leaving their barracks with rifles and wounding the battalion commander, Colonel Aleksandr Nikolaevich Eksten, but their revolt was suppressed by the soldiers of the Preobrazhensky Regiment, and the 4th Company soldiers were forced to return to their barracks. He ended his report: "The information is received that on February 27, a part of the workers will return to work. Moscow is quiet."[39] Khabalov reported: "Today, February 26, the city is quiet since morning."[40]

Protopopov's information was largely responsible for the complacency with which Nicholas and his entourage reacted to the unrest in the capital. Witnessing the incompetence and chaos of the security authorities, especially the lack of leadership of Khabalov, Major General Aleksandr Spiridovich, who served as Nicholas's secret personal guard before he was appointed city governor of Yalta, was visiting Petrograd at that time. Witnessing the disturbance in the capital, he invited himself into Voeikov's house in Tsarskoe Selo to access the direct telephone line to the Stavka in order to get in touch with the palace commandant at the Stavka. A gendarme guarding Voeikov's house knew Spiridovich and let him use the direct line. Spiridovich alerted Voeikov of the alarming situation in the capital. He also told Voeikov of the strong recommendation that the Duma should be dissolved and the disorder be suppressed by armed forces, insisting that in order to carry out these measures, the tsar should return to the capital immediately: "Let the Sovereign carry out his affair, as he should. Without the Sovereign, nothing will be done."[41] Voeikov does not appear to have paid much attention to Spiridovich's plea, and the whole of the Stavka continued in their state of blissful ignorance about the storm that was gathering in the capital. On this Bloody Sunday, when demonstrators were massacred, the tsar peacefully took a walk and played dominos. His diary did not include a single word about the events in the capital. Only in a letter to Alexandra that day did he comment on the crisis for the first time: "I hope Khabalov will know how to stop those street rows quickly. Protopopov ought to give him clear and categorical instructions. Only that old Golitsyn does not lose his head."[42]

On the day of the mass shootings, Golitsyn called a meeting of the Council of Ministers. Earlier on that day, before the shootings, the government representatives, Pokrovsky and Rittikh, met with the Duma representatives to negotiate for the formation of a new government.[43] With the government's offensive against the demonstrators, the atmosphere changed. The cabinet decided to discontinue negotiations with the Duma and adopted the resolution to prorogue the Duma as of February 27. The imperial decree of prorogation of the Duma, which Golitsyn had obtained from Nicholas earlier, was now dated February 26, and was handed to Rodzyanko that evening. Earlier, when the First Duma and the Second Duma had been dissolved, the government had taken precautionary measures to secure the area around the Duma to prevent any demonstrations.[44] But in February 1917 it never occurred to Golitsyn, Khabalov, or Protopopov that such precautions were necessary, even in light of the massive demonstrations still under way.

Since the beginning of the strike movement on February 23, the Duma had taken a cautious attitude toward the strikes. While criticizing the government for causing the bread shortage that provoked the workers' strike movement, the Duma liberals were hesitant to throw their support behind the strikes and demonstrations. The Duma chairman, Rodzyanko, had to restrain inflammatory speeches by socialist deputies Aleksandr Kerensky, Nikolai Semyonovich Chkheidze, and Matvei Ivanovich Skobelev, who called on their liberal colleagues to support the revolution that had begun in the streets. On February 26, before he received the news that the tsar was proroguing the Duma, Rodzyanko wrote a telegram to Nicholas appealing for urgent change.

Addressed to "His Imperial Majesty, Headquarters of the Commander in Chief," it began: "Popular uprisings, having begun in Petrograd, are taking on uncontrollable and threatening dimensions." The cause was a shortage of bread, but "the main reason is the absolute distrust of the authorities, who are not competent to lead the country out of its difficult situation." He warned that the outbreaks would spread to railways, which would lead to factory shutdowns, leaving workers unemployed and hungry; this would lead to the "path of elemental and uncontrollable anarchy." The economic crisis was causing a "major reduction in the production of shells" as well as a food shortage that was "threatening the army and the rest of the population." But "state authority is totally paralyzed and utterly unable to reimpose order." Here Rodzyanko was talking not about the government's inability to deal with the current disturbances in the capital but about the broader economic crisis.[45] Then he recommended the formation of a ministry of confidence to avoid the movement getting out of control:

> Your Majesty, save Russia; she is threatened with humiliation and disgrace. In these circumstances, the war cannot be brought to a victorious conclusion because the ferment has already spread to the army and threatens to grow if a decisive end cannot be put to anarchy and government disorder. Your Majesty, urgently summon a person in whom the whole country can have faith and entrust him with the formation of a government that all the people can trust. Having been re-inspired by faith in themselves and their leaders, all of Russia will heed such a government. In this terrible hour, unprecedented in its ghastly consequences, there is no other way out and to delay is impossible.[46]

Rodzyanko also sent almost identical telegrams to Generals Alekseev, Brusilov, Ruzsky, and Evert. In the telegram that he sent to Alekseev, he added five sentences: "Procrastination means death. Your Excellency, the fate of the honor and victory of Russia are in your hands. Unless the decision indicated by me is not taken immediately, there cannot be such [honor and victory]. Help save Russia from the catastrophe with your government. I implore you from the bottom of my heart."[47]

Alekseev received Rodzyanko's telegram to him at 10:22 p.m. and the telegram addressed to the tsar at 10:40 p.m. on February 26.[48] Because of the lateness of the hour, however, Alekseev decided not to convey this telegram to the tsar that night. When Nicholas read Rodzyanko's telegram the next morning, he immediately dismissed the Duma chairman's recommendation and told Count Fredericks: "That fat Rodzyanko wrote to me all kinds of nonsense, to which I will not even reply."[49] Given Nicholas's unyielding commitment to autocracy, this reaction to Rodzyanko's telegram may have been flippant, but it was not surprising.

Feeling that the government had the upper hand after shooting demonstrators on Nevsky Prospect during the day, Golitsyn had decided that conditions had improved sufficiently that he could move to prorogue the Duma. Protopopov had reported that order was being restored. Even the militant revolutionary leaders thought that the movement had come to an end.[50] Contrary to what Rodzyanko had described, the government was not "powerless" to restore order on February 26. If the tsar had found it unnecessary to grant political concessions in the past, there was no reason he should suddenly change course on the basis of Rodzyanko's information.

Neither did Rodzyanko seem to expect Nicholas to accept his recommendation. The real purpose of his telegram was to influence the high command. It was an unprecedented move for Rodzyanko to send a copy of the telegram addressed to the tsar to Alekseev and the three front commanders. As noted earlier, he added five sentences in the telegram addressed to Alekseev. In those additional sentences the chairman of the Duma was attempting to convince the high command to prevail upon Nicholas to allow a ministry of confidence. For this purpose, the telegram specifically mentioned the disruption of the railways and war production, emphasizing that the food supply crisis was threatening not only the civilians in the city but the army as well.

Rodzyanko's telegram to the commander of the northern front, General Ruzsky, was dated February 27, rather than February 26, as the others were dated. Ruzsky wrote this comment on the margin of the telegram: "It was a pity that there was no information about what went on in Petrograd from February 24 to 27. By 24th there must have been signs of growing dissatisfaction, threatening disturbances, also about agitation among workers and the garrison [soldiers] in Petrograd. They did not take the trouble to inform the front about this, perhaps, intentionally."[51]

Brusilov, commander of the southwestern front, and Ruzsky, commander of the northern front, responded favorably to Rodzyanko's telegram. Brusilov sent his own telegram to Alekseev: "In view of the approaching storm, I do not see any other alternative."[52] The Stavka received this telegram at 1 a.m. on February 27, before the soldiers' insurrection that would take place later that morning. The hero of the Brusilov Offensive displayed sympathy with the Duma liberals, and he was to maintain this position consistently throughout the abdication drama. It should be remembered that Grand Duke Mikhail had already written to Alekseev on February 25 about the serious situation in Petrograd.

Ruzsky sent a telegram to the tsar giving an even more startling warning. He wrote that since the army was now composed of all classes and professions with various persuasions, its sentiments could not be separated from the sentiments of the population. Therefore, he recommended that the tsar take immediate measures that could calm the people, "give them confidence, courage of spirit, and faith in themselves and in their future," adding at the end: "Under the existing conditions repressive measures could rather make the situation worse than could give the necessary long-lasting satisfaction."[53]

Evert had a different reaction to Rodzyanko's telegram than Ruzsky and Brusilov. Evert's response to Rodzyanko's telegram reached the Stavka at around 2 p.m. on February 27. The commander of the western front refused to comment on political matters, but recommended that appropriate measures should be taken to improve the transport and the food supply question, the two important issues that would directly affect the army.[54]

Alekseev was irritated that Rodzyanko had sent his telegram directly to the front commanders without going through him, especially when the telegrams were not encoded and sent not through military channels but through the regular telegraphic line. But Rodzyanko's violation of military protocol succeeded in planting the seed for the subsequent defection of Ruzsky and Brusilov from the emperor's side. Alekseev was also well aware of the conservative leanings of General Evert. Alekseev had a history of serious disagreements on strategy with Brusilov, Ruzsky, and Evert in the past, so he had to tread carefully regarding their recommendations. It is also important to note that there was a large information gap between the front commanders and the fast-developing events in Petrograd. The Stavka and the front commanders lacked vital real-time information on the events in the capital and had to rely on information given by the chairman of the State Duma and, subsequently, the information given by the Petrograd Telegraph Agency, which was controlled by the Duma. The means of communications available thus had profound consequences for the events that would unfold.

Rodzyanko took advantage of this information gap. His machinations to use the high command to force political concessions on the tsar had begun.

# CHAPTER 6

# Suppressing the Revolution

On the morning of February 27, mutiny broke out among the soldiers of Petrograd.

Bloody Sunday on February 26 seemed to have given the government the upper hand against the strikers and demonstrators. The troops dutifully obeyed the order to shoot in order to control the crowds. But this temporary victory for the government produced unexpected, fateful consequences. As noted in Chapter 5, the 4th Company of the Pavlovsky Regiment attempted a revolt on February 26, angry because other soldiers in their regiment had participated in the shootings of demonstrators earlier in the day. The rebels killed their commander, but soon the soldiers of the Preobrazhensky Regiment, quartered in barracks on Millionnaya Street next to the Winter Palace, were sent to put down the revolt among their fellow troops. The 4th Company's revolt fizzled out, and its ringleaders were sent to the dungeon of the Peter and Paul Fortress. The security authorities let out a sigh of relief, but the calm did not last long.

Around eight o'clock in the morning on February 27, soldiers in the Volynsky Regiment, led by Sergeant Timofei Ivanovich Kirpichnikov, mutinied in protest against their orders to shoot demonstrators, killing the company commander, Major Ivan Stepanovich Lashkevich. The rebel soldiers moved to the nearby compounds of the Lithuanian Regiment, the Preobrazhensky Regiment, quartered in the barracks near the Tauride Palace, and the 6th Sapper Battalion, and the soldiers they encountered there joined in the mutiny. In five days, the workers' movement had snowballed into a genuine insurrection involving the garrison soldiers.

Meanwhile, contrary to Aleksandr Protopopov's optimistic prediction, the workers of the Vyborg district continued with their strikes and demonstrations. They now attacked large state munitions factories, seized enormous quantities of weapons, and overwhelmed the police. The insurgent soldiers crossed the Liteinyi Bridge to the Vyborg district and merged with the demonstrators, burning the police station and occupying the Finland railway station by 2 p.m. Around the same time, another contingent of insurgents, a motley group of workers and soldiers, attacked the notorious Kresty prison, releasing political prisoners and common criminals alike. The insurgents, workers, and rebel soldiers mingled, crossed the Liteinyi Bridge back into the city center, burned the Circuit Court, and attacked the Main Artillery Administration and the arsenal attached to it. Before the day was over, the Vyborg district and the northeastern part of the city around the Tauride Palace were occupied by an unorganized crowd of armed insurgents.[1]

While the conflagration of insurgency was spreading with astonishing speed in the capital, the emperor and the Stavka were still unaware of the gravity of the crisis.

In his regular morning report to the tsar on February 27, Vladimir Voeikov conveyed the telegram from Protopopov that he had received on the previous night, which stated that the situation was under control and that order would be restored by the following day.[2] Nicholas then went to the Stavka headquarters to receive General Mikhail Alekseev's daily report. Alekseev had fallen ill with a high temperature, but he gave his regular report. After the news about the front, General Alekseev apprised the tsar of two telegrams he had received on the previous night. One was a telegram from the chairman of the Council of Ministers, Prince Nikolai Golitsyn, informing the tsar that he had issued the imperial decree of prorogation of the legislative chambers.[3] Then the chief of staff gave Nicholas a telegram from Colonel Vladimir Pavlenkov, Sergei Khabalov's assistant, addressed to the tsar, which read: "Colonel Eksten, commander of the Pavlovsky Regiment, was seriously injured by the crowd on February 26."[4] Pavlenkov failed to mention that prior to this incident the 4th Company of the Pavlovsky Regiment had revolted and that Eksten had been killed, not injured, by his own soldiers. Since the revolt had been suppressed, Pavlenkov must have concluded that there was no reason to report the incident. Protopopov did mention the revolt of the 4th Company of the Pavlovsky Regiment, but reported that the mutiny had been nipped in the bud; however, the Stavka did not seem to pay much attention.

Alekseev then gave the tsar Mikhail Rodzyanko's February 26 telegram, which he had received the previous night. In this telegram Rodzyanko had asked Alekseev to persuade the tsar to grant a ministry of confidence (that is, to replace large numbers of personnel within the existing governmental structure, as a way of placating the liberals). The chief of staff explained that identical telegrams had been sent to the front commanders, and Aleksei Brusilov had already sent Alekseev his response: "*Fulfilling faithfully my oath to the tsar*, under the approaching stormy hour I do not see any other exit" (italics added).[5] Alekseev did not report Nikolai Ruzsky's stronger recommendation not to take any repressive measures against the disturbance in the capital, presumably because Ruzsky's recommendation conflicted with the measures Alekseev himself intended to suggest.[6]

The tsar was not pleased to hear such "abominable" news, and the usually very punctual emperor was upset that Alekseev's reports kept him longer than usual, making him late for breakfast.[7] Over the course of the meeting, Nicholas categorically rejected the idea of replacing the current cabinet with a ministry of confidence, but he seems to have accepted Alekseev's suggestion to appoint someone to be in charge of the food supply and another to be in charge of transport. It seems that at least Rodzyanko's February 26 telegram had some influence, though, as expected, Nicholas did not accept a ministry of confidence. The meeting concluded without a final decision.[8]

Breakfast passed in complete silence. News about the soldiers' mutiny began to filter into the Stavka. Everyone's mind appeared to be transfixed by the disturbing news from the capital. Invitees to the breakfast later remarked that Nicholas's face was pale and he did not talk to anyone. The usual conversational "circle" did not take place after breakfast, and the tsar went to his office with Adjutant General Nikolai Ivanov.[9] But even in the midst of a revolution, Nicholas would never break his daily routine. He made sure to take his daily walk on Orsha Highway.[10]

After breakfast, Voeikov caught up with the assistant naval chief of staff at the Stavka, Rear Admiral Aleksandr Bubnov, and asked a question: "Can you guarantee the safety of the imperial family in Livadia [in the Crimea]?" Apparently Voeikov was considering the possibility of transporting the imperial family to the Crimea after the children recovered from the measles. Bubnov answered: "We can guarantee their safety from the external enemy, but not from the internal enemy." Voeikov, shrugging, said: "Rubbish! We will deal with them."[11]

The Duma deputies hurried to assemble in the Tauride Palace. Besides the soldiers' uprising, some deputies had already learned from Rodzyanko that the tsar had issued a decree of prorogation of the Duma. The Duma liberals now had to make a choice. Would they choose to support the insurgency or to accept the prorogation of the Duma?

Rodzyanko decided to appeal to the tsar one final time. He locked himself in his office and composed another telegram to Nicholas urging him to establish a ministry of confidence. The chairman of the Duma deplored the imperial decree of prorogation that deprived Petrograd of "the last bulwark of order" in the face of the total powerlessness of the government "to suppress the disturbances." As a result, a civil war had broken out in the streets, where soldiers were killing their officers. Rodzyanko begged the tsar to withdraw the decree to prorogue the Duma and to grant a ministry of confidence. He pleaded: "Sire, do not delay. . . . The hour that will decide the fate of Yourself and of the fatherland has come. Tomorrow it may already be too late."[12] It would be Rodzyanko's last attempt to reach a compromise, suggesting the formation of a ministry of confidence.

After he sent this letter, Rodzyanko summoned the Council of Elders (Senioren Konvent), which consisted of senior representatives of the parties in the Duma. Unable either to submit meekly to the imperial decree of prorogation or to defy it, the Council of Elders attempted to thread the needle: they passed a resolution accepting the imperial decree of prorogation but stipulating that the deputies should not disperse. It marked the Duma's first step on the side of the revolution, although it was a tiny step. Since the official session could not be held due to the imperial decree, the Duma deputies held an unofficial private session at 2 p.m. Then, at a private meeting that lasted from 2 to 5 p.m., the deputies debated how they should replace the current government.

By this time, a group of insurgents were headed toward the Tauride Palace, the seat of the Duma, most likely hoping to obtain legitimacy from the Duma for their revolt. Seeing the crowd gathering outside the Tauride Palace, the socialist deputies Aleksandr Kerensky, Nikolai Chkheidze, and Matvei Skobelev opened the gate and invited the insurgents into the building. A decisive moment for the revolution had arrived.[13]

Insurgents from all over the city now marched to the Tauride Palace and poured into it. Soon the Tauride Palace was occupied by insurgents who wanted to know whether the Duma would support the mutiny. Still unwilling to take power into its own hands by decisively supporting the insurgency, the private meeting of the Duma deputies decided at around 5 p.m. to create a Temporary Committee of the State Duma (hereafter the Duma Committee). It was a second step toward seizing power, though according to Kadet representative Pavel Milyukov, Rodzyanko was still afraid of siding openly with the insurrection, which would mean breaking his oath to the tsar.[14]

The chaos prompted even foreign diplomats to appeal for decisive action. At 11:30 a.m., the French and British ambassadors went to the Foreign Ministry and advised the minister, Nikolai Pokrovsky, to establish a new ministry to restore order. Pokrovsky responded that the Council of Ministers had agreed to form a new government but that the proposal had met with opposition from Protopopov. "Couldn't anyone persuade the emperor?" the ambassadors asked. The foreign minister answered: "The emperor is blind!"[15]

Nicholas's usual routine of a walk after breakfast was interrupted by Alekseev, who brought even more alarming news about the soldiers' revolt in Petrograd.

It is difficult to understand why Nicholas and the Stavka did not pay more attention to the news they had already received. The first news of the soldiers' uprising in Petrograd reached the Stavka at 12:20 p.m. on February 27. Khabalov reported that soldiers involved in the revolt of the 4th Company of the Pavlovsky Regiment on February 26 had been "disarmed and arrested," but he added word of the spiraling mutiny that had begun with the Volynsky Regiment on February 27. Khabalov concluded his report with these disturbing words: "I consider it necessary to request the immediate dispatch of reliable units from the front."[16]

The Stavka, however, did not take the matter seriously as yet, since an hour later a telegram from war minister Mikhail Belyaev optimistically assured the Stavka that every conceivable measure had been taken to suppress the disorder and that the government maintained complete calm.[17] Belyaev's telegram countermanded Khabalov's request that the Stavka dispatch reliable troops.

To be sure, Belyaev was the war minister, but he was not directly in charge of implementing security measures, and it was a serious mistake on the part of Alekseev and the Stavka that they did not act immediately on Khabalov's request. Perhaps Alekseev and the Stavka latched on to the optimistic judgment of the war minister out of reluctance to deploy troops from the front. Preparations for the spring offensive had been carefully mapped out, and Alekseev and the high command did not wish to disrupt the plan they had made in consultation with the Allied powers. Nonetheless, the least Alekseev and other commanding officers could have done was to verify the accuracy of the information given by Khabalov and Belyaev, respectively, by contacting the naval and/or army General Staff in Petrograd. This Alekseev did not do.

Together with the telegrams from Khabalov and Belyaev, Alekseev also brought Rodzyanko's second telegram to the tsar, begging him to form a ministry of confidence and urging, "Sire, do not delay." Not realizing the seriousness of the crisis yet, Nicholas treated this telegram, too, as a nuisance.

Some of the tsar's entourage, however, were alarmed by the news of the disturbances in the capital. The day before, February 26, court historian Dmitry Dubensky and the tsar's physician, Dr. Sergei Fyodorov, had hatched the idea of dispatching General Ivanov, the former commander of the southwestern front, to suppress the disturbance in the capital.[18]

After Dubensky and Fyodorov returned to the Stavka, they went straight to General Ivanov and told him that the emperor was likely to appoint him as the commander of a punitive detachment against the insurrection in Petrograd, assuring the general that his seat was arranged for a meeting with the emperor at dinner so that they could discuss this matter.[19] After they left Ivanov, they went back to the governor's house. As they walked on Dneprovsky Prospect, they saw Voeikov coming out of one of the houses. Even as the crisis in Petrograd was escalating, the palace commandant was still busily looking for a house in Mogilev for his wife to purchase.[20]

That evening, Nicholas made two decisions: to leave the Stavka for Tsarskoe Selo the next morning and to send reliable troops to Petrograd to suppress the disorder. Originally he had not intended to leave the Stavka until March 1. But sometime in the afternoon he received a telephone call from Pavel Benckendorff at Tsarskoe Selo, informing the tsar that Alexandra was toying with the idea of leaving Tsarskoe Selo, to ensure the safety of the children. Benckendorff's call must have been a decisive factor, as Nicholas made the decision to leave Mogilev immediately. At 7 p.m., following afternoon tea, he sent a telegram to Alexandra telling her that he planned to leave Mogilev for Tsarskoe Selo on the following morning, February 28, at 2:30.[21] He hoped that by sending reinforcements from the cavalry units in Novgorod, "disorders among the troops would be soon ended." In addition, he sent a letter to the empress to be delivered by a courier on the next train:

After the news of yesterday from town [Petrograd] I saw many faces here with frightened expressions. Luckily Alekseev is calm, but finds a very energetic man must be named to make the ministers work for the food situation, coal, railways etc.[22]

Sometime in either late afternoon or early evening, he made another decision: to suppress the disorder in the capital by sending the expeditionary forces from the front. It is not known exactly how and when the decision to send punitive detachments to the capital was made, but it appears that the appointment of General Ivanov as commander was decided upon prior to seven o'clock in the evening, before the news of the further deterioration of the situation in Petrograd had made its way to the Stavka.[23]

Alekseev begged Nicholas not to take this trip to Tsarskoe Selo, giving multiple reasons. The two trains needed to transport the emperor and his entourage would hinder the movement of the expeditionary forces. He would endanger his personal safety. And his journey would make it difficult to have efficient communication between the tsar and the Stavka. Alekseev may also have hoped to keep the tsar far from the empress's influence. Nicholas told the general that he would think about it and let him know of his decision. Alekseev returned to his office and told a subordinate in the operation divisions: "Thank God, he changed his mind. He is not going to leave and stay here." But Alekseev was mistaken. At midnight, Nicholas had Voeikov make arrangements for departure behind Alekseev's back.[24] The commandant of the railway regiment, Colonel Georgy Aleksandrovich von Thal, received the order from Voeikov to make preparations so that the imperial trains could leave at 2:30 a.m. on February 28 for the emperor to return to Tsarskoe Selo.[25] When they were informed of this sudden decision, Nicholas's entourage had to pack things in a hurry to prepare for the journey. It should be noted that his decision to return to Tsarskoe Selo was prompted by his desire to be with his family, not to deal with the disturbances in the capital. As Nikolai Bazili sarcastically remarked later: "He was first of all an excellent husband and a good father. In these moments of anguish, he was anxious about his own family and desired above all to be with them."[26] The fate of his family mattered more to the tsar than the fate of the state at that moment.

Having formed the Duma Committee, as evening fell on February 27 Rodzyanko and other Duma deputies made one last attempt to negotiate with Prince Nikolai Golitsyn's government for the transfer of power. Earlier that day Rodzyanko had called Grand Duke Mikhail in Gatchina and urged him to come to the capital; Mikhail and his personal secretary, Nikolai Johnson, took the express train and arrived in Petrograd at 5 p.m. At 6 p.m., Rodzyanko, Nikolai Nekrasov, and two other Octobrist Duma deputies (Ivan Ivanovich Dmitryukov, who was also secretary of the Duma, and Nikanor Vasilievich Savich) met Mikhail, Golitsyn, and Belyaev at the Mariinsky Palace, the seat of the government. According to the minutes of the Duma Committee, two members of the Duma delegates demanded that the grand duke take over as regent and advise Nicholas to step down as tsar.[27] This is important because it indicates that already on February 27, some Duma leaders were entertaining the idea of Nicholas's abdication. It is doubtful, however, that Rodzyanko supported this position at that time. Rodzyanko did demand the resignation of the Golitsyn government and the transfer of power to the Duma Committee, and he urged Grand Duke Mikhail to assume a temporary regency to head a military dictatorship in Petrograd. It appears that the discussions at the Council of Elders and the private meeting indicated radicalization of the Duma members, who were not satisfied with Rodzyanko's insistence on a ministry of confidence and instead demanded the establishment of a responsible ministry or even the abdication of Nicholas II. As we will see later, Grand Duke Mikhail suggested to his brother that Prince Lvov, not Rodzyanko, should head the Council of Ministers after the resignation of the Golitsyn government. Rodzyanko had to be mindful of the pressure from his colleagues, and plot a way to recover his power among the Duma liberals. It is possible to surmise that he had to accept the establishment of a responsible ministry to retain his power in the face of his colleagues' pressure.[28] As for Golitsyn, who refused to transfer power to the Duma Committee, Rodzyanko warned him that the entire cabinet would be arrested. Rodzyanko returned to the Tauride Palace having failed in his final attempt to negotiate the formation of a ministry of confidence. Finally, at 11 p.m., under pressure from his colleagues, Rodzyanko, as chairman of the Duma Committee, decided to seize power from the current tsarist government. He solemnly declared: "I consent to take power only on one condition, I demand—and this refers especially to you, Aleksandr Fyodorovich [Kerensky]—that all members of the committee . . . unconditionally and blindly subordinate themselves to my command." In addition to naming Kerensky, Rodzyanko's speech was addressed to his rival Milyukov without specifically mentioning him by name. The members of the Duma Committee, embarrassed by Rodzyanko's pompous speech, kept silent, but Kerensky reminded Rodzyanko that he was still vice chairman of the Petrograd Soviet.[29]

The Duma Committee now clearly stood for the revolution. It created a Military Commission and began to take measures not only to restore order but also to remove pockets of resistance from the old regime; consequently, they began to arrest the former tsarist ministers and officials.

In the meantime, the tsar's Council of Ministers had had an eventful afternoon. At a meeting at Golitsyn's apartment, the ministers had unanimously decided to place Petrograd under martial law and transfer all power temporarily to the commander of the Petrograd Military District, Khabalov. But Khabalov had no combat experience, and both his immediate subordinates, Lieutenant General Aleksandr Chebykin, and Chebykin's replacement, Colonel Vladimir Pavlenkov, were ill. Not knowing what to do without more experienced officers, Khabalov completely lost his nerve. Appalled by the paralysis of the security authorities, the war minister, Belyaev, on his own initiative dismissed the sick and absent Chebykin and appointed Major General Mikhail Ippolitovich Zankevich, head of the army General Staff, to assist Khabalov.

The Council of Ministers met again at 7 p.m., this time at the Mariinsky Palace, since Golitsyn's apartment was dangerously close to the center of the insurgency. At this meeting, the Council of Ministers decided to send the tsar a telegram requesting the formation of a dictatorship headed by a popular general, a change of composition for the cabinet, the dismissal of Protopopov, and a negotiated settlement with the Duma. The council delegated all authority to Golitsyn temporarily, and forced Protopopov to resign on the pretext of "illness."[30] It was the last cabinet meeting of the Golitsyn government.

The Duma Committee had taken power in the capital. Some ministers awaited their arrests by the insurgents, and others, including Protopopov, slipped out of the Mariinsky Palace. They were now hunted men.

News of the accelerating crisis in Petrograd finally convinced the Stavka and Nicholas of the gravity of the situation. At 7:35 p.m. on February 27, Alekseev received two telegrams from Belyaev. Earlier that morning, the minister of war had assured the Stavka that the security authorities were taking energetic measures to suppress the mutiny. The war minister's telegrams that evening showed a striking shift in tone. In the first, Belyaev informed the Stavka that "the situation in Petrograd is becoming extremely serious." The soldiers' mutiny was spreading to other units. The war minister requested the immediate dispatch of "truly reliable units in substantial numbers." A second telegram immediately followed, reporting that the Council of Ministers had now declared Petrograd to be in a state of siege, and that in view of General Khabalov's confusion, Belyaev had been compelled to appoint General Zankevich to assist the commander of the Petrograd Military District.[31]

By this time, Alekseev had received two contradictory telegrams from front commanders. A telegram sent by General Aleksei Evert of the western front, who at that point was still unaware of the soldiers' revolt, expressed concern with the disruption of transport of food to the front due to the railway strikes, and recommended military action to restore order to the rails.[32] General Ruzsky, who was aware of the soldiers' insurrection, sent the tsar a telegram that advised urgent measures but not violence. "Under existing circumstances," Ruzsky wrote, "repressive measures could only aggravate the situation rather than accomplish the necessary, lasting peace."[33] Alekseev was confronted with the difficult task of navigating between these two contradictory recommendations. In an urgent audience with the tsar, he reported on the dire situation in Petrograd. The idea of sending a punitive detachment, headed by General Ivanov, had already been suggested to the tsar, and Belyaev's telegrams must have solidified Nicholas's resolve to put down the mutiny.

Supper was served at 8 p.m. When the tsar entered the dining room, his face was pale, and to Dubensky his eyes were not the same as usual. Clearly, Alekseev's latest reports had alarmed him. He walked behind the dinner guests silently. During the supper, General Ivanov sat next to the tsar, and the two were talking in whispers to each other and ignoring the other guests. After supper, the tsar bowed and quickly disappeared into his office.[34]

Nicholas then summoned General Ivanov and appointed him commander of the Petrograd Military District, to replace Khabalov. It was an appointment Nicholas made without consultation with Alekseev, who had no choice but to accept the decision.[35]

General Ivanov, a stocky man of sixty-six who had a massive beard, came from humble origins. During the Russo-Japanese War he had been assigned to the Siberian Army in Manchuria. In 1907 he had mercilessly suppressed a revolt by sailors in Kronstadt. At the beginning of World War I he became a commander on the southwestern front, with Alekseev as his chief of staff, and carried out successful operations against the Austrian army, but his plan to carry forward the operation was thwarted by General Ruzsky, who took command of the northwestern front. Directly responsible for the great retreat of the Russian army in 1915, Ivanov was relieved of his post as commander of the southwestern front (replaced by General Brusilov) and since then had worked in a sinecure at Mogilev. Ivanov and Alekseev, who had never been close to begin with, were no longer on speaking terms. Ivanov confided to his closest friends that he had been dismissed because of Alekseev's intrigues.[36]

The imperial couple liked the old general for his unflagging devotion to the throne and his simplicity, which they considered represented the character of the simple Russian people. Ivanov may have been Nicholas's favorite general, but he did not command the respect of his peers. Shortly after the appointment, while Lieutenant General Nikolai Mikhailovich Tikhmenev, chief of military communications of theaters of military operations, was delivering a report in Alekseev's office, Ivanov came in. As Tikhmenev recounted later, "Alekseev stood straight, tightened himself up, and in an imposingly official tone told Ivanov: 'Your Highness, the sovereign-emperor ordered you to head the St. George Battalion and cavalry units to Petrograd to . . . suppress the revolt.'" Ivanov immediately replied, "The sovereign's will is sacred for me, and I will fulfill his order." Tikhmenev left the room before he could overhear Alekseev's conversation with Ivanov, but he had the distinct impression that Alekseev had some serious misgivings about Ivanov's mission.[37]

Alekseev was not alone in this opinion. Learning about the appointment, Quartermaster General Aleksandr Lukomsky blurted out to Alekseev: "How could you consent to such an appointment?!" Lukomsky considered Ivanov to be totally incompetent and inappropriate for the task assigned to him. "He was absolutely not the person who should be entrusted with such authority," Lukomsky continued, "and who could not be expected to do anything."[38] According to Bubnov, Ivanov lived in his railcar without doing anything, and his main concern was to sit at the dinner table with the tsar.[39] Nor did General Yury Danilov, chief of staff of the northern front, mince words in describing Ivanov's petty ambition, distrustfulness, narrow-mindedness, and obsequiousness. "He was called to suppress the insurrection in the capital," Danilov remarked; "that would require will, resoluteness, and authority, the qualities that were missing in General Ivanov."[40]

As for Ivanov himself, the old general must have been elated, for this appointment would give him a chance to shine. Resentful of Alekseev, Ruzsky, and Brusilov, he was eager to fulfill his task without consulting any of his personal enemies, whether those at the Stavka or the commanders of the northern and southwestern fronts. He would outshine his detractors by scoring a major victory against the insurgents. But the other officers' distrust of Ivanov portended his ultimate failure.

During the meeting with Ivanov, Alekseev granted the general extraordinary power to enforce martial law by overriding civil authority.[41] After his meeting with Alekseev, Ivanov came to see Tikhmenev to arrange the details of his mission. Tikhmenev agreed that he would inform Ivanov directly of the movements of additional units sent from the northern front for his command, but requested that Ivanov should send telegrams directly to him in turn. He warned that it was likely not all the telegrams would go through, for they would be intercepted. This turned out to be true. Only after the revolution did it become clear that Tikhmenev had received just one telegram from Ivanov.[42]

News of the spiraling revolution in Petrograd reached Tsarskoe Selo on February 27. Belyaev called Major General Pavel Pavlovich Groten, assistant commandant of the palace, and warned that the empress and her children might be in danger. This must have been around 7 p.m., about the same time the war minister sent the alarming telegram to the Stavka. Benckendorff, grand marshal of the imperial court, then called Voeikov again, informing the palace commandant that the empress was on the verge of nervous exhaustion and sought her husband's advice again as to the advisability of her leaving Tsarskoe Selo with her sick children for Mogilev.[43] Voeikov intruded into the telephone room of the headquarters and, to the annoyance of the telephone operators, monopolized the telephone connection between Tsarskoe Selo and the Stavka for three hours. Going back and forth from the governor's office and the Stavka headquarters, he served as the intermediary in the exchange between Nicholas and Alexandra.[44] Soon after this, the telephone connections between Tsarskoe Selo and the Stavka were cut off.[45]

Nicholas thought that it was out of the question that the empress would travel by train to the Stavka with sick children, as the security of the railways was not ensured. It would be better and safer for him to return to Tsarskoe Selo rather than the other way around.[46] General Tikhmenev, who as communications head at the Stavka was responsible, along with Thal, for coordinating the movements of the imperial train, had to scramble to get the trains ready without the careful inspections usually given for any movement of imperial trains and without coordinating with the schedule of the military trains. To make sure that the trains were prepared, Tikhmenev had to go to the station personally in the middle of the night, something he had never done before.[47]

At 11:12 p.m. on February 27, the empress telegraphed to Nicholas: "The revolution yesterday [today?] took a frightening turn. I learned that other units had joined. The information was worse than ever." Then at 1:05 a.m. on February 28 she sent another: "Concessions are necessary. Many troops took the side of the revolution. Alix." The revolution in the capital was clearly tightening the noose in Tsarskoe Selo, as even the intransigent Alexandra was talking about concessions.[48] Yet it was Nicholas who opted for firmness this time.

At half past ten in the evening on February 27, Grand Duke Mikhail requested a direct conversation with the tsar through the Hughes telegraphic apparatus (which allowed two-way communications, though not simultaneously). The grand duke suggested that to bring the anarchy to an end, it would be necessary to dismiss the present ministry and to organize a new cabinet that would both enjoy the trust of the emperor and command the respect and confidence of the nation. He requested the tsar's permission to issue a manifesto to that effect in the tsar's name, and suggested that Prince Georgy Lvov would be the most suitable candidate for the head of the future cabinet.[49] He stopped short of suggesting that a military dictatorship should be established in the capital under his regency, as had been urged by Rodzyanko.

When Nicholas received his brother's message, he refused to communicate directly with him, as Mikhail requested, and instead ordered General Alekseev to convey his reply. Although in his diary he noted his meeting with General Ivanov, he mentioned nothing about his brother's plea.[50] Nicholas's refusal to speak to his own brother at this time of crisis showed the intensity of his intransigence. He did not have an iota of intention to seek a political solution; he would suppress the revolution through military means alone.

Though ill, Alekseev delivered the tsar's message to his brother, bluntly rejecting his suggestions one by one. First, the tsar did not consider it possible to postpone his departure for Tsarskoe Selo, and would leave Mogilev for Tsarskoe Selo at 2:30 in the morning on the following day. Second, concerning the dismissal of the Council of Ministers, the tsar himself would decide on this matter pending his return to the capital. Third, with regard to the suppression of the disorder in the capital, General Ivanov would be sent to Petrograd for that purpose. Fourth, on the next day, reliable troops would be sent to the capital from the northern and western fronts.[51]

Alekseev intimated his agreement with Mikhail's recommendation to seek a political solution acceptable to the Duma liberals, and promised to urge the emperor to "take some measures" when he reported to the tsar the next morning.[52] Importantly, despite his support of Nicholas's policy for military suppression of the revolution, Alekseev considered it necessary to combine coercive measures with a political concession—replacing the current government with a ministry of confidence.

Shortly after this conversation was over, a telegram from Golitsyn arrived, reporting to the emperor that the cabinet found itself unable to function in the face of the prevailing anarchy and imploring the tsar to relieve the ministers of their duties and appoint a new ministry that enjoyed the confidence of the nation. Despite the high fever from which he was suffering, Alekseev implored the tsar "on his knees" to seek the political solution recommended by Golitsyn.

He did not succeed. Alekseev reported to General Lukomsky that the emperor was displeased with Golitsyn's telegram, and added with a sigh of resignation that the emperor did not want to talk to Alekseev. The unwell Alekseev went back to his quarters to rest, though his night was not yet over. A few hours later Nicholas appeared in person in Lukomsky's room and handed him a copy of his imperial order to the chairman of the Council of Ministers. He made sure that Lukomsky conveyed this message to Alekseev. The order rejected Golitsyn's resignation and informed him of the appointment of General Ivanov as the new commander of the Petrograd Military District. The tsar declared: "This is my final decision, which I shall not change, and therefore, it is useless to report to me further on this issue."[53] Nicholas was acting as firmly as his wife had earlier insisted.

The telegram to Petrograd containing the tsar's order was sent at 11:25 p.m., but no one was there to receive it. The government had already disappeared. Foreign Minister Pokrovsky had notified the British, French, and Italian ambassadors that the revolution had been completed and that the government had no military means to suppress it.[54]

Unhappy as they were with Ivanov's appointment, military leaders clearly meant to give him access to the most reliable forces available in order to move against the insurgents in the capital. General Alekseev was understandably reluctant to commit forces from the front for the suppression of an internal disorder, given that the scheduled spring offensive was approaching. Moreover, he was not at all sure of the morale of the soldiers, who would be ordered to fire not upon the enemy but upon their fellow countrymen. Perhaps his wife's experience of looking down from her window on Bloody Sunday in 1905 and seeing the troops shooting demonstrators crossed his mind. Despite this reluctance, however, Alekseev endorsed Nicholas's decision for a counterrevolutionary offensive.

By late at night on February 27, Alekseev had taken measures to move sizable numbers of troops from the front. In his conversation with General Danilov, Alekseev instructed him to dispatch two infantry regiments and two cavalry regiments, selected from the "strongest and most reliable units" and commanded by the "strongest generals, because apparently Khabalov lost his head, and it is necessary to have reliable, capable, and bold assistants at the disposal of General Ivanov." In addition to these four regiments, the northern front was instructed to send one machine gun detachment and two artillery batteries. Alekseev further stated: "The situation demands the immediate arrival of troops. . . . It is a threatening moment, and it is necessary to do everything to speed up the dispatch of strong troops. The problem of our future depends on this."[55]

The western front was ordered to dispatch one brigade from the Ural Cossack Division or the 2nd Cavalry Division equipped with machine guns, commanded by bold and energetic generals.[56] The Stavka further instructed the main administration of the General Staff in Petrograd to form a staff for Ivanov's forces, and made arrangements to install a field radio station between Orsha and Tsarskoe Selo to coordinate information and the activities of Ivanov's forces, the northern front, the western front, and the Stavka.[57] Alekseev then ordered the addition of one infantry and one cavalry battery each from the northern and western fronts to be sent to the capital.[58] Furthermore, Alekseev instructed General Iosif Ivanovich Mrozovsky, commander of the Moscow Military District, to declare martial law in his military district.[59] All military preparations for the spring offensive were pushed to secondary importance next to the suppression of revolt in the capital.[60] General Ruzsky, commander of the northern front, had been skeptical of coercive measures to suppress the revolution, but he had no choice other than to obey Alekseev's order to dispatch troops from his front.[61]

Before he talked with Grand Duke Mikhail through the Hughes apparatus, Alekseev learned that the tsar had changed his mind and planned to
leave Mogilev for Tsarskoe Selo to join his family. Shortly after midnight,
despite his high fever, he rushed to the governor's house as the emperor
was preparing for his departure. He brought a telegram Khabalov had sent
at 8:10 p.m. on February 27, which was received at 12:55 a.m. on February
28. In it, Khabalov informed the Stavka of the total disintegration of the
loyal troops. All the units had taken the side of the rebels, and only small
units were assembled in the Winter Palace under the command of Major
General Zankevich. Khabalov flatly confessed: "It is now impossible to
fulfill the order to suppress the revolt in the capital."[62]

According to his daughter, Alekseev again implored the emperor to
stay in Mogilev, but the tsar was determined to join his family.[63] Alekseev
saw that Count Vladimir Fredericks, Voeikov, and aide-de-camp Anatoly
Mordvinov were already dressed for the journey. Alekseev made a last-ditch
appeal to Mordvinov: "It is a mistake for the Sovereign to leave the Stavka. At
this time, it is better to stay here. I tried to dissuade him from leaving here,
but His Majesty is very worried about the empress and the children, and
I decided not to insist." Mordvinov asked Alekseev what should be done.
The chief of staff answered: "I just told the Sovereign that there now remains
one thing: assemble reliable units somewhere near Tsarskoe Selo and take
the offensive against the mutinied Petrograd. I have already taken all the
measures, but of course, it will take time, at least five or six days, before all
the units assemble. Until that time no measure is worth taking with small
forces."[64] To Mordvinov's question as to whether Petrograd would be quiet,
the general shrugged and said: "Things will become worse there. Sailors will
join the mutiny, and it will spread to Tsarskoe Selo."[65]

Nicholas left the governor's house, bidding farewell to Alekseev at the
Stavka headquarters. He and Fredericks got into an automobile and drove

to the station, with the entourage following.[66] At 2 a.m. on February 28, Ivanov was summoned to the tsar's railcar. Apparently not satisfied with the power granted by Alekseev, the general requested that he be given absolute power over four ministries: internal affairs, agriculture, trade and industry, and transport. Nicholas went far beyond his request and granted him dictatorial power over all ministries.[67] According to Ivanov's later testimony to the Provisional Government's Investigation Committee, the old general offered the opinion that military means alone would not solve the crisis and suggested a political concession in the form of a ministry of confidence be granted. To this Nicholas replied: "Yes, yes. General Alekseev just mentioned it." Ivanov had the distinct impression that the tsar had made up his mind to make this concession. However, Nicholas took no such action and continued to reject all suggestions of political concessions.[68] Ivanov's testimony with regard to the political concession should be taken with a grain of salt: it is contradicted by Ivanov's determination to assume a dictatorship in Petrograd. The possibility of bloodshed was from the beginning inherent in undertaking the expedition.[69]

As Ivanov was leaving the tsar's railcar, the emperor addressed the general: "Good-bye. We will most likely see you tomorrow in Tsarskoe Selo." The tsar went to sleep. The imperial trains began to move slowly in the darkness at 5 a.m. on February 28.[70]

CHAPTER 7

# Imperial Train
# and Information Blockade

When Nicholas left Mogilev at 5 a.m. on February 28 with his entourage, officers assembled on the platform to see the tsar off with enthusiastic hurrahs and the imperial Russian anthem, "God Save the Tsar." Nicholas had no inkling of what was in store for him on this fateful journey.[1]

The straightest, shortest route from Mogilev to Tsarskoe Selo was to take the Vindavo–Rybinskaya Line through Orsha and Dno. Instead, the tsar and his entourage decided to take a longer, roundabout route, from Orsha through Smolensk to Vyazma, then north from Vyazma through Rzhev to Likhoslavl. They would transfer to the Nikolaevskaya Line at Likhoslavl and travel through Bologoe, Malaya Vishera, and Tosno, and finally take the branch line from Tosno through Gatchina and Aleksandrovskaya before arriving at last in Tsarskoe Selo. The distance of this roundabout route was 1,013 kilometers, compared with 810 kilometers for the shorter, more direct route. Besides, their choice meant that the imperial trains would travel along five different railway lines instead of just one.[2]

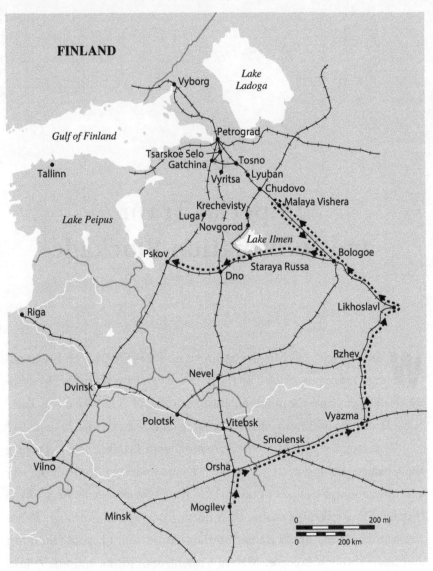

*Nicholas's Train Journey, February 28–March 1*

Part of the reason for the choice of route had to do with the military's needs. The first priority for the Stavka was getting General Nikolai Ivanov and his troops to Petrograd. Furthermore, the reinforcements from the northern and the western fronts would need to travel to Petrograd. Therefore, the traffic on the Vindavo–Rybinskaya Line was expected to be heavy. The speed of the imperial trains was limited, and the security regulations along the way for the imperial trains would be rigorous and cumbersome, disrupting other railway movements.[3] It was quite understandable that the Stavka did not want the tsar to travel the shortest route. But if the tsar wanted to reach Tsarskoe Selo as quickly as possible, he could have directed the palace commandant, Major General Vladimir Voeikov, to choose the Vindavo–Rybinskaya Line over the objections of the Stavka's transport authority. That would have had an added advantage of having the St. George Battalion to protect the imperial trains. He did not. That would turn out to be a fatal mistake.

For security reasons the tsar and his entourage always traveled in two identical trains—the suite train and the imperial train.[4] The suite train, known as train B, carried the entourage and led the way, clearing the route and relaying information in code back to the imperial train, train A, which followed one hour behind the suite train. Tsar Nicholas was on train A, along with Voeikov and the minister of the imperial court, Count Vladimir Fredericks.

The two trains moved slowly through the snow-covered countryside, where there was no hint of the insurrection roiling the capital. Colonel Georgy von Thal, commandant of the railway regiment, on board the suite train, noted: "There was absolutely no sign of disturbance or confusion either along the railway or in the cities we passed through. Everything was quiet and calm."[5] Gendarmes and troops were stationed at all the major railway stations, where the imperial trains were, as ever, greeted with cheers and bands playing "God Save the Tsar."[6] The information about the movement of the imperial trains was relayed from station to station through the Ministry of Transport via telegraph. As the trains went by, all the people except railway workers, soldiers of the railway regiments, gendarmes, and police were cleared from the stations and nearby areas. All passenger and freight trains were moved to the sidings as the imperial trains went through.

As the imperial trains rumbled through the serene countryside, they began to receive disturbing news of the deteriorating situation in Petrograd transmitted from the Stavka through the military communication line. Just after the imperial train passed Orsha, a telegram arrived. Twenty State Council deputies had signed a joint petition asking the emperor to reopen the Duma and the State Council and appoint a new government that would enjoy the confidence of the country. This was the same request that Mikhail Rodzyanko had asked the tsar to accept on the previous day, and which Nicholas had turned down. But seeing that the petition came from State Council members, who were usually more conservative than the Duma members, had a sobering effect on the tsar. Voeikov entered the emperor's salon car and found him standing in a reflective mood with the telegram in his hands.[7] In addition, war minister Mikhail Belyaev had sent a telegram to Voeikov via the Stavka with the news that the Mariinsky Palace was occupied by insurgents, and all ministers except foreign minister Nikolai Pokrovsky and transport minister Edvard Bronislavovich Kriger-Voinovsky had run away.[8] Another telegram from Belyaev reported that the mutiny had spread to the entire city and confirmed that the government had ceased its normal function.[9]

At 3 p.m. on February 28, upon arrival at Vyazma, the emperor received yet another telegram from Belyaev, reporting that as of noon of that day, the number of loyal troops had shrunk to four companies, two batteries, and one machine gun company.[10] Shortly after they passed Vyazma, Nicholas sent the first telegram to Alexandra: "Left this morning at 5. Thoughts always together. Glorious weather. Hope [you] are feeling well and quiet. Many troops sent from front. Fondest love. Niki."[11] The alarming situation in the capital described by Belyaev's telegrams still did not seem to have registered in Nicholas's mind.

The situation in Petrograd was swiftly changing from bad to worse. Around 8:30 a.m. a telegram from Major General Sergei Khabalov arrived at Mogilev, informing the Stavka that the number of loyal troops had shrunk to 600 infantry and 500 cavalry soldiers, who had 15 machine guns, 12 larger guns, and 80 shells. Khabalov commented, with astonishing understatement, "The situation is extremely difficult."[12] Urgent measures were necessary to prevent further deterioration of the situation prior to the arrival of Ivanov's troops.

Adjutant General Mikhail Alekseev ordered Adjutant General Nikolai Ruzsky to send the "most reliable battalion" from the Vyborg Fortress Artillery, 112 kilometers northwest of Petrograd. In addition, he ordered the navy minister, Ivan Konstantinovich Grigorovich, to send the "two most reliable battalions" of the Kronstadt Fortress to Petrograd immediately. The Kronstadt Fortress was on an island only 25 kilometers west of Petrograd.[13] It is important to note that Alekseev phrased this not as his own direct order; rather, he prefaced it with the words "The imperial majesty directed me to order"—evidently making an effort to camouflage the order, as if it had emanated from the emperor, not from him. He knew that Ruzsky and Grigorovich had been opposed to military intervention, so these words were necessary to compel the commander of the northern front and the navy minister to obey. But since Nicholas had already departed the Stavka, there was no way that Alekseev could have consulted the supreme commander on these orders. These orders came from Alekseev alone. At this point he was endorsing and actively formulating the policy of military suppression of the revolution.

By late morning the situation had become even more hopeless. The Stavka received a telegram from Belyaev reporting that the rebels "had occupied the most important institutions in all parts of the city" and the "normal life of the government had stopped."[14] In order to assess the situation in Petrograd, General Ivanov contacted Khabalov via the Hughes apparatus in the Admiralty. Khabalov's answers to Ivanov's questions revealed that the government and all the institutions in the capital were near collapse. At 11:30 a.m., Khabalov's answers to Ivanov were transmitted to Alekseev. According to this information, only a small number of troops remained at Khabalov's disposal; the revolutionaries had taken all the railway stations as well as all artillery and munitions factories and depots into their own hands, and had arrested the ministers; no food supplies were available to Khabalov, who had also lost contact with all technical and economic institutions connected with military operations.[15] Finally, just after 2 p.m., the Stavka received news that the loyal troops had completely disintegrated. The remaining loyal soldiers surrendered their arms on the orders of their commanders and quietly returned to their barracks.[16]

Between 1 and 3 p.m. on February 28, Alekseev sent a telegram to all the front commanders, outlining the development of the revolution in Petrograd from February 26 until February 28, based on the information from Khabalov's and Belyaev's telegrams. This was the first comprehensive report of the revolution in the capital that the front commanders received. "According to private information," Alekseev wrote, "the revolutionary government had taken over the administration of Petrograd, declaring its manifesto, capturing four guard regiments on its side, occupying the arsenal of the Peter and Paul Fortress, [and] the main artillery administration." The insurgents were also taking over major government buildings. The troops, under the influence of propagandists, were abandoning their weapons, either having taken the side of the insurgency or remaining neutral. Random shootings were happening everywhere, and rebels were disarming officers in the streets. All the ministers were safe, but the ministerial work had ceased. Shcheglovitov had apparently been arrested. Alekseev reported the outcome he feared most: "In the State Duma, a Soviet of leaders of the [left-wing] parties was formed for [establishing] relations with institutions and persons, and additional elections from the workers and the rebel troops have been called for." Having just received a telegram from Khabalov saying that he no longer had any control over the events in Petrograd, Alekseev concluded his message to the front commanders:

> Informing all this, I add that we all must fulfill our *sacred duty to the sovereign* and the motherland, maintain *our faithful obligation to our oath* . . . , and secure railway movement and food supply reserves. (Italics added)[17]

If Nicholas's telegram to Alexandra from Vyazma around 3 p.m. betrayed the tsar's indifference to the dire situation in the capital, Alekseev's telegram to the front commanders, sent around the same time, revealed a sharp grasp of the reality that Petrograd was under the control of mutineers influenced by radical elements. The "private" information he cited might refer to information he received from the Naval Staff in Petrograd, telling him that the workers' organization was planning to "raise the banner of socialism and crush the Duma."[18]

Alekseev's understanding was not wholly correct in one crucial respect, however. The proclamation for "the establishment of relations with institutions and persons" had been issued by the Duma Committee, not by the Soviet. The radical Soviet leaders had not actually taken power. Yet the gap between Alekseev's understanding and the actual situation began to influence the process of the revolution, allowing Rodzyanko and the Duma Committee the chance to manipulate information for their own political purposes. It is worth noting that this was the only document in which Alekseev referred to the obligation to be faithful to the oath. His treatment of the oath would start to change as his policy began to diverge from the tsar's.

The latest alarming news about the revolution only hardened Alekseev's resolve to crush the rebellion with overwhelming force. In addition to the sizable reinforcements from the northern front and the western front, as discussed in Chapter 6, he ordered Ruzsky (commander of the northern front) and Aleksei Evert (commander of the western front) to send additional reinforcements; he even requested that Aleksei Brusilov (commander of the southwestern front) prepare three guard battalions for possible use by Ivanov.[19]

Each time the Stavka received information that the situation was worsening in Petrograd, it stepped up the military commitment to Ivanov's attempt to suppress the revolution in the capital. This response stemmed from the belief that Petrograd had fallen into the hands of irresponsible, anarchic masses, influenced by left-wing elements—an alarming situation that, if allowed to develop further, would inevitably undermine the integrity of the army and seriously hamper military operations at the front. The Stavka was given to understand that no forces were at work to restore peace and order in Petrograd. Even worse, they believed—mistakenly—that the radical left-wing elements were forming a revolutionary government.[20]

It is interesting to note that according to Colonel Boris Sergeevsky, chief of communications at the Stavka, early on the morning of March 1 Alekseev instructed Sergeevsky to hand-carry a packet of papers to Grand Duke Sergei, presumably with the intention to persuade him to be the military dictator in the capital.[21] Perhaps Alekseev was contemplating replacing the unreliable Ivanov with the more trusted grand duke after the suppression of the revolution.

The military commanders had a variety of reactions to Alekseev's news. General Ruzsky appeared to have his own sources informing him about events in Petrograd. Early on the morning of March 1, Ruzsky received a telegram from Rodzyanko informing the general that the Duma Committee had seized power. The Stavka, in contrast, would not receive word until 6 a.m.[22] Ruzsky knew more than Alekseev about the nature of the Duma Committee, having received a telegram from the Petrograd Telegraph Agency about its membership, although the inclusion of the two socialists, Nikolai Chkheidze and Aleksandr Kerensky, were of concern to him.[23] For the moment, Ruzsky complied with Alekseev's order to send troops from the northern front, but besides his vocal reservations about the use of force to suppress disorder, he also agreed with Rodzyanko's recommendation that the tsar grant a ministry of confidence, which would involve retaining the existing governmental structure but replacing many of the personnel.

General Evert had a different reaction to Alekseev's order to send reinforcement troops. He considered it totally unacceptable for workers in the cities to stage strikes when Russia was waging war. He believed that his troops would demonstrate "unswerving loyalty to the tsar and the motherland" and take the measures necessary to fulfill their "sacred" obligation.[24] He wholeheartedly endorsed Alekseev's plan for military suppression of the revolution.

In the afternoon of February 28, the Stavka ordered the western front to set up a field radio station at Nevel so that Ivanov could remain in contact with the Stavka and with the northern front headquarters at Pskov. The western front immediately complied with this request, promising to send two sets of radio station equipment to Nevel.[25] It is interesting to note that the Stavka assigned this task to the western front rather than the northern front, which was closer to Nevel and Ivanov's forces. Alekseev did not trust Ruzsky.


In the meantime, Ivanov was organizing his expedition. Before his departure from Mogilev (eight hours after the imperial trains), Ivanov had instructed Ruzsky and Evert to assemble reinforcements from the northern front at Aleksandrovskaya, near Tsarskoe Selo, and those from the western front at Tsarskoe Selo itself, where he planned to arrive around 8 a.m. on March 1.[26] The first reinforcements from the northern front were expected to arrive at Aleksandrovskaya by late night on February 28 through March 1, and the last troops from the western front not earlier than March 2.[27] Based on what he had learned from his conversation with Khabalov through the Hughes apparatus, Ivanov concluded that suppression of the revolution would not be achieved quickly with only three companies of the St. George Battalion from the Stavka alone, and that he had no choice but to wait for massive reinforcements before initiating military action against Petrograd.

Nicholas was not happy with Ivanov's sluggishness.[28] But taking into consideration the total collapse of the loyal forces in the capital, Ivanov must have concluded that the punitive operation against the revolutionary capital would not be easy, contrary to what Nicholas and Voeikov seem to have believed. It would be a large-scale military operation, and without the reinforcements from the front, Ivanov could do little. But given the transport arrangements made for the reinforcements, the tsar and the entourage could actually have taken the Vindavo–Rybinskaya Line, as at the time of their departure the reinforcements would not yet be traveling. Had they done so, that would have changed the course of the revolution.

Ivanov caught up with the St. George Battalion on the way and arrived at Dno, approximately 210 kilometers south of Tsarskoe Selo, around 7 a.m. on March 1—at about the same time that the imperial trains were approaching Bologoe, where they would change direction and head toward Pskov, as will be discussed later. However, from Dno, Ivanov's troops proceeded at an excruciatingly slow speed. It took eleven hours for them to travel from Dno to Vyritsa, some 180 kilometers. By the time they arrived at Vyritsa, about 32 kilometers south of Tsarskoe Selo, it was already 6 a.m. on March 2.[29]

After attempting in vain to convince his brother to grant a ministry of confidence on the night of February 27, Grand Duke Mikhail found it impossible to return from Petrograd to Gatchina, as the route to the railway station was blocked by mutinying soldiers. The grand duke and his secretary, Nikolai Johnson, decided instead to spend the night in the Winter Palace. After they arrived, they found that the palace became the place where the troops that remained loyal to the government began assembling.

But the loyal soldiers were not allowed to stay for long. The palace commandant, General Vladimir Aleksandrovich Komarov, more concerned with protecting the treasures in the Winter Palace than with protecting the government, frantically urged the grand duke to force the dirty soldiers out of the palace. Mikhail complied; instead of thanking the troops who remained to defend the monarchy, he evicted them. The soldiers were outraged. They felt that they were being "kicked out like dogs" by the person they thought they were defending. No wonder many of them deserted their position after they left the Winter Palace.[30] Those who did not desert went back to the Admiralty (from where they had been ordered to move to the Winter Palace) and surrendered their arms; then they went back to the barracks.

The defense of the Winter Palace was entrusted to a unit of the Preobrazhensky Regiment, whose barracks stood nearby. This unit, unlike some of the others in the barracks near the Tauride Palace, did not join the revolt. Uncertain of their loyalty, however, the grand duke and Johnson decided to leave the Winter Palace at 5 a.m. on February 28. They snuck into Princess Olga Pavlovna Putyatina's apartment a couple of buildings down, via the backyard, to avoid the street, where sporadic gunfire could still be heard. For the rest of that day, the grand duke did not venture outside of his hideout, as automobiles filled with soldiers wearing red armbands and carrying red banners drove around shooting in the air and shouting.[31]

While the tsar and his entourage were traveling through the quiet countryside on February 28, there were new developments in Petrograd and

Tsarskoe Selo. On the morning of February 28, Rodzyanko ordered a huge gold-framed portrait of Nicholas II to be removed from the walls of the Tauride Palace. A blank space was left on the wall. Soldiers pierced the portrait with bayonets, and the torn portrait was tacked up behind Rodzyanko's couch. The tsar's former palace security chief, Aleksandr Spiridovich, writes: "What happened eloquently speaks about what the Duma Committee was thinking about the Sovereign."[32]

Nevertheless, he was not on board with the demand for Nicholas's abdication—at least, not yet. Late on February 27, Rodzyanko had reluctantly agreed, under pressure from his colleagues, to elevate their demand from a ministry of confidence to a responsible ministry. But on February 28, he now faced two challenges to his power. First, there was a growing consensus among his colleagues to demand Nicholas's abdication. Second, the soldiers' mutiny had now engulfed not only the entire Petrograd garrison but also the garrisons in surrounding areas. Since the tsar had rudely rejected his brother's plea to accept a ministry of confidence, this potential moderate path was now closed. Yet Rodzyanko was afraid of the high command's reaction were he to demand Nicholas's abdication. As we will see later, he had already rejected a proposal made by one of his colleagues to distribute a nationwide statement declaring: "The old regime has fallen." He knew that the revolution in the capital would collapse immediately if organized army units were employed against it. Even Kerensky, a staunch supporter of the revolution, admitted: "One well-disciplined regiment, equipped with machine-guns . . . could have exterminated the entire Duma—its Left and its Right together."[33]

In the meantime, Nicholas's relatives were increasingly alarmed that the revolution might topple the entire monarchical system. The three senior grand dukes—Pavel (the most senior), Mikhail (second in the line of succession), and Kirill (third in the line of succession)—composed a collective petition to Nicholas, recommending that he issue an imperial manifesto granting the country a responsible ministry, essentially a constitutional monarchy. The draft of this petition was written by Prince Sergei Mikhailovich Putyatin, a minister of the imperial court, and approved by Grand Duke Pavel, who at the time was in charge of the guard units in Tsarskoe Selo. Rodzyanko received this draft petition from a barrister, Nikolai Nikitich Ivanov. (In order to distinguish Nikolai Nikitich Ivanov from General Nikolai Iudovich Ivanov, who commanded the counterrevolutionary forces, I identify the former as Barrister Ivanov here.) Barrister Ivanov was vice chairman of the organization Aid to German POWs, for which Grand Duke Pavel's wife, Princess Olga Paley, was chair. Barrister Ivanov had close connections with Grand Duke Pavel and Princess Paley, while through his work he established a close relationship with Rodzyanko. The grand dukes' petition provided Rodzyanko with a golden opportunity to resolve the dilemma he was facing. The demand for a responsible ministry would more likely be acceptable to the high command than the demand for the abdication of the tsar. Under pressure from the high command, Nicholas might be compelled to accept that demand and grant a responsible ministry. While that would fall far short of what Rodzyanko's colleagues in the Duma Committee wanted, it might meet with wide acceptance among the populace, blunt the radicalism of his colleagues, and mollify the insurgents.[34]

On March 1, Barrister Ivanov brought back to Petrograd the draft manifesto that had been signed by Grand Duke Pavel. The grand duke provided a car for him to make the trip, and an escort of two officers. In Petrograd Barrister Ivanov secured the signature of Kirill first, then went to see Mikhail in his hideout at Princess Putyatina's home on Millionnaya Street. Mikhail asked Ivanov to give him time to think about it, but Barrister Ivanov bluntly told the grand duke that there was no time for deliberation; he could have five or ten minutes to think about it, but no more. Under this pressure, Mikhail signed the draft manifesto.[35]

The draft manifesto signed by the three grand dukes stated:

> We grant the Russian Empire a constitutional system and enjoin
> to continue the interrupted session of the State Duma and the
> State Council by Our decree. We entrust the chairman of the
> State Duma with the immediate formation of a temporary cabinet
> which relies on the confidence of the country and which in agree-
> ment with Us is concerned with the convocation of the legislative
> assembly which is necessary for the urgent reexamination . . . of
> the draft of the new Fundamental Laws of the Russian Empire.[36]

The draft manifesto granted Rodzyanko the power to form a ministry, a
power previously only the emperor's prerogative. This elevated Rodzyanko's position to be almost equal to the tsar's, above the chairman of the
Council of Ministers. The Council of Ministers was to be responsible to the
legislative chambers. The draft manifesto would also rescind the decision
to prorogue the legislative chambers, and envisaged that the Duma would
propose a new set of Fundamental Laws. In other words, the draft manifesto proposed a genuine constitutional monarchy. Rodzyanko and the
grand dukes must have hoped that this manifesto, like the October Manifesto in the 1905 revolution, would ultimately contribute to ending the
revolution and opening a new era. Grand Duke Mikhail noted in his diary
that Barrister Ivanov came at 12:30 p.m. He asked him to sign the draft
manifesto that had already been signed by Grand Dukes Pavel and Kirill.
The manifesto was to grant a complete constitution. On this day, he wrote
a letter to his wife, Natasha Brasova: "I signed the [draft of the] manifesto,
which was already signed by Pavel Aleksandrovich and Kirill, and now by
me, as the senior grand dukes. A new era will begin with this manifesto.
The Sovereign will arrive today, or possibly tomorrow."[37] This was the
grand dukes' last-ditch, desperate attempt to save the monarchy, as they
were frightened that the popular uprising would sweep aside the monar-

chical system itself. Rodzyanko, who was facing the ever-radicalizing revolutionary situation in the capital on the one hand, and a possibility of military intervention on the other, stepped up his demand from a ministry of confidence to a responsible ministry. He also saw the grand dukes' manifesto as a way of restoring his eroding prestige among his colleagues.

Despite the hope shared by Rodzyanko and the grand dukes, Nicholas not only failed to sign the manifesto but did not even receive a copy. By the time the draft was signed by the grand dukes, Nicholas was traveling in the train, and all communications along the railway were under the control of the Duma Committee.

While the tsar and the entourage were traveling by train, the revolution in Petrograd accelerated with astonishing speed. Insurgent soldiers attacked not just units that remained loyal to the government but also those that stood neutral; they did not tolerate neutrality. By the end of February 28, Petrograd had fallen completely into the hands of the insurgents, and the revolt spread all the way to the outskirts of the capital.

The Duma Committee's Military Commission, headed by Colonel Boris Engelgardt, an Octobrist deputy in the Fourth Duma, organized revolutionary units from the insurgents assembled in the Tauride Palace and set to work. With Rodzyanko's approval, the Military Commission created under the Duma Committee swiftly occupied strategically important positions and buildings, including the railway stations, the State Bank, the Central Telephone Station, the Central Telegraph Office, the Central Post Office, military supply facilities, munitions depots, and armament factories. Significantly, the Admiralty, where the Naval Staff and the Navy Ministry were located, remained untouched, as did the headquarters of the army's General Staff. The Military Commission disarmed the police and attempted to combat lawlessness in the streets. It also began to arrest the ministers.[38] Most importantly, by the end of February 28, the Duma Committee had succeeded in controlling all means of communications and transport. The most important factor in establishing this control was the occupation by the Duma Committee of the Ministry of Transport (more accurately the Ministry of Ways and Communications [Ministerstvo Puti i Soobshcheniia]).

This action was led by Aleksandr Aleksandrovich Bublikov, an elected member of the Fourth Duma in 1912 from Perm province who belonged to the Progressive Party.[39] Supported by a detachment of fifty soldiers he randomly picked up and two trucks furnished by the Military Commission, Bublikov marched into the Ministry of Transport around 3 p.m. on February 28 and declared that the ministry was being occupied by the Duma Committee. The soldiers Bublikov assembled included Sosnovsky, an ex-con who had just been released from prison and whose real name was Iosif Rogalsky, and a Bolshevik named E. N. Rulevsky.

Bublikov placed all the ministry's officials under arrest, including the minister of transport, Kriger-Voinovsky, who refused to pledge allegiance to the Duma Committee. The deputy transport minister, General Vladimir Nikolaevich Kislyakov, decided to cooperate with Bublikov under one condition: that he would not take any measures against the tsar.[40] Sosnovsky was given the assignment of guarding the ministry.[41]

Control of the railways and communications was a crucial factor in determining the fate of the revolution. Belyaev, who was still free in the early afternoon of February 28, before Bublikov took over the Ministry of Transport, sent a telegram to Alekseev at 12:25 p.m., recommending that the Stavka take over the administration of the railways and communications. When Alekseev received this telegram, he transferred the railway administration to Kislyakov, who worked under General Nikolai Tikhmenev, the railway and communication chief of the military theater.[42] According to Aleksandr Spiridovich, Kislyakov recommended to Alekseev that he rescind this decision, and Alekseev accepted the recommendation.[43]

Historians would later argue that ceding control of the railways to the Duma Committee was a grave mistake.[44] It would have been impossible, however, for the Stavka to have effectively controlled railway movements and communications from Mogilev. Even if the Stavka had ordered Kislyakov to take over the administration, he would not have been able to do so single-handedly. Kislyakov's job was to coordinate railway communications with military communications, and the latter was Tikhmenev's jurisdiction. Kislyakov was stationed at the Stavka, and because he was sympathetic to the Duma Committee he kept in close touch with Bublikov and his assistant, Professor Yury Lomonosov, behind the back of his superior, General Tikhmenev.[45] Prior to the revolution, railway communications operated in two ways: the Ministry of Transport oversaw communications relayed to stationmasters, and the military communications network connected the military commandants at major stations. During the revolution, however, the Ministry of Transport network took over the military communications channel for the railways.[46] This meant that the imperial trains effectively found themselves under an information blockade, with all communications to and from the trains controlled by the Duma Committee. (It should be noted that the Stavka did attempt to keep the military communications network under the jurisdiction of the communications officer in the army General Staff, although this officer faced constant harassment and obstruction from the Duma Committee.)[47]

Bublikov's first act after taking over the Ministry of Transport was to dispatch a telegram to all railway stations in Russia informing them of the revolution in Petrograd. The text read:

Railroad workers! The old regime, which created chaos in all aspects of state affairs, has proved powerless. The State Duma took the formation of a new government into its own hands. I appeal to you in the name of the fatherland that it now depends on you to save our native land, that it expects from you more than fulfillment of your duties, and that it expects sacrifices from you. The movement of trains must be carried on without interruption and with doubled energy. Technical weaknesses and insufficiencies must be offset by your selfless energy, love for your native land, and your awareness of the importance of transport for the war and the welfare of the rear.[48]

Bublikov's original draft, when submitted to Rodzyanko, had begun with the phrase "The old regime has fallen." Rodzyanko vetoed this sentence, asking Bublikov: "How is it possible that 'the old regime' has fallen? Has it really fallen?" He reminded Bublikov that the tsar was still alive and well, and that the attitude of the high command remained unknown.[49] Rodzyanko was being careful not to alienate the military leaders with unnecessarily inflammatory words, and so he forced Bublikov to soften his tone.

When the revised statement was sent at 1:50 p.m. on February 28, it amounted to the first nationwide statement by the Duma Committee regarding the transfer of power. The impact of Bublikov's telegram was far-reaching. Every single railway station in Russia, "from the front of the war to Vladivostok, from Murmansk to the Persian border," received this news, and all Russia now accepted the revolution as an accomplished fact. According to Lomonosov, "From Bublikov's telegram all knew that by February 28, power was actually in the hands of the Duma." He adds: "Was this really the way it was? Of course not. Bublikov acted as Bismarck had done with the Ems telegram."[50] That is, the telegram Bublikov sent was calculated to appease those, particularly military leaders, who feared the destructive elements of the revolution. It assured them that power was now in responsible hands. Bublikov's telegram would prove one of the most important factors motivating a change of attitude by military leaders. But the Stavka did not know that Bublikov followed this message with another that prohibited any military trains from coming closer to

Petrograd than 270 kilometers, in order to block any counterrevolutionary forces sent from the front.[51]

The intention of the Duma Committee in sending Bublikov's first telegram to the railway workers is made even clearer by the committee's subsequent telegram to the commanders of all fronts and to the Stavka. In that message Rodzyanko informed them that the resignation of the cabinet ministers compelled the Duma Committee to assume power, and he assured them that no change in external or internal policy would be implemented. The telegram continued, "The Duma Committee in cooperation with the military units and the population in the capital will in the immediate future restore peace in the rear and resume the normal activity of governmental institutions."[52] A difference in emphasis between Bublikov's public announcement and Rodzyanko's classified telegram to the military leaders illustrated the predicament of the Duma Committee in trying to steer through the narrow passage between the two opposing forces.

Another important move that Bublikov made was to choose Lomonosov as his assistant. Lomonosov was an eminent engineer, an inventor of the combustion engine for locomotives and later electrical engines. When he taught at the Kiev Polytechnic Institute, he was involved in the socialist movement and became acquainted with a Bolshevik, Leonid Krasin. In 1912, he had been appointed by transport minister Sergei Vasilievich Rukhlov to the post of assistant chief of railway administration of all Russian railways, and at the same time taught at the Petersburg Institute of Railway Engineers of Ways and Communications. In early 1917 he was named the assistant to the minister of transport.[53] Bublikov's choice of Lomonosov was a brilliant move. Lomonosov was sympathetic to the revolution, so he gladly offered his assistance, and through his work he was thoroughly familiar with the personnel of the railways. Together, Bublikov and Lomonosov sought to manipulate the railway movements of General Ivanov's expeditionary forces as well as the movements of the imperial trains.[54]

Because Lomonosov was fully acquainted with the ministry personnel, he knew who was in favor of the old regime and who supported the
Duma Committee. Lomonosov appointed his own men to key positions
that controlled railway movement. In addition, the Ministry of Transport
under Bublikov and Lomonosov controlled two city telephone lines and
one ministerial telephone line, and through Kislyakov it placed the military communication line under its control as well.[55]

In Tsarskoe Selo on the morning of February 28, Princess Olga Paley,
Grand Duke Pavel's wife, woke up and glanced out of the window: "a pure
blue sky, the snow sparkling and scintillating in the sun's rays, and not a
sound to disturb the calm of the nature."[56] Within the palace walls, however, the anxiety was growing overwhelming. The children were more
feverish than before. Alexandra wrote to Baroness Sofia Karlovna Buxhoeveden to report their temperatures: "Olga 39'9 [degrees C], Tatiana 39'3,
Aleksei 40, Anya [Anna Vyrubova] 40'3." Tatiana developed abscesses in
the ears, and Olga's pericarditis had to be monitored. Shortly thereafter
Anastasia joined her sisters in the sickroom. Only Maria remained well
for a few days longer, serving as her mother's reliable helper. Buxhoeveden
noted of Maria: "These days, in which she was her mother's sole support,
turned her from a child into a woman."[57] Alexandra was debating whether
she should evacuate to Gatchina with the children or wait for the arrival of
Nicholas in Tsarskoe Selo. At 9:30 in the morning, she asked Aleksei's tutor,
Pierre Gilliard, to arrange a train for Gatchina. Count Pavel Benckendorff
and Major General Pavel Groten, assistant commandant of the palace, also
urged the empress to leave. But she changed her mind, fearing that leaving
the palace would have catastrophic consequences for her sick children.

Count Pyotr Apraksin, marshal of the court, had walked all the way
from Petrograd to Tsarskoe Selo on foot, 25 kilometers, and when he
arrived at the palace he informed the empress that the capital had been

completely taken over by the revolution. The count attempted to persuade the empress to go to Novgorod, where she would be able to assemble loyal troops to protect her and her children. While the empress was wavering, Groten warned that all the railway movements would be stopped in two hours. As it was impossible to arrange for the departure of the entire family in just two hours, they decided to remain in the palace.[58]

There were two types of armed units stationed at Tsarskoe Selo. The first was the Tsarskoe Selo garrison troops, who were steadily abandoning their posts and heading to Petrograd.[59] The second group of military units, those assigned to protect the palace and the imperial family, remained loyal. These units included two battalions of His Majesty's Convoy, one battalion of the Guard Regiment, two squadrons of the Cossacks of the Emperor's Escort, one company of the 1st Railway Regiment, and one heavy artillery battery. They were under the command of General Groten in the absence of his superior, Voeikov.[60]

By the afternoon those at Tsarskoe Selo heard still worse news from Petrograd. The Okhrana headquarters in Petrograd had been destroyed, and its chief, General Konstantin Globachev, fled to Tsarskoe Selo during the afternoon of February 28. He reported to Colonel Boris Andreevich Gerardi, director of the palace police, about the genuine revolution engulfing the capital, warning that it might sweep away the monarchy. The powerful secret police chief must have been more in tune with the real situation than any government and palace officials, having heard the extent of popular sentiment against Nicholas and Alexandra through countless reports from his spy agents. Gerardi answered: "So what? If there is no Nicholas, there will be Mikhail."[61]

After 3 p.m. the situation suddenly changed. Rumors of an impending attack on the palace began spreading, and the palace was consumed by panic. Gerardi's wife was the first one to abandon their apartment and evacuate with their two children to the military hospital, where she openly made remarks critical of the empress and Anna Vyrubova.[62]

The telegram Nicholas had sent from Vyazma arrived shortly before 7 p.m., but his optimism regarding the "many troops sent from the front" must have struck even Alexandra as oddly unrealistic. Around 8 p.m., insurgent soldiers from the garrison approached the palace, singing the revolutionary song "La Marseillaise" and shouting "Hurrah!," but they never launched an attack, out of fear of the guns that had been set up in the courtyard. To prevent a clash between the loyal troops and the insurgents, which would endanger the lives of the imperial family, the military authorities in the palace entered into negotiations with the insurgents. The delegates from the insurgents promised not to attack the palace if the loyal troops agreed not to use the artillery against the insurgents, and the palace military authorities promised to send emissaries from the loyal troops to the Duma. The insurgents promised to remain neutral until the emissaries returned.[63]

Although the Cossacks and the emperor's personal convoy remained loyal, the morale of the guard regiment, the artillery unit, and the railway regiment deteriorated. In an attempt to steel them in their duties, Alexandra, accompanied by Maria, went to the courtyard to inspect the troops, many of whom they knew personally. She told the soldiers that she trusted their loyalty to the emperor and the heir, but she warned them that no blood should be shed. As Buxhoeveden recalled, "The scene was unforgettable. It was dark, except for a faint light thrown up from the snow and reflected on the polished barrels of the rifles. The troops were lined up in battle order in the courtyard. . . . The figures of the Empress and her daughter passed like dark shadows from line to line, [with] the white Palace looming as ghostly mass in the background."[64] As the empress spoke, "some of the troops answered in a surly fashion."[65]

The empress's concern was for her children's safety above anything else. At 10 p.m. on February 28 she received a second telegram from Nicholas, which said that he hoped to be home the next morning. Benckendorff and Apraksin began to worry that the presence of Anna Vyrubova would endanger the empress and the imperial family, and suggested to the empress that her friend should be moved out of the palace. Alexandra categorically refused to abandon her ailing friend.[66] Count Benckendorff and his wife, together with other officials, spent the night in the palace, and the empress went to sleep fully clothed.[67]


After the imperial trains left Vyazma, they headed north to Likhoslavl. The suite train, which arrived at Rzhev at 5 p.m. on February 28, learned that in Petrograd a "provisional government" (actually the Duma Committee) had been formed. This news should have caused alarm for the emperor and the others in train A.[68] In fact, Nicholas did not appear to attach any significance to it at all. At Rzhev the emperor strolled back and forth on the platform while the locomotive was refilled with water and coal.[69] At 8 p.m. he had supper with his entourage, but they did not talk about the revolution.[70]

Train B switched tracks to the Nikolaevskaya Line at Likhoslavl. A new locomotive was attached, a new team came on board, and the train took off. When train B was between Likhoslavl and Bologoe, sometime after 9 p.m., those aboard learned of Bublikov's telegram that had been sent to all the railway stations, announcing that the Duma Committee had taken over the capital.[71] Bublikov's telegram was relayed to the imperial train, train A. Half an hour later, train A arrived at Likhoslavl.

To change the locomotive, a new team of locomotive engineers entered the train, accompanied by two gendarme generals, who came from Petrograd. One of the officers must have been General Pyotr Illich Fursa. Aide-de-camp Anatoly Mordvinov asked the gendarme general about the situation in Petrograd, and learned that the soldiers had mutinied, the insurgents were running around madly in the street, and people were frightened. The gendarme general told Mordvinov that he had made arrangements to make sure that Tosno would be safe enough to transfer the imperial trains to Gatchina and from there to Tsarskoe Selo. Gatchina was quiet, but before he left Petrograd, Nikolaevsky station had been taken over by the rebels, and what happened afterward he did not know. While this conversation was going on in the service wagon, one of the railway engineers brought a telegram that the station had received from Bublikov. Now everyone in train A knew about Bublikov's telegram.[72]

Paying little attention to the disturbing news about the insurrection in the capital or Bublikov's telegram, Nicholas sent another telegram to the empress: "Am glad all is well with you [all]. Hope to be home tomorrow morning. Embrace you and the children. God bless you, Niki."[73] This was Nicholas's last telegram that went through to Tsarskoe Selo. After this, the imperial trains were placed under the information blockade enforced by the Duma Committee.

After train A departed from Likhoslavl, Nicholas retired to his sleeping car. As usual, he wrote his diary entry for that day before he went to sleep. The entry for February 28 simply states:

> I went to bed at 3:25 since I talked for a long time with N. I. Ivanov, whom I am sending to Petrograd with troops in order to restore order. I slept until 10. I left Mogilev at five in the morning. The weather is frosty and sunny. During the day we went through Vyazma, Rzhev, and Likhoslavl at nine.[74]

Nicholas remained confident that General Ivanov would put down the insurrection by force. He did not seem aware that he might not even be able to count on safe passage to his family.

Bublikov and Lomonosov had to prevent the imperial trains from reaching either Petrograd or Tsarskoe Selo. The Duma Committee did not want the tsar to be confronted by insurgents it could not control, who might arrest him or, even worse, lynch him on the spot; this would likely provoke military action. Nor did it want the tsar to be reunited with

Alexandra in Tsarskoe Selo, as they expected Nicholas would be bombarded by his wife's pleas to stand firm for the autocracy. Bublikov and Lomonosov also had to prevent Ivanov and his forces from joining the strongholds of loyal troops. It was important, therefore, to block Ivanov's path to Gatchina, Aleksandrovskaya, and Tsarskoe Selo.

At 9:45 p.m., as the suite train arrived at the small station of Vyshny Volochek, near Bologoe, it unexpectedly received an order signed by Lieutenant Konstantin Fyodorovich Grekov, the new commandant of Nikolaevsky station in Petrograd. Grekov's order was sent to all the stationmasters and commandants of the Nikolaevskaya Line. This order demanded that the stationmasters reroute the imperial trains directly to Petrograd, not allowing them to proceed to Tsarskoe Selo.[75]

Upon hearing of this order, Thal immediately understood that continuing along the Nikolaevskaya Line would be dangerous, as they risked being diverted toward Petrograd rather than being able to go to Tsarskoe Selo. Thal, in train B, sent a telegram to Voeikov in train A, requesting further instruction as to whether to proceed to Tsarskoe Selo, ignoring Grekov's order.[76] Also, in consultation with General Sergei Aleksandrovich Tsabel, General Dmitry Dubensky wrote a note in pencil and sent it to Dr. Sergei Fyodorov in train A, recommending that the imperial trains reroute from Bologoe to Pskov. This handwritten letter was given to an officer in train B, who disembarked from the train before it reached Bologoe, waited for the arrival of train A, and gave it to Fyodorov.[77]

Train B arrived at Bologoe at 10:15 p.m. There, Staff Captain Kun, of His Majesty's Railway Regiment, on guard duty at the Bologoe station, informed Thal that, according to the information he had received, Tosno had been occupied by the rebels; therefore, it would be dangerous to venture into Tosno. From Bologoe to Tosno the railway regiment could provide a secure route with armed guards, but beyond Tosno, no armed guards protected the railway. If the imperial trains ventured into Tosno, they might be rerouted to Petrograd instead of being allowed to go to Tsarskoe Selo.[78] Where Kun obtained this information is not clear. By this point, however, Thal had received a response from Voeikov, who, in answer to Thal's request for instructions, said, "Proceed to Tsarskoe Selo, no matter what." So Thal left a packet of reports with Kun to give to Voeikov, and also instructed Kun to tell Voeikov to leave specific instructions at the next station, Malaya Vishera, as to what to do, given the danger of going farther toward Tosno.[79] In the meantime, Thal sent an advance party to Malaya Vishera—an officer and three soldiers of His Majesty's Railway Regiment who had been on duty to protect the locomotive of the suite train—to see if the station was occupied by the rebel soldiers.

Thal relayed the thinking of those in train B to Voeikov on train A: "By rumors, an order was received to direct the imperial trains from Tosno to Nikolaevsky station in Petrograd. If the route to Gatchina is closed, we decided to stop the trains at Tosno. I request that you give us your order at Malaya Vishera."[80] At 11 p.m., train A arrived at Vyshny Volochek, and Voeikov gave Thal's report to Fredericks and the emperor. After he consulted with them, the palace commandant telegraphed to Thal: "Must move on to Tsarskoe Selo."[81] Nicholas's desire to join his family outweighed his concerns with the risk of venturing into the area close to the revolution in Petrograd.

Neither those on train B nor those on train A were aware of the circumstances surrounding Grekov's order to stationmasters to divert the imperial train to Petrograd. Grekov had been appointed commandant of Nikolaevsky station by Lieutenant Vasily Nikolaevich Filippovsky of the Duma Committee's Military Commission.[82] It appears likely that the order to redirect the imperial train to Petrograd initially originated with Kerensky, who harbored the ambition to arrest the emperor. But this order contradicted the aim of other members of the Duma Committee, who wanted to divert the imperial train away from Petrograd to avoid the possibility of the tsar being arrested by the insurgents, and away from Tsarskoe Selo to prevent Nicholas from joining Alexandra. When the goal of the Duma Committee was explained to Kerensky, he immediately realized his shortsightedness, and instructed Grekov to ignore his previous order. Subsequently, Lomonosov contacted Engelgardt of the Military Commission and complained about the commission's orders related to railway movements, insisting that any decision about railway movements had to be cleared with the Ministry of Transport under Bublikov as the central authority. Engelgardt agreed. Grekov, though reluctantly, cooperated with Bublikov and Lomonosov, rescinding his previous order.[83] But those on train B had no knowledge of this change of order. They did not know who Grekov was, and this uncertainty enhanced their fear that the imperial trains would be confronted by an anarchic mob if they continued along the Nikolaevskaya Line.

At midnight, imperial train A arrived at Bologoe. One of the officers of His Majesty's Railway Regiment gave Fyodorov the message from General Dubensky in train B, recommending that the imperial trains change direction at Bologoe and head toward Pskov rather than risk falling into the hands of the rebels. To go to Tosno, Dubensky warned, would expose the emperor to danger.[84]

Dr. Fyodorov showed Dubensky's letter to Voeikov and Flag Captain Konstantin Nilov, but they did not heed his recommendation; Voeikov did not change his earlier instructions to go straight to Tsarskoe Selo. As train A moved along, other members of the entourage in that train talked about the situation in Petrograd. "This is nothing," said Vasily Dolgorukov, marshal of the court; "we will deal with it." "Ivanov is going with two and three good units," agreed Mordvinov. "The mere appearance of one of them will restore order." Voeikov and Dr. Fyodorov agreed with Mordvinov, believing that Ivanov's forces would crush the revolution.[85]

Despite the misgivings of Thal and Dubensky, the imperial trains continued moving along the Nikolaevskaya Line as planned. The suite train arrived in Malaya Vishera at 1:55 a.m. on March 1. Accompanied by the officer and soldier sent earlier, Thal walked into the stationmaster's office and high-handedly told him: "I am Commandant of the Imperial Train B. Do you obey my orders?" The stationmaster promptly replied, "Aye, aye, sir." Then the stationmaster handed Thal an encoded telegram sent by Staff Captain Kun. It contained the decision by Voeikov to proceed to Tsarskoe Selo.[86]

Despite misgivings about Voeikov's decision, Thal ordered the suite train to proceed north toward Tosno.[87] But just as the train was about to depart, an unexpected event took place. A new drama was about to unfold at Malaya Vishera—one that would change the fate of the imperial trains, the fate of the emperor, and the fate of the monarchy.

# CHAPTER 8

# To the Pskov Station

A t 1:55 a.m. on March 1 the suite train arrived at Malaya Vishera. As the stationmaster received instructions on the route that the locomotives would be taking next, an officer of the railway regiment, one Lieutenant Gerliakh, arrived at the station bearing grave news. The stations of Lyuban and Tosno had been captured by revolutionary troops led by companies of the Lithuanian Regiment. Armed with machine guns, these rebels had completely overwhelmed the railway regiment soldiers guarding those stations, and they were now on their way to Malaya Vishera.[1] Receiving this alarming news, Colonel Georgy Thal and General Sergei Tsabel, of His Majesty's Railway Regiment in train B, decided to wait for the arrival of train A before deciding where train B should go. It was a clear, quiet, and frosty night. Everywhere there was deathly silence.[2]

Train A arrived fifteen minutes after this frightening news was brought to the entourage. Though General Vladimir Voeikov was asleep upon arrival, some of the entourage from the suite train went into Voeikov's railcar and loudly knocked at the door of his sleeping compartment until he woke. As soon as the grumpy palace commandant got dressed,

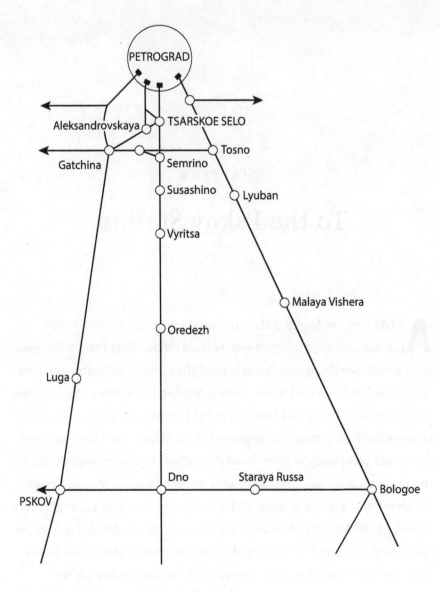

*Schematic Railway Map, Petrograd, Pskov, Bologoe*

General Tsabel went into his compartment and reported the news about the occupation of Tosno and Lyuban stations by revolutionary troops. Finally, Voeikov came out into the corridor, still with messy, uncombed hair, and summoned the other members of the entourage to discuss what course should be taken. Some, like the court historian General Dmitry Dubensky, advocated going to Pskov, and others proposed returning to Mogilev. But no one advocated going further, to Tosno.

Voeikov went to the emperor's sleeping car, woke up the sovereign, and asked for his opinion. Nicholas had not abandoned his wish to join his family—rather, he hoped to approach Tsarskoe Selo from Dno, a station on the way to Pskov, from where he could change to the Vindavo–Rybinskaya Line north to Tsarskoe. This choice had another advantage. If it turned out to be impossible to go to Tsarskoe, they could proceed to Pskov, as Dubensky advocated, where the emperor would have access to a Hughes apparatus.[3]

He reacted to the news about the occupation of the stations "with unusual calmness." Dubensky, who earlier had handwritten a letter recommending that the trains be rerouted to Pskov and had attempted to send it to the tsar's physician, Dr. Sergei Fyodorov, on train A, learned that his letter had not been given to the tsar, because the palace commandant considered the incident insignificant and decided not to pass along the missive.[4] Later on that day, Nicholas wrote in his diary: "At night we turned back from M. Vishera, since Lyuban and Tosno turned out occupied by the insurgents. . . . Shame and disgrace! Could not go to Tsarskoe. My thoughts and feelings are all the time there! How poor Alix must be painfully living through all these events by herself! Help us Lord!"[5]

Up north in Petrograd, Aleksandr Bublikov and Yury Lomonosov were busy tracing the movement of the imperial trains and of General Nikolai Ivanov. Nikolai Nekrasov, of the Duma Committee, learned that General

Ilya Leonidovich Tatishchev of the Life Guard Hussar Regiment had left Tsarskoe Selo and had arranged for a train to go to Tosno so that he could meet the emperor. The Duma Committee decided that it had to stop Tatishchev's train.[6]

At the Ministry of Transport, Lomonosov received the news before 2 a.m. that the imperial trains were approaching Malaya Vishera. He also received information from the railway officials at Lyuban that the trains would soon reach Tosno, the point at which they would have to switch to the route to Tsarskoe Selo, and that the commander of the corps of gendarmes had already instructed railway authorities at Tosno to switch locomotives for the imperial trains for the last leg of their journey to Tsarskoe Selo. Lomonosov knew he would have to act quickly if he hoped to prevent the imperial trains from reaching Tsarskoe Selo.

When Lomonosov received this news, Bublikov was fast asleep. Lomonosov called Duma Committee chairman Mikhail Rodzyanko, asking for his instructions. Rodzyanko told him to wake up Bublikov. When Bublikov came to the telephone, Lomonosov heard only Bublikov's end of the conversation: Bublikov asked Rodzyanko what he wanted to do with the imperial trains—whether to let them go to Tsarskoe Selo, or divert them to Petrograd, or detain them at Malaya Vishera. Rodzyanko could not decide, however, and so Bublikov and Lomonosov waited for further instructions.[7]

While waiting, Bublikov and Lomonosov received a telegram sometime between 2:10 and 3:20 a.m. on March 1 from Malaya Vishera: "Malaya Vishera. General Fursa and Assistant Chief Kern on the imperial train. Having a meeting."[8] Major General Pyotr Fursa served in the Corps of Gendarme Police for Railways. Having been actively involved in the shooting of demonstrators on February 26, he had been hunted by the insurgents, and had hurriedly escaped from Petrograd before the insurgents captured Nikolaevsky station.[9] Fursa must be one of the two gendarme officers who boarded train A at Likhoslavl, as the aide-de-camp

Colonel Mordvinov mentioned. According to Aleksandr Spiridovich, news of the capture of Tosno by the insurgents came from Fursa.[10] Mordvinov, however, recalls that Fursa told him that he had made arrangements to ensure that Tosno would be safe enough to transfer the imperial trains to Gatchina and from there to Tsarskoe Selo.[11] According to Voeikov, what he learned from the gendarme officer was information about the revolution in Petrograd; Fursa said nothing about the capture of Tosno.[12] According to Lomonosov, Tosno was under the control of the gendarmes, and the railway workers were preparing to change the route of the imperial trains from the Nikolaevskaya Line to the Northwestern Line, which would take them toward Gatchina and ultimately Tsarskoe Selo. Fursa may have known about the situation in Petrograd and the danger of having the imperial trains approach the capital, but it is doubtful that the information about the capture of Tosno by the rebels came from Fursa. It seems certain, however, that Fursa was on board train A to Malaya Vishera and from there back to Bologoe, giving advice to the entourage.[13]

More important was the role of Ivan F. Kern, an engineer who was the assistant to the director of the Nikolaevskaya Line.[14] It is not clear why Kern was at Malaya Vishera. The possibility that Kern was acting on behalf of Bublikov and Lomonosov cannot be excluded, as he later reported to them.[15]

Upon receiving the telegram from Malaya Vishera that the imperial trains had arrived there, Lomonosov called the Duma, hoping to find out what they had decided regarding whether to allow the imperial trains to continue to Tsarskoe Selo, but learned that they had not yet reached a decision. In the meantime, another telegram arrived: "Malaya Vishera. Following the instructions of engineer Kern, Train A left here at 4:50 to return to Bologoe." Why Kern instructed that the trains return to Bologoe is not clear. If we assume that Kern was acting on behalf of Bublikov and Lomonosov, Kern was following their directive to prevent the trains from going to Tosno.

The stationmaster's two cryptic messages to Lomonosov, however, did not tell the whole story. The decision to turn the trains back to Bologoe must have been made at a higher level than Kern and Fursa, involving Voeikov and even Nicholas. As discussed above, Voeikov made the decision to turn the trains back to Bologoe and then redirect them to Dno. It makes more sense to think that Fursa and Kern served as consultants to Voeikov, providing technical advice that informed Voeikov's political decision. The stationmaster was secretly reporting to Lomonosov what he knew, and he knew only what Fursa and Kern instructed him to do, without knowing that the decision was made by Voeikov.

Lomonosov immediately called the Duma again. "Should we detain them?" he asked. The person at the other end of the line, most likely Rodzyanko, answered: "It has not been decided. Follow the train. When the situation becomes clear, you will receive the instruction."[16]

The trains turned around and left Malaya Vishera, reversing order, with the imperial train going first, leaving the station at 3:35 a.m., and the suite train leaving twenty minutes later. The trains returned to Bologoe at 6:40 and 7 a.m., respectively, on March 1, and changed direction, heading west on the Vindavo–Rybinskaya Line.[17]

As soon as the imperial trains left the Nikolaevskaya Line, no further new information arrived from the capital, even as the emperor's company noticed no signs of disturbance along the route.[18] When train A stopped at Staraya Russa at 1:35 p.m. to take on water for the locomotive, the entourage received the news that a bridge was destroyed somewhere on the Vindavo–Rybinskaya Line north of Dno, making it impossible to change the direction of the train from Dno to Tsarskoe Selo. Therefore, they decided to proceed to Pskov from Dno. They hoped that the imperial trains would take the Warsaw Line to Tsarskoe Selo through Luga.[19] Voeikov sent a telegram from Staraya Russa to General Nikolai Ruzsky, commander of the northern front, instructing him to take all measures necessary to secure passage from Dno to Pskov.[20] Before they left the station, Voeikov received word that General Ivanov had gone through Dno only that morning. This information did not please Nicholas. He had been counting on Ivanov already having reached Tsarskoe Selo to command the expeditionary forces against the revolution.[21]

The trains resumed their journey, now moving more slowly.[22] This slowness was not a coincidence: Bublikov and Lomonosov had telegraphed orders to the railway officials to slow down the movement of the imperial trains by jamming the routes with freight trains. Noncompliance with this order would be treated as treason to the fatherland.[23] The Stavka intercepted this telegram at 11 a.m. on March 1, signaling the military command's first awareness of the Duma Committee's attempts to manipulate the movement of the imperial trains.[24]

However, Voeikov's decision to reroute the imperial trains from Malaya Vishera to Bologoe and then to Dno was not relayed to the Stavka. It was not until 12:30 p.m. that Colonel Ivan Aleksandrovich Barmin, chief of the military movement division at the Stavka, learned from Colonel Amir Batyrgareevich Karamyshev, assistant for military communication on the northern front, that the imperial trains had turned back and were moving toward Pskov through Bologoe.[25] This means that from the time the imperial trains arrived at Malaya Vishera at 1:55 a.m. on March 1 until 12:30 p.m. later that day, the Stavka was in the dark as to the whereabouts of the imperial trains. Interestingly, the northern front received this information from Colonel Nikolai Sergeevich Shikheev, commandant of the Warsaw Line. How Shikheev obtained this information and how it was relayed to the northern front is not clear, but Shikheev must have intercepted telegraph communications between stationmasters and the Ministry of Transport under Bublikov and Lomonosov. The tsar and his entourage had no means of communicating with the Stavka for almost ten hours. At Staraya Russa Voeikov was able to send a telegram to Ruzsky, mentioned above, asking for his help ensuring safe passage.[26] But only when the imperial trains arrived at Dno did Voeikov report to the Stavka that they intended to move to Pskov. At this point Alekseev suggested that they return to Mogilev, but the tsar rejected this recommendation. He was anxious to get to Tsarskoe Selo.

It is important to highlight that Nicholas and the entourage decided to redirect the trains from Malaya Vishera back to Bologoe and thence to Dno and Pskov solely based on the information given to them by Lieutenant Gerliakh. Strangely, this information is not corroborated by any other firsthand evidence; all the documentary evidence of the capture of Lyuban and Tosno comes from the memoirs of Nicholas's entourage on the trains.

The information that those on the imperial trains had received about the capture of Tosno by the revolutionaries is suspicious. According to Lomonosov, Tosno was firmly controlled by gendarmes, and the railway workers were preparing the locomotives to switch the trains from the Nikolaevskaya Line to the Northwestern Line, toward Gatchina.[27]

As for Lyuban, the only incident that took place there was minor. An echelon of troops arrived at the station, although it is not known what military unit they belonged to or where they came from. The commander of the unit commandeered a locomotive and four railcars from the railway authorities. The armed soldiers got on board and left for Petrograd.[28]

But this was hardly an occupation of the station by insurgents, as reported by Lieutenant Gerliakh. After their departure, no troops remained at the station, and the soldiers had gone in the direction of Petrograd, not in the direction of Malaya Vishera, as Gerliakh stated.

While there is no evidence to prove the seizure of Lyuban and Tosno by insurgents, archival materials reveal that railway authorities, in cooperation with Bublikov and Lieutenant Konstantin Grekov, commandant of Nikolaevsky station, had firm control of the communications network on the Nikolaevskaya Line. P. P. Karelin, an engineer with the Ministry of Transport whom Bublikov had appointed as his assistant, informed Grekov that Malaya Vishera had sworn allegiance to the new government and that all the stations from Petrograd to Bologoe were following its directions for control of the railways.[29] Thus the Ministry of Transport had a monopoly on information along the Nikolaevskaya Line. Lomonosov received a telephone call from Malaya Vishera after the imperial trains left the station.[30] Another telegram from Bolshaya Vishera to Grekov reported that both trains had been redirected from Malaya Vishera back to Bologoe.[31]

About Lieutenant Gerliakh we know little. He was a duty officer of His Majesty's Railway Regiment at Lyuban, and he used a railroad handcar to get from Lyuban to Malaya Vishera. But there is much else that is not known. Who ordered him to go to Malaya Vishera? Did Tsabel or Thal verify his identity? What happened to Gerliakh after he reported the occupation of Tosno and Lyuban? Did he leave Malaya Vishera on his own? Did he have any connection with Bublikov and Lomonosov or with Lieutenant Grekov? Was his information derived from his own experience and observation at Lyuban? Gerliakh mysteriously showed up at Malaya Vishera and mysteriously disappeared after he provided the information. But his information was consequential: had the imperial trains not changed direction based on his information, there was a strong possibility they would have reached Tsarskoe Selo without being stopped at either Lyuban or Tosno. Had Nicholas joined Alexandra in Tsarskoe Selo on March 1, instead of going to Pskov, it would have changed the course of the abdication drama drastically. The course of the February Revolution thus hinged on this mysterious Lieutenant Gerliakh, now lost in the murk of history.

The imperial trains reached Bologoe shortly before 7 a.m. on March 1.[32] The news of their arrival at Bologoe was immediately relayed to Lomonosov, who called up Rodzyanko for further instructions. Rodzyanko instructed Lomonosov to detain the trains at Bologoe and arrange a special train for him to take to Bologoe. Lomonosov dispatched a telegram to Voeikov on Rodzyanko's behalf, which requested that the emperor await the chairman of the Duma at Bologoe station, since the latter wished to talk with him about "the critical situation of the throne."[33]

The chief of the Vindavo–Rybinskaya Line, Mikhail Elevferievich Pravosudovich, telephoned from his office in Petrograd to Lomonosov at the Ministry of Transport, saying that the stationmaster at Bologoe, K. F. Baranov, had been ordered by Voeikov to direct the imperial trains from Bologoe to Pskov. Lomonosov, guessing that Nicholas was heading toward the army units there, ordered: "Never, in any case!" Pravosudovich responded: "Yes, sir, your order will be fulfilled." Apparently Pravosudovich then contacted Baranov at Bologoe to convey Lomonosov's order. But the station chief, supported by Fursa and his gendarme officers, defied that order and let the imperial trains be redirected to the Vindavo–Rybinskaya Line toward Dno.[34]

Usually when a train changes from one railway line to another, the locomotive and the brigade to man the locomotive change, too, because each brigade specializes in a particular line—they are familiar with local conditions, the route, and the signals on that line.[35] But in this case, the imperial trains changed from the Nikolaevskaya Line to the Vindavo–Rybinskaya Line but continued using the Nikolaevskaya Line locomotive and its brigade. This suggests that the rerouting of the trains must have been done in a hurry. General Fursa, who must have accompanied the imperial train from Malaya Vishera, likely played a role in this hasty shift. Fursa knew that the Nikolaevskaya Line was under the control of either Grekov or Bublikov and Lomonosov. He must have advised the entourage to transfer from the Nikolaevskaya Line to the Vindavo–Rybinskaya Line and change direction from Bologoe to Dno in a hurry without changing the locomotive and the locomotive brigade. As a result, the imperial trains were not detained at Bologoe, as Bublikov and Lomonosov had intended. The tsar slipped out of their hands.

Ten minutes later, Pravosudovich called Lomonosov and reported that the imperial trains had already left Bologoe. Rodzyanko's telegram sent via Lomonosov did not reach Voeikov. As the imperial trains moved toward Dno, Rodzyanko feared that they might reroute from Dno to Tsarskoe Selo, where the emperor would join General Ivanov's troops as well as his family—or, even worse, the imperial trains might return to Mogilev. In a panic, Bublikov issued an order to send freight trains from Dno to jam the track, causing the imperial trains to travel very slowly, as we have seen.[36] The intention was to turn the trains back to Bologoe so that Rodzyanko would be able to meet the tsar there. At one point the stationmaster at Polonka, a small station 12 kilometers east of Dno, had to take measures to avert a collision between a freight train and the imperial trains.[37]

In the meantime, Lomonosov had personally gone to Nikolaevsky station to arrange a train for Rodzyanko, as at that point the plan was still to detain the tsar's train at Bologoe and for Rodzyanko to meet the tsar there. He encountered no resistance from the insurgent soldiers who had occupied the station, and readied a train for Rodzyanko. Lomonosov succeeded in persuading Grekov that he was in charge of the security of the station and that Grekov should not interfere in railway movements, as that task had to be done only by experts.[38] Nevertheless, despite Lomonosov's repeated inquiries to the Duma, Rodzyanko did not come to the station. In the meantime, Lomonosov received the news that the imperial train had already left Bologoe and had passed Staraya Russa. Rodzyanko then decided to travel to Dno to meet the tsar there, so Lomonosov arranged a train for the Vindavo–Rybinskaya Line at Warsaw station.[39]

When the imperial trains arrived at Dno, the emperor and his entourage had three options: proceed to Tsarskoe Selo, return to Mogilev, or go to Pskov. As noted earlier, after learning that the imperial trains had arrived at Dno, the Stavka recommended that the tsar return to Mogilev, but Voeikov did not even respond to this recommendation.[40] The Duma leaders did not want the imperial trains to return to Mogilev, where the emperor, protected by loyal troops, might reinforce his resolve to suppress the revolution. Also, the Duma Committee was anxious to isolate Nicholas from Alexandra as well as General Ivanov; thus, it was interested in preventing the imperial trains from heading to Tsarskoe Selo. The best option, the Duma Committee concluded, was to let the imperial trains proceed to Pskov, the headquarters of the northern front, commanded by Ruzsky, who the Duma Committee expected was sympathetic to the Duma liberals. Nicholas, as noted earlier, was anxious to go to a place where he would have access to the Hughes apparatus, and therefore he agreed with Voeikov's idea of going to Pskov. Lomonosov heard from Pravosudovich that at Dno station the gendarmes arrested unreliable railway workers and secured the station for the safety of the tsar.[41] It became impossible for Bublikov and Lomonosov to block the imperial trains from going from Dno to Pskov.

When train A arrived at Dno at 4:25 p.m., Rodzyanko's telegram was waiting for the tsar: "Your Majesty the Emperor, a special train is leaving now for Dno station to deliver a report to you, Sire, concerning the general situation and measures necessary for the salvation of Russia. I earnestly implore you to wait for my arrival, for each moment is precious."[42] Lomonosov's trusted aide Inspector Vladimir Pavlovich Nekrasov (not to be confused with Duma Committee member Nikolai Vissarionovich Nekrasov) walked to Warsaw station to accompany Rodzyanko on the train. Once at the station Nekrasov waited and waited, but—precious though each moment might be—Rodzyanko failed to come to the station.[43]

In the meantime, Nicholas waited patiently at Dno for Rodzyanko's arrival, pacing on the platform with some of his entourage. The appointed hour came and went, but still Rodzyanko did not show up. Voeikov telegraphed Petrograd and finally learned, through Lomonosov, that the

Duma chairman had had to cancel the appointment because "extenuating circumstances" made it impossible for him to leave the capital. Bublikov called the Duma and got more of an explanation: "An important meeting is going on now between the Duma Committee and the Soviet of Workers' Deputies. Rodzyanko cannot leave now, but asks to let the train wait. We have received an answer from General Ruzsky that he will fulfill his duty for the fatherland. The army is with us."[44] The last part of this message is significant, indicating that there was some contact between the Duma Committee and Ruzsky, and that the Duma Committee had obtained assurances from the general that he would support the Duma Committee. Ruzsky said he would fulfill his duty to the fatherland, not to the tsar, as his oath required.[45]

As we have seen, at Staraya Russa the entourage had received the disturbing news about the safety of the Vindavo–Rybinskaya Line north of Dno, and Voeikov had requested that the northern front ensure that the route from Dno to Pskov was clear. When he arrived at Dno, Voeikov learned that the railway line connecting the Vindavo–Rybinskaya Line and Tsarskoe Selo had been seized by revolutionary troops and that Ivanov had stopped at Vyritsa, unable to continue to Tsarskoe Selo. After receiving this information, the tsar finally abandoned his plan to go to Tsarskoe Selo from Dno. He decided to proceed to Pskov and wait there for Rodzyanko.[46]

The tsar's entourage hoped that Pskov would afford the emperor safety, under the protection of loyal troops of the northern front. Yet, as we know, the northern front was headed by General Ruzsky, who was overtly sympathetic to the Duma liberals, as were his chief of staff, General Yury Danilov, and the quartermaster general, Lieutenant General Vasily Georgievich Boldyrev. Indeed, Ruzsky had already petitioned the tsar to grant a ministry of confidence on February 27, as Rodzyanko had recommended.[47] According to Duma Committee member Nikolai Nekrasov, "He was allowed to travel there because it was safe for us—we were sure of the mood in Pskov."[48] Rodzyanko gave Lomonosov permission to let the imperial trains proceed to Pskov without obstruction.

Rodzyanko's behavior on March 1 has puzzled historians who have wondered why he first sought a special audience with the emperor and then canceled the trip. The prevailing view has held that by the evening of February 28 the Duma Committee had decided to send Rodzyanko and Sergei Shidlovsky to force Nicholas to accept his abdication in favor of his son under the regency of Mikhail, but this plan was obstructed by the Petrograd Soviet and its chairman, Nikolai Chkheidze, forcing Rodzyanko to cancel his trip.[49] The evidence, however, points to another explanation.

The Duma Committee never actually met formally to adopt this policy. According to Vasily Shulgin, a monarchist member of the Nationalist Party, the idea of abdication "had matured in the minds and hearts on its own. It grew from the hatred to the monarch" by March 1. Everyone had come to the conclusion that Nicholas could no longer reign, but it was not made into policy—in Shulgin's words, "I do not remember that this question was discussed by the Duma Committee as such. The decision was made at the last minute."[50]

The idea of seeking Nicholas's abdication had already been floating around among members of the Duma Committee on February 27, and once a tacit consensus emerged, the idea of sending someone to the tsar to extract this concession was raised. This "someone" had to be Rodzyanko. Rodzyanko was the only person who was in contact with military leaders. As we have seen, a train for Rodzyanko had already been prepared at Nikolaevsky station, but then Bublikov had a telephone conversation with Rodzyanko that indicated that there was internal dissension within the Duma Committee about his trip to Bologoe.

It should be remembered that Rodzyanko was seeking the option to gain a concession from Nicholas to establish a constitutional monarchy in cooperation with the grand dukes. As the Soviet-era historian Edvard Burdzhalov argues, Rodzyanko was pursuing a dual-track policy. He bowed to the Duma Committee's consensus to seek Nicholas's abdication, but he did not abandon the possibility of limiting the political reform to the establishment of a constitutional monarchy. He remained afraid that seeking Nicholas's abdication might invite the high command's reaction in support of the sovereign against the revolution.

Rodzyanko's dual-track policy provoked suspicion among the Duma Committee. They thought that if they allowed the chairman of the Duma to negotiate with Nicholas, he might settle for a constitutional monarchy without forcing the tsar's abdication. As émigré historian Sergei Melgunov states, "It is impossible to attribute to Rodzyanko the idea of going to the tsar with the proposal of abdication from the throne, as is done by Shidlovskii. During the day of March 1, he was not yet psychologically prepared to make such a radical decision."[51] In his memoirs, Pavel Milyukov sums it up thus: "Rodzyanko clearly stalled and wavered to somehow outwit us in the final account."[52]

It is likely that as a result of this suspicion, the Duma Committee members opted to send Shidlovsky, an Octobrist and an avowed enemy of Nicholas, to accompany Rodzyanko and ensure that he would fulfill the mission to seek Nicholas's abdication. Shidlovsky recalled that Rodzyanko told him "to get ready within one hour to travel with him to the sovereign to propose his abdication from the throne."[53] But Shidlovsky commented that the idea of Rodzyanko's mission to see the tsar was not well thought out. The plan did not take into account the possibility of the Duma delegates being arrested by loyal troops. Neither did it have any provision to arrest the tsar in case he refused to agree to abdicate. If the Duma Committee believed that simply sending Rodzyanko to the tsar would achieve Nicholas's abdication, it was indeed incredibly lacking in foresight. How could these Duma Committee members expect Rodzyanko to extract the concession of abdication only by persuasion? For Rodzyanko to travel to see the tsar without any military protection would have made far more sense if he sought the tsar's acceptance of a constitutional monarchy, in accordance with the grand dukes' manifesto, rather than his abdication outright.[54]

This leads us to the question of why Rodzyanko canceled his trip. Historians have largely accepted the explanation that Chkheidze and the Petrograd Soviet intervened to prevent his leaving the city. But this does not stand up to scrutiny either.[55]

According to Shidlovsky, Chkheidze, who was both chairman of the Petrograd Soviet and a member of the Duma Committee, showed up at a meeting of the Duma Committee and declared that the Petrograd Soviet would let Rodzyanko travel under two conditions. First, Chkheidze himself would accompany Rodzyanko and Shidlovsky, and second, after Nicholas's abdication, no successor should be designated. Since Rodzyanko could not accept such conditions, he canceled the trip.[56]

Nevertheless, Chkheidze's opposition does not seem to be a decisive factor in the cancellation of Rodzyanko's trip. Nikolai Nikolaevich Sukhanov, who chronicled the revolution, recalls that at first the Executive Committee decided not to allow Rodzyanko's trip to see the tsar. After that decision, however, Kerensky burst into the room in extreme anger and accused the members of the Executive Committee of playing into the hands of the monarchy, since Rodzyanko's mission was to force Nicholas's abdication. As a result of Kerensky's flamboyant performance, all those present "gave in to Kerensky's hysteria."[57] After that, the Executive Committee did not actively exert influence on the matter. According to another Executive Committee member, Matvei Skobelev, as long as the Duma Committee would be getting rid of autocracy, the Executive Committee preferred to let it decide on the question of Nicholas's abdication. "We ourselves did not undertake any aggressive steps or decisive measures," Skobelev confided later, "fearing that we might go too far and do too much."[58]

So the Soviet's opposition was not the reason for Rodzyanko's cancellation of his trip to Dno. Then why did he cancel the trip?

On February 27 and 28, Rodzyanko was the undisputed leader of the Duma Committee. But by March 1, his authority had already greatly diminished. A key reason for the shift was a decision by the head of the Duma Committee's Military Commission, Colonel Boris Engelgardt, to issue an order asking the soldiers to return to their barracks and restore order under their officers. On February 28, he sent the order out in the name of Rodzyanko.[59] The insurgent soldiers interpreted the order as an attempt to restore the military discipline that had existed before and disarm those who had mutinied. The resulting outburst of anger against Rodzyanko peaked at the Petrograd Soviet plenary session on March 1, which was taken over by the angry insurgent soldiers. This led to the Petrograd Soviet's adoption of Order No. 1 on March 1. This order abolished the old requirements for how soldiers were to address officers and how officers addressed soldiers. Order No. 1 further advised soldiers to obey the Duma Committee's orders only as long as these orders did not contradict the policy of the Petrograd Soviet, virtually denying soldiers' allegiance to the Provisional Government.[60]

In the meantime, Milyukov, not Rodzyanko, began composing a list of ministers for the Provisional Government. He pointedly excluded Rodzyanko as the prime minister, instead nominating Prince Lvov for that position. The leaders of the Petrograd Soviet Executive Committee, partly because of their Marxist ideological belief that the "bourgeoisie" should take power and partly fearful that the radicalized masses would compel them to take power, were anxious to negotiate with the Duma Committee and the potential ministers of the Provisional Government that was being formed. The negotiations began shortly after midnight and lasted until 3 a.m. on March 2. During the negotiations, it was Milyukov who did most of the talking, while Rodzyanko sat silently.[61]

As Rodzyanko's authority suffered erosion, Milyukov's prestige rose. The dynastic question—what would happen after the abdication of Nicholas II—was placed in the context of this shift of power relations between the two leaders. David Osipovich Zaslavsky and Vladimir Abramovich Kantorovich, two Mensheviks who keenly observed the course of the revolution, noted: "The Octobrist [Rodzyanko] who created the Duma Committee was eliminated from power in the first two days, and Milyukov, who had been in Rodzyanko's shadow on the 27th, became on the 28th the unquestionable leader, and already, on March 1, had bid farewell to Rodzyanko without regret."[62]

When was the final decision of the Duma Committee taken on the abdication? Shulgin writes that that decision was not made until the last moment. According to this monarchist, after 3 a.m. on March 2, Aleksandr Guchkov came to the Duma Committee after having gone around the city. There were only a handful of members there at that time—Rodzyanko, Milyukov, Shulgin, and some others he does not remember—but he distinctly remembers that Kerensky and Chkheidze were not there. In other words, this small circle was a group of like-minded members, and Guchkov could speak freely. The conspiratorial Octobrist informed those who remained in the room that his trusted aide Prince Dmitry Vyazemsky had been shot and killed by a stray bullet fired by the soldiers because he was an officer. Similar incidents were taking place everywhere, and many officers came to the Duma to save their lives. Guchkov said that something extraordinary had to be done to find ways to prevent the further spread of anarchy. The first and foremost task was to save the monarchy. "Without the monarchy Russia cannot survive. But it is apparent that the current sovereign can no longer reign. We must face the established fact. We need a new tsar." They must act immediately—secretly, quickly, and decisively—to force Nicholas's abdication, Guchkov insisted, before the revolution swept away the monarchy itself once and for all. "OK, but what exactly do you propose that we should do?" someone asked. To which Guchkov answered: "I propose that we go to the tsar immediately and bring about abdication in favor of the heir." Guchkov then volunteered: "I will go if you authorize me to do it. But I would like to have someone to accompany me." The attendees looked at each other. After a pause, Shulgin said: "I will go with you."[63]

Shulgin's account on the whole appears to be accurate. The Duma Committee did not adopt a formal policy to seek Nicholas's abdication during a full-scale meeting or through an explicit vote. The idea to seek the abdication had grown to be an informal consensus among the Duma Committee members as the revolution unfolded, and it became the committee's semi-formal position only on the morning of March 2, when Guchkov joined the conservative members of the Duma Committee minus Kerensky and Chkheidze.

The validity of this account is also confirmed by the Duma Committee's minutes, which recorded a meeting "around 6 o'clock" on the morning of March 2, at which Guchkov presented a view that was more or less similar to what Shulgin describes. This record states: "We must accomplish what was decided on February 28, namely, to go to the tsar and obtain his abdication. . . . Guchkov said that until the voluntary abdication of the sovereign is obtained, there remains a danger of bloody internecine war. As long as the oath of allegiance is not removed from many people, these people will be compelled to remain under the oath to the old order, and a huge bloodshed will become inevitable, and an aggravated situation will result." Then Guchkov requested that he be authorized to go to the tsar to obtain his abdication, and if he was not authorized, he would act on his own.[64] Only the note about the timing of this meeting is wrong. The negotiations between the Duma Committee, the Provisional Government, and the Petrograd Soviet leaders for the transfer of power to the Provisional Government were not over until 3 a.m. on March 2. The historic conversation between Rodzyanko and Ruzsky (discussed in Chapter 10) began at 3:30 a.m. This meeting must have happened between these two events—that is, between 3 and 3:30 a.m. on March 2, not at 6 a.m.

At this point the Duma Committee was seeking the abdication of Nicholas in order to preserve the monarchy, not to overthrow the monarchical system itself.

As all of this drama was playing out, General Ivanov and his forces were continuing their excruciatingly slow journey toward Tsarskoe Selo. By the time they arrived at Vyritsa, 32 kilometers south of Tsarskoe Selo, it was already 6 p.m. on March 1.[65]

It is often argued—and it was an accepted view of Russian historians during the Soviet period—that Ivanov's eventual safe arrival at Tsarskoe Selo was possible only because of the connivance of the Duma Committee, which wished to use Ivanov's forces to suppress the revolution in Petrograd.[66] There is, however, no basis to support this contention. When the Duma Committee first learned of the dispatch of the counterrevolutionary forces under Ivanov late on the evening of February 27, there was great apprehension, even panic, among its members. The Duma Committee had already taken decisive steps to support the revolution against the old regime, and it was determined to prevent the military suppression of the revolution. As we saw in Chapter 7, Bublikov had given the railway authorities instructions to obstruct any military train coming within 270 kilometers of Petrograd.[67]

But Ivanov, at Vyritsa, was determined to proceed to Tsarskoe Selo, if necessary with the use of force, so Bublikov had no choice but to let him go. It certainly did not represent the Duma Committee's tacit approval of Ivanov's forces.

Ivanov and his troops finally arrived at Tsarskoe Selo at 9 p.m. on March 1. The assistant commandant of the palace, Major General Pavel Groten, and the Tsarskoe Selo police chief, Nikolai Vasilievich Osipov, greeted him, but the news they brought was not pleasant. They reported that the Tsarskoe Selo garrison had taken the side of the Duma, although the palace itself was protected by loyal troops. Ivanov immediately issued an order: he announced his position as dictator of the Petrograd Military District and demanded that all citizens, military personnel, and clergy subordinate themselves to him. He would take measures to assemble all available troops in the headquarters he established in Tsarskoe Selo.[68]

It was a bold exercise of the dictatorial power granted by the emperor, but it was not destined to continue very long. Soon Colonel Vladimir Nikolaevich Domanevsky and Lieutenant Colonel Nikolai Nikolaevich Tilli arrived at Tsarskoe Selo station. They had been dispatched by Major General Mikhail Zankevich, chief of the main administration of the General Staff in Petrograd, on the instructions of General Alekseev, to create a staff for Ivanov.[69] Until the previous day Zankevich had hopelessly attempted to command loyal troops against the insurgents; after their disintegration, he returned to the General Staff. In the meantime, Engelgardt and Guchkov from the Duma Committee's Military Commission had succeeded in recruiting several officers from the General Staff to join their side.[70] His failed experience with troop loyalty must have convinced Zankevich of the necessity of reaching a compromise with the Duma Committee. That opinion was now widely shared by officers in the General Staff in Petrograd.

Late on the night of February 28, Domanevsky went to the Tauride Palace to tell Engelgardt that he had been appointed chief of staff for Ivanov's forces. To Engelgardt, the aim of Ivanov's mission was clear: "Ivanov went to Petrograd to restore tsarist power. On this matter, my lot was cast: I openly acted against the tsar and no excuse nor any agreement could be possible here." He later recalled what he said to Domanevsky:

Ivanov could also . . . help to contain the revolution within those limits that seemed at that time acceptable. We could become allies and co-workers only on that basis. However, for the agreement, it was necessary to obtain a concession from Ivanov. He must recognize the accomplished fact, recognize the legal power of the Temporary Committee of the State Duma.

Domanevsky "allowed a possibility of agreement on the part of Ivanov," but he expressed doubt that restoring tsarist power and imposing order could be separated in the minds of the soldiers. In general, "faith in the success of Ivanov's mission did not exist in him."[71]

Though many officers were coming around to the belief that an agreement must be made with the Duma Committee to restore order, few wanted to be seen officially recognizing the committee as long as they were under the Stavka's order to cooperate with Ivanov's counterrevolutionary mission. The Domanevsky-Engelgardt conversation was, therefore, a delicate diplomatic negotiation, during which the true intentions of both sides were camouflaged in carefully worded opinions. But the fundamental intention of the Duma Committee's Military Commission was unambiguous: to stop Ivanov's counterrevolutionary offensive and seek a peaceful settlement to solve the crisis.[72]

After the meeting with Engelgardt, Domanevsky and Tilli went to Tsarskoe Selo to meet General Ivanov. In the name of the chief of the General Staff, Domanevsky reported to Ivanov that all troops as well as officers in Petrograd had fallen under the influence of the "provisional government" formed by the Duma. This "provisional government" was making efforts to restore order, and "the reserve battalions support only the orders issued by the provisional government."[73] Some ministers had been arrested, Domanevsky continued, but most of the ministries, including the war ministry, continued to function only in agreement with the "provisional government." In Domanevsky's opinion, "it is difficult to restore order by force in the armed struggle against the insurgents and the Provisional Government." Armed intervention would require an enormous

number of troops, and it would encounter difficulties in provisioning, bil-
leting, and transportation that could not be resolved without the cooperation of the "provisional government."

Domanevsky also presented the political realities. There were two
points of view among the insurgents: one group, which swore allegiance
to the "provisional government," remained faithful to the monarchical
principle, supported only limited internal reforms, and intended to eradicate disorder as quickly as possible in order to continue the war. The other
group, which supported the Petrograd Soviet, was willing to overthrow
the existing state structure and to end the war. "Until March 1, the prestige
of the Duma government stood high and in fact it looked like the master
of the situation, at least in the capital," Domanevsky continued. "But it is
clear that with each day the situation of the Duma government, which is
not supported by law, is getting more difficult and that there is an increasing possibility that power could go to the extreme left." All this would lead
to the conclusion that "at the present moment an armed struggle would
only complicate and worsen the situation," and therefore an agreement with
the Duma was "the only means to restore order." Ivanov dutifully heard
Domanevsky out, though he did not seem to attach much importance to
his recommendations.[74] A staff was never established for Ivanov. But he proceeded to assemble reinforcements as they arrived over the coming hours.


The empress and her entourage still held out hope that the situation would
improve with Nicholas's expected arrival at Tsarskoe Selo on March 1 at 6
a.m. But an hour before she expected to see Nicholas, she learned that the
imperial trains had been detoured. Around 8 a.m., General Groten told
Count Pavel Benckendorff that the emperor's trains had turned around
at Malaya Vishera and that he would not arrive until noon even under
the most favorable conditions. Shortly afterward, Benckendorff learned
from the officers of the railway regiment that trains were allowed to go

to Petrograd only, because the path to Tsarskoe Selo was blocked.[75] Alexandra sent a telegram to Nicholas without knowing where it should be directed: "The thoughts of prayers will not desert you. Lord will save. The temperatures of the children are still high. They are coughing badly. All firmly kiss you." Her intransigent stance to preserve the principles of the monarchy had disappeared. She was now just a mother concerned with the safety of her children. The telegram never reached the emperor; it fell into the hands of the Military Commission.[76]

Alone and helpless, the empress instructed Groten to enter into negotiations with Rodzyanko to prevent bloodshed and to learn the whereabouts of her husband. As noted in Chapter 7, after negotiating with the rebels, Groten gained the insurgents' assurance that they would not attack the palace by promising that the palace guard would send two truce emissaries to the Duma. It was arranged on both sides that troops wearing white armbands should not attack one another, that the Alexander Palace should not come under attack, and that the garrison of the palace should take no part in the events happening in the town.[77]

On the night of February 28–March 1, a delegation from the Tsarskoe Selo palace's royal troops arrived at the Tauride Palace to announce that they had transferred their allegiance to the Duma Committee, but they would protect the property and safety of the imperial family to the end.[78] Rodzyanko in turn gave the military units in Tsarskoe Selo the Duma Committee's new assignment: to protect the property of the imperial palace and the security of the imperial family. They also sent two Kadet members of the Duma, Igor Platonovich Demidov and Vasily Aleksandrovich Stepanov, to make sure that these orders would be obeyed.[79] Despite her hatred of Rodzyanko, the empress was beginning to look upon him as "the only person who could do a lot."[80] At 11 a.m. on March 1, however, telephone and radio communications between Tsarskoe Selo and the Stavka were cut off on the order of Engelgardt, rendering Alexandra a virtual prisoner of the Duma Committee.[81]

On the afternoon of March 1, Demidov and Stepanov arrived at Tsarskoe Selo.[82] They succeeded in calming the insurgents at the barracks by having them pledge their allegiance to the Duma. The empress and palace authorities had surrendered the entire garrison to the Duma Committee to secure the safety of the imperial family by the time General Ivanov arrived.

The change in the direction of the imperial trains had a significant consequence for the grand dukes' manifesto. The tsar was scheduled to arrive at Tsarskoe Selo at 6 a.m. on March 1. Grand Duke Pavel was planning to meet the emperor at the station and get Nicholas to sign the manifesto.

Grand Dukes Kirill and Mikhail were supposed to go to the Duma to pressure Rodzyanko to issue the manifesto once Nicholas had signed it. But as it turned out, only Kirill made it to the Duma. Kirill's arrival at the Duma, allegedly "wearing a red rosette on his chest," resulted in a widespread story that he led his troops to swear allegiance to the Provisional Government; he was praised by some and blamed by others for being the first member of the royal family to support the revolution. But these stories are patently false. Kirill went to the Duma, as agreed with Grand Dukes Pavel and Mikhail, to persuade Rodzyanko to implement the grand dukes' draft manifesto, preserving Nicholas's position as tsar and saving the monarchy.[83] He did not arrive at the Tauride Palace wearing a red rosette on his chest. He could not have sworn allegience to the Provisional Government, since on that day there was not yet a Provisional Government.[84] Rodzyanko asked Kirill to make his units available to protect the Duma, but after his initial brief meeting with Kirill, he avoided the grand duke for the rest of the day. Was this because Rodzyanko had already agreed to accept Nicholas's abdication, as Andrei Nikolaev argues, or because he did not wish to have his colleagues see him plotting with the grand dukes? It is not clear.[85] Either way, he must have been held up in the discussion with his colleagues about the dynastic question—the same meeting that Lomonosov learned of when he inquired about Rodzyanko's intention about the imperial trains.

As noted earlier, Mikhail was supposed to join Kirill at the Duma. But when his administrative secretary, Aleksei Sergeevich Matveev—after having had some difficulty navigating through streets filled with insurgents—managed to find the grand duke's hideout on Millionnaya at 2 p.m., he reported that a general who had been staying in Miechen's palace nearby had been murdered during a search by insurgent soldiers. Mikhail's safety became precarious. Johnson arranged for twenty cadets from the military school, led by five officers, to serve as a security detail for Mikhail. Officers took turns walking to the Tauride Palace to contact Rodzyanko.[86]

When Grand Duke Pavel learned that Nicholas would not be arriving at Tsarskoe Selo as scheduled, as a last resort he decided to approach the empress for her endorsement of the draft manifesto. Pavel went to the palace at 5 p.m. The empress met the grand duke with hostility, castigating his inaction and blaming his insufficient supervision over the loyal battalion as the reason those soldiers had joined the mutiny. When Grand Duke Pavel gave the empress the draft of the manifesto, according to one account, she declared the manifesto "idiotic" and adamantly refused to endorse it, shouting: "There is no revolution here. What we have is a revolution concocted by the Duma, and it is treason!"[87] This version is contradicted by Baroness Bux-hoeveden's account. According to this lady-in-waiting, the empress considered it necessary to make a political concession to stave off the revolution, but she thought that for her to sign the petition would look "as if I did just the things that I am accused of doing." She was not a regent and therefore had no right to take any initiative in the emperor's absence.[88] Perhaps a constitutional monarchy was more of a concession than she could accept.

The news that the grand dukes' attempt to institute a constitutional monarchy had failed must have been relayed to Barrister Ivanov, who was waiting for Grand Duke Pavel's signal. Ivanov brought the failed draft to the Duma Committee and told Rodzyanko, "I think that this was too late." Rodzyanko answered, "I am of the same opinion." Milyukov received the document and stuffed it in his pocket, commenting: "This is an interesting document."[89]

After 10:30 p.m. on March 1, Bublikov informed the Duma Committee on the phone that the St. George Battalion had arrived, accompanied by artillery, at Tsarskoe Selo station. The Duma Committee swiftly told General Ivanov to abandon any intention to transport the troops via railway to Petrograd, since measures had been taken to physically obstruct movement on the railways.[90]

Ivanov had no intention of giving up, and he contacted Lomonosov, peremptorily ordering him to arrange a train to Petrograd. Lomonosov answered that he had not received any order to that effect from the Stavka. Furthermore, he warned Ivanov that if he ventured toward Petrograd, there would be no guarantee of the safety of the train, since four batteries of artillery and 20,000 infantry troops had already been deployed less than 6 kilometers from Petrograd. This was completely made-up information, but Ivanov had no way of verifying it.[91]

The conversation ended, and forty minutes later Lomonosov received a telephone call from the Vindavo–Rybinskaya Line saying that Ivanov was at Tsarskoe Selo station and was insisting on going to the palace; he had arrested a number of railway employees and was threatening to shoot them. Lomonosov relented, allowing the general to make his way to the palace.

Ivanov arrived at midnight. From the point of view of the empress and her entourage, the general was an unwelcome visitor. After a dreadful night where the imperial family's security had been hanging by a thread, they had barely managed to achieve a precarious peace with the insurgents. The arrival of Ivanov's troops could shatter this peace at any moment. For this reason, the empress strongly hinted to Ivanov that his forces were not welcome.

Ivanov had a mission to attend to, however, and asked the empress to authorize him to use the troops guarding the palace to protect his rear while his battalion marched on Petrograd. Alexandra answered that she could not give any orders on military matters. "The Emperor gave you the mission," the empress said. "You must obey him, but not me. Act according to your conscience."[92] The empress was only interested in speaking to Ivanov for a single reason: to learn Nicholas's whereabouts. Ivanov revealed that Nicholas's train had been diverted from Bologoe to Dno, from where he was to proceed to Pskov. Alexandra asked the general if he might find a personal carrier to send a message on her behalf to her husband, since she was deprived of any other means of communicating with him. Ivanov refused, insisting he did not possess enough personnel to send one off with such a message. The empress otherwise spoke of her sick children and complained bitterly about the proposed solution of a responsible ministry.[93]

When General Ivanov left the palace after talking to the empress and returned to the station, he received word that insurgents from the Tsarskoe Selo garrison were approaching. Though the source of this information is unknown, it is most likely that someone connected with the Duma Committee fed the general this information in order to remove the St. George Battalion from Tsarskoe Selo.

If the source's goal was to force Ivanov to retreat, the move was a success. Upon receiving this information, Ivanov immediately withdrew his troops to Vyritsa to avoid confrontation with the insurgents. There he was informed that only fifteen minutes after their withdrawal, insurgent soldiers and crowds had occupied Tsarskoe Selo station, though this may have been misinformation as well.[94] Though it has often been argued that the withdrawal was caused by the dissolving loyalty of his troops, there were no signs of faltering loyalty in the ranks until the very end.[95] As long as the presence of his troops might endanger the safety of the imperial family and as long as his duty did not specifically include defense of the palace and the imperial family, Ivanov had no desire to defy the wish of the empress.[96]

One hour later, Lomonosov learned that Ivanov had proceeded to Semrino and now wanted to go to Gatchina. It was a dangerous moment: the station chief at Gatchina had refused to obey Lomonosov's order to break the switches (to prevent Ivanov from traveling by rail), and troops in Gatchina remained loyal to the old regime. But the locomotive brigade obtained two machine guns and installed them at the Gatchina depot to deter Ivanov from venturing in that direction. Soon Lomonosov received news that Ivanov had abandoned his intention to go to Gatchina and returned to Vyritsa. Lomonosov sighed with relief and ordered the railways to remove all the switches north of Vyritsa as Ivanov moved to the south.[97]

On March 1, Mikhail was busy receiving a host of guests and writing letters. As we have seen, Barrister Ivanov came in the morning to ask for his signature on the grand dukes' manifesto. In the afternoon and evening, his close advisers came, including Grand Duke Nikolai Mikhailovich (Bimbo) and British ambassador George Buchanan. We have no record of what they discussed, but their talk must have centered around the consensus in the Duma favoring Nicholas's abdication under Mikhail's regency. Earlier that morning the grand duke had sent a letter to Rodzyanko; Rodzyanko was supposed to come to see Mikhail, but he did not show up.[98] According to Matveev, Mikhail took his name off the grand dukes' collective manifesto. Perhaps he realized that it had no chance of being implemented.[99]

Ivanov did not know it, but by the time he withdrew to Vyritsa, the Stavka had decided to halt his operation. Until at least 9 p.m. on February 28,

Alekseev was determined to send reinforcement troops from the front to support Ivanov's counterrevolutionary expedition.[100] But sometime on March 1, he sent a telegram ordering Ivanov to halt his operations:

> According to the latest information, on February 28, complete peace was restored in Petrograd. The troops that had joined the Provisional Government in entire composition have been brought in order. The Provisional Government under the chairmanship of Rodzyanko, meeting in the State Duma, asked the commanders of the military units to obey orders for the restoration of peace. The proclamation to the populace issued by the Provisional Government mentions *the immutability of the monarchical basis of Russia*, necessity of a new basis for election and appointment of a government. They are waiting with impatience for the arrival of His Majesty, to present the aforementioned demands and to request his acceptance of the aspirations of the people. If this information is correct, then the method of your action will be changed, and the negotiations will lead to pacification, to avoid disgraceful fratricide, which our enemy has long awaited, and to preserve institutions and to get the factories operating. The proclamation of the new minister of transport, Bublikov, to the railway workers, which I received in a roundabout way, appeals to all to intensify work to remedy the disorganization of transportation. Let His Majesty know all this and also the conviction that it is possible to bring everything to a peaceful end, which will strengthen Russia. (Italics added)[101]

The Stavka's determination to organize a counterrevolutionary offensive had been based on its judgment that Petrograd had been consumed by a state of complete anarchy, from which the radical elements were emerging to control the insurgents. Therefore, the news of the Duma Committee's control over the situation—what Alekseev erroneously referred to as the "provisional government"—immediately produced a change of policy.

Military leaders had sympathized with the moderate wing of the liberals well before the revolution, so it would be difficult to direct arms against those with whom the military leaders had no substantial disagreement. Taking up arms against these figures, even if successful, would most likely isolate the army from the rest of the population, rendering the continuation of the war impossible. In the eyes of the public, the army and its leaders would inevitably be associated with the reactionary "dark forces." Moreover, if the Stavka involved the army in a counterrevolutionary attempt not only against the insurgents but also against the Duma, it could no longer count on the reliability of the officers, not to mention the soldiers. Thus, the Stavka welcomed with a sigh of relief the news that the Duma Committee was exerting its influence to restore order in the capital, with some measure of success.

There was no question that the Duma Committee had revolted against legitimate authority, and as long as the supreme commander's order to suppress the revolt remained in effect, the Stavka should have been bound to obey. Seeing nothing but catastrophe for the country and for the army in following the imperial order, the Stavka chose another path. By 12:30 p.m. on March 1, the Stavka had obtained information that the imperial train had changed its route and moved from Bologoe to Dno, but there were no direct communications from the imperial trains to the Stavka.[102] Even if Alekseev had wanted to obtain Nicholas's permission to halt Ivanov's operations, he would not have been able to do so. So with his telegram Alekseev defied the imperial order and halted Ivanov's offensive, decisively aligning the Stavka with the Duma Committee and against the supreme commander, Nicholas.

What made Alekseev switch the policy from suppressing the insurrection in the capital to halting this operation? And when did he make this decision? Though reports from Khabalov and Belyaev ceased to reach the Stavka after the collapse of the loyal forces, the Stavka kept in touch with the army General Staff and the Naval Staff in Petrograd. But their information remained fragmentary and did not give the Stavka an accurate picture of the situation in the capital. Only on the morning of March 1 did the Petrograd Telegraph Agency, now under the control of the Duma Committee, began delivering comprehensive information to the editor of *Voennyi Vestnik* [*Military Herald*], a military publication, at the Stavka.

The picture that emerged showed the Duma Committee acting decisively to take control of a chaotic situation. The Stavka received its first update from the Petrograd Telegraph Agency at 1:10 a.m. on March 1, learning that the Duma's Council of Elders had decided not to disperse despite the tsar's order of prorogation, and that it had passed a resolution that the current task of the Duma was to overthrow the old regime and replace it with a new one. The dispatch also indicated that Rodzyanko had issued a proclamation to restore order, but it did not say anything about the contents of the proclamation.[103]

The most important and detailed information, however, came at 4:30 a.m. on March 1. The telegram described the Duma Committee's two appeals along with the Petrograd Soviet's appeal for restoring and maintaining order. It described speeches by Rodzyanko, Milyukov, and Kerensky appealing for order among the insurgent soldiers who came to the Tauride Palace. It mentioned Bublikov's proclamation to the railway workers, urging them to restore and maintain railway service. It stated that telephone connections had been restored and the state bank had been reopened, while the railway was functioning normally between Moscow and Petrograd. On the whole, this information gave the impression that order was being restored thanks to the Duma Committee. Alekseev stamped his name on this document, showing that he had read this dispatch by 11:30 a.m. on March 1.[104]

It seems certain that the information Alekseev received from the Petrograd Telegraph Agency played a crucial role in his decision to halt

Ivanov's counterrevolutionary expedition. If this assumption is correct, then Alekseev's telegram ordering Ivanov to cease operations must have been sent at 1:15 p.m., after he read this report.[105]

There were other sources of information bolstering the Stavka's understanding of the situation. Rodzyanko sent two telegrams to the Stavka and the commanders at the front on the morning of March 1. The first telegram informed Alekseev at 5:51 a.m. that "due to the removal of all the former Council of Ministers from administration, governmental power was transferred at the present moment to the Provisional Committee of the State Duma."[106] The other was a copy of Rodzyanko's appeal to the army and the navy, informing them of the transfer of power to the Duma Committee, whose task was to "create normal conditions of life and administration" in the capital. It appealed to them to maintain discipline and order and fulfill their duty to fight against the enemy. Aleksandr Lukomsky received a copy and instructed army units to distribute it widely.[107]

Bublikov's message to the railway workers urging them to restore and maintain rail service was mentioned in the information given by the Petrograd Telegraph Agency as well, but Alekseev's telegram to Ivanov noted that he had obtained a copy of Bublikov's telegram "in a roundabout way," and it appeared to influence his change in position. Though Bublikov's telegram ensured the smooth functioning of the railways and made it clear that the Duma Committee would stand for the restoration of order, its overriding tone was markedly hostile to the old regime. A conversation between Lukomsky and General Mikhail Fyodorovich Kvetsinsky, chief of staff of the western front, may hint at how the Stavka interpreted this striking document. While Kvetsinsky was alarmed by Bublikov's telegram, Lukomsky said: "The telegram is known to us, but it is not bad, since it is calling for order."[108] The Stavka was already aware that Bublikov had been attempting to obstruct the movement of the imperial train from Bologoe to Dno by sending freight trains. Despite this, the Stavka was willing to accept the authority of the Duma Committee.[109]

In the pronouncements passed along by the Petrograd Telegraph Agency, nothing was said about the formation of a "provisional government," nor was any reference made to "the immutability of the monarchical basis of Russia." These references suggest that Alekseev's position toward the Duma Committee was buttressed by the Naval Staff and the army General Staff in Petrograd. Not only was the Stavka's contact with these staffs maintained without interruption, but the reference to the "provisional government" is identical to the term that Domanevsky used in his discussions with Ivanov, and it is conceivable that Alekseev inferred the "immutability of monarchical principles" from those who were closely associated with Guchkov. The position taken by Alekseev's telegram to Ivanov was thus well in line with the preferences of Zankevich, Domanevsky, and other officers of the General Staff, not to mention Rodzyanko himself. They all believed that halting the counterrevolutionary expedition was justifiable in the name of upholding the monarchical principle. Even so, it is unlikely that Alekseev's order reached Ivanov before he arrived at Tsarskoe Selo.[110]

Now that he had decided to halt Ivanov's operations and support the Duma Committee, Alekseev had to tread carefully as he handled the commanders in the field. From the western front General Aleksei Evert complained to Lukomsky that he had received two telegrams from Rodzyanko. He had no intention of accepting the authority of the Duma Committee and abrogating his oath to the tsar, but he wanted to know how Alekseev would respond before making a decision about how to answer.

Alekseev wrote a telegram sternly protesting Rodzyanko's decision to send his dispatches directly to front commanders without due consideration for the normal chain of command in the army, and he strongly warned that this practice should be immediately discontinued.[111] This telegram had dual purposes. On the one hand, it was intended to assuage Evert's anger by protesting Rodzyanko's unwelcome intervention in the military chain of command. On the other, it was also intended to exclude the troublemaking western front from the decision-making process. But Alekseev had to tread carefully between Evert and Ruzsky.

At the same time, Alekseev's telegram to Ivanov had a decisive influence on General Ruzsky, who had up to that point followed the Stavka's instructions to send troops for Ivanov's operations. From the beginning Ruzsky had believed that a political solution was the only way to cope with the revolution in the capital, and with this telegram in hand, he now moved to recall those troops without the approval of the Stavka.[112] During the night of March 1–2, the Tarutin Company, which had already arrived at Aleksandrovskaya, and the battalion of the Vyborg Fortress Artillery—the two units located closest to Ivanov—were the first to be recalled. At the same time, without seeking prior approval from Alekseev, Ruzsky requested that the western and southwestern fronts detain the dispatched troops at the nearest railway stations.[113] It is not clear what communications were exchanged between the Stavka and the northern front, but it is hard to imagine that Alekseev was happy with Ruzsky's unauthorized actions. Nevertheless, the Stavka accepted them. Ruzsky's collusion with the Duma Committee ahead of Alekseev would have far-reaching consequences in determining the fate of the monarchy.

The northern front learned during the night of March 1–2 that the Luga garrison had taken the side of the Duma Committee. In his telegraphic conversation with Ruzsky, which will be discussed in more detail in Chapter 10, Rodzyanko informed the commander of the northern front that troops dispatched from the northern front had revolted at Luga, occupied the station, and pledged to stop military trains.[114] If this information proved to be true, it would be ominous, the first sign that revolution had spread to the very troops sent to suppress it. Furthermore, the occupation of Luga posed a serious question about effective transportation of the reinforcements, since Luga was situated in the middle of the line between Pskov and Petrograd. It would also make it impossible for the tsar to return to Tsarskoe Selo. The "mutiny at Luga" was another decisive turning point for the military.

Luga, situated halfway from Petrograd to Pskov on the Warsaw Line, was a garrison city, whose fifteen thousand soldiers significantly outnumbered the civilian population. After the news of the soldiers' uprising in the capital reached Luga, the garrison's commander, Lieutenant General Georgy Georgievich Mengden, told the commanding staff that he was convinced that his soldiers would faithfully fulfill their oath of allegiance and put down any disturbances. Some on the staff were not so sure and recommended that the commanding staff isolate the soldiers from Petrograd by not issuing any permission to travel outside the barracks.[115]

But they couldn't keep the soldiers from learning about the insurrection in Petrograd. A soldier named Grigory Krivenko was sent to Petrograd and returned to Luga at 11 p.m. on February 27. He brought with him a document signed by Rodzyanko urging the Luga garrison to support the new regime.

On March 1, the soldiers held a meeting at which they decided to create a temporary revolutionary committee, with a noncommissioned officer, A. P. Zaplavsky, as its head. They formed fighting units and seized control of the railway station and the telegraph/post station, and took measures to prevent any military units from passing through Luga to Petrograd. They decided to disarm their officers.[116]

As the revolution took hold, the officers' corps was split into two groups. One group, led by Captain Nikolai Vladimirovich Voronovich (a member of the Socialist Revolutionary Party), advocated supporting the Duma Committee and organizing the insurgent soldiers along this line. The other, represented by the commander of the garrison, Mengden, refused to join the revolution. It was at the initiative of the first group of officers that a Military Committee was formed, which immediately established contact with the Duma Committee. This managed to subdue the flaring temper of the insurgents, who, having shot to death several officers, including Mengden, had already tasted blood. As chair of the Military Committee, Voronovich managed to disarm the insurgents and convince them to return to their barracks.[117]

The Luga Military Committee soon received their first mission. The Borodin Company, consisting of two thousand disciplined soldiers with eight machine guns, was on its way to Petrograd to join General Ivanov's expedition to suppress the revolution. The Luga Military Committee received an order from Nikolai Nekrasov of the Duma Committee: "You have promised to discontinue the movement of the troops for the pacification of Petrograd. I request that you report the details."[118] It appeared a difficult task. The Luga Military Committee could gather only 300–400 undisciplined, untrained soldiers. Moreover, the available guns in the reserve artillery division were for training purposes only and of no use in actual battle. Nevertheless, machine guns with no cartridge belts and training weapons were arranged on the platform, and as soon as the train entered the station, three members of the Military Committee issued a strict order to the soldiers on the train to remain inside. They then hurried into the officers' car and solemnly handed to the commanders an ultimatum demanding unconditional surrender and voluntary disarmament of officers and soldiers. If they did not comply, the artillery would open up on the trains without mercy.

The Borodin Company made no effort to resist. The commanders easily gave in, surrendered their arms, and ordered their soldiers to do the same. In fifteen minutes, the entire company was disarmed.[119] It will never be known whether the commanders of the Borodin Company really believed the threat of the Luga Military Committee or pretended to believe it so as to have a good excuse not to fulfill the onerous obligation of putting down the revolution. The commander of the Borodin Company told the Military Committee that they would wait for the arrival of the Duma

Committee's representatives. Fearing that the approaching dawn would reveal the dummy weapons ostentatiously displayed on the platform, the Military Committee rejected the proposal and ordered the Borodin Company to return to the northern front immediately.[120]

There never was a mutiny at Luga by the reinforcement troops sent from the northern front. The northern front learned before 1 a.m. on March 2 that the Luga garrison had taken the side of the Duma Committee. At 1:10 a.m., Boldyrev, quartermaster general of the northern front, sent a telegram to Lukomsky at the Stavka saying that the northern front had the information that the Luga garrison had transferred its allegiance to the side of the Duma Committee.[121] The Luga garrison pledged its support of the Duma Committee, and it received instructions from its Military Commission, but no mutiny of the troops sent from the front was reported.

The tsar finally arrived at Pskov at 7:30 p.m. on March 1, with the suite train catching up at 7:53 p.m.[122] The entourage was immediately struck by the eerie lack of ceremony. There was no official reception, no guard of honor present. The governor of Pskov and his subordinates welcomed the emperor on the platform, but the commander of the northern front, General Ruzsky, and his staff were conspicuously absent.[123]

Nicholas had spent two days traveling the railways through the countryside of Russia, and the political atmosphere that greeted him in Pskov on the evening of March 1 was radically different from the one he had left behind in Mogilev. The Duma Committee and the military leadership had redefined their attitudes toward the revolution during those crucial two days, and Nicholas's failure to intervene actively had consequences.[124] While he was traveling leisurely in the snow-covered countryside, important forces were at work to ruin Nicholas's power.

CHAPTER 9

# Responsible Ministry

Adjutant General Mikhail Alekseev was in the hot seat. As news of the revolution spread to the front, local commanders flooded Alekseev with questions concerning his attitude toward the Duma Committee. Whether these local commanders should support the Duma Committee or remain loyal to the emperor more or less depended on Alekseev's decision.[1] By halting General Nikolai Ivanov's operation at around 11 a.m. on March 1, Alekseev took the first major step toward recognition of the Duma Committee. On the afternoon of March 1, several disheartening news dispatches had arrived at Mogilev. Now Moscow had fallen into the hands of the insurgents, and mutiny was already spreading to the Baltic Fleet and Kronstadt. Admiral Adrian Nepenin of the Baltic Fleet urged the tsar to come to terms with Duma Committee chairman Mikhail Rodzyanko immediately: he himself had unilaterally recognized the authority of the Duma Committee without sanction from the Stavka. Meanwhile, Adjutant General Aleksei Brusilov, commander of the southwestern front, urged the tsar to recognize "the accomplished fact" and emphasized "the necessity of solving the terrible situation peacefully and quickly."[2]

Such news hastened Alekseev's efforts to seek a compromise with the Duma Committee. In the late afternoon, Alekseev sent the tsar a telegram that reached Pskov before the tsar's arrival there. This telegram reported on the spread of the revolution to Moscow. "It can be said with certainty that a disturbance in the rear will provoke the same throughout the army," Alekseev wrote. With a revolution breaking out in the rear, it would be impossible to ask the army to keep fighting, since due to the social composition of the soldiers and officers, there "will not be any basis to consider that the army will not react to what goes on in Russia." Alekseev concluded: "The suppression of the disorders by force is dangerous under the present conditions and will lead Russia and the army to ruin."

It would be necessary to take measures that would quiet the population and restore normal life in the country. If the Duma Committee's attempt to restore order was not accompanied by the emperor's "act quieting the population," then power would inevitably go to the "hands of the extreme elements tomorrow." Thus, Alekseev recommended:

I beg you, for the sake of salvation of Russia and *the dynasty*, place at the head of the government a person whom Russia would believe and entrust him with the formation of a cabinet. At the present moment, this is the only salvation. It is impossible to delay, and it has to be done immediately. To report Your Majesty otherwise will unconsciously and criminally bring Russia to ruin and shame, and create a danger for *the dynasty of Your Imperial Majesty*. (Italics added)[3]

By the time Nicholas arrived at Pskov, however, Alekseev's position had drastically changed. Previously all he had asked for was the formation of a ministry of confidence—that is, changes in key personnel, but no changes in governmental structure. But sometime by late afternoon of March 1 he had come to advocate for the establishment of a responsible ministry—in essence, a constitutional monarchy. At 4:05 p.m., General Yury Danilov, chief of staff of the northern front, sent a telegram asking what instructions the Stavka would give Adjutant General Nikolai Ruzsky when he met with the emperor in a few hours.[4] Assistant chief of staff General Vladislav Napoleonovich Klembovsky's response reinforced Alekseev's recommendation to establish a ministry of confidence, and specifically mentioned Rodzyanko as the candidate to head the ministry of confidence.[5] This exchange ended at 5:40 p.m.

By 10:20 p.m., Alekseev would change course.[6] The key shift must have come shortly before Nicholas arrived at Pskov. Around that time, General Klembovsky, under Alekseev's instruction, began sending telegrams to the front commanders regarding the spread of the revolution to Moscow, Kronstadt, and the Baltic Fleet. Through Klembovsky, Alekseev explained that the worsening situation had forced the Stavka to request that the tsar "issue an act capable of calming the population and ending the revolution." Klembovsky then continued:

> General Alekseev reports that the salvation of Russia and the possibility of continuing the war will be achieved only when at the head of the government stands a person who can enjoy the confidence of the population and who can form a corresponding [*sootvestvuyushchii*] cabinet.[7]

The telegram's use of the word "corresponding" to describe the cabinet is worthy of closer examination. *Sootvestvuyushchii* can be translated as "corresponding" or "appropriate." It is not clear, however, to what the cabinet should correspond or how the cabinet should be appropriate. However, though it makes no sense translated literally, *sootvestvuyushchii* is phonetically close to *otvestvennyi*, which means "a responsible ministry." It is possible to view this wording as an intentional attempt to obfuscate the Stavka's real intention. It should also be noted that this telegram was sent to the western front at 6:09 p.m., to the Rumanian front at 8:20, and to the Caucasian front at 9:15 p.m., and not to the northern front (where Ruzsky was in command) or to the southwestern front (Brusilov's command) at all. In the margins of Klembovsky's copy of the telegram, there is a note that the commander of the northern front was separately "oriented."[8] When Klembovsky wanted to talk to Ruzsky before 5:40, he was told that Ruzsky had already gone to the station to meet the tsar—yet, as we will see, Ruzsky was not at the platform when the tsar arrived two hours later. Where was Ruzsky between 5:40 and 7:30? We can speculate that Ruzsky left his office at 5:40 but stopped by the telegraph office. It is likely that the possibility of seeking a political solution to the crisis by granting a responsible ministry was discussed by Alekseev and Ruzsky through the Hughes apparatus or via telegraph exchanges between the Stavka and the northern front between 5:40 and 7:30 p.m. In this unrecorded but crucial conversation, both military leaders must have agreed to pursue the formation of a responsible ministry.

Though General Brusilov did not receive Klembovsky's telegram either, he sent a telegram of his own to Count Vladimir Fredericks at Dno giving his opinion and asking that it be conveyed to the tsar. "With honor and love to the tsar and the fatherland," Brusilov asked the tsar to "accept the completed fact and conclude the horrible situation peacefully and immediately" in order to avoid at any cost an internecine war.[9] It is likely that Alekseev had already contacted Brusilov as well to alert him to his change of policy toward seeking a responsible ministry.

The task of actually convincing the emperor to accept the policy now fell on the shoulders of General Ruzsky.

From the very beginning of the revolution, Ruzsky's sympathy lay with the liberal opposition. He later stated that he was neither right nor left politically, but that he believed it was impossible for a tsar like Nicholas to reign over such a vast empire as Russia.[10] As early as February 27, when the outcome of the disturbances in the streets was not yet clear, Ruzsky implored the tsar to take measures to quiet the country. He was the first military leader to align himself with the Duma opposition during the crisis, and recommended that the tsar not take military measures but instead grant political concessions.[11] As long as he believed Petrograd to be in chaos, he fully cooperated with the Stavka in its military intervention, but once Alekseev called a temporary halt to Ivanov's operation, Ruzsky recalled the troops he had dispatched to Petrograd—and recalled them without the Stavka's prior approval. Nicholas thus spent the most crucial two days of his life under the influence of the military commander who most decisively opposed him.[12]

On the station platform at Pskov on the evening of March 1, General Ruzsky, his chief of staff, Danilov, and his aide-de-camp, Count Dmitry Aleksandrovich Sheremetev, arrived a few minutes after the tsar. According to an eyewitness: "Stooping, gray, and old, Ruzsky walked in rubber galoshes; he was in the uniform of the General Staff. His face was pale and sickly, and his eyes under the glasses revealed hostility."[13] Maintaining his usual calm, Nicholas received the general in his favorite Circassian coat with a dagger at the side and a dahlia on the chest.

The tsar told Ruzsky that he expected to meet Rodzyanko at Pskov, because the chairman of the Duma had failed to come to Dno as he had promised. He explained that he had left Mogilev since the situation was serious and he hoped that he could be closer to the scene, where he could talk personally with the necessary people. He did not say that he was most anxious to rejoin his family and sick children. Ruzsky then asked for an audience before Rodzyanko arrived so that he could give the tsar an important report entrusted to him by Alekseev. The appointment was set for nine o'clock. In the meantime, Ruzsky spoke with the emperor's entourage and discovered that they were oblivious to the seriousness of the situation. The entourage blamed Major General Sergei Khabalov (commander of the

Petrograd Military District) and Major General Aleksandr Balk (Petrograd city governor) for incompetence, but hoped that General Ivanov, with reliable troops, would soon put down the revolt.[14]

Isolated from events in Petrograd while traveling through the countryside for two days, Nicholas still had no knowledge of the Stavka's decision to halt Ivanov's operation or its recognition of the Duma Committee. When he read the piles of telegrams that awaited him in Pskov, his shock must have been profound. For the first time he learned of the revolution's spread to Moscow, the Baltic Fleet, and Kronstadt. Alekseev, who had strongly endorsed Nicholas's plan to suppress the revolution by force, now urged the tsar to formally halt Ivanov's operations, thus reversing his previous policy to suppress the revolution by force. General Brusilov and Grand Duke Sergei Mikhailovich appealed to the tsar to accept Alekseev's recommendations. There was no news from his wife or from Tsarskoe Selo.[15]

Ruzsky was well aware that convincing the emperor of the necessity of the concession to the Duma Committee would be difficult. Thinking nervously of the historical role he was to play, he felt himself extremely ignorant of events in Petrograd and of the Stavka's intentions, although he had had conversations with Alekseev before Nicholas's arrival. He finally went to the tsar's salon car but had to wait another hour in the corridor, since palace commandant General Vladimir Voeikov, "busy with smoking a cigar and straightening out pictures on the wall," neglected to tell the emperor of Ruzsky's arrival. Finally, at 10 p.m., Nicholas admitted him.

Ruzsky began with a general outline of events as reported by the Stavka. He made it clear that what he intended to report was concerned not with military matters but with matters of state structure, which went beyond his competence. He expressed fear that the emperor might not wish to listen to his report, since he might not have much confidence in the commander of the northern front, accustomed as he was to the perspective of General Alekseev, with whom Ruzsky had had many disagreements. But Nicholas told Ruzsky to state his opinion frankly.

Immediately getting to the point, Ruzsky urged the tsar to grant a responsible ministry. As expected, the tsar rejected this suggestion "quietly, coolly, but with the feeling of a deep conviction." However, Ruzsky persisted. As he later recalled, he mustered "all nerves to tell the emperor all that I thought about individual persons who occupied responsible posts in the last years, and who seemed to me the greatest mistakes . . . both in the government and in the Stavka." Nicholas told Ruzsky that he was opposing a responsible ministry not from personal interests nor for any concealed purposes, but rather because "he was not entitled to give up the whole matter of governing Russia to the hands of those who, today in the government, could cause such blunders to the fatherland and tomorrow wash their hands, and send in their resignations from the cabinet."

Ruzsky reminded Nicholas that under the existence of the State Council and the State Duma, autocracy was merely a fiction.

Nicholas declared: "I am responsible before God and Russia for everything that has happened and will happen. Whether ministers are responsible before the Duma and the State Council, it is all the same to me." To Nicholas, autocracy with the emperor at its head was not a "fiction" but the essence of his moral and religious responsibility. He still clung to his mythical understanding of the Russian state as an autocracy headed by the tsar, whose responsibility was not to the nation but to God.

Ruzsky insisted that Russia was a state, governed by the legal institution to which the emperor himself should be subordinated. Ruzsky emphasized: "The emperor reigns, but a government governs." But Nicholas retorted that he could not understand such a formula and that he would have had to be brought up differently to understand it. He repeated that he was not clinging to power for personal interest, but he simply could not take measures against his own conscience. The conference had grown stormy. And Ruzsky's attempts at persuasion seemed to no avail.[16]

It was here that the fundamental contradictions of the state structure since 1905 were laid bare. Nicholas rejected the new state structure instituted in 1906 by the Fundamental Laws, and reverted to the archaic notion of autocracy that had existed before 1905—the autocracy that he had inherited from his father, Alexander III. This concept of autocracy had become solidified through his intimate consultations with Alexandra, and for him it developed into a mythical and religious conviction. Autocracy was his essence. At his coronation he had sworn before God to uphold autocracy, and he had endured all the terrible experiences of the 1905 revolution and the war, even as his detractors spoke against him. He deeply believed that the tsar and the people were united by the love of God and fatherland and that any change to autocracy would mean betrayal of the trust that the people extended to the autocrat. That was the world he firmly believed in, the world he had strived all his life to maintain and that he intended to bequeath to his son. Nicholas resisted, objected, disagreed, and disputed, mustering what strength and indignation he could.

At about 11 p.m., a telegram from Alekseev arrived at Pskov. In this new telegram Alekseev suggested to the tsar that, given the "disorganization of the army and the impossibility of continuing the war," the only possible solution would be to "recognize a responsible ministry, the composition of which should be entrusted to the chairman of the State Duma."[17] According to Alekseev, the Duma Committee could still stop the complete breakdown of authority. But any further loss of time would diminish the chances for restoration and maintenance of order and create circumstances favorable to the extreme radical elements. Finally, Alekseev proposed that the emperor sign a manifesto drafted by Nikolai Bazili, a legal specialist attached to the diplomatic section at the Stavka, for a responsible ministry. The draft manifesto stated:

In the desire to unite all the forces of the people for the purpose of achieving victory as soon as possible, I have considered it necessary to call a Ministry which would be *responsible before the representatives of the people*, entrusting its formation to the Chairman

of the State Duma Rodzyanko; the Ministry should be composed
of persons enjoying the confidence of all Russia. (Italics added)[18]

The manifesto concluded: "We strongly hope that all faithful sons of
Russia, *closely united around the throne and people's representatives*, will
help together our brave army to complete the great task" (italics added).
This expression referred both to the oath to the tsar and to the Duma.
The recommendation—establishment of a ministry responsible to the
Duma, appointed by Rodzyanko—was consistent with the policy that
Rodzyanko pursued after he abandoned the effort to form a ministry
of confidence, and with the policy he had pursued with the grand dukes
until March 1.

Though there is no direct evidence to show that Alekseev and Ruzsky
knew about the grand dukes' manifesto, indirect evidence indicates that
they knew about it and that they acted in collaboration with Rodzyanko
and the grand dukes. Early in the morning of March 1, between 9 and
10:30 a.m., Colonel Ivan Barmin, in the military theater communications
section at the Stavka, had a conversation with Colonel Amir Karamyshev,
in charge of military communications for the northern front. Karamyshev
told Barmin that Grand Duke Georgy had left for Petrograd on the night
of February 27.[19] Georgy was close to his brothers, Sergei (artillery inspector at the Stavka) and Aleksandr (Sandro). It would be inconceivable to
think that during his sojourn in Petrograd he did not learn about the
grand dukes' draft manifesto and in some way communicate this to Sergei, a steadfast supporter of Alekseev. It is possible to believe that through
these brothers, Alekseev had caught wind of the attempts by Rodzyanko
and the grand dukes to persuade the tsar to accept this manifesto.

For Nicholas, Alekseev's desertion was a great blow. The telegram
revealed that what Ruzsky was advocating was not merely the personal
opinion of an untrustworthy commander but was shared by Alekseev, and
behind him stood the entire army. If such a view was so widely held, it

would be impossible for Nicholas, during a time of war, to purge all officers who agreed with it.

Nevertheless, it is important to note that Alekseev had not consulted
on this matter with all the commanders. He did not consult General Aleksei Evert, General Vladimir Viktorovich Sakharov, or Grand Duke Nikolai
Nikolaevich (Nikolasha). Alekseev gambled that he and Ruzsky, possibly
with the support of Brusilov, could overwhelm Nicholas before he thought
to communicate with his most loyal commanders. This is why Klembovsky
had sent those three the obscure telegram about the necessity to accept an
ambiguously phrased "corresponding" ministry. It was Alekseev's attempt
to prepare those three front commanders to accept a responsible ministry.
His strategy must have been to obtain the consent of the tsar first, and then
present those three commanders with a fait accompli.

Nicholas finally surrendered. He consented to issue the manifesto sent
by Alekseev without the slightest change and without studying it carefully,
at least for that moment. Ruzsky himself later confessed: "I do not know if
I would have been successful in convincing the emperor, had it not been
for Alekseev's telegram."[20] Alekseev was the one who wrote the script and
Ruzsky played his part as written.

After retiring to his office, Ruzsky immediately dispatched a telegram
to let Alekseev know of Nicholas's consent to the manifesto. Meanwhile,
Nicholas summoned Voeikov to the salon car to share the news. The palace commandant was stunned by Nicholas's concessions and advised him
to change the contents of the telegram he was to send to Rodzyanko, in
order to preserve his prerogative as the supreme leader to appoint the
war, navy, and foreign ministers. Agreeing immediately with this recommendation, Nicholas instructed Voeikov to send the amended telegram
to Rodzyanko via the Hughes apparatus.[21] This action was tantamount to
Nicholas's rescinding his agreement to accept a responsible ministry.

When Voeikov returned to his train car, Danilov came to receive the emperor's intended telegram to Rodzyanko granting a responsible ministry. Voeikov refused to hand it over and instead asked Danilov if he could use the Hughes apparatus to transmit Nicholas's telegram to Rodzyanko by himself. Upon learning of this request, Ruzsky rushed to Voeikov's train car. Ruzsky and Voeikov launched into a heated argument as other members of the entourage gathered around. Voeikov argued that he was fulfilling the emperor's order, while Ruzsky insisted that he, as the commander of the northern front, had sole control of the Hughes apparatus, and he did not intend to grant Voeikov access. Ruzsky was effectively overruling the decision of the supreme commander, in a clear act of insubordination.

Ruzsky and Voeikov went to Nicholas's salon car to resolve the conflict. The emperor was "surprised" at Ruzsky's refusal to let Voeikov use the Hughes apparatus. Nicholas told Voeikov to present the draft telegram to Fredericks, who then gave the draft telegram to Ruzsky.[22] Ruzsky was shocked to discover that the draft mentioned nothing about a responsible ministry and merely authorized Rodzyanko to form a cabinet with the exceptions of the ministers of war, navy, and foreign affairs. All his persuasion and Alekseev's pressure had been overturned. Dumbfounded, Ruzsky asked Voeikov to tell the emperor that this telegram would not be acceptable. He asked for another audience.[23] If Ruzsky talked to Rodzyanko, as a duty officer reported to the Stavka, it must have been at this time, to explain that he had to meet the tsar once more to finalize the deal.[24]

It was already past midnight when Ruzsky was summoned to the emperor's salon car again. This time Nicholas asked him about the details of the manifesto. A dreadful suspicion crossed Ruzsky's mind that Nicholas had changed his mind. He asked the emperor if he had acted in an unacceptable way by having already informed the Stavka of the emperor's agreement with the manifesto. This was another way of telling the tsar that his acceptance of a responsible ministry was already an established fact. Nicholas answered that he had made up his mind to grant a responsible ministry for the good of Russia, since Ruzsky and Alekseev, who could hardly agree on anything, were of the same opinion.[25] Having secured the tsar's final acceptance of a responsible ministry, Ruzsky made arrangements to speak directly to Rodzyanko through the Hughes apparatus rather than sending him a telegram.

When Nicholas finally accepted the manifesto, it meant that the world that he had maintained all his life had been destroyed. Nicholas and the entourage had chosen Pskov as their destination so that the emperor would be protected by troops loyal to the tsar and to allow the tsar access to the Hughes apparatus. When he arrived, however, the tsar was deprived of freedom to contact the outside world and barred from using the Hughes apparatus. Not only that, but the northern front troops under Ruzsky were there not to protect the emperor but to force him to accept the manifesto. The tsar had become a prisoner of the northern front. It is important to note that behind the scene enacted at Pskov, it was Alekseev who was directing the play.

Alekseev's previous order halting the counterrevolutionary expedition belatedly received the approval of the commander in chief. According to Aleksandr Spiridovich, after Nicholas accepted the manifesto to grant a responsible ministry, Ruzsky came to the emperor's car once more and requested that he agree with the suspension of Ivanov's operations.[26] Accepting this recommendation, the emperor sent a telegram to General Ivanov shortly after midnight to halt his operations until Nicholas's arrival at Tsarskoe Selo. The telegram was addressed to General Ivanov: "Hope you arrived safely. I ask you not to take any measures until my arrival and report. Nicholas."[27] It is not known whether Ivanov received this telegram, and if he did, when and where he received it. It is possible that when he left Tsarskoe Selo and moved to Vyritsa, he still did not know that his operations had been suspended.

Ruzsky was so exhausted by the evening's efforts that he could hardly stand. He went to sleep with the conviction that this hard-won concession of a responsible ministry would once and for all calm the nation.

Nicholas wrote a telegram to Alexandra afterward: "Arrived here before supper. Hope that everyone's health is better, and that I will see you soon. Lord with you, and tightly embrace."[28] He did not breathe a word about the catastrophic concessions he had just made to Ruzsky. Perhaps he feared her disapproval. He did not have to, since this telegram never reached Tsarskoe Selo.

Nicholas lay awake until 5 a.m. Spiridovich writes: "He was defeated. Ruzsky broke the moral foundation that had sustained the emperor, who was tired and worn out and without any serious support around him. . . . To the emperor, surrendering to Ruzsky and Alekseev was almost tantamount to admitting his mistake of the past, and by that ruined his authority as the ruler and the autocrat."[29] It would not be the last concession he made.

# CHAPTER 10

# Abdication

Though Adjutant General Nikolai Ruzsky and Adjutant General Mikhail Alekseev had succeeded in forcing Nicholas to accept a responsible ministry, something that had previously been utterly unacceptable, the revolution continued to transform the political landscape in Petrograd. Upon learning of Mikhail Rodzyanko's move to seek an audience with the tsar and his secret dealings with the grand dukes in composing a manifesto on the establishment of a responsible ministry, some members of the Duma Committee, led by Pavel Milyukov, suspected that he was "plotting a conspiracy with the military leaders, considering himself dictator of the Russian Revolution."[1]

Pointing to mounting anger by insurgent soldiers at Rodzyanko's order to return to their barracks and restore order under their officers, Aleksandr Kerensky, Nikolai Nekrasov, and Aleksandr Konovalov—the Masonic trio—had declared that they considered Rodzyanko unacceptable as the prime minister of the Provisional Government.[2] Confronted with such strong opposition, Rodzyanko could no longer pursue his independent course of seeking a compromise with the tsar. When the Duma

Committee decided to seek Nicholas's abdication and to send Aleksandr Guchkov and Vasily Shulgin as emissaries to Pskov, rather than Rodzyanko, his position became untenable.[3] Moreover, leaving Petrograd in this precarious situation would mean the loss of his authority as a leader of the liberals. To regain his power, he now found it necessary to back the majority opinion and seek Nicholas's abdication. He would do so by establishing direct contact with the military, preempting the Duma Committee's delegates.

In the early hours of March 2, Rodzyanko called Ruzsky through the Hughes apparatus at the war minister's residence. Their conversation began at 3:30 a.m. on March 2 and lasted until 7:30.[4] Already exhausted by his fateful conversations with Nicholas, Ruzsky slumped on the bench in the telegraph room and read sheets of tape of the conversation, handed to him by his chief of staff, General Yury Danilov. As soon as the tape was decoded, it was also sent to Alekseev from the next room by Quartermaster General Vasily Boldyrev.[5]

Ruzsky first asked Rodzyanko about the real reason he had cancelled his trip to Pskov, since "the knowledge of this reason is essential for our further talk." Rodzyanko explained:

Frankly speaking, there are two reasons why I did not go: in the first place, the troops you dispatched mutinied, ran out of the train at Luga, declared that they were going to associate themselves with the State Duma, and decided to take the weapons and not to let anybody pass, not even the imperial trains. Immediately, I took measures so that the track for the train of His Majesty could be freed, but I do not know if I shall succeed or not.

The second reason is that I received the information that my leaving the capital would cause an undesirable result. It was impossible to leave the pent-up anger of the people without my presence, because until that time they believed in me and carried out only my instructions.[6]

This explanation opened with a bald-faced lie. The troops sent from the northern front never mutinied at Luga, although the Luga garrison revolted and pledged its support for the Duma, as Ruzsky was well aware.[7] But the general did not challenge Rodzyanko on this point.

Rodzyanko does not fare well in the second explanation, either. The reaction of the masses, particularly of the insurgent soldiers, to Rodzyanko's order to return to the barracks and submit themselves to their officers contributed to the erosion of his authority. This development puts the lie to his claim that the people "believed in me and carried out only my instructions." What is most important about Rodzyanko's words are not how he concealed the truth from Ruzsky but why he attempted to mislead him. As the historian George Katkov has argued, Rodzyanko was in a difficult plight. On the one hand, he had deeply committed himself to seeking a compromise with the tsar, a policy for which he had succeeded in mobilizing the support of the high command and the grand dukes until the early morning of March 1. It was partly because of Rodzyanko's persuasion that the high command had agreed to induce the tsar to grant the political concession prescribed by Rodzyanko's project. However, he could no longer go to Pskov to present the old demand for the establishment of a responsible ministry, since this would be regarded by his colleagues in the Duma Committee as unacceptable intrigue behind their backs. But he could not go to Pskov to demand Nicholas's abdication, either, since he did not know how the high command would react to the new demand. Cultivating the military's favor was the only path to regaining political influence among his colleagues.

Since, in Katkov's summation, he would not gain anything from the trip to Pskov, Rodzyanko "thought it preferable to wait and see how matters would develop in Pskov after the meeting between the emperor and Ruzsky, and then try to persuade the army commanders that an immediate abdication was both desirable and necessary."[8] Rodzyanko's conversation with Ruzsky was a desperate maneuver to escape from this predicament.

Rodzyanko was aware that his colleagues had selected Prince Lvov as the candidate to head the Provisional Government, pushing his candidacy aside. For the past two days, he had maneuvered to restore his authority by supporting the grand dukes' manifesto. This draft manifesto envisaged a constitutional monarchy in which the Duma was the parent body of the Provisional Government, and the chairman of the Duma would appoint the chairman of the Council of Ministers. But this would mean that Nicholas would continue as tsar, retaining some imperial prerogatives that would restrict the power of the Duma chairman. On the other hand, Nicholas's abdication in favor of his son would mean greater power for Rodzyanko, since the new child tsar would be a figurehead without power; nevertheless, Rodzyanko would have to figure out a way to maintain the power to appoint the cabinet. Thus Rodzyanko had to weigh the pros and cons of the two options: to pursue the grand dukes' manifesto or to seek Nicholas's abdication. He knew there was a growing consensus in the Duma to seek Nicholas's removal from the throne, and for that reason he was leaning toward supporting this radical position. But first he had to see how the high command would react to his probing question about the abdication.[9]

Ruzsky reported to Rodzyanko that the tsar had finally agreed to grant a responsible ministry, the formation of which would be entrusted to Rodzyanko. The manifesto for a responsible ministry would be made public on March 2, and Ruzsky promised he would send it to Rodzyanko. Ruzsky must have expected that Rodzyanko would be jubilant at receiving this news.

The Duma chairman's reply must have hit the unsuspecting Ruzsky like a bolt out of the blue: "It is obvious that His Majesty and you did not take into account what was going on here." Rodzyanko went on to impart a completely new picture of the situation in Petrograd, where, he said, "one of the most terrible revolutions is approaching, the course of which is impossible to reverse." Soldiers were roaming about in the streets, randomly killing officers. The ugly passions of the insurgents had been unleashed to such an extent that it would be almost impossible to control them. Rodzyanko was forced to take the side of the insurgents "to avoid anarchy and demoralization, which might bring the state to a downfall . . . Hatred towards the empress has reached to the extreme." He was obliged even to "imprison all the ministers except for the ministers of war and navy in the Peter and Paul Fortress, to avoid bloodshed." Agitation was now directed against anyone who tried to counsel moderation. Rodzyanko then concluded, "I consider it necessary to tell you that what you have proposed is not enough; *the problem of the dynasty has been put point blank*" (italics added).

One can imagine Ruzsky's shock. Only hours before, Ruzsky had received a telegram from Rodzyanko himself assuring him that order was being restored.[10] But now he said that there was widespread violence against officers by insurgent soldiers in the streets, claiming: "Hatred to the empress" had "reached to the extreme."[11]

The perception of the Duma Committee's control of the situation had been the most important factor behind the Stavka's decision to suspend counterrevolutionary action and seek a peaceful settlement. Both Ruzsky and Alekseev had believed that the manifesto granting a constitutional government could bring the crisis to a peaceful end. But the situation Rodzyanko described was totally different from what Ruzsky had been led to believe.

Most astonishing was Rodzyanko's reference to the fate of the dynasty being "put point blank." The question was no longer whether the emperor should grant a ministry of confidence (a change of personnel within the existing structure) or a responsible ministry (a constitutional monarchy).

Either of these solutions would assume Nicholas II continuing to rule as the emperor. Rodzyanko had now put on the table the fate of the tsar.

Before tackling the dynastic question, Rodzyanko paused to assure General Ruzsky of the patriotism of the revolutionaries. "All the people I talked to, when I went out to the crowds and to the troops, are firmly in favor of continuing the war to a victorious end and not surrendering to the Germans. Not only the entire Petrograd and the Tsarskoe garrisons but also people all over the cities supported the Duma." This was not completely accurate. There were signs of antiwar sentiments among the insurgents, though they were not dominant, and the radical revolutionary propagandists had distributed inflammatory antiwar leaflets among the garrison soldiers. Still, Rodzyanko was well aware that the first and foremost concern of the high command was to maintain the cohesion of the army and to continue the war to a victorious end, so he made sure to say what the high command wanted to hear.

Then he came to the crucial point: "People are presenting the threatening demand for the abdication of Nicholas in favor of his son under the regency of Mikhail Aleksandrovich and this is becoming a definite demand." Here Rodzyanko was again twisting the truth a bit. Anti-dynastic feelings were high among the masses, especially against those whom they considered to be German agents and German sympathizers, and the target of their hatred was above all the empress. Nevertheless, this definite formula—Nicholas's abdication in favor of his son under his brother's regency—cannot be said to have been widely known and popular among the masses of insurgents. Rodzyanko knew that Soviet leaders were seeking the overthrow (*nizlozhenie*) of the monarchical system entirely, something far beyond Nicholas's abdication. It might be accurate to say that the idea of a regency was "becoming a definite demand" among his Duma Committee colleagues, but that was not the case among the masses nor among the Petrograd Soviet leaders. Still, that is how Rodzyanko presented it. It is also important to note that Rodzyanko presented this formula—Nicholas's abdication in favor of his son under Mikhail's regency—as the demand gaining popularity, but not as his own demand.

Finally, Rodzyanko warned against General Nikolai Ivanov continuing his counterrevolutionary operations. Violence would surely pour fuel on the fire; furthermore, such an attempt would provoke revolts among the soldiers sent to suppress the revolution. This would lead to an internecine war.

Ruzsky answered that the emperor had already consented to halt Ivanov's operation and to recall the other troops sent from the front. Furthermore, he said, the emperor had agreed to sign the manifesto granting a responsible ministry, entrusting its formation to Rodzyanko himself. He then read the manifesto prepared by the Stavka and accepted by the emperor. To Ruzsky's desperate effort to limit the concession to the formation of a responsible ministry, Rodzyanko replied:

> Power is slipping from my hands. The anarchy has reached such a degree that I am compelled tonight to announce the formation of the Provisional Government. Unfortunately, the manifesto was too late; it should have been issued immediately after my first telegram. . . . Time was wasted and there is no return.

Rodzyanko's statement was a strange yet shrewd juxtaposition of two contradictory positions. He said that anarchy had reached the point that "power was slipping from [the] hands" of the chairman of the Duma, and that the Duma Committee's effort to restore order was "far from successful." And yet, he said, "all the troops joined the State Duma" and "there was no disagreement" between the Duma and the people. On the one hand, chaos prevailed in which "soldiers are killing officers," but on the other, there was order and unity in which "everywhere the troops remain on the side of the Duma and the people."[12] Furthermore, he stated that he, as the Duma chairman, had appointed the Provisional Government. This power, according to the Fundamental Laws, belonged only to the tsar. Rodzyanko was thus usurping this power and claiming himself to be endowed with this power.

Ruzsky responded by asking Rodzyanko what would happen to the motherland if anarchy suffused the army, destroying the leadership's authority. "In essence," he continued, "the ultimate goal is only one: a responsible ministry answerable to the people, and that is the only path for achieving the change of order of administering the state." Ruzsky seemed to make the point that he preferred to limit the tsar's concessions to a responsible ministry, short of abdication. Then he asked: "Is it necessary to make the manifesto public?" This was tantamount to asking directly where Rodzyanko stood: for a responsible ministry or for abdication. Rodzyanko demurred: "Frankly, I don't know how to answer. Everything depends on events that are flying with head-spinning speed." Ruzsky answered that he had received instructions from the Stavka to make the manifesto public, and that he would follow those instructions and see what would follow. Rodzyanko said that he had nothing against that; in fact, he would request that Ruzsky should follow the Stavka's instructions.

It is important to note that while Rodzyanko presented the abdication as the aspiration of the masses, he himself remained outwardly noncommittal, although he was already leaning toward seeking Nicholas's abdication, as clearly revealed in the letter he had sent to Grand Duke Mikhail prior to this conversation with Ruzsky. His was a probing move, to see if the high command would take the bait. If it did, the abdication drama would then be the high command's responsibility. If not, he would retreat.

Although Ruzsky possessed ample grounds to question Rodzyanko's truthfulness, he showed no hint of such suspicions. His silence on Rodzyanko's contradictions reflected his own political calculations. As soon as he learned of the existence of the Duma Committee in Petrograd, he had drawn the conclusion that counterrevolutionary measures should be avoided at all costs and that a political settlement should be reached through the Duma Committee. Considering the political reality facing the military, he may have thought that the compromise of a responsible ministry might be the best option available, although at heart he would prefer Nicholas to abdicate. Though he never openly supported that outcome during his conversation with Rodzyanko, he never forcefully rejected the idea, either. Pointing out Rodzyanko's contradictions served no purpose for him; it would be better to pretend to believe in Rodzyanko and to let him initiate the demand for abdication.

Totally exhausted, Ruzsky went back to his train car and took a nap before he was scheduled to meet Nicholas to report what Rodzyanko had said in the fateful conversation.


After a sleepless night, at 5:15 a.m. on March 2, Nicholas finally sent a telegram to Alekseev, giving permission to make the manifesto public.[13] Needless to say, he had no idea that Rodzyanko was firing the first salvo for his abdication at the time.

The grand dukes sensed the Duma Committee's shift almost as soon as it began happening. The doyen of the grand dukes, Pavel, wrote a letter to Kirill on March 2 reflecting on the disturbing consensus that was forming in the Duma Committee. The grand dukes' draft manifesto had been intended to save the dynasty under Nicholas. Disturbed by the "tendency" to want to appoint Mikhail as a regent, Pavel instructed Kirill to get in touch with Rodzyanko to try to solve the crisis along the lines outlined in the manifesto signed by the grand dukes. "We must do everything to keep Niki on the throne," he concluded.[14]

Kirill responded to "Uncle Pavel," stating that all he had heard so far was a rumor. But he complained that despite his plea to Mikhail to work together with the "family," "Misha" was hiding and consulting only Rodzyanko.[15]

The united front among the three senior grand dukes seemed to crumble as soon as they sensed a tilt among the Duma liberals toward seeking Nicholas's abdication.

Mikhail received a letter from Rodzyanko on the morning of March 2. Rodzyanko had written it prior to his conversation with Ruzsky:

> Everything was too late now. Only the abdication from the throne in favor of the heir under your regency can calm the country. I ask you to exert influence so that this can be done voluntarily, then everything will be immediately calmed down. I am personally hanging by a hair, and can be arrested and hanged every minute. Do not take any steps and do not go anywhere. You must not avoid the regency. God help you to fulfill my advice to persuade the Sovereign.[16]

This letter indicates that despite his wavering on abdication in his conversation with Ruzsky, Rodzyanko had resigned himself to accepting the Duma Committee's consensus for abdication. That day Mikhail had a couple of visitors, including Rear Admiral Aleksei Pavlovich Kapnist of the Naval Staff, who was close to Navy Minister Admiral Ivan Grigorovich. In the evening, Grand Duke Nikolai (Sandro's older brother, Bimbo) came in civilian clothes. There is no doubt that they talked about the consensus among the leading Duma Committee members for demanding Nicholas's abdication under Mikhail's regency.[17]

The Rodzyanko-Ruzsky conversation threw Alekseev totally off balance. His strategy had been to obtain the concession of a responsible ministry from the tsar, then jam the manifesto down the throats of Generals Aleksei Evert, Vladimir Sakharov, and Nikolai Nikolaevich as a fait accompli. But now this strategy had to be discarded.

Before the conversation between Ruzsky and Rodzyanko through the Hughes apparatus was even completed, Danilov sent a telegram to Alekseev summarizing the gist of the conversation. Danilov relayed Rodzyanko's words to Ruzsky: that the dynastic question was being put point blank, and that the manifesto to grant a responsible ministry was no longer acceptable. Danilov suggested that the Stavka should not make the manifesto for the responsible ministry public until Ruzsky met with the tsar at 10 a.m. on March 2.[18]

Alekseev then sent a telegram to the front commanders outlining what Rodzyanko had told Ruzsky. He conveyed Rodzyanko's opinion that it was now too late for the manifesto, that hatred of the empress had reached an extreme level, and that the question of the dynasty was being raised explicitly. He summarized Rodzyanko's "demand" as the abdication of Nicholas in favor of his son under Mikhail's regency. He relayed Ruzsky's sense that in view of the great difficulty that the general had encountered in wringing from Nicholas the concession of a responsible ministry, it would be difficult to make the emperor acquiesce to an abdication. Alekseev added one piece of information that had not been included in the Rodzyanko-Ruzsky conversation: that the Tsarskoe Selo garrison soldiers had transferred their allegiance to the Duma Committee and that the lives of the imperial family were now in danger. He concluded that Nicholas's refusal to accept Rodzyanko's demand for his abdication would lead to an internecine conflict and bring Russia to ruin.[19]

The telegram he sent to front commanders sometime between 3:30 and 10:15 a.m. is important for several reasons. First, Alekseev took Rodzyanko's probing action as a definite demand for Nicholas's abdication. Second, he informed the front commanders that the life of the imperial family was in danger. Third, he claimed that rejecting Rodzyanko's "demand" would lead to a civil war. All these points indicate that Alekseev and the Stavka had decided to seek Nicholas's abdication. Furthermore, this telegram was sent to all the front commanders except Ruzsky at the northern front. This strongly suggests that Alekseev had already talked with Ruzsky separately, and discussed how to approach the dynastic question.

At 9 a.m., Alekseev told Aleksandr Lukomsky to talk to Danilov, who had access to both Alekseev and the emperor. Alekseev wanted Ruzsky to dispense with etiquette, wake up the emperor, and convey the sense of the Rodzyanko-Ruzsky conversation without further delay. In his conversation with Danilov, Lukomsky said: "We are going through an extremely serious moment when the problem was not only the emperor alone but the entire reigning house and Russia." Alekseev and the Stavka had already understood the implications of Rodzyanko's suggestion for abdication: that it went beyond Nicholas's abdication alone, and would result in an existential crisis for the dynasty. Further, Lukomsky explained to Danilov that Alekseev thought it was necessary to immediately give the army "necessary information" from the high military authorities, "since uncertainty on this issue would be worse than anything else and threaten that anarchy would spread to the army." What was this "necessary information"? Lukomsky explained: "It is my deep conviction that there is no other way and the abdication must be obtained. We must remember that all the imperial family is in the hands of the mutinied troops. . . . If it [the abdication] cannot be obtained, further excesses would likely result, which will threaten the tsar's children, and then an internecine war will begin and Russia will perish under the blows of Germany and the dynasty will perish."[20]

It appears certain that upon receiving the contents of the Rodzyanko-Ruzsky conversation, the Stavka had decided to seek Nicholas's abdication. To make their argument persuasive to Nicholas, they included the new information that "the imperial family was in the hands of the mutinied troops." Where the Stavka received this information from is not clear, since the telephone connection between the Stavka and Tsarskoe Selo had been cut off. Clearly this information was added to buttress the Stavka's case for seeking Nicholas's abdication.

Danilov was reluctant to disturb either the emperor or Ruzsky; he responded that Ruzsky was scheduled to report to the emperor within the hour, and that therefore there was no need to wake him. He reminded Lukomsky how hard it had been for Ruzsky to persuade Nicholas to accept a responsible ministry, and he predicted that it would be well nigh impossible to get Nicholas to accept abdication. "I repeat," he added, "I do not expect any definite decision to come out of General Ruzsky's report." To this, Lukomsky replied: "May God help General Ruzsky succeed in convincing the Sovereign. The fate of Russia and the tsar's family are now in his hands."

It seems likely that due to the gravity of the issue, Danilov did actually wake his commander, and that there was direct contact between Alekseev and Ruzsky as to how to approach the dynastic question. Colonel Boris Sergeevsky, head of communications at the Stavka, refers to the conversation between Alekseev and Ruzsky, though it may have taken place between 5:30 and 10:15 (not while the Ruzsky-Rodzyanko conversation was still going on, as he recalls).[21] Alekseev further informed all the front commanders that in order to maintain calm among the army units, he had decided to allow the distribution of all the Duma Committee's pronouncements in the army units, overruling the protest by the western front headquarters.[22] The manifesto to grant a constitutional monarchy that Nicholas had signed was kept secret. This hard-won document would turn out to be a hindrance to the policy that the Stavka was about to embark on.

All military personnel in the imperial Russian armed forces, whether officers or soldiers, pledged the same oath of allegiance:

## OATH OF ALLEGIANCE

I, [name of the person], promise and swear to the Almighty God before his sacred Gospels that I want and am obligated to serve faithfully and sincerely His Imperial Majesty, my true and innate Most Gracious Great Sovereign Emperor Nikolai Aleksandrovich, All-Russian Tsar and His Imperial Majesty's lawful Heir of All-Russian Throne, without regard for my own health and to the last drop of blood, and to obey, to the best of my understanding, might, and possibilities, all enacted and to be enacted laws and privileges that belong to the power and authority of His High Imperial Majesty Monarch.

To the enemies of His Imperial Majesty Realm and lands, in the field and in fortresses, on land and at sea, in battles, detachments, sieges and charges and other military events [I shall] offer brave and strong resistance, with my body and blood, and assist in all matters that might arise in regard to loyal service to His Imperial Majesty and national advantage. . . .

If I learn about any damage to His Majesty's interests, harm and disadvantage, I shall not only report in good time, but [also] by all means avert and prevent; I shall keep any secret confided in me, and I shall dutifully obey all my superiors in everything that concerns the advantage and service of the State and honestly rectify; shall not act against service and allegiance upon my self-interest, character, friendship or animosity; shall not violate command or banner to which I belong, whether in field, in transport or garrison; but I shall follow them as long as I live, and shall act and behave as an honest, faithful, obedient, brave and deft soldier ought to. Let Almighty God help me in all this.

In conclusion of this oath I am kissing the words and cross of the Savior. Amen.

They pledged to serve not the fatherland but Tsar Nicholas and his heir, Aleksei.[23] This pledge was consecrated by "Almighty God before the Gospels," and the ceremony of oath concluded by kissing the "words and cross of the Savior." Much as the peasant soldiers resented Nicholas II for his weakness, the oath of allegiance to Nicholas II and his heir, sworn in front of almighty God and the sacred scriptures, had a spiritual and psychological hold on the army. The mutinied soldiers revolted not only against the rigid military discipline enforced by their officers but also against the tsar, to whom they had pledged their allegiance in front of almighty God. Guchkov was aware of this; in lobbying his colleagues in the Duma Committee to seek Nicholas's abdication, he emphasized that the mutinied soldiers should be freed from their oath to Nicholas II, in order to relieve their fears that they would be punished for violating their oath of allegiance.

Though the officers, too, were bound by the oath of allegiance to Tsar Nicholas II and the heir, the democratization of the officers' corps and the difficult experience of fighting a war for "the fatherland" and a "war for national survival" for two and a half years had gradually instilled a "national consciousness" among many officers.[24] Many officers had come to feel that their allegiance was to the "fatherland" rather than Nicholas—and certainly not to the "German woman." Many officers began to feel that any continuation of rule by Nicholas II, influenced as he was by Alexandra and Rasputin, would be detrimental to the prosecution of the war.

Nevertheless, the oath of allegiance to the tsar imposed a heavy burden on the officers. For the commanders to violate the oath would inevitably lead to the destruction of the army they commanded. Neither Ruzsky nor Alekseev wanted to be the first one to break the oath of allegiance to the tsar, but one of them would need to act to persuade Nicholas to abdicate.

Nikolai Bazili recommended that Alekseev call Rodzyanko, come to "an agreement," and then announce that agreement to the front commanders, in the name of the Duma and the army. Bazili does not say specifically what that agreement might be, but clearly he had Nicholas's abdication in mind. Rejecting this suggestion, Alekseev asked Bazili to prepare for him a short legal brief on the problems that would arise with a possible abdication.[25] In his report, the lawyer did not answer the question of whether the tsar had the right to abdicate while in power. But he stated that although the law did not envision abdication of the tsar in power, it stipulated the order of succession to the throne, according to which the oldest son of the emperor should succeed him. This answer implied that the tsar could abdicate. "This order of succession," Bazili added, "could not be modified by Emperor Nicholas."[26] Since Aleksei was still a minor, a regency would be required until he reached maturity. As for the regent, the Fundamental Laws left the emperor free to choose whomever he wished. Thus, Nicholas's abdication in favor of the heir apparent, Aleksei, would be legally possible, and taking an oath of allegiance to the new tsar, Aleksei, would not violate the oath that all had previously pledged to Nicholas. The trick was to persuade Nicholas to abdicate voluntarily and have him transfer the throne to Aleksei.

According to Major General Sergei Vilchkovsky, who became Ruzsky's confidant after the October Revolution, Ruzsky still held out hope that the manifesto for the responsible ministry might lead to the resolution of the crisis, yet it was the Stavka that came to the conclusion that Nicholas's abdication was the only possible way out of the crisis.[27] Alekseev could have insisted that a responsible ministry was the maximum concession that the military could accept, and rejected the idea of abdication. After all, he had sworn allegiance to the tsar and the heir. The ease and the speed with which Alekseev switched from seeking a responsible ministry to seeking abdication revealed how little sense of loyalty he maintained to Nicholas. It is most likely that he welcomed Nicholas's abdication as the way in which the country could remove the pernicious influence of Alexandra.

Aleksandr Solzhenitsyn has depicted Alekseev's relationship with Nicholas II as amicable, bonded with trust and mutual affection, but the archives tell a different story. Russian historian Oleg Airapetov recently discovered Alekseev's handwritten remarks about Nicholas, whom he referred to merely as "N.," in the manuscript division of the National Library in St. Petersburg. Alekseev writes:

> N. is passive and has no energy. He lacks the courage and confidence to seek out honorable people, and constantly fears people who are forceful or too easy-going. . . . He does not trust his own intellect and his own heart, and delegates too much to others' designs. . . . He lacks the power of intellect in order to seek truth tenaciously, and he lacks conviction in order to accomplish his decisions by overcoming all obstacles and beating the will of those with whom he disagrees. . . . His goodness—tender heart—comes from his weakness, and it inevitably leads to dubiousness and mendacity. . . . Perhaps he does not possess deep feelings, and is incapable of having long-lasting convictions. . . . He is incapable of inspiring his people to act excellently and forcefully. . . . He is secretive and deceitful. People who know him well are afraid to trust him. . . . He lacks internal excitement. He lacks a character and a real temperament. He does not possess an iota of creativity. It is difficult for him to come up with an original idea. . . . His mental forces are readily channeled into triviality, and he is incapable to rising above triviality to something higher. . . . He loves flattery; he never forgets malice and insult. . . . Among unimportant people, he has a special kind of arrogance, somewhat mixed with awkwardness and suspicions. . . . His egoism turns into distrust, contempt, and hatred of people. He is scornful and envious.

At the end, Alekseev asks the most damning question of all: "Does he really passionately love the motherland?"[28]

These short, cryptic notes were written in the wake of the February Revolution, between March and August. Having worked closely with

Nicholas for eighteen months, Alekseev had had ample opportunity to observe his character. These devastating remarks show that behind Alekseev's outward respect, courteousness, and deference lurked a sense of profound contempt for the supreme commander he served. Alekseev had deserted Nicholas long before he came out in favor of his abdication.

Alekseev, however, did not wish to be the one to force the tsar to abdicate, as he had done to have him accept the concession of a responsible ministry. He concluded that the only way to effect Nicholas's abdication would be through collective pressure from the front commanders.[29] This would exonerate Alekseev of the accusation that he had dethroned Nicholas.

At 10:15 a.m. on March 2, Alekseev sent a telegram to all the commanders—General Evert (western front), General Brusilov (southwestern front), General Sakharov (Rumanian front), Admiral Nepenin (Baltic Fleet), Admiral Aleksandr Vasilievich Kolchak (Black Sea Fleet), and Grand Duke Nikolai Nikolaevich (Caucasian front)—conveying the substance of the Ruzsky-Rodzyanko conversations that morning, and requesting their reactions to Rodzyanko's proposal for Nicholas's abdication. The key was the inclusion of Nicholas's cousin Grand Duke Nikolai Nikolaevich, who had been supreme commander before Nicholas II took over, and who was a powerful figure in the House of Romanov. This telegram was not sent to Ruzsky, indicating that Alekseev and Ruzsky had already reached an agreement on this procedure.[30]

It should be remembered that in his conversation with Ruzsky, Rodzyanko had not "demanded" Nicholas's abdication. He merely had said that the dynastic question was now being raised explicitly and that there was increasing popular support for Nicholas's abdication in favor of his son under Mikhail's regency. But in his telegram to the front commanders, Alekseev went one step further and argued that Rodzyanko was presenting the abdication demand as a necessary measure to continue the war.

Thus misrepresenting what Rodzyanko had proposed, Alekseev's telegram went on to make his preferred option known to the commanders:

> It is necessary to save the active army from disintegration; to continue the fight against the external enemy until the end; to save the independence of Russia and *the fate of the dynasty*. This needs to be put into the highest priority even at the sacrifice of costly concessions. If you share my views, then kindly telegraph through the Commander in Chief of the Northern Front your petition as faithful subjects to His Majesty, advising me of it. (Italics added)[31]

Alekseev did not recommend Nicholas's abdication outright. He was merely introducing Rodzyanko's proposal, emphasizing that according to Rodzyanko, Nicholas's abdication was the only hope to restore order in the capital, and then leaving the rest to the collective decision of the commanders. This was a carefully crafted strategy. Like a skillful conductor, he knew exactly how to bring the orchestra to the grand finale. With the deft movements of his conductor's baton he coordinated the actions of all the front commanders, elevating his supporters (Ruzsky and Brusilov) and limiting the potential troublemakers (Evert, Sakharov, and Nikolai Nikolaevich). He was careful to instruct the commanders to send their recommendation to Ruzsky *only if* they agreed with him. They were not to consult each other without going through Alekseev. That way, if they did not agree, Alekseev would suppress these dissenting voices, preventing them from reaching Nicholas or delaying the delivery of their opinions until after the job was accomplished.

It is important to note that to Alekseev the cohesion and unity of the army and the continuation of the war had higher priority than the preservation of the dynasty. Also, it is important to note that the meaning of "dynasty" underwent a significant change compared with its previous usage. Previously, "dynasty" had been used to mean the dynasty headed by Nicholas II, but in this new usage, he implied that the continuity of the "dynasty" could be ensured only by Nicholas's voluntary abdication in favor of his son, Aleksei. Alekseev further emphasized the necessity of maintaining unity among the commanders of the active army and of saving the army from "instability and possible treason of duty." There was a danger of a split within the army in its attitude toward abdication, between those who supported the abdication and those who remained faithful to the tsar.

After Alekseev had received the contents of the Rodzyanko-Ruzsky conversations, he invited Admiral Aleksandr Rusin, chief of the Naval Staff at the Stavka, to his office, and explained what Rodzyanko had said.

"What do they demand? A responsible ministry?" asked the admiral.

"No. More than that. They demand abdication," answered Alekseev.

"What horror! What misfortune!" exclaimed Rusin.

Alekseev remained silent. They did not talk further, but understood each other perfectly. Rusin stood up and walked out of the room.[32]

Rusin was by no means a reactionary admiral blindly following the tsar. He shared the liberal-leaning politics of Aleksandr Bubnov and Nikolai Bazili.[33] But the fact that even Rusin was not eager to break his oath must have convinced Alekseev that he had to tread carefully. Alekseev had to be concerned that there might be many Rusins. To prevent their resistance, he had to obtain the unanimous consent of all the front commanders, not allowing them to consult with their subordinate officers.

While Ruzsky's willingness to cooperate with the Duma Committee was apparent to Alekseev because of Ruzsky's hasty recall of his northern front troops without Alekseev's permission, the communications with Evert and Sakharov in the past few days had indicated that they were not enthusiastically disposed toward the Stavka's support of the "rebel" Duma Committee. Alekseev had to make sure that they were on board.[34]

Alekseev's message was now conveyed again to the front commanders, this time in personal telegraphic communications from the representatives of the Stavka. At the same time, Alekseev reversed his earlier position and requested that they send their recommendations to him so that he could collate the responses in one telegram.

General Vladislav Klembovsky dealt with Evert, who expressed his general agreement with Alekseev that the issue should be resolved only from above by the imperial decision to abdicate. He feared that otherwise there would be some elements hostile to either the abdication or its refusal, and probably "those who wish to fish in troubled waters." He then asked Klembovsky if he had time to consult other commanders on this matter. Klembovsky categorically rejected that possibility: there was no time for consultation. Only the unanimous opinion of the front commanders, and the front commanders alone, he emphasized, would be able to overcome Nicholas's hesitation.[35]

It was Lukomsky who sent Alekseev's telegram regarding the Ruzsky-Rodzyanko conversations that morning and a potential abdication to another potential troublemaker, General Sakharov of the Rumanian front. Sakharov was at first reluctant to express his view, and cut off the Hughes apparatus connecting his headquarters to the Stavka. Angered by this action, Lukomsky ordered his telegraph officers to connect with the Rumanian front to talk to that "scoundrel."[36] Sakharov asked Lukomsky first whether what had been conveyed was Alekseev's opinion, to which Lukomsky answered yes. The commander of the Rumanian front conceded that then it had to be accepted, however sad it might be—presumably because this was the chain of command—and agreed to send a telegram to the tsar at the northern front. But he raised the question of whether it might be better for all the commanders to come to a consensus and send this united view to the tsar, and that it was most important to have the agreement of Nikolai Nikolaevich from the Caucasus. The quartermaster general answered that General Ruzsky "was apparently in agreement" with that view. Lukomsky then insisted that Sakharov should send his own view separately and directly to the tsar, and promised that as soon as he received an answer from Nikolai Nikolaevich, he would let Sakharov know.[37]

In a follow-up communication, Alekseev himself asked Brusilov to send the tsar a telegram to persuade him to accept abdication.[38] As Alekseev expected, Brusilov completely agreed and promised to send his recommendation directly to the tsar at the northern front. Brusilov added: "Clearly we both must have complete solidarity. I consider you legally the supreme commander in chief, until other measures are taken."[39] This was a bold assertion: Nicholas II had not abdicated, and therefore, legally, there was no supreme commander but him.

The biggest challenge was how Nikolai Nikolaevich would respond. Individual follow-up telegrams were sent to Evert, Sakharov, and Brusilov around 11 a.m., to ensure that everyone was on board. Therefore, we can assume that a similar telegram was also sent to Nikolai Nikolaevich around the same time. But neither the Stavka nor the northern front received an answer from the grand duke for a long time. At 12:14 p.m., Lukomsky had to contact Nikolai Nikolaevich Yanushkevich, the grand duke's chief of staff, and tell him to have the grand duke send his reply to Alekseev rather than to the tsar directly. Alekseev may have been concerned that Nikolai Nikolaevich might not agree with his recommendation for abdication. At 12:28, Yanushkevich informed Lukomsky: "The answer that has been edited to the final version will be sent soon. It is in the spirit of General Alekseev's wish." Alekseev and the Stavka breathed a sigh of relief. Klembovsky received the answer from the Caucasian front at 12:40.[40] All the commanders' answers arrived by 2:30 p.m. except that from Sakharov, which was sent to Pskov directly.[41]

Nicholas spent the morning alone, without any close advisers. The person he could trust was Alexandra, but she was far away in Tsarskoe Selo, and he had not received any news from her for three days. Isolated and lonely, the emperor was surrounded by military leaders who were plotting his removal from the throne behind his back.

Nicholas came to morning tea later than usual. He looked pale and tired, but he was as cordial as ever. He smoked incessantly, then retired to his private car to meet with Ruzsky around 10 a.m.[42] According to Ruzsky, the emperor carefully read the transcript of the Ruzsky-Rodzyanko conversation and Evert's telegram recommending abdication without saying a word.

Ruzsky consoled the emperor by saying that there was still hope that the manifesto for establishing a responsible ministry might settle the situation, and he urged the tsar to wait for the instructions from General Alekseev, although he did not conceal Lukomsky's opinion, which indicated that the Stavka was already leaning toward accepting the abdication. At about 10:30, the telegram Alekseev had sent to all the commanders at 10:15 finally arrived. Turning pale, Ruzsky read the telegram aloud to the tsar, and then said: "The problem is so serious and so dreadful that I ask Your Majesty to think over this dispatch before answering it. This is a circular telegram. Let us see what the other commanders would say. Then the situation will become clear."

Nicholas stood. Looking at Ruzsky with an air of attentive sadness, he said: "Yes, I have to think." Declining the tsar's invitation to breakfast, which was taken around noon, Ruzsky returned to his headquarters. On the way, he saw Vladimir Voeikov and told him to wait for the emperor on the platform. Ruzsky also gave Voeikov a brief synopsis of the conversation he had had with Rodzyanko, then told the palace commandant that the only way to solve the crisis was Nicholas's abdication, and added that all the front commanders agreed with this view.[43]

The emperor did not say a word at breakfast, and the meal passed in total silence. Afterward he walked silently on the platform.[44] Voeikov wrote later: "When I returned to His Highness, I was struck by the change in the expression on his face in such a short time. It appeared that the emperor surrendered himself to the chain of events after going through the devastating trauma and blamed his tragic fate. My conversation with Ruzsky did not give me any basis to say any words to console His Majesty, although I had the most sincere and heartfelt wish to do so."[45]

Ruzsky was summoned back to the emperor shortly before 2 p.m. Anticipating that this would be the most decisive moment for Nicholas's reign, Ruzsky asked permission to be accompanied by Danilov and General Sergei Sergeevich Savvich, chief of supplies in the northern front.[46] Ruzsky needed witnesses to prove that Nicholas abdicated of his own volution. In addition to these three generals, Count Vladimir Fredericks attended the meeting.[47]

The fateful meeting began in Nicholas's cabinet in his car. Nicholas constantly smoked cigarettes, and suggested the generals do the same. Only Ruzsky complied.[48]

Ruzsky first made a short, routine report about all the telegrams he had received since he had left the tsar that morning. Then, at 2:30 p.m., a new telegram from Alekseev arrived. Ruzsky put this telegram on the desk and asked the tsar to read it for himself.[49]

In his message, Alekseev first quoted Nikolai Nikolaevich's response. The grand duke wrote:

Adjutant-General Alekseev reports to me on the unprecedentedly fateful situation that has developed and asks me to support his view that a victorious end to the war, so very necessary for the happiness and future of Russia and the salvation of the dynasty, calls for the adoption of extraordinary measures. I as a loyal subject think, in accordance with the *duty to the oath* as well as *the spirit of my oath of allegiance*, consider it necessary to implore on my knees Your Imperial Majesty to save Russia and your heir, knowing your sacred love to Russia and to him. Having made the sign of the cross, transfer to him your legacy. There is no other way out. As never before in my life, with particularly fervent prayer, I beseech God to fortify and to guide you. —Nikolai. (Italics added)[50]

With this recommendation, the grand duke shifted his allegiance from the tsar to "the spirit of allegiance."

Alekseev then cited Brusilov's telegram, which began, "As a most faithful subject, based on my loyalty and love for the fatherland and *the tsar's throne . . .*" (italics added). Nevertheless, Brusilov declared to the emperor:

At the present moment, the only solution that could save the situation and make possible the continuation of the struggle with the external enemy . . . is the abdication of the throne in favor of the Heir Tsarevich under the regency of Grand Duke Mikhail Aleksandrovich. There is no other way out. But it is necessary to hurry in order that the flames of popular unrest, which have already grown large, may be more quickly extinguished; otherwise, this situation will have no end of catastrophic consequences. *This act will save the dynasty itself in the person of the rightful heir.* (Italics added)

Professing his loyalty to the throne, Brusilov was urging Nicholas to abdicate in order to save the dynasty.

Then Alekseev cited Evert's telegram. Evert stated that he had been informed by Alekseev about the situation in Petrograd, Tsarskoe Selo, the Baltic Sea, and Moscow, and about the conversation between Ruzsky and Rodzyanko. "Your Majesty, counting upon the army, as presently constituted, to repress internal disorders is impossible," Evert said, then continued, "I am taking all measures to prevent information about the real state of affairs in the capital cities from penetrating into the army in order to guard against the otherwise unavoidable unrest." Then he also asked Nicholas, "in the name of saving the fatherland and *the dynasty*" (italics added), to make the decision "advocated by" Ruzsky and Rodzyanko "as the only effective way to stop the revolution and save Russia from the horrors of anarchy."[51]

Alekseev now urged Nicholas to accept the abdication that all three commanders had implored him to accept:

> Procrastination threatens Russia with death. So far, we have managed to save the army from the disease that has overtaken Petrograd, Moscow, Kronstadt, and other cities. But one cannot vouch for the further preservation of the highest discipline. Any involvement of the army in the business of internal politics will mean an unavoidable end to the war, Russia's disgrace, and her collapse. Your Imperial Majesty passionately loves the motherland, and for the sake of her unity and independence, for the sake of achieving victory, deign to make a decision that can lead to a peaceful and favorable way out of the more than grave situation that has arisen. I await your decision.[52]

There are a couple of important points in Alekseev's telegram. First, Alekseev introduced Nikolai Nikolaevich's reply first, although that was the last telegram he had received. Clearly, the tsar's chief of staff presented the most damaging telegram to the emperor as a first strike to break the tsar's resistance. Second, Nikolai Nikolaevich, Brusilov, and Evert begged the tsar to accept abdication not only to maintain the unity of the country and to fight the enemy but also to save the dynasty. But saving the dynasty was not mentioned in Alekseev's own recommendation, indicating that in his mind, the maintenance of the dynasty was a lower priority. Third, Alekseev did not include Sakharov's telegram, which the commander of the Rumanian front had sent directly to Ruzsky. Sakharov's telegram to Ruzsky stated:

> My passionate love to His Majesty does not permit my soul to make peace with the possibility to implement the vile proposal given to you by the chairman of the Duma. I am convinced that no Russian people would conceive this criminal act to their own tsar, but a villainous small gang of bandits, who called themselves as the State Duma, are treacherously exploiting a convenient moment to carry out their criminal designs. I am convinced that the army and the navy will unswervingly stand for their auto-cratic leader [*derzhavnyi vozhd'*], if they were called to defend the fatherland from the external enemy and if there were not the state criminals who seize into their hands the sources of life of the army. Such is the impulse of my heart and soul.

This almost sounded like a rejection of Alekseev's recommendation for abdication. Nevertheless, in the next paragraph, Sakharov retreated and recommended, "in tears, that the least painful way out for the country and for the preservation of the possible chance to fight the external enemy would be to meet the conditions already stated."[53]

Knowing Sakharov's monarchist convictions, Alekseev must have thought that it was better to present the telegrams from the other three commanders without Sakharov's. Apparently Ruzsky did not hide Sakharov's telegram, but he likely placed it at the bottom of the pile of telegrams without calling the emperor's attention to it. It may well be that Nicholas did not even read Sakharov's telegram.[54]

The reply from Admiral Nepenin of the Baltic Fleet, which would come only later that evening—at 8:40 p.m., long after the tsar had made the decision to abdicate—said: "If this solution is not accepted within the next hours, it will bring about a catastrophe with incalculable calamities for our fatherland."[55] Nepenin's view had been known to Ruzsky and Alekseev, but his explicit statement of that view, in his role as representing the navy, would have buttressed their opinion further. We don't know why Nepenin's answer was delayed, but presumably he was too busy dealing with the revolt in the Baltic Fleet. As for Kolchak, there is no record that he responded to Alekseev.

Nicholas carefully read Alekseev's long telegram twice, then read it a third time quickly. Then Ruzsky asked him to listen to the opinion of the two other generals who had accompanied him. Nicholas granted Danilov and Savvich permission to express their frank opinions. First, Danilov stated that he saw no way out except for his abdication to save the fatherland and the dynasty. Savvich was entirely confused, and so he answered: "I am a simple person, and therefore, I entirely agree with what General Danilov has said."[56]

Without saying a word, the emperor stood up and looked out the window. There was a dreadful silence. Danilov observed that the tsar's usually expressionless face was somehow distorted, with his lips lowered on one side, a facial expression that Danilov had never seen before.[57] Returning to his desk, Nicholas gestured to Ruzsky to sit down. He quietly told Ruzsky that he was born for unhappiness and that even last night he had been convinced that no manifesto would help. He then said:

If it is necessary that I should abdicate for the good of Russia, I am ready for it. But I am afraid that the people will not understand it. Old Believers would not forgive me for the breach of the oath taken on the day of the Holy Coronation. The Cossacks will blame me for abandoning the front.[58]

It was 2:45 p.m. It had not taken more than three-quarters of an hour for him to decide to abdicate. In comparison, earlier it had taken three and a half hours for him to decide to grant a responsible ministry.[59] The scenes of his people's enthusiastic cheers repeated time and time again in front of him must have crossed his mind. He was concerned about the wrath that he might incur from those faithful subjects by breaking their trust, not knowing that their trust had long since deserted him. The positions of the autocrat and the people had been reversed: now it was the autocrat who feared the people, not the other way around. And that itself was the repudiation of autocracy.

But Nicholas was a patriot, deeply committed to the war. When five adjutant generals and Nikolai Nikolaevich presented their unanimous view that his staying in power would divide the military, making it impossible to continue the war and achieve victory, and when monarchist generals such as Nikolasha, Alekseev, and Evert argued that his holding the throne would imperil the existence of the dynasty, he had no alternative but to abdicate.

For a few minutes there was dead silence. Then the emperor spoke. "I have made up my mind. I have decided to abdicate from the throne in favor of my son, Aleksei." After finishing his words, Nicholas crossed himself. The generals followed his example. The emperor turned to Ruzsky, thanked the general—who, like Judas, had betrayed him—for his "valorous and faithful service," and kissed him.[60]

He then retired to his car, where he wrote two messages to be sent by telegraph, one to Alekseev and the other to Rodzyanko. To Alekseev, he wrote: "In the name of the good, peace, and salvation of Russia, which I passionately love, I am ready to abdicate from the Throne in favor of my son. I ask you all to serve him loyally and sincerely."[61] He did not say anything about Mikhail's regency. Perhaps he remembered that he had revoked Mikhail's right to become regent in 1912, or perhaps he could not bear the thought of trusting his son to the care of Mikhail's wife, Natasha Brasova, whom the imperial couple detested. In the margins of the telegram, Ruzsky noted that Nicholas had written this at 3 p.m. in his imperial car and that this telegram was sent after the tsar read Alekseev's telegram and the telegrams of other front commanders.[62]

The message to Rodzyanko, however, set one condition for his abdication: "I am ready to abdicate from the Throne in favor of my son on the condition that he can remain with me until he comes of age."[63] To this, Ruzsky added a phrase: "under the regency of my brother Mikhail Aleksandrovich." Ruzsky's addition virtually nullified Nicholas's condition that Aleksei would remain with him. Nicholas's condition and Ruzsky's amendment were contradictory, and this contradiction would have a fatal consequence for the monarchy.

At exactly 3 p.m., the emperor returned to the salon car and handed Ruzsky the text of the telegrams to be sent to Alekseev and Rodzyanko.[64] Ten minutes later, the commandant of Pskov station reported to Ruzsky that he had received a telegram from Petrograd informing him that an express train had been arranged for Guchkov and Shulgin to come to Pskov. Having received this information, Ruzsky decided to withhold Nicholas's telegram to Rodzyanko.[65]

Around this time, Milyukov announced the formation of the Provisional Government at Catherine Hall in the Tauride Palace, in front of the insurgents who had packed the hall.[66] Milyukov declared triumphantly that the Provisional Government would seek Nicholas's abdication and that the throne would be transferred to Aleksei under Mikhail's regency. What followed were not cheers but an outburst of protest at the return of the old monarchy. The rage of the insurgent masses hinted at the next chapter of the abdication drama. Milyukov had to retract that statement, saying instead that this was only his personal view and did not represent the view of the Provisional Government.[67]

We can imagine a possible alternative. If Ruzsky had sent Nicholas's telegram to Rodzyanko that afternoon rather than holding it back, the mood in Petrograd might have been very different. Had the news of Nicholas's abdication coursed through the streets, spreading like wildfire among the people, there might have been a wave of jubilation. There might have been rallies celebrating the boy tsar, Aleksei II. There was little question that the masses hated Nicholas and Alexandra, but did they hate the monarchy? Guchkov confessed that he had been counting on the people being sympathetic to the boy emperor. This sentiment cannot easily be discounted. If so, Ruzsky's failure to send the telegram to Rodzyanko reporting on the transfer of the throne to Aleksei on the afternoon of March 2 may have determined the fate of the monarchical system itself. It ended up yet another path not taken.

The entourage learned from Fredericks that the tsar had abdicated. Having heard from the count that the tsar had prepared two telegrams, one to Alekseev and another to Rodzyanko, they sent Kirill Naryshkin, head of the Military-Field Chancellery, to see Ruzsky and demand that those telegrams be held back, at least until Guchkov and Shulgin met with the tsar.[68]

Ruzsky refused.[69] Furthermore, he told Naryshkin a lie. By this time, Ruzsky had already sent the tsar's telegram to Alekseev, but when he learned that the two delegates of the Duma Committee were headed to Pskov to negotiate with the emperor, he decided to hold on to the telegram to Rodzyanko until their arrival.[70]

The entourage intervened once again. They sent Dr. Sergei Fyodorov to see the tsar. Fyodorov had a long discussion with the tsar in which he made Nicholas understand that there was no guarantee that Aleksei would live long, and that it would be impossible for Nicholas to live with Aleksei after his abdication. This prompted Nicholas to send Naryshkin again to Ruzsky in another effort to retrieve the telegrams, in an attempt to prevent them from being sent.[71] Ruzsky refused once again.

Instead of giving the telegrams to Naryshkin, Ruzsky went to speak to Nicholas in person. The general told the tsar: "Your Highness, I feel that you are not trusting me, but allow me to serve you for the last time and negotiate with Guchkov and Shulgin and explain the general situation." Nicholas conceded, saying: "All right, let everything stand as it is." The commander of the northern front left the salon car with the telegram to Rodzyanko in his pocket, and he told the railway commandant to bring Guchkov and Shulgin to him as soon as they arrived.

We do not know what argument Ruzsky presented at the audience with the tsar, but he may have informed Nicholas that both telegrams, the one to Alekseev and the one to Rodzyanko, had already been sent, and that his abdication was now known not only to the high command but also to the Duma Committee. If so, this was a deception on Ruzsky's part, since he had not yet sent Nicholas's telegram to Rodzyanko. But it caused Nicholas to believe that he could not rescind his decision to abdicate.[72]

In the meantime, the Stavka anxiously waited for news from Pskov. At 4:50 p.m., Klembovsky sent a telegram to Danilov inquiring how Ruzsky's negotiations with the emperor were going. He informed Danilov that the Stavka was withholding the announcement of Nicholas's manifesto to grant a responsible ministry while Ruzsky was meeting with the emperor. He asked Danilov to make sure the imperial trains were still in Pskov. He had received information from an engineer of the Northwestern Line that an order had been given to arrange for the imperial trains to go to Dvinsk, where the reinforcement troops were to be assembled. The Stavka was worried that the tsar would flee Pskov without agreeing to abdicate and resume military operations against the revolution.[73]

At 4:30 p.m., twenty minutes before Klembovsky sent his telegram, Danilov sent the following telegram to Alekseev: "Sovereign Emperor in the long conversation with Adjutant-General Ruzsky with the presence of myself and General Savvich, stated that there is no sacrifice that His Highness will not make for the true good for the motherland. Your and front commanders' telegrams were all achieved."[74] This news was what the Stavka was waiting for.

Lukomsky sent a circular telegram informing the chief of staff of each front of the publication of the emperor's impending act of abdication, instructing each to take all necessary measures to calm the population and prevent the horrors of revolutionary excesses. It would be essential for the front officers to be aware of all the events that had led to this decision. This telegram was sent to all the front headquarters between 4:43 and 6:40 p.m., except for the Caucasian front; Alekseev planned to contact Nikolai Nikolaevich personally.[75]

As soon as the Stavka received the emperor's telegram consenting to abdicate, Alekseev instructed Bazili to write an act of abdication. Alekseev told Bazili: "Put all your heart into it." The diplomatic representative at the Stavka shut himself up in his office and one hour later submitted his draft to Alekseev.[76] It read:

We have deemed it Our duty in conscience to help Our people to draw closer together and to unite all the forces of the nation for a speedier attainment of victory, and, in agreement with the State Duma, We have judged it right to abdicate the Throne of the Russian State and to lay down the Supreme Power. In conformance with the order established by the Fundamental Laws, We hand over Our succession to Our beloved Son, the Tsar Successor Tsarevich and Grand Duke Aleksei Nikolaevich, and bless Him on his accession to the Throne of the Russian State. We entrust to Our brother the Grand Duke Mikhail Aleksandrovich the duty of Regent of the Empire until the coming of age of Our Son. We enjoin Our Son and also, until His coming of age, the Regent of the Empire, to conduct the affairs of the state in complete and inviolable union with the representatives of the people in the legislative bodies on the principles to be established by them.[77]

This draft was notable for emphasizing that the emperor had made this decision in consultation with the State Duma, and further that the new tsar and regent were to conduct the affairs of the state "in complete and inviolable union with the representatives of the people in the legislative bodies." The idea of a constitutional monarchy was clearly enunciated in this document. It met with Alekseev's agreement, and the draft of the abdication "manifesto" was sent to Pskov at about 7:40 p.m. for the approval of the emperor. Danilov received this draft at the staff headquarters and immediately hand-delivered it to Ruzsky, who was in his railcar at the station.[78]

Throughout the drama that played out in Pskov, Nicholas II displayed an amazing degree of indifference to the catastrophe that had struck him. In fact, throughout the tragedy of the events at Pskov, Nicholas impressed the participants in the drama with his serenity at this grave historic moment.[79] He was acting like a ghost of a man, like someone from whom the spirit had been taken away.

Vilchkovsky also noted that the first round of negotiations with the tsar, when he finally accepted a responsible ministry, had been stormy, but that Ruzsky's audience with the tsar, when Nicholas decided on abdication, was marked by the emperor's air of resignation. Katkov contends that Nicholas's abdication seemed "a solution far more morally acceptable" than a responsible ministry that restricted his autocratic power.[80] It seems that to Nicholas, abdication was the logical conclusion of the concession of a responsible ministry. He had breached his sacred duty, ordained by God and sworn to on his father's deathbed. His personal and moral world had already been shattered by this concession.

He must have felt compelled to seek absolution of his sin by willingly accepting his abdication.

Could Nicholas have refused to abdicate? Had he decided to cling to power, he would have needed the military, or at least some reliable units, to back him up. But the entire high command, not only his trusted chief of staff but also Evert and Nikolai Nikolaevich, had deserted him. Alekseev's strategy for collective pressure had succeeded in isolating Nicholas. The king was checkmated.

On the afternoon of March 2, Grand Duke Mikhail, who was still staying at Princess Putyatina's house on Millionnaya Street, was informed by Rodzyanko that Nicholas had abdicated in favor of Aleksei under his regency. Nicholas had not been in contact with his brother on this matter. In the evening, Mikhail received a letter from Rodzyanko confirming this news.[81]

After 10 p.m. on March 1, Alekseev received information that the Luga garrison had pledged allegiance to the Duma Committee and that the Duma Committee had issued an order to the insurgent soldiers not to let loyal troops pass beyond Luga. He ordered the northern front to appoint an officer to be dispatched to Ivanov by going through Dno, since he had received information that Ivanov had been at Tsarskoe Selo earlier.[82] Finally, at noon on March 2, Danilov informed Alekseev that Nicholas had agreed to recall the troops sent to Petrograd.[83] That made all the previous orders to recall the reinforcement troops retroactively legal. Still, the Stavka was nervous about Ivanov's actions. Boldyrev, of the northern front, inquired about the earlier order to send an officer to Ivanov, and asked exactly what task this officer was to perform. Lukomsky responded that Alekseev was anxious to determine Ivanov's location in order to make sure that he did not approach Tsarskoe Selo and wanted to find out precisely what Ivanov's intention was.[84] Lukomsky urged again that the northern front send an officer to contact Ivanov urgently.[85] Both the Stavka and the northern front were interested in canceling Ivanov's operations. And Alekseev and Ruzsky were racking their brains in order to figure out how to control Ivanov. Alekseev requested that Nicholas recall Ivanov and order him to return to Mogilev.[86] The hapless Ivanov was hung out to dry, abandoned by the Stavka, the northern front, and even the tsar.

Finally, at 9 p.m. on March 2, Danilov informed Alekseev that Nicholas had agreed to dismiss Ivanov and replace him with General Lavr Georgievich Kornilov as the commander of the Petrograd Military District.[87] (We will discuss this appointment in the next chapter.) Late on March 2, Ivanov sent a telegram to Alekseev complaining that he had received no information and that his ability to travel by rail had been disrupted—clearly by the "provisional government." The Stavka received this telegram at 1:30 a.m. on March 3. General Nikolai Tikhmenev later noted that Ivanov and the St. George Battalion left Vyritsa at 3:30 p.m. on March 3.[88] That was the end of the tragicomedy of Ivanov's counterrevolutionary expedition.

All the while, the imperial palace in Tsarskoe Selo had been living in fear and apprehension. A company of the Railway Regiment that guarded the palace's pavilion had mutinied during the night, killing two officers, and deserted to Petrograd. Furthermore, those at the palace heard rumors that the insurgents in town meant to launch an attack on the palace.

On March 2, Alexandra wrote a rambling letter to Nicholas, commenting on many random subjects. She praised the telegram Nicholas had sent two days earlier as "the first ray of sunshine in this swamp." She blamed Rodzyanko for "pretending he did not know why one stopped you." "It is clear," she continued, "[he] does, only not to get you to join with me before you have signed some paper of theirs, constitution or some such horror. And you, who are alone, no army behind you caught like a mouse in a trap, what can you do? That's the lowest, meanest thing unknown in history, to stop one's sovereign." "If you are forced into concessions," she advised, "you are *never* required to keep them." She then commented about the grand dukes' collective manifesto recommending the establishment of a responsible ministry on the previous day: "Paul, after getting a colossal reprimand for doing nothing with the guard, tries to work hard now, & he is going to save us by means which all very grand & foolish. He wrote an idiotic manifesto about constitution after the war etc."[89]

In between comments about the condition of the children, she made scattered but astute political comments: "Two currents—the Duma & revolutionists—two snakes who I hope will eat off each other[']s heads, that would be the saving of the situation." She longed for Nicholas: "Heart aches very much, but I don't heed it, my spirits are quite up, and I am like a cock. Only suffer too hideously for you." She concluded: "If you have to give into things, God will help you to get out of them. Oh my suffering Saint. I am one with you, inseparably one." She added in a postscript: "Wear his [Rasputin's] cross the whole time even if uncomfortable—for *my* peace's sake."[90]

Since there was no way to deliver this letter, she had the outlandish idea of using an airplane to drop the letter, but no airplane was available to her. Even if one had been available, she did not know where her husband was.[91] She then surreptitiously asked two trusted young officers, named Soloviev and Gramotin, to carry the letter to Mogilev, hoping that at least one of them could smuggle it to Nicholas. The empress was resorting to methods used by underground revolutionary organizations.

This time, the holy devil's cross seemed to have lost its magic power. Nicholas had already agreed to abdicate "voluntarily." But what came next was much worse than everyone had expected.

CHAPTER 11

# A Fateful Change of Mind

Nicholas's telegram to Adjutant General Mikhail Alekseev stated that he was "prepared to abdicate," but nothing was truly official until he signed the abdication manifesto. With General Nikolai Ruzsky holding off on circulating further information about the abdication for the moment, it was now up to the Duma Committee to secure the signature of an indecisive and unpredictable autocrat. What they would ultimately receive for their efforts would have startling consequences for Russia's future.

Following the Duma Committee's decision early in the morning on March 2 to seek Nicholas's abdication, Aleksandr Guchkov volunteered to travel to Pskov and present the demand to the tsar. The Duma Committee considered Guchkov a perfect emissary for the job. In stark contrast to Mikhail Rodzyanko's shifty maneuvering, Guchkov had been working toward a palace coup for months before the revolution. Now that even Duma Committee members like Pavel Milyukov and Vasily Shulgin, who had rejected the plot before the revolution, strongly advocated its implementation, Guchkov volunteered to plunge into the lion's den to confront the tsar with the demand for abdication.

The only problem was that Guchkov was not technically a member of the Duma Committee. To make it official, Guchkov suggested that someone from the Duma Committee should accompany him. The members of the Duma Committee did not dare send Rodzyanko to Pskov, fearing that he might make a deal with the military leaders, and if Nikolai Chkheidze, chairman of the Petrograd Soviet and a member of the Duma Committee, had been chosen, his radicalism would have prompted a major confrontation with the high command. Those seeking Nicholas's abdication needed to be monarchists. Shulgin volunteered, and the committee settled on him and Guchkov as its best hope for besting Nicholas.[1] The only terms that were to be specifically secured were that of Nicholas's abdication for his son under the regency of Grand Duke Mikhail. Beyond that, the Duma Committee did not even discuss a draft act of abdication, which was composed by Shulgin in a hasty manner on the train while on the way to Pskov.

The Duma Committee's delegates left Petrograd around 5 a.m. on March 2, while Rodzyanko was still carrying on his historic conversation with Ruzsky.[2] We should assume, therefore, that the Duma Committee's delegates did not know that Rodzyanko had already stolen their thunder by saying that the question of dynasty was now being "raised point-blank," and that this conversation had set in motion a chain of events among the high command that eventually led to Nicholas's acceptance of his abdication. Like Nicholas, who had been traveling in the train ignorant of the fast-developing events in Petrograd, Guchkov and Shulgin spent fifteen hours in the train not knowing that the objective of their trip had already been accomplished without their intervention.[3]

There were only two passengers in the car, Guchkov and Shulgin; in another car, five soldiers wearing red armbands served as security for the Duma Committee's delegates.[4] Yury Lomonosov had his trusted aide, Vladimir Nekrasov, an official of the Ministry of Transport's record-keeping office, board the train, so that he would receive detailed reports about the Duma Committee's delegates on the way to Pskov and their movements once they had arrived in Pskov to meet the emperor.[5] From Guchkov's and Shulgin's accounts and testimonies given after the February Revolution, it appears that they did not anticipate danger. But both delegates were nervous at the thought of a possible violent encounter with Nicholas as well as what they thought would be the nearly insurmountable difficulty of obtaining his consent for his abdication. During the journey Shulgin wrote a rough draft of the abdication manifesto but did not spend any time improving it. Both were preoccupied with the enormous challenge ahead. According to Shulgin, they traveled as if they were "doomed convicts" surrounded by blind walls, seeking a small spot of light as the only hope.[6] Yet Guchkov must have been excited by the opportunity to put into practice the idea of a palace coup, something he had harbored for a long time.

Along the way, the train stopped at various stations and Guchkov and Shulgin had to deliver short speeches before the people who gathered on the platforms. At Gatchina, General Nikolai Ivanov was trying to contact the Duma Committee delegates, but they refused to see him, limiting communications with him only to telegrams.[7] The train stopped for a long time at Luga, where the soldiers who had joined the revolution welcomed the Duma delegates with enthusiasm. However, not confident of the soldiers' allegiance, the Duma delegates did not come out of the train.[8] Because of these interruptions the Duma Committee's emissaries arrived at Pskov two hours later than scheduled.[9]

Ruzsky had instructed the railway commandant to escort the Duma Committee's delegates to his car immediately upon their arrival at Pskov station. Ruzsky needed to inform Guchkov and Shulgin that the emperor had already agreed to abdicate, and Guchkov and Shulgin would need Ruzsky's advice on Nicholas's attitude and disposition before their historic meeting.[10]

The tsar, in the meantime, had already changed his mind. As mentioned in the previous chapter, after he agreed to abdicate, his private physician, Dr. Sergei Fyodorov, came to see him around 4 p.m. Nicholas asked the doctor for his opinion about the possible length of Aleksei's life. Fyodorov frankly answered that given the powerlessness of modern medicine in curing hemophilia, he was pessimistic. "Thanks to the care and precautions, it might be possible to prolong his life," the doctor stated, "but he would never be a perfectly healthy man." Nicholas remarked that he hoped to stay with his family in Livadia and that he could not be separated from his son. Fyodorov expressed his skepticism about the possibility of Nicholas living with his son. If Aleksei become the tsar, he would most likely live with his regent, Mikhail.

Such a separation from his beloved son was unbearable for Nicholas. Moreover, the possibility of Aleksei living with Natasha Brasova, Mikhail's wife, whom Nicholas and Aleksandra loathed, was unacceptable. Nicholas loved his son dearly, and if he was forced to choose between his desire to live with his son and the need to relinquish his long-cherished dream to bequeath him the Russian Empire, there was no question of his preference. Nothing could tear him away from twelve-year-old Aleksei. Nicholas now decided to abdicate not only for himself but also for Aleksei in favor of his brother Mikhail, and he was certain that his wife would approve that decision.[11]

In preparing for Nicholas's meeting with the Duma Committee's delegates, the tsar's entourage intended to outmaneuver Ruzsky. They meant to direct the Duma delegates straight to Nicholas without giving Ruzsky a chance to talk to them first, and to that end they stationed the duty officer, Colonel Anatoly Mordvinov, on the platform as a scout.[12]

The special train for the Duma delegates, with the locomotive draped with red flags, arrived at Pskov station at 9:32 p.m.[13] Even before the train came to a complete stop, Mordvinov quickly stepped aboard and asked the Duma delegates to follow him to where the emperor was waiting in the imperial train, while Ruzsky and his chief of staff, General Yury Danilov, were waiting in the general's car for the arrival of the tsar.[14] The Duma delegates were not in presentable shape: they had not shaved or bathed for several days, their collars were limp, their suits rumpled, their shirts dirty, and their ties not tied straight. According to Shulgin, they looked like convicts who had just been released from prison.[15] They would have preferred to change before the historic meeting. But Mordvinov, paying no attention to their shabby attire and foul smell, led them across the platform, only several steps, to the imperial train, and took them straight to the dining car. As was the custom for an audience with the emperor, the footman there took their sheepskin overcoats and opened the door to the salon car. As they entered the well-lighted salon car, the minister of the imperial court, Count Vladimir Fredericks, impeccably dressed with three diamond-framed portraits of the emperor on his chest and a blue aiguillette from shoulder to waist, greeted them punctiliously. Next to Fredericks stood Major General Kirill Naryshkin, chief of the Military-Field Chancellery.[16]

Courteously and formally greeting the deputies, Fredericks told them that the emperor would come in a moment, and asked them about the situation in Petrograd. Guchkov answered: "Petrograd is becoming quieter, Count. But your house on Pochtamskaya Street was completely razed to the ground by the rebels, and what happened with your family is not clear." The count was shaken by this news.[17]

At last Nicholas entered the salon car. He was wearing his favorite Circassian Cossack coat. He was calm but pale. According to Guchkov, "His expression was calm; as usual, his eyes were clear; his gestures tranquil and measured. There was no trace of agitation."[18] The Duma delegates bowed to the emperor. The emperor shook hands with the delegates and asked: "Where is Ruzsky?" Naryshkin answered: "He will come in a moment." The emperor sat on one side of a four-cornered table, a green silk-covered wall behind him. Guchkov was invited to sit on his right at the table, and across from the emperor sat Shulgin and Fredericks. At the corner of the room there was another small table, where Naryshkin sat and took notes.[19]

After pleasantries were exchanged, Guchkov began to make his case.[20] He was nervous. He gazed down at the table, holding his brow with his left hand, and avoided looking the emperor straight in the face.[21]

Guchkov began his speech by offering the emperor a view of the dire situation in Petrograd that had brought him and Shulgin to the emperor's train. To prevent the further spread of anarchy, the Duma Committee had been formed. But along with the Duma Committee, "the committee of workers has also convened in the Duma [building] and we find ourselves under its control and censorship." The first danger was that anarchy led by these extremists, who espoused the concept of a socialist republic, might sweep away the moderate elements. Second, the revolution might spread to the armed forces at the front.[22]

At that moment Ruzsky and Danilov arrived. Mordvinov had attempted to block their entrance to the train, but Ruzsky and Danilov pushed him aside, took off their overcoats, and entered the salon car.[23] Bowing to the emperor, Ruzsky sat in between Fredericks and Shulgin, and Danilov sat on a sofa in the corner of the room. Ruzsky reprimanded the footman for not having obeyed his order to bring the delegates to him first.[24]

After the short pause caused by the entrance of Ruzsky and Danilov, Guchkov continued. Troops dispatched from the front had mutinied and declared their allegiance to the Duma Committee. Ruzsky interjected at this point in support of Guchkov and declared that the army could no longer afford to send a single soldier from the front for suppression of the revolution.[25] By then Ruzsky and Guchkov should have known that no revolt of troops from the front had occurred at Luga, but they both considered the claim convenient leverage to exert on the tsar.

Guchkov then hit hard where the tsar was most concerned: the situation at Tsarskoe Selo.

Yesterday, representatives of the Combined Infantry Regiment, the Railway Regiment, Your Majesty's Convoy, and court police appeared at the Duma and announced that they had joined the movement. They were told that they must continue to guard the persons they were assigned to protect, but the danger still exists, for the mob is now armed.[26]

Nicholas, leaning against the wall, looked straight into the air as Guchkov spoke. His face was calm and impassive, as Shulgin remembered; he seemed to be bored.[27]

Guchkov reached the climax of his impromptu speech:

The only path is to transfer the burden of supreme rulership to other hands. Russia can be saved, the monarchical principle can be saved, the dynasty can be saved. If you, Your Majesty, announce that you transfer your power to your little son, if you assign the regency to Grand Duke Mikhail Aleksandrovich, and if in your name or in the name of the regent instructions are issued for a new government to be formed, then perhaps Russia will be saved.[28]

"Of course, before deciding to do this, you should think it over well, and pray," Guchkov added, "but make a decision no later than tomorrow, because by that time we will no longer be in a position to give advice if you ask it of us, since there is reason to fear the aggressive outbreaks of the mob."[29] When Guchkov referred to praying, Nicholas for the first time stared at him.[30]

According to Shulgin, at this point Ruzsky whispered to Shulgin, who was sitting next to him, that trucks of armed soldiers were moving toward Pskov along the highway from Petrograd. The general asked Shulgin if they had been sent by the Duma Committee. Shulgin whispered back indignantly: "How could this idea come into your head?" The general answered: "Thank God. Forgive me. I ordered them to be detained."[31] This information, seeming proof that the anarchy might be spreading not only in Petrograd but approaching Pskov as well, must have provoked a sense of urgency to settle the matter.

Ruzsky now interrupted to tell the Duma Committee's delegates that the emperor had already made his decision, and handed to Nicholas the still unsigned draft manifesto. Guchkov's speech had just taken an ominous turn toward intimidation, and Ruzsky may have intended to stop it before it went too far. Ruzsky hoped that by handing Nicholas the draft manifesto, he would preclude further discussion. But he was astonished to see Nicholas fold the draft manifesto and put it in his pocket.[32] Neither Guchkov nor Shulgin seems to have appreciated the importance of the draft of the original abdication manifesto returning to Nicholas's hands.[33]

Paying no mind to Ruzsky, Nicholas spoke. According to Shulgin, his voice and manners were calm and businesslike.

> Through the morning, before your arrival and after Adjutant-General Ruzsky's conversation with the Duma chairman over the direct line, I thought it over, and for the sake of the good, peace, and preservation of Russia, I was ready to abdicate from the throne in favor of my son.

Ruzsky must have felt sick with the premonition that his worst fear was coming to pass: that the tsar had changed his mind and decided not to abdicate. As for Guchkov and Shulgin, this was the first time they had heard about the conversation between Rodzyanko and Ruzsky.

Nicholas continued:

> But now, having again thought the situation over, I have come to the conclusion that, in light of his illness, I should abdicate in my

name and his name simultaneously, as I cannot be separated from him. I changed my mind that I abdicate in favor of my brother Mikhail.

He added softly: "I hope you will understand the feelings of a father."[34]

This answer was so unexpected that the Duma delegates were left utterly speechless. They looked at each other with incredulity. Ruzsky and Danilov too looked at each other, having no words. Guchkov then broke the silence: "We were hoping that the tender age of Aleksei Nikolaevich would have a softening effect on the situation at the transfer of power."

The formula of Nicholas's abdication in favor of his son under the regency of Mikhail had been the idée fixe that had been nurtured by the plotters of a palace coup and widely shared in liberal circles. No one had ever thought of the possibility of a double abdication.

Shulgin saved his colleague from making any further embarrassing remarks by requesting a recess for fifteen minutes.[35]

The ghost of Nicholas's ancestors cast a dark shadow on the final drama of the Romanov monarchy. Though succession in Muscovy was never legally formalized, in 1722 Peter the Great (r. 1682–1725) issued a new Law of Succession, authorizing the ruler to nominate anyone he or she desired as his or her successor. This led to confusion, intrigue, and palace coups in the eighteenth century. When Catherine the Great (Catherine II, r. 1762–1796) came to power by having her feeble and deranged husband, Peter III (r. 1761–1762), killed, she assumed the throne and designated her son, Paul, as the heir. But Catherine hated her son and came to favor her grandson, Alexander, who was kept from his father and groomed under Catherine's careful tutelage. The hatred between the son and the mother was mutual. For his part, Paul believed that the throne belonged to him and should have been passed to him when his father died but that it had been snatched by his mother. He languished during the long reign of Catherine, brooding and counting the days and years he was deprived of becoming the emperor.

When Paul (r. 1796–1801) was crowned on Easter Day, 1797, the first thing he did was issue his own Law of Succession and a Statute on the Imperial Family. Paul's succession law established a clear path of succession, following the male line of descent. The accompanying statute determined honors, titles, marriage, divorce, and the age of majority, among other elements, of the Romanov dynastic house. The emperor was the head of the monarchy. Grand dukes and grand duchesses were to marry only members of European royal families, with the approval of the emperor. Morganatic marriages had to be approved by the emperor and meant that their male offspring would lose their place in the line of succession. The heir was to reach maturity at sixteen. The wife of the emperor had to convert to Orthodoxy; she became the empress but had no right to rule. If an abdication should occur and there was the possibility that the throne would be passed to a minor, the outgoing ruler had the right to designate a regent until the minor reached sixteen years of age.[36] The succession law was slightly modified under Alexander III and Nicholas II, and incorporated into the Fundamental Laws of the Russian Empire enacted in 1906.

The succession law clearly stipulated that succession to the throne went to the eldest son of the emperor. The Duma Committee's formula—Nicholas's abdication in favor of his son, Aleksei, who until he reached age sixteen would be under the regency of Nicholas's brother Grand Duke Mikhail—was a perfectly legal proposal. It is presumed that the composition of the regent council would have been heavily influenced and even dictated by the Provisional Government without any influence from Nicholas II. It would have been a perfect prescription for a constitutional monarchy, where a nominal tsar under a weak regent who was sympathetic to the cause of the liberals would not exert any influence in actual policies other than rubber-stamping the decisions made by the Provisional Government. Nonetheless, the monarchy would be preserved, and legal continuity from the old regime to the new would be guaranteed.

Nicholas's decision threw a monkey wrench into this scheme. The succession law was clear that the throne was to be transferred to the eldest son. Although Nicholas had the right to designate a regent for his heir, he had no right to skip over Aleksei. Transferring the throne to Mikhail by skipping over the rightful heir was a violation of the succession law. Furthermore, by abdicating on his behalf, Nicholas illegally deprived Aleksei of his rightful claim to the throne.[37] Thus Nicholas's decision was illegal twice over.

It appears unlikely that Nicholas was unaware of the illegality of this succession. All his relatives knew it, and it is impossible to believe that the head of the imperial house was not aware of the succession law. But in view of the great sacrifice he had made by giving up the throne, he must have felt that the illegality could be justified. He was demanding merely "a small concession" to fulfill his last personal wish. To Nicholas, his personal concerns trumped legality; after all, he was the autocrat, and so he could do whatever he wanted, as Alexandra time and again had reminded him. His overriding desire to live with his son and with his family took priority.

Milyukov commented:

Nicholas II did not wish to risk the fate of his son, preferring to risk his brother and Russia to an unknown future. As always, thinking first of himself and his loved ones, even in this critical moment, and rejecting a course of action which, though painful, was to some degree prepared, he once again laid open the entire question of the monarchy just at the moment when it could only be decided in a negative manner. This was Nicholas II's final act of service to his fatherland.[38]

Milyukov's last sentence is not quite accurate, however. When Nicholas transferred the throne to Mikhail, he assumed that Mikhail would accept the throne. It never occurred to him that his decision spelled the doom of the monarchy.

From a corner of the salon car, Guchkov and Shulgin spent the recess discussing what to do with Nicholas's unexpected proposal. For Guchkov, it would be out of the question for Aleksei to continue to live with Nicholas and Alexandra after Nicholas's abdication, since "no one could agree to entrust the fate and the education of the future emperor with those who had brought the country to the present condition."[39] Ruzsky joined the consultation and asked if it was even possible for the tsar to legally abdicate for his son. Neither Guchkov nor Shulgin knew the answer.[40] The general exploded: "How could you come here to decide on such an important matter of the state without bringing a single volume of the Fundamental Laws or even a jurist!?" Shulgin lamely protested that they had not expected such an answer from the emperor. Even so, it was a cardinal and inexcusable oversight on the part of the Duma deputies, who had not even thought about bringing a legal expert with them.

Returning to the issue at hand, Shulgin argued: "Whether or not the tsar had the right does not matter." He argued that they should accept Nicholas's formula, since the most important point at the moment was not the legality of the abdication but the fact of abdication. Besides, Shulgin continued, if Aleksei was separated from his parents, he would blame the Provisional Government for the separation. In addition, Aleksei would not be able to swear allegiance to the constitution until he reached maturity, while Mikhail as the new tsar could become a constitutional monarch immediately.[41]

It is worth pausing to consider what would have happened if the Duma Committee had refused to accept Nicholas's amended abdication. Would

Nicholas then have withdrawn his agreement to give up the throne? Knowing the emperor's stubbornness and intransigence, Guchkov and Shulgin must have shuddered at the notion. They did not know how the high command would react to such a development, and they did not have the time to renegotiate the matter. Any delay might trigger the anti-Romanov sentiments that had already boiled over in response to Milyukov's speech at the Tauride Palace earlier that day. Confusion and division threatened to further consume the armed forces. Guchkov gave in.

The Duma Committee's delegates returned to the tsar's salon car.[42] Guchkov gave the emperor his consent: "Your Majesty, human feelings of a father have spoken in you, and politics has no place in it. Therefore, we cannot object to your proposal." Shulgin hastened to inject politics immediately: "It is important only that the act of Your Majesty declare that your successor is obligated to give allegiance to the constitution." Nicholas sarcastically asked him: "Do you want to think more about it?" Guchkov replied: "No, I think we can immediately accept your proposal."[43]

The emperor wanted to know if there was any guarantee that his abdication would not lead to bloodshed and that the whole of Russia would accept it. Guchkov answered that not Nicholas's abdication but rather the declaration of a republic had the potential to provoke an internecine war. Shulgin said that although there were extremists who would not accept the new order and would attempt to fight, they should not fear this, since, judging from the sentiment in Kiev, which he knew best, the people remained solidly monarchist.[44]

By yielding to Nicholas's paternal feelings, Guchkov and Shulgin exceeded the charge the Duma Committee had entrusted them with. The two monarchists did not seem to realize the grave consequences of their concession. It was a decision made on the spur of the moment, during a fifteen-minute break in the negotiations, without serious thought to the consequences of an illegal succession.[45]

As the historian Vitaly Startsev argues, the Duma deputies could have insisted on the original formula. They could have promised Nicholas that he and Alexandra could continue to live with their son—a promise that could be broken, citing a change in circumstances. But the Duma deputies did not insist on the original formula. And it was Guchkov who made the final decision to accept Nicholas's double abdication. At this crucial moment, Guchkov, the leader of the conspiratorial palace coup, failed to exercise "the moral coercion" that he had insisted on for many years, and in so doing he lent his hand to slay the monarchical system that he wanted to save.[46]

To Nicholas, the whole process must have been intolerably humiliating. The abdication itself was bad enough, but a situation in which he had to beg for his personal enemy to accept its terms added insult to injury, though he must have felt a sense of satisfaction by throwing a monkey wrench back at his sworn opponents. If he felt humiliated, however, he disguised his emotions. He occasionally lobbed oblique sarcasm at his opponents but on the whole maintained quiet dignity throughout the meeting. This struck Guchkov, who later testified:

Such an important act in the history of Russia . . . was conducted in such a simple, ordinary form. And I would say that there was such a profoundly tragic lack of understanding of all the events by the very person who was the main character of this scene that I even wondered if we were dealing with a normal person.[47]

Guchkov then told Nicholas that since they could not stay more than an hour and a half in Pskov, they needed to have in their hands the signed "manifesto" of Nicholas's abdication.[48] Shulgin presented his version of the manifesto, the one he had prepared on the train, but Nicholas offered his draft as a point of departure. This was the draft manifesto that had been composed by Bazili on Alekseev's instructions and sent to Pskov around 7 p.m. on March 2 but was handed to the emperor by Ruzsky during the meeting with the Duma delegates. Reading the highly polished, dignified draft, Shulgin immediately withdrew his own inferior effort. Nicholas went to his car and made revisions to the original in pencil with his own hand. Bazili's original formula—Nicholas's abdication in favor of his son, Aleksei, under Mikhail's regency—was now corrected, in Nicholas's own handwriting, to abdicate not only for himself but also for his son and to transfer power to his brother Mikhail.[49]

Guchkov and Shulgin requested one change: a phrase should be inserted to the effect that the new emperor would pledge allegiance to the constitution. Nicholas accepted the change, though, as we will see, he avoided using the word "constitution."[50]

The draft "manifesto" stated that Russia was going through a difficult time of war, when national unity was most needed and internal popular disturbances were threatening this unity. It went on to say:

> In these decisive days in the life of Russia We deem it Our duty in conscience to help Our people [to keep] the close and unbroken unity of all popular forces for the speedy achievement of the victory and in agreement with the State Duma, We consider it best to abdicate from the throne of the Russian state and to renounce the supreme power.

Thus far the tsar's words were in agreement with what the State Duma wanted, though what followed diverged significantly:

> Not wishing to be separated from Our beloved son, We hand Our succession to Our brother, Grand Duke Mikhail Aleksandrovich, and bless him for ascending on the throne of the Russian State, and enjoin Our brother to rule the state affairs in the complete and unbroken unity with the representatives of the people in the legislative institutions on the foundations on which they were

established, *taking the inviolable oath* in the name of [Our] passionately beloved homeland. (Italics added)[51]

Here again, Nicholas stressed unity with the legislative power, but refused to use the cursed word he hated to the last moment, "constitution," and instead using an ambiguous phrase without specifying to whom people would have to take the inviolable oath. Even at the last minute, Nicholas was trying to resist.

At 11 p.m. Colonel Vsevold Vasilievich Stupin of the Operation Division of the northern front was summoned to the station. Danilov gave him a draft "manifesto" of abdication and ordered Stupin to go back to headquarters to make two clean copies of the "manifesto." Stupin summoned a typist, A. K. Loginov, who typed two copies of the "manifesto" that was dictated. The copies were brought back to the imperial train, and Naryshkin hand-delivered them to the tsar's car, where Nicholas signed those two copies in pencil. Before he signed the "manifesto," at the request of the Duma Committee delegates Nicholas appointed Prince Georgy Lvov as the chairman of the Council of Ministers and Grand Duke Nikolai Nikolaevich as the supreme commander.[52] This was intended to make those appointments legal and institutionally legitimate.

Then Naryshkin came to the salon car and asked Fredericks to countersign the two copies of the document. Fredericks complained there was no space to countersign, but in a trembling hand he signed his name below "Pskov" and the date. It was 11:48 p.m. on March 2.[53] One copy was to remain with Ruzsky, and another was for Guchkov and Shulgin to bring back to Petrograd. At Shulgin's request, it was backdated to 3 p.m.[54] The fate of the throne, monarchy, and the state would hang on this unnecessary change.

Also backdated were the appointments of Lvov and Nikolai Nikolaevich to 2 p.m., one hour before the tsar accepted his abdication on behalf of his son. Lvov had already been selected as the prime minister of the Provisional Government, but this document used the term "Chairman of the Council of Ministers," as if the tsar had appointed him as such before he abdicated. These minor acts of fraud would cast a dark shadow over the legitimacy of the Provisional Government.

When Nicholas signed the "manifesto," and Fredericks countersigned as the witness, everyone present was moved. Shulgin said: "Alas, Your Majesty, if you had done this sooner . . ." Nicholas answered: "You think that would have turned out all right [*oboshlos'*]?" He told Shulgin that he planned to go to the Stavka to say farewell and then go see his mother before he returned to Tsarskoe Selo. At that point the deputies, the generals, and the tsar shook hands and parted ways.[55]

The salon car, where the last act of Nicholas's reign was played, was now empty. The antique clock on the wall showed 11:45 p.m.[56]

Thus ended Nicholas II's twenty-two-year reign.

Guchkov and Shulgin sent a telegram to Rodzyanko via the chief of the General Staff:

The Sovereign has given the agreement for the abdication from the throne in favor of Grand Duke Mikhail Aleksandrovich with the obligation for him to swear allegiance to the constitution. The charge to form a new government was given to Prince Lvov. Simultaneously, Grand Duke Nikolai Nikolaevich has been appointed as the supreme commander in chief. The manifesto will be sent immediately. Inform immediately Pskov the situation of affairs in Petrograd.[57]

As the Duma delegates went out of the salon car, Guchkov saw a crowd gathering. He said to them: "Gentlemen, rest assured. The sovereign gave more than we hoped." In a subsequent interview with Grand Duke Andrei, Ruzsky stated:

These last words of Guchkov remained to me totally incomprehensible. What did he want to say, "more than we hoped"? Did they come to demand from the tsar a responsible ministry or abdication, I don't know. They did not bring with them any documents. They had no certificates that proved they acted on behalf of the State Duma, and no draft of abdication. I did not see any documents, I swear. If they came to ask for the abdication and obtained it, then, why did Guchkov say that they obtained more than they had hoped? I think . . . they both did not expect the abdication.[58]

It is possible to interpret Guchkov's words differently, however. They had expected strenuous resistance from the tsar. But Nicholas agreed, though not exactly with the formula they had prepared for. Still, acceptance of any kind was more than they had anticipated.

Guchkov and Shulgin were invited to Ruzsky's car, where they had a light meal while they waited for their train to be ready. General Sergei Sergeevich Savvich joined them. Guchkov later reflected that he was "troubled by the excessive satisfaction displayed by the two generals [Ruzsky and Savvich]; while Shulgin and I were tormented by a thousand worries, they were overflowing with joy."[59]

The Duma delegates departed for Petrograd around 3 a.m. on March 3. The "manifesto" of Nicholas's abdication and two decrees to the Senate were sent to the Stavka and the chairman of the Provisional Government by telegraph. The Duma delegates took one copy of the original "manifesto," and another copy was kept with Danilov at the headquarters of the northern front.[60]

As this whole drama played out, it seems that no one thought of alerting Mikhail that the throne was being transferred to him. Amid all of these discussions on who should take the throne, not a word was conveyed to the person who had been selected.[61]

Most of the entourage gathered in the dining car after Guchkov and Shulgin left. They talked only in whispers, and many wept. No one blamed anyone for anything; they just wanted to be together, as if to mourn a dead man they loved.[62] But the rats would swiftly desert the ship. Count Aleksandr Grabbe, chief of the convoy, requested the tsar's permission to be transferred under the new commander in chief, Nikolai Nikolaevich, at the Stavka. Lieutenant Nikolai Pavlovich Sablin, Alexandra's favorite officer at the Stavka, quickly disappeared, and Baron Rudolf von Stackelberg, chief of the Field Chancellery, deserted.[63]

Nicholas scarcely revealed his opinions and feelings either in his letters or in his diary. On the day of his abdication, he wrote in his diary:

March 2. Thursday. In the morning, Ruzsky came and read to me the long conversation by direct wire with Rodzyanko. In his words, Petrograd was in such a state that a cabinet [formed] from the members of the State Duma will be powerless to do anything, for the SR-Socialist-Democratic parties are competing with it in the form of a workers' committee. My abdication is necessary. Ruzsky transmitted this conversation to Alekseev in the Stavka and to all General Headquarters. At 12:30 the answers came. For the salvation of Russia and the preservation of the army at the front, I decided to take this step. I conceded, and from the Stavka a draft for the manifesto was sent. In the evening, from Petrograd came Guchkov and Shulgin, with whom I had a talk and to whom I handed the manifesto, which was drawn up and signed. At one o'clock at night I left Pskov with gloomy feelings.

Treachery, cowardice, and deception all around.[64]

The last six words were a rare window into his inner feelings, but to whom these words should be applied he did not spell out.

At 6 p.m. on March 2, Rodzyanko informed Alekseev in a telegram that the Duma Committee had transferred power to the Provisional Government headed by Prince Lvov. All the troops in Petrograd and Tsarskoe Selo had now pledged allegiance to the Provisional Government. Rodzyanko considered it essential to appoint a new commander for the Petrograd Military District in order to restore order and avoid anarchy, and after consultation with the General Staff officers, he recommended for that position Lieutenant General Lavr Kornilov of the 25th Army Corps, commanded by Vasily Gurko of the southwestern front.[65]

Rodzyanko's request was clearly an unprecedented intervention in military affairs, since any appointment for the commanding position was the prerogative of the emperor. Furthermore, recalling Ivanov would have meant a further step of retreat by the high command from military suppression of the insurrection in the capital. Rodzyanko's telegram was sent not only to Alekseev but also to Gurko and Adjutant General Aleksei Brusilov.

Brusilov opposed this appointment, considering Kornilov too "straightforward and extremely hot-tempered."[66] Yet without any hesitation or protest, Alekseev accepted the recommendation. He expressed his hope that "this would be the first step toward restoring order in the military units in the garrison of Petrograd and the surrounding areas," and requested that Nicholas approve this appointment and recall General Ivanov to Mogilev. Alekseev's telegram to the tsar was supposedly sent at 6:55 p.m., just before he sent the draft "manifesto" of abdication. On the margin of the telegram there was a note written by Nicholas: "Implemented, N." It must have been one of the last acts Nicholas performed before he abdicated.[67] Danilov reported to Alekseev that the emperor approved the decision recommended by Alekseev.[68] Danilov's telegram was sent at 9:21 p.m., in the middle of Nicholas's meeting with Ruzsky, Danilov, and Savvich about his abdication. It is not known how and when Ruzsky interrupted the talk with the tsar and slipped Alekseev's telegram to the tsar for his approval. In any case, not a word of protest against Rodzyanko's interference in military appointments was voiced, and no discussion was conducted about the implications of Kornilov's appointment as the new commander of the Petrograd Military District, who would also control the security of the imperial family in Tsarskoe Selo. Alekseev sent a telegram to Rodzyanko informing him of the tsar's appointment of Kornilov. He said that he did not know where Ivanov was, so he asked Rodzyanko to inform Ivanov that the tsar had relieved him of the command of the Petrograd Military District and that Ivanov should return immediately to Mogilev.[69]

Although Ivanov had retreated to Vyritsa and received the orders from the Stavka and from the tsar to halt his operations, Yury Lomonosov and Aleksandr Bublikov continued to monitor the general's every move. They had succeeded in keeping him out of Gatchina, although a part of his echelons had managed to reach Gatchina and Aleksandrovskaya. They continued to intercept telegraph traffic as they surveilled the situation. This allowed them to intercept the news first of the appointment of Lvov as the chairman of the Council of Ministers and of Nikolai Nikolaevich as the new commander in chief, then the news about Nicholas's abdication.

Armed with this information, they continued to torment General Ivanov. When Ivanov contacted Lomonosov demanding that he and his echelons be allowed to go to Petrograd, by imperial order, Lomonosov answered: "Under the order of what emperor, General? Nicholas II has abdicated." After a long silence, Ivanov asked Lomonosov to arrange a train for him to return to the Stavka.

Lomonosov gave the illusion of compliance, ordering the Vindavskaya authorities to make two tenders available for Ivanov, but instructed them to drain all the water from them, sabotaging the locomotive. Thus, Ivanov was able to leave Vyritsa, but without water for the steam engine, he had to stop only 7.5 kilometers from the station and was stuck there all night.[70] Bublikov then sent Ivanov the following telegram:

It became clear to me that you are arresting and terrorizing the employees of the railways who are under my jurisdiction. With the authority of the Temporary Committee of the State Duma, you will bear with these actions grave responsibility. I advise you that you do not move out of Vyritsa, otherwise according to the information I have, your regiment will meet artillery fire.[71]

The tragicomedy of Ivanov's counterrevolutionary expedition finally came to an end.

CHAPTER 12

# Mikhail's Renunciation
# of the Throne

It was after midnight on March 3, and the mood at the Stavka was anxious. Nikolai Bazili, Grand Duke Sergei Mikhailovich, and a few officers had gathered in the room of the officer on duty, just below Adjutant General Mikhail Alekseev's office and next to the telegraph office housing the Hughes apparatus. They smoked incessantly as they waited for news. From time to time General Aleksandr Lukomsky looked in to see if anything had changed.[1] At 1:30 a.m., the nervous atmosphere was punctured by the arrival of a fateful telegram from chief of staff General Yury Danilov.[2]

All eyes in the small duty officer's room were glued to the tape of paper as it was printed. Bazili was puzzled to read this crucial sentence: "The Sovereign Emperor then signed the act of abdication from the throne to be transferred to Grand Duke Mikhail Aleksandrovich." Though Bazili did not initially grasp what he was seeing, the shock of recognition soon came as he realized that all references to regency had been deleted from the draft of the "manifesto" and that Aleksei's name had been replaced with Mikhail's. As the "manifesto" reached its end, the officers took in a newly added passage referring to the swearing of an "inviolable oath" in the name of the "beloved homeland." In Bazili's words, "In the case of little Prince Alexei there would have been no reason for addition, as a minor cannot take an oath."[3]

The machine had finished its work. The officers reeled. Grand Duke Sergei shouted, "Why on earth, Mikhail?! This is such a joke!" He collapsed on the sofa, exclaiming: "This is the end!" Frantic questions swirled among those packed into the smoke-filled little room. Was this succession even legal? Could Mikhail, who preferred to remain in the shadows, ever secure the people's respect? Had Alekseev been at the scene instead of Nikolai Ruzsky, could he, or would he, have prevented Nicholas from taking this inexplicable course of a double abdication?[4]

Alekseev said nothing, though Bazili noticed that he was visibly "overwhelmed." At 2 a.m., Alekseev sent the text of the "manifesto" that Nicholas had signed to Mikhail Rodzyanko.[5] Around an hour after that, he sent a message to Nikolai Nikolaevich, informing him that the grand duke had been appointed as the supreme commander and requesting that the chief of staff at Mogilev serve as interim supreme commander until Nikolai Nikolaevich could arrive at the Stavka. Though in this message Alekseev included Danilov's telegram with the news of the double abdication in favor of Mikhail, in his immediate response Nikolai Nikolaevich merely granted Alekseev's request and did not address this most shocking turn of events.[6]

Having informed Nikolai Nikolaevich, and trusting Ruzsky to know what to do, Alekseev proceeded to break the news to the rest of the military leadership. He dispatched a telegram to Generals Aleksei Evert, Aleksei Brusilov, and Vladimir Sakharov and to Admiral Aleksandr Rusin (again excluding Nikolai Nikolaevich) informing them of the text of the tsar's "manifesto" of abdication and instructing them to send it to all the army and navy units by telegraph, as well as printing and distributing it widely.[7]

Now Alekseev's most urgent task was to secure the loyalty of the armed forces to the new tsar. He fired off another telegram to Prince Georgy Lvov, now chairman of the Council of Ministers, asking him to make the "manifesto" of Nicholas's abdication public as soon as possible so that the army and the navy would swear allegiance to the new tsar.[8] He sent another telegram to Lvov and the new foreign minister, Pavel Milyukov, urging them to let the Allied representatives know about the abdication "manifesto."[9] Left unanswered was the question of whether the illegality of Nicholas's double abdication doomed these efforts; that was now the Duma's problem.

As soon as Aleksandr Guchkov and Vasily Shulgin left the imperial train, they sent an encoded telegram to the Duma Committee. But those in the Tauride Palace did not receive the official message until 3 a.m.[10] Alekseev had already sent a telegram to Rodzyanko at 2 a.m. with the text of Nicholas's abdication "manifesto," though we do not know whether or when Rodzyanko received it. But word very likely reached them earlier, in a telephone call from Aleksandr Bublikov to Rodzyanko, since the original message was sent via the Ministry of Transport channel, which Bublikov was carefully monitoring.[11] The Duma members must have scratched their heads at the claim by Guchkov and Shulgin that Nicholas had abdicated in favor of Mikhail. Bublikov made a telephone call from his office in an attempt to prod Guchkov to follow through with the "manifesto." After he ended the call and came out of his office, he told those who were waiting: "I congratulate you. Nicholas has abdicated, but remember that the act of the abdication has so far not been received. This is a secret. Not a word should be said."[12] But because Guchkov had decided to send the "manifesto" text through the military line rather than the more open Ministry of Transport line, they were left in suspense about the precise terms under which Nicholas had abdicated.

Nicholas's double abdication placed the Duma Committee and the Provisional Government in a thicket of legal and political dilemmas. For

Nicholas's abdication "manifesto" to take effect officially, it would need to be approved by the Senate, signed by the minister of justice, and then printed for the public. Because Nicholas had appointed Prince Lvov as the chairman of the Council of Ministers, it would be Lvov's task to obtain the original copy, certify it as the official document, stamp it with the official seal of the minister of justice, send it to the Senate, and have it print the manifesto in its official notice.[13] The original abdication manifesto was addressed to the Stavka and to the chief of staff of the supreme headquarters, as if it was a telegram. The intention must have been that the Stavka, where the draft of the manifesto had been composed, should rewrite this into the draft of the official manifesto with the heading "Imperial Manifesto" ("Vysochaishii Manifesto," ) which had been the title of the October Manifesto in 1905). Then Lvov, as the prime minister of the Provisional Government, or Kerensky, as the minister of justice, would cosign and send it to the Senate to make it the official manifesto, with Nicholas's signature. But the Stavka, to which this "telegram" was addressed, would not and could not write a manifesto, since Alekseev, Bazili, and Grand Duke Sergei were well aware of the illegality of the double abdication. So it was up to the political leaders to break out of this logjam.

However, the Duma Committee and the Provisional Government, facing a quickly moving revolutionary situation, did not have the luxury of following this legal procedure. Still, in order to announce to the public that the tsar had abdicated, they needed to obtain an authentic copy of the manifesto, although the document Nicholas signed could hardly be considered an official, legally binding document, even if it was signed by Nicholas himself, dated, and countersigned by Fredericks. It was at best the document that signaled Nicholas's intention to abdicate, which would need to be legally validated later.[14] But the emergency situation called for emergency measures. The Duma leaders thus treated this document as an official "manifesto" and even elevated it to an official "act," though it was hardly either a manifesto or an act.[15] As for the Stavka, it was anxious to have the armed forces swear allegiance to the new tsar, legal or illegal, by treating this document as the official manifesto.

The devious attempt to treat the document that Nicholas signed as the official manifesto, or even as the official act of abdication, had serious problems. Nicholas signed two copies, but these two copies are not quite identical. One copy was signed by Nicholas in pencil, but the other was signed in ink. There were discrepancies regarding the precise time of the document. These questions have provoked a swirl of debates for contemporary historians, prompting forensic examination of the two copies, and leading to a host of conspiracy theories that claim that the document was a forgery.[16]

More importantly, the time given in this document, 3 p.m., was a back-dated time, not the real time when Nicholas signed. At 3 p.m. Nicholas was going to transfer the throne to Aleksei, but at 11 p.m., when he signed this document, he committed a double abdication, not only for himself but also for his son, and transferred the throne to Mikhail. These discrepancies raised a series of tricky legal questions. Was the tsar considered to have abdicated when he agreed to abdicate? If so, was the throne automatically transferred to Aleksei at that moment, at 3 p.m.? Or did he abdicate when he signed the document? In that case it was at 11 p.m. If we ignore the backdating trick and assume that Nicholas intended to transfer the throne to Mikhail, did Mikhail become Tsar Mikhail II without knowing it, even if it violated the succession law? If the "abdication manifesto" was published and widely distributed, the transfer of power to Mikhail would become an established fact that would be difficult to reverse. Should the Duma Committee and the Provisional Government persuade the grand duke to assume the throne, thereby asserting the legitimacy of the Provisional Government by being anointed by the illegally installed new emperor? Or should they persuade the grand duke to renounce the throne? In that case, the premature publication of Nicholas's abdication manifesto would have to be prevented. These were weighty issues, and they had to make a decision quickly—within several hours.

At this point someone from the Duma, most likely Rodzyanko, called Yury Lomonosov and pressed him to locate and send the text of the abdication manifesto as soon as possible. This caller said that the document would have to be published urgently, explaining that due to the strike of printing workers, the government had very limited resources. Lomonosov offered the services of the printing press of the Ministry of Transport, which could accomplish the highly secretive and urgent task. The caller from the Duma urged Lomonosov to send a copy to the Duma and begin typesetting as soon as he received the text, and again exhorted him to hurry up.[17]

Before 3 a.m. on March 3, Rodzyanko and Lvov left the Tauride Palace to retrieve a copy of the "abdication manifesto" from the General Staff, and then went to the War Minister's residence to use the Hughes apparatus there to contact Ruzsky and Alekseev. Before they returned nearly six hours later, a stormy debate had already begun among the members of the Duma Committee and the Provisional Government.[18] A rapid political realignment was afoot.

The group that had sought and won Nicholas's abdication (as opposed to Rodzyanko's limited constitutional reform) consisted of two groups with differing positions on the role of the monarchy. The first was represented by Milyukov, who considered it crucial that the Provisional Government obtain its legitimacy from the monarchy, without relying on the State Duma. The second group, who claimed to represent the insurgent masses, was headed by Aleksandr Kerensky, supported by his Masonic colleagues Nikolai Nekrasov, Mikhail Tereshchenko, and Aleksandr Konovalov. They were republicans and wished to abolish the monarchical system, but they had gone along with the first group's plan to retain the monarchical system when the Duma Committee was seeking Nicholas's abdication, and they supported the Milyukov-led majority of the Duma Committee. This coalition was now riven by the problem of the illegal double abdication.

For Kerensky's republicans, Nicholas's double abdication offered an opportunity to put a knife into the monarchical system once and for all. If Kerensky could persuade Mikhail to renounce the throne, he could enhance his own authority as the pivotal link between the Provisional Government (for which he was minister of justice) and the Petrograd Soviet (for which he was vice chairman). He claimed to represent the masses of insurgents, and said that he was joining the Provisional Government as "the hostage" of the insurgent masses.[19]

Ironically, it was Milyukov, Nicholas's personal enemy, who fought the lonely fight to preserve the monarchy. For Milyukov, it was necessary that the Provisional Government be anointed by the new tsar, who would be reduced to a figurehead after transferring his power. Milyukov realized that it would be necessary to consolidate the new order for it to have sufficiently strong power, and that such consolidation would need to be based on a symbol that could attract the support of the masses. The monarchy was just such a symbol. "Without the fulcrum of this symbol," Milyukov predicted, the Provisional Government "could not survive until a Constituent Assembly. It will turn out to be a fragile boat that will sink in the ocean of mass disturbances."[20] Milyukov understood that support for the Provisional Government needed to come from the vast majority of the Russian people who had remained neutral to the revolution in Petrograd, not just from the outspoken, radicalized Petrograd masses. Milyukov also understood that political power was not merely a legal and institutional issue; ceremonies and rituals, culture, and history also had vital roles to play in the people's consciousness.[21] Milyukov then suggested that the Provisional Government should abandon Petrograd and establish its headquarters in Moscow, where, he assumed, the situation was calmer.

The problem with this argument was that if the double abdication was illegal, the grand duke would have no right to succeed Nicholas, and hence no right to bestow power on the Provisional Government. For Milyukov, political expediency superseded legal niceties. Although he was in the minority among the Duma leaders, he had the support of an officers' group that had presented to the Duma Committee a petition urging that the Provisional Government not take any position on the form of the government until the Constituent Assembly decided what that form would be.[22]

Milyukov went so far as to threaten to resign from the Provisional Government if Mikhail refused to assume the throne. The rest of the Provisional Government and Duma Committee members managed to talk him out of resigning by promising that he would be able to present his views fully to Mikhail when they met with him later.[23] At any rate, the discussion was deadlocked, and they decided to leave the decision to the grand duke himself.

After the joint meeting of the Duma Committee and the Provisional Government, Kerensky telephoned Grand Duke Mikhail at 5:55 a.m. on March 3 and requested that he be good enough to receive representatives of the Duma Committee and the Provisional Government.[24] Even the fact that Kerensky, rather than Milyukov, delivered this request was a sign of how much Kerensky's stature had been enhanced within the Duma Committee and the Provisional Government by the drama of the past few hours.

During those same hours, to everyone's surprise, the faction that sought to end the monarchy acquired a new ally: Rodzyanko. He had begun the night frantically working to preserve the monarchy, and upon receiving news of the double abdication, he had even called Barrister Ivanov to his office and asked him to persuade Mikhail to assume the throne.[25] But the experiences of the previous days were catching up with him. His dealings with Grand Duke Mikhail on the evening of February 27 had disappointed him. He now viewed the grand duke as lacking the willpower and charisma necessary to lead. The violent reaction of the insurgents to Milyukov's announcement that Russia would retain the monarchy had frightened him. By the time he left the Tauride Palace for the war minister's residence to receive the abdication manifesto, he had already changed his mind. It seemed to the chairman of the Duma "that it was quite obvious to us that the grand duke would not have reigned more than a few hours and that terrible bloodshed, marking the beginning of a general civil war, would have immediately started within the walls of the capital."[26] Also, his political calculations played an important role. In order to elevate the Duma and the Duma Committee as legitimate institutions in the post-revolutionary era and to reduce the influence of his rival Milyukov, Rodzyanko made a decision to side with Kerensky, thus hatching an unholy alliance.[27]

There is a huge difference between the political system envisioned by a responsible ministry and a system without the monarchy. Although both envisioned that the chairman of the Duma would be endowed with the power to appoint the government, in the former the tsar would continue to exist, wielding some power as defined by the revised Fundamental Laws. But without the tsar, the Duma chairman would acquire power unlimited by any higher authority. The political power of the state would emanate from him as the expression of the will of the people, not from the tsar. It is no wonder Rodzyanko jumped to grab this opportunity.

Rodzyanko and Lvov left the Tauride Palace at 3 a.m. to retrieve Nicholas's "abdication manifesto" at the General Staff headquarters. He and Lvov went to the war minister's residence to talk with Ruzsky at 5 a.m. What were they doing after they retrieved the abdication manifesto at the General Staff headquarters and before they went to the war minister's residence to talk with Ruzsky? According to historian Semion Lyandres, both took a catnap, Lvov at the apartment of his longtime associate Dmitry Mitrofanovich Shchepkin and Rodzyanko at the home of his old friend M. Vonlyarlyarsky.[28] According to Andrei Nikolaev, however, Rodzyanko, Lvov, and Kerensky met where Lvov was staying, presumably in Shchepkin's apartment, where they agreed to persuade Mikhail to decline the throne.[29] The unholy alliance among Rodzyanko, Lvov, and Kerensky must have been concluded there.

At 4:40 a.m. Rodzyanko dispatched a telegram to Alekseev and to all the front commanders informing them that "the Duma Committee had appointed the Provisional Government," and introducing the names of the ministers.[30] This telegram had a double purpose. First, Rodzyanko underscored that it was not the emperor but the Duma Committee that had appointed the Provisional Government; thus the legitimacy of the Provisional Government emanated from the Duma, not from the emperor. Second, the Duma chairman conveyed to the high command that the establishment of the Provisional Government was now a fait accompli. This was a necessary step before his next move: to block the transfer of the throne to Mikhail. He must have sent this telegram only after he concluded the unholy alliance with Lvov and Kerensky.

Immediately after he sent this telegram to the high command, he sought to talk with Ruzsky. This talk began at 5 a.m. and lasted until 6.[31] Having just forged an alliance with Kerensky and Lvov to persuade Mikhail to renounce the throne, Rodzyanko sought to prevent Nicholas's "abdication manifesto" from being widely publicized. He feared that wide circulation of the "manifesto" might be accompanied by the joyous celebration of Nicholas's abdication and the acceptance of the new tsar, Mikhail II, among the people, especially among the soldiers at the front. To prevent this, Rodzyanko first sought to convince Ruzsky to withhold Nicholas's manifesto of abdication.

Standing before the Hughes apparatus at the war minister's residence alongside Lvov, with Ruzsky at the northern front on the other end of the line, Rodzyanko delivered his request: "It is extraordinarily important not to publish the manifesto about [Nicholas's] abdication and the transfer of power to the Grand Duke Mikhail Aleksandrovich until I will notify you." The reason for this request was that "we succeeded in confining the revolutionary movement within more or less reasonable limits, but the situation has not returned to normal and a civil war is still possible." Rodzyanko continued: "It might be possible that they can reconcile themselves to the regency of the grand duke and the accession of the throne to Aleksei, but his [Mikhail's] accession to the emperor is absolutely unacceptable." The chairman of the Duma Committee asked Ruzsky to take all possible measures to postpone the publication of Nicholas's abdication manifesto.

Ruzsky promised that he would do his best, but warned that he could not guarantee that he would be able to stop the dissemination of the document after so much time had already elapsed. Why, Ruzsky asked, had Guchkov and Shulgin not informed them of the real conditions in the capital? Rodzyanko said that the Duma deputies should not be blamed. It was only after their departure that, "unexpectedly," another soldiers' mutiny had broken out, this one with a destructive force the likes of which had not been seen before. The mutineers were no longer soldiers but muzhiks—simple, ignorant peasants—who had found a good opportunity to make muzhiks' demands. The crowds were shouting: "Land and liberty!" "Down with the dynasty!" "Down with the Romanovs!" "Down with the officers!" Officers were massacred in many army units, workers joined the soldiers, and anarchy had reached its climax.

To prevent the further development of anarchy, "we had to come to an agreement with the deputies of the workers . . . at night today" and were forced to promise the convocation of a Constituent Assembly "in due course" to enable the people to express their opinion about the form of government. "Only then did Petrograd take a long breath and the night passed relatively peacefully and the troops little by little came to order through the night." The proclamation of Grand Duke Mikhail as emperor, however, would pour oil onto the fire and touch off the merciless destruction of everything that could be destroyed. In that event, "power will slip out of our hands and no one could possibly allay the popular unrest."

Rodzyanko assured Ruzsky that the possibility of a return to the monarchy was not completely lost, since the people would be able to voice their opinion in its favor in the Constituent Assembly. But in the meantime, until the end of the war, the "Supreme Council" and the

Provisional Government "that is now acting with us" should continue to act. Rodzyanko was convinced that under these conditions it would be possible to restore peace, and that a decisive victory in the war would be secured, since "there is no doubt that there will be a resurgence of patriotic feeling and everyone would work with the intensified tempo, and I repeat that victory could be guaranteed."

This was the first time that Rodzyanko mentioned the "Supreme Council." It was the first hint that this Supreme Council and the Provisional Government would now rule, and the monarchy was no more, at least until the Constituent Assembly that would not be convened until the war was over.

However, Ruzsky did not seem to grasp this implication. He reiterated that although he would take measures to delay the publication of the "abdication manifesto," it would be difficult to prevent its dissemination, since its dissemination was meant to maintain peace in army units. He stated that since the tsar had already left for Mogilev the night before, further discussion about this issue would have to take place with the chief of staff of the supreme general headquarters. If the formula of abdication had to change, then this would have to be negotiated at the Stavka after the tsar arrived there.

Ruzsky then said that he had taken measures to postpone the performance of the oath at the northern front, and he promised to keep Rodzyanko informed about the performance of the oath at his front as well as at the Stavka. Here is a mystery. Why did Ruzsky postpone the ceremony of the oath of allegiance, when Alekseev had ordered front commanders to disseminate the information of Nicholas's abdication and have the military units take the oath to the new tsar, Mikhail II? Did he have any communications with someone who persuaded him to do so, or did he postpone it on his own? If the latter, what was his motivation? We have no clear answer to this mystery. Perhaps he had already concluded that the enthronement of Mikhail would not be a viable option, especially given the questionable legality of his succession.

Ruzsky then asked Lvov, at the other end of the Hughes apparatus, if he had anything to add. But Lvov did not come to the apparatus. Rodzyanko spoke for him: "Everything has been said already, and Prince Lvov has nothing to add." Did Lvov willingly concede Rodzyanko's authority above his? Was Rodzyanko afraid that Lvov might spill the beans about their intention to persuade Mikhail to refuse the throne? Did Rodzyanko want to demonstrate that the chairman of the Duma outranked the head of the Provisional Government? Or was Lvov really present with Rodzyanko at all? We have no answer to these questions either.

Though Rodzyanko attempted to end the conversation at that point, Ruzsky was unsettled. He asked one more question:

Mikhail Vladimirovich. Tell me, for the sake of clarity, whether I have understood you correctly. It means that for the present everything remains as before, as if there has been no manifesto, and likewise, there was no appointment of Prince Lvov to form a ministry? As for the appointment of Grand Duke Nikolai Niko-laevich as the supreme commander in chief by the order of His Majesty, given yesterday by the separate decree of the sovereign emperor, I would like to know also your opinion. These decrees were reported yesterday very widely, by the request of the depu-ties, even in Moscow, and of course to the Caucasus.[32]

Ruzsky must have believed that Rodzyanko's objections lay in the for-mula of transferring the throne to Mikhail and that Rodzyanko wanted to revert to the original formula of transferring the throne to Aleksei under Mikhail's regency. He had no idea that the question was not who would be the next tsar but the fate of the monarchy itself.

Rodzyanko was caught off guard, and answered evasively:

Today we have formed a government with Prince Lvov as its head, about which we sent telegrams to all the front commanders. Everything remains as follows: the Supreme Council, the responsible ministry and the legislative chambers to be active until the question of the constitution is solved by the Constituent Assembly.

Ruzsky persisted: "Tell me, who was the head of the Supreme Council?" Rodzyanko replied, "I misspoke. It was not the Supreme Council but the Temporary Committee of the State Duma [Duma Committee] under my chairmanship."[33] Still, he referred to the "Supreme Council" [*Verkhovnyi sovet*] twice in this conversation. He meant to elevate the position of the Duma Committee as the parent body of the Provisional Government.

Did Rodzyanko convey the situation in Petrograd accurately, stressing that the accession of Mikhail to the throne was likely to be the prelude to anarchy and a civil war? It is true that after Milyukov's speech, a number of incidents of illegal searches, arrests, and reprisals were carried out against officers by soldiers; as we have seen, Milyukov was forced to state that what he said was merely his personal view.[34] Colonel Lev Tugan-Baranovsky of the army General Staff, who offered his services to the Duma Committee's Military Commission, was in charge of the liaison between the Duma Committee and the insurgent soldiers. Testifying to the radical mood of the insurgents on March 2, he described how placards with the inscription "Down with the Romanovs" suddenly appeared in the Tauride Palace. According to the colonel, "a crisis was brewing; slaughter was becoming a real possibility." Anti-Romanov sentiments were so dangerous that Tugan-Baranovsky, together with other officers, suggested to Nikanor Savich, Milyukov, and Andrei Shingarev that the idea of continuing the monarchical system be abandoned.[35] Although Rodzyanko's warning about another imminent soldiers' uprising was an exaggeration, there existed the danger of further radicalization of insurgents, fanned by the news of the preservation of the monarchy.

Nevertheless, it is important to point out the source of this radicalism. Rodzyanko mentioned that the demand for "land and liberty" was growing, but this was certainly an exaggeration. In the Soviet plenary sessions, some delegates talked about landlords, and leaflets put out by the radical SR-Mezhraiontsy denounced the landlords, but the demand for land was not pronounced among the radicalized insurgents.[36] It is plausible that Rodzyanko took these inflammatory statements as a personal attack directed at him as a landlord and was frightened by them. But the discontent was centered on the insurgent soldiers, who had revolted in violation of the oath they had pledged—the oath to the tsar. They feared the officers' reprisals against them for breaking this oath. Thus, the sentiment against the Romanovs was not necessarily against the Romanovs in general, but rather against Tsar Nicholas II. It is difficult to assess the Petrograd crowds' sentiments regarding the maintenance of the monarchy, not to speak of the reaction of people in other parts of the country, and more importantly the reaction of military units. Although Milyukov was isolated within the Duma Committee and the Provisional Government, his argument for gambling on people's tsar worship had a point that should not be dismissed outright.

In any case, Rodzyanko's purpose in this conversation was to persuade Ruzsky to refrain from distributing Nicholas's "abdication manifesto." By exaggerating the danger of further radicalizing insurgents, he partially accomplished his goal: Ruzsky agreed to withhold the publication of the "manifesto" and to hold off on securing oaths from the army until further instructions from the Stavka.[37]

At 6 a.m., Rodzyanko used the Hughes apparatus to call Alekseev, awakening the chief of staff of the supreme general headquarters from only a few hours of rest; he still had a high fever. Rodzyanko said that "the events here are far from being calmed down, the situation is still alarming and unclear." He asked Alekseev not to publish any kind of manifesto until he sent along further instructions, which, he claimed, "alone can immediately stop the revolution."

Irritated with Rodzyanko's domineering tone, Alekseev answered that the Stavka had already sent the "abdication manifesto" to all the front commanders, Nikolai Nikolaevich, and commanders of armies under the front commanders. This had been a necessity, since the total lack of information had already raised many inquiries as to where their loyalty lay, what directives should be followed, and what they should uphold in the life of the troops. After he received the "manifesto" transferring the throne to Mikhail, Alekseev had sent a telegram to the chairman of the Council of Ministers to make preparations to swear the oath of allegiance to the new tsar. If this did not correspond to Rodzyanko's views, Alekseev wanted to know what Rodzyanko expected him to do, because the army needed clarity.

Rodzyanko immediately came to the point: "Wouldn't it be possible to withhold the publication of the manifesto, because the proposed combination may provoke a civil war, as the candidacy of Mikhail Aleksandrovich as emperor is unacceptable to anyone?" He explained it to Alekseev as he had explained it to Ruzsky: "What had been agreed upon before Guchkov and Shulgin's departure was the accession to the throne by Aleksei under Mikhail's regency. But this solution was not adopted, and therefore the question of what kind of government should be adopted would have to wait for the decision of the Constituent Assembly"; during the interim "the Supreme Committee [*Verkhovnyi komitet*] and the Council of Ministers" were to assume power. Rodzyanko asked Alekseev not to publish the "manifesto" until he received further instructions from Rodzyanko, hastening to add: "The decision of the Constituent Assembly does not exclude the possibility of the return of the dynasty to power, because for the further development of Russia, it is necessary for all the people to acknowledge this solution. The indignation against the regime cannot be calmed down by anything else."

Alekseev agreed, promising that he would send a supplementary telegram to withhold the publication and dissemination of the "manifesto," although he was afraid that despite his efforts the contents of the "manifesto" would become known sooner or later. "Obviously, Aleksandr Ivanovich [Guchkov] telegraphed to you the essence [of the 'manifesto'] from Pskov," the chief of staff added. "I would have preferred to have been informed by you earlier as to what should have been detained." Though he had previously been anxious to have the army swear allegiance to the new tsar, he raised no further questions or objections to Rodzyanko's request.

It was the first time that Rodzyanko had mentioned the Constituent Assembly to Alekseev. Moreover, his description of the future form of government depending on the decision of the Constituent Assembly was tantamount to saying that the monarchy had already been suspended. Rodzyanko suggested that in the interim, the "Supreme Committee" would govern. Only after Alekseev asked what this body was did Rodzyanko correct himself, saying that he meant the Duma Committee by that term. This was an intentional "mistake," just as he had done with Ruzsky earlier. Rodzyanko wished to elevate the Duma Committee as a sort of regent body, coequal with the Provisional Government, which he intentionally called the "Council of Ministers" to underscore the continuity from the old regime to the Provisional Government.

The implication of his suggestion was so stunning, sudden, and unexpected that Alekseev did not seem to grasp its magnitude. Instead, Alekseev assured Rodzyanko that, as a soldier, he concentrated all his thoughts on the struggle with the external enemy, and promised: "I will take all necessary measures to have the manifesto go no further than the commanders in chief and the commanders of the district troops."[38]

The fate of the monarchy hung on this conversation. Up to this point, Alekseev had justified Nicholas's abdication not only in the name of maintaining the cohesion of the armed forces but also as necessary for preserving the dynasty. If the monarchy was the principle that he wanted to preserve, he could have refused Rodzyanko's request and proceeded with publishing the "abdication manifesto" and administering the swearing of oaths of allegiance in all the military units. Alekseev did not seem to realize that what confronted him was the fate of the monarchy itself. He decided to accept Rodzyanko's request for the time being, and in so doing to leave the fate of the monarchy in the hands of the Duma Committee.

Before the conversation with Rodzyanko had even concluded, Alekseev sent a telegram to the front commanders. He explained that Rodzyanko had "convincingly" asked him to stop the public announcement of Nicholas II's "abdication manifesto." He asked the commanders to discuss the manifesto only with the senior commanding staff.[39] The term "convincingly" was key. Rodzyanko had successfully won Alekseev over, and the chief of staff's instructions were followed by all the fronts.[40] In response, Nikolai Nikolaevich went so far as to tell Alekseev that it had never occurred to him to make the "manifesto" public, "since it has not been published according to the legal procedure"— effectively questioning the legality of the "manifesto" itself. Later the grand duke stated that he had expected the "manifesto" to transfer the throne to Aleksei under Mikhail's regency, but that he believed the transfer of power to Mikhail would "inevitably lead to bloodbath."[41] Although Evert, of the western front, also followed Alekseev's order to withhold the distribution of the manifesto, he expressed displeasure and demanded more explanation, since already its contents had become known in some units.[42] Later that same day Alekseev would begin to harbor suspicions that Rodzyanko had come under the influence of left-wing parties.[43] But his early-morning decision to hold back news of the abdication had already granted Rodzyanko the time he needed.

At 8 a.m., the Duma delegates Guchkov and Shulgin arrived at Warsaw station in Petrograd after an overnight train ride from Pskov to find a waiting crowd alive with revolutionary energy. Though Rodzyanko had somewhat exaggerated the level of unrest to Alekseev, the reception of political figures in public could vary wildly, sometimes dangerously. The two delegates would have to be cautious, especially as they were carrying an original copy of the tsar's "abdication manifesto." Because Guchkov was a better-known public figure, he handed the document to Shulgin before the welcoming crowds surrounded them at the station and they were separated.

The stationmaster conveyed a message from Rodzyanko to Guchkov advising him not to read the "abdication manifesto" and to go straight to Princess Putyatina's apartment at Millionnaya 12 to join a meeting with Grand Duke Mikhail.[44] Unaware of Rodzyanko's message, Shulgin proceeded to deliver a passionate speech to the crowds of mostly insurgent soldiers, making a point of reading from the "abdication manifesto." He ended his speech with the words: "Long live Emperor Mikhail II!" The crowd responded to his speech with shouts of "Hurrah!"[45]

Guchkov was not so fortunate. After receiving the stationmaster's message from Rodzyanko, he was waylaid by a railway worker, who asked him to join a workers' meeting at the depot to inform them about the most recent developments. He dutifully joined the meeting but met an extremely hostile reception. A speaker, clearly a left-leaning activist, accused the Provisional Government of consisting of rich capitalists and landlords. For these radical workers, the abdication was not enough. They wanted the annihilation of the monarchy. The speaker went as far as to propose Guchkov's arrest. The crowd demanded: "Arrest him! Arrest him!"[46]

One of Lomonosov's most trusted helpers, Vladimir Nekrasov, of the Ministry of Transport's record-keeping office, intervened to rescue Guchkov. He stood on a stool and gave a passionate speech defending Guchkov and informing the crowd that he was the hero who had obtained Nicholas's abdication. The organizers of the meeting then held a conference, while Guchkov and Nekrasov were detained for twenty minutes. The workers were looking for the original abdication manifesto so that they could confiscate it and nullify the abdication. Unable to find the document on Guchkov, in the end they decided to release him and the inspector.[47] It is not clear if the organizer of this meeting had any connection with the anti-monarchist faction in the Duma Committee or in the Petrograd Soviet—for instance, with Aleksandr Kerensky, Nikolai Chkheidze, or Matvei Skobelev. But their knowing that the Duma Committee delegates possessed the original document strongly indicates some connection. Back at the station, Guchkov and Shulgin reunited, and rushed away in a car made available by a sympathetic soldier.[48] The different reactions to Shulgin and Guchkov illustrate the volatility of the crowds and the differences in the attitudes of different groups toward the monarchical system.

At 9:15 a.m. the members of the Duma Committee and the Provisional Government gathered at the luxurious apartment of Princess Putyatina at Millionnaya 12. The sumptuously furnished residence, just across the street from the Hermitage, now opened its doors to "an unspeakably strange company of people—dirty and unwashed, with creased faces, eyes red and bloodshot from sleepless nights, uncombed hair and wrinkled collars," noted Nikolai Nekrasov, a member of the Duma Committee and the Provisional Government.[49] These rumpled newcomers included several representatives of the Provisional Government (Prince Georgy Lvov, Milyukov, Kerensky, Nikolai Nekrasov, Tereshchenko, Konovalov, Ivan Vasilievich Godnev, and Vladimir Nikolaevich Lvov) and several representatives from the Duma Committee (Rodzyanko, Ivan Efremov, Mikhail Aleksandrovich Karaulov, Sergei Shidlovsky, and Vladimir Aleksandrovich Rzhevsky). Mikhail greeted them in his uniform with its lieutenant general's epaulets, emperor's monogram, and adjutant general's aiguillettes.[50] Guchkov and Shulgin, waylaid at the Warsaw station, had not yet arrived by the time the meeting started in earnest.

The majority faction spoke first, making the case that Mikhail would be safest if he rejected the throne that Nicholas had thrust upon him. Prince Lvov and Rodzyanko warned of the great personal danger he would face if he took over the throne. All the while, according to Nekrasov, "Mikhail Aleksandrovich was very calm, reserved, and proper." Nekrasov then read out the proposed text of an abdication statement that he had prepared for Mikhail.[51]

Next, Milyukov delivered the minority opinion, urging the grand duke to accept the throne. To the annoyance of everyone at the meeting, he delivered a lengthy lecture on constitutional law and the necessity of Mikhail's participation for the survival of the Provisional Government. His was the lone voice supporting this option, and his intention was clearly to prolong the meeting in order to allow Guchkov and Shulgin to arrive and give their support.

Guchkov and Shulgin finally arrived as these speeches were still ongoing, though the arguments that they walked in on were completely unfamiliar to them. Guchkov could not believe his ears; something must have happened during the night. The participants called for a recess, and Guchkov took Godnev out of the room to ask what had happened. Godnev caught him up on the overnight meetings, at which revolutionary tempers had grown tense and all kinds of deputations had been sent to the Duma Committee. Now Milyukov was the only one who still insisted on Mikhail assuming the throne.[52]

After the recess, Kerensky was first to mount a rebuttal against Milyukov's position, and he did not mince words:

Your Highness. I am by conviction a republican. I am against a monarchy. . . . Permit me to speak to you as a Russian to a Russian. Pavel Nikolaevich [Milyukov] is wrong. By assuming the throne, you do not save Russia. I know the mood of the masses—the workers and the soldiers. At present sharp dissatisfaction is directed at the monarchy. Precisely this issue will become the cause for bloodshed.

At the end of his peroration Kerensky threateningly reminded the grand duke: "I cannot vouch for the life of Your Highness."[53] Of all of the participants, he was the only one who could speak on behalf of the insurgents. He claimed that he represented the insurgent masses, unlike all the others there, who belonged to the propertied class. And the menace he expressed was unmistakable, as if he had pointed a gun at the grand duke's temple.[54]

When Guchkov spoke, his words were far from what Milyukov would have hoped for. He acknowledged that there were reasons to fear assuming the throne, but if the grand duke was afraid to take up the burden of the imperial crown, then he should at least agree to exercise supreme authority as the regent during the vacancy of the throne.[55] It was a proposition that no one took seriously—it would have been nearly impossible to renegotiate the matter with Nicholas, and if Mikhail assumed the regency, ignoring the "abdication manifesto," the effect would still be to suspend the monarchy and vacate the throne. Milyukov had counted on Guchkov's support, and his change of heart revealed that the pro-monarchist camp was weak and divided. Unlike the unholy alliance of Rodzyanko, Lvov, and Kerensky, the pro-monarchist camp had had no time for prior consultation.

Mikhail then asked for Shulgin's opinion. The leader of the Nationalist Party replied that with the majority of the Provisional Government members opposed to Mikhail's assumption of the throne, he did not dare to advise the grand duke otherwise.[56] Having already accepted Nicholas's change of heart on the spur of the moment at Pskov, Guchkov and Shulgin turned on a dime once again.

Deserted by his erstwhile allies, Milyukov attempted a final response. He acknowledged the risks to Mikhail's personal safety but offered that there was still the possibility of gathering the military force necessary to protect the grand duke. The government could move to Moscow, assemble reliable military forces, and march against revolutionary Petrograd. With his white hair disheveled and his face gray from lack of sleep, Milyukov "croaked" in a hoarse voice for a long time, more than an hour, without anyone interrupting him.[57] What he was describing, to the alarm of his colleagues, was nothing less than a civil war—something that everyone wanted to avoid.

Mikhail grew impatient before Milyukov's remarks had concluded, and now asked for half an hour to deliberate the matter quietly by himself. As he retired, Kerensky leaped up and called out: "Promise us not to consult your wife." The grand duke answered with a smile: "Don't worry, Aleksandr Fyodorovich, my wife isn't here at the moment. She stayed behind at Gatchina."[58] In fact, Mikhail was living under virtual house arrest, with only his secretary, Nikolai Johnson, and an administrator, Aleksei Matveev. As he spent a half hour contemplating the fate of the Russian monarchy, he could not consult his wife, his brother, any of his other relatives, the Stavka, or any other military leaders.[59]

A few minutes later the grand duke invited Rodzyanko and Prince Lvov to his room. As Rodzyanko headed toward the grand duke's private room, he already knew the decision that was coming, and whispered, "He cannot reign, and he knows it."[60] During the minutes that followed, Guchkov attempted to telephone his wife to assure her of his safe return from Pskov, but in a reflection of the tension that filled the apartment, he was immediately interrogated by a suspicious Kerensky, who demanded to know whom he was trying to call and why.[61]

There are two versions of what happened in the room between Mikhail, Rodzyanko, and Lvov as Mikhail decided whether he would save the monarchy or let it fall. Rodzyanko's version, perhaps unsurprisingly, is more critical. He claimed that Mikhail had a single question: whether his life would be guaranteed if he accepted the throne. Rodzyanko bluntly answered in the negative. In his telling, Mikhail then and there made up his mind to refuse the throne.[62] Milyukov laconically commented: "At the base of it one did not sense love or anxiety for Russia, but only the grand duke's fear for himself."[63] This is a patently unfair interpretation. Mikhail's courage in battle was well known; he had been decorated with a St. George's Cross for it.

A kinder telling of this exchange comes to us from Countess Lyudmila Nikolaevna Vorontsova-Dashkova, who spoke directly with the grand duke after this momentous meeting. She heard from Johnson that when Mikhail asked Rodzyanko if he could count on the Petrograd garrison if he took the throne, Rodzyanko answered negatively. She explained that it was not Mikhail's desire to save his own life alone but the fear of civil war and the accompanying bloodshed that might result from the decision to take power that weighed on him. She believed that no one who surrounded him had the iron determination to persuade him to take power. For good measure, Mikhail was suffering from a stomach ulcer, and his health played a role as well.[64]

With his two closest political contacts—Rodzyanko and Prince Lvov—recommending against assuming the throne, and even speaking openly of civil war, it is hard to imagine Mikhail deciding otherwise. He was fully aware that the succession was illegal, that the other grand dukes opposed his assumption of power, and that he could not rally the nation with personality alone.[65] Most of all, neither he nor his wife wanted him to become tsar.[66]

At one o'clock in the afternoon on March 3, Mikhail reentered the room where the members of the Duma Committee and the Provisional Government were anxiously waiting. He announced: "Under these circumstances I cannot assume the throne." According to Shulgin, he could not finish the sentence, because he was crying.[67]

The 304-year Romanov rule had come to an end.

Technically, Mikhail did not renounce the throne, but merely refused to assume the throne until it was determined whether the will of the people was to preserve the monarchical system—a decision that would have to have been made at the Constituent Assembly. After this decision, his close friend Countess Vorontsova-Dashkova consoled him: "I am sure that the Constituent Assembly will call you back." Mikhail responded: "I don't think so." Later Mikhail told Shulgin: "My brother abdicated for himself. But I, it turned out, abdicated for everyone."[68] He knew that his decision marked the end of the monarchy.[69]

Kerensky, overwhelmed with joy, said to the grand duke: "Your Royal Highness, you have acted nobly and like a patriot. I assume the obligation of making this known and of defending you."[70] It was not the last time Kerensky made a promise that he could not keep.

The rest of the assembled group did not share in Kerensky's happiness. Nekrasov confessed: "I was a passionate supporter of abdication, but when the moment came, I felt all the weight of this decision fall on my shoulders."[71]

Already, concerns about Rodzyanko's dishonesty were coming to a head. As all of this was playing out, Alekseev instructed the Stavka's Naval Staff to assess the veracity of Rodzyanko's information. The Naval Staff in Petrograd returned with astonishing information that strongly contradicted Rodzyanko's depiction of the situation in the capital. According to the chief of naval administration, Flag Captain Vasily Mikhailovich Altfater, in Petrograd "the situation is rather quiet, and everything is gradually returning to normal." At the Stavka, Senior Lieutenant V. G. Goncharov asked about the rumor that a slaughter of officers had taken place on the previous day. Altfater answered: "It is all sheer nonsense." Altfater further told the Stavka that the authority of the Duma Committee was increasing rather than diminishing.[72]

Alekseev had already harbored suspicions that Rodzyanko was not altogether candid, but because of the lack of contradictory information, he had accepted his recommendations on the withdrawal of General Ivanov's troops and Nicholas's abdication. Although he had been skeptical about Rodzyanko's further demand to withhold the "manifesto" of Nicholas's abdication, he had nonetheless complied by ordering all the front commanders not to make it public.[73] Now it was clear that Rodzyanko had been manipulating information all along and that Alekseev and the military had been duped.

Shortly after noon, the Stavka received the information that Mikhail had decided not to assume the throne.[74] Alekseev took immediate action. Between 1:27 and 1:40 p.m. on March 3, he dispatched a telegram to the commanders of all fronts except Nikolai Nikolaevich. In this telegram, Alekseev began by outlining the conversation he had had with Rodzyanko and the conversation between Rodzyanko and Ruzsky, a copy of which he had just received. Alekseev pointed out that the "manifesto" had already been widely distributed, and insisted that such an important document, intended for the public, should not be kept secret. Indeed, he informed them, the alleged "concealment" of the document—an action Admiral Adrian Nepenin, commander of the Baltic Fleet, did not desire—had already led to an uprising of sailors against the officers in the Baltic Fleet.[75]

Alekseev then unloaded on Rodzyanko. He first reported that there was no unity within the Duma or within the Duma Committee, as Rodzyanko had claimed, and that the radicals of the Petrograd Soviet were acquiring strong influence. Second, "the left-wing parties and the workers' deputies are exerting tremendous pressure on Rodzyanko" and that "Rodzyanko has provided information without frankness or sincerity." Third, the political solution proposed by Rodzyanko emanated from the aims of the left-wing parties, who had essentially taken Rodzyanko as their hostage. Fourth, the troops of the Petrograd garrison had finally fallen completely under the influence of the propaganda of the workers' deputies and had become "harmful and dangerous to all, including the moderate elements of the Provisional Committee." Clearly, Alekseev considered Rodzyanko's deception to be motivated solely by left-wing influence, failing to recognize or choosing not to recognize that it stemmed from the Duma chairman's own political calculations. Further, characterizing Rodzyanko's information as deceptive, Alekseev concluded that "the outlined situation constituted a danger more serious than any other for the active army," since he expected that the uncertainty resulting from Rodzyanko's meddling would deprive the army of "the fighting capacity," resulting in "the hopeless misery of Russia, territorial loss, and the takeover by the extreme left elements." Conspicuous was the absence of any reference to the preservation of the monarchy, which up to this time he had repeatedly emphasized as the core principle that the army should uphold.

He concluded by demanding the implementation of Nicholas's "abdication manifesto" and calling for a conference of the front commanders on March 8 or 9.[76] This proposal for a military conference appears to suggest that his intention was, ostensibly, to revive the plan of military intervention or establishment of a military dictatorship against Petrograd. He concluded by once again condemning Rodzyanko as untrustworthy, warning of the influence of extreme elements, and urging the front commanders to consult with the heads of army groups under their authority about the situation.[77]

Ruzsky later noted, on a copy of this telegram, Lukomsky's words: "Adjutant General Alekseev, after dispatching this telegram, went back to his office, and said: 'I will never forgive myself for having believed the sincerity of some people, for listening to them, and for sending the telegram to the front commanders with regard to the emperor's abdication from the throne.'"[78]

Remarkably, though Mikhail's decision to refuse the throne had prompted Alekseev to dispatch this telegram, the telegram said nothing to the front commanders about that fact. He could have ordered the front commanders to release Nicholas's "abdication manifesto" widely and have the military units swear allegiance to the new tsar, Mikhail II. He did not do that.

Why did Alekseev withhold crucial information about Mikhail's decision, and why did his orders go no further than proposing a conference to discuss next steps? Most likely, he knew that his front commanders were divided, and he feared that unilateral action would lead to further disagreements. Pitting the monarchist faction against the anti-monarchist faction would doom the armed forces. And Alekseev considered the cohesion of the armed forces more important than anything else, even the preservation of the monarchy. He would try to salvage the monarchical system, but if his choice was between the integrity of the armed forces and the monarchy, he would jettison the monarchy itself.

But he would not do it alone. As chief of staff, Alekseev had spent the past few extraordinary days crafting a consensus among the front commanders: first to shift from advocating a ministry of confidence to supporting the idea of a responsible ministry, and then to urging Nicholas's abdication. But if events demanded that the commanders betray their oath of allegiance and bury the monarchy for good, they would have to bear the blame collectively. In the end, Alekseev's telegram to the front commanders was a cleverly constructed attempt to shift the blame of slaying the monarchical system from himself to the collective action of the high command.

At 3 p.m. Alekseev asked Rodzyanko to talk to him directly through the Hughes apparatus.[79] But the Duma Committee chairman refused to talk to Alekseev. Presumably Alekseev was going to ask Rodzyanko to release Nicholas's "abdication manifesto," as he had promised in his telegram to the front commanders. But he already knew that Mikhail had refused to assume the throne, and therefore he must have anticipated the negative reaction from Rodzyanko. Then what would he do? Had he insisted on the release of the "manifesto," it would have meant a major confrontation with the Provisional Government, and he would likely back down again.

In the meantime, Alekseev received the responses from the front commanders. Their reactions to Alekseev's proposal were largely negative.

Ruzsky sent a telegram to his army commanders strictly forbidding them to make the "manifesto" public and, above all, forbidding them to conduct the oath of allegiance under any circumstances.[80] He opposed Alekseev's proposal to convene a military conference to consider military action against the Provisional Government. In his opinion, the military should come to terms with the Provisional Government. Since the military was the only authoritative power in places other than Petrograd, the front commanders should remain at their posts.[81]

Though Sakharov agreed with Alekseev's proposal to convene a conference, he was the only commander to do so. He remained silent about the wisdom of military intervention, although he pointed out the danger of making further concessions to the liberals.[82]

The Stavka did not receive Evert's telegram until 8 p.m., by which time he must have learned of Mikhail's decision to decline the throne. In the telegram Evert summarized the views expressed by his three army commanders, who were unhappy with the tsar's "abdication manifesto" but also displeased with the available options. Commander Vladimir Vasilievich Smirnov of the Second Army believed that any suppression of information would negatively affect the army. Nikolai Nikolaevich's attendance at the conference would be essential. Commander Leonid Vilgelmovich Lesh of the Third Army considered the front commanders' meeting of March 8 or 9 too late, arguing that it was necessary to determine right away the form the government would take and inform the army frankly about this decision. Although the news of Nicholas's abdication was announced in some places, it would be nonetheless better to withhold it for the time being. According to Commander Vladimir Nikolaevich Gorbatovsky of the Tenth Army, the transfer of the throne to Mikhail would not lead to peace in the army and the country. It would be better to transfer the throne to Aleksei under the regency of Nikolai Nikolaevich instead of Mikhail. The commanders' responses made clear that Mikhail would have little chance of being accepted by the army if he agreed to take the throne.

Evert spelled his view out plainly: The election of a Constituent Assembly would plunge the country into prolonged anarchy, since the troops would no doubt demand their voice, disrupting the urgent task of fighting against the external enemy. Nevertheless, the absence of an official announcement would also lead to unrest in the army. Under the pressing circumstances, the only alternative would be to appeal to the emperor to change the form of government by imperial decree and to have this change accepted by the Duma and the Provisional Government. If this could not be done, Evert continued, the commanders should ask the tsar to free the front commanders from the responsibility to conduct war against the enemy. The collective declaration to this effect should be issued right away, at least not later than the following morning.

This was unrealistic in the extreme. There was no possibility of Alekseev, Ruzsky, and Brusilov voluntarily resigning from their posts. Evert further suggested that in any case, he too thought that the proposed conference on March 8 or 9 would be too late.[83] Alekseev censored Evert's telegram, since "it was no longer appropriate to the newly established state order at the time when we received it."[84] Clearly, Alekseev was never serious about his proposal for a military conference or making the "manifesto" public. He had already accepted the authority of the Provisional Government, and this exchange of telegrams with the commanders was merely cover.

In a direct conversation with Alekseev, Brusilov dismissed the notion of a conference, since the army could not remain in uncertainty any longer. He advocated for the Stavka to announce that the emperor had abdicated and that the Duma Committee had taken over the governing of the state. It was time for the military to accept the end of the monarchy and pledge allegiance to the Provisional Government.[85] Despite Alekseev's advice to the front commanders to consult army commanders under their command, Brusilov kept all the information about Nicholas's double abdication and Mikhail's refusal to assume the throne from his army commanders, including General Gurko.

Brusilov's objections virtually put an end to discussion of Alekseev's idea of rallying the front commanders to accept Nicholas's "abdication manifesto," acknowledge Mikhail as the new tsar, and hold a military conference to decide whether to return to the policy of military intervention against Petrograd or establish a military dictatorship. It is likely that this was what Alekseev had expected all along. Once Mikhail renounced the throne, Alekseev had no choice but to accept the end of the monarchy. Now he had convincing proof that the armed forces were united behind that decision. Alekseev could rest assured that history would not remember him as the gravedigger for autocracy.

The final obstacle was Grand Duke Nikolai Nikolaevich. Nicholas's last act had been to appoint the grand duke as the military's supreme commander. But when Nikolai Nikolaevich received the text of Nicholas's "abdication manifesto," he grew concerned and asked the Stavka to have Rodzyanko explain the circumstances behind this document.[86] He knew that the double abdication was a violation of the succession law. Besides, he did not think much of Mikhail. Perhaps he may have thought that if the throne was to be transferred to someone, he should have it.

The Stavka learned early in the afternoon that Mikhail had decided to refuse to accept the throne, and Alekseev had been attempting to reach Rodzyanko all day to ascertain the accuracy of this information, but Rodzyanko refused to come to the Hughes apparatus. Finally, at 6 p.m., it was Guchkov, not Rodzyanko, who appeared at the Hughes apparatus in the war minister's residence. Alekseev demanded that the "manifesto" of Nicholas's abdication be made public immediately and that the Provisional Government promptly take measures to enable the soldiers of the active army to take an oath of allegiance to the new emperor. Alekseev was making a last-ditch attempt to save the monarchy by having the army swear allegiance to the new tsar, Mikhail II. To this, Guchkov replied:

The manifesto of March 2 was given to me by the emperor last night at Pskov. Its promulgation met with difficulties in Petrograd because Grand Duke Mikhail Aleksandrovich, who consulted with the members of the Council of Ministers, decided to renounce the throne despite my and Milyukov's opinions. It is supposed that the manifestos of March 2 and March 3—the refusal of Mikhail Aleksandrovich—will be promulgated simultaneously. The promulgation of the two manifestos will be made during the night. The Provisional Government will remain in power with Prince Lvov at its head and with the composition which is already known to you until the convocation of a constituent assembly.[87]

Alekseev attempted to change Guchkov's mind: "Is it not possible to persuade the grand duke to accept the power temporarily until the convocation of the Constituent Assembly?" He emphasized that to maintain the cohesion and morale of the army, the retention of the monarchical system would be essential. Guchkov agreed with Alekseev but stated that no one else believed him and that the decision of the grand duke was voluntary and final.[88]

It appears that at this point Alekseev finally gave up. It should be remembered that while Alekseev was negotiating with the Duma Committee, he was receiving news about the Baltic Fleet, where the insurrection was spreading to all ships. Furthermore, the Petrograd Telegraph Agency informed the Stavka that one city after another had declared allegiance to the Duma Committee. In addition, he had to worry about the pro-monarchy officers starting a movement to defend the deposed tsar. He needed to make a quick decision to avert the crisis and saw no other way out except to submit to the authority of the Duma Committee and the Provisional Government. Alekseev decided to concentrate all his energy on a single goal—the preservation of the active army.[89]

Later in the evening, at 6:22 p.m., Nikolai Nikolaevich sent a telegram to Alekseev. He argued that it should be he, as the supreme commander, not any collective meeting of the front commanders, who should serve as the voice of the army and the navy. But after this brave pronouncement, the grand duke said that he could not attend the meeting suggested by Alekseev, since he would need several days for orientation as the new supreme commander under the new government. Now fully aware of Rodzyanko's formation of the Provisional Government, he said that he had already made contact with "the chairman of the Council of Ministers to let him know the course of events so that he could express his views on what measures, acceptable to both, should be taken in the front and the rear." In reference to the abdication, he was dismissive: "As far as the information given by you this morning about the manifesto of transferring the throne to Grand Duke Mikhail Aleksandrovich, it would inevitably provoke bloodshed [*reznia*]. In addition, its revision and no mention of the heir to the throne could undoubtedly cause complications." As for the Constituent Assembly, the grand duke considered it completely unacceptable.[90]

Certainly there would be no military conference, and no military action against the Provisional Government, if they did not have Nikolai Nikolaevich's support. It would be impossible to save the Romanovs if the most important remaining member of the dynasty refused to participate in the effort.

It is possible that Nikolai Nikolaevich may not have recognized that he had co-signed the death knell of the monarchy. He issued Order No. 1 on the evening of March 3, which pronounced: "As far as you are concerned, you miraculous heroes, super-valiant knights of the Russian land, I know how much you are ready to give for the good of Russia and the *Throne*" (italics added).[91]

Having received Nikolai Nikolaevich's order, at 8:25 p.m. on March 3 Alekseev notified the front commanders and chief of Naval Staff of the grand duke's appointment as supreme commander, of the names of ministers of the Provisional Government, and of the news that the emperor, Nicholas II, in agreement with the Duma, would announce a new form of government.[92] This still did not say anything about the "manifestos" of Nicholas's abdication or of Mikhail's renunciation of the throne. But at 9:16 p.m. Alekseev sent a copy of Nikolai Nikolaevich's telegram to Rodzyanko and let the Duma Committee chairman know that the grand duke had accepted the authority of the new government.[93] This represented the final capitulation of Nikolai Nikolaevich and Alekseev to the authority of the Provisional Government.

On March 4, Alekseev would send another telegram to Nikolai Nikolaevich. Outlining his conversation with Rodzyanko, the chief of staff would tell Nikolai Nikolaevich that Grand Duke Mikhail had agreed to convene the Constituent Assembly and that the two "manifestos" of abdication would be published. He would add: "I believe that although the second manifesto referring to the Constituent Assembly is pregnant with danger and adverse consequences, it was impossible to reverse what had happened."[94] It is interesting to note that Alekseev was referring to Mikhail's "manifesto" as the document that called for the convocation of the Constituent Assembly without making the point that it was the document in which the grand duke declined to accept the throne, and thus it marked the end of the monarchy. He also said that Mikhail agreed to convene the Constituent Assembly, which was not exactly true. What was true was that Mikhail refused to assume the throne until the Constituent Assembly made a decision on the form of the government. This crucial difference obscured the importance of Mikhail's decision: suspension of the monarchical system until the Constituent Assembly. Alekseev was trying his best to minimize the implication of Mikhail's refusal to assume the throne.

As the March 3 meeting in Princess Putyatina's apartment broke up, the members of the Duma Committee and the Provisional Government had yet to make some sort of public statement announcing Mikhail's refusal to assume the throne. After so many sleepless nights, no one was in any physical or mental condition to compose a coherent statement. Most of the meeting's participants had already declined the princess's invitation to breakfast and left. The responsibility now fell to two jurists: Vladimir Dmitrievich Nabokov (father of famous writer Vladimir Nabokov), of the General Staff at Petrograd, and Baron Boris Emmanuilovich Nolde, in the Ministry of Foreign Affairs. Shulgin remained behind to assist them in composing the proclamation.

At a tiny desk in the children's room in the apartment, the three set out to write a draft for Mikhail's signature. The most important question that occupied the attention of the three was its political implication. Nabokov stated elliptically:

Under the conditions of the moment, it appeared to be essential to utilize this act, without limiting ourselves to its negative aspect, to confirm solemnly *the plenitude of power of the Provisional Government and its continuing tie with the State Duma*. (Italics added)

Nabokov's reference to the "negative aspect" surely meant the clear illegality of the succession. The most important task for these two lawyers was to ignore the law and endow the Provisional Government with a legal and institutional link to the monarchical regime that it had replaced. For this purpose, they crafted a crucial phrase: "I ask all citizens of the Russian State to pledge allegiance to the Provisional Government, which came into being at the initiative of the State Duma and which is endowed with full power." A handwritten note in French survives, revealing that Bazili, at the Stavka, was also consulted during the composition of this document, though his proposed revisions were not accepted. That he was consulted at all attests to the fact that Alekseev's maneuverings in the afternoon and evening of March 3 were prompted by his knowledge that the monarchy was endangered.[95]

When the final draft was sent to the grand duke for approval, he asked for only three revisions. The royal "We" was changed to "I," since the grand duke insisted that he had not assumed the throne. The verb "command" was changed to "ask." Lastly, Mikhail inserted a reference to God, whom Shulgin and the two jurists had forgotten all about.[96]

After the draft was approved by Mikhail and the Provisional Government at the Tauride Palace, Nabokov handwrote a final copy and Mikhail signed it, though there was no countersignature to certify Mikhail's signature. The death certificate of the Romanov monarchy was written at a child's desk in Princess Putyatina's apartment. It is important to note that this handwritten document, with no official certification, no official seal, and no countersignature, could hardly be considered a legally binding, official document, although the Provisional Government and the Duma Committee treated it as if it were.

The Duma Committee and Provisional Government settled on a plan for breaking the news to the public. They would issue the two "manifestos," Nicholas's and Mikhail's, side by side without any reference to what agency or institution had issued them. Before all was said and done, Milyukov and Nabokov had a heated argument over whether Mikhail should be identified as the emperor. Milyukov insisted that the moment Nicholas abdicated, the throne had been transferred to Mikhail. To him it was important that the Provisional Government was anointed by the emperor and that the printed "manifesto" should identify Mikhail as such. Nabokov countered that doing so would not only invite suspicion from the members of the imperial family but also highlight the illegal decision by Nicholas II to transfer supreme power to Mikhail. After a long discussion, Milyukov finally yielded, accepting that Mikhail's statement simply declined the assumption of the throne.[97] Mikhail's "manifesto" was not to be the manifesto of his abdication.

Late on the night of March 3, the two newspapers in Petrograd— *Izvestiya of the Petrograd Soviet* and *Izvestiya of the Committee of Petrograd*

*Journalists*—printed special issues in which large Gothic headlines told the sensational news of the "abdications" of Nicholas and Mikhail.

The two "manifestos" were sent to the Ministry of Transport printing press, where typesetters had been waiting for the text to arrive. They had grown frustrated by the long wait for this unexplained assignment, but Lomonosov bought their patience by giving them extra payment for a free lunch. When Lomonosov went to the printing press and read the "manifesto" to the waiting typesetters, they listened to him intently. One old man crossed himself.[98]

All of Lomonosov's care mattered little, however, since by 3 p.m. the Petrograd Soviet had already circulated leaflets announcing: "Nicholas II abdicated in favor of his brother, and the latter in turn abdicated in favor of the people."[99] The Petrograd Soviet beat the Duma Committee and the Provisional Government once again on this issue.

Wasting no time, on the afternoon of March 3 the Provisional Government had its first official meeting, pointedly not including any Duma Committee members, nor even Rodzyanko.[100] Aware of the need to settle the complex relationship between the Provisional Government, the Fundamental Laws, and the Duma Committee, the ministers were not shy, and resolved that "the entire plenitude of power that belonged to the monarch must be considered transferred, not to the State Duma, but to the Provisional Government." Further, it resolved:

There is no basis to suppose that the Provisional Government can take measures of legislative character [only] when the Duma is not in session by applying Article 87 of the Fundamental Laws, since after the just completed revolution in the state the Fundamental Laws of the Russian State must be considered invalid.[101]

In a stroke, the Provisional Government had established itself as a dictatorship answering to no other institution or law. Not only had the Provisional Government declared itself the inheritor of the emperor's power, but by denouncing the Duma and the State Council as relics of the old regime, it dismissed the limits previously imposed by the legislative chambers. As mentioned above, Nabokov and Nolde inserted two principles: the Provisional Government was endowed with "the plenitude of power," and it had been created at the initiative of the Duma. The resolution of the Provisional Government's first meeting amounted to accepting only the first principle and throwing away the second.

The boldness of the Provisional Government would not stand. The Provisional Government could not disregard the Fundamental Laws, and under Rodzyanko, the Duma continued to function for a while longer. Yakov Vasilievich Glinka, who was the administrative secretary of the Duma Committee and took over the administrative secretaryship for the Provisional Government, refused to endorse this decision, and the resolution made at the first meeting was not printed in the official publication of the Provisional Government. But in attempting to sever institutional continuity with the Duma in its very first meeting, the Provisional Government had embarked upon treacherous waters without any compass or ballast.[102]

March 3 brought a blizzard to Tsarskoe Selo, where the empress took care of her sick children and fretted about Nicholas. The day before, the troops that guarded the imperial palace had deserted, and electricity and water were cut off. Olga's and Tatiana's conditions were growing worse.[103] As household servants arrived by foot from Petrograd, rumors started to spread about the abdication. By four o'clock, Benckendorff felt that it was his duty to tell the empress about the rumor on everyone's lips. Alexandra did not believe it. No one else in the entourage had the courage to tell her, even when, at five o'clock in the afternoon, the printed newspaper sheets announcing Nicholas's abdication and Mikhail's renunciation of the throne first arrived at the palace.

Only at 7 p.m. did Grand Duke Pavel arrive and give Alexandra the grim news. The empress received him in a hospital nurse's uniform, and when he told her the facts, "the Empress trembled and bent down her head, as though she were uttering a prayer."[104]

Having prodded her husband all along to stand firm for autocracy, she now accepted Nicholas's decision without question. Her heart broke that he had had to take this agonizing decision by himself, without her. Not yet familiar with the details of Nicholas's abdication, she trembled at the thought that Aleksei would be taken away from her "under some kind of 'regency.'"[105] When Count Benckendorff, Baroness Buxhoeveden, and Count Apraksin came to see her later that evening, she was in tears. She told them that "the Emperor had preferred to abdicate the crown rather than to *break the oath which [he had taken] at his coronation to maintain and to transfer to his heir the autocracy such as he had inherited it from his father*" (emphasis in original). In French, she went on: "It is for the better. It was the will of God. God has given what saves Russia. That is the only thing that matters."[106]

She wrote a memo to Baroness Buxhoeveden: "There is nothing I would not do! Let them kill me, put me in a convent--only that the Emperor should be safe and should be with his children again."[107]

The children's conditions got worse. Tatiana was suffering terribly from earaches and had temporarily become deaf. Anastasia developed abscesses, and her ears throbbed with pain. And finally, Maria, who had assisted her mother heroically, succumbed to the measles, with a high fever and a rash all over her body. She became so seriously ill that Dr. Evgeny Sergeevich Botkin feared that she might not survive. She lay in bed imagining that soldiers were coming to kill her mother. In a way, the children's illnesses kept Alexandra busy, distracting her from her distress over Nicholas's abdication.

As the servants and court officials one by one deserted the empress and her family, a few loyal subjects came to support the imperial family in distress. Count Adam Stanislavovich Zamoisky, the emperor's aide-de-camp, whom the empress hardly knew, came all the way from Petrograd, part of the way on foot. Colonel Aleksandr Linevich, another aide-de-camp for the emperor, also came to protect the imperial family. He was sent to negotiate with Rodzyanko to secure the safety of the imperial family, but on the way to Petrograd, he was arrested. A squadron of horse guards traveled two days from Novgorod to Tsarskoe Selo in the bitter cold. At the gate of the palace, they were told that they had come too late; there was no emperor anymore to defend. Dejected, they left quietly. These exceptions aside, those who came to support the former holders of the monarchy were few and far between.[108]

CHAPTER 13

# Arrests and Reunion

After Nicholas signed the manifesto of his abdication, he set out on yet another railway journey. Leaving Pskov at 2 a.m. on March 3, he would pass through Dvinsk, Polotsk, Vitebsk, and Orsha over the course of the nearly twenty-one hours he spent en route to Mogilev. On his first day as a former emperor, he woke to a sunny but frosty day. In his diary he wrote, "Had a long and sound sleep," and spent the hours reading a book about Julius Caesar and talking with his entourage about "yesterday."[1]

From a small station, Sirotino, near Vitebsk, he sent a telegram to Mikhail:

To Your Imperial Highness Mikhail, Petrograd.

The events of the past days forced Me to take this irreversible extreme step. Forgive Me if this grieved you and for not forewarning you. We will forever be your faithful and devoted Brother. Am returning to the Stavka, and hope from there in a few days to get back to Tsarskoe Selo. Fervently pray may God help You and Your Fatherland. Niki[2]

The last time he had communicated with Mikhail, it was when his brother had begged him to grant a ministry of confidence, a suggestion he rejected outright. Now he had thrust the throne at Mikhail without any prior consultation with him, without one iota of doubt that he was going to accept it. In any event, this telegram never reached Mikhail.[3] Still focused on isolating the grand duke, the Provisional Government intended to confiscate all communications between Nicholas and Mikhail.

Having maintained decorum and civility throughout the painful negotiations with the Duma Committee delegates, not even revealing his true feelings in his diary, the former tsar could only keep his self-composure for so long. After the train left Sirotino, when Vladimir Voeikov entered Nicholas's dark salon, Nicholas seized the opportunity to embrace the man and bury his head in his chest.[4] One can imagine how much he wished to be in the embrace of Alexandra instead at that moment.

On Adjutant General Mikhail Alekseev's instructions, Bazili met with Nicholas sixty-eight kilometers north of Mogilev, two hours before his long journey's end.[5] After boarding the gold-trimmed blue car of the imperial train at Orsha, Bazili was led to the emperor's compartment. "His face and his small beard were as carefully groomed as ever," Bazili wrote. "His expression was absolutely calm, and betrayed no trace of emotion. The look in his fine blue eyes was affable as always."[6]

Alekseev's intention in arranging this meeting between Bazili and Nicholas was surely to be certain that Nicholas grasped that with Mikhail's refusal to assume the throne, the monarchy had ended.[7] The general wanted to make sure that Nicholas would not change his mind again.[8] The former tsar received the news from Bazili impassively, responding to each piece of information with the words "But yes, naturally [Nu da, konechno]." He did not express any astonishment at the turn of events. In the end, when Bazili ventured to say that he should have accepted Alekseev's recommendation and abdicated in favor of his son, Nicholas simply replied: "You know that my son is ill. I could not separate myself from him."[9]

Bazili left, impressed by Nicholas's "dignity" and "stoicism." But this demeanor was a misdirection. Bazili did not realize that Nicholas had indeed changed his mind again. He now decided to abdicate only for himself in favor of his son, Aleksei—the formula that the Duma Committee had advocated before Nicholas changed his mind during the talks with Aleksandr Guchkov and Vasily Shulgin. According to General Anton Ivanovich Denikin, who later worked closely with Alekseev in the White Army during the Civil War, Nicholas wrote this decision out on a piece of paper with a pencil. If this is true and Nicholas did change his mind, it is likely that this decision was prompted by Bazili's news about Mikhail's renunciation of the throne.[10]

As the imperial trains approached Mogilev, the higher echelon of officers of the Stavka assembled at the railway station. All the generals, staff officers, and ranked administrators of the Stavka were invited to greet the former tsar. On that gray, cold, and depressing March 3, when snowflakes were falling, about thirty officers of the Stavka waited in the massive imperial pavilion. As soon as they received the news that the imperial train had left the station closest to Mogilev, they went out on the platform, with the senior officer at the front. The train slowly moved into the station. When it stopped, Alekseev stepped into Nicholas's salon car.[11]

The deposed emperor handed the general a piece of paper on which he had penciled his new decision to transfer the throne to Aleksei after all. He asked Alekseev to send it to Mikhail Rodzyanko. Alekseev must have been stunned. He had sent Bazili to the imperial train precisely to make sure that the deposed tsar realized that he could not change his mind again. The two "manifestos"—Nicholas's abdication and Mikhail's refusal to assume the throne—had been published in two newspapers, and they had already been widely circulated in the form of broadsheets.[12] Events had moved quickly, and it was impossible to turn the clock back now. Alekseev took the paper Nicholas had given him and put it in his pocket.[13]

Alekseev then descended from the car first, and Nicholas followed. They embraced on the platform. But, for the first time, no one sang "God Save the Tsar." Then the deposed tsar walked past the senior officers assembled on the platform. According to Bazili:

> In silence he saluted each one of us with a handshake, looking into our eyes. All were greatly moved, and stifled sobs could be heard. The emperor kept his apparent calm. From time to time, he threw back his head in a movement customary to him. A few tears formed in the corners of his eyes and he brushed them away with a gesture of his hand.[14]

A waiting car then drove him to the governor's house, which remained as it had been when he was the emperor.[15] After Nicholas had tea, Alekseev brought him the two "manifestos," and the scope of what was happening finally dawned on the former tsar. He wrote in his diary:

> Alekseev brought the latest news from Rodzyanko. It turned out that Misha abdicated. His manifesto ends with four-tailed voting in 6 months for the election of the Constituent Assembly. God knows who forced him to sign such rubbish! In Petrograd the disturbance has stopped. Only hope that this will last further.[16]

He blamed his brother. But nowhere was there any sign of regret or reflection on his own responsibility for bringing about this tragic end.

While Alekseev was reporting to the deposed tsar, at 10 p.m. Rodzyanko finally called the Stavka on the Hughes apparatus. Alekseev's quartermaster general, Aleksandr Lukomsky, told Rodzyanko that "if the Chairman of the State Duma can transmit to me what he wants to tell General

Alekseev, I can take your call." Rodzyanko answered: "The situation is serious. When will General Alekseev return and come to the apparatus?" Lukomsky answered that Nicholas had arrived in Mogilev and summoned Alekseev to his car at the station. "But I could answer all the questions," Lukomsky continued, "if it is all right for you to ask me these questions you want him to answer." Lukomsky's tone indicated the depth of anger that Alekseev and his subordinate officers at the Stavka felt against Rodzyanko.

Eager to offset his loss of influence in the Provisional Government by appealing to the military, Rodzyanko reported to Lukomsky that things were getting calmer and order was more or less being restored. He explained the reason for this as follows: "[We] had to enter into agreement with the left-wing parties, and, having established general positions, secured their assurance to stop the disorder." There had been "a genuine anarchy, senseless and unstoppable, which is significantly more intense than that in 1905. These disorders are so huge that they threatened wholesale slaughter [*pogolovnaia reznia*] and a large-scale fight [*potasovka*] among the population and soldiers." After describing the extent of the anarchy, he detailed the substance of the agreement with the left-wing parties. In addition to the convocation of a Constituent Assembly, they had to agree to a series of freedoms that had not been given in the Manifesto of October 17 (the October Manifesto of 1905), freedoms that "the Russian people had earned by making sacrifices and spilling blood on the battlefields." Because of these concessions, Rodzyanko told Lukomsky, "today is considerably calmer, and the soldiers' mutiny [*bunt*] is being liquidated, and soldiers are returning to the barracks, and the city is by and by restoring a decent appearance." He then added that two "acts" of abdication, Nicholas's and Mikhail's, would be published "tomorrow."

Although the "acts" of the abdications had not yet been published, the rumors had been spread and the news had been received by the population with rejoicing. The Peter and Paul Fortress greeted the new government with a 101-gun salute. Rodzyanko promised to send the new oath of allegiance to the new government through the Hughes apparatus.

Rodzyanko's statement is a juxtaposition of contradictions, exaggerations, ambiguities, and untruths. The description of the "anarchy" was contradictory. If the anarchy had been "senseless and unstoppable," larger than what they had experienced in 1905, how was this anarchy "liquidated" and order restored overnight by merely coming to an agreement with "extreme left-wing parties"? If by "left-wing parties" he meant the Petrograd Soviet, the agreement reached by its Executive Committee members and the Duma Committee/Provisional Government members on March 2 was not forced upon the latter by the "left-wing parties" but voluntarily offered by the liberals, including calling the Constituent Assembly and the promise of fundamental rights. Moreover, this agreement had been reached even before the conversation between Rodzyanko and Nikolai Ruzsky on March 2. This reveals that Rodzyanko was emphasizing or diminishing the danger of the anarchy depending on the political situation, and rearranging the chronology of events to fit his purposes—deceptions that Alekseev had become well aware of by then. Furthermore, Rodzyanko presented the draft manifesto signed by Nicholas and the handwritten, unwitnessed "manifesto" signed by Mikhail as legally binding, official "acts."

At that point Alekseev returned and joined the conversation. He gave alarming updates about how knowledge of the "manifestos" had spread among military units, a military rebellion in the Baltic Sea, and the dissemination of the latest news to the army. He further stated that the Petrograd garrison was out of commission as a result of propaganda by the workers, "against whom apparently no measures have been taken." All the other reserve regiments, which were infested with the spirit of rebellion, might as well be written off until the restoration of order and discipline. All efforts now, he said, should be concentrated on restoring strict discipline, and he expressed his hope that the new government would assist the army in carrying out this task. He did not show outward anger, but briskly tried to end the conversation with "I have nothing further to add except the words: Lord, save Russia!"[17]

"I sincerely regret," Rodzyanko responded, "that Your Excellency is in such a gloomy and depressed mood. . . . Here we are all in a bold, decisive mood." According to Rodzyanko, the information he possessed about the Baltic Fleet was not as gloomy as Alekseev had indicated, and the army commanders were as bold and decisive as the Duma Committee. He was convinced that the people would come around and unite themselves again with the army. He then insisted upon the necessity of publishing the two "manifestos" immediately. He added: "Here we also explain: Lord, save Russia, but we also add: Long live strong, great mother Russia, and her glorious, brotherly army and great Russian people!"[18]

Provoked by Rodzyanko's paternalistic smugness, Alekseev introduced two telegrams from the Baltic Fleet, which had informed the Stavka that the revolt had spread to all ships, and that the killing of officers had begun. "You see how quickly events are developing," Alekseev added, "and how careful we must be in evaluating events." He sharply pointed out that both senior and junior officers were doing their utmost to maintain the cohesion of the army.

> As for my mood, it has resulted from the fact that I have never allowed myself to be led to an error by those on whom at this moment lies the responsibility before the country. To say that everything was all right and that serious work would not be necessary for recovery would mean to say the untruth.[19]

Even this flash of anger at Rodzyanko in the telegraphic conversation was restrained. To save the army from disintegration, he did not accuse nor remonstrate with the person who was most responsible for having made a fool of him.

Rodzyanko replied: "Your Highness, don't be angry with me." And he belatedly asked how Alekseev's health was and if his stay in Sevastopol had helped to improve it. In the many conversations Rodzyanko had had with Alekseev, this was the first time he had asked about the health of the general. Alekseev bluntly responded that he was fine, and concluded the conversation wishing Rodzyanko health in return.[20]

The revolution moved quickly to tie a noose around the necks of the fallen imperial family. Before March 3 was over, the Executive Committee of the Petrograd Soviet passed a resolution to arrest the deposed Nicholas II, place Grand Duke Mikhail under house arrest, and transport Grand Duke Nikolai Nikolaevich to Petrograd to keep him under surveillance. Arrests of the female members of the Romanov dynasty would be made depending on the degree of their involvement in the old regime. This implied the arrest of the empress. The Soviet Military Commission was to carry out the arrests, and Nikolai Chkheidze and Matvei Skobelev were entrusted with informing the Provisional Government of what would come to pass.[21]

Interestingly, it was not the extremists, Bolsheviks, the leftist SRs, or the bomb-throwing anarchists of the Petrograd Soviet who made these decisions, but the moderate socialists. Here one can hear the echo of Louis-Antoine Saint-Just, who made a plea for the death sentence against King Louis XVI at the king's trial during the French Revolution:

> What is at issue is not the guilt or innocence of a citizen, someone within the body politic, but the natural incompatibility of someone, by definition, outside of it. Just as Louis could not help but be a tyrant, since one cannot reign innocently, so the Republic whose very existence is predicated on the destruction of tyranny cannot help but eliminate him. All that is needed is the surgical removal of this excrescence from the body of the Nation. A king must die so a republic can live.[22]

The following day, the Provisional Government took up the question of how to treat the tsar and the grand duke. At the Provisional Government meeting, Pavel Milyukov reported that the Petrograd Soviet was in favor of exiling the imperial family abroad, considering it necessary for political reasons as well as their security. The Provisional Government did not find it necessary to extend this measure to all the members of the Romanovs, but as far as Nicholas II and Grand Duke Mikhail and their families were concerned, if they wanted to remain in Russia, it would be necessary to restrict their place of residence as well as their movements.[23]

Aleksandr Kerensky's position was delicate: while he was in favor of exiling the imperial family, he could not openly defy the radical resolutions adopted by various workers' meetings. Later, on March 7, appearing at the Moscow Soviet and responding to the demand for the execution of the imperial family, Kerensky defended his position, which was that they should "guarantee the safety of the deposed emperor's personal life and exile the family to England."[24] In the end, it was Kerensky, as the minister of justice and the vice chairman of the Petrograd Soviet, who proved most responsible for determining the fate of the imperial family and their relatives.

When he reported to work at the Stavka on March 4, Lieutenant Colonel Vasily Mikhailovich Pronin saw a huge red flag hanging at the entrance of the building that housed the Mogilev City Duma. Portraits of Nicholas and Alexandra that had decorated the streetlamps had been torn down. The St. George Battalion marched to the headquarters with the orchestra playing "La Marseillaise." The abdicated tsar watched from his window as these decorated soldiers, who had been sent to suppress the revolution only a few days ago, were now celebrating the overthrow of the monarchy.[25] Even at the Stavka, the world was turned upside down.

As soon as she received the news of Nicholas's abdication from her son-in-law Sandro on March 3, Dowager Empress Maria Fyodorovna left

Kiev for Mogilev to see her son. Grand Duchess Olga Aleksandrovna, Nicholas's younger sister, who was with her mother in Kiev, noted: "My mother was in a terrible state. She kept telling me that it was the greatest humiliation of her life. . . . She blamed Alicky for . . . everything."[26] Sandro accompanied the dowager empress, but Olga stayed behind.

At 10 a.m. on March 4, after his usual morning tea, Nicholas went to the quartermaster's office at the Stavka to receive Alekseev's reports, as if nothing had happened. As usual, he sat in the armchair in front of Alekseev's desk and received his report in the presence of Lukomsky and Vladislav Klembovsky, raising questions and giving instructions to Alekseev. At the end of the report, the deposed tsar told the generals quietly that it was painful to receive the report for the last time (this practice was being discontinued after a protest from the Provisional Government and the Petrograd Soviet).[27] He shook hands with the generals and walked out of the office with Alekseev.[28] With the end of these reports, his usual routine was progressively falling by the wayside. Invitations for breakfast and supper were discontinued except for the grand dukes.

Just before 3 p.m. on March 4, the dowager empress's train glided up to the imperial platform. The weather was stormy and cold. Descending from her car, the dowager empress embraced her son, and greeted Alekseev and other officers on the platform. Then mother and son went into a small wooden shed on the platform and spoke alone for two hours. Alekseev stood outside the shed. All the entourage and staff officers stood in complete silence at a distance on the other end of the platform.[29] The dowager empress wrote in her diary:

It was a mournful meeting. He opened to me his bleeding heart, and we both wept. . . . Poor Niki told me all about the tragic events that happened for two days. In the beginning a telegram from Rodzyanko came in which he was told that he had to take everything with the Duma in order to restore order and stop the revolution; then in order to save the country, it was suggested to form a new government and to abdicate from the throne in favor of his son (unbelievable!). But Niki, naturally, could not part with his own son, and handed the throne to Misha! All the generals telegraphed and advised him the same, and he . . . signed the manifesto. Niki was unusually quiet and majestic in this terribly humiliating situation.[30]

When Sandro entered the shed, "he found the Dowager Empress collapsed in a chair, sobbing aloud, while Nicholas stood smoking quietly and staring at his feet."[31] Did she blame Alexandra for bringing catastrophe not only to her son but also to the legacy of the proud autocratic tradition she had shared with her husband? Did Nicholas mount any defense of his wife? We cannot know for sure. The picture of Nicholas smoking, with his eyes downcast, while his mother sobbed in her chair is the sad finale of the Romanovs.

Leaving the rest behind at the station, the three drove to the governor's house. "We embraced," Sandro wrote. "I did not know what to say to him. He was calm, firmly convinced that he had made the right decision, although he blamed his brother Mikhail Aleksandrovich for his decision to abdicate and to leave Russia without the emperor. 'Misha should not have done this,' he firmly insisted, 'I am surprised [at] who gave him such advice.'"[32] So it was Mikhail's fault, not his, that the monarchy had ended.

He gave Sandro his reasons for abdicating: the avoidance of civil war, the need to avoid weakening the army with politics, and his belief that the Provisional Government would rule Russia better than he could. He did not give the only true reason: his desire to live together with his son and the other members of his family. Then he showed the piles of telegrams he had received from commanders urging the tsar to abdicate. He showed the telegram from Nikolai Nikolaevich. "Even he," said Nicholas, his voice breaking for the first time.[33]

Night descended on Mogilev. It was quiet, and only a few people were seen in the streets. Light was seen coming from the tsar's office for a long time. To Dmitry Dubensky, it seemed as if what he experienced that day, the final day of the 304-year Romanov monarchy, was only a bad dream.[34]

After he finished the Hughes apparatus conversation with Rodzyanko, Alekseev sent a telegram to all the front commanders between 1:45 and 3:40 a.m. on March 4, instructing them that the two "manifestos of abdication should be immediately published to the army and fleet and the population under the area of the front." Alekseev reminded them that since the unity of the armed forces was essential to fight against the enemy to the victorious end, no dissension should be tolerated.[35]

Alekseev's capitulation to Rodzyanko did not go without objections, however. Immediately after Alekseev sent instructions to promulgate the two "manifestos," Lieutenant General Mikhail Kvetsinsky of the western front questioned the authenticity of Mikhail's "manifesto," which was neither countersigned nor ratified by the Senate. Furthermore, that document contradicted Nikolai Nikolaevich's Order No. 1, which called for the army and the navy to be "faithful to the throne." It was, therefore, necessary to ascertain whether Nikolai Nikolaevich really accepted this "manifesto," and, further, to come to a consensus among the front commanders as to what to do regarding the "manifesto."

Another objection came from unexpected quarters. At 4:37 a.m. on March 4, Yury Danilov of the northern front and Aleksandr Lukomsky at the Stavka had a conversation through the Hughes apparatus. Danilov questioned the title of Nicholas's manifesto, which Alekseev had promised to send in the "supplementary telegram." The original "manifesto" he was familiar with was merely addressed to the chief of the supreme headquarters. Clearly Danilov wanted to know why the draft manifesto that was sent to the Stavka was not made into the official manifesto, how the manifesto of Nicholas's abdication referred to Mikhail, and how the grand duke had referred to himself in the subsequent manifesto that Alekseev was supposed to send. Presumably the question was whether Mikhail was considered the tsar, Mikhail II, before he renounced the throne. Furthermore, like Kvetsinsky, Danilov questioned the legality of Mikhail's "manifesto" since it was merely handwritten, it had not been countersigned, and there was no title. Furthermore, it was contradictory with Nikolai Nikolaevich's appeal to the military units to "be faithful to the throne." This also showed that the western front and the northern front communicated with each other without going through the Stavka.

To these questions, Lukomsky responded that Mikhail's "manifesto" was indeed authentic, vouched for by Rodzyanko and Guchkov. He did not respond to the question of the title of Nicholas's "manifesto," but simply emphasized that the two "manifestos" had already been promulgated in Petrograd. As for Nikolai Nikolaevich's order, that had been issued before the supreme commander learned about Mikhail's renunciation of the throne. Delaying the publication of the "manifestos" would result in dire consequences, as such delay had led to the mutiny in the Baltic Fleet. Alekseev strongly believed that it was essential to abide by the consequences of the two "manifestos." The Stavka's argument was that the military should accept the established facts without questioning the legal minutiae. Otherwise, the cohesion and the unity of the armed forces would collapse, as had already begun to occur in the Baltic Fleet.[36]

The Stavka saw the situation as dire. Not only in the Baltic Fleet but also in other places, the disturbances were spreading widely.[37] The first news of the Petrograd Soviet's Order No. 1 to the soldiers reached the northern front, causing dismay among the commanding staff about the relationship between the soldiers and the officers.[38] The Stavka was busy trying to deal with these trouble spots. Despite Rodzyanko's manipulation of information, which had led the Stavka to accept Nicholas's abdication and ultimately the end of the monarchy, Alekseev and the Stavka were moving decisively in cooperation and collaboration with the Provisional Government in order to save the armed forces from disintegration.

And for that purpose, they had to suppress the objections raised by General Aleksei Evert and forestall the potential alliance between the western front and the northern front.

To quash this potentially dangerous coalition, the Stavka chose to mobilize Nikolai Nikolaevich. It persuaded the grand duke to issue an order to senior and junior commanders in the army and navy. This order, dated March 4, instructed them to accept the two "manifestos" and to instruct the troops under their command to "await quietly the expression of the Russian people's will and maintain their sacred duty to obey the lawfully established superiors."[39] The phrase "the expression of the Russian people's will" indicated that Nikolai Nikolaevich had accepted the convocation of the Constituent Assembly despite his initial objections.

Between 4:34 and 5:55 a.m. on March 4, Alekseev sent the front commanders a telegram that included the latest telegram from Nikolai Nikolaevich, accepting Alekseev's decision to approve the double abdication and Mikhail's refusal to take the throne—in fact, the decision to end the monarchy. Alekseev asked the front commanders to publish all the pertinent documents to the company-level units of the army and the navy.[40] Having received the supreme commander's approval, Alekseev issued an order officially announcing five documents: the appointment of Prince Georgy Lvov as the chairman of the Council of Ministers, the appointment of Nikolai Nikolaevich as the supreme commander, the two "abdication manifestos," and Nikolai Nikolaevich's order to accept these "manifestos." This telegram was tantamount to pounding the last nail in the coffin of the monarchy, a final outcome that Alekseev could not have dreamed of five days earlier but in which he had played a vital role. Shortly after noon, Alekseev notified Guchkov that the Stavka and the front commanders had published the two "manifestos."[41]

In the meantime, the revolutionary air had infiltrated the Stavka itself. Soldiers held meetings and celebrated "freedom." Red flags were hung in various buildings. News from local commanders about self-appointed delegates who claimed to have been dispatched from the Petrograd Soviet disarming railway gendarme officers and arresting local commanding officers began to be reported to the Stavka. Alekseev had to be mindful of the revolutionary fever that was catching among his own soldiers at the Stavka. Afraid of "unfriendly" sentiment among the soldiers, Alekseev decided to expel Voeikov and Count Vladimir Fredericks from the ranks of the entourage and send them away from Mogilev.[42] Alekseev dutifully reported this action to Guchkov, tacitly accepting the war minister's right to appoint and dismiss imperial court officials, the right that formerly had belonged to the emperor. Sometime between March 3 and March 10, the Stavka requested that the war ministry change the titles of military units that bore the names of the Romanov household members and the uniforms of the members of the emperor's suite. As soon as the monarchy ended, the Stavka was quick to shed any traces of the monarchy. Alekseev took these measures without Nikolai Nikolaevich's approval.[43]

The size of the tsar's entourage dwindled. At the gate to the governor's house, Bubnov met a man in a civilian overcoat with his lambskin hat pulled down to cover his face. Fearfully looking around, he asked Bubnov: "No one would recognize me, right?" That was Voeikov, who was plotting to escape from Mogilev incognito to avoid arrest.[44]

On March 3, the same day that Nicholas returned to Mogilev, General Ivanov with the St. George Battalion also returned to the Stavka from Vyritsa, where he had been stuck for three days. General Ivanov was unable to return to his old railcar due to the soldiers' protest, and he had to seek a hotel to accept him.[45]


On March 4, Nicholas wrote down a list of requests in pencil that he wanted to give to the Provisional Government: (1) unobstructed passage to Tsarskoe Selo for him and the accompanying personnel; (2) a safe stay at

Tsarskoe Selo until the recovery of his children and other persons from illness; (3) unobstructed passage to Murmansk with accompanying personnel and from there to exile in England; (4) return to Russia for permanent residence in the Crimea upon the end of the war.[46] Clearly, the deposed tsar had finally accepted the authority of the Provisional Government and resigned himself to the thought of exile to England. He had not the faintest inkling that he was about to be arrested.

Alekseev met with Nicholas at 10 a.m., then immediately sent a telegram to Lvov with the first three requests on Nicholas's wish list. Lukomsky explained later that Alekseev wisely thought that it would be better not to talk about something in the very distant future, given how quickly events had developed over the last few days, and instead wait to see if the Provisional Government would allow the imperial family to go into exile to England.[47] Or Alekseev may have thought that Nicholas's return to Russia would not be a politically wise idea, wishing to keep the former tsar abroad and far away.

Considering the deposed tsar's presence at the Stavka to be inconvenient and even dangerous, the Provisional Government was eager to grant this permission.[48] Alekseev, too, must have been growing concerned about the safety of the deposed tsar, as soldiers at the Stavka were showing signs of influence by the revolution in the capital. He wanted to get rid of Nicholas as soon as possible.[49]

Despite the inclement weather, Nicholas took his daily walk as usual. Even amid the tragic circumstance, he was unable to break his habits. He had tea as usual, and after tea he received first Alekseev and then Fredericks, who came to bid farewell before he left the Stavka. The old servant, who had served three tsars faithfully, now wept. As for Voeikov, he never bothered to come see Nicholas before he left Mogilev.[50]

Having experienced the most difficult ordeal in his life, Grand Duke Mikhail left Petrograd early in the morning on March 4 for his home in Gatchina and rejoined his wife, Natasha Brasova.[51]

The "manifesto" of Nicholas's abdication and Mikhail's "manifesto" declining the throne were published in the first issue of the official bulletin of the Provisional Government, *Vestnik vremennogo pravitelstva* [*Herald of the Provisional Government*], on March 5. The two "manifestos" were brought to the Governing Senate by the minister of justice, Kerensky, and duly registered.[52] Nicholas's abdication and Mikhail's renunciation of the throne became official without a legally proper manifesto being issued, signed, and certified.

On a cold, windy Sunday, March 5, the third day after Nicholas's abdication, there was a mass at the Cathedral of Three Saints in Mogilev, on the bank of the Dniepr. All the generals, including General Alekseev, officers, and soldiers packed the cathedral. Nicholas and Maria Fyodorovna attended the service, occupying the imperial seat. The prayer offered by the priest no longer referred to "the Autocrat Great Sovereign of Our Emperor Nikolai Aleksandrovich," as had been the case before. By the order of the Holy Synod, the prayer for the sovereign had been abolished. This change caused consternation and audible murmurs among the attendees. When the service was over, Nicholas and his mother entered their automobile. The public, officers, and soldiers surrounded the car. Many saluted, and others took off their hats.[53] But once again, no one sang "God Save the Tsar."[54] As they returned to the governor's house, they saw two huge red flags flying at the city hall across from Nicholas's residence.[55]

By this point the foreign missions of the Allies, having learned of Nicholas II's abdication, had become worried that Russia would conclude a separate peace with Germany. At the initiative of John Hanbury-Williams of the British military mission, the Allies' foreign missions composed a collective letter that they sent to all the front commanders as well as to Alekseev, pleading for Russia to continue fighting in the war. They immediately received answers from Ruzsky, Sakharov, Evert, and Nikolai Nikolaevich, as well as from Alekseev, confirming that in conjunction with the Allies they would continue the war to its victorious end. Nevertheless, Alekseev must not have been happy that the Allies took that action without consulting him.[56]

Furthermore, sensing the spread of revolution and hostility among common soldiers toward the deposed tsar and tsarina, the foreign missions of the Allies had become concerned about the tsar's safety after his departure from Mogilev, assuming that Nicholas would be returning to Tsarskoe Selo by train. To ensure his safe passage, Hanbury-Williams suggested that he and several other Allied military representatives be allowed to accompany Nicholas in the train.

On the evening of March 6, Hanbury-Williams was summoned to Nicholas's office. The former emperor was sitting at the table in khaki uniform, as he had done before, though he was "tired, white, with big black lines under his eyes." But he smiled as he shook Hanbury-Williams's hand. He talked about his decision to abdicate not only for himself but also for Aleksei, since he could not bear to be parted from his son. He said that he did not wish to leave Russia, and wanted to live in the Crimea, but if that was not allowed he would go to England. Hanbury-Williams did not record that Nicholas said anything about the end of the monarchy. Nicholas had no inkling that he and his wife were to be arrested and that he and his beloved family would become prisoners of the Provisional Government.[57]

On March 5, Alekseev sent a supplementary telegram to Prince Lvov and Rodzyanko, requesting that the Provisional Government send its authorized representatives to ensure the safe passage of the abdicated tsar to Tsarskoe Selo.[58] He sent Bazili to Petrograd to see foreign minister Milyukov to inquire about the possibility of the imperial family's exile in England. Milyukov responded that although he was working hard to secure the imperial family's exile, it was not up to him. He had managed to gain the support of Kerensky, but the Petrograd Soviet was adamantly opposed.[59] The Petrograd Soviet, which had sat quietly on the sidelines during the abdication drama, proved quick to rear its head and show its vicious fangs. That was the first sign of the troubles that blocked the exile of the imperial family. The moderate members of the Petrograd Soviet were not the only ones opposed to his exile. His cousin King George V of Britain, under political pressure, refused to accept the imperial family as exiles.

Also on this day, the troops stood in line in front of the Stavka's headquarters. The priest read the oath, replacing the phrase "the Most Gracious Great Sovereign Emperor Nikolai Aleksandrovich, All-Russian Tsar and His Imperial Majesty's lawful Heir of All-Russian Throne" with a much simpler phrase: "the Provisional Government." The *Te Deum* followed. For the first time in 304 years, the emperor was not mentioned in the prayer at the official ceremony. Nicholas was in his room until the ceremony was over; he must have seen it.[60] Few bothered to wonder how they could swear allegiance to a government that was provisional.

Just before midnight on March 5, the Provisional Government's war minister, Guchkov, and the new commander of the Petrograd Military District, General Lavr Kornilov, came to visit the now deposed empress. The ostensible purpose of the visit was to ensure the security of the palace and the imperial family given the riotous Tsarskoe Selo garrison troops. Guchkov and Kornilov were accompanied by about twenty individuals—officers, soldiers, and workers—who formed part of the new city government in Tsarskoe Selo. The grand marshal of the court, Count Pavel Benckendorff, met the visitors at the entrance of the palace and informed them that the empress had gone to bed. But after the visitors insisted, Benckendorff led them to the waiting room. Bracing herself for arrest, Alexandra donned her Red Cross nurse's uniform to meet the uninvited guests. Behind her was Grand Duke Pavel, standing in as a bodyguard to protect the deposed empress just in case.[61]

Initially, the empress was understandably cold and even haughty, refusing to shake hands with her long-standing enemy and the new commander of the Petrograd Military District. She talked only with Kornilov, ignoring Guchkov. But Guchkov's offer to extend assistance to the sick children broke the ice. The empress requested that the hospitals she had established and where she had worked be maintained as before, a request that Guchkov promised to honor. After this, she came around to addressing the uninvited guests with a modicum of civility, though she still refused to shake hands with them when they left.[62]

On March 6, Nicholas was allowed to use the telephone to talk to his wife for the first time since the beginning of the revolution. After lunch, when the valet informed the empress that Nicholas was on the phone, the empress jumped up "with the alacrity of a girl of sixteen," as if the constant pain of which she had complained had suddenly vanished, and rushed out of the room to receive the call.[63] Nicholas said only: "You know?" Alexandra answered, "Yes." With these few words, all was understood between husband and wife. They then talked about the children's illnesses. They could not talk about anything else, since the telephone was obviously bugged by the Provisional Government.[64] When she returned to the mauve boudoir, she was both all smiles and tearful. She was relieved to hear that Nicholas was alive and that he would join the family soon.[65]

It was a lucky day for Nicholas. He was delighted to receive two letters from "dear Alix" and two letters from Maria. These letters had been surreptitiously carried by Captain Golovkin of the Finland Regiment. And later, before 8 p.m., his chauffeur drove him 2.4 kilometers to see his mother, who was living in her special train car at the train station. Without Alexandra there, the dowager empress had lent crucial support to the disgraced former tsar.[66]

On March 7, Nikolai Nikolaevich left Tiflis for Mogilev to assume the post of supreme commander.[67] Masses of people saw him off at the railway station, though, perplexingly, they sang "La Marseillaise" and waved red flags. People greeted the grand duke at every station on the way. At the Stavka in Mogilev, his portrait with the words "Beloved and Respected Leader [*vozhd*]" was hung in his office in the governor's house, which was still used by Nicholas, awaiting his arrival. The term *vozhd* had never been used for Nicholas II during the war. To avoid an awkward encounter between these cousins who hated each other, Alekseev had to remove Nicholas from Mogilev before the popular grand duke's arrival.

Alekseev, characteristically, knew more than he let on. The day before, Prince Lvov, the prime minister of the Provisional Government, and Guchkov, the war minister, had informed Alekseev that the Provisional Government had decided to deny Nikolai Nikolaevich the supreme commandership because of how negatively the populace viewed the Romanovs. Alekseev nevertheless recommended that Lvov appoint the grand duke to the post anyway, suggesting that the popularity the grand duke enjoyed in the army would serve to enhance the authority of the Provisional Government. The possibility of the popular military leader leading the army was precisely what the Provisional Government feared, Lvov candidly admitted. One month earlier, Nikolai Nikolaevich might have been accepted as leader of the nation, Lvov argued, but after the revolution, the positions of the army and the rear had flipped, with the rear now deciding the fate of the nation. The Provisional Government had to take into account the overwhelming sentiment of the masses against the Romanov family. Lvov and his colleagues feared Bonapartism—a situation in which the possibility of counterrevolution with a popular military leader with close dynastic connections at its head might arise to challenge the authority of the Provisional Government. The Provisional Government, with the Stavka's cooperation, had removed all members of the Romanov house from military service. But Nikolai Nikolaevich was an exception. Alekseev, whose priority was firmly set on maintaining the cohesion and morale of the armed forces, was counting on the popularity of the grand duke to rally the armed forces.[68] But Alekseev caved under the pressure of

Lvov and Guchkov and promised to give the grand duke the letter from the Provisional Government recommending his resignation from the supreme commandership.[69]

It was an ironic twist. Before the February Revolution, Lvov and Guchkov had been involved in the palace coup to depose Nicholas and had attempted to recruit Nikolai Nikolaevich and Alekseev to this plot. Now that Nicholas II had been deposed, Lvov and Guchkov no longer needed the grand duke. On the contrary, they were anxious to prevent Nikolai Nikolaevich's accession to the powerful position of supreme commander.

While Nikolai Nikolaevich was still en route to Mogilev, Kerensky, the Provisional Government's minister of justice, declared in Moscow that the grand duke would not be appointed as the supreme commander. Kerensky aspired to have that position reserved for the *vozhd* of the revolution, and he saw himself as filling that role.[70] Though the grand duke did not know that the Petrograd Soviet had already ordered his deportation, he confessed to Grand Duke Andrei, who had come to Tiflis to meet him, that he might be arrested at any moment. He recommended that Andrei stay in Kislovodsk, a spa in southern Russia, with his mother and not go anywhere. He could not guarantee Andrei's safety, but at least Kislovodsk would be safer.[71]

According to Andrei, Nikolasha expressed his low opinion of Nicholas. Although "he was a nice, sympathetic boy," wherever he went he left a stinking trail. Referring to the deposed emperor as a "boy" reflected the grand duke's contempt for Nicholas. And he savagely mocked Nicholas's naive affection for the Cossacks, whose uniform he had loved to don on ceremonial occasions. Based on what Nikolasha had heard, Nicholas could not be the ataman of the Cossacks, as he had always claimed. When Nicholas's name was mentioned, the grand duke said, the Cossacks used a swear word referring to him.

In Kharkov, Nikolai Nikolaevich also met Adjutant General Husein Khan Gussein-Nakhichevansky, who was one of the few officers who strongly opposed Nicholas's abdication. He, Feliks Yusupov, and Count Feliks Sumarokov-Elston (the father of Feliks Yusupov) tried to dissuade the grand duke from going to Mogilev. They correctly guessed that Mogilev was under the thumb of the Provisional Government and that the new government would oppose the grand duke's assumption of the supreme commandership. Nikolai Nikolaevich consulted his brother Pyotr, General Nikolai Yanushkevich, and his entourage, and decided to move on to Mogilev.[72] He must have judged that any pro-monarchist armed resistance would stand no chance of winning.

On March 7, the Provisional Government passed a resolution to deprive Nicholas and Alexandra of freedom, to transport Nicholas to Tsarskoe Selo, and to entrust General Alekseev with making arrangements for the former tsar's arrest. For this purpose, the Provisional Government was to send a delegation of four Duma members, headed by Aleksandr Bublikov, for the protection of the abdicated emperor.[73] This decision passed with no opposition from the Petrograd Soviet. Perhaps at least some members of the Provisional Government had become concerned with the safety of the imperial couple; considering the passionate hatred that hotheaded radical soldiers and workers had for the imperial couple, they thought it would be safer to arrest the pair in the palace in Tsarskoe Selo, where they could keep them safely quarantined under guard. It must be noted that the arrest order was not extended to the former tsar's children. It never occurred to Nicholas and Alexandra to send the children abroad to be safe. To live without their children was the farthest thing from their minds. They could not fathom the impending danger for the family.

Before Bublikov departed for Mogilev to arrest the deposed tsar, he requested a written order, and it was Rodzyanko, not anyone in the Provisional Government, who provided it. This indicated that Rodzyanko still wielded tremendous authority and influence.

On the night of March 6, the deposed tsar drafted his last "order of the day," a farewell address to the army. This put Alekseev in a delicate situation. Nicholas was no longer the supreme commander and had no right to issue an order. But Alekseev agreed to print it as his own order and distribute it to all the army units. "I address you, my troops I passionately love," it began, and continued: "After my abdication for myself and for my son from the Russian Throne, power has been transferred to the Provisional Government, which was created by the State Duma." He asked the soldiers and officers "to submit yourselves to the Provisional Government and obey your commanders." He appealed to the officers and soldiers to continue their patriotic duty to carry out the war to a victorious end, and concluded: "Fulfill your duty, defend valiantly our Great Motherland, obey the Provisional Government, listen to your superiors, and remember that the slightest weakening of order serves only the hands of the enemy."[74]

Immediately after Alekseev received a copy of Nicholas's farewell address, however, the general received an order from Guchkov, prohibiting him from printing and disseminating Nicholas's farewell address. Although the address appealed to the officers and soldiers to support the Provisional Government, the war minister did not wish to elevate the prestige of the deposed tsar.[75] Alekseev obeyed the order, as preserving the integrity of the armed forces was his primary focus now. For the last few days, the Stavka had been inundated by incidents of arrested officers, soldiers' unilateral actions, and the breakdown of discipline in various units. Two new orders from the Petrograd Soviet, Order No. 1 and Order No. 2, reached army units, disrupting the relationship between soldiers and officers. The new way of addressing officers and soldiers and the creation of soldiers' committees were greeted by soldiers with excitement but caused consternation among old-fashioned officers. The old order of the imperial army and the navy was beginning to crumble. The Stavka was desperate to prevent the decomposition of the armed forces, and for that purpose, Alekseev's cooperation with the Provisional Government was a sine qua non.

On March 7, Major General Vladimir Kislyakov came to see General Nikolai Tikhmenev. Kislyakov was the deputy minister of transport in charge of military operations, stationed at the Stavka. General Tikhmenev was his superior officer. Early on February 28, Kislyakov had taken the side of the revolution, and kept in close touch with Bublikov and Nikolai Nekrasov behind Tikhmenev's back; apparently, Kislyakov's loyalty wavered between his sympathy for the Duma Committee and his loyalty to the deposed tsar. Now Kislyakov told Tikhmenev that he had received an encoded telegram from Bublikov or Nekrasov informing him that four commissars, headed by Bublikov, would come to Mogilev to arrest the tsar and take him to Petrograd. He revealed that he was forbidden to divulge this information to anyone, and that he had been ordered to prepare a train and a locomotive secretly for this purpose.

Tikhmenev sternly told Kislyakov that he should immediately go see Alekseev at the Stavka headquarters to reveal this information. Later, Tikhmenev learned that when Kislyakov began to reveal this secret, Alekseev cut him off, saying that he knew what to do with the information. Alekseev himself had previously asked the Provisional Government to provide an escort for the deposed tsar's safe journey to Tsarskoe Selo, and he had been informed that four commissars would be sent to Mogilev for this purpose. Now he learned that the four commissars would come to the Stavka to arrest the deposed tsar, not to secure his safe journey to Tsarskoe Selo. Though Alekseev held a very low opinion of Nicholas, his arrest was something that the chief of staff had never anticipated. But either he did not have the heart to tell Nicholas this terrible news or he feared what Nicholas and pro-monarchist officers would do when they learned of his impending arrest. So Alekseev kept this secret for the moment. It would be better to wait until the last minute, he thought, to give Nicholas this bad news.[76]

It is possible to speculate that the Provisional Government prohibited Alekseev from organizing a huge farewell gathering of officers, soldiers, and foreign military representatives on the train platform when the arrested tsar departed the Stavka. Or perhaps it was Alekseev himself who thought it would not be advisable to have hundreds of officers come to the platform to see Nicholas off, as he feared how they might react to news of the arrest. And surely Hanbury-Williams's earlier offer to have several members of the Allied countries' military missions accompany the deposed emperor on the train to Tsarskoe Selo must have placed Alekseev in an awkward position, knowing that Nicholas was to be arrested before he left Mogilev. So Alekseev decided to arrange a ceremonial farewell gathering for the departing former tsar in the hall of the duty general's headquarters, which previously had been used for the circuit court. Each unit was asked to bring twenty-five soldiers, to be selected by the unit's commanding officer, and assemble at the hall by 10 a.m.[77] He sent Hanbury-Williams a message saying that the Allied military representatives were not going to be invited to the gathering in the hall (though they would get a chance to say farewell privately), nor would they be allowed to accompany Nicholas in the train as he left Mogilev.[78]

As soon as Lieutenant Colonel Pronin entered the hall on the morning of March 7, he noticed that the life-size portrait of Nicholas that once had hung on the wall had been removed, leaving a huge empty space.[79] Alekseev was in the middle of the hall, awaiting the arrival of the deposed tsar. Grand Dukes Aleksandr Mikhailovich, Sergei Mikhailovich, and Boris Vladimirovich stood behind Alekseev. The atmosphere in the hall was nervous and tense. Exactly at eleven o'clock, Nicholas entered the hall in Circassian uniform, holding the hilt of a sword in his left hand. His right hand was lowered but visibly trembling. He exchanged greetings with Alekseev, then turned to the right to greet the soldiers in a soft voice, as if he was speaking with them in a small room.

The soldiers answered in full, loud voices: "We wish you health, Your Majesty!"

Nicholas's face was completely pale, somewhat convulsed, and nervous-looking. He remained silent for a moment, then quickly moved to the center of the hall and began to speak, still in a soft voice: "Today . . . I see you . . . for the last time. . . . Such is the will of God and the following is my decision." Soon his voice grew louder and he spoke distinctly, but he was terribly nervous, often pausing in the middle of sentences. The speech was the same as the last address that he had wished to have published but that had been confiscated. He talked about his decision to abdicate in favor of Mikhail, who, however, also had "abdicated." The fate of Russia was now entrusted to the Provisional Government, he said. He thanked the assembled officers and soldiers for their faithful service to him and the motherland. He asked them to serve the Provisional Government and to fight the war against the enemy.

Dead silence filled the room. All eyes were fixed on the former emperor. Many wept and wiped away tears.

Nicholas turned and walked among the officers, exchanging a few words and shaking hands with some. Two officers fainted and fell to the ground. Suddenly pandemonium erupted in the hall, with shrieking and wailing. Tears welled up in Nicholas's eyes. He could no longer keep his composure and hurriedly walked toward the exit. Alekseev rushed to him and said: "Your Highness, allow me to wish you a happy journey, and a happy life!" Given that Alekseev already knew that Nicholas would be arrested, we do not know what he meant by wishing him "a happy journey, and a happy life."

The former supreme commander embraced his chief of staff, kissed him three times, and quickly left.[80] But no one asked him to change his mind.[81]

As he went outside, the stairs and all the surrounding area were packed with the soldiers who were not invited inside. Nicholas addressed them: "Greetings, brothers!"

The soldiers responded: "We wish you health, Your Imperial Majesty!"

"Farewell, brothers!" responded Nicholas.

"Happy journey, Your Majesty!" responded the soldiers.

Witnessing the scene, an officer whispered to Sergeevsky: "Are we really having a revolution?"

As soon as Nicholas's car turned the corner, however, two huge red flags could be seen hanging on the city administration building, an unmistakable sign of the revolution.[82]

Nicholas went back to the governor's house, where the representatives of foreign military missions had gathered to say their last farewell. The usually unperturbable John Hanbury-Williams, head of the British military mission, wept uncontrollably. The head of the Serbian military mission, Branislav Lontkevich, was so distressed that he could not even kneel and kiss Nicholas's hand. He muttered: "Russia without the tsar—this is impossible. This can never be!"[83] Nicholas later noted in his diary: "My heart was almost broken!"[84]

Afterward, the former tsar had his driver take him to meet the dowager empress in her imperial train, and he spent his last hours in Mogilev with his mother in the railway station. The deposed tsar had breakfast with his mother and her entourage there in her car. After breakfast, the son and the mother talked until 4:30 in the afternoon. He then bid farewell to Sandro, Sergei, and Boris.[85]

At 3 p.m. Bublikov's train arrived at Mogilev. Although Nicholas and the imperial train were at the railway station, Bublikov and the Duma commissars immediately drove to Alekseev's headquarters, where Bublikov asked Alekseev to give Nicholas the Provisional Government's order of arrest. He claimed that it would be better for a person close to Nicholas to give him this order. Later he confessed that he did not even want to see the deposed emperor, though he had volunteered for this task.[86] Arresting the former emperor was a weighty undertaking, and at the last moment he lost his nerve and passed on the onerous task to Alekseev.[87]

After they dropped off the arrest warrant with Alekseev, Bublikov and his company went back to the railway station. The imperial train A stood on the right side of the platform, while on the opposite side stood train M, that of Maria Fyodorovna. Dr. Sergei Fyodorov and another member of the entourage approached Bublikov to offer him tea with the former emperor. The commissar refused the invitation. Bublikov's sharp eyes noticed that the emperor's personal physician had torn off the imperial monogram from his overcoat.[88]

Bublikov ordered the imperial train to be coupled with his train. Then he selected the members of Nicholas's entourage who would be allowed to accompany him. He excluded Flag Captain Konstantin Nilov from the list. The purpose was to eliminate anyone who could give the deposed tsar dangerous military advice.[89]

Prince Vasily Dolgorukov invited the Duma delegates to join the supper in the dining car, but the commissars declined. They did not wish to eat their prisoner's meal as the prisoner's guests. Their rude refusal dismayed Nicholas. No one had ever rejected his invitation to join him for supper before. The former emperor still did not grasp the grave danger he was in, still believing that the commissars had been sent to escort him for his protection.[90]

After Nicholas and the dowager empress made their farewells to each other—Bublikov could see their silhouettes through the windows of the train car—Nicholas came out of his mother's car. He glanced back for one last look at his mother as he stepped onto the platform. He saluted to the twenty or thirty people surrounding him, then walked hurriedly to his train. Bublikov noted: "On his face absolutely nothing was shown reflecting the tragic events that he had gone through. Apparently, those who surrounded him were more agitated than he."[91] General Alekseev followed him into his car on the imperial train. This was the point at which Alekseev told Nicholas about the Provisional Government's arrest order. A few minutes passed. The general came out of Nicholas's car and handed Bublikov back the Provisional Government's arrest order.

We have no information as to how Nicholas responded to his arrest order, nor how Alekseev felt about handing it to him. According to one telling, when Nicholas heard of the arrest order, he became pale and turned his back to Alekseev.[92] But there was no one except Nicholas and Alekseev in the car to witness the scene. As for Alekseev, the task of conveying the arrest order to the former supreme commander must have been excruciatingly painful. Rodzyanko, Guchkov, Kerensky, Bublikov—none of them had the courage to give Nicholas the arrest order. All of these actors, who played important roles as the gravediggers for the monarchy, copped out at the last moment when it came time to arrest the autocrat they so hated. Did Alekseev accept this last task as the inevitable consequence of his actions? Or did he take it on to spare the former emperor the humiliation of being arrested by his enemy Bublikov? We don't know the answer.

As for Nicholas, he wrote in his diary: "Painful, sick, and depressed [*tiazhelo, bol'no i tosklivo*]."[93] When he abdicated, he must have thought that he would spend his life in exile, together with his family, in England. Had he known he would be arrested, would he have willingly abdicated from the throne? Would he have fought tooth and nail against his abdication? Had Alekseev known that the emperor would be arrested, would he have worked for his abdication? We don't know the answer to these questions, either.

Bublikov ordered the train to depart. The locomotive whistled, and the train slowly started moving at 4:45 p.m. The deposed tsar, now under arrest, stood before the large window of his car in absolute silence. He was wearing a simple khaki shirt. He smiled and waved.[94] Even at this moment, the former emperor had to go through the ceremonial performance expected of a tsar, a habit that had become his second nature.

As the train began to move, Alekseev took off his hat, bowed low, and then stood in salute on the platform. Many thoughts, mingled with pity, regret, and remorse, must have crossed his mind. His salute was the last farewell not only to the former emperor but also to the dying monarchy. His salute was also his atonement for the decisive role he had played in the destruction of the emperor and the monarchical system, something for which he could not forgive himself.

In tears, Maria Fyodorovna watched the train depart. As soon as her son's train disappeared from view, the dowager empress ordered her train to leave for Kiev. Mother and son never saw each other again.[95]

On March 8, one day after the Provisional Government resolved to arrest the former emperor and empress, General Kornilov, accompanied by the commandant of the Tsarskoe Selo garrison, Colonel Evgeny Stepanovich Kobylinsky; the new palace commandant, Captain Pavel Pavlovich Kotsebu; and several officers, came to place the former empress under house arrest. Why the military authority and not officials of the Ministry of Internal Affairs, headed by Lvov, handled the arrest is not known, but it is possible to surmise that Lvov simply did not have the courage to do it.

The empress met Kornilov in her Red Cross uniform, refusing to shake hands with the man who had come to arrest her. The new commander of the Petrograd Military District assembled the commander and officers of His Majesty's Combined Regiment and declared that their duties at the palace had come to an end, that they would be replaced by the troops of the Tsarskoe garrison, and that Captain Kotsebu would be appointed commandant of the palace. He then ordered all the servants and employees to assemble and told them that they could leave now, but if they decided to stay, they would be under the order of the new commandant. All telephone use was forbidden except for the telephone in the duty office, and all correspondence would be subject to inspection. All the exterior doors would be locked and sealed except for the one to the kitchen, where entry and exit would be monitored, and another at the main entrance, through which official visitors would arrive and leave. All correspondence was to pass through the new palace commandant, and all letters were to remain unsealed until the commandant had inspected them, after which he would seal them. Count Benckendorff, some ladies-in-waiting, the doctors, and the tutors decided to remain in the palace.[96] The palace was virtually turned into a prison.

General Kornilov then requested a meeting with the empress alone. At this meeting, Kornilov assured her that the arrest was only a precaution to protect the imperial family. He told her that her husband had been arrested and would be returning to Tsarskoe Selo the next day. He promised also that as soon as the children recovered from their illness, the Provisional Government intended to send the entire family to Murmansk, from where a British cruiser would take them to England. When Kornilov left, she held out both hands to say goodbye.[97]

At 2 p.m. a corps of the Guards of the First Regiment of the garrison came to Tsarskoe Selo to relieve His Majesty's Combined Infantry Regiment. Before 3 p.m. the company of the Combined Regiment, which had always guarded the emperor's palace, lined up in formation before the front entrance and received the colors of the regiment. The officers and soldiers of the regiment refused to be reassigned outside the palace and were determined to welcome the former tsar upon his return. But the empress persuaded them to disband, so as not to repeat the example of the French Revolution, where the Swiss Guard was massacred on the marble stairs of the Tuileries palace. The Combined Regiment disbanded.[98]

After Kornilov left, Alexandra asked the tutor Pierre Gilliard to tell Aleksei about Nicholas's abdication. She would tell her daughters the news by herself. Both Tatiana and Anastasia were still suffering from painful ear infections. Tatiana could not hear and had to read notes written down by her sisters. We don't know their reactions, but in all likelihood they accepted the news as God's will without question. Gilliard told Aleksei about Nicholas's abdication and Mikhail's renunciation of the throne. Aleksei asked: "But who's going to be Tsar, then?" Gilliard answered: "I don't know. Perhaps nobody now." Gilliard wrote, "Not a word about himself. Not a single allusion to his rights as the Heir. He was very red and agitated." Then Aleksei said: "But if there isn't a tsar, who's going to govern Russia?"[99] Aleksei, twelve years of age, the rightful heir to the throne, had grown up believing that he would be the tsar one day, and he raised a pertinent question: What was going to happen to the state (*gosudarstvo*) without the sovereign (*gosudar*)?

On March 9, Nicholas arrived in Tsarskoe Selo. Bublikov dropped him off at the imperial pavilion at the station and turned him over to his escort.[100] The escort, consisting of guards sent by the Petrograd Soviet, drove him, accompanied only by Dolgorukov (Benckendorff's son), to the palace. A humiliating kabuki-like ceremony was enacted at the locked gate. The sentry at the gate asked who was in the car. "Citizen Romanov," answered the driver. The sentry telephoned the officer, who came and asked again: "Who is in the car?" The sentry answered: "Citizen Romanov." Only then was the gate opened.[101]

Nicholas entered the palace. The antechamber was full of people. The deposed emperor walked through the crowd, saluting and shaking hands with Pavel Benckendorff and Pyotr Apraksin, and entered the empress's apartment without saying a word.[102] Alone, in her room, they fell into each other's arms. With tears in her eyes, Alexandra assured him that to have him back as husband and father was infinitely more precious to her than to have him back as the tsar whose throne she had fought all her life to preserve. Nicholas finally broke down. Laying his head on his wife's breast, he sobbed like a child.[103]

Nikolai Nikolaevich was scheduled to arrive at Mogilev on March 10. Alekseev invited Lvov and Guchkov to come to Mogilev and negotiate with the grand duke on "the delicate matters" involving his appointment to the supreme commandership, but Lvov and Guchkov chose not to make the trip, preferring to "negotiate" with the grand duke via telegrams.[104] In a telegram to Lvov and Guchkov sent on March 7, Alekseev reported that the appointment of Nikolai Nikolaevich as the supreme commander had been greeted with enthusiasm everywhere, including the Baltic Fleet and the Black Sea Fleet, and strongly urged Lvov and Guchkov to support the grand duke, who would, in Alekseev's view, help restore the cohesion of the army and boost the prestige of the Provisional Government.[105] But, as we have seen, the popularity of the grand duke was precisely what the Provisional Government feared.

Lvov sent a letter to the Stavka demanding that the grand duke resign from the supreme commandership, due to the popular sentiment against any member of the Romanov dynasty taking government positions, and instructed Alekseev to convey this letter.[106] Once again it fell upon Alekseev to force another Romanov from the supreme commandership. Once again Alekseev raised no objections.

When Nikolai Nikolaevich arrived in Mogilev on March 10, he was welcomed by the crowds enthusiastically. He then issued seven orders, but none was conveyed to the army, since Alekseev confiscated them.

On March 11, Nikolai Nikolaevich received Lvov's letter and accepted the Provisional Government's demand to step down from the supreme commandership, "for the good of the motherland." Alekseev was to be appointed supreme commander, and Klembovsky temporary chief of staff. Then Nikolai Nikolaevich submitted his letter of resignation to Lvov and pledged allegiance to "the fatherland and the new state order."[107] In turn, the grand duke requested the Provisional Government's guarantee of safe passage to the Crimea, and Alekseev requested that the Provisional Government's commissar or a member of the State Duma accompany him there. He urged Lvov and Guchkov to arrange for the departure of the grand duke from the Stavka as quickly as possible, the sooner the better.[108]

Before he stepped down, Nikolai Nikolaevich made one decision: to replace General Evert with General Gurko as the commander of the western front. General Evert, who had supported Nicholas and resisted the end of the monarchy, had no place in the new era of revolutionary Russia under the Provisional Government.

When Nicholas II was finally reunited with Alexandra and his children for the first time since leaving Tsarskoe Selo on February 22, he was no longer the tsar, and Aleksei was no longer the heir. They were united as prisoners of the Provisional Government and the Petrograd Soviet.

Grand Duke Mikhail retired to his private life in Gatchina to join his wife, but under close surveillance.

Nikolai Nikolaevich, the most powerful member of the Romanovs, accepted his dismissal as the supreme commander, and left Mogilev on March 13.

Thus ended Romanov rule in Russia.

# Epilogue

While it is impossible to see a clear path that could have fully restored the power of the Romanov autocrat after his accession to the throne, it is almost as difficult to imagine how Nicholas could have done a worse job as steward of the monarchy. At every turn, among each key constituency, he undermined his support. Even so, up until he decided to abdicate on his son's behalf, there was a real chance for the preservation of the Romanov monarchy in some form. Ultimately, every key support for his rule turned against him, and yet the one most to blame for the sputtering finale of a three-hundred-year regime is Nicholas himself—through intransigence, inaction, weakness, stupidity, and, oddly enough, fatherly love.

The German sociologist Max Weber conceptualized three types of authority: traditional, charismatic, and legal-rational. Tsarist authority had a traditional element, where power passed through hereditary succession and as part of a cultural mythology of mutual dependence between the sovereign and his people. Nevertheless, for the tsarist authority to be accepted by those people and retain legitimacy, the tsar also had to demonstrate charisma commensurate with his power.

Legal-rational authority played its role too, even in an autocracy. As historian Marc Raeff argues, many German monarchies in the seventeenth and eighteenth centuries evolved into a *Rechtsstaat*, where monarchical power itself became subject to the rule of law and well-ordered norms of the implementation of policies.[1] The Romanovs might have salvaged a similar, diminished position through the institution of a ministry of confidence or a responsible ministry had Nicholas acted sooner. But Nicholas ultimately defied tradition, projected no charisma, and failed to accept a legal-rational compromise until it was too late.

Nicholas II was obstinately committed to an archaic notion of autocracy, where the tsar's power was absolute and unencumbered by any laws or institutions. As American historian Richard Pipes observes, his notion of autocracy was also patrimonial, making little distinction between matters of state and his private affairs.[2] He and his wife, Empress Alexandra, devoted their entire life to the task of preserving the view of autocracy that Nicholas had inherited from Alexander III so that they might bequeath it to their hemophiliac son, Aleksei. Nicholas's commitment to autocracy was also a religious conviction. His autocratic power was anointed by God at his coronation, when he swore a holy vow to uphold his duty as ruler. It was a covenant with almighty God, a religious conviction binding him with his people. He deeply believed that the tsar and the people (*narod*) were one. Time and again he witnessed simple folk bowing, kneeling, and making the sign of the cross after catching just a glimpse of him at his coronation, at the canonization of Seraphim in Sarov, at the commemorations of the battles of Poltava and Borodino, at the tercentenary celebration, and at the announcement of the declaration of war against Germany and Austria at the Winter Palace.[3]

Such a notion of autocracy was ill-suited to be the principle by which to govern a dynamically changing state, society, and empire at the turn of the century. Any autocratic ruler would have encountered difficulties in balancing the need for change demanded by the modern era and upholding the monarchical principle, but Russia had the misfortune to have Nicholas II, who possessed neither the charisma with which to garner the support of his subjects nor the intellectual capacity to comprehend the need to accommodate the monarchical system to the demands of a changing society and empire. Immediately after he ascended to the throne, he dismissed, as a "senseless dream," the collective petition from the zemstvo activists to "crown the edifice" by granting a constitution. To ensure the survival of the monarchy following the 1905 revolution, he was forced to grant a quasi-parliamentary system that limited his autocratic power. But rather than developing this system into a genuine constitutional monarchy and transforming Russia into a *Rechtsstaat*, he regarded this concession with regret, considering the Duma an irritant that encroached on his autocratic power. His tutor Konstantin Pobedonostsev had taught him that "constitution and autocracy are irreconcilable." Despite his generally mediocre showing as a student, or perhaps because of it, he learned this lesson, forever tainting his view of the very word "constitution."

World War I put the inadequacy of Nicholas's notion of autocracy on full display. Despite the problems that confronted the country, there was a possibility of creating a united front among the tsarist elite that would harness the bureaucracy and the society for national defense. Instead, Nicholas made everything worse. He had a chance to create a government, inviting the liberals and the voluntary organizations to mobilize for the defense of the country. He missed this chance at the outbreak of the war, the very moment when the country seemed to be united. The summer of 1915 was another crucial turning point, when he could have established a ministry of confidence, inviting representatives of the liberals into the government. The leading figures in the bureaucracy were eager to accept such a government. Nicholas refused. In August 1915, he abandoned any cooperation with the liberals, inciting their hostility against the monarchy. He dismissed capable ministers, initiating a ministerial leapfrog that incapacitated the bureaucracy and made it impossible for the government to function as one body. The government became dysfunctional, demoralized, and uncoordinated. Despite concerted opposition inside and outside the government, Nicholas assumed the supreme commandership of the military, abandoning the capital and thereby allowing the pernicious influence of Alexandra and Rasputin to expand. Although there was no truth to the widespread rumors that Rasputin and Alexandra were plotting a separate peace with Germany or even that they were German agents, such rumors penetrated deeply into all layers of society and undermined the authority of the tsar.

One may ask: what's wrong with a separate peace? In retrospect, it would have been a possible way out of the quagmire of the war, thus saving the monarchy. It would have been greeted with joy among the soldiers and among the common people, who were going through unprecedented suffering—as historian William Rosenberg describes it, "unimaginable losses and excessive shortages."[4] Nevertheless, the elite core—aristocracy, bureaucracy, high command, and liberals—were solidly behind the continuation of the war, and a separate peace was anathema to them. Had the tsar opted for peace, he would have met with rebellion from the united forces of the Russian elite. The elite turned against Nicholas's government not because it was "conspiring for a peace," as Milyukov wrongly accused, but because it was not prosecuting the war as it should. Besides, Tsar Nicholas was too faithful to the commitment he had made to Russia's ungrateful allies.

Sensing the danger to the monarchy, members of the House of Romanov and the monarchists began to put pressure on Nicholas to rid himself of the cancerous influence of Alexandra and Rasputin. It was the monarchists who assassinated Rasputin, but the removal of Rasputin pushed the imperial couple further into a cocoon where, isolated and detached from reality, they more adamantly clung to the principle of autocracy, rejecting all advice for political concessions as an infringement of the tsar's personal prerogatives as the autocrat. No one, including the dowager empress, the grand dukes, Nicholas's own sisters, or even Alexandra's sister, Ella, could shake the imperial couple's conviction. In the meantime, the country drifted into crisis. While the tsar and tsarina were clinging to the notion that the *narod* was faithfully united with the tsar, his prestige sank to its nadir. Not only could Nicholas not demonstrate an iota of charismatic leadership to lead the country at war, but disapproval, mockery, and ridicule of him permeated every layer of society. Historian Boris Kolonitskii assembled numerous uncensored comments from common people, replete with criticism and ridicule, some even suggesting regicide. Instead of being called a "bloodsucker," as before the war, he was now often called a "fool" (*durak*).[5] The imperial couple could not comprehend that those who made such savage comments against them were the same *narod* who knelt to pray for them when they saw them.

Almost all layers of society became hostile to the imperial couple. Rumors of a palace coup became rampant even in aristocratic salons and officers' clubs, and some, like Aleksandr Guchkov and Prince Georgy Lvov, seriously contemplated implementing such a coup against Nicholas and Alexandra. Adjutant General Mikhail Alekseev and Grand Duke Nikolai Nikolaevich, who were consulted about the coup, did not support it, but they did nothing to prevent it. Many sensed a storm approaching from below. The liberals were afraid of an anarchic popular uprising that might sweep away not only the tsarist government but also civil society itself, but they were prepared to move swiftly to intervene against the government once a popular uprising began. The protracted war, two and a half years old, had a profound influence on people's consciousness. The war, for which the entire country was mobilized, injected a sense of national consciousness in people, including soldiers and officers. This sentiment was often expressed in the form of anti-German and anti-Jewish pogroms. But soon people began to sense how their willingness to sacrifice for the motherland was divorced from their oath of allegiance to the tsar. What Crane Brinton calls the transfer of allegiance had taken place in all layers of society—not only the lower strata of society and the liberal opposition but also the aristocracy, including some members of the reigning dynasty, as well as many officers at the highest rank in the armed forces, the very men tasked with propping up the regime.[6] To many, the sovereign (*gosudar*) became divorced from the state (*gosudarstvo*).

When the women workers in the workers' quarter of the capital went out into the streets demanding bread on February 23, 1917, marking the beginning of the February Revolution, and even when on February 27 a soldiers' uprising paralyzed the government in Petrograd, no one thought that the monarchy would actually come to an end. But only five days later, when Grand Duke Mikhail refused to assume the throne vacated by Nicholas, the Romanov dynasty fizzled out.

Contrary to the once accepted interpretation that it was the uprising of the masses of workers and soldiers that toppled the monarchical system, the most decisive factor in ending the monarchy was high politics. While the insurgency provided the background and a framework, the specific ways by which the abdications took place were instigated by actors at the highest level, including liberal politicians, military leaders, and a coterie of aristocrats including the tsar's own relatives.

Nevertheless, those players in high politics did not act in concert, coordinating their designs, contrary to what contemporary Russian monarchist historians claim.[7] They acted independently, following their own respective interests and goals. The end of the monarchy was not a preordained, inevitable outcome but a contingent process. The most important players involved were the Duma liberals and the generals of the high command. Within each group, there were divisions. Contrary to a widely accepted interpretation that the Duma liberals were reluctant revolutionaries who joined the revolution only to suppress it, from the moment the soldiers' insurrection began on the morning of February 27, the Duma liberals acted as revolutionaries against the government. Mikhail Rodzyanko played one of the most decisive roles in the abdication drama, but even he was challenged by other members of the Duma Committee. The dynamic of the power struggle within the Duma's leadership, especially among Rodzyanko, Pavel Milyukov, and Aleksandr Kerensky, greatly influenced the course of events. As the chairman of the Duma and the head of the Duma Committee, created on February 27, Rodzyanko enjoyed unquestionable authority on February 27 and 28. On February 27, before the Duma Committee virtually took over control of Petrograd, he recommended that the tsar grant a ministry of confidence. As the insurgency spread to the entire Petrograd garrison and its environs on February 28 and March 1, he and the senior grand dukes of the Romanov dynasty attempted to solve the crisis by persuading Nicholas to accept the grand dukes' manifesto calling for the establishment of a responsible ministry appointed by Rodzyanko and answerable to the Duma. Rodzyanko and the grand dukes considered the situation dire enough to demand a full constitutional monarchy, which would entail revising the Fundamental Laws. Such a manifesto would save the monarchy, as the October Manifesto had in 1905. To Rodzyanko this was also a means to maintain his power among his liberal colleagues.

On February 27, when Nicholas learned of the soldiers' insurrection in the capital, he made two decisions. First, he rejected Rodzyanko's plea to grant a ministry of confidence, although this recommendation was supported by Generals Mikhail Alekseev, Nikolai Ruzsky, and Aleksei Brusilov and by his brother Grand Duke Mikhail. He was determined to suppress the soldiers' insurrection by dispatching a counterrevolutionary expedition, composed of soldiers sent from the fronts and led by General Nikolai Ivanov. Second, he decided to leave the Stavka to join his family in Tsarskoe Selo. He was above all a family man, and he could not leave his wife alone to take care of their sick children, who were suffering from measles.

The tsar left the Stavka early on February 28. In the meantime, it was the Duma Committee that controlled movements and communications on the railway network. The Duma Committee—led by Aleksandr Bublikov, the Duma Committee's commissar of the Ministry of Transport, and his assistant, Yury Lomonosov—blocked the imperial trains from reaching

Tsarskoe Selo by imposing an information blockade and changed their route to Pskov, the headquarters of the northern front, where the tsar arrived late in the evening of March 1. Bublikov and Lomonosov also made arrangements to prevent General Ivanov's expeditionary forces from approaching the capital.

During these two days, while the tsar was traveling in the snow-covered countryside without any communication with the Stavka, the situation in Petrograd drastically changed. Rodzyanko faced challenges from his colleagues in the Duma Committee, who advocated Nicholas's abdication in favor of his son, Aleksei, under the regency of his brother Grand Duke Mikhail. With his authority already eroding due to the insurgent soldiers' hostility to his order that they return to their barracks and obey their officers, Rodzyanko had to cancel his trip to see the tsar to appeal for a responsible ministry, reluctantly accepting the Duma Committee's emerging consensus to seek Nicholas's abdication.

Rodzyanko was the point man who served as the liaison between the Duma Committee and the military leaders, who relied on information given by Rodzyanko about the situation in the capital and were fed information by the Petrograd Telegraph Agency that the Duma Committee wanted them to hear. In addition to Rodzyanko, the Naval Staff and the army General Staff provided information about the situation in the capital, but on the whole they took positions favorable to the Duma Committee.

If the Duma liberals were divided on the fate of the monarchy, the high command was not a united body, either. The nominal head of the armed forces, Nicholas II, was not present at the Stavka during these crucial two days; he was traveling in the countryside. His chief of staff, General Alekseev, had to lead the high command's policy by navigating the different views of the front commanders—General Ruzsky of the northern front, General Brusilov of the southwestern front, General Aleksei Evert of the western front, General Vladimir Sakharov of the Rumanian front, and Grand Duke Nikolai Nikolaevich of the Caucasian front. Each general ruled what was essentially a fiefdom, and the generals' relation-ships during the military operations of the war prior to the February Rev-olution had created hostility, rivalry, and distrust among them. Although Alekseev remained a monarchist, he leaned heavily toward accepting the demand of the moderate wing of Duma liberals, who advocated for politi-cal reforms while insisting on the maintenance of monarchical principles.

On February 27, Alekseev supported Nicholas's determination to sup-press the revolution in the capital by dispatching an expeditionary force led by General Ivanov. He was clear about his intention to fulfill his oath to the tsar, but as soon as he learned that it was the Duma Committee that had taken control in the capital, he suspended Ivanov's operations without Nicholas's approval. As for Ruzsky, he recalled the troops that had been sent from the northern front as reinforcements for Ivanov even before Alekseev halted Ivanov's operations. The possibility of a military interven-tion against the revolution in the capital receded.

On February 27 and 28, Alekseev supported Rodzyanko's recom-mendation to grant a ministry of confidence, but as the revolution spread to Moscow, Kronstadt, and the Baltic Fleet by March 1, he switched to advocating a responsible ministry, which would have required a larger concession of power by Nicholas. Alekseev, Ruzsky, and Brusilov were in agreement on this. Their policy was to gain Nicholas's consent for a con-stitutional monarchy and impose this decision on the rest of the high command. It fell to General Ruzsky, commander of the northern front, to wring this concession from the reluctant tsar. Nicholas resisted, objected, disagreed, and disputed, mustering what he could of his strength and indignation. He said that granting this concession would violate his sacred oath to God. But when he saw a telegram from Alekseev, who proposed a responsible ministry as the only possible way to save the dynasty, he finally relented. Even if he was an autocrat, anointed by God, and even if his wife's constant harangue that he should act like an autocrat was ringing in his ears, he seemed to have no choice but to succumb to the demands of the generals. At this moment, the world that Nicholas had clung to all his life and had aspired to maintain for his son was shattered.

By the time Ruzsky succeeded in obtaining Nicholas's acceptance of a responsible ministry, however, a majority of the Duma Committee had begun to push instead for Nicholas's abdication in favor of his son under the regency of Grand Duke Mikhail. Rodzyanko was forced to cancel his trip to meet the tsar at Dno and then at Pskov, since his colleagues suspected that Rodzyanko might negotiate with Nicholas to limit the concession to a responsible ministry. Instead, the Duma Committee decided to send Aleksandr Guchkov and Vasily Shulgin, both monarchists, to Pskov to demand Nicholas's abdication.

Had Nicholas remained at the Stavka instead of wasting two valuable days on his railway journey, could he have avoided abdication? Had he accepted a ministry of confidence and withdrawn his decision to prorogue the Duma on February 28, it might have calmed the situation in the capital and enhanced the prestige of the Duma Committee, helping to restore order. This also might have widened the cleavage between the Duma liberals and the socialist leaders who headed the Petrograd Soviet. Had he stayed at the Stavka and had Alekseev and Rodzyanko coordinated their pressure on Nicholas to accept a constitutional monarchy on February 28 or on the afternoon of March 1, when the Stavka learned of the spread of the revolution to Moscow, Kronstadt, and the Baltic Fleet, the situation in the capital might have improved considerably. But by the time Nicholas finally agreed to a constitutional monarchy, late at night on March 1, it was too late. By then, granting a constitutional monarchy would have had little chance of quelling the radicalized insurgents in the capital. Rodzyanko's order instructing the insurgent soldiers to return to their barracks and submit themselves to their officers was issued on February 28, and it provoked violent reactions from the insurgent soldiers, who occupied the Soviet plenary session to air their grievances at noon on March 1; it was this session that eventually led to the issuance of Order No. 1 by the

Petrograd Soviet late at night on March 1. This event contributed to the general consensus among the Duma Committee members that Nicholas's abdication was necessary. Even monarchists like Guchkov and Shulgin were already solidly behind this consensus at this point.

Had Nicholas stayed at the Stavka, Alekseev might have obtained concessions from the tsar by the afternoon of March 1. Had the manifesto granting a constitutional monarchy been announced at that time, this concession might have dulled the radicalism of the insurgent soldiers. In this sense, Nicholas's decision to leave Mogilev for Tsarskoe Selo on February 28, a journey that wound up taking two days, had fatal consequences.

In the early hours of March 2, in a historic conversation with Ruzsky, Rodzyanko suggested to the commander of the northern front that in order to prevent further anarchy in the capital, Nicholas's abdication might be necessary. All military personnel, from the highest-ranking generals to the lowest privates, swore allegiance "in the presence of God and on the Bible" to serve the sovereign and his heir "to the last drop of blood." The garrison soldiers in Petrograd revolted against this oath and feared that returning to their barracks and submitting themselves to their officers would mean severe punishment for breaking it. It was necessary to remove this fear to contain the insurgent soldiers' rebellions. But the generals in the high command were well aware that demanding Nicholas's abdication could be construed as a violation of this oath. Neither Alekseev nor Ruzsky was willing to push for abdication alone, so Alekseev worked to obtain the consent of other front commanders to put pressure on Nicholas to abdicate "to save the active army from disintegration; to continue the fight against the external enemy until the end; to save the independence of Russia and the fate of the dynasty." Previously, Alekseev had insisted that the army's obligation was to fulfill the oath to the tsar. But now the high command demanded the sacrifice of Nicholas in order to save the dynasty. This was the device they concocted to break the oath to the tsar while still adhering to their oath to the reigning dynasty.

The Last Tsar

Why did the front commanders, including Nikolai Nikolaevich, so readily accept this concoction? The answer is that they had wished to remove Nicholas from the throne all along. Alekseev and Nikolai Nikolaevich had been aware of a conspiracy for a palace coup to remove Alexandra from proximity to power, although at that time they hesitated to support the idea of removing the tsar from the throne. But they did not strongly raise objections to the idea, and they did nothing to forestall it. Had such a coup come to pass, they likely would have endorsed it. Brusilov was vaguely aware of the conspiracy and supported it. Ruzsky admitted later that had he known of the conspiracy to remove Nicholas, he would have joined it. When Rodzyanko presented Nicholas's abdication as the only option to avoid the conflagration of an anarchic revolt of the masses, Alekseev, Ruzsky, and Brusilov welcomed Rodzyanko's recommendation in order to actualize their own secret wish to remove Nicholas from the throne. Despite his outward respect, courteousness, and deference, Alekseev had no confidence in Nicholas. It was Alekseev who skillfully orchestrated the collective pressure of the high command to bear on Nicholas. Nicholas II's abdication was not the result of the deception and manipulation engineered by Rodzyanko, but rather was the result of the concerted action of the high command generals. It was Alekseev, not Rodzyanko, who was the chief engineer of Nicholas's abdication.

This did not mean, however, that Alekseev, Ruzsky, Brusilov, and Nikolai Nikolaevich colluded with Rodzyanko and Guchkov and the members of the Masonic organizations, headed by Kerensky, nor that each step they took was a cleverly calculated and coordinated move by these "conspirators," as contemporary Russian monarchist historians argue.[8] They shared the view that Nicholas II should be removed and that the empress should be banished from a position of influence. They did not present this demand from the very beginning of the revolution, because at any given point they believed such a demand would not be achievable because of the various urgent crises they were facing at that point.

Each reacted to the task each faced at the moment. After all, as Bismarck famously said, politics is the art of the possible.

At 2:45 p.m. on March 2, Nicholas agreed to abdicate in favor of his son under the regency of Mikhail. Witnesses observed that he accepted his abdication more calmly and more easily than he had accepted a constitutional monarchy. Accepting his abdication was for him a logical conclusion, a sort of atonement for the sin that he had committed by accepting a constitution.

Could Nicholas have had the option of rejecting the demand for his abdication? The high command was telling him that the rejection of the abdication would make it impossible to continue the war, and hence would lead to Russia's defeat. Second, if he rejected abdication, the safety of his family would not be guaranteed. And third, this demand was the unanimous opinion of the high command, led by Alekseev, whom he trusted. He had no choice but to agree to abdicate.

The two Duma Committee delegates, Guchkov and Shulgin, who did not know that Rodzyanko had stolen their thunder, arrived at Pskov late in the evening of March 2 to demand the tsar's abdication. But Nicholas had already changed the formula he had earlier accepted, deciding to abdicate not only for himself but also for his son, passing the throne to Mikhail. Nicholas feared he would not be allowed to live with his sickly son during Mikhail's regency, and he could not bear to be parted from Aleksei. Abdicating on Aleksei's behalf seemed like the only way to keep his family together, a touching display of fatherly love. Guchkov and Shulgin were stunned by Nicholas's change of mind, but in the end they accepted the double abdication in favor of Mikhail. When Nicholas made this decision, he took it for granted that his brother would accept the throne thrust upon him. He never consulted the grand duke, and never even attempted to contact him. The "abdication manifesto," penned by Nikolai Bazili and amended by Nicholas, was sent to Alekseev and Rodzyanko in the early hours of March 3.

Nicholas's double abdication clearly violated the succession law, which stipulated that the throne should pass to the heir, Aleksei. His decision to transfer the throne to Mikhail was thus illegal. Moreover, Nicholas had no right to abdicate on his son's behalf. Thus, Nicholas's double abdication was doubly illegal. It was Nicholas, the head of the Romanov house himself, who violated the rules of the house, with which every member was familiar. His action also touched on the fundamental nature of Russian autocracy. Was the emperor obligated to observe the law or, as an autocrat, could he ignore it? At heart, Nicholas was betraying the mythic continuity of the monarchy, the sense of fate and holy obligation, prioritizing his own desire to live with Aleksei over the fundamental rite of succession. By flouting this rite, Nicholas signaled to the world that the throne was a flimsy thing, a hand-me-down, easily discarded, and not a sacred duty born of an inviolable principle. With the double abdication, Nicholas further undermined what little remained of the tsar's traditional authority.

The double abdication also triggered a realignment of the Duma Committee members. New options were now on the table, and various forces rallied to advance their own interests. Rodzyanko, a monarchist, and Kerensky, a republican, formed an unlikely marriage of convenience to conspire to force Mikhail to renounce the throne. Rodzyanko believed that with Mikhail's renunciation of the throne, the prestige of the Duma would be enhanced, as it was the only institution that linked the new regime with the old. The Duma would serve as the legislature and the Provisional Government as the executive. The Duma Committee would function as a board of regency. Also, we have to keep in mind that the nature of the Duma was transformed during the revolution, becoming the center of the revolution, which boosted its prestige. Kerensky, on the other hand, believed that with the end of the monarchy, his power would be enhanced, as he was the only link between the Provisional Government and the insurgent masses that supported the Petrograd Soviet. He was the minister of justice in the Provisional Government and the vice chairman of the Petrograd Soviet. Only

Milyukov advocated for Mikhail's assumption of the throne so that the Provisional Government would maintain its legal continuity from the old regime. Mikhail II would then anoint the Provisional Government with his authority and exit from all political decisions, granting the Provisional Government sole authority to govern Russia without relying on the Duma. Milyukov was keen on undermining Rodzyanko's authority as well as the authority of the Duma so that the Provisional Government would have the sole authority to govern.

The "manifesto" of Nicholas's abdication in favor of Mikhail was sent to Rodzyanko and Alekseev around 1 a.m. on March 3. This was not an official, legally binding manifesto, certified by the Governing Senate, but only a draft, though it was signed by Nicholas and countersigned by his imperial household minister, Count Vladimir Fredericks. Still, the high command, the Duma Committee, and the Provisional Government all treated this draft as the "manifesto." As soon as Alekseev received the news, he sent the "manifesto" to the front commanders, excepting Nikolai Nikolaevich, with instructions to publicize the document among the military units. Alekseev was anxious to have the army and the navy swear allegiance to the new tsar, but he did not know how Nikolai Nikolaevich would react to Nicholas's abdication. He would handle Nikolai Nikolaevich by limiting the information the grand duke received, so as to influence his decision.

At 5 a.m. on March 3, Rodzyanko contacted Ruzsky and asked him to withhold the publication and dissemination of the "manifesto" of Nicholas's abdication. Without detecting the true motivation behind this request, Ruzsky agreed to postpone the publication of the "manifesto." The moat was filled before the attack on the castle, so to speak. At 6 a.m., Rodzyanko attacked the castle by contacting Alekseev and asking him to withhold the "manifesto" of Nicholas's abdication on the grounds that the transition of the throne to Mikhail would inflame popular resentment of the monarchy, throwing the country into uncontrollable anarchy. The only way to avoid this was to wait until the Constituent Assembly, which would determine the form of the government. But the Constituent Assembly would not be convened until after the war. Thus, the "suspension" of the monarchy was virtually tantamount to the end of the monarchy. The question was no longer merely who was to assume the throne; rather, the issue shifted to whether the monarchical system itself should be preserved. This was a decisive moment. Had Alekseev been committed to the preservation of the monarchy, as he had professed he was when he recommended Nicholas's abdication, he could have insisted on the publication of Nicholas's abdication "manifesto" immediately and unilaterally, rejecting Rodzyanko's request to withhold the document, and had the military units swear allegiance to the new tsar, Mikhail II. Nonetheless, Alekseev accepted, though reluctantly, Rodzyanko's request to withhold the announcement of the "manifesto" of Nicholas's abdication.

At 9 a.m. on March 3, the representatives of the Duma Committee and the Provisional Government met with Grand Duke Mikhail. Rodzyanko, Prince Lvov, and Kerensky presented the argument that Mikhail should not assume the throne, while Milyukov argued that he should. In the end, warned by Rodzyanko, Lvov, and Kerensky that his assumption of the throne would invite a catastrophic civil war, Mikhail decided not to take the throne thrust on him by his brother.

Mikhail never wanted to be the tsar. He was aware of the illegality of his succession to the throne, and he was equally aware that he too lacked the charisma to steer the nation in this turbulent period. Most importantly, he did not have the backing of the high command. He was never given the chance to consult anyone. His wife, Natasha Brasova, was dead set against her husband assuming the throne. Mikhail's decision not to assume the throne meant the end of the dynasty and the end of the monarchical system in Russia. The Romanov monarchy, which had begun with a Mikhail, ended with another Mikhail.

Alekseev learned of Mikhail's decision sometime in the early afternoon on March 3. Immediately Alekseev sent a telegram to the front

commanders. The chief of staff stated that "the outlined situation constituted a danger more serious than any other for the active army," because
"uncertainty, vacillation, and the change of the 'manifesto'" would have
staggering effects and deprive the army of "fighting capacity." He then
made two recommendations. The first was to demand that Rodzyanko
make the "manifesto" of Nicholas's abdication public "in the name of salvation of the homeland and of the active army." The second was to convene a meeting of front commanders at Mogilev on March 8 or 9.

The front commanders reacted to Alekseev's proposal coldly. Ruzsky
and Brusilov strongly opposed Alekseev's proposal to convene a military
conference and recommended that the high command cooperate with the
Provisional Government. Sakharov was the only commander who agreed
with Alekseev's proposal to convene a military conference, but even he
did not support military intervention. Evert was not in favor of Nicholas's
abdication and leaned toward resolving the crisis by establishing a responsible ministry, withdrawing his earlier consent for Nicholas's abdication.
In any case, the proposed conference on March 8 or 9 would be too late.
He too did not advocate military intervention to restore the dynasty.

The response of the front commanders revealed that the high command was hopelessly divided in their attitudes toward the Provisional
Government and the preservation of the monarchical system. The only
policy that they agreed on was the avoidance of military intervention
against the revolution in the capital. Once events had progressed to a
certain point, they were unanimous in the opinion that it was too late to
revive the idea of military intervention.

The most decisive blow to Alekseev's proposal came from Grand Duke
Nikolai Nikolaevich. He argued that the most sacred duty of the army and the
navy was to fight against the enemy. However, he did not say anything about
the duty to preserve the monarchical system. He further stated that he could
not attend the military conference suggested by Alekseev, since he would
need several days for orientation as the new supreme commander under the

new government. He had already made contact with the Provisional Government to familiarize himself with the "course of events." He made it clear that he was against Mikhail assuming the throne, as it would inevitably lead to bloodshed. The only member of the Romanovs who might conceivably have resurrected the Romanov dynasty willingly accepted its pitiful end.

Late on the night of March 3, the two newspapers in Petrograd printed special issues in which bold headlines told the sensational news of the abdications of Nicholas and Mikhail. After learning about Mikhail's refusal to assume the throne, however, Nicholas did change his mind again, and attempted to abdicate only for himself and transfer the throne to Aleksei. When he arrived at Mogilev, he asked Alekseev to transmit this change to Rodzyanko, but Alekseev refused, saying that it was too late.

The major players in the abdication drama did not act in concert or in coordination. Each actor operated independently, but these actions provoked the actions of others in a dazzling sequence of toppling dominoes that culminated in the fall of the monarchy. These major players shared one idea: the need to remove Nicholas from the throne and banish Alexandra from proximity to power. They would have accepted a ministry of confidence or a constitutional monarchy under the circumstances that confronted them at certain junctures. But in the end, they achieved what they had desired in their heart: Nicholas's abdication. And yet all these actors, except for Kerensky, would have preserved the monarchical system without Nicholas. Why, then, did Nicholas's abdication wind up ending the monarchy? The crucial turning point came when Nicholas changed the original formula of his abdication in favor of his son under the regency of Mikhail and instead abdicated not only for himself but also for Aleksei, transferring the throne to Mikhail.

The most essential characteristic of Russian autocracy was that the autocrat and the autocracy were integrally connected, in contrast to the

Japanese monarchy or the British monarchy. From the Meiji period to the end of World War II, the Japanese emperor was shielded from the vagaries of politics, while his position was revered as the essence of Japanese nationhood. Through the Imperial Rescript on Education and the Imperial Rescript on Soldiers and Sailors, emperor worship penetrated deeply every corner of Japanese society. The Japanese emperor did not need to prove his charisma to be revered. In fact, the Taisho emperor was believed to be mentally deficient. Ironically, the nature of autocracy in Russia, where the autocrat preserved power, unencumbered by any laws and institutions, was the death knell for the monarchy and autocracy itself. The Russian state (*gosudarstvo*) could not survive without the sovereign (*gosudar*).

To Vladimir Nabokov and Boris Nolde, who wrote the "manifesto" of Mikhail's renunciation of the throne, the most important points were to confirm, first, the plenitude of power of the Provisional Government and, second, its continuing tie with the Duma. Thus, the most important point of this "manifesto" was the phrase "I ask all citizens of the Russian State to pledge allegiance to the Provisional Government, which came into being at the initiative of the State Duma and which is endowed with full power."

In the late afternoon or early evening of March 3, the first meeting of the Provisional Government was held. Neither Rodzyanko nor the rest of the Duma Committee was invited. At this meeting, Lvov, now the prime minister, "raised the question about the need to precisely determine the scope of power possessed by the Provisional Government and the Fundamental Laws of the Russian State," as well as the relationship between the Provisional Government and the Duma Committee. The meeting resolved that "the entire plenitude of power that belonged to the monarch must be considered transferred, not to the State Duma, but to the Provisional Government." Further, it resolved that the Fundamental Laws be considered invalid. When Milyukov announced the formation of the Provisional Government in front of the insurgent masses in Catherine Hall of the Tauride Palace, someone in the audience asked Milyukov: "Who elected you?"

Milyukov answered: "It was the revolution that elected us." The second part of the Provisional Government's March 3 decision acknowledged that the Provisional Government would have to take the opinion of the Petrograd Soviet into serious consideration. Although to allow its views to play a role in the formal decisions made by the Provisional Government would not be acceptable, the Provisional Government would consult the Petrograd Soviet through a liaison committee, composed of the representatives of the Provisional Government and the Petrograd Soviet. This was the tacit acceptance of dual power, admitting that the Provisional Government did not actually hold power completely on its own. Although it claimed to be endowed with a plenitude of power, it was in reality not the sole occupier of state power.

The Soviet Executive Committee had stood on the sidelines while the abdication drama ran its course, deciding to let the Duma Committee play the major role in "overthrowing" the monarchy. They feared that their involvement in the abdication drama would provoke the military leaders to take action against the revolution. But as soon as the monarchy was dead at Mikhail's refusal to assume the throne on March 3, the Executive Committee of the Petrograd Soviet was quick to rear its head and pass a resolution to arrest Nicholas and Alexandra, place Grand Duke Mikhail under house arrest, and transport Grand Duke Nikolai Nikolaevich to Petrograd and place him under surveillance.

On March 7, the Provisional Government passed a resolution to deprive Nicholas and Alexandra of freedom and to transport Nicholas to Tsarskoe Selo. Alekseev was tasked with carrying out this order, and he did so without protest. On the following day, former empress Alexandra was arrested by General Lavr Kornilov, the new commander of the Petrograd Military District, appointed by Rodzyanko and approved by Alekseev. Nicholas and Alexandra were reunited on March 9 in the Alexander Palace in Tsarskoe Selo, now as prisoners of the Provisional Government and the Petrograd Soviet.

On March 4, the new supreme commander, Grand Duke Nikolai Niko-laevich, instructed the armed forces to swear allegiance to the Provisional Government. He arrived in Mogilev on March 10, but the Provisional Government unceremoniously stripped him of the supreme commandership. The grand duke accepted this verdict meekly in return for the Provisional Government's assurance of his safe passage to the Crimea.

This was only the beginning of the Romanovs' descent down the hills of Golgotha, ending in the brutal execution of Nicholas's entire family in Ekaterinburg in July 1918 by Bolshevik executioners. Each member of the Romanovs suffered a tragic end of one kind or another, some in brutal murders by the Bolsheviks and others fleeing from Russia with torturous difficulties.[9] Those fates were sealed in March 1917 as the Romanovs exited the world-historical stage not with a bang but with a whimper.

# ACKNOWLEDGMENTS

This book is the outcome of my lifelong research on the February Revolution of 1917 in Russia. Its origin goes way back to my undergraduate thesis at Tokyo University in 1964, which eventually became the book *The February Revolution: Petrograd, 1917* (Seattle: University of Washington Press, 1981). In this book I presented the view that the February Revolution in Petrograd consisted of two revolutions: the revolution of insurgent workers and soldiers against the established order and the revolution of the liberal political elite against the tsarist autocracy. The second part of this interpretation did not receive much credit either in the Soviet Union or in the West, failing to make much of a dent on the prevailing view that the tsarist regime was swept away by the mass revolt.

After the publication of this book, I took a leave of absence from the February Revolution for many years. In the meantime, the world changed drastically, especially prompted by the collapse of the Soviet Union. This epoch-making event was placed in the broader perspective of transition from authoritarianism to democracy by scholars as well as by the general public. Scholarly work on the Soviet Union/Russia went in two different directions. In post-Soviet Russia, finally freed from the rigid straitjacket of Marxist-Leninist interpretation of the Russian Revolution, historians in the post-Soviet era began to explore the revolution from various perspectives. The place of the February Revolution, which had been overshadowed during the Soviet period merely as a prelude to the October Revolution led by the Bolsheviks, has been restored to its rightful place, and a new vista of research that had hitherto been suppressed became wide open, with an abundance of new sources that previously had been buried in the archives. In contrast, however, interest in the Russian Revolution among specialists on Russian/Soviet history in the West significantly waned, and a small legion of researchers who continued to study the Russian Revolution shifted their gaze to examine different aspects of the revolution, such as culture, gender, and regional and ethnic studies. Such new research has undoubtedly enriched our understanding of the Russian Revolution, but the February Revolution itself was largely pushed back onto the back burner as an issue that did not require careful reexamination, as if the question of the end of the monarchy had already been settled.[1]

Prompted by the changing world, as well as by new scholarship and new sources that became available, I returned to the February Revolution and published a revised edition of my first book, *The February Revolution: Petrograd, 1917: The End of the Tsarist Regime and the Birth of Dual Power* (Leiden: Brill, 2017). By incorporating new scholarship and new sources, especially about the liberal elite and centering around the Duma Committee, I reinforced my previous position on the two separate but interrelated revolutions, the popular insurrection and the Duma liberals' revolt against Tsar Nicholas II and his government. I argued more forcefully than in the first book that the liberal elite played a decisive role in the abdication of Nicholas II and the end of the monarchy.

Since I published this book, however, the world has been going through a new challenge: the rise of authoritarianism globally, which is challenging democracy, including our own in the United States. I went back to reexamine the vigorous debates among Russian historians about

Nicholas II's abdication and the sources that I had overlooked in revising my book. I also benefited a great deal from new research and new sources on the role of the high command in the abdication drama. I became convinced that the full story of how Russian autocracy functioned during World War I and how it ended in the February Revolution, involving not only the Duma liberals but also the high command and Nicholas II's own relatives, deserved to be told. This book is the fulfillment of a dream that began a long time ago: to tell the full story of the abdication drama that ended the tsarist autocratic system.

Many scholars, colleagues, and friends in Japan, the United States, Britain, and Russia/the Soviet Union have provided me with help, advice, and inspiration along the way. They are too numerous to be listed individually. I merely mention here three scholars to whom I owe intellectual debts: Wada Haruki, Donald W. Treadgold, and Vitalii Ivanovich Startsev. To single out those who have most helped with this book: I thank a host of Russian scholars whom I have not met or corresponded with, but who have provided numerous new sources and insightful interpretations on the abdication drama, although I may disagree with some of their views. Especially I would like to thank Andrei Borisovich Nikolaev, whose books and numerous articles on the February Revolution are undoubtedly the most authoritative works on the revolution, and I benefited a great deal from his encyclopedic knowledge about it. He has also unstintingly provided me with numerous sources that were otherwise unavailable to me. Ekaterina Sergeevna Gabroeva provided me with invaluable help on my numerous inquiries. I also thank Boris Ivanovich Kolonitskii, whose pioneering works on Nicholas and Alexandra, Kerensky, and language and culture during the Russian Revolution influenced my work in various aspects.

In the United States and Britain, I would like to thank Semion Lyandres, who has organized numerous workshops on the Russian Revolution, which facilitated connections with many scholars in Russia and in the West working on the Russian Revolution. Discussions and correspondence I have had with my fellow colleagues on the Russian Revolution, including Michael Hickey, Daniel Orlovsky, Rex Wade, Sarah Badcock, Aaron Retish, and Ian Thatcher, among others, provided me with inspiration. Hickey, Orlovsky, Lyandres, and Nikolaev read a portion of this book and gave me their critical comments. Nicholas Nicholson has also given me helpful advice, shared sources, and corrected my errors on Nicholas II's relatives, especially Grand Duke Mikhail, Grand Duke Kirill Vladimirovich, and the succession laws. In addition to answering my numerous queries and sharing source materials, Bruce Menning gave me permission to use his unpublished paper on the high command during World War I. Margaret Herzen and Robert Nichols have given me valuable insight into Orthodox rituals and Nicholas's religiosity.

The archivists at the Hoover Institution at Stanford University and the Bakhmeteff Archive at Columbia University extended their generous help. So did the archivists at the former TsGIA (now RGIA), TsGAOR (now GARF), TsGAORSS (now TsGA SPb), and the Manuscript Division of the Russian National Library, which I used during the Soviet period. Unfortunately, the war in Ukraine that began in February 2022 has prevented me from using Russian archives since.

I am grateful for the general fellowships I have received for this book: the Silas Palmer Fellowship at the Hoover Institution at Stanford University and the Research Fellowship from the Academic Senate at the University of California at Santa Barbara.

Above anyone else, I owe a great debt to Brandon Proia of Basic Books, who believed in the value of my book and transformed my rough, long-winded manuscript with patience, care, and impeccable professional editorial skills. The sharp eyes of Sue Warga, my copy editor, caught numerous inconsistencies and errors, tolerated numerous last-minute changes, and made my book much better. Patti Isaacs created a complicated genealogical table and made wonderful maps. Annie Chatham of

Basic Books patiently shepherded the manuscript through production. Thomas LeBien of Moon and Company has assisted me with helpful advice for navigating the publishing world.

I also thank Alexandra Noi, my indefatigable research assistant, who has tracked down obscure books, deciphered seemingly illegible hand-written archival materials, and answered numerous queries regarding translation.

The Interlibrary Loan office at the Davidson Library at UC Santa Barbara provided invaluable service in obtaining materials from all over the world. Letters and Science Information Technology (LSIT) at UCSB was a lifesaver for resolving all kinds of technical issues.

Needless to say, I am solely responsible for any mistakes that might slip into the book.

Last but not least, I thank my wife, Debbie, for her patience, for her reading of numerous drafts, and for giving me her candid comments. Without her encouragement and constant support, this book would not have been written. It is to Debbie that this book is dedicated.

SANTA BARBARA, MAY 2024

# BIBLIOGRAPHY

**Abbreviations**

Anan'ich, *Fevral'skaia revoliutsiia*: B. V. Anan'ich, ed., *Fevral'skaia revoliutsiia: Pervaia mirovaia voina i konets Rossiiskoi imperii.* Vol. 3. St. Petersburg: Liki Rossii, 2014.

*ARR: Arkhiv russkoi revoliutsii*

Bakhmeteff Archive: Bakhmeteff Archive of Russia and East European Culture, Columbia University

d.: delo

Dokumenty Lukomskago: "Dokumenty k 'Vospominaniiam' gen. Lukomskago." *ARR* 3 (1921).

f.: fond

Fuhrmann: J. T. Fuhrmann, ed., *The Complete Wartime Correspondence of Tsar Nicholas II and the Empress Alexandra, April 1914–March 1917.* Westport, CT: Greenwood Press, 1999.

GARF: Gosudarstvennyi arkhiv Rossiiskoi Federatsii, Moscow

*Gibel' monarkhii*: A. Liberman and S. Shokarev, eds., *Gibel' monarkhii: Istoriia Rossii i doma Romanovykh v memuarakh sovremennikov XVII–XX.* Moscow: Fond Sergeia Dubova, 2000.

*Guchkov rasskazyvaet*: A. I. Guchkov, *Aleksandr Ivanovich Guchkov rasskazyvaet: vospominaniia predsedateli Gosudarstvennoi dumy i voennogo ministra Vremmenogo pravitel'stva.* Moscow: TOO, 1993.

HIA: Hoover Institution Library and Archives

*KA: Krasnyi arkhiv*

*KA* (1): "Fevral'skaia revoliutsiia 1917 goda: Dokumenty Stavki verkhovnogo glavnokomanduiushchego i shtaba glavnokomanduiushchego armiiami severnogo fronta." *Krasnyi arkhiv* 21, no. 2 (1927).

*KA* (2): "Fevral'skaia revoliutsiia 1917 goda: Dokumenty Stavki verkhovnogo glavnokomanduiushchego i shtaba glavnokomanduiushchego armiiami severnogo fronta." *Krasnyi arkhiv* 21, no. 3 (1927).

*KL: Krasnaia letopis'*

l: list

ll: listy

Matveev, *Memoirs*: Aleksei Sergeevich Matveev Papers, Box 1, Bakhmeteff Archive, Columbia University.

ob: obratna

op.: opis'

OR RGB: Otdel Rukopisei, Rossiiskaia Gosudarstvennaia Biblioteka

*Otrechenie: Otrechenie Nikolaia II: Vospominaniia ochevidtsev i dokumenty.* Moscow/Berlin: Direct Media, 2017.

*Permskaia Golgofa: Permskaia Golgofa Mikhaila II: sbornik dokumentov o poslednem perioda zhizni i ubiistva v gorode Permi Velikogo Kniazia Mikhaila Aleksandrovicha.* Vol. 1. Edited by L. A. Lykova, V. M. Khrustalev, et al. Perm': Pushka, 2018.

*PR: Proletarskaia revoliutsiia*

"Protokol sobytii": "Protokol sobytii," Document 43, in O. A. Shashkova, ed., *Fevral'skaia revoliutsiia 1917: Sbornik dokumentov i materialov.* Moscow: Rossiiskii gosudarstvennyi gumanitarnyi universitet, 1996.

"Protokol zasedanii": "Protokol zasedanii: soveshchaniia Gosudarstvennoi dumy s predstaviteliami fraktsii, chastnogo soveshchaniia chlenov Gosudarstvennoi dumy i Vremennogo komiteta Gosudarstvennoi dumy 27 fevralia–3 marta 1917 goda, vvedenie, tekst i komentarii." In A. B. Nikolaev, ed., *Tavricheskie chteniia 2011.* St. Petersburg, 2012.

RGIA: Rossiiskii gosudarstvennyi istoricheskii arkhiv, St. Petersburg

*RL: Russkaia letopis'*

Shashkova, *Fevral'skaia revoliutsiia*: O. A. Shashkova, ed., *Fevral'skaia revoliutsiia 1917: Sbornik dokumentov i materialov.* Moscow: Rossiiskii gosudarstvennyi gumanitarnyi universitet, 1996.

*Stavka i revoliutsiia: Stavka i revoliutsiia: Sbornik dokumentov v dvukh tomakh: Shtab verkhovnogo glavnokomanduiushchego i revoliutsionnykh sobytiia 1917–nachala 1918 goda po dokumentam Rossiiskogo gosudarstvennogo-*

*istoricheskogo arkhiva, 18 fevralia–18 iunia 1917*. Vol. 1. Edited by I. O. Garkusha et al. Moscow: Fond "Sviaz' Epokha" Kuchkogo Pole, 2019.

Tal', *Chronology: Chronology of Abdication*, handwritten manuscript in Russian, Georgii Aleksandrovich Tal' Papers, Bakhmeteff Archive.

Tal', *Memuary*: Memuary ob otrechenii ot prestola Rossiiskogo Gosudaria Imperatora Nikolaia II, Von Thal Memoirs, HIA.

Tal', *Mysl' ob otrechenii*: Georgii Aleksandrovich Tal' Papers, Bakhmeteff Archive.

Telegrammy Ruzskago: "Telegrammy i razgovory po telegrafu mezhdu Pskovom, Stavkoiu i Petrogradom, otnosiashchiesia k obstoiatel'stvam otrecheniia Gosudaria Imperatora, s primechaniiami k nim general-ad"iutanta N. V. Ruzskago." *Russkaia letopis'* 3 (1922).


## Archives

**GARF:** Rossiiskii gosudarstvennyi arkhiv Rossiiskoi Federatsii, Moscow
f. 6: Chancellery of the Provisional Government
f. 601: Nicholas II
f. 1467 (ChSK): Extraordinary Investigation Commission
**RGIA:** Rossiiskii gosudarstvennyi istoricheskii arkhiv, St. Petersburg
f. 1278: State Duma
**OR RGB:** Otdel Rukopisei, Rossiiskaia Gosudarstvennaia Biblioteka
f. 15: P. A. Bazilevskii, papka IV, ed. kh. Dnevnik P. A. Bazilevskogo
f. 218: B.A. Engel'gardt, "Potonuvshii mir: Vospominaniia"
**Hoover Institution Archives**
Mikhail Vasil'evich Alekseev Papers
A. Balk, "Poslednie piat' dnei tsarskago Petrograda: Dnevnik posledniago Petrogradskago gradonachal'nika," Belgrade, 1929, typewritten
Nikolai I. Bazili Papers
Vera Catell Papers
Grand Duchess Ksenia Aleksandrovna Papers
Alexandre Tarsaidze Papers
Von Thal Memoirs
**Bakhmeteff Archive**
Petr L'vovich Bark Papers
Benckendorff Family Papers
K. I. Globachev, "Pravda o russkoi revoliutsii, byvshego nachal'nika Petrogradskogo Okhrannogo otdeleniia"

Arkadii Nikolaevich Iakhontov Papers
Nikolai Nikitich Ivanov Papers
Aleksei Sergeevich Matveev Papers
Georgii Aleksandrovich Tal' Papers

**Works Cited**

Abraham, Richard. *Alexander Kerensky: The First Love of the Revolution.* New York: Columbia University Press, 1987.

Airapetov, O. R. *Generaly, liberaly i predprinimateli: rabota na front i na revoliutsiiu, 1907–1917.* Moscow: Izd-vo "Trikvardata," 2003.

Akaemov, N. F. "Agoniia starago rezhima." *Istoricheskii vestnik* 148 (1917).

Akhmatova, Anna. "Iul' 1914." In Dmitri Obolensky, ed., *The Heritage of Russian Verse.* Bloomington: Indiana University Press, 1962.

Alekseeva-Borel', V. *Sorok let v riadakh russkoi imperatorskoi armii: General M. V. Alekseev.* St. Petersburg: Izd-vo Bel'beder, 2000.

Alexander Mikhailovich. *Once a Grand Duke.* New York: Farrar & Rinehart, 1932.

Almedingen, E. M. *The Empress Alexandra, 1872–1918: A Study.* London: Hutchinson, 1961.

Anan'ich, B. V., ed. *Fevral'skaia revoliutsiia: Pervaia mirovaia voina i konets Rossiiskoi imperii.* Vol. 3. St. Petersburg: Liki Rossii, 2014. [Anan'ich, *Fevral'skaia revoliutsiia*]

Andrei Vladimirovich. "Dnevniki." In *Gibel' monarkhii.*

Andrei Vladimirovich. "Iz dnevnika A. V. Romanova, 1916–1917 gg." *KA* 26 (1928).

Andrei Vladimirovich. *Voennyi dnevnik Velikogo kniazia Andreiia Vladimirovicha Romanova (1914–1917).* Ed. V. M. Osin and V. M. Khrustalev. Moscow: Izd-vo im Sabashnikovykh, 2008.

Arkhipov, I. L. *Rossiiskaia politicheskaia elita v fevrale 1917: Psikhologiia nadezhdy i otchainii.* St. Petersburg: Izd-vo St. Peterburgskogo universiteta, 2000.

Azar, H., ed. *The Diary of Olga Romanov.* Yardley, PA: Westholme, 2014.

Badcock, S. "Autocracy in Crisis: Nicholas the Last." In I. Thatcher, ed., *Late Imperial Russia: Problems and Prospects.* Manchester: Manchester University Press, 2005.

Balk, A. *Poslednie piat' dnei tsarskago Petrograda: Dnevnik posledniago Petrogradskago gradonachal'nika.* Belgrade, 1929, typewritten manuscript, HIA.

Bark, Peter. *Memoirs* (typewritten memoirs in English). Petr L'vovich Bark Papers, Bakhmeteff Archive.

Basily, Nicolas de. *Memoirs: Diplomat of Imperial Russia, 1903–1917*. Stanford, CA: Hoover Institution Press, 1973.

Basily, Nicolas de. *The Abdication of Emperor Nicholas II of Russia: A Memoir by Nicolas de Basily*. Princeton, NJ: Kingston Press, 1984.

Benckendorff, P. *Last Days at Tsarskoe Selo*. London: W. Heinemann, 1927.

Blok, A. A. *Poslednie dni imperatorskoi vlasti*. Moscow: Progress, 2012.

Boldyrev, V. G. "Iz dnevnika gen. V. G. Boldyreva." *KA* 23, no. 4 (1927).

Boltunova, E. M. "Stavka Nikolaia II v Mogileve i pamiat' o nei v Sovetskoe i poslesovetskoe vremia." *Voennaia letopis otechestva* 10 (2016).

Botkin, Gleb. *The Real Romanovs*. London, New York: Putnam, 1932.

Brinton, Crane. *The Anatomy of Revolution*. New York: Random House, 1965.

Browder, R. P., and A. F. Kerensky, eds. *The Russian Provisional Government: Documents*. Vol. 1. Stanford, CA: Stanford University Press, 1961.

Brusilov, A. A. *A Soldier's Notebook, 1914–1918*. Westport, CT: Greenwood Press, 1930.

Brusilov, A. A. *Moi vospominaniia*. Moscow: Voenno-izd-vo, 1943.

Brusilov, A. A. *Moi vospominaniia*. Moscow: ROSSPEN, 2001.

Bublikov, A. "K istorii otrecheniia Nikolaia II." *Solntse Rossii* 9, no. 367 (April 1917). Bazili Papers, Box 27, File 8:5, HIA.

Bublikov, A. A. *Russkaia revoliutsiia: Vpechatleniia i mysli ochevidtsa i uchastnika*. New York, 1918.

Bublikov, A. A. *Russkaia revoliutsiia: Vpechatleniia i mysli ochevidtsa i uchastnika*, with introductory essay by V. M. Khrustalev, "Fevral'skaia revoliutsiia i vospominaniia deputata Gosudarstvennoi dumy Aleksandra Aleksandrovicha Bublikova (1875–1941)." Moscow: Kuchkovo Pole, 2016.

Bubnov, A. D. *V tsarskoi Stavke: Vospominaniia Admirala Bubnova*. New York: Chekhov Publishing House, 1955.

Bubnov, A. D. "V tsarskoi Stavke." In *Konets Rossiiskoi monarkhii*. Moscow: Voennoe izdatel'stvo, 2002.

Buchanan, George. *My Mission to Russia and Other Diplomatic Memories*. Vol. 2. London: Cassell and Co., 1923.

Buchanan, Meriel. *The Dissolution of an Empire*. London: John Murray, 1932.

Buchanan, Meriel. *Petrograd*. London: Collins, 1918.

Buknin, B. "Fevral'skoe dni v Bologoe: Iz vospominanii." *Stalinits* 35, no. 405 (1935).

Bulygin, Paul. *The Murder of the Romanovs: The Authentic Account*. Westport, CT: Hyperion Press, 1935.

Buranov, Iu., and V. Khrustalev. *Gibel' imperatorskogo doma, 1917–1919 gg.* Moscow: Progress, 1992.

Burdzhalov, E. N. *Vtoraia russkaia revoliutsiia: Vosstanie v Petrograde.* Moscow: Nauka, 1967.

Burdzhalov, E. N. *Vtoraia russkaia revoliutsiia: Moskva, front, periferiia.* Moscow: Nauka, 1971.

Buxhoeveden, Sofia. "Gosudar' Imperator Nikolai II: iz vospominanii, Chast' II." Typewritten memoirs, Bazili Papers, Box 23, File 3, HIA.

Buxhoeveden, Sophie. *The Life and Tragedy of Alexandra Feodorovna, Empress of Russia: A Biography.* London: Longmans, Green, 1929.

Cantacuzene, Julia. *Revolutionary Days: Recollections of Romanoffs and Bolsheviki, 1914–1917.* Boston: Small, Maynard, 1920.

Chamberlin, William Henry. *The Russian Revolution, 1917–1921.* Vol. 1. New York: Macmillan, 1935.

Chebotareva, Valentina. "V dvortsovom lazarete v Tsarskom Sele: Dnevnik 14 iulia 1915–5 ianvaria 1918." *Novyi zhurnal* 181 (1990), 182 (1991).

Chermenskii, E. D., *IV gosudarstvennaia duma i sverzhenie tsarizma v Rossii.* Moscow: Mysl', 1976.

Cherniaev, V. Iu. "Vosstanie Pavlovskogo ploka 26 fevralia 1917 g." In O. N. Znamenskii et al., eds., *Rabochii klass Rossii, ego soiuzniki i politicheskie protivniki v 1917 godu: Sbornik nauchnykh trudov.* Leningrad: Nauka, 1989.

Cherniavsky, Michael. *Prologue to Revolution: Notes of A. N. Iakhontov on the Secret Meeting of the Council of Ministers, 1915.* Englewood Cliffs, NJ: Prentice-Hall, 1967.

Crawford, Donald. *The Last Tsar: Emperor Michael II.* New York: Emperor Michael Foundation, n.d.

Crawford, Rosemary, and Donald Crawford. *Michael and Natasha: The Life and Love of Michael II, the Last of the Russian Tsars.* New York: Avon Books, 2000.

Danilov, Iu. N. "Moi vospominaniia ob Imperatore Nikolae II-om, o Vel. Kniaze Mikhaile Aleksandroviche." *ARR* 19 (1928).

Danilov, Iu. N. "Na puti k krusheniiu: ocherki iz poslednego perioda Russkoi monarkhii." In V. A. Avdeev, ed., *Konets Rossiiskoi monarkhii.* Moscow: Voennoe izdatel'stvo, 2002.

Dehn, L. *The Real Tsaritsa.* London: Butterworth, 1922.

Demidov, I. "Tsarskoe Selo 1-go marta 1917 goda." *Poslednie novosti,* March 12, 1927.

Denikin, A. I. *Ocherki russkoi smuty: krushenie vlasti i armii, fevral'-sentiabr'* 1917. Vol. 1, Part 1. Paris: J. Povolozky, 1921.

Diakin, V. S. *Russkaia burzhuazia i tsarizm v gody pervoi mirovoi voiny.* Leningrad: Nauka, 1967.

"Dokumenty k 'Vospominaniiam' gen. Lukomskago." *ARR* 3 (1921). [*Dokumenty Lukomskago*]

Dubenskii, D. N. "Kak proizoshel perevorot v Rossii: Zapiski-dnevniki." *RL* 3 (1922).

Elizaveta Fedorovna. "Pis'ma k imperatritse Marii Fedorovne, 1883–1916 gg." *Rossiiskii arkhiv* 11 (2001).

Engel'gardt, B. A. "Potonuvshii mir: Vospominaniia." OR RGB, f. 218, No. 306, ed. kh, 1–3.

Engelstein, Laura. *Russia in Flames: War, Revolution, Civil War, 1914–1921.* New York: Oxford University Press, 2018.

Fabritskii, S. S. *Iz proshlogo: Vospominaniia fligel'-ad"iutanta gosudaria imperatora Nikolaia II.* In V. M. Khrustalev, ed., *Imperator Nikolai II: Tainy Rossiiskogo Imperatorskogo dvora.* Moscow: AST, 2013.

Fallows, Thomas. "Politics and the War Effort in Russia: The Union of Zemstvos and the Organization of the Food Supply, 1914–1916." *Slavic Review* 37, no. 1 (1978).

"Fevral'skaia revoliutsiia 1917 goda: Dokumenty Stavki verkhovnogo glavnokomanduiushchego i shtaba glavnokomanduiushchego armiiami severnogo fronta." *KA* 21, no. 2 (1927). [*KA* (1)]

"Fevral'skaia revoliutsiia 1917 goda: Dokumenty Stavki verkhovnogo glavnokomanduiushchego i shtaba glavnokomanduiushchego armiiami severnogo fronta." *KA* 21, no. 3 (1927). [*KA* (2)]

"Fevral'skaia revoliutsiia i okhrannoe otdelenie." *Byloe* 29, no. 1 (1918).

*Fevral'skaia revoliutsiia ot novykh istochnikov k novomu osmyshleniiu.* Moscow: Institut Rossiiskoi istorii RAN, 1997.

"Fevral'skaia revoliutsiia v dokumentakh: politicheskie svodki i donesheniia." *PR* 13, no. 1 (1923).

"Fevral'skaia revoliutsiia v Petrograde: Materialy voennoi komissii vremennogo komiteta gosudarstvennoi dumy." *KA* 41–42, nos. 4–5 (1930).

Fleer, M. G. *Rabochee dvizhenie v Rossii v gody imperialisticheskoi voiny.* Leningrad: Priboi, 1926.

Florinsky, M. T. *The End of the Russian Empire.* New Haven, CT: Yale University Press, 1931.

Fuhrmann, J. T., ed. *The Complete Wartime Correspondence of Tsar Nicholas II and the Empress Alexandra, April 1914–March 1917*. Westport, CT: Greenwood Press, 1999. [Fuhrmann]

Gaida, N. A. *Liberal'naia oppozitsiia na putiakh k vlasti (1914–1917 gg.)*. Moscow: ROSSPEN, 2003.

Ganelin, R. Sh. "Proekt Manifesta Nikolaia II, podgotovlennyi velikimi kniaz'-iami 1 marta 1917 g.," in Anan'ich, *Fevral'skaia revoliutsiia*.

Ganelin, R. Sh. "23 Fevralia," "24 Fevralia," "25 Fevralia," and "26 Fevralia." In Anan'ich, *Fevral'skaia revoliutsiia*.

Ganelin, R. Sh. "Velikii kniaz' Mikhail Aleksandrovich v martovskie dni 1917 g.: Vospominaniia N. N. Ivanova." In Anan'ich, *Fevral'skaia revoliutsiia*.

Ganin, A. V., "Genshtabisty i Fevral'skaia revoliutsiia." In V. V. Kalashnikov, ed., *Fevral'skaia revoliutsiia 1917 goda: problemy istorii i istoriografii; sbornik dokladov*, St. Petersburg: Izd-vp SPbGETU "LETI," 2017.

Gatrell, Peter. *A Whole Empire Walking: Refugees in Russia During World War I*. Bloomington: Indiana University Press, 1999.

Gavriil Konstantinovich. *V Mramornom dvortse*. Moscow: Zakharov, 2001.

Genkina, E. "Fevral'skii perevorot." In *Ocherki po istorii Oktiabr'skoi revoliutsii*, vol. 2, ed. M. N. Pokroskii. Leningrad, 1927.

*Gibel' monarkhii: Istoriia Rossii i doma Romanovykh v memuarakh sovremennikov XVII–XX*. Eds. A. Liberman and S. Shokarev. Moscow: Fond Sergeia Dubova, 2000. [*Gibel' monarkhii*]

Gilliard, Pierre. *Thirteen Years at the Russian Court*. New York: D. H. Dolan, 1921.

Gippius, Z. N. *Dnevniki*. Vol. 1. Moscow: NFK Intervak, 1999.

Gippius, Z. N. *Siniaia kniga: Peterburgskii dnevnik, 1914–1918*. Belgrade: Radenkovicha, 1929.

Gleason, William E. "The All-Russian Union of Towns and the Politics of Urban Reform in Tsarist Russia." *Russian Review* 35, no. 3 (1976).

Glinka, Ia. V. *Odinatsat' let v gosudarstvennoi dume, 1906–1917: Dnevnik i vospominaniia*. Moscow: Novoe literaturnoe obozrenie, 2001.

Globachev, K. N. "Pravda o russkoi revoliutsii: vospominaniia byvshego nachal'nika Petrogradskogo Okhrannogo Otdeleniia." Bakhmeteff Archive.

Globachev, K. N. *Pravda o russkoi revoliutsii: vospominaniia byvshego nachal'nika petrogradskogo okhrannogo otdeleniia*. Moscow: ROSSPEN, 2009.

Golovin, N. N. *The Russian Army in the World War*. New Haven, CT: Yale University Press, 1931.

Gray, Pauline. *The Grand Duke's Woman*. London: Macdonald and Jane's, 1976.

Gronsky, Paul F., and Nicholas J. Astrov. *The War and the Russian Government*. New Haven, CT: Yale University Press, 1929.

Guchkov, A. I. *Aleksandr Ivanovich Guchkov rasskazyvaet: vospominaniia predsedateli Gosudarstvennoi dumy i voennogo ministra Vremmenogo pravitel'stva.* Moscow: TOO, 1993. [*Guchkov rasskazyvaet*]

Guchkov, A. I. Bazili's interview with Guchkov. Bazili Papers, Box 22, File 10, HIA.

Guchkov, A. I. "Vospominaniia." *Poslednie novosti*, September 13, 1936.

Gurko, V. I. *Tsar' i tsaritsa: O tsarstvovanii Nikolaia II.* Moscow: Veche, 2008.

Haimson, Leopold. "The Problem of Social Stability in Urban Russia, 1905–1917." *Slavic Review* 23, no. 4 (1964); 24, no. 1 (1965).

Hall, Coryne. *Imperial Dancer: Mathilde Kschessinska and the Romanovs.* Gloucestershire: Sutton, 2005.

Hanbury-Williams, J. *The Emperor Nicholas II as I Knew Him*. London: A. A. Humphreys, 1922.

Hasegawa, Tsuyoshi. "Rodzianko and the Grand Dukes' Manifesto of March 1917." *Canadian Slavonic Papers* 18, no. 2 (1976).

Hasegawa, Tsuyoshi. *The February Revolution: Petrograd 1917.* Seattle: University of Washington Press, 1981.

Hasegawa, Tsuyoshi. *The February Revolution of Petrograd, 1917: The End of the Tsarist Regime and the Birth of Dual Power.* Leiden: Brill, 2017.

Hasegawa, Tsuyoshi. "Aleksandr Fedorovich Kerenskii in the February Revolution of 1917." *Journal of Modern Russian History and Historiography* 13 (2020).

Hasegawa, Tsuyoshi. "The Duma Committee, the Provisional Government, and the Birth of 'Triple Power' in the February Revolution." In Daniel Orlovsky, ed., *A Companion to the Russian Revolution.* Hoboken, NJ: John Wiley & Sons, 2020.

Iablonovskii, A. N. "Vstrecha s v. kn. Mikhailom Aleksandrovichem." *Golos minuvshago na chuzhoi storone* 14, no. 1, 1926.

Iakhontov, A. N. Minutes of the Council of Ministers meetings. Arkadii Nikolaevich Iakhontov Papers, Bakhmeteff Archive.

Iakobii, I. P. *Imperator Nikolai II i revoliutsiia.* Tallinn: Kirj-Uh, 1938.

Ioffe, G. Z. *Velikii Oktiabr' i epilog tsarizma.* Moscow: Nauka, 1987.

Ioffe, G. Z. *Revoliutsiia i sem'ia Romanovykh.* Moscow: Respublika, 1992.

Ioffe, G. Z. *Revoliutsiia i sud'ba Romanovykh.* Moscow: Algoritm, 2012.

Isaev, A. *Imperatorskii poezd: Khronika trekh dnei, 28 fevralia–2 marta 1917 goda.* St. Petersburg: Alteiia, 2023.

Ivanov, N. N. Prilozhenie k delu Generala N. I. Ivanov. GARF, f. 1467, d. 643.

Ivanov, N. N. Grand dukes' manifesto, draft with handwritten revisions, and Miliukov's receipt. Bakhmeteff Archive.

Ivanov, N. N. "Otrechenie Vel. K. Mikhaila Aleksandrovicha." Handwritten manuscript. Bakhmeteff Archive.

Ivanov, N. N. "Velikii kniaz' Mikhail Aleksandrovich v nachale marta 1917 g." Handwritten manuscript. Bakhmeteff Archive.

Johnson, Chalmers. *Revolutionary Change.* Boston: Little, Brown, 1966.

Kafafov, K. D. "Vospominaniia o vnutrennikh delakh Rossiiskoi Imperii." *Voprosy istorii* 7, 2005.

Kanishchev, V. V. *Russkii bunt—besmyslennyi i vesposhchadnyi: Pogromnoe dvizhenie v gorodakh Rossii v 1917–1918 gg.* Tambov: Gosudarstvennyi komitet Rossiiskoi federatsii po vyshemu obrazovaniiu, Tambovskii Gosudarstvennyi universitet im. G. R. Derzhavina, 1995.

Karrik, V. "Voina i revoliutsiia: Zapiski, 1914–1917 gg." *Golos minuvshego* 7–9 (1918).

Katkov, George. *Russia 1917: The February Revolution.* New York: Harper & Row, 1967.

Kerensky, Alexander F. *The Catastrophe: Kerensky's Own Story of the Russian Revolution.* New York: Appleton, 1927.

Kerensky, Alexander F. "The Road to the Tragedy." In Paul Bulygin, *The Murder of the Romanovs: The Authentic Account.* Westport, CT: Hyperion, 1935.

Kerensky, Alexander F. *Russia and History's Turning Point.* New York: Duell, Sloan, and Pearce, 1965.

Khodnev, D. I. "Fevral'skaia revoliutsiia i zapasnoi batal'on leib-gvardii Finliandskogo polka." In *Fevral'skaia revoliutsiia ot novykh istochnikov k novomu osmyshleniiu.* Moscow: Institute Rossiiskoi istorii RAN, 1997.

Khrisanfov, V. I. "Luga v 1917 g." *Vestnik Sankt-Peterburgskogo Universiteta* 2, no. 2 (2007).

Khrustalev, Vladimir. *Velikii kniaz' Mikhail Aleksandrovich: Skorbnyi put' ot prestola do golgofy.* Moscow: Izd-vo TONCHU, 2018.

Khrustalev, V. M. "Brati'a Gurko v istorii Rossii: zhiznennyi put' generala Vasiliia Iosifovicha Gurko (1864–1937)." In V. I. Gurko, ed., *Tsar' i tsaritsa.* Moscow: Veche, 2008.

Khrustalev, V. M. "Fevral'skaia revoliutsiia i vospominaniia deputata Gosudarstvennoi dumy Aleksandra Aleksandrovicha Bublikova (1875–1941)." In Bublikov, *Russkaia revoliutsiia* (2016).

Khrustalev, V. M. *Petrograd: rasstrel Velikikh kniazei*. Moscow, 2010.

Khrustalev, V. M. *Skorbnyi put' Romanovykh (1917–1918): Gibel' tsarskoi sem'i: sbornik dokumentov i materialov*. Moscow, 2001.

Khrustalev, V. M. *Velikii kniaz' Mikhail Aleksandrovich*. Moscow: Veche, 2008.

Khrustalev, V. M., ed. *Dnevnik i perepiska Velikogo Kniazia Mikhaila Aleksandrovicha, 1915–1918*. Moscow: Prozaik, 2012.

Khrustalev, V. M., and L. A. Lykova, eds. *Skorbnyi put' Mikhaila Romanova: Ot prestola do Golgofy: Dokumenty, materialy sledstvia, dnevniki, vospominaniia*. Perm', 1996.

King, Greg. *The Last Empress: The Life and Times of Alexandra Feodorovna, Tsarina of Russia*. New York: Birch Lane Press, 1994.

King, G., and P. Wilson. *The Fate of the Romanovs*. Hoboken, NJ: John Wiley and Sons, 2003.

Kir'ianov, Iu., comp. "Pravye v 1915-m—fevrale 1917 g. (Po perliustrirovannym departamentom politsii pis'mam)." *Minuvshee* 14 (1993).

Kirill Vladimirovich. *Vospominaniia*. Moscow: Zakharov, 2006.

"K istorii poslednikh dnei tsarskogo rezhima (1916–1917 gg.)." *KA* 14, no. 1 (1926).

Knox, Sir Alfred. *With the Russian Army*. 2 vols. London, 1921.

Kochakov, B. M. "Sostav Petrogradskogo garnizona v 1917 g." *Uchenye zapiski Leningradskogo universiteta* 205 (1956).

Kokovtsov, V. *Iz moego proshlogo*. Moscow: Nauka, 1992.

Kokovtsov, V. *Out of My Past: The Memoirs of Count Kokovtsov*. Stanford, CA: Stanford University Press, 1935.

Kolonitskii, Boris. *Tragicheskaia erotika: obrazy imperatorskoi sem'i v gody pervoi mirovoi voiny*. Moscow: Novoe literaturnoe obozrenie, 2010.

Kolonitskii, Boris. *"Tovarishch' Kerenskii": anti-monarkhicheskaia revoliutsiia, formirovanie kul'ta "vodzhia naroda," mart-iiul' 1917 god*. Moscow: Novoe literaturnoe obozrenie, 2017.

Kolonitskii, Boris. *"Comrade Kerensky": The Revolution Against the Monarchy and the Formation of the Cult of "the Leader of the People" (March–June 1917)*. Cambridge, MA: Polity Press, 2021.

Kryzhanovskii, S. E. *Vospominaniia: iz bumag S. E. Kryzhanovskogo, poslednego gosudarstvennogo sekretaria Rossiiskoi imperii*. St. Petersburg: Izd-vo Rossiiskaia national'naia biblioteka, 2009.

Kschessinska, Mathilde. *Dancing in Petersburg*. Alton, NH: Dance Books, 1960.

Kudrina, Iu. V., ed. *Imperatritsa Mariia Fedorovna: Dnevniki, pis'ma, vospominaniia*. Moscow: Olma-Press, 2001.

Kulikov, S. V. *Biurokraticheskaia elita Rossiiskoi imperii nakanune padeniia starogo poriadka (1914–1917)*. Riazan', 2004.

Kulikov, S. V. "Otrechenie Nikolaia II." In Anan'ich, *Fevral'skaia revoliutsiia*.

Kulikov, S. V. "Sovet ministrov i padenie monarkhii." In Anan'ich, *Fevral'skaia revoliutsiia*.

Kulikov, S. V. "Stavka: 23 fevralia–1 marta." In Anan'ich, *Fevral'skaia revoliutsiia*.

Lemke, M. K. *250 dnei v tsarskoi stavke, 1914–1915: Vospominaniia memuary*. Minsk: Kharvest, 2003.

Lieven, D. C. B. *Nicholas II: Twilight of the Empire*. New York: St. Martin's Press, 1994.

Lieven, D. C. B. *Russia and the Origins of the First World War*. London: Macmillan, 1983.

Lincoln, W. Bruce. *Passage Through Armageddon: The Russians in War and Revolution, 1914–1918*. New York: Oxford University Press, 1986.

Lohr, Eric. *Nationalizing the Russian Empire: The Campaign Against Enemy Aliens During World War I*. Cambridge, MA: Harvard University Press, 2014.

Lohr, Eric. "Tsarism, Tsarist Autocracy, and the Russian *Sonderweg*." *Journal of Modern History* 95, no. 1 (2023).

Lomonosov, Iu. V. "Podlinik manifesta ob otrechenii v Petrograde." *Otrechenie*.

Lomonosov, Iu. V. *Vospominaniia o martovskoi revoliutsii 1917 g.* Stockholm and Berlin, 1921.

Lomonosov, Iu. V. *Vospominaniia o martovskoi revoliutsii 1917 goda*. In V. B. Stankevich and Iu. V. Lomonosov, *Vospominaniia o martovskoi revoliutsii 1917 goda*. Moscow: Rossiskii gosudarstvennyi gumanitarnyi universitet, 1994.

Loukianov, Mikhail. "The First World War and the Polarization of the Russian Right, July 1914–February 1917." *Slavic Review* 75, no. 4 (2016).

Lukomskii, A. S. "Iz vospominanii." *ARR* 2 (1921).

Lukomskii, A. S. *Vospominaniia*. 2 vols. Berlin, 1922.

Lyandres, Semion. "On the Problem of 'Indecisiveness' Among the Duma Leaders During February Revolution: Imperial Decree of Prorogation and Decision to Convene the Private Meeting of February 27, 1917." *Soviet and Post-Soviet Review* 24, nos. 1–2 (1997).

Lyandres, Semion. "Progressive Bloc Politics on the Eve of the Revolution: Revisiting P. N. Miliukov's 'Stupidity or Treason' Speech on November 1, 1916." *Russian History/Histoire Russe* 31, no. 4 (2004).

Lyandres, Semion. *The Fall of Tsarism: Untold Stories of the February 1917 Revolution*. Oxford: Oxford University Press, 2013.

Lyandres, Semion. "Conspiracy and Ambition in Russian Politics Before the February Revolution of 1917: The Case of Prince Georgii Evgen'evich L'vov." *Journal of Modern Russian History and Historiography* 8 (2015).

Maklakov, V. A. "Introduction." In V. A. Maklakov et al., *La chute du regime tsariste*. Paris, 1927.

Maria Fedorovna. *Dnevniki imperatritsy Marii Fedorovny (1914–1920, 1923 gg.)*. Moscow, 2005.

Maria Fedorovna. *Dnevniki*. Moscow, 2006.

Marie, Grand Duchess of Russia. *Education of a Princess: A Memoir*. New York, 1931.

Martin, Russell E. "'For the Firm Maintenance of the Dignity and Tranquility of the Imperial Family': Law and Familial Order in the Romanov Dynasty." *Russian History* 37 (2010).

Martin, Russell E. "Law, Succession, and the Eighteenth-Century Refounding of the Romanov Dynasty." In *Dubitando: Studies in History and Culture in Honor of Donald Ostrowski*, ed. Brian J. Boeck, Russell E. Martin, and Daniel Rowland. Bloomington, IN: Slavica, 2012.

Martynov, E. I. *Tsarskaia armiia v fevral'skom perevorote*. Leningrad: Voennaia Tipografiia Upravleniia delami Narkomvoenmori RVS SSSR, 1927.

Massie, Robert K. *Nicholas and Alexandra: The Classic Account of the Fall of the Romanov Dynasty*. New York: Random House, 1967.

Matveev, A. S. *Memoirs*. Bakhmeteff Archive, Columbia University. [Mateev, *Memoirs*]

Matveev, A. S. "Vel. Kniaz' Mikhail Aleksandrovich v dni perevorota." *Vozrozhdenie* 24 (1952).

Mawdsley, Eva. *The Russian Revolution and the Baltic Fleet: War and Politics, February 1917–April 1918*. New York: Barnes and Noble, 1978.

McKean, Robert B. *St. Petersburg Between the Revolutions: Workers and Revolutionaries, June 1907–February 1917*. New Haven, CT: Yale University Press, 1990.

Mel'gunov, S. P. *Na putiakh k dvortsovomu perevorotu*. Paris: Knizhnoe delo "Rodnik," 1931.

Mel'gunov, S. P. *Sud'ba Imperatora Nikolaia II posle otrecheniia: istoriko-kriticheskie ocherki*. Paris: Editions "La Renaissance," 1951.

Mel'gunov, S. P. *Martovskie dni 1917 goda*. Paris: Sklad izd. "Les Éditeurs réunis," 1961.

Menning, Bruce W. "The Russian High Command at War, 1914–1917: Tsar–Stavka–Government." Paper presented at the 55th ASEEES Convention, Philadelphia, December 2023.

Miliukov, P. N. *Istoriia vtoroi russkoi revoliutsii*. Vol. 1. Sofia: Rossiisko-Bolgarskoe izd-vo, 1921.

Miliukov, P. N. "Pervyi den'," *Poslednye novosti*, March 12, 1927.

Miliukov, P. N. *Vospominaniia, 1859–1917*. 2 vols. New York: Chekhov Publishing, 1955.

Miliukov, P. N. *Political Memoirs, 1905–1917*. Ann Arbor: University of Michigan Press, 1967.

Miliukov, Paul N. *The Russian Revolution*. Vol. 1. Ed. Richard Stites. Gulf Breeze, FL: Academic International Press, 1978.

Mints, I. I. *Istoriia Velikogo Oktiabria*. Vol. 1, *Sverzhenie samoderzhaviia*. Moscow: Akademiia nauk SSSR, 1967.

Mints, I. I., ed. *Oktiabr' i grazhdanskaia voina v SSSR: Sbornik statei*. Moscow: Institut istorii Akademii nauk SSSR, 1966.

Mints, I. I., L. M. Ivanov, et al. *Sverzhenie samoderzhaviia: Sbornik statei*. Moscow: Institut istorii Akademii nauk SSSR, 1970.

Montefiore, Simon Sebag. *The Romanovs: 1613–1918*. New York: Vintage Books, 2017.

Mordvinov, A. "Poslednie dni imperatora: Otrechenie Nikolaia II: Otryvki iz vospominanii." *RL*, 1923.

Mordvinov, A. "Poslednie dni imperatora: Otrechenie Nikolaia II: Otryvki iz vospominanii." *Otrechenie*.

Mosolov, A. A. *Pri dvore poslednego imperatora: zapiski nachal'nika kantseliarii ministra Dvora*. St. Petersburg, 1992.

Mossolov, A. A. *At the Court of the Last Tsar*. Ed. A. A. Pilenco. London, 1935.

Mul'tatuli, P. V. *Nikolai II: Otrechenie, kotorogo ne bylo*. Moscow: Astrel', 2010.

Nabokov, V. "Vremennoe pravitel'stvo." *ARR* 1 (1921).

Nekrasov, N. V. "N. V. Nekrasov v Kieve." *Poslednie Novosti* (Kiev), morning edition, May 16, 1917.

Nicholas II. *Dnevnik Imperatora Nikolaia II*. Ed. K. F. Shatsilo. Moscow: Orbita, 1991.

Nicholas II. *Letters of the Tsar to the Tsaritsa, 1914–1917*. Stanford, CA: Hoover Institution Press, 1973.

Nichols, Robert L. "The Friends of God: Nicholas II and Alexandra at the Canonization of Seraphim of Sarov, July 1903." In Charles E. Timberlake, ed., *Religious and Secular Forces in Late Tsarist Russia: Essays in Honor of Donald W. Treadgold.* Seattle: University of Washington Press, 1992.

Nicholson, Nicholas, ed. *Michael Romanov: Brother of the Last Tsar: Diaries and Letters, 1916–1918.* Washington, DC: Academica Press, 2020.

Nicolas Mikhailovich. *La fin du tsarisme: Lettres inédites à Frédéric Masson (1914–1918).* Paris: Payot, 1968.

Nikitin, B. V. *Rokovye gody: novye pokazaniia uchastnika.* Paris: Sklad izd. "Éditeurs réunis," 1937.

Nikolaev, A. B. *Revoliutsiia i vlast': IV Gosudarstvennaia duma 27 fevralia–3 marta 1917 goda.* St. Petersburg: Izdatel'stvo RGPU im. A. I. Gertsena, 2005.

Nikolaev, A. B. *Dumskaia revoliutsiia: 27 fevralia–3 marta 1917 goda,* 2 vols. St. Petersburg: Izdatel'stvo RGPU im. A. I. Gertsena, 2017.

Nikolaev, A. B. "Lidery Fevral'skoi revoliutsii 1917 goda: Pochemu M.V. Rodzianko?" *Journal of Modern Russian History and Historiography* 13 (2020).

Nikolaev, A. B. "A. A. Bublikov–Komissar Vremennogo Komiteta Godusarstvennoi Dumy v Ministerstve Putei Soobshcheniia," *Tavrichekie chteniia* 2021. St. Petersburg, 2022.

Nikolaevskii, B. I. *Russkie masony i revoliutsiia.* Ed. Iu. G. Fel'shtinskii. Moscow: Terra-Terra, 1990.

Nol'de, B. E. *Dalekoe i blizkoe: Istoricheskie ocherki.* Paris: Izd-vo 'Sovremennyia zapiski', 1930.

Nol'de, B. E. "V. N. Nabokov v 1917 g." *ARR* 7 (1924).

Oberuchev, K. M. *Ofitsery v russkoi revoliutsii.* New York: Izd. pervoe izdatel'stvo v Amerike, 1928.

Oberuchev, K. M. *V dni revoliutsii: Vospominaniia uchastnika russkoi revoliutsii 1917 goda.* New York: Izd. "Narodopravstva," 1919.

Obolenskii, V. A. *Moia zhizn', moi sovremenniki.* Paris: YMCA Press, 1988.

Ol'denburg, S. S. *Tsarstvovanie Imperatora Nikolaia II.* Vol. 2. Washington, DC: Obshchestvo rasprostraneniia russkoi natsional'noi i patrioticheskoi literatury, 1949.

*Otrechenie Nikolaia II: Vospominaniia ochevidtsev i dokumenty.* Moscow/Berlin: Direct Media, 2017. [*Otrechenie*]

Oznobishin, D. V. "Vremennyi komitet gosudarstvennoi dumy i Vremennoe pravitel'stvo." *Istoricheskie zapiski* 75 (1965).

*Padenie tsarskogo rezhima: Stenograficheskie otchety doprosov i pokazanii dannykh v 1917 g. v Chrezvychainoi Sledstvennoi Komissii Vremennogo Pravitel'stva.* 7 vols. Ed. P. E. Shchegolev. Moscow: Gosizdat, 1924–1927.

Paléologue, Maurice. *An Ambassador's Memoirs.* 3 vols. New York: George H. Doran, 1924.

Paley, Princess Olga. *Memories of Russia, 1916–1919.* London: Herbert Jenkins, 1924.

Pares, Bernard. *The Fall of the Russian Monarchy.* New York: Vintage Books, 1961.

Pearson, Raymond. *The Russian Moderates and the Crisis of Tsarism, 1914–1917.* New York: Barnes and Noble, 1977.

Perets, G. P. *V tsitadeli russkoi revoliutsii: Zapiski komendanta Tavricheskogo dvortsa 27 fevralia–23 marta 1917 g.* Petrograd: Prosveshchenie, 1917.

*Permskaia Golgofa Mikhaila II: Sbornijk dokumentov o poslednem perioda zhizni i ubiistva v gorode Permi Velikogo Kniazia Mikhaila Aleksandrovicha.* Vol. 1. Eds. L. A. Lykova, V. M. Khrustalev, et al. Perm': Pushka, 2018. [*Permskaia Golgofa*]

Perry, John Curtis, and Constantine Pleshakov. *The Flight of the Romanovs: A Family Saga.* New York: Basic Books, 1999.

Peshekhonov, A. V. "Pervyia nedeli: Iz vospominanii o revoliiutsii." *Na chuzhoi storone* 1 (1923).

*Petrogradskii Sovet rabochikh i soldatskikh deputatov v 1917 godu: Dokumenty i materialy.* Vol. 1, *27 fevralia–31 marta 1917 goda.* Leningrad: Nauka, 1991.

Phenix, Patricia. *Olga Romanov: Russia's Last Grand Duchess.* Toronto: Viking Press, 1999.

Pipes, Richard, ed. *Revolutionary Russia.* Cambridge, MA: Harvard University Press, 1967.

Pipes, Richard. *Russia Under the Old Regime.* New York: Scribner's, 1974.

Pipes, Richard. *The Russian Revolution.* New York: Random House, 1990.

Polner, T. E. *Zhiznennyi put' Kniaziia Georgiia Evgen'evicha L'vova.* Paris, 1932.

*Posledniaia voina Rossiiskoi imperii: Rossia, mir nakanune, v khode i posle Pervoi mirovoi voiny po dokumentam Rossiiskikh i zarubezhnykh arkhivov: materialy Mezhdunarodnoi nauchnoi konferentsii, Moskva, 7–8 sentiabria 2004 goda.* Moscow: Nauka, 2006.

"Programma soiuza russkogo naroda pered Fevral'skoi revoliutsii," *KA* 20, no. 1, 1927.

"Progressivnyi blok, 1915–1917." *KA* 50–51, nos. 1–2 (1932); 52, no. 3 (1932); 56, no. 1 (1933).

Pronin, V. M. *Poslednie dni Tsarskoi Stavki*. Belgrade, 1929.

"Protokol sobytii." Document 43 in Shashkova, *Fevral'skaia revoliutsiia 1917: Sbornik dokumentov i materialov*. ["Protokol sobytii']

"Protokol zasedanii: soveshchaniia Gosudarstvennoi dumy s predstaviteliami fraktsii, chastnogo soveshchaniia chlenov Gosudarstvennoi dumy i Vremennogo komiteta Gosudarstvennoi dumy 27 fevralia–3 marta 1917 goda, vvedenie, tekst i komentarii." In *Tavricheskie chteniia*, ed. A. B. Nikolaev. St. Petersburg, 2012. ["Protokol zasedanii"]

Protopopov, A. D. "Alerksandr Dmitrievich Protopopov, Pokazaniia Chrezvychainoi sledstvennoi komissii Vremennogo pravitel'stva," *Gibel' monarkhii*.

"Proval popytki Stavki podavit' Fevral'skuiu revoliutsiiu 1917 goda v Petrograde." *Voprosy arkhivovedeniia* 1 (1962).

Raeff, Marc. "The Well-Ordered Police State and the Development of Modernity in Seventeenth- and Eighteenth-Century Europe: An Attempt at a Comparative Approach." *American Historical Review* 80, no. 5 (1975).

Raeff, Marc. *The Well-Ordered Police State: Social and Institutional Change Through Law in the Germanies and Russia, 1600–1800*. New Haven, CT: Yale University Press, 1983.

Raeff, Marc. *Understanding Imperial Russia: State and Society in the Old Regime*. New York: Columbia University Press, 1986.

Rappaport, Helen. *The Race to Save the Romanovs: The Truth Behind the Secret Plans to Rescue the Russian Imperial Family*. New York: St. Martin's Press, 2018.

Rengarten, I. I. "Fevral'skaia revoliutsiia v Baltiiskom flote: iz dnevnika I. I. Rengartena." *KA* 32, no. 2 (1929).

Riha, Thomas. "Miliukov and the Progressive Bloc in 1915." *Journal of Modern History* 32, no. 1 (1960).

Riha, Thomas. *A Russian European: Paul Miliukov in Russian Politics*. Notre Dame, IN: University of Notre Dame Press, 1969.

Robinson, Paul. *Grand Duke Nikolai Nikolaevich: Supreme Commander of the Russian Army*. DeKalb: Northern Illinois University Press, 2014.

Rodichev, F. I. *Vospominaniia i ocherki o russkom liberalizme*. Ed. K. E. McKenzie. Newtonville, MA, 1983.

Rodzianko, M. V. "Gosudarstvennaia duma i fevral'skaia 1917 goda revoliutsiia." *ARR* 4 (1922).

Rodzianko, M. V. "Krushenie imperii." *ARR* 17 (1926).

Rodzianko, M. V. *The Reign of Rasputin: An Empire's Collapse*. Gulf Breeze, FL: Academic International Press, 1973.

Rosenberg, William G. *Liberals in the Russian Revolution*. Princeton, NJ: Princeton University Press, 1974.

Rosenberg, William G. "Po tu storonu Velikoi Metaistorii." In *Epokha voin i revoliutsii, 1914–1922: Materialy mezhdunarodnogo kollokviuma*. St. Petersburg: Nestor-Istoriia, 2017.

Rosenberg, William G. *States of Anxiety: Scarcity and Loss in Revolutionary Russia*. New York: Oxford University Press, 2023.

*Rossiia v mirovoi voine 1914–1918 goda (v tsifrakh)*. Moscow: TsSU, 1925.

Ruzskii, N. V. "Beseda s zhurnalistom V. Samoilovym ob otrechenii Nikolaia II." In *Otrechenie Nikolaia II: Vospominaniia ochevidtsev, dokumenty*, ed. P. E. Shchegolev. Leningrad: Krasnaia gazeta, 1927.

Safonov, M. M. "General Ruzskii fal'sifitsiruet istoriiu." In *Revoliutsiia 1917 goda v Rossii: sobytiia i kontseptsii, posledstviia i pamiat': Materialy mezhdunarodnoi nauchno-prakticheskoi konferentsii, 1917–2017: K 100-letiiu Rossiiskoi revoliutsii*, St. Petersburg: Gosudarstvennyi muzei politicheskoi istorii Rossii; Sankt-Peterburgskii institut istorii RAN, Severo-Zapadnoe otdelenie Sektsii "Istoriia sotsial'nykh reform, dvizhenii i revoliutsii," 2017.

Safonov, M. M. "Lozh' i pravda ob otrechenii Nikolaia II." *Nestor* 3 (2005).

Safonov, M. M. "Spetssluzhby i otrechenie Nikolaia II." *Peterburgskii istoricheskii zhurnal*, no. 4 (2017).

Safonov, M. M. "'Stavka, Nachal'niku Shtaba': Vokrug otrecheniia Nikolaia II." In *Velikaia voina*, 2014.

Salisbury, Harrison. *Black Night, White Snow: Russia's Revolutions 1905–1917*. New York: Doubleday, 1978.

Sanborn, Joshua. "The Mobilization of 1914 and the Question of the Russian Nation: A Reexamination." *Slavic Review* 59, no. 2 (2000).

Sanborn, Joshua. *Drafting the Russian Nation: Military Conscription, Total War, and Mass Politics, 1905–1925*. DeKalb: Northern Illinois University Press, 2003.

Sanborn, Joshua. "When the Front Came Home: The Great Retreat of 1915 and the Transformation of Russian Society." In *Russia's Home Front in War and Revolution, 1914–22, Book 4, Reintegration—The Struggle for the State*, ed. Adele Lindenmeyer, Christopher Read, and Peter Waldron. Bloomington, IN: Slavica, 2018.

Saul, Norman E. *Sailors in Revolt: The Russian Baltic Fleet in 1917*. Lawrence: Regents Press of Kansas, 1978.

Savich, N. V. *Vospominaniia*. Ed. N. H. Rutych. Düsseldorf: Goluboi vsadnik, 1993.

Savvich, S. S. "Priniatie Nikolaem II resheniia ob otrechenii ot prestola." In *Otrechenie*.

Savvich, S. S. "Priniatie Nikolaem II resheniia ob otrechenii ot prestola." In *Otrechenie Nikolaia II: Vospominaniia ochevidtsev, dokumenty*, ed. P. E. Shchegolev. Leningrad: Krasnaia gazeta, 1927.

Sazonov, S. *Fateful Years*. London: Jonathan Cape, 1928.

Schama, Simon. *Citizens*. New York: Knopf, 1989.

Schapiro, Leonard. "The Political Thought of the First Provisional Government." In *Revolutionary Russia*, ed. Richard Pipes. Cambridge, MA: Harvard University Press, 1967.

Semennikov, V. P., ed. *Nikolai II i velikie kniaz'ia: Rodstvennye pis'ma k poslednemu tsariu*. Moscow: Gos. izd-vo, 1925.

Semennikov, V. P., ed. *Monarkhiia pered krusheniem, 1914–1917 gg.: bumagi Nikolaia II i drugie dokumenty*. Moscow: Gos. izd-vo, 1927.

Sergeevskii, Boris Nikolaevich. *Otrechenie (perezhitoe) 1917*. New York: Izd-vo voennyi vestnik, 1969.

Service, Robert. *The Last of the Tsars: Nicholas II and the Russian Revolution*. New York: Pegasus Books, 2017.

Shashkova, O. A., ed. *Fevral'skaia revoliutsiia 1917: Sbornik dokumentov i materialov*. Moscow: Rossiskii gosudarstvennyi gumanitarnyi universitet, 1996. [Shashkova, *Fevral'skaia revoliutsiia*]

Shavel'skii, Otets Georgii. *Vospominaniia poslednego protopresvitera russkoi armii i flota*. 2 vols. New York: Izd-vo imeni Chekhova, 1954.

Shchegolev, P. E., ed. *Otrechenie Nikolaia II: Vospominaniia ochevidtsev i dokumenty*. Leningrad: Krasnaia gazeta, 1927.

Shchegolev, P. E. *Poslednii reis Nikolaia vtorogo*. Moscow: Gos. izd-vo, 1928.

Shidlovskii, S. I. *Vospominaniia*. 2 vols. Berlin: O. Kirchner, 1923.

Shklovskii, Viktor. *Sentimental'noe puteshestvie: Vospominaniia, 1917–1922*. Moscow: Gelikon, 1923.

Shklovskii, Viktor. *A Sentimental Journey: Memoirs, 1917–1922*. Trans. Richard Sheldon. Ithaca, NY: Cornell University Press, 1970.

Shliapnikov, A. *Kanun semnadtsatogo goda*. 2 vols. Moscow: Gosizdat, 1923.

Shliapnikov, A. *On the Eve of 1917: Reminiscences from the Revolutionary Underground*. Chapel Hill: University of North Carolina Press, 1982.

Shliapnikov, A. *Semnadtsatyi god*. Vol. 1. Moscow: Gosizdat, 1923.

Shul'gin, V. V. *Dni*. Belgrade: Novoe Vremia, 1925. (Also in *Otrechenie*.)

Shul'gin, V. V. *Dni: 1920*. Moscow: Sovremennik, 1989.

Shulgin, V. V. *Days of the Russian Revolution: Memoirs from the Right, 1905–1917*. Gulf Breeze, FL: Academic International Press, 1990.

Sidorov, A. L. *Ekonomicheskoe polozhenie Rossii v gody pervoi mirovoi voiny*. Moscow, 1973.

Sidorov, A. L. "Otrechenie Nikolaia II i Stavka." In *Problemy obshchestvenno-politicheskoi istorii Rossii i slavianskikh stran: Sbornik statei*, ed. V. I. Shunkov. Moscow, 1963.

Sidorov, A. L., L. M. Ivanov, et al., eds. *Pervaia mirovaia voina, 1914–1918*. Moscow: Nauka, 1968.

Siegelbaum, L. H. *The Politics of Industrial Mobilization in Russia, 1914–1917: A Study of the War-Industries Committees*. New York: St. Martin's Press, 1983.

Siegelbaum, L. H. "Russian Industrialists and the First World War: The Failure of the National Bourgeoisie." *Slavic and Soviet Series* 2, no. 1 (1977).

Skobelev, M. "Gibel' tsarizma: Vospominaniia M. I. Skobeleva." *Ogonek* 11 (1927).

Slonimskii, M. *Kniga vospominanii*. Moscow, 1966.

Smith, Nathan. "The Role of Russian Freemasonry in the February Revolution: Another Scrap of Evidence." *Slavic Review* 27, no. 4 (1968).

Smith, Douglas. *Rasputin: Faith, Power, and the Twilight of the Romanovs*. London: Macmillan, 2016.

Sobolev, G. L. *Petrogradskii garnizon v bor'be za pobedu Oktiabria*. Leningrad: Nauka, 1985.

Sokolov, N. D. "Kak rodilsia prikaz No. 1." *Ogonek* 11 (1927).

Solzhenitsyn, Aleksandr. *March 1917: The Red Wheel. Node III (8 March–31 March)*. Trans. Martin Schwartz. Notre Dame, IN: University of Notre Dame Press, 2017–2021.

Spiridovich, A. I. *Velikaia voina i fevral'skaia revoliutsiia, 1914–1917 gg.* 3 vols. New York: Vseslavianskoe izd-vo, 1962.

Stankevich, V. B. *Vospominaniia, 1914–1919*. Berlin: Izd-vo I. P. Ladyzhnikova, 1920.

Startsev, V. I. *Vnutronniaia politika vremennogo pravitel'stva pervogo sostava*. Leningrad: Nauka, 1980.

Startsev, V. I. "Russkie politicheskie masony v praviashchei elite Fevral'skoi revoliutsii 1917 goda." In *Rossiia v 1917 godu: novye podkhody i vzgliady*, ed. I. L. Afanas'ev, A. Iu. Davydov, and V. I. Startsev. St. Petersburg: Izdatel'skaia gruppa kafedry russkoi istorii Rossiiskogo gosudarstvennogo pedagogicheskogo universiteta imeni A. I. Gertsena, 1994.

Startsev, V. I. "Tshchetnye usiliia Rodzianko." *Nestor* 3 (2005).

Startsev, V. I. "Deklaratsiia Vremennogo pravitel'stva ot 3 marta 1917 g." *Nestor* 4 (2005).

*Stavka i revoliutsiia: Sbornik dokumentov v dvukh tomak: Shtab verkhovnogo glavnokomanduiushchego i revoliutsionnykh sobytiia 1917–nachala 1918 goda po dokumentam Rossiiskogo gosudarstvennogo-istoricheskogo arkhiva, 18 fevralia–18 iunia 1917.* Vol. 1. Ed. I. O. Garkusha et al. Moscow: Fond "Sviaz' Epokha" Kuchkogo Pole, 2019. [*Stavka i revoliutsiia*]

Steinberg, Mark D., and Vladimir M. Khrustalev. *The Fall of the Romanovs: Political Dreams and Personal Struggles in a Time of Revolution.* New Haven, CT: Yale University Press, 1995.

*Stenograficheskii otchet zasedaniia chlenov Gosudarstvennoi Dumy, chetvertago sozyvov, 1917.* St. Petersburg: Gosudarstvennaia tipografiia, 1917.

Stone, Norman. *The Eastern Front.* London: Hodder and Stoughton, 1975.

Storozhev, V. N. "Fevral'skaia revoliutsiia 1917 goda." *Nauchnye izvestiia: Sb. 1, ekonomika, istoriia, pravo* 1 (1922).

Sukhanov, N. N. *Zapiski o revoliutsii.* Vol. 1. Berlin: Z. I. Grzhebin, 1922.

Sworakowski, Witold S. "The Authorship of the Abdication Documents of Nicholas II." *Russian Review* 30, no. 3 (1971).

Szeftel, Marc. *The Russian Constitution of April 23, 1906: Political Institutions of the Duma Monarchy.* Brussels: Éditions de la libraire encyclopédique, 1976.

Tal', G. A. von. n.d. *Memuary ob otrechenii ot prestola Rossiiskago gosudarstva Imperatora Nikolaia II.* Handwritten manuscript. HIA. [Tal', *Memuary*]

Tal', G. A. von. *Mysl' ob otrechenii.* Bakhmeteff Archive. [Tal', *Mysl' ob otrechenii*]

Tal', G. A. von. *Chronology of Abdication.* Handwritten manuscript in Russian. Bakhmeteff Archive. [Tal', *Chronology*]

"Telegrammy i razgovory po telegrafu mezhdu Pskovom, Stavkoiu i Petrogradom, otnosiashchiesia k obstoiatel'stvam otrecheniia Gosudaria Imperatora, s primechaniiami k nim general-ad"iutanta N. V. Ruzskago." *RL* 3 (1922). [*Telegrammy Ruzkago*]

Tikhmenev, N. M. *Iz vospominanii o poslednikh dniakh prebyvaniia Imperatora Nikolaia II v Stavke.* Nice: Kruzhok Revnitelei Russkogo Proshlogo, 1925.

Tikhmenev, N. M. "Poslednii priezd Nikolaia II v Mogileve." In *Otrechenie.*

Tiutiukin, S. V. *Voina, mir, revoliutsiia: Ideinaia bor'ba v rabochem dvizhenii Rossii, 1914–1917 gg.* Moscow: Mysl', 1972.

"V ianvare i fevrale 1917 g. Iz donesenii sekretnykh agentov A. D. Protopopova." *Byloe* 13, no. 7 (1918).

Van Der Kiste, John, and Coryne Hall. *Once a Grand Duchess: Xenia, Sister of Nicholas II.* Gloucestershire: Sutton, 2002.

*Velikaia Oktiabr'skaia sotsialisticheskaia revoliutsiia: Khronika sobytii.* Vol. 1. Moscow, 1957.

*Velikaia Oktiabr'skaia sotsialisticheskaia revoliutsiia: Revoliutsionnoe dvizhenie v Rossii posle sverzheniia samoderzhaviia. Dokumenty i materialy.* Moscow, 1957.

*Velikie dni Rossiiskoi revoliutsii 1917 g.* Petrograd: Biuro Rossiiskoi pressy, 1917.

Velikie kniaz'ia v Gosudarstvennoi Dume, *Russkoe Slovo*, March 2, 1917.

"Verkhovnoe komandovanie v pervye dni revoliutsii." *ARR* 16 (1925).

Verkhovskii, A. I. *Na trudnom perevale.* Moscow: Voennoe izd-vo, 1959.

Verner, Andrew M. *The Crisis of Russian Autocracy: Nicholas II and the 1905 Revolution.* Princeton, NJ: Princeton University Press, 1990.

Vil'chkovskii, S. N. "Prebyvanie Gosudaria Imperatora v Pskove, 1–2 marta 1917 goda, po rasskazu general-ad"iutanta N.V. Ruzskago." *RL* 3 (1922). Reprinted in Shchegolev, *Otrechenie Nikolaia II*, and *Otrechenie.*

Vitenberg, B. M. "Iakov Vasil'evich Glinka: zhizn' v epokhu peremen." *Al'manek* 10 (1998).

Voeikov, V. N. *S tsarem i bez tsaria: Vospominaniia posledniago dvortsovago Komendanta gosudaria Imperatora Nikolaia II.* Helsingfors: Tip. O Liter, 1936.

Voronovich, N. "Zapiski predsedatelia soveta soldatskikh deputatov." *Arkhiv grazhdanskoi voiny* 2 (1921).

Vorres, Ian. *The Last Grand Duchess.* Toronto: Key Porter Books, 1964.

Vyrubova, A. *Memories of the Russian Court.* London: Macmillan, 1923.

Wada, Haruki. *Roshia kakumei: Petorogurado, 1917nen 2gatsu.* Tokyo: Sakuhin-sha, 2018.

Wildman, Allan K. *The End of the Russian Imperial Army: The Old Army and the Soldiers' Revolt (March–April 1917).* Princeton, NJ: Princeton University Press, 1980.

Williams, Stephen F. "Antidote to Revolution: Vasilii Maklakov's Advocacy of the Rule of Law and Constitutionalism." In *Russia's Home Front in War and*

*Revolution, 1914–22*, Book 4, *Reintegration—The Struggle for the State*, ed. Adele Lindenmeyer, Christopher Read, and Peter Waldron. Bloomington, IN: Slavica, 2018.

Williams, Stephen F. *The Reformer: How One Liberal Fought to Preempt the Russian Revolution*. New York: Encounter Books, 2017.

Wortman, Richard S. *Scenarios of Power: Myth and Ceremony in Russian Monarchy from Peter the Great to the Abdication of Nicholas II*. Abridged ed. Princeton, NJ: Princeton University Press, 2006.

Zaslavskii, D., and V. A. Kantorovich. *Khronika fevral'skoi revoliutsii*. Petrograd, 1924.

Zavadskii, S. V. "Na velikom izlome." *ARR* 8 (1923).

"Zhurnal zasedanii Vremennogo pravitel'stva, Mart–Oktiabr' 1917 goda," vol. 1, in *Arkhiv noveishei istorii Rossii*. Moscow: ROSSPEN, 2000.

# NOTES

## Chapter 1: Nicholas II: Autocracy, Family, Religion

1. Pipes, *Russian Revolution*, 57.
2. Wortman argues that Romanov emperors alternated between European and Russian values to enhance their authority. See Wortman, *Scenarios of Power*.
3. Montefiore, *Romanovs*, 459.
4. Verner, *Crisis of Russian Autocracy*, 24.
5. King and Wilson, *Fate of the Romanovs*, 31.
6. Ibid., 31.
7. Perry and Pleshakov, *Flight of the Romanovs*, 55–56. For Nicholas's love affair with Matilda Kshesinskaya, see Hall, *Imperial Dancer*; Kschessinska, *Dancing in Petersburg*.
8. Baroness Sofia Karlovna Buxhoeveden, "Gosudar' Imperator Nikolai II: iz vospominanii, Chast' II," 8, Bazili Papers, Box 23, File 3, HIA.
9. Alexander Mikhailovich, *Once a Grand Duke*, 168–169.
10. Pares, *Fall of the Russian Monarchy*, 30.
11. Ibid., 29.
12. King, *Last Empress*, 14–26.
13. Ibid., 39.
14. Almedingen, *Empress Alexandra*, 8–9.
15. Ibid., 23.
16. Quoted in Verner, *Crisis of Russian Autocracy*, 35–36; Almedingen, *Empress Alexandra*, 31.
17. Massie, *Nicholas and Alexandra*, 45. For the wedding, Montefiore, *Romanovs*, 493–494.
18. Buxhoeveden, *Life and Tragedy*, 45–46; King, *Last Empress*, 90; Rappaport, *Race to Save the Romanovs*, 27.
19. Massie, *Nicholas and Alexandra*, 47; King, *Last Empress*, 82.
20. King, *Last Empress*, 92–93.
21. Buchanan, *Dissolution*, 36.

22. Paléologue, *Ambassador's Memoirs*, vol. 1, 229.

23. Buxhoeveden, *Life and Tragedy*, 170–173.

24. V. A. Kantororovich, *Aleksandra Fedorovna (Opyt khrakteristki)*, Leningrad, 1927, 3, quoted in Kolonitskii, *Tragicheskaia erotika*, 242.

25. Massie, *Nicholas and Alexandra*, 55.

26. Ibid., 56. For the coronation, see ibid., 52–62; Wortman, *Scenarios of Power*, 334–343.

27. Buxhoeveden, *Life and Tragedy*, 69; Montefiore, *Romanovs*, 498–500.

28. Nichols, "The Friends of God," 219–220.

29. Shavel'skii, *Vospominaniia*, vol. 2, 296.

30. Vyrubova, *Memories*, 151.

31. For Philippe of Lyon, see Smith, *Rasputin*, 32–45; Paléologue, *Ambassador's Memoirs*, vol. 1, 203–207.

32. Militsa was married to Grand Duke Pyotr Nikolaevich, Nicholas II's cousin. Stana, after her divorce from Prince George of Leuchtenberg, found a lover in Grand Duke Nikolai Nikolaevich (Nikolasha), Pyotr's brother and Nicholas's cousin and the future supreme commander of the Russian armed forces at the beginning of World War I.

33. Smith, *Rasputin*, 38.

34. Ibid., 43.

35. Ibid., 44.

36. Nichols, "The Friends of God," 215.

37. Wortman, *Scenarios of Power*, 359.

38. King, *Last Empress*, 157.

39. Ibid., 158.

40. Buxhoeveden, *Life and Tragedy*, 153–156; Massie, *Nicholas and Alexandra*, 132–133; Gilliard, *Thirteen Years*, 73–75; Rappaport, *Race to Save the Romanovs*, 2; Montefiore, *Romanovs*, 540.

41. Gilliard, *Thirteen Years*, 43.

42. Ibid., 43; Massie, *Nicholas and Alexandra*, 144–145.

43. Lieven, *Nicholas II*, 50.

44. The first son, Alfonso, lived from 1907 to 1938, and renounced the crown. The fourth son, Gonzalo, lived from 1914 to 1974, despite hemophilia. It was possible, though not guaranteed, that Aleksei could have enjoyed a long life. For Alfonso XIII, see en.wikipedia.org/wiki/Alfonso_XIII; for Alfonso, Prince of Asturias, see en.wikipedia.org/wiki/Alfonso_Prince_of_Asturias; for Gonzalo, see en.wikipedia.org/wiki/Infante_Gonzalo_of_Spain, all accessed September 19, 2020.

45. Lieven, *Nicholas II*, 50.

46. Van Der Kiste and Hall, *Once a Grand Duchess*, 78.

47. For Olga Aleksandrovna, see Phenix, *Olga Romanov*, and Vorres, *Last Grand Duchess*.

48. Nicholson, *Michael Romanov*, 2.

49. Khrustalev, *Velikii kniaz' Mikhail Aleksandrovich* (2018), 138–232; Crawford, *Last Tsar*, 29–34; Nicholson, *Michael Romanov*, 2–3; Gray, *Grand Duke's Woman*, 19–28.

50. Khrustalev, *Velikii kniaz' Mikhail Aleksandrovich*, 188–209; Crawford, *Last Tsar*, 34–43; Nicholson, *Michael Romanov*, 2–3; Gray, *Grand Duke's Woman*.

51. For the details of Mikhail's correspondence with Nicholas and Maria Fyodorovna, and Ksenia's diary on this affair, see Khrustalev, ed., *Dnevnik i perepiska Velikogo Kniazia Mikhaila Aleksandrovicha*, 31–41.

52. Nicholas Nicolson's email message to the author, March 25, 2024. For Alexandra's objections, see Alexandra to Nicholas, No. 460/No. 354, 11/IX, 1915, in Fuhrmann, 228; Gray, *Grand Duke's Woman*, 36–44.

53. Alexander Mikhailovich, *Once a Grand Duke*, 136–137.

54. Information on Kirill's morganatic marriage from Nicholas Nicolson's email to the author, April 5, 2024.

55. Nicholson, *Michael Romanov*, 2.

56. Perry and Pleshakov, *Flight of the Romanovs*, 37–38.

57. Alexander Mikhailovich, *Once a Grand Duke*, 137–138.

58. Kolonitskii, *Tragicheskaia erotika*, 379–380. For his biography, see Robinson, *Grand Duke Nikolai Nikolaevich*.

59. It is not necessary to provide a long list of biographical works on Rasputin here. The best biography, which is based on a wide array of archival sources and makes numerous corrections regarding widely spread false stories of Rasputin, is Smith, *Rasputin*. For an extensive bibliography on Rasputin, see Smith, *Rasputin*, 682–715.

60. Lieven, *Nicholas II*, 164.

61. Massie, *Nicholas and Alexandra*, 199.

62. Ibid., 199–200.

63. Gilliard, *Thirteen Years*, 128.

64. The theory that Vyrubova administered poison to make Aleksei's bleeding worse is outlandish and should be discarded. Another theory, that Rasputin used hypnosis, is also doubtful. See Smith, *Rasputin*, 289–290.

65. Ibid., 294–295.

66. Wortman, *Scenarios of Power*, 362.

67. Ibid., 364.

68. Bark, *Memoirs*, chap. 1, 12.

69. For the Fundamental Laws, see Szeftel, *Russian Constitution*.

70. Verner, *Crisis of Russian Autocracy*, 299.

71. Wortman, *Scenarios of Power*, 365. Also see Verner, *Crisis of Russian Autocracy*, 245.

72. Historians debate the nature of the structure after 1906. See Verner, *Crisis of Russian Autocracy*; Lieven, *Nicholas II*; Lohr, "Tsarism, Tsarist Autocracy, and the Russian Sonderweg."

73. Verner, *Crisis of Russian Autocracy*, 350.

74. Lieven, *Nicholas II*, 110.

75. Menning, "Russian High Command," 9.

76. Lieven, *Russia and the Origins of the First World War*, 57.

77. See Guchkov, *Guchkov rasskazyvaet*.

78. See Rosenberg, *Liberals*.

79. See Abraham, *Alexander Kerensky*. See Nikolaevskii, *Russkie masony*; Startsev, "Russkie politicheskie masony."

80. See Kolonitskii, *Tragicheskaia erotika*.

81. Smith, *Rasputin*, 137–138.

82. Ibid., 258.

83. Ibid., 273. For Guchkov's speech, see ibid., 272–273, and for Rodzyanko's reports to Nicholas, see ibid., 165–270.

84. King, *Last Empress*, 193.

85. Wortman, *Scenarios of Power*, 377–378, 380–382, 394–395.

86. Lieven, *Nicholas II*, 191.

87. Ibid., 192–193; Lieven, *Russia and the Origins of the First World War*, 35–37.

88. Lieven, *Nicholas II*, 193.

89. Ibid., 197.

90. Gilliard, *Thirteen Years*, 97.

91. Smith, *Rasputin*, 331–336.

92. Paléologue, *Ambassador's Memoirs*, vol. 1, 122; Massie, *Nicholas and Alexandra*, 282–283.

93. Massie, *Nicholas and Alexandra*, 282; Vyrubova, *Memories*, 104; Montefiore, *Romanovs*, 576.

94. Bark, *Memoirs*, chap. VII, 1–2.

95. Lieven, *Nicholas II*, 199–200.

96. Paléologue, *Ambassador's Memoirs*, vol. 1, 46.

97. Bark, *Memoirs*, chap. VII, 35–36.

98. Lieven, *Nicholas II*, 201–202; for Nicholas's diary entries for this period, see Nicholas II, *Dnevnik Imperatora*, 475–477; also see Montefiore, *Romanovs*, 572.

99. For the Council of Ministers meeting on July 11, see Lieven, *Russia and the Origins of the First World War*, 141–144; Bark, *Memoirs*, chap. VII, 7–19.

100. Bark, *Memoirs*, chap. VII, 3–4; Lieven, *Nicholas II*, 199.

101. Kaiser Wilhelm to Tsar Nicholas, July 31, 1914, "The Willy-Nicky Telegrams," World War I Document Archive, wwi.lib.byu.edu/index-php/The_Willy_Nicki_Telegrams.

102. Bark, *Memoirs*, chap. VIII, 4–7; Cantacuzene, *Revolutionary Days*, 69–70, based on what Bark confided to her.

103. Gilliard, *Thirteen Years*, 105–106.

104. Kaiser Wilhelm to Tsar Nicholas, August 1, 1914, "The Willy-Nicky Telegrams."

105. Paléologue, *Ambassador's Memoirs*, vol. 1, 196–197.

## Chapter 2: Russia Enters the War

1. Akhmatova, "Iul' 1914," 318–320.

2. Kolonitskii, *Tragicheskaia erotika*, 73.

3. Ibid., 73–75; Cantacuzene, *Revolutionary Days*, 14–15. Princess Cantacuzene, née Julia Dent Grant, was a granddaughter of Ulysses Grant. In 1896 she married Prince Mikhail Cantacuzene, who became an aide-de-camp for Nicholas II.

4. Kolonitskii, *Tragicheskaia erotika*, 77; Cantacuzene, *Revolutionary Days*, 18–19.

5. Cantacuzene, *Revolutionary Days*, 19.

6. Almedingen, *Empress Alexandra*, 134.

7. Rodzianko, *Reign of Rasputin*, 109–111; Kolonitskii, *Tragicheskaia erotika*, 83–87; Rodichev, quoted in Mel'gunov, *Na putiakh*, 14; Miliukov, *Vospominaniia*, vol. 2, 190; Miliukov, *Political Memoirs*, 306.

8. Fleer, *Rabochee dvizhenie*, 5–8; McKean, *St. Petersburg*, 318.

9. For different interpretations of the workers' reaction to the war, see McKean, *St. Petersburg*, 357–358.

10. Akhmatova, "Iul' 1914," 318–320.

11. "Na Issakskaia ploshchad'," *Birzhevyia vedomosti*, July 23, 1914, 3; Kolonitskii, *Tragicheskaia erotika*, 82. The city governor (*gradonachalnik*), appointed by and directly responsible to the minister of internal affairs, was entrusted with the task of securing peace and order in the city. He controlled the police, the gendarmerie, and the secret police network, known as the Okhrana.

12. Sanborn, "Mobilization of 1914," 275–279; Sanborn, *Drafting the Russian Nation*, 30–31; Kanishchev, *Russkii bunt*, 36–43.

13. Stone, *Eastern Front*, 45, 50.

14. Engelstein, *Russia in Flames*, 37.

15. Menning, "Russian High Command," 3–4.

16. Menning, "Russian High Command," 19–27. The British military attaché, Sir Alfred Knox, characterizes Yanushkevich as "a courtier rather than the soldier," and said that he owed his position to Alexandra's influence. In his opinion, the brain at the Stavka was General Yury Danilov. Knox, *With the Russian Army*, vol. 1, 42, 331.

17. Menning, "Russian High Command," 11.

18. Lincoln, *Passage*, 63.

19. Engelstein, *Russia in Flames*, 47.

20. Lincoln, *Passage*, 71–72.

21. For the details of the Battle of Tannenberg and the Masurian Lakes, see Lincoln, *Passage*, 63–76; Knox, *With the Russian Army*, vol. 1, chaps. 2–5.

22. Pipes, *Russian Revolution*, 197–199.

23. Lincoln, *Passage*, 78–89.

24. Ibid., 89, 129.

25. Stone, *Eastern Front*, 45, 146; Pipes, *Russian Revolution*, 206; Sidorov, *Ekonomicheskoe polozhenie*, 11–12.

26. Lincoln, *Passage*, 145; *Rossiia v mirovoi voine, 1914–1918 (v tsifrakh)*, 32.

27. Pipes, *Russian Revolution*, 202–203.

28. Ibid., 203.

29. Gippius, *Siniaia kniga*, 17, 21–23; Lincoln, *Passage*, 143–144.

30. Lincoln, *Passage*, 119–121.

31. Ibid., 123.

32. Engelstein, *Russia in Flames*, 33, quoting Golovin, *Russian Army*, 221.

33. Lincoln, *Passage*, 125–127.

34. Engelstein, *Russia in Flames*, 53.

35. Lincoln, *Passage*, 127–129; Knox, *With the Russian Army*, vol. 1, 282.

36. Menning, "Russian High Command," 33–34; Knox, *With the Russian Army*, vol. 1, chap. 8.

37. Gatrell, *Whole Empire*, 31.

38. Engelstein, *Russia in Flames*, 56.

39. Ibid., 58.

40. Menning, "Russian High Command," 21.

41. Gatrell, *Whole Empire*, 62–63.

42. Quoted in Lincoln, *Passage*, 157. See Gatrell, *Whole Empire*, 15–32.

43. Rosenberg, "Po tu storonu Velikoi Metaistorii," 409–431; also see Rosenberg, *States of Anxiety*, 21–26.

44. Nicholas II, *Dnevnik Imperatora*, 10/VIII, 18/VIII, 21/VIII, 30/VIII, 8/IX, 1914.

45. Nicholas to Alexandra, No. 18/No. 57, Stavka, 22/IX, 1914, in Fuhrmann, 20.

46. Kolonitskii, *Tragicheskaia erotika*, 99–101.

47. Nicholas to Alexandra, No. 19/No. 237, 23/IX, 1914, in Fuhrmann, 22; Nicholas to Alexandra, No. 21/No. 158, 23/IX, 1914, in Fuhrmann, 23; Alexandra to Nicholas, No. 24/No. 238, 24/IX, 1914, 23. For Rasputin's backing of Alexandra, see Kolonitskii, *Tragicheskaia erotika*, 101–102.

48. Nicholas II, *Dnevnik Imperatora*, 25/IX, 1914, 488.

49. Kolonitskii, *Tragicheskaia erotica*, 123.

50. Ibid., 103.

51. Ibid., 115.

52. Ibid., 134.

53. Ibid., 134.

54. Cherniavsky, *Prologue to Revolution*, 77–78; also Kolonitskii, *Tragicheskaia erotika*, 134–135.

55. Quoted in Kolonitskii, *Tragicheskaia erotika*, 265.

56. Ibid.

57. Alexandra to Nicholas, No. 10/No. 235, 20/IX, 1914, in Fuhrmann, 17.

58. Alexandra to Nicholas, No. 164/No. 273, 29/I, 1915, in Fuhrmann, 79.

59. Alexandra to Nicholas, No. 196/No. 282, 5/III, 1915, in Fuhrmann, 91.

60. Alexandra to Nicholas, No. 218/No. 287, 4/IV, 1915, in Fuhrmann, 100.

61. Alexandra to Nicholas, No. 231/No. 291, 7/IV, 1915, in Fuhrmann, 106.

62. Nicholas to Alexandra, No. 233/No. 172, 7/IV, 1915, in Fuhrmann, 107.

63. Alexandra to Nicholas, No. 320/No. 313, 10/VI, 1915, in Fuhrmann, 135.

64. Fuhrmann, 137n94.

65. Alexandra to Nicholas, No. 323/No. 314, 11/VI, 1915, in Fuhrmann, 136.

66. Pearson, *Russian Moderates*, 12–13.

67. Ibid., 30.

68. The composition of the Fourth Duma was (viewed on an ideological spectrum beginning from the left): Bolsheviks, 5; Mensheviks, 7; Trudoviks, 10; Progressists, 47; Kadets, 57; Octobrists, 85; Centrists, 33; Progressive Nationalists, 20; Nationalists, 60; and Rightists, 64. The Bolsheviks and the Mensheviks were Marxist revolutionaries, and the

Trudoviks, led by Aleksandr Fyodorovich Kerensky, formed an independent Duma faction that stood close to the Socialist Revolutionary Party. The Centrists, Nationalists, and Rightists constituted the right wing of the Duma and stood for the monarchist principle. Pearson, *Russian Moderates*, 15.

69. Katkov, *Russia 1917*, 3–11; Diakin, *Russkaia burzhuazia*, 68. See also Gleason, "All-Russian Union of Towns," 290–302; Fallows, "Politics and War Effort," 70–90.

70. Rodzianko, *Reign of Rasputin*, 130–134.

71. Ibid., 134.

72. Diakin, *Russkaia burzhuazia*, 91–94; Siegelbaum, "Russian Industrialists," 40–41; Pearson, *Russian Moderates*, 34–35; Gaida, *Liberal'naia oppozitsiia*, 73–79.

73. Chermenskii, *IV gosudarstvennaia duma*, 87; Pearson, *Russian Moderates*, 41.

74. Stone, *Eastern Front*, 17–43, 197–198; Mel'gunov, *Martovskie dni*, 20–29; Katkov, *Russia 1917*, 119–132.

75. Alexandra to Nicholas, No. 325/No. 315, 12/VI, 1915, in Fuhrmann, 138.

76. For Alexandra's and Rasputin's opposition to firing Shcheglovitov and Sabler, see Alexandra to Nicholas, No. 340/No. 319, 15/VI, 1915, in Fuhrmann, 146; for Nicholas's decision for the dismissals, see Nicholas to Alexandra, No. 338/No. 178, in Fuhrmann, 145.

77. Alexandra to Nicholas, No. 340/No. 319, 15/VI, 1915, in Fuhrmann, 146.

78. Pearson, *Russian Moderates*, 42–43.

79. Chermenskii, *IV gosudarstvennaia duma*, 85; Arkhipov, *Rossiiskaia politicheskaia elita*, 26; Kulikov, *Biurokraticheskaia elita*, 95–96. For debates about a ministry of confidence and a responsible ministry, see Gaida, *Liberal'naia oppozitsiia*, 82–101.

80. Quoted in Diakin, *Russkaia burzhuazia*, 82–83, 85–86. Milyukov reversed the Kadets' previous policy of nonparticipation in the Special Council for Defense after Sukhomlinov's dismissal. In protest, Nekrasov resigned from the party central committee. Pearson, *Russian Moderates*, 47. See also Miliukov, *Russian Revolution*, vol. 1, 13.

81. Diakin, *Russkaia burzhuazia*, 96; Milyukov quoted in Chermenskii, *IV gosudarstvennaia duma*, 90, 91; Pearson, *Russian Moderates*, 47–48; Gaida, *Liberal'naia oppozitsiia*, 88–101.

82. Konstantin Konstantinovich was an accomplished poet and translator of Shakespeare. He struggled with his sexuality, revealing his homosexuality in his diary. His family experienced numerous tragic events. His sons were given the title of prince but not grand duke. His son Oleg was killed in action in the beginning of the war. His sons Konstantin, Igor, and Georgy were executed by the Bolsheviks in a gruesome manner in 1918.

83. Kolonitskii, *Tragicheskaia erotika*, 123.

### Chapter 3: Parting Ways

1. Menning, "Russian High Command," 37–38, 42–45.

2. Quoted in Kolonitskii, *Tragicheskaia erotika*, 478.

3. Quoted in Menning, "Russian High Command," 23.

4. Kolonitskii, *Tragicheskaia erotika*, 138–139, 416–463. For the disparaging remarks on the tsar and contrasting effusive praise of the grand duke among peasants, see Kolonitskii, *Tragicheskaia erotika*, 452–453.

5. Pearson, *Russian Moderates*, 49–50; Chermenskii, *IV gosudarstvennaia duma*, 96, 109; Diakin, *Russkaia burzhuazia*, 110; Menning, "Russian High Command," 39. For the Council of Ministers meeting during the political crisis in the summer of 1915, see Cherniavsky, *Prologue to Revolution*; Bark, *Memoirs*, chap. XVI, 4–11.

6. Quoted in Riha, *Russian European*, 227.

7. Shul'gin, *Dni* (1925), 147; Arkhipov, *Rossiiskaia politicheskaia elita*, 30. For heated discussion among the liberals who met at Konovalov's villa in Moscow on August 16, 1915, see Gaida, *Liberal'naia oppozitsiia*, 111–112.

8. See Hasegawa, *February Revolution* (2017), chap. 5.

9. Bark, *Memoirs*, chap. XVI, 11–18; for letter, see 16–17. Also see Pearson, *Russian Moderates*, 56; Kulikov, *Biurokraticheskaia elita*, 89–92.

10. Bark, *Memoirs*, chap. XVI, 20–25; Shidlovskii, *Vospominaniia*, vol. 2, 37–40; Chermenskii, *IV gosudarstvennaia duma*, 117–118; Diakin, *Russkaia burzhuazia*, 115; Pearson, *Russian Moderates*, 53–54; Miliukov, *Russian Revolution*, vol. 1, 13–14; Kulikov, *Biurokraticheskaia elita*, 91–92; Gaida, *Liberal'naia oppozitsiia*, 119.

11. Chermenskii, *IV gosudarstvennaia duma*, 111; Kulikov, *Biurokraticheskaia elita*, 90.

12. Alexandra to Nicholas, No. 383/No. 330, 22/VIII, 1915, in Fuhrmann, 171–172.

13. Nicholas to Alexandra, No. 385, Telegram 1 in Russian, 23/VIII, 1915, in Fuhrmann, 175.

14. Chermenskii, *IV gosudarstvennaia duma*, 114–115; Diakin, *Russkaia burzhuazia*, 117; Kulikov, *Biurokraticheskaia elita*, 132–133.

15. Alexandra to Nicholas, No. 383/No. 330, 22/VIII, 1915, in Fuhrmann, 172.

16. Alexandra to Nicholas, No. 383/No. 330, 22/VIII, 1915, in Fuhrmann, 173.

17. Alexandra to Nicholas, No. 469/No. 354, 14/IX, 1915, in Fuhrmann, 235.

18. Quoted in Kolonitskii, *Tragicheskaia erotika*, 482.

19. Bubnov, *V tsarskoi Stavke*, 77.

20. Nicholas to Alexandra, No. 395, 25/VIII, 1915, in Fuhrmann, 182.

21. Andrei Vladimirovich, "Dnevnik Velikogo Kniazia Andreia Vladimirovicha," *Gibel' monarkhii*, 294.

22. Alexandra to Nicholas, No. 389/No. 332, 24/VIII, 1915, in Fuhrmann, 176.

23. For the Council of Ministers meeting on September 2, 1915, see Cherniavsky, *Prologue*, 226–243.

24. Mosolov, *Pri dvore*, 7.

25. Mosolov, *Pri dvore*, 7; Cantacuzene, *Revolutionary Days*, 68. For Orlov's role, see Cantacuzene, *Revolutionary Days*, 48–49; Paléologue, *Ambassador's Memoirs*, vol. 2, entry for September 5, 1915, 69.

26. Dnevnik b. Velikogo Kniazia Andreia Vladimirovichma, 70, cited by Mul'tatuli, *Nikolai II*, 42; Velikii Kniaz' Kirill Vladimirovich, *Moia zhizn' na sluzh be Rossii*, 234, cited in Mu'tatuli, *Nikolai II*, 57.

27. Kolonitskii, *Tragicheskaia erotika*, 160–162.

28. *Dnevnik L. A. Tikhomirova*, ed. A. V. Repnikov (Moscow, 2008), 145–146, quoted in Kolonitskii, *Tragicheskaia erotika*, 159.

29. Riha, *Russian European*, 235.

30. Chermenskii, *IV gosudarstvennaia duma*, 120; Diakin, *Russkaia burzhuazia*, 119, 121; Pearson, *Russian Moderates*, 58–59.

31. Bark, *Memoirs*, chap. XVI, 36–37; Diakin, *Russkaia burzhuazia*, 121–122, 125; Chermenskii, *IV gosudarstvennaia duma*, 125, 127, 130; Pearson, *Russian Moderates*, 60–61; Gaida, *Liberal'naia oppozitsiia*, 130–132.

32. Aleksandr Alekseevich Khvostov briefly assumed the post from July 9 to September 16, 1916, but for the sake of convenience, I have treated this period as a part of the Stürmer period, since Stürmer continued to dominate the political scene as chairman of the Council of Ministers.

33. Kulikov, *Biurokraticheskaia elita*, 235, 246–248; Cantacuzene, *Revolutionary Days*, 81.

34. For Vasily Maklakov's satirical fable "Tragic Situation," see Katkov, *Russia 1917*, 178–179; Gaida, *Liberal'naia oppozitsiia*, 161.

35. For Alexandra's references to Khvostov, see the index in Fuhrmann, 746. On Alexandra's doubt about Khovstov, Alexandra to Nicholas, No. 839/No. 449, 2/III, 1916, in Fuhrmann, 393.

36. The Union of Zemstvos and the Union of Towns were united into a loose association, Zemgor, in 1915, with G. E. Lvov as its head, while each maintained its separate organization.

37. Riha, *Russian European*, 238; Pearson, *Russian Moderates*, 66; Gaida, *Liberal'naia oppozitsiia*, 159–160; Bark, *Memoirs*, chap. XVIII, 3–16. Kulikov rejects the "myth" of Rasputin's influence on Nicholas; Kulikov, *Biurokraticheskaia elita*, 100.

38. Diakin, *Russkaia burzhuazia*, 128–139, 140–143; Pearson, *Russian Moderates*, 70.

39. Boltunova, "Stavka," 50–51. For the Stavka at Baranovichi, see Perry and Pleshakov, *Flight of the Romanovs*, 119.

40. Dubenskii, "Kak proizoshel perevorot," 24.

41. Lemke, *250 dnei*, 39; Boltunova, "Stavka," 51.

42. Boltunova, "Stavka," 51.

43. Menning, "Russian High Command," 61; Knox, *With the Russian Army*, vol. 1, 331.

44. Menning, "Russian High Command," 61.

45. Solzhenitsyn, *March 1917*, Book 3, 177, 520, 537, 567, 568.

46. Shavel'skii, *Vospominaniia*, vol. 2, 201, quoted in Menning, "Russian High Command," 76.

47. Dubenskii, "Kak proizoshel perevorot," 77.

48. Bubnov, *V tsarskoi Stavke*, 84.

49. Pearson, *Russian Moderates*, 75–76.

50. For Aleksei Khvostov and his sordid intrigues, see Globachev, *Pravda o russkoi revoliutsii*, 97–103.

51. Gaida, *Liberal'naia oppozitsiia*, 186.

52. Diakin, *Russkaia burzhuazia*, 163–170; Arkhipov, *Biurokraticheskaia elita*, 37–38.

53. Lincoln, *Passage*, 238–257; Menning, "Russian High Command," 73–75; Knox, *With the Russian Army*, vol. 2, chap. 12.

54. Lincoln, *Passage*, 255–256.

55. Alekseev's memorandum to Nicholas, "Dokladnaia zapiska Generala Alekseeva Imperatoru Nikolaiu Vtoproiu, June 15, 1916," Alekseev Papers, Box 1, File 6, HIA; Alekseeva-Borel', *Sorok let*, 439–444; Menning, "Russian High Command," 57–58.

56. Alekseeva-Borel', *Sorok let*, 445; Rodzianko, *Reign of Rasputin*, 194–195.

57. Rodzianko, *Reign of Rasputin*, 194–195; Alekseeva-Borel', *Sorok let*, 445.

58. Alekseeva-Borel', *Sorok let*, 445–446.

59. See Arkhipov, *Biurokraticheskaia elita*, 38–56; Kolonitskii, *Tragicheskaia erotika*, 228–240, 289–313; Bark, *Memoirs*, chap. XX, 18–28.

60. Shavel'skii, *Vospominaniia*, vol. 2, 61, quoted in Menning, "Russian High Command," 53.

61. Denikin, *Ocherki russkoi smuty*, vol. 1, 34.

62. Menning, "Russian High Command," 55–56.

63. Ibid., 66.

64. Kolonitskii, *Tragicheskaia erotika*, 177.

65. Ibid., 207.

66. Ibid., 207.

67. Ibid., 194.

68. Ibid., 210.

69. Ibid., 220.

70. Ibid., 286–287; Montefiore, *Romanovs*, 541.

71. Numerous examples of false rumors are given in Kolonitskii, *Tragicheskaia erotika*, 289–313; Rappaport, *Race to Save the Romanovs*, 29–31.

72. For more details, see Kolonitskii, *Tragicheskaia erotika*, 313–326; Chebotareva, "V dvortsovom lazarete," *Novyi zhurnal*, No. 181, 212.

73. Alexandra to Nicholas, No. 1430/No. 595, 20/IX, 1916, in Fuhrmann, 592.

74. Nicholas to Alexandra, No. 1431, 20/IX, 1916, in Fuhrmann, 594.

75. For Alexandra's campaign to appoint Protopopov, see Alexandra to Nicholas, No. 1380/No. 583, 7/IX, 1916, in Fuhrmann, 574.

76. Nicholas to Alexandra, No. 1386, 9/IX, 1916, in Fuhrmann, 577.

77. Alexandra to Nicholas, No. 1390/No. 585, 10/IX, 1916, in Fuhrmann, 578.

78. Nicholas to Alexandra, No. 1391, 10/IX, 1916, in Fuhrmann, 579; Alexandra to Nicholas, No. 1461/No. 602, 27/IX, 1916; Nicholas to Alexandra, No. 1467/Telegram 77, 27/IX, 28/IX, 1916, in Fuhrmann, 610, 613. Nicholas thanked Alexandra for "tidy instructions for my talk with Protopopov." Nicholas to Alexandra, No. 1466, 28/IX, 1916, in Fuhrmann, 613.

79. Alexandra to Nicholas, No. 1487/No. 607, 12/X, 1916, in Fuhrmann, 619.

80. Shliapnikov, *Kanun semnadtsatogo goda*, 115–124. Also see GARF. f. 102, d. 307a, t. 2, 1916 g., ll. 41–43.

81. Diakin, *Russkaia burzhuazia*, 239–240; Chermenskii, *IV gosudarstvennaia duma*, 201; Kulikov, *Biurokraticheskaia elita*, 287.

82. "Progressivnyi blok," 87, 114. For the discussions in the Progressive Bloc in October, see "Progressivnyi blok," 82–117; Pearson, *Russian Moderates*, 108–115; Arkhipov,

*Rossiiskaia politicheskaia elita*, 44–45; Kulikov, *Biurokraticheskaia elita*, 286–287; Gaida, *Liberal'naia oppozitsiia*, 220–252.

83. For the background of Milyukov's speech, see Gaida, *Liberal'naia oppozitsiia*, 230–232; Lyandres, "Progressive Bloc," 447–464.

84. Arkhipov, *Rossiiskaia politicheskaia elita*, 45–46; Lyandres, "Progressive Bloc," 457–460.

85. Iakobii, *Imperator Nikolai II*, 93–94.

86. Arkhipov, *Rossiiskaia politicheskaia elita*, 48–51. Also see Katkov, *Russia 1917*, 190–193; Miliukov, *Vospominaniia*, vol. 2, 276–277; Pearson, *Russian Moderates*, 115, 117. For the reactions to Milyukov's speech, see Gaida, *Liberal'naia oppozitsiia*, 232–237.

87. Chermenskii, *IV gosudarstvennaia duma*, 214–215; Lyandres, "Conspiracy," 99–133.

88. Kudrina, *Imperatritsa*, 149–150, 154.

89. Alexander Mikhailovich, *Once a Grand Duke*, 272–273.

90. Bark, *Memoirs*, chap. XVIII, 35.

91. Gilliard, *Thirteen Years*, 178; Kudrina, *Imperatritsa*, 154–155.

92. See Bark, *Memoirs*, chap. XVIII, 33–34.

93. Alexandra to Nicholas, No. 1556/No. 622, 4/XI, 1916, in Fuhrmann, 640.

94. Andrei Vladimirovich, "Iz dnevnika" (1928), 197; Diakin, *Russkaia burzhuazia*, 244; Kulikov, *Biurokraticheskaia elita*, 358–372.

95. Shavel'skii, *Vospominaniia*, vol. 2, 223.

96. Almedingen, *Empress Alexandra*, 180; Cantacuzene, *Revolutionary Days*, 99.

97. Alexander Mikhailovich, *Once a Grand Duke*, 275–276.

98. Quoted in Khrustalev, "Sud'ba pretendenta," in *Permskaia Golgofa*, 53–54. The draft of this letter was written by Nikolai Wrangel, his trusted aide-de-camp, and Vasily Maklakov.

99. Alexandra to Nicholas, No. 1569/No. 625, 7/XI, 1916, Nicholas to Alexandra, No. 1574, 8/XI, 1916, in Fuhrmann, 645, 647.

100. Nicholas to Alexandra, No. 1584, 10/XI, 1916, in Fuhrmann, 650.

101. Shavel'skii, *Vospominaniia*, vol. 2, 23.

102. Diakin, *Russkaia burzhuazia*, 246, 261; Pearson, *Russian Moderates*, 116–117; Arkhipov, *Rossiiskaia politicheskaia elita*, 49–50.

103. Diakin, *Russkaia burzhuazia*, 373. For Trepov's tenure, see Kulikov, *Biurokraticheskaia elita*, 304–318.

104. RGIA, f. 1276, op. 10, d. 7, l. 386. For Purishkevich's position, see Arkhipov, *Rossiiskaia politicheskaia elita*, 56–57; Gaida, *Liberal'naia oppozitsiia*, 244–245.

105. Chermenskii, *IV gosudarstvennaia duma*, 228–229; Pearson, *Russian Moderates*, 125–126. The government also recognized that it was losing the support of the conservative majority in the State Council. See RGIA, f. 1276, op. 10, d. 7, l. 413.

106. For the division of the conservative right, see Loukianov, "First World War," 872–895.

107. Paley, *Memories of Russia*, 24–27.

108. Alexandra to Nicholas, No. 1591/No. 630, 12/XI, 1916, in Fuhrmann, 653–654.

109. Alexandra to Nicholas, No. 1600/No. 632, 5/XII, 1916, in Fuhrmann, 658.

110. Alexandra to Nicholas, No. 1606/No. 633, 6/XII, 1916, No. 1620/No. 636, 9/XII, 1916, in Fuhrmann, 660, 665.

111. Alexandra to Nicholas, No. 1637/No. 639, 13/XII, 1916, No. 1642/No. 640, 14/XII, 1916, in Fuhrmann, 672, 675; Diakin, *Russkaia burzhuazia*, 261.

112. Paléologue, *Ambassador's Memoirs*, vol. 3, 107–108.

113. Shavel'skii, *Vospominaniia*, vol. 2, 244–248.

114. Ibid., 249.

115. Diakin, *Russkaia burzhuazia*, 259.

116. Chermenskii, *IV gosudarstvennaia duma*, 231–232; Gaida, *Liberal'naia oppozitsiia*, 251–252.

## Chapter 4: The Bullet That Killed Rasputin

1. Smith, *Rasputin*, 572–574.

2. Ibid., 590–592; Montefiore, *Romanovs*, 605–610; Wada, *Roshia kakumei*, 102–109.

3. Smith, *Rasputin*, 595.

4. Blok, *Poslednie dni*, 7; Spiridovich, *Velikaia voina*, vol. 2, 197.

5. Alexandra to Nicholas, No. 1655/No. 643, 17/XII, 1916, in Fuhrmann, 684; Alexandra to Nicholas, No. 1657/Telegram 110, 17/XII, 1916, in Fuhrmann, 685; Nicholas II, *Letters of the Tsar to the Tsaritsa*, 31; Spiridovich, *Velikaia voina*, vol. 2, 208–209. General Alekseev returned to Mogilev on December 17. Although he was not completely recovered from illness, he was urged to return in preparation for the spring offensive, scheduled on April 18. He did not attend the meeting with the Allied representatives on that day. G. Orlov, "General M. V. Alekseev—K tritsatipiatiletiiu osnovaniia Dobrovol'skoi Armii," Bern, 1952, Alekseev Papers, Box 1, File 3, 15, HIA.

6. Nicholas II, *Dnevnik Imperatora*, 615.

7. Nicholas to Alexandra, No. 1658/Telegram 123, 17/XII, 1916, in Fuhrmann, 685; Spiridovich, *Velikaia voina*, vol. 2, 209.

8. Shavel'skii, *Vospominaniia*, vol. 2, 249.

9. Spiridovich, *Velikaia voina*, vol. 2, 210; Shavel'skii, *Vospominaniia*, vol. 2, 249.

10. Azar, ed., *Diary of Olga Romanov*, 74.

11. No. 1663/Telegram 0770, Orsha train station, 18/XII, 1916, in Fuhrmann, 686; Nicholas II, *Letters of the Tsar to the Tsaritsa*, 312; Spiridovich, *Velikaia voina*, vol. 2, 212.

12. Spiridovich, *Velikaia voina*, vol. 2, 212–213.

13. Ibid., 203.

14. Dehn, *Real Tsaritsa*, 118–119.

15. Smith, *Rasputin*, 606; Spiridovich, *Velikaia voina*, vol. 2, 208.

16. Alexandra to Nicholas, No. 1664/Telegram No. 119, 19/XII, 1916, 13:50 > 14.00, in Fuhrmann, 686.

17. Spiridovich, *Velikaia voina*, vol. 2, 208.

18. Nicholas II, *Dnevnik Imperatora*, 616.

19. Spiridovich, *Velikaia voina*, vol. 2, 215–216; Voeikov, *S tsarem*, 179–180.

20. Spiridovich, *Velikaia voina*, vol. 2, 216.

21. Ibid.; Voeikov, *S tsarem*, 182.

22. A rumor spread that he was buried in the middle of the night in secrecy. This is one of the myths that were circulated even after Rasputin's death. See Andrei Vladimirovich, "Dnevniki," *Gibel' monarkhii*, 322.

23. Vyrubova, *Memories*, 183.

24. Dehn, *Real Tsaritsa*, 123; Vyruvoba, *Memoirs*, 183; Smith, *Rasputin*, 612.

25. Voeikov learned that Nicholas himself had ordered two motorcars, an arrangement that was usually handled by Voeikov. This means that Nicholas did not want Voeikov to know that he defied his recommendation. According to Douglas Smith, in addition to the imperial family and their close confidants, Aklina Laptinskaya, Colonel Vladimir Maltsev (commander of Tsarskoe air defenses), and one or two others attended. Smith, *Rasputin*, 612.

26. Quoted in Almedingen, *Empress Alexandra*, 182–183.

27. Paléologue, *Ambassador's Memoirs*, vol. 3, 135.

28. Shavel'skii, *Vospominaniia*, vol. 2, 249; A. S. Pireiko, *V tyli i na fronte imperialisticheskoi voiny*, 65, quoted in Kolonitskii, *Tragicheskaia erotika*, 344.

29. Lomonosov, *Vospominaniia* (1994), 220.

30. Gilliard, *Thirteen Years*, 187.

31. Ibid., 183.

32. See diary entries of Olga in Azar, ed., *Diary of Olga*, 74–77; Spiridovich, *Velikaia voina*, vol. 3, 17.

33. Chebotareva, "V dvortsovom lazarete," *Novyi zhurnal*, No. 182, 207.

34. Chebotareva, "V dvortsovom lazarete," *Novyi zhurnal*, No. 181, 212.

35. Ibid., 242.

36. Spiridovich, *Velikaia voina*, vol. 3, 17–18.

37. Paléologue, *Ambassador's Memoirs*, vol. 3, 172.

38. Spiridovich, *Velikaia voina*, vol. 3, 17–18.

39. Nikolai Mikhailovich, "Zapiski," in *Gibel' monarkhii*, 12; Alexander Mikhailovich, *Once a Grand Duke*, 278.

40. Kudrina, *Imperatritsa*, 160; Smith, *Rasputin*, 615–616.

41. Andrei Vladimirovich, "Dnevniki," *Gibel' monarkhii*, 321; Spiridovich, *Velikaia voina*, vol. 2, 220; Gavriil Konstantinovich, *V Mramornom dvortse*, 291.

42. Alexander Mikhailovich, *Once a Grand Duke*, 279.

43. Spiridovich, *Velikaia voina*, vol. 2, 224.

44. Nikolai Mikhailovich, "Zapiski," in *Gibel' monarkhii*, 71, also quoted in Kolonitskii, *Tragicheskaia erotika*, 349–350.

45. Cantacuzene, *Revolutionary Days*, 101.

46. Those who came were Olga (Queen of Greece), Miechen, Kirill, Ducky, Boris, Andrei, Pavel, Maria Pavlovna the Younger, Nikolai Mikhailovich (Bimbo), Sergei Mikhailovich, and K.R.'s widow, Elizabeth Mavrikievna (Marva), Ioan, Gavriil, Konstantin, and Igor. Perry and Pleshakov, *Flight of the Romanovs*, 136; Wada, *Roshia kakumei*, 114.

47. Paley, *Memories*, 32–35; Andrei Vladimirovich, "Iz dnevnika" (1928), 186, 191–192; Andrei Vladimirovich, "Dnevniki," *Gibel' monarkhii*, 326–327; Gavriil Konstantinovich, *V Mramornom dvortse*, 293–294; Voeikov, *S tsarem*, 182–183; Spiridovich, *Velikaia voina*, vol. 2, 225–226.

48. Azar, ed., *Diary of Olga*, 77.

49. Spiridovich, *Velikaia voina*, vol. 2, 233.

50. Andrei Vladimirovich, "Dnevniki," *Gibel' monarkhii*, 324–325; Paléologue, *Ambassador's Memoirs*, vol. 3, 167. For Nikolai Mikhailovich's letter and Nicholas's reply, see Andrei Vladimirovich, "Dnevniki," *Gibel' monarkhii*, 328. According to Perry and Pleshakov, Bimbo (Nikolai Mikhailovich) and Sandro also went to see Dmitry off at the station. Perry and Pleshakov, *Flight of the Romanovs*, 136.

51. Paley, *Memories*, 39–40; Andrei Vladimirovich, "Dnevniki," *Gibel' monarkhii*, 139–140.

52. Nicolas Mikhailovich, *La fin du tsarisme*, 138.

53. Quoted in Kudrina, *Imperatritsa*, 160.

54. Quoted in ibid., 160.

55. Perry and Pleshakov, *Flight of the Romanovs*, 141.

56. Smith, *Rasputin*, 622–623.

57. Paléologue, *Ambassador's Memoirs*, vol. 3, 140.

58. Rodzianko, *Reign of Rasputin*, 245–247; Diakin, *Russkaia burzhuazia*, 264.

59. Paléologue, *Ambassador's Memoirs*, vol. 3, 168.

60. Nicholson, *Michael Romanov*, 21–22; Khrustalev, *Dnevnik i perepiska*, 377.

61. Rodzianko, *Reign of Rasputin*, 248–250.

62. Paléologue, *Ambassador's Memoirs*, vol. 3, 172.

63. Nicholson, *Michael Romanov*, 37–38.

64. Brusilov, *Soldier's Notebook*, 286.

65. Mul'tatuli, *Nikolai II*, 316–317.

66. Alexander Mikhailovich, *Once a Grand Duke*, 284–285.

67. Quoted in Kudrina, *Imperatritsa*, 161.

68. Ibid., 161.

69. Ibid., 160–161.

70. Deposition of Golitsyn, *Padenie*, vol. 2, 1925, 256.

71. For the series of meetings between the representatives of the liberals and the bureaucracy, see GARF, f. DPOO, d. 307a, t. 2, 1916 g., ll. 76v–76g; ibid., d. 341, ch. 57/1917 g., l. 1; ibid., f. DPOO, 1917 g., d. 669a, ll. 2–3; Maklakov's letter to Konovalov, ibid., f. DPOO, op. 343, ZS 57, ch/1917 g., ll. 20–22.

72. "Programma soiuza russkogo naroda," 243–244. For Nikolai Maklakov's memorandum, see Mul'tatuli, *Nikolai II*, 314–315.

73. GARF, f. 1276, op. 10, d. 7, ll. 449–450.

74. Spiridovich, *Velikaia voina*, vol. 3, 28–29, 40.

75. Ibid., 37–39; see "Aleksandr Dmitrievich Protopopov, Pokazaaniia Chrezvychainoi sledstvennoi komissii Vremennogo pravitel'stva," *Gibel' monarkhii*, 356–366; Paléologue, *Ambassador's Memoirs*, vol. 3, 173.

76. Spiridovich, *Velikaia voina*, vol. 3, 40–41.

77. Alexandra to Nicholas, No. 853/No. 453, 6/III, 1916, in Fuhrmann, 401.

78. Balk, *Poslednie piat' dnei*, 5.

79. Andrei Vladimirovich, "Dnevniki," *Gibel' monarkhii*, 324.

80. For Alexandra's push for Belyaev, see Alexandra to Nicholas, No. 1329/No. 572, 13/VIII, 1916, No. 1336/No. 574, 14/VIII, 1916, No. 1345/No. 576, 17/VIII, 1916, in Fuhrmann, 558, 561, 564.

81. Verkhovskii, *Na trudnom perevale*, 145; Martynov, *Tsarskaia armiia*, 61.

82. Akaemov, "Agoniia starago rezhima," xi; Khodnev, "Fevral'skaia revoliutsiia," 260.

83. The court shared their hostility to Ruzsky. Not only Khabalov and Belyaev but also the imperial court demanded that Ruzsky release meat—the highest quality of meat—and sugar in his possession to the court. Ruzsky refused. Andrei Vladimirovich, "Dnevniki," *Gibel' monarkhii*, 342–343.

84. GARF, f. 1467 (ChSK), d. 460, l. 164; Andrei Vladimirovich, "Iz dnevnika" (1928), 202–203; Andrei Vladimirovich, "Dnevniki," *Gibel' monarkhii*, 343–344.

85. GARF, f. 1467 (ChSK), d. 460, l. 164.

86. Wildman, *End of the Russian Imperial Army*, 124; Martynov, *Tsarskaia armiia*, 58; Shliapnikov, *Semnadtsatyi god*, vol. 1, 160; Kochakov, "Sostav Petrogradskogo garnizona," 61; Burdzhalov, *Vtoraia russkaia revoliutsiia*, 96–97.

87. Shklovskii, *Sentimental Journey*, 7.

88. Engel'gardt, OR RGB, f. 218, ed. khr. 3, 101–102.

89. See Hasegawa, *February Revolution* (2017), 189–192. See slso "Fevral'skaia revoliutsiia i okhrannoe otdelenie."

90. Semennikov, ed., *Monarkhiia pered krusheniem*, 97–98.

91. GARF, f. 601, op. 1, d. 1003, ll. 1–2; Chermenskii, *IV gosudarstvennaia duma*, 247.

92. Diakin, *Russkaia burzhuazia*, 269.

93. Ibid., 275.

94. Buchanan, *My Mission to Russia*, vol. 2, 42–49; Paléologue, *Ambassador's Memoirs*, vol. 3, 163–164.

95. Rodzianko, *Reign of Rasputin*, 252–254; "Krushenie Imperii," *ARR* 17 (1926): 163.

96. Rodzianko, *Reign of Rasputin*, 244–245.

97. Ibid., 245–247.

98. Ibid., 259–261; Deposition of Rodzianko, *Padenie*, vol. 7, 163–165; Startsev, "Tshchetnye usiliia Rodzianko," 201; Lyandres, *Fall of Tsarism*, 285.

99. Rodzianko interview in Lyandres, *The Fall of Tsarism*, 106.

100. Bazili's statement in his interview with Vasily Vasilievich Vyrubov, 9 December 1933, 11, Bazili Papers, 22:12, HIA.

101. Mel'gunov, *Na putiakh*, 94–102; Denikin, *Ocherki russkoi smuty*, vol. 1, pt. 1, 37–39. The meeting between Alekseev and Lvov was confirmed by Alekseev's wife, Anna Nikolaevna Alekseeva, who confided in Lukomsky later about their secret meeting. See Bazili's interview with Lukomskii, 24 February 1933, Box 22, File 11, Bazili Papers, HIA.

102. Bazili's interview with Vyrubov, Box 22, File 12, Bazili Papers, HIA.

103. Mel'gunov, *Na putiakh*, 105–117.

104. Ibid., 108–109. Also see what Khatisov told Spiridovich, in Spiridovich, *Velikaia voina*, vol. 3, 15–16. According to Spiridovich, Nikolai Nikolaevich was worried about the reaction of *muzhik*—by this he meant the reaction of peasants and soldiers. V. V. Vyrubov, a Union of Zemstvos representative at the Stavka, questions the reliability of this story. Bazili's interview with Vyrubov, 9 December 1933, 3–5, Box 22, File 12, Bazili Papers, HIA.

105. Spiridovich, *Velikaia voina*, vol. 3, 16; Airapetov, *Generaly, liberaly i predprinimateli*, 192.

106. Kolonitskii, *Tragicheskaia erotika*, 507.

107. Guchkov, *Guchkov rasskazyvaet*, 15–17.

108. Unpublished paper by Semion Lyandres presented at the Jerusalem Workshop on the Russian Revolution, May 2013, 7–8. Its revised version, "A Nice Little Family: The Romanov Brothers and the Fate of Russian Monarchy in 1917," is forthcoming.

109. Guchkov, *Guchkov rasskazyvaet*, 17. In another part of this interview, he raised the question: "If there were a regicide . . ." and then immediately added: "But we were against it." Ibid., 18.

110. Mul'tatuli, *Nikolai II*, 166–167; Mel'gunov, *Na putiakh*, 102.

111. Guchkov, *Guchkov rasskazyvaet*, 22.

112. Tereshchenko interview, Lyandres, *Fall of Tsarism*, 251.

113. Airapetov, *Generaly*, 192–193; Voeikov, *S tsarem*, 187; Guchkov, *Guchkov rasskazyvaet*, 9. Airapetov's source is from Arkhiv voenno-istoricheskogo muzeia artillerii, inzhenernykh voisk i voisk sviazi (SPb), f. 13, op. 87/1, d. 137, l. 58ob.

114. Engel'gardt interview, Lyandres, *Fall of Tsarism*, 58.

115. Tereshchenko interview, Lyandres, *Fall of Tsarism*, 252.

116. Alexander Mikhailovich, *Once a Grand Duke*, 281.

117. Voeikov, *S tsarem*, 187; Khrustalev, "Brati'a Gurko," 97–98.

118. Denikin, *Ocherki russkoi smuty*, vol. 1, 37–38.

119. Mel'gunov, *Na putiakh*, 156.

120. GARF, f. DPOO, op. 1917, d. 669a, ll. 10, 14.

121. GARF, f. 1467 (ChSK), d. 460, l. 158.

122. Zavadskii, "Na velikom izlome," 40–41.

123. Dnevnik Z. V. Arapova, OR RGB, f. 12, papka 1, d. 9, 85–87, quoted in Chermenskii, *IV gosudarstvennaia duma*, 1976, 274.

124. Spiridovich, *Velikaia voina*, vol. 3, 24.

125. Khrustalev, "Brati'a Gurko," 97.

126. Almedingen, *Empress Alexandra*, 189; Spiridovich, *Velikaia voina*, vol. 3, 56–57. For a conspiratorial theory that Alekseev, Gurko, and Mikhail had conspired to keep the tsar out of Tsarskoe Selo to attain his abdication, see Mul'tatuli, *Nikolai II*, 334.

127. Khrustalev, "Brati'a Gurko," 97.

128. Nicholas's diary from February 16 to February 22, *Dnevnik Imperatora*, 623–624; "Dnevniki Nikolaia II," *Otrechenie*, 32–39; Nicholson, *Michael Romanov*, 43–44.

129. Spiridovich, *Velikaia voina*, vol. 3, 57.

130. Alexandra to Nicholas, No. 1665/No. 644, 22/II, 1917, in Fuhrmann, 686–687.

131. Nicholas to Alexandra, No. 1666/Telegram 205, Bologoe > Tsarskoe Selo, 22/II, 1917, in Fuhrmann, 688; *Letters of the Tsar to the Tsaritsa*, 312.

132. "Dnevnika Nikolaia II," *Otrechenie*, 34.

133. Nicholas II, *Dnevnik Imperatora*, 624.

### Chapter 5: Revolution Erupts in Petrograd

1. Alexandra to Nicholas, No. 1668/No. 645, 23/II, 1917, in Fuhrmann, 688. Nicholas to Alexandra, No. 1670, 23/II, in Fuhrmann, 689. From here on, the year 1917 is omitted.

2. Alexandra to Nicholas, No. 1665/No. 644, 22/II, in Fuhrmann, 687.

3. Nicholas to Alexandra, No. 1670, 23/II, in Fuhrmann, 689.

4. Mordvinov, "Poslednie dni," *Otrechenie*, 86, 113. For Nicholas's daily schedule see Tal', *Memuary*, 4–5.

5. Dubenskii, "Kak proizoshel perevorot," 24–25.

6. Hasegawa, *February Revolution* (2017), 201–211.

7. Ibid., 220–235.

8. Golitsyn to Nicholas II, 24/II, RGIA, f. 472, d. 605, l. 16, quoted in Kulikov, "Otrechenie Nikolaia II," 167; Ganelin, "24 Fevralia," 95; Voeikov, *S tsarem*, 196.

9. Dubenskii, "Kak proizoshel perevorot," 28.

10. Alexandra to Nicholas, No. 1673/No. 646, 24/II, in Fuhrmann, 690.

11. Hasegawa, *February Revolution* (2017), 236–261.

12. Quoted in Arkhipov, *Rossiiskaia politicheskaia elita*, 81–82.

13. Hasegawa, *February Revolution* (2017), 247.

14. Alexandra to Nicholas, No. 1675/No. 647, 25/II, in Fuhrmann, 693; No. 5, Steinberg and Khrustalev, *Fall of the Romanovs*, 75.

15. Spiridovich, *Velikaia voina*, vol. 3. 98.

16. Alexandra to Nicholas, No. 1675/No. 647, 25/II, in Fuhrmann, 692; Steinberg and Khrustalev, *Fall of the Romanovs*, 73; Nos. 73, 75 in Shashkova, *Fevral'skaia revoliutsiia*, 203–204, 205; Spiridovich, *Velikaia voina*, vol. 3, 102.

17. Spiridovich, *Velikaia voina*, vol. 3, 102.

18. Ibid.

19. Alexandra to Nicholas, No. 1675/No. 647, 25/II, in Fuhrmann, 693; Alexandra to Nicholas, 25/II, No. 5, Steinberg and Khrustalev, *Fall of the Romanovs*, 75.

20. Spiridovich, *Velikaia voina*, vol. 3, 99.

21. Spiridovich, *Velikaia voina*, vol. 3, 157. I cannot verify the accuracy of this information, since these telegrams are not included in the Stavka's documents in either *KA* (1) or *Stavka i revoliutsiia*.

22. Khabalov to Alekseev, No. 486, sent 17:40, received 18:08, 25/II, *KA* (1), 4–5; No. 2, *Stavka i revoliutsiia*, 133–134.

23. Khabalov to Alekseev, No. 486, sent 17:40, received 18:08, 25/II, *KA* (1), 5; No. 2, *Stavka i revoliutsiia*, 133–134.

24. Footnote 1, for Khabalov's telegram to Alekseev, *KA* (1), 4.

25. Deposition of Khabalov, *Padenie*, vol. 1, 220, 221; GARF f. 1467 (ChSK), d. 460, l. 69. See also Spiridovich, *Velikaia voina*, vol. 3, 100; Blok, *Poslednie dni*, 39.

26. Deposition of Khabalov, *Padenie*, vol. 1, 220.

27. Dubenskii, "Kak proizoshel perevorot," 30.

28. Hasegawa, *February Revolution* (2017), 259–260.

29. Dubenskii, "Kak proizoshel perevorot," 30. Dubensky repeatedly mentions that Nicholas was prepared to grant a responsible ministry on February 26, and certainly on February 27 when he talked with General Ivanov. Dubenskii, "Kak proizoshel perevorot," 30, 38, 40. Russian historian S. V. Kulikov takes the view, based on Dubensky's memoirs, that not only the tsar's entourage but also Nicholas himself was inclined to make political concessions. Dubensky's testimony, given in 1922, is not reliable, and it contradicts other pieces of evidence I give in the narrative, especially his rejection of Mikhail's recommendation.

30. Sergeevskii, *Otrechenie*, 7–8.

31. Andrei Vladimirovich, "Dnevniki," *Gibel' monarkhii*, 345.

32. Matveev, *Memoirs*, 2–4, Bakhmeteff Archive; Nicholson, *Michael Romanov*, 44–45.

33. Dubenskii, "Kak proizoshel perevorot," 31.

34. Nicholas to Alexandra, No. 1679, 26/II, 1917, in Fuhrmann, 696.

35. Hasegawa, *February Revolution* (2017), 262–266.

36. Spiridovich, *Velikaia voina*, vol. 3, 110.

37. Alexandra to Nicholas, No. 677/No. 648, 26/II, in Fuhrmann, 694–695; No. 7, Steinberg and Khrustalev, *Fall of the Romanovs*, 79; Spiridovich, *Velikaia voina*, vol. 3, 110–111.

38. According to Spiridovich, Alexandra wrote a telegram to Nicholas, saying, "I am really worried about the city." Spiridovich, *Velikaia voina*, vol. 3, 111–112. I cannot find this passage in Fuhrmann. It is unlikely that she became worried about the situation on that day.

39. Protopopov to Stavka, 26/II, No. 1, *Permskaia Golgofa*, 76–77; Spiridovich, *Velikaia voina*, vol. 3, 160–161.

40. Khabalov to Alekseev, No. 3703, sent 13:05, received 13:40, 26/II, *KA* (1), 5; No. 3, *Stavka i revoliutsiia*, 134.

41. Spiridovich, *Velikaia voina*, vol. 3, 112.

42. Nicholas to Alexandra, No. 1679, 26/II, 696; No. 8, Steinberg and Khrustalev, *Fall of the Romanovs*, 80.

43. The Duma representatives included Nikanor Vasilievich Savich, Vasily Alekseevich Maklakov, Pyotr Nikolaevich Balashov, and Ivan Ivanovich Dmitryukov. See Hasegawa, *February Revolution* (2017), 272.

44. Voeikov, *S tsarem*, 125.

45. Introducing this telegram in abridged form, Browder and Kerensky (*Russian Provisional Government*, 40) state that the telegram says, "There is wild shooting in the streets. In places troops are firing at each other." These passages are not found in the original telegram.

46. Rodzianko to Nicholas, 26/II, 1917, "Pervaia telegramma M. V. Rodzianko Tsariu," *Izvestiia Komiteta Petrogradskikh zhurnalistov*, No. 1, February 27, 1917; "Protokol sobytii," 110; "Protokol zasedanii," 238; No. 6, Steinberg and Khrustalev, *Fall of the Romanovs*, 76–77.

47. Rodzianko to Nicholas, sent 21:53, received 22:22, 26/II, *KA* (1), 5–6; No. 4, *Stavka i revoliutsiia*, 135–136; No. 1, Telegrammy Ruzskago, 8–9; Spiridovich, *Velikaia voina*, vol. 3, 165. To the telegram to Ruzsky, he added merely, "Procrastination means death."

48. No. 6, in Steinberg and Khrustalev, *Fall of the Romanovs*, 76.

49. Spiridovich, *Velikaia voina*, vol. 3, 163; Blok, *Poslednie dni*, 43.

50. Hasegawa, *February Revolution* (2017), 266–269.

51. Rodzianko to Ruzskii, 27/II, No. 1, Telegrammy Ruzskago, 113; Dokumenty Lukomskago, 247.

52. Brusilov to Alekseev, 27/II, *KA* (1), 7; No. 5, *Stavka i revoliutsiia*, 136.

53. Ruzskii to Tsar, No. 1147/B, sent 27/II, 21:15, received 27/II, 21:35, *KA* (1), 13; No. 2, Telegrammy Ruzskago, 114; No. 15, *Stavia i revoliutsiia*, 144.

54. Evert to Alekseev, No. 6081, received 27/II, 13:59, *KA* (1), 8–9; No. 11, *Stavka i revoliutsiia*, 139–140.

## Chapter 6: Suppressing the Revolution

1. Hasegawa, *February Revolution* (2017), 277–284. The units of the Preobrazhensky Regiment that were quartered in Millionnaya did not join the mutiny in the morning.

2. Sipridovich, *Velikaia voina*, vol. 3, 169.

3. Golitsyn to tsar, sent 1:58, 27/II, received 2:05, 27/II, *KA* (1), 7; No. 7, *Stavka i revoliutsiia*, 137.

4. Pavlenkov to tsar, sent 01:40, 27/II, received 02:05, 27/II, *KA* (1), 7; No. 6, *Stavka i revoliutsiia*, 136–137.

5. Brusilov to Alekseev, received 11:01, 27/II, *KA* (1), 7; No. 5, *Stavka i revoliutsiia*, 136; Spiridovich, *Velikaia voina*, vol. 3, 170. In response to Rodzyanko's telegram on February 26, Ruzsky recommended a political solution, but it did not reach Alekseev until late evening on February 27. Ruzskii to Nicholas, sent 21:15, received 21:55, 27/II, *KA* (1), 13; No. 15, *Stavka i revoliutsiia*, 144.

6. Spiridovich, *Velikaia voina*, vol. 3, 178–179; Bubnov, *V tsarskoi Stavke*, 151.

7. "Dnevniki Nikolaia II," *Otrechenie*, 35; Nicholas II, *Dnevnik Imperatora*, 625.

8. Spiridovich, *Velikaia voina*, vol. 3, 170. According to Spiridovich, Nicholas rejected the idea of a responsible ministry, but what Rodzyanko demanded was a ministry of confidence; therefore, what Nicholas rejected was likely a ministry of confidence, not a responsible ministry.

9. Bubnov, *V tsarskoi Stavke*, 151.

10. "Dnevniki Nikolaia II," *Otrechenie*, 35; Nicholas II, *Dnevnik Imperatora*, 625.

11. Bubnov, *V tsarskoi Stavke*, 151.

12. "Vtoraia telegramma predsedatelia Gos. Dumy Tsariu," *Izvestiia Komiteta Petrogradskikh zhuranalistov*, no. 1, February 27, 1917; Rodzianko to the tsar, *KA* (1), 6–7; Browder and Kerensky, *Russian Provisional Government*, 42; "Protokol sobytii," 111; "Protokol zasedanii," 240; No. 9, *Stavka i revoliutsiia*, 138. This telegram was not sent until 12:40 p.m. Belyaev refused to send it through the Hughes apparatus, so Rodzyanko had it sent by direct wire in the telegraph office. Rodzyanko interview, Lyandres, *Fall of Tsarism*, 108.

13. Hasegawa, "Aleksandr Fedorovich Kerenskii," 13–18.

14. Miliukov, "Pervyi den'," *Poslednye novosti*, March 12, 1927.

15. Paléologue, *Ambassador's Memoirs*, vol. 3, 223.

16. Khabalov to tsar, No. 56, sent 12:10, 27/II, received 12:20, 27/II, *KA* (1), 8; No. 8, *Stavka i revoliutsiia*, 137–138.

17. Beliaev to the tsar, No. 196, sent 13:15, received 13:20, 27/II, *KA* (1), 8; No. 10, *Stavka i revoliutsiia*, 139.

18. Spiridovich, *Velikaia voina*, vol. 3, 163–164; Dubenskii, "Kak proizoshel perevorot," 33.

19. Spiridovich, *Velikaia voina*, vol. 3, 172–173; Dubenskii, "Kak proizoshel perevorot," 33–34, 36–37.

20. Dubenskii, "Kak proizoshel perevorot," 37.

21. Nicholas to Alexandra, No. 1682/Telegram 12, 27/II, 19.06 > 20.02, in Fuhrmann, 697. Palace Commandant Voeikov instructed Colonel von Thal to prepare the imperial trains so as to be able to leave by 2:30. Tal', *Memuary*, 7.

22. Nicholas to Alexandra, No. 1681, 27/II, in Fuhrmann, 696.

23. According to Vladimir Cherniaev, the news about the abortive revolt of the Pavlovsky Regiment had a decisive influence on Nicholas's decision. At lunch, Alekseev reported about the revolt of the Pavlovsky Regiment, and after lunch, General Ivanov was summoned by the tsar; Cherniaev, "Vosstanie," 165. Katkov's assertion that this decision was made late at night appears to be inaccurate; Katkov, *Russia 1917*, 307. Ivanov clearly stated that this appointment was made before dinner, which took place usually at seven-thirty. See Mel'gunov, *Martovskie dni*, 143–144.

24. Mikhail Borel', "Stavka v miatezhnye dni," Alekseev Papers, Box 1, File 20, 3, HIA; G. Orlov, "General M. V. Alekseev—K tritsatipiatiletiiu osnovaniia Dobrovol'skoi Armii," Bern, 1952, Alekseev Papers, Box 1, File 3, 16, HIA.

25. Tal', *Memuary*, 7.

26. Basily, *Abdication*, 118–119.

27. "Protokol sobytii," 115–116; "Protokol zasedanii," 244–245; Khrustalev, *Velikii kniaz' Mikhail Aleksandrovich* (2008), 347. Even on February 28, Rodzyanko greeted the cadets of the Mikhailovsky Artillery School, calling for the government of "people's confidence." Nikolaev, "Lidery," 78.

28. Mikhail-Alekseev conversation, *KA* (1), 11–12; No. 19, *Stavka i revoliutsiia*, 147–148; Khrustalev, *Dnevnik i perepiska*, 396–397; Nicholson, *Michael Romanov*, 46; No. 4, *Permskaia Golgofa*, 78–79; "Iz dnevnika Velikogo Kniazia Mikhaila Aleksandrovicha," No. 8, *Permskaia Golgofa*, 82–83.

29. Engel'gardt, "Potonuvshii mir," ll. 105–106; Miliukov, *Vospominaniia*, vol. 2, 298; Engel'gardt interview in Lyandres, *Fall of Tsarism*, 59.

30. GARF f. 1467 (ChSK), d. 466, ll. 178; Kulikov, "Sovet ministrov," 181–182; Hasegawa, *February Revolution* (2017), 304–305. According to Matveev, Golitsyn recommended the formation of a new government headed by Prince Lvov when he handed the imperial decree of prorogation to Rodzyanko. But he may have been confusing the two separate events. See Matveev, *Memoirs*, 5, Bakhmeteff Archive.

31. Beliaev to Alekseev, No. 197, sent 19:22; received 19:35, 27/II; Beliaev to Alekseev, No. 198, sent 19:29, received 19:35, 27/II, *KA* (1), 9; Nos. 12 and 13, *Stavka i revoliutsiia*, 140, 141; Browder and Kerensky, *Russian Provisional Government*, 83.

32. Evert to Alekseev, No. 6081, received 13:59, 27/II, *KA* (1), 8–9; No. 11, *Stavka i revoliutsiia*, 139–140.

33. Ruzskii to tsar, No. 1147/B, 21:15, 27/II, *KA* (1), 13: No. 15, *Stavka i revoliutsiia*, 144: Andrei Vladimirovich, "Dnevniki," *Gibel' monarkhii*, 345.

34. Dubenskii, "Kak proizoshel perevorot," 37–38.

35. Mordvinov, "Poslednie dni," *Otrechenie*, 120.

36. Martynov, *Tsarskaia armiia*, 7, 130–131; Kulikov, "Stavka," 358–359; Basily, *Abdication*, 116–117.

37. Tikhmenev, "Poslednii priezd," *Otrechenie*, 277. For Ivanov's complaint about Alekseev, see Shavel'skii, *Vospominaniia*, vol. 2, 16–17.

38. Bazily's interview with Lukomskii, 24 February 1933, 18, Bazili Papers, Box 22, File 11, HIA.

39. Bubnov, *V tsarskoi Stavke*, 85.

40. Danilov, "Na puti," 367.

41. GARF, f. 1467 (ChSK), d. 643, ll. 1–2; GARF, f. 1467 (ChSK), d. 466, l. 130.

42. Tikhmenev, "Poslednii priezd," *Otrechenie*, 278.

43. Voeikov, *S tsarem*, 202; Benckendorff, *Last Days*, 2.

44. Sergeevskii, *Otrechenie*, 14–15.

45. Dehn, *Real Tsaritsa*, 150.

46. Benckendorff, *Last Days*, 2; Voeikov, *S tsarem*, 200–201; Kulikov, "Stavka," 356.

47. Tikhmenev, "Poslednii priezd," *Otrechenie*, 277–278.

48. Spiridovich, *Velikaia voina*, vol. 3, 176. These telegrams are not included in Fuhrmann. If these telegrams were sent from Tsarskoe Selo, they may never have reached Stavka.

49. Alekseev-Mikhail Aleksandrovich conversation, *KA* (1), 11–12; No. 19, *Stavka i revoliutsiia*, 146–147; No. 4, *Permskaia Golgofa*, 78–80; Browder and Kerensky, *Russian Provisional Government*, 86–87; Nicholson, *Michael Romanov*, 46; Khrustalev, *Dnevnik i perepiska*, 396–397; "Iz dnevnika Velikogo Kniazia Mikhaila Alekandrovicha," No. 8, *Permskaia Golgofa*, 82–83; Matveev, *Memoirs*, Prilozhenie, Bakhmeteff Archive. Where the recommendation of Lvov came from is still mysterious. According to Matveev, his name came up when the Golitsyn cabinet decided to prorogue the Duma. This is highly unlikely, but it is possible that the Golitsyn cabinet had decided to recommend Lvov after its resignation. It followed the negotiations between Rittikh/Pokrovsky and Vasily Maklakov/Dmitriukov in the Duma on February 26. See Matveev, *Memoirs*, 5, Bakhmeteff Archive.

50. "Dnevniki Nikolaia II," *Otrechenie*, 35; Nicholas II, *Dnevnik Imperatora*, 625.

51. Alekseev-Mikhail Aleksandrovich conversation, *KA* (1), 12; No. 79, Shashkova, *Fevral'skaia revoliutsiia*, 209–210; No. 19, *Stavka i revoliutsiia*, 146–147; Browder and Kerensky, *Russian Provisional Government*, 86–87.

52. Alekseev-Mikhail Aleksandrovich conversation, *KA* (1), 12; No. 79, Shashkova, *Fevral'skaia revoliutsiia*, 10; Browder and Kerensky, *Russian Provisional Government*, 87; No. 19, *Stavka i revoliutsiia*, 147.

53. Lukomskii, *Vospominaniia*, 1922, vol. 1, 126–127; Basily, *Abdication*, 111; Nicholas to Golitsyn, 23:25 27/II, *KA* (1), 13; No. 20, *Stavka i revoliutsiia*, 147–148; Mikhail Borel', "Stavka v miatezhnye dni," Alekseev Papers, Box 1, File 20, 3, HIA.

54. Borel', "Stavka v miatezhnye dni," Alekseev Papers, Box 1, File 20, 4, HIA.

55. Alekseev-Danilov conversation, 0:15, 28/II, *KA* (1), 9–10; Alekseev-Danilov conversation, 21:00, 27/II; No. 4, Telegrammy Ruzskago, 115; No. 16, *Stavka i revoliutsiia*, 143–144; Danilov to Alekseev, No. 1161/B, *KA* (1), 14; Alekseev-Lukomskii conversation, Dokumenty Lukomskago, 249; Spiridovich, *Velikaia voina*, vol. 3, 174–175.

56. Lukomskii-Kvetsinskii conversation, No. 17, *Stavka i revoliutsiia*, 44; Alekseev-Danilov conversation and Evert to Alekseev, No. 6144, 28/II, *KA* (1), 9–10, 17; Danilov to Alekseev, No. 1161/B, sent 0:15, received 0:33, 28/II, *KA* (1), 14; No. 22, *Stavka i revoliutsiia*, 149; Boldyrev, "Iz dnevnika," 251; GARF, f. 1467, d. 466, l. 130.

57. Alekseev to Beliaev, No. 1789, 11:22, 27/II, *KA* (1), 10–11; No. 18, *Stavka i revoliutsiia*, 145; Lukomskii to Lebedev, No. 1817, 15:55, 28/II, *KA* (1), 28; No. 78, Shashkova, *Fevral'skaia revoliutsia*, 208.

58. Alekseev to Ruzskii and Evert, No. 1805, 2:12 to northern front, 2:27 to western front, 28/II, *KA* (1), 17; No. 29, *Stavka i revoliutsiia*, 153.

59. Alekseev to Mrozovskii, No. 1806, 3:45, 28/II, *KA* (1), 17; No. 32, *Stavka i revoliutsiia*, 155.

60. G. Orlov, "General M. V. Alekseev: Osnovaniia Dobrovol'skoi armii," 13, Alekseev Papers, Box 1, File 3, HIA.

61. Andrei Vladimirovich, "Dnevniki," *Gibel' monarkhii*, 345; Danilov, "Na puti," 365–366.

62. Khabalov to Alekseev, sent 20:10, 27/II, received 0:55, 28/II, *KA* (1), 15–16; No. 14, *Stavka i revoliutsiia*, 141.

63. According to his daughter, Alekseev recommended that if he was determined to go, he should be accompanied by a guard unit. Alekseeva-Borel', *Sorok let*, 475. Her account is not supported by other evidence.

64. Mordvinov, "Poslednie dni," *Otrechenie*, 123; Spiridovich, *Velikaia voina*, vol. 3, 183.

65. Mordvinov, *Otrechenie*, 122.

66. Mordvinov, "Poslednie dni," *Otrechenie*, 123.

67. Ivanov to Alekseev, *KA* (1), 18–19; No. 31, *Stavka i revoliutsiia*, 154–155.

68. Ivanov's deposition, *Padenie*, 1926, vol. 5, 317–318; "Proval," 104; Dubenskii, "Kak proizoshel perevorot," 30–31; Basily, *Abdication*, 108–109; Blok, *Poslednie dni*, 55. Mel'gunov and Katkov, and most recently Kulikov, take this as evidence to show that Nicholas and Ivanov intended to avoid bloodshed. Mel'gunov, *Martovskie dni*, 159; Katkov, *Russia 1917*, 308–309; Kulikov, "Stavka," 344–345. For the counterargument, see Ioffe, *Velikii Oktiabr'*, 61–62.

69. Kulikov takes Ivanov's words at face value and argues that Ivanov had no intention of bringing the troops to Petrograd. Kulikov, "Stavka," 359. According to Dubenskii, Nicholas intended to grant a responsible ministry and told Alekseev about this intention before his departure from Mogilev. But considering his conversation with Grand Duke Mikhail, it seems unlikely that he was already leaning toward granting a responsible ministry. Dubenskii, "Kak proizoshel perevorot," 39.

70. The precise time of his departure was given by telegram, Tikhmenev to Alekseev, No. 42, 9:10, 28/II, *KA* (1), 17; Spiridovich, *Velikaia voina*, vol. 3, 183–184.

## Chapter 7: Imperial Train and Information Blockade

1. Tikhmenev to Alekseev, 9:10, 28/II, *KA* (1), 17; No. 34, *Stavka i revoliutsiia*, 156.

2. Isaev, *Imperatorskii poezd*, 58; Spiridovich, *Velikaia voina*, vol. 3, 225.

3. Katkov, *Russia 1917*, 309.

4. The emperor's entourage consisted of the following: minister of the imperial court, General Count V. B. Fredericks; Flag Captain Admiral K. D. Nilov; Palace Commandant Major-General V. N. Voeikov; head of military campaign chancellery, Major-General K. A. Naryshkin; commander of the convoy of His Majesty, Major-General Count A. N. Grabbe; Count Nitikin; court historian, Major-General D. N. Dubenskii; commander of the railway regiment, Major-General Tsabel'; imperial physician, Professor S. P. Fyodorov; military ceremony, Baron Rudolf A. Stackelberg; aide-de-camp to the emperor, Colonel A. A. Mordvinov; and marshal of the court, V. A. Dolgorukov. Dubenskii, "Kak proizoshel perevorot," 22. Voeikov, Fredericks, Nilov, Dolgorukov, and Mordvinov were in Train A, and Dubenskii, Stackelberg, and Tsabel were in Train B, according to von Thal. Tal', *Memuary*, 15.

5. Tal', *Memuary*, 19; Tal', *Chronology*, 13–14. Colonel von Thal was, as commandant of the railway regiment, responsible for the technical details of the movement of the trains as well as for general information. His handwritten manuscripts in the Hoover Institution and Bakhmeteff Archive are the most important and accurate sources of information regarding the movement of the imperial trains from February 28 to March 1. Thal was the commandant for the imperial train B, and the commandant of the imperial train A was the assistant chief of the Palace Police, Gomzin. Spiridovich, *Velikaia voina*, vol. 3, 225.

6. Tal', *Memuary*, 19; Spiridovich, *Velikaia voina*, vol. 3, 226.

7. Telegram of elected members of the State Council, *KA* (1), 18; Spiridovich, *Velikaia voina*, vol. 3, 226–227; No. 14, Steinberg and Khrustalev, *Fall of the Romanovs*, 84–85.

8. Beliaev to Voeikov, No. 200, sent 1:55; received at Stavka, 1:59, 28/II, *KA* (1), 16; No. 27, *Stavka i revoliutsiia*, 152.

9. Beliaev to Alekseev, No. 201, sent at 11:32, 28/II, *KA* (1), 20; No. 41, *Stavka i revoliutsiia*, 160–161; Spiridovich, *Velikaia voina*, vol. 3, 228.

10. Beliaev to Alekseev, No. 9157, received at Stavka 11:45, 28/II, *KA* (1), 27; Spiridovich, *Velikaia voina*, vol. 3, 228–229.

11. Nicholas to Alexandra, No. 1683, Telegram 1, 15:00–16:49, 28/II, in Fuhrmann, 697; No. 15, Steinberg and Khrustalev, *Fall of the Romanovs*, 85. The original is in English without periods, and with spelling errors; he used both "Niki" and "Nicky."

12. Khabalov to Alekseev, No. 415, sent 8:21, received 8:25, 28/II, *KA* (1), 19; No. 33, *Stavka i revoliutsiia*, 156.

13. Alekseev to Ruzskii, No. 1807, 11:13, 28/II, *KA* (1), 19; No. 36, *Stavka i revoliutsiia*, 157; Alekseev to Grigorovich, No. 1809, 11:05, 28/II, *KA* (1), 19; No. 35, *Stavka i revoliutsiia*, 157.

14. Beliaev to Alekseev, No. 201, 11:32, 28/II, *KA* (1), 20; No. 41, *Stavka i revoliutsiia*, 161.

15. Khabalov to Alekseev, 11:30, 28/II, *KA* (1), 20–21; No. 39, *Stavka i revoliutsiia*, 159.

16. Beliaev to Alekseev, No. 9157, sent 13:30, 28/II, received 14:25, 28/II, *KA* (1), 27; No. 51, *Stavka i revoliutsiia*, 170.

17. Alekseev's circular telegram, No. 1813, sent to northern front, 13:10, western front, 14:00, southwestern front, 14:00; Rumanian front, 14:58, Caucasian front, 19:15, 28/II, *KA* (1), 22–24; No. 5, Telegrammy Ruzskago, 116–119; Dokumenty Lukomskago, 250–251; Browder and Kerensky, *Russian Provisional Government*, 89; No. 48, *Stavka i revoliutsiia*, 166–168. Alekseev did not send this telegram to Nikolai Nikolaevich until 7:25 p.m., 28/II. By this time the situation had changed considerably.

18. Kapnist to Rasin, No. 2704, 0:35, 28/II, *KA* (1), 14–15; direct conversation between the Naval Staff at the Stavka and the main Naval Staff in Petrograd, 18:00, 28/II, *KA* (1), 29; No. 44, *Stavka i revoliutsiia*, 163; Basily, *Abdication*, 121.

19. Beliaev to Alekseev, No. 9157, sent 13:30, received 14:25, 28/II, *KA* (1), 27; Alekseev to Ruzskii and Evert, No. 1819, 19:21 (northern front), 18:00 (western front), 28/II, *KA* (1), 29; Alekseev to Brusilov, No. 1912, *KA* (1), 24; No. 45, *Stavka i revoliutsiia*, 163–164. The total composition of the reinforcements from the northern, western, and southwestern fronts was given in his telegram to Beliaev, No. 1816, sent at 6:30 p.m. Alekseev to Beliaev, No. 1816, 18:30, 28/II, *KA* (1), 27–28; No. 60, *Stavka i revoliutsiia*, 175.

20. Orlov, "General M. V. Alekseev," 13, Alekseev Papers, Box 1, file 3, HIA.

21. Sergeevskii, *Otrechenie*, 18–19; Alekseeva-Borel', *Sorok let*, 479. The packet referred to has not been found in the archives.

22. Vil'chkovskii, "Prebyvanie," 165; Rodzianko to Ruzskii, No. 8, Telegrammy Ruzskago, 120; Rodzianko to Alekseev, 5:51, 1/III, *KA* (1), 36; No. 74, *Stavka i revoliutsiia*, 194.

23. Telegram from the Petrograd Telegraph Agency, No. 11, Telegrammy Ruzskago, 121.

24. Evert to Loshunov (commander of the 9th Infantry regiment)/Gen. Prince Trubetskoi (commander of the 2nd Cavalry regiment), No. 6121, 13:09, 28/II, *KA* (1), 26–27; No. 42, *Stavka i revoliutsiia*, 161–162; Evert to commanders of the 2nd, 3rd, and 10th Armies, No. 6126, 14:20, 28/II, *KA* (1), 27; No. 40, *Stavka i revoliutsiia*, 160.

25. Lukomskii to Lebedev, No. 1817, 15:55, 28/II; Lebedev to Lukomskii, No. 6143/99, 1:20, 1/III, *KA* (1), 28–29; No. 70, *Stavka i revoliutsiia*, 28–29.

26. GARF, f. 1467 (ChSK), d. 643, l. 14; GARF, f. 1467 (ChSK), d. 466, l. 127; Ivanov to Ruzskii, No. 2, 11:24, 28/II, *KA* (1), 21; No. 47, *Stavka i revoliutsiia*, 165; Ivanov to Evert, No. 1, 11:26, 28/II, *KA* (1), 16.

27. GARF, f. 1467 (ChSK), d. 643, l. 18.

28. Voeikov, *S tsarem*, 205.

29. Ivanov's deposition, *Padenie*, 1926, vol. 5, 321.

30. Hasegawa, *February Revolution* (2017), 307–308.

31. Nicholson, *Michael Romanov*, 47; No. 8, *Permskaia Golgofa*, 84.

32. Spiridovich, *Velikaia voina*, vol. 3, 191–192.

33. Kerensky, "Road to Tragedy", 80.

34. Ivanov, "Velikii kniaz'," Bakhmeteff Archive; Ganelin, "Proekt Manifesta," 369–374, 378–381. For Rodzianko and the grand dukes' manifesto, see Ioffe, *Velikii Oktiabr'*, 53–58.

35. Ivanov, "Velikii kniaz'," 9, Bakhmeteff Archive.

36. *Ogonek*, no. 1, 1923; Hasegawa, "Rodzianko and the Grand Dukes' Manifesto," 154–155; Prilozhenie No. 1 and No. 2 in Ganelin, "Proekt Manifesta," 376–378; No. 12, *Permskaia Golgofa*, 86–87; Nicholson, *Michael Romanov*, 49–50. According to Matveev, Grand Duke Dmitry Konstantinovich also signed the draft manifesto. Matveev, *Memoirs*, 10, Bakhmeteff Archive.

37. Nos. 11, 13, *Permskaia Golgofa*, 85, 87–88; Nicholson, *Michael Romanov*, 47–48, 50–51.

38. Hasegawa, *February Revolution* (2017), 382–385, 390–394, 396–399.

39. Isaev, *Imperatorskii poezd*, 79–80; Khrustalev's introduction in Bublikov, *Russkaia revoliutsiia* (2016), 31–32.

40. Bublikov, *Russkaia revoliutsiia* (1918), 21–22; Bublikov, *Russkaia revoliutsiia* (2016), 58; Lomonosov, *Vospominaniia* (1994), 229–230; Spiridovich, *Velikaia voina*, 240–241. The exact time of Bublikov's occupation of the Ministry of Transport is not clear. See Nikolaev, "A. A. Bublikov," 221–222.

41. Nikolaev, *Dumskaia revoliutsiia*, vol. 1, 483–484.

42. Beliaev to Alekseev, No. 202, 12:25, 28/II, *KA* (1), 25; No. 46, *Stavka i revoliutsiia*, 164. The document in the latter states that Alekseev gave a copy of this telegram to Kislyakov, and ordered the transfer of railway administration to Kislyakov.

43. Spiridovich, *Velikaia voina*, vol. 3, 240–241.

44. Spiridovich, *Velikaia voina*, vol. 3, 240–241; Katkov, *Russia 1917*, 315.

45. Isaev, *Imperatorskii poezd*, 70–72.

46. Isaev, *Imperatorskii poezd*, 30.

47. As for the Stavka's concerns with the security of railway movements, see the Stavka's communications with Colonel S. V. Liubi, in charge of military transportation in the Moscow Junction, *KA* (1), 32; No. 49, *Stavka i revoliutsiia*, 168; Alekseev to all the military districts, No. 1810, *KA* (1), 32; No. 50, *Stavka i revoliutsiia*, 169. Both telegrams were sent early in the afternoon, on February 28. Responding to Alekseev's request, Evert immediately deployed reserve forces with machine guns to secure the railway. Kvetsinskii to army commanders, 15:35, 28/II, *KA* (1), 19; No. 53, *Stavka i revoliutsiia*, 171.

48. "Obrashchenie k zheleznodorozhnikam," *Izvestiia Komiteta Petrogradskikh zhurnalistov*, No. 2, 28 February 1917; *KA* (1), 32–33; "Protokol sobytii," 120; "Protokol zasedanii," 250; ; No. 6, Telegrammy Ruzskago, 119. For the Duma Committee's attempts to maintain the normal function of the railway movement, see also RGIA, f. 1278, op. 10, d. 3, ll. 7–8.

49. Bublikov, *Russkaia revoliutsiia* (1918), 20–21; Bublikov, *Russkaia revoliutsiia* (2016), 56.

50. Lomonosov, *Vospominaniia* (1921), 27; Nikolaev, "A. A. Bublikov," 232–235, 248.

51. Lomonosov, *Vospominaniia* (1994), 230; Nikolaev, "A. A. Bublikov," 240.

52. "Protokol sobytii," 119; "Protokol zasedanii," 248–249.

53. "Yury Lomonosov," Wikipedia, accessed May 9, 2024, https://en.wikipedia.org/wiki/Yury_Lomonosov.

54. Lomonosov, *Vospominaniia* (1994), 224–228; Nikolaev, "A. A. Bublikov," 229, 230.

55. Lomonosov, *Vospominaniia* (1994), 227, 231–232, 234; Nikolaev, "A. A. Bublikov," 230–231.

56. Paley, *Memories*, 48–49.

57. Buxhoeveden, *Life and Tragedy*, 251.

58. Spiridovich, *Velikaia voina*, vol. 3, 196–197; Benckendorff, *Last Days*, 4–5; Buxhoeveden, *Life and Tragedy*, 251–252.

59. Hasegawa, *February Revolution* (2017), 311.

60. Benckendorff, *Last Days*, 6–7; Buxhoeveden, *Life and Tragedy*, 254; Tal', *Memuary*, 3–4.

61. Spiridovich, *Velikaia voina*, vol. 3, 198; Globachev, *Pravda o russkoi revoliutsii*, 127.

62. Spiridovich, *Velikaia voina*, vol. 3, 198; Lomonosov, *Vospominaniia* (1994), 223–224.

63. Spiridovich, *Velikaia voina*, vol. 3, 200.

64. Buxhoeveden, *Life and Tragedy*, 255.

65. Benckendorff, *Last Days*, 8.

66. Spiridovich, *Velikaia voina*, vol. 3, 202; Benckendorff, *Last Days*, 13–14.

67. Benckendorff, *Last Days*, 8–9.

68. Dubenskii, "Kak proizoshel perevorot," 40.

69. Isaev, *Imperatorskii poezd*, 11–12.

70. Dubenskii, "Kak proizoshel perevorot," 40; Spiridovich, *Velikaia voina*, vol. 3, 229; Mordvinov, "Poslednie dni," *Otrechenie*, 127.

71. Tal', *Memuary*, 23–25; Dubenskii, "Kak proizoshel perevorot," 40.

72. Mordvinov, "Poslednie dni," *Otrechenie*, 127–128.

73. Nicholas to Alexandra, No. 1684, Telegram 88, Likhoslavl > Tsarskoe Selo, 28/II, 21.2>22.10, in Fuhrmann, 697; Spiridovich, *Velikaia voina*, vol. 3, 229.

74. Nicholas II, *Dnevnik Imperatora*, 625.

75. Tal', *Memuary*, 27–28; Tal', *Chronology*, 16–18; Tal', *Mysl' ob otrechenii*, 12; Spiridovich, *Velikaia voina*, vol. 3, 230; Isaev, *Imperatorskii poezd*, 65.

76. Tal', *Memuary*, 28–30; Tal', *Chronology*, 18–20.

77. Dubenskii, "Kak proizoshel perevorot," 41.

78. Tal', *Memuary*, 30–31.

79. Dubenskii, "Kak proizoshel perevorot," 41.

80. Tal', *Memuary*, 28–29; Tal', *Mysl' ob otrechenii*, 12; Spiridovich, *Velikaia voina*, vol. 3, 230.

81. Tal', *Mysl' ob otrechenii*, 12; Spiridovich, *Velikaia voina*, vol. 3, 230.

82. Katkov believes that Grekov was a Cossack subaltern. Melgunov states that Grekov, appointed by the Petrograd Soviet, issued the order "despite the instruction given by the railway engineers under the influence of the Duma." Katkov, *Russia 1917*, 311; Mel'gunov, *Martovskie dni*, 169.

83. Hasegawa, *February Revolution* (2017), 481.

84. Dubenskii, "Kak proizoshel perevorot," 41; Mordvinov, "Poslednie dni," *Otrechenie*, 131; Spiridovich, *Velikaia voina*, vol. 3, 230–231.

85. Spiridovich, *Velikaia voina*, vol. 3, 231; Tal', *Memuary*, 23–32; Dubenskii, "Kak proizoshel perevorot," 41; Voeikov, *S tsarem*, 204; Mordvinov, "Poslednie dni," *Otrechenie*, 131–132.

86. Tal', *Memuary*, 32–34; Tal', *Chrolonogy*, 21–22; Tal', *Mysl' ob otrechenii*, 21–22.

87. Tal', *Memuary*, 34; Tal', *Chronology*, 22; Tal', *Mysl' ob otrechenii*, 22.

### Chapter 8: To the Pskov Station

1. Dubenskii, "Kak proizoshel perevorot," 1922, 41–42; Tal', *Memuary*, 34; Tal', *Chronology*, 22; Tal', *Mysl' ob otrechenii*, 12.

2. Dubenskii, "Kak proizoshel perevorot," 42; Spiridovich, *Velikaia voina*, vol. 3, 232.

3. Tal', *Memuary*, 36–37; Tal', *Chronology*, 22–24; Tal, *Mysl' ob otrechenii*, 12–13; Dubenskii, "Kak proizoshel perevorot," 42–43; Voeikov, *S tsarem*, 204–205, Spiridovich, *Velikaia voina*, vol. 3, 232–233.

4. Dubenskii, "Kak proizoshel perevorot," 43.

5. "Dnevniki Nikolaia II," *Otrechenie*, 36; Nicholas II, *Dnevnik Imperatora,* 625.

6. Nekrasov interview, Lyandres, *Fall of Tsarism*, 151–152.

7. Lomonosov, *Vospominaniia* (1994), 233.

8. Lomonosov, *Vospominaniia* (1994), 233. Train A arrived at Malaya Vishera at 2:10 and left at 3:35 a.m. Tal', *Memuary*, 76.

9. Nikolaev, *Dumskaia revoliutsiia*, vol. 1, 74–75. According to Spiridovich, the news of the capture of Tosno by the insurgents came from Fursa. He informed the entourage of this news at Likhoslavl. But it is doubtful that he had any knowledge about the situation of Tosno. Spiridovich, *Velikaia voina*, vol. 3, 229.

10. Spiridovich, *Velikaia voina*, vol. 3, 229.

11. Mordvinov, "Poslednie dni," *Otrechenie*, 127–128.

12. Voeikov, *S tsarem*, 203.

13. According to Thal, Fursa boarded at Rzhev. Tal', *Memuary*, 20. He must subsequently have disembarked from the imperial train at Dno and taken the train to Mogilev. Fursa was at the Stavka when Bublikov ordered his arrest. He was brought back to Petrograd for investigation by the Military Commission on March 6. Nikolaev, *Dumskaia revoliutsiia*, vol. 2, 74–75.

14. Lomonosov, *Vospominaniia* (1994), 283n43.

15. Ibid., 283.

16. Ibid., 283. Acording to Tal', train A left Malaya Vishera at 3:35.

17. Timetable in Tal', *Memuary*, 76.

18. Tal', *Memuary*, 41; Tal', *Chronology*, 26.

19. Mordvinov, "Poslednie dni," *Otrechenie*, 36.

20. No. 90, Voeikov to Ruzskii, No. 95, 13:05, 1/III, *Stavka i revoliutsiia*, 206; No. 9, Telegrammy Ruzskago, 120; Dokumenty Lukomskago, 252.

21. Voeikov, *S tsarem*, 205.

22. Dubenskii, "Kak proizoshel perevorot," 45.

23. Bublikov to chief of movements of Vindavskaya Railway, 1/III, *KA* (1), 36; No. 80, *Stavka i revoliutsiia*, 197–198.

24. Tal', *Memuary*, 41–42, 76.

25. Conversation via direct line between Barmin and Karamyshev, 12:30, 1/III, *KA* (1), 34; No. 83, *Stavka i revoliutsiia*, 200–201.

26. No. 90, Voeikov to Ruzskii, No. 95, 13:05, 1/III; *Stavka i revoliutsiia*, 206; No. 9, Telegrammy Ruzskago, 120, Dokumenty Lukomskago, 252. Georgii Orlov's letter to Alexandre Tarsaidze, March 24, 1953, Tarsaidze Papers, Box 16, File 1, HIA.

27. Nikolaev, *Dumskaia revoliutsiia*, vol. 1, 375; his source is V. Isakov, *Vospominania o 1917 g*, TsGAIPD SPb, f. 4000, op. 5, d. 1347, l. 1. Kulikov, "Stavka," 362; Spiridovich, *Velikaia voina*, vol. 3, 198–199; GARF, f. 1779, op. 1. d. 1922, l. 8, cited in Isaev, *Imperatorskii poezd*, 98.

28. GARF, f. 3348, d. 129, l. 20; GARF, f. 6, op. 1, d. 1722, ll. 8–9.

29. GARF, f. 3348, d. 129, ll. 17, 21; GARF, f. 6, op. 1, d. 1722, ll. 3–5, 7, 9. As for Karelin, see Nikolaev, *Dumskaia revoliutsiia*, vol. 1, 483.

30. Lomonosov, *Vospominaniia* (1921), 43.

31. GARF, f. 3348, d. 129, l. 18.

32. According to Lomonosov, the imperial train reached Bologoe at 9 in the morning. Lomonosov, *Vospominaniia* (1994), 234.

33. Lomonosov, *Vospominaniia* (1921), 33; Lomonosov, *Vospominaniia* (1994), 234.

34. B. Biknin, "Fevral'skoe dni v Bologoe: Iz vospominanii," *Staliomets*, No. 35, 1935, quoted in Isaev, *Imperatorskii poezd*, 102–104.

35. Isaev, *Imperatorskii poezd*, 102–103.

36. Lomonosov, *Vospominaniia* (1921), 34; Bublikov, *Russkaia revoliutsiia* (1918), 24; Kulikov, "Stavka," 364–365.

37. Isaev, *Imperatorskii poezd*, 116–136; Nikolaev, *Dumskaia revoliutsiia*, vol. 1, 494–495; Nikolaev, "A. A. Bublikov," 242.

38. Lomonosov, *Vospominaniia* (1994), 235.

39. Lomonosov, *Vospominaniia* (1921), 35–38; Lomonosov, *Vospominaniia* (1994), 237.

40. Borel', "Stavka v miatezhnye dni," Alekseev Papers, Box 12, file 20, 5, HIA.

41. Lomonosov, *Vospominaniia* (1994), 237.

42. Shchegolev, *Poslednii reis*, 1928, 45–46; Voeikov, *S tsarem*, 205.

43. Lomonosov, *Vospominaniia* (1994), 238.

44. Ibid., 238.

45. Ibid., 238–239; Nikolaev, "A. A. Bublikov," 242.

46. Voeikov, *S tsarem*, 205–206; Tal', *Memuary*, 42–43.

47. Spiridovich, *Velikaia voina*, vol. 3, 247–248.

48. Nekrasov interview, Lyandres, *Fall of Tsarism*, 132.

49. Katkov, *Russia 1917*, 297, 299; Burdzhalov, *Vtoraia russkaia revoliutsiia*, 311; Nikolaev, *Revoliutsiia i vlast'*, 548–549; Nikolaev, *Dumskaia revoliutsiia*, vol. 2, 205–206.

50. Shul'gin, *Dni* (1989), 232; Shul'gin, "Dni," *Otrechenie*, 238–239. According to the Duma Committee's minutes, the Duma Committee decided on February 28 to seek Nicholas's abdication in favor of his son under the regency of Mikhail. But I do not believe that the Duma Committee had the formal meeting and made its decision. "Protokol zasedanii," 254, 316; "Protokol sobytii," 124. Shulgin's explanation is more plausible.

51. Mel'gunov, *Martovskie dni*, 57; Ioffe, *Velikii Oktiabr'*, 57.

52. Quoted in Arkhipov, *Rossiiskaia politicheskaia elita*, 68.

53. Shidlovskii, *Vospominaniia*, vol. 2, 83.

54. Burdzhalov, *Vtoraia russkaia revoliutsiia*, 311.

55. For instance, see Nikolaev, *Revoliutsiia i vlast'*, 549; Burdzhalov, *Vtoraia russkaia revoliutsiia*, 311.

56. Shidlovskii, *Vospominaniia*, vol. 2, 84–85; Shul'gin, "Dni," *Otrechenie*, 237.

57. Sukhanov, *Zapiski*, vol. 1, 248; Skobelev interview, Lyandres, *Fall of Tsarism*, 179–180; Kerensky interview, Lyandres, *Fall of Tsarism*, 234.

58. Skobelev interview, Lyandres, *Fall of Tsarism*, 192.

59. Burdzhalov, *Vtoraia russkaia revoliutsiia*, 275.

60. For detailed analysis of this issue, see Hasegawa, *February Revolution* (2017), 422–437.

61. According to Andrei Nikolaev, on the night of March 1–2, prior to the negotiations with the delegates of the Petrograd Soviet, Rodzyanko, Prince Lvov, and Kerensky struck a deal by which they made an alliance to put an end to the monarchy and install Rodzyanko as the supreme leader. See Nikolaev, "Lidery," 97. But in his previous book, Nikolaev dates this meeting to the night of March 2–3. Nikolaev clarified to me in an email message on May 26, 2024, that Nekrasov had clearly stated that the agreement had been reached on the night of March 2–3, but he would not exclude the possibility that Nekrasov was in error and that these three had struck a deal on the night of March 1–2. See Nekrasov's interview in *Poslednie novosti* (Kiev), morning edition, May 16, 1917.

62. Zaslavskii and Kantorovich, *Khronika*, 38.

63. Shul'gin, "Dni," *Otrechenie*, 240–241. See also A. I. Guchkov, "V tsarskom poezde," *Otrechenie*, 257–258.

64. "Protokol zasedanii," 266.

65. Ivanov's deposition, *Padenie* (1926), vol. 5, 321.

66. Chamberlin, *Russian Revolution*, vol. 1, 86; Martynov, *Tsarskaia armiia*, 146. This is the accepted opinion of Soviet-era historians. See Diakin, *Russkaia burzhuazia*, 345; Chermenski, *IV gosudarstvennaia duma*, 297.

67. Bublikov, *Russkaia revoliutsiia* (1918), 40.

68. Ivanov's deposition, *Padenie* (1926), vol. 5, 321–322; GARF, f. 6, op. 1, d. 1722, l. 1; Spiridovich, *Velikaia voina*, vol. 3, 221.

69. Alekseev to Beliaev, No. 1789, *KA* (1), 10–11; No. 18, *Stavka i revoliutsiia*, 145.

70. GARF, f. 6, op. 1, d. 1722, l. 26.

71. Engel'gardt, "Potonuvshii mir: Vospominaniia," OR RGB, f. 218, l. 112.

72. GARF, f. 1278, op. 10, d. 19, l. 4.

73. GARF, f. 1467 (ChSK), d. 643, l. 24. Although Domanevsky used the term "provisional government," he must have meant the Duma Committee, since the Provisional Government was not formed until March 2. Hence I use quotation marks when indicating what Domanevsky was referring to.

74. Ibid., l. 29; Deposition of Ivanov, *Padenie* (1926), vol. 5, 323.

75. Benckendorff, *Last Days*, 9–10.

76. GARF, f. 3348, d. 129, l. 19. This telegram is not included in Fuhrmann.

77. Spiridovich, *Velikaia voina*, vol. 3, 219; Benckendorff, *Last Days*, 14–15.

78. "Protokol sobytii," 126–127: "Protokol zasedanii," 257.

79. "Protokol sobytii," 126–127; "Protokol zasedanii," 257–258.

80. Spiridovich, *Velikaia voina*, vol. 3, 218–219.

81. Spiridovich, *Velikaia voina*, vol. 3, 219; Nos. 78, 79, *Stavka i revoliutsiia*, 195–197. It should be noted that the Stavka had obtained the information by 11 a.m. on March 1 that the Duma Committee had control of the telephone operations between Petrograd and Tsarskoe Selo.

82. I. Demidov, "Tsarskoe Selo 1-go marta 1917 goda," *Poslednie novosti*, March 12, 1927.

83. For such allegations see Kerensky, "Road to Tragedy," 88; Paléologue, *Ambassador's Memoirs*, vol. 3, 232–234.

84. See Iakobii, *Imperator Nikolai II*, 134–135; Spiridovich, *Velikaia voina*, vol. 3, 216–217; Nicholas Nicholson's email messages to the author, September 12, 2023, April 5, 2024, and April 12, 2024. Later, Grand Duke Nikolai Mikhailovich and Princess Elizabeta Mavrikovna joined Kirill. "Velikie kniaz'ia v Gosudarstvennoi dume," *Russkoe slovo*, March 2, 1917.

85. Nikolaev, "Lidery," 87.

86. Matveev, *Memoirs*, 7, Bakhmeteff Archive.

87. Spiridovich, *Velikaia voina*, vol. 3, 219–220; Alexandra to Nicholas, No. 1686/650, 1/III, 1917, in Fuhrmann, 698; Benckendorff, *Last Days*, 12–13, 15; Ivanov, "Velikii kniaz'," 11, Bakhmeteff Archive.

88. Buxhoeveden, *Life and Tragedy*, 259.

89. Ivanov, "Velikii kniaz'," 10, Bakhmeteff Archive; Burdzhalov, *Vtoraia russkaia revoliutsiia*, 310; Ganelin, "Proekt Manifesta," 374.

90. "Protokol sobytii," 130.

91. Lomonosov, *Vospominaniia* (1994), 244.

92. Buxhoeveden, *Life and Tragedy*, 259.

93. Ivanov's deposition, *Padenie* (1926), vol. 5, 322–323.

94. Ibid., 323.

95. Chamberlin, *Russian Revolution*, vol. 1, 86.

96. A commander of the St. George Battalion, Major General Iosif Fomich Pozharskii, however, testified at the Extraordinary Investigation Commission that he had declared that he would not give his soldiers an order to shoot at the people, even if Ivanov had given him instructions to do so. Blok, *Poslednie dni*, 57, 64; "Proval," 105. But this testimony made after the revolution may not be reliable.

97. Lomonosov, *Vospominaniia* (1994), 244.

98. For Mikhail's letter to Rodzyanko, see Nicholson, *Michael Romanov*, 48. For Buchanan's visit, see Matveev, *Memoirs*, 10, Bakhmeteff Archive. For Rodzyanko's failed visit, see No. 11, *Permskaia Golgofa*, 86.

99. Matveev, *Memoirs*, 10, Bakhmeteff Archive.

100. See Alekseev to Ruzskii and Evert, No. 1819, 18:00, 28/II, *KA* (1), 29; No. 58, *Stavka i revoliutsiia*, 174; Alekseev to Beliaev, No. 1816, 18:30, 28/II, *KA* (1), 27–28; No. 60, *Stavka i revoliutsiia*, 175–176; No. 61, *Stavka i revoliutsiia*, 176.

101. Alekseev to Ivanov, No. 1833, 1:15, 1/III, *KA* (1), 31; No. 7, Telegrammy Ruzskago, 119–120; No. 52, *Stavka i revoliutsiia*, 170–171. This telegram was sent to Generals Klembovsky, Ruzsky, Evert, Brusilov, Sakharov, and Yanushkevich between 13:35 and 14:59 p.m. on March 1. *Stavka i revoliutsiia* made an error on the date of this telegram, dating it "no later than 13:35 on February 28," but the date of dispatch of this telegram is identified as March 1 in the *Krasnyi arkhiv* collection.

102. Conversation between Barmin and Novosokol'niki railway station, 10 a.m., 1/III, *KA* (1), 37; No. 77, *Stavka i revoliutsiia*, 195.

103. Document No. 69, *Stavka i revoliutsiia*, 181. It gave the wrong date for the private meeting of the Duma members as February 26, which was actually on February 27, after the soldiers' insurrection.

104. No. 73, Petrograd Telegraph Agency to editors of *Voennyi Vestnik*, 4:30, 1/III, *Stavka i revoliutsiia*, 185–191. This important information is not included in the *KA* collection of documents of the Stavka.

105. *Stavka i revoliutsiia* gives 13:35 on February 28 for the time of Telegram 1833. It was clearly an error, since the Stavka was determined to follow the military suppression of the revolution until at least 9 p.m. on that day. *Krasnyi arkhiv* gives 1:15 a.m. on March 1 as the time of dispatch of this telegram. It raises the question of why Alekseev waited until 1:35 p.m. to send a copy of this telegram to the front commanders. On the margin of the information given by the Petrograd Telegraph Agency, Alekseev noted the time of receipt of the information as 11:30 a.m. on March 1. Thus, it makes more sense to argue that the time indicated in the *Krasnyi arkhiv* collection was an error. It should be 1:35 p.m., not 1:35 a.m.

106. Rodzianko to Alekseev, 5:52, 1/III, *KA* (1), 21; No. 74, *Stavka i revoliutsiia*, 192.

107. No. 74, Rodzianko's appeal to Army and Navy, 5:59, 1/III, *Stavka i revoliutsiia*, 192–193. This is not included in *KA* collection.

108. Lukomskii-Kvetsinskii conversation, *KA* (1), 33; No. 71, *Stavka i revoliutsiia*, 182–183. This conversation took place no later than 1:40 a.m. on March 1. This meant that the Stavka had already received Bublikov's telegram before the Petrograd Telegraph Agency's information reached the headquarters.

109. Bublikov to Chief of Moscow–Vindavskaia Line, 11 a.m. 1/III, *KA* (1), 36; No. 812, *Stavka i revoliutsiia*, 198–199.

110. Mul'tatuli argues without citing any source that Ivanov had received Alekseev's order to halt his operation at Vyritsa. Mul'tatuli, *Nikolai II*, 508.

111. Alekseev to Rodzianko, No. 1845, 14:30, 1/III, *KA* (1), 44–45; No. 96, *Stavka i revoliutsiia*, 211–212.

112. Vil'chkovskii, "Prebyvanie," 165.

113. Danilov to commander of the 42nd Corps, No. 1221/b, *KA* (1), 54; No. 20, Danilov to commander of the 5th Army, No. 1216/b, Telegrammy Ruzskago, 126; No. 24, Danilov to Alekseev, No. 1220, ibid., 127.

114. Boldyrev to Lukomskii, 1215/B 1:10, 1/III, *KA* (1), 61; Ruzskii-Rodzianko conversation, *KA* (1), 55–56; No. 21, Telegrammy Ruzskogo, 126.

115. Khrisanfov, "Luga," 35–36.

116. Ibid., 36–37.

117. Voronovich, "Zapiski," 17–18, 23–30.

118. RGIA, f. 1278, op. 10, d. 5, ll. 5, 6; Voronovich, "Zapiski," 31.

119. Voronovich, "Zapiski," 32–33.

120. Ibid., 32–33, 92.

121. Boldyrev to Lukomskii, No. 1215/B, 01:10, 2/III, *KA* (1), 61; No. 159, *Stavka i revoliutsiia*, 257.

122. Tal', *Memuary*, 45.

123. Dubenskii, "Kak proizoshel perevorot," 46–47. Ruzsky states that he made the arrangements so that the tsar's arrival would not be noticed. Ruzskii, "Besada s Samoilovym," 192.

124. Borel', "Stavka v miatezhnye dni," 5, Alekseev Papers, Box 1, File 223, 5, HIA.

## Chapter 9: Responsible Ministry

1. Gulevich to Alekseev, No. 525, *KA* (1), 35; No. 65, *Stavka i revoliutsiia*, 178–179; Evert-Lukomskii conversation, *KA* (1), 36–37; No. 81, *Stavka i revoliutsiia*, 198–199.

2. Brusilov to Fredericks, No. 744, *KA* (1), 47; No. 120, *Stavka i revoliutsiia*, 228.

3. Alekseev to Nicholas, No. 1847, *KA* (1), 39–40. No. 89 in *Stavka i revoliutsiia*, 204–205, erroneously states that Alekseev demanded the establishment of a responsible ministry in its heading. This telegram was written before the news of the revolution in Kronstadt and the Baltic Fleet reached the Stavka.

4. Danilov to Klembovskii, sent 15:45, received 16:05, *KA* (1), 38; No. 101, *Stavka i revoliutsiia*, 214.

5. Klembovskii to Boldyrev, *KA* (1), 41–42; No. 110, *Stavka i revoliutsiia*, 220–220; Dokumenty Lukomskago, 253; No. 14, Telegrammy Ruzskago, 122–123.

6. Alekseev to Nicholas, No. 1865, *KA* (1), 53–54; No. 133, *Stavka i revoliutsiia*, 239–240. In Lukomsky's telegram to Danilov at 6 p.m. on March 1, Alekseev merely recommended that the tsar meet the demand of the Duma. Lukomskii to Danilov, *KA* (1), 45–46; No. 106, *Stavka i revoliutsiia*, 217–218; No. 91, Shashkova, *Fevral'skaia revoliutsiia*, 217.

7. Klembovskii to commanders, No. 1854/718, *KA* (1), 40–41; No. 114, *Stavka i revoliutsiia*, 223–224. This telegram was sent to the western front at 6:09 p.m., at 8:20 p.m. to the Rumanian Front, and at 9:15 p.m. to the Caucasian front.

8. *KA* (1), 40, No. 114, *Stavka i revoliutsiia*, 223.

9. Brusilov to Fredericks at Dno, No. 744, 19:36, 1/III, *KA* (1), 47; No. 120, *Stavka i revoliutsiia*, 228. This telegram reached Dno station after the imperial trains had already left, and it was not delivered to the tsar.

10. Andrei Vladimirovich, "Iz dnevnika" (1928), 208.

11. Ruzskii to Nicholas, No. 1147/b, *KA* (1), 13; No. 15, *Stavka i revoliutsiia*, 144; Vil'chkovskii, "Prebyvanie," 163–164; Martynov, *Tsarskaia armiia*, 90–91.

12. Kulikov, "Stavka," 385–387.

13. Dubenskii, "Kak proizoshel perevorot," 46–47.

14. Vil'chkovskii, "Prebyvanie," 167; Andrei Vladimirovich, "Iz dnevnika" (1928), 204.

15. For Sergei Mikhailovich's endorsement of Alekseev's recommendation, see Klembovskii conversation with Boldyrev, 17:40, 1/III, *KA* (1), 42; No. 110, *Stavka i revoliutsiia*, 220–223, No. 14, Telegrammy Ruzskago, 122.

16. Vil'chkovskii, "Prebyvanie," 167–170. Kulikov defends Nicholas's argument as "rational"; Kulikov, "Stavka," 389. I find this argument unconvincing.

17. According to Bazili, his original draft included the expression: "But this result can be obtained only by the constitution of a responsible ministry whose formation would be entrusted to the president of the Duma." After Bazili submitted the draft message, Alekseev consulted with Lukomsky. The quartermaster made two minor word alterations; one of the alterations was to delete the word "constitution." Basily, *Abdication*, 125.

18. Alekseev to Nicholas, No. 1865, *KA* (1), 53; Browder and Kerensky, *Russian Provisional Government*, 91; Steinberg and Khrushalev, *Fall of the Romanovs*, 89; Basily, *Abdication*, 124–125.

19. No. 76, Karamyshev-Barmin conversation, *Stavka i revoliutsiia*, 194. This document is not included in the *Krasnyi arkhiv* collection.

20. Vil'chkovskii, "Prebyvanie," 170; Andrei Vladimirovich, "Iz dnevnika" (1928), 204.

21. Voeikov, *S tsarem*, 206.

22. Ibid., 208–209.

23. Andrei Vladimirovich, "Iz dnevnika" (1928), 204.

24. Shcherbatov-Sergeevskii conversation, 23:25, 1/III, *KA* (1), 52; No. 142, *Stavka i revoliutsiia*, 245–246.

25. Vil'chkovskii, "Prebyvanie," 170–171. Kulikov argues that none of the emperor's entourage objected to the concession of a constitutional system; Kulikov, "Stavka," 397. Earlier in the same chapter (387–389) he argues that the entourage was in favor of a concession to grant a ministry of confidence, responsible to the tsar but not to the Duma, a "semi-parliamentarism." Kulikov does not explain when and how the entourage switched their position from the concession of a ministry of confidence to a responsible ministry.

26. Spiridovich, *Velikaia voina*, vol. 3, 252–253.

27. Nicholas to Ivanov, 0:20, 2/III, *KA* (1), 53; No. 154, *Stavka i revoliutsiia*, 253; No. 18, Telegrammy Ruzskago, 125; Dokumenty Lukomskago, 254; Spiridovich, *Velikaia voina*, vol. 3, 252–253.

28. No. 155, *Stavka i revoliutsiia*, 253; Nicholas to Alexandra, No. 1685/Telegram No. 23 (in Russian), Pskov > Tsarskoe Selo, 2/III, in Fuhrmann, 667.

29. Spiridovich, *Velikaia voina*, vol. 3, 253.

### Chapter 10: Abdication
1. Miliukov, *Vospominaniia*, vol. 2, 309.

2. Skobelev interview, Lyandres, *Fall of Tsarism*, 187–188.

3. Deposition of Guchkov, *Padenie*, vol. 6, 262–263; "Protokol sobytii," 136; "Protokol zasedanii," 266.

4. Ruzskii-Rodzianko conversation, 1/III, *KA* (1), 55–59; No. 170, *Stavka i revoliutsiia*, 263–268; No. 25, Telegrammy Ruzskago, 127–133; Dokumenty Lukomskago, 255–258.

5. Andrei Vladimirovich, "Dnevniki," *Gibel' monarkhii*, 347; Danilov, "Moi vospominaniia," *ARR* 19 (1928): 225.

6. Rodzianko-Ruzskii conversation, *KA* (1), 55–56; No. 170, *Stavka i revoliutsiia*, 264; No. 25, Telegrammy Ruzskago, 128; Browder and Kerensky, *Russian Provisional Government*, 92.

7. See Chapter 8.

8. Katkov, *Russia 1917*, 320.

9. See Nikolaev, "Lidery," 97–98.

10. Rodzianko to Ruzskii, 1/III, *KA* (1), 52. This document is not included in *Stavka i revoliutsiia*.

11. Rodzyanko's statement includes numerous points of misinformation. For instance, his statement that all ministers except for the ministers of war and navy were arrested is not accurate. Navy Minister Grigorovich was not arrested, but war minister Belyaev was. Foreign Minister Pokrovskii and Finance Minister Bark were not arrested.

12. Vil'chkovskii points out these contradictions in "Prebyvanie," 174. Rodzianko's explanations for the situation in Petrograd had numerous misleading and deceptive points. For instance, he was not forced to arrest the ministers because of the demands of insurgents; rather, he actively sought their arrests. He sent them not to the Peter and Paul Fortress but rather to the Ministerial Pavilion in the Tauride Palace.

13. Nicholas to Alekseev, No. 1223B, 05:25, 2/III, *KA* (1), 62; No. 172, *Stavka i revoliutsiia*, 270; No. 26, Telegrammy Ruzskago, 133.

14. Letter from Pavel Aleksandrovich to Kirill Vladimirovich, No. 18, *Permskaia Golgofa*, 95; Paley, *Memories of Russia*, 55–56; Spiridovich, *Velikaia voina*, vol. 3, 272.

15. Kirill Vladimirovich to Pavel Aleksandrovich, 2/III/1917, *Poslednie Novosti*, 26/XII/1922, in email message from Nicholas Nicolson to the author, 15/II/2021.

16. Nikitin, *Rokovye gody*, 202; Matveev, *Memoirs*, Prilozhenie, 2, Bakhmeteff Archive.

17. No. 22, *Permskaia Golgofa*, 97.

18. Danilov to Alekseev, No. 1224B, 05:48, 2/III, *KA* (1), 62–63; No. 173, *Stavka i revoliutsiia*, 270–271. This telegram is not included in Telegrammy Ruzskago.

19. No. 171, Alekseev to Evert, Brusilov, Sakhalov, and Ianushkevich, 3:30–10:15, 2/III, *Stavka i revoliutsiia*, 268–269. The exact timing of this telegram is not indicated. This document is not included in the *Krasnyi arkhiv* collection.

20. Danilov-Lukomskii conversation, 2/III, *KA* (1), 74–75; No. 176, *Stavka i revoliutsiia*, 273–274; No. 27, Telegrammy Ruzskago, 133–135; Dokumenty Lukomskago, 258–259; Vil'chkovskii, "Prebyvanie," 177; Bazili's conversation with Paléologue in Paléologue, *Ambassador's Memoirs*, vol. 3, 249–250.

21. Sergeevskii, *Otrechenie*, 57; Ganin, "Genshtabisty," 242.

22. Alekseev to Evert, Brusilov, Sakharov, Ianushkevich, No. 1870, 8:52, 1/III, *KA* (1), 64–65; No. 175, *Stavka i revoliutsiia*, 271–273. As for the western front's protest, see Kvetsinskii to Danilov, No. 680, 1:30, 2/III, *KA* (1), 62; No. 162, *Stavka i revoliutsiia*, 259.

23. The oath of allegiance is often erroneously referred to as allegiance to "the tsar and fatherland." For instance, Rosenberg, *States of Anxiety*, 40. But nowhere is there any reference to "fatherland" in the oath. Instead it was the oath to the tsar, tsarevich, and to the state, not the fatherland.

24. See Eric Lohr, *Nationalizing the Russian Empire*.

25. Basily, *Abdication*, 127.

26. Ibid., 128.

27. Vil'chkovskii, "Prebyvanie," 172. Vilchkovsky was chief of police for the Tsarskoe Selo buildings. He became a confidant to Ruzsky afer the October Revolution in Kislovodsk, before the Bolsheviks occupied the city. Ruzsky entrusted his papers to Vilchkovsky. The documents in Telegrammy Ruzskago come from Vilchkovsky's collection. While Vilchkovsky argues that the initiative for Nicholas's abdication came from Alekseev and the Stavka, Alekseev's daughter, citing Lukomsky, Sergeevsky, and Bazili, insists that it was Ruzsky who took the initiative. See Alekseeva-Borel', *Sorok let*, 484–485.

28. Airapetov, *Generaly*, 201–203. His source: OR RGB, f. 855, kart. 4, ed. khr. 18, ll. 1ob–2.

29. Spiridovich, *Velikaia voina*, vol. 3, 277.

30. Alekseev to Evert, Brusilov, Sakharov, and Ianushkevich, No. 1872, 10:15, 2/III, *KA* (1); No. 178, *Stavka i revoliutsiia*, 276–277; Dokumenty Lukomskago, 259–260; No. 28, Telegrammy Ruzskago, 135–136; Basily, *Abdication*, 130.

31. Alekseev to Evert, Brusilov, Sakharov, and Ianushkevich, No. 1872, 10:15, 2/III, *KA* (1), 67–68, 68–69; No. 178, *Stavka i revoliutsiia*, 276–277; Dokumenty Lukomskago, 259–260; No. 28, Telegrammy Ruzskago, 135–136.

32. Rusin talked about this episode personally to Spiridovich. Spiridovich, *Velikaia voina*, vol. 3, 283.

33. Bubnov, *V tsarskoi Stavke*, 57, 83; Basily, *Abdication*, 116–117.

34. Alekseev to Evert, No. 1872, in Evert-Klembovskii conversation, *KA* (1), 67; No. 179, *Stavka i revoliutsiia*, 277–278; Alekseev-Brusilov conversation, *KA* (1), 68–69; No. 183, *Stavka i revoliutsiia*, 280–281.

35. Evert-Klembovskii conversation, ended at 11:07 March 2. According to Lukomsky, Evert telegraphed him that he would postpone his response after he knew how Ruzsky and Brusilov would answer. But we have no record of this communication. Lukomskii, "Otrecheniie Nikolaia II (vospominaniia)," *Otrechenie*, 265.

36. Sergeevskii, *Otrechenie*, 38–39; Ganin, "Genshtabisty," 244.

37. Lukomskii-Sakharov conversation, 11:07, 2/III, *KA* (1), 69–70; No. 184, *Stavka i revoliutsiia*, 281–282.

38. Alekseev-Brusilov conversation, 11:00, 2/III, *KA* (1), 69; No. 183, *Stavka i revoliutsiia*, 280–281.

39. Alekseev-Brusilov conversation, 11:00, 2/III, *KA* (1), 69; No. 183, *Stavka i revoliutsiia*, 280–281.

40. Ianushkevich to Lukomskii, 12:28, March 2, *KA* (1), 72; No. 191, *Stavka i revoliutsiia*, 286.

41. Basily, *Memoirs*, 121. Acording to Dubensky, Alekseev's telegram caught Grand Duke Nikolai Nikolaevich by surprise. The urgent situation described by Alekseev prompted the grand duke to send his reply without verifying the accuracy of the facts. Dubenskii, "Kak proizoshel perevorot," 108. As for Nikolai Nikolaevich's reply to Alekseev, see No. 196, Nikolai Nikolaevich to Alekseev, 13:39, 2/III, *Stavka i revoliutsiia*, 290.

42. The precise time of this meeting was not definitely established. According to Ruzsky's interview with Andrei Vladimirovich, it was 9:30, according to Danilov it was 10, but according to Vilchkovsky it was 10:15. Martynov, who used archival materials of Spiridovich, said it was 10:45. Vil'chkovskii, "Prebyvanie," 177; Andrei Vladimirovich, "Iz dnevnika" (1928), 206; Martynov, *Tsarskaia armiia*, 152; Danilov, "Moi vospominaniia," 227–228. If Martynov is correct, Ruzsky could have received Alekseev's telegram before he met the emperor. Either Martynov's time was wrong or the telegram was not delivered until Ruzsky began his meeting with Nicholas.

43. Voeikov, *S tsarem*, 210–211.

44. Mordvinov, "Poslednie dni" (1923), 141.

45. Voeikov, *S tsarem*, 211.

46. It is not clear why Ruzsky chose General Savvich. His daughter was married to Baron B. E. Nolde, who later composed the "manifesto" for Grand Duke Mikhail to refuse to take the throne. Baron Nolde had close connections with the Kadets.

47. Savvich, "Priniatie Nikolaem II," *Otrechenie*, 269.

48. Ibid., 270.

49. Danilov, "Moi vospominaniia," 230.

50. Alekseev to tsar, No. 1878, 14:30, 2/III, *KA* (1), 72–73; No. 30, Steinberg and Khrustalev, *Fall of the Romanovs*, 89–90; No. 30, Telegrammy Ruzskago, 137. Steinberg and Khrustalev's translation omitted the crucial phrase put in italics: "duty to the oath." This is exactly the telegram he received at 13:39, which is missing in the *Krasnyi arkhiv* collection. See No. 196, *Stavka i revoliutsiia*, 290.

51. Alekseev to tsar, No. 1878, 14:30, 2/III, *KA* (1), 72–73; No. 20, Steinberg and Khrustalev, *Fall of the Romanovs*, 90–91; No. 30, Telegrammy Ruzskago, 137–138; No. 202, *Stavka i revoliutsiia*, 293–295.

52. Alekseev to tsar, No. 1878, 14:30, 2/III, *KA* (1), 73; No. 20, Steinberg and Khrustalev, *Fall of the Romanovs*, 91; No. 30, Telegrammy Ruskago, 138–139; No. 202, *Stavka i revoliutsiia*, 293–295.

53. Sakharov to Ruzskii, 2/III, *KA* (1), 74; No. 31, Telegrammy Ruzskago, 139; No. 204, *Stavka i revoliutsiia*, 296.

54. Andrei Vladimirovich, "Dnevniki," *Gibel' monarkhii*, 348.

55. Dokumenty Lukomskago (1922), 264; No. 235, *Stavka i revoliutsiia*, 320; No. 39, Telegrammy Ruzskago, 143–144; Browder and Kerensky, *Russian Provisional Government*, 97.

56. Danilov, "Moi vospominaniia," 230; Danilov, "Na puti," 388–389; Savvich, "Priniatie Nikolaem II," in Shchegolev, *Otrechenie*, 177.

57. Danilov, "Na puti," 389.

58. Vil'chkovskii, "Prebyvanie," 178; Danilov, "Na puti," 388.

59. Andrei Vladimirovich, "Dnevniki," *Gibel' monarkhii*, 349.

60. Savvich, "Priniatie Nikolaem II," *Otrechenie*, 270.

61. Nicholas to Alekseev, No. 33, Telegrammy Ruzskago, 140; No. 205, *Stavka i revoliutsiia*, 297; Mordvinov, "Poslednie dni," *Otrechenie*, 148.

62. Nicholas to Alekseev, No. 33, Telegrammy Ruzskago, 140–141; No. 205, *Stavka i revoliutsiia*, 297; Dokumenty Lukomskago, 262; Danilov, "Moi vospominaniia," 231.

63. Nicholas to Rodzianko, No. 32, Telegrammy Ruzskago, 140; No. 206, *Stavka i revoliutsiia*, 297–298; No. 25, *Permskaia Golgofa*, 100; Mordvinov, "Poslednie dni," *Otrechenie*, 148.

64. Andrei Vladimirovich, "Dnevniki," *Gibel' monarkhii*, 349.

65. Vil'chkovskii, "Prebyvanie," 179.

66. Milyukov's speech was conveyed to the Stavka in the afternoon of March 3 by the Petrograd Telegraph Agency, see Nos. 274, 275, 277, 278, 279, 280, *Stavka i revoliutsiia*, 347–350, 351–354. For Milyukov's speech at the Tauride Palace, see "Protokol zasedanii," 282–286; Browder and Kerensky, *Russian Provisional Government*, 129–133.

67. Browder and Kerensky, *Russian Provisional Government*, 133.

68. Mordvinov, "Poslednie dni," *Otrechenie*, 141–143; Voeikov, *S tsarem*, 212–213. Dubenskii, "Kak proizoshel perevorot," 49, 58.

69. Mordvinov, "Poslednie dni," *Otrechenie*, 144.

70. Danilov, "Moi vospominaniia" (1928), 233–234.

71. Mordvinov, "Poslednie dni," *Otrechenie*, 145.

72. Andrei Vladimirovich, "Dnevniki," *Gibel' monarkhii*, 349–350; Vil'chkovskii, "Prebyvanie," 179.

73. Klembovskii to Danilov, No. 1886, 16:50, 2/III, *KA* (1), 77; No. 34, Telegrammy Ruzskago, 141; No. 214, *Stavka i revoliutsiia*, 303–304.

74. Danilov to Alekseev, No. 1230/B, sent 16:30, received 16:50, 2/III, *KA* (1), 77; No. 35, Telegrammy Ruzskago, 143; No. 212, *Stavka i revoliutsiia*, 302.

75. Lukomskii to front chiefs of staff, No. 1884, 16:43, 2/III, *KA* (1), 76; No. 213, *Stavka i revoliutsiia*, 303.

76. Basily, *Abdication*, 131.

77. Ibid.; Nikolai Bazili Papers, Box 27, File 6, Nicholas II, Abdication, photocopies of Bazili's drafts of abdication, HIA; "Proekt manifesta Nikolaia II ob otrechenie," attached to Alekseev's Telegram No. 1896, sent 19:40, 2/III, *KA* (2), 7. For Bazili's original draft and Alekseev's revisions, see Basily, *Abdication*, between 132 and 133.

78. Alekseev to Danilov, 19:40, 2/III, *KA* (2), 7; No. 231, *Stavka i revoliutsiia*, 317; Nicholas II's Abdication Manifesto, *KA* (2), 7; No. 232, *Stavka i revoliutsiia*, 317–318; Danilov, "Moi vospominaniia," 232–233, 242–243; Danilov, "Na puti," 390–391; Sworakowski, "Authorship," 282.

79. Andrei Vladimirovich, "Iz dnevnika" (1928), 181.

80. Katkov, *Russia 1917*, 323.

81. Matveev, *Memoirs*, 12, Bakhmeteff Archive; Nikolaev, "Lidery," 101.

82. Alekseev to Danilov, No. 1871, 10:00, 2/III, *KA* (1), 65; No. 177, *Stavka i revoliutsiia*, 275.

83. Danilov to Alekseev, No. 1277/B, 12:00, 2/III, *KA* (1), 64; No. 186, *Stavka i revoliutsiia*, 283.

84. Boldyrev to Lukomskii, No. 1229/B, 13:15, 2/III, *KA* (1), 85; No. 194, *Stavka i revoliutsiia*, 288–289.

85. Lukomskii to Boldyrev, No. 1881, 15:50, 2/III, *KA* (2), 65; No. 209, *Stavka i revoliutsiia*, 300.

86. Alekseev to Nicholas, No. 1890, 18:55, 2/III, *KA* (2), 10.

87. Danilov to Alekseev, No. 1241/B, 21, 2/III, *KA* (2), 10; No. 237, *Stavka i revoliutsiia*, 321.

88. No. 225, Ivanov to Alekseev, No. 9, *Stavka i revoliutsiia*, 335.

89. No. 1686/No. 650, 2/III, No. 1687/No. 651, 2/III, in Fuhrmann, 698, 700.

90. Alexandra to Nicholas, No. 1686/No. 650, 2/III, 1917, in Fuhrmann, 698–699; No. 24, Steinberg and Khrustalev, *Fall of the Romanovs*, 93–95.

91. Spiridovich, *Velikaia voina*, vol. 3, 273.

## Chapter 11: A Fateful Change of Mind

1. Shul'gin, "Dni," *Otrechenie*, 241.

2. Skobelev interview in Lyandres, *Fall of Tsarism*, 188–189. According to Skobelev, the Executive Committee let Guchkov and Shulgin's train depart from Warsaw station. The regency of Mikhail that was revealed in Milyukov's speech was not yet a hot issue. According to Spiridovich, the train did not leave until 5 in the morning.

3. Mul'tatuli argues that Guchkov and Shul'gin knew about Nicholas's decision to abdicate from Alekseev. It is unlikely that Alekseev had contacted the Duma Committee before their departure. Mul'tatuli, *Nikolai II*, 577.

4. Startsev, *Vnutrenniaia politika*, 75.

5. Lomonosov, *Vospominaniia* (1994), 248.

6. Shul'gin, "Dni," *Otrechenie*, 244.

7. Ibid.; Guchkov, "V tsarkom poezde," *Otrechenie*, 259.

8. Guchkov's statement to Bazili, quoted in Basily, *Abdication*, 127; Shul'gin, *Dni* (1925), 243–244.

9. Spiridovich, *Velikaia voina*, vol. 3, 307.

10. Guchkov statement in Basily, *Abdication*, 154.

11. Mordvinov, "Poslednie dni," *Otrechenie*, 144–145; Dubenskii, "Kak proizoshel perevorot," 56–57; Benckendorff, *Last Days*, 46–48; Danilov, "Moi vospominaniia," 234; Martynov, *Tsarskaia armiia*, 160; Gilliard, *Thirteen Years*, 165; Spiridovich, *Velikaia voina*, vol. 3, 297–298.

12. Mordvinov, "Poslednie dni," *Otrechenie*, 149–150.

13. Tal', *Memuary*, 50; Tal', *Chronology*, 32–33.

14. Tal', *Memuary*, 53; Mordvinov, "Poslednie dni," *Otrechenie*, 152–153.

15. Shul'gin, "Podrobnosti otrecheniia," in *Otrechenie*, 231.

16. Mordvinov, "Poslednie dni," *Otrechenie*, 153; Shul'gin, "Dni," *Otrechenie*, 245; Guchkov, "V tsarkom poezde," *Otrechenie*, 259; Spiridovich, *Velikaia voina*, vol. 3, 307; Voeikov, *S tsarem*, 223; Basily, *Abdication*, 134; Guchkov statement in Basily, *Abdication*, 134; Danilov, "Moi vospominaniia," 235–236; Dubenskii, "Kak proizoshel perevorot," 60.

17. Mordvinov, "Poslednie dni," *Otrechenie*, 154; Spiridovich, *Velikaia voina*, vol. 3, 307.

18. Guchkov statement in Basily, *Memoirs*, 134. See also Shul'gin, *Dni* (1925), 267; Shul'gin, *Dni* (1989), 250.

19. Guchkov statement in Basily, *Abdication*, 135; Spiridovich, *Velikaia voina*, vol. 3, 308; Shul'gin, "Podrobnosti," *Otrechenie*, 231. According to Shul'gin, he sat next to Guchkov.

20. The meeting has been recounted by the participants of the meeting, but their stories differ in details. They differ, first, on when Ruzsky and Danilov joined the meeting and, second, on whether there was a recess. Here I reconstruct what I believe is the most likely process of the meeting, mostly relying on the record in GARF. f. 601, o. 1, d. 2099, ll. 1–30ob, No. 25, Steinberg and Khrustalev, *Fall of the Romanovs*, 96–100, 424, supplemented by the memoirs of the participants (Guchkov, Shul'gin, Ruzsky, Danilov, and Fredericks).

21. Basily, *Abdication*, 138–139; Shul'gin, "Podrobnosti," *Otrechenie*, 231; Shul'gin, *Dni* (1989), 251; Shulgin, "Dni," *Otrechenie*, 246.

22. No. 25, Steinberg and Khrustalev, *Fall of the Romanovs*, 96–97.

23. Mordvinov, "Poslednie dni," *Otrechenie*, 155.

24. Shul'gin, "Dni," *Otrechenie*, 247; Voeikov, *S tsarem*, 224. Exactly when Ruzsky entered the room is not certain. According to Spiridovich, he came about the time Guchkov was about to finish his speech; Spiridovich, *Velikaia voina*, vol. 3, 308. According to Guchkov, he entered the room before he began to speak; Guchkov statement in Basily, *Abdication*, 135. See also Andrei Vladimirovich, "Dnevniki," *Gibel' monarkhii*, 350; Shul'gin, *Dni* (1989), 252. No. 25 in Steinberg and Khrustalev, *Fall of the Romanovs*, did not mention anything about Ruzsky's joining the meeting. In fact, it treats the subject as if Ruzsky was present from the very beginning.

25. Guchkov's deposition in *Padenie*, vol. 6, 264; Guchkov statement in Basily, *Abdication*, 135. This part is not included in No. 25 in Steinberg and Khrustalev, *Fall of the Romanovs*.

26. This account is based on No. 25, Steinberg and Khrustalev, *Fall of the Romanovs*, 96–100, which comes from GARF, f. 601, d. 2099, ll. 1–3ob; also Storozhev, "Fevral'skaia revoliutsiia," 1, 139; Mel'gunov, *Martovskie dni*, 190–191; No. 97, in Shashkova, *Fevral'skaia revoliutsiia*, 223. Storozhev's account is based on the record taken by Naryshkin. Mel'gunov uses this document.

27. Shul'gin, "Dni," *Otrechenie*, 247; Spiridovich, *Velikaia voina*, vol. 3, 308; Basily, *Abdication*, 134.

28. No. 25, Steinberg and Khrustalev, *Fall of the Romanovs*, 97, with slight modifications.

29. Ibid.; Guchkov statement in Basily, *Abdication*, 135; Storozhev, "February Revolution," 140; Mel'gunov, *Martovskie dni*, 191; No. 97, Shashkova, *Fevral'skaia revoliutsiia*, 224–225.

30. Spiridovich, *Velikaia voina*, vol. 3, 309.

31. Shul'gin, "Dni," *Otrechenie*, 247.

32. Andrei Vladimirovich, "Iz dnevnika" (1928), 207; Andrei Vladimirovich, "Dnevniki," *Gibel' monarkhii*, 350.

33. Neither Guchkov nor Shulgin mentions anything about the transfer of the original abdication "manifesto" from Ruzsky to Nicholas. Guchkov statement in Basily, *Abdication*, 135; Shul'gin, "Dni," *Otrechenie*, 248–249.

34. No. 25, Steinberg and Khrustalev, *Fall of the Romanovs*, 97; Storozhev, "February Revolution," 140; Guchkov statement in Basily, *Abdication*, 135; Mel'gunov, *Martovskie dni*,

192; No. 97, Shashkova, *Fevral'skaia revoliutsiia*, 225; Shul'gin, *Dni* (1925), 269; Shul'gin, *Dni* (1989), 252; Shul'gin, "Podrobnosti," *Otrechenie*, 232. The last sentence of the quote is missing in Document 25. Shul'gin described Nicholas's speech slightly differently in his March 3 article; Shul'gin, "Podrobnosti," *Otrechenie*, 232. For the slightly different wording, see Shul'gin, "Dni," *Otrechenie*, 248.

35. Storozhev, "Fevral'skaia revoliutsiia," 139-140; Mel'gunov, *Martovskie dni*, 192; No. 97, Shashkova, *Fevral'skaia revoliutsiia*, 225; Shul'gin, "Podrobnosti," *Otrechenie*, 232. Naryshkin's note cited by Storozhev does not make clear when Shulgin proposed a recess. This version, widely accepted by historians, is challenged by the contemporary Russian historian Kulikov. The prevailing view is based on the note attributed to Naryshkin, who attended the crucial meeting, and Storozhev, who first introduced this version, exclusively relying on Naryshkin's note. Kulikov argues that Naryshkin's note, without signature, is not reliable. Kulikov argues, based on Mordvinov's account, that Nicholas's change of mind took place during his talk with the Duma delegates. According to Kulikov, Nicholas was prepared to abdicate in favor of his son and wanted to spend his retirement in the Crimea. Guchkov rejected this proposal and told him that Nicholas would be exiled abroad. Nicholas then requested that his son join him abroad until he reached maturity. Guchkov rejected this request as well, saying the new emperor would have to remain in Russia. It was only then that Nicholas decided to abdicate not only for himself but also for his son in favor of his brother. Lukomsky also writes in his memoirs that Nicholas's change of mind took place during the meeting with Guchkov and Shulgin. Lukomsky bases this version on the talk he had with Ruzsky later. This version is difficult to accept. Naryshkin was in the salon car and took notes, but Mordvinov, whom Kulikov relies on, did not attend the meeting. Lukomsky's version is merely hearsay. The accuracy of Naryshkin's note is confirmed by Guchkov and Shulgin. Guchkov statement in Basily, *Abdication*, 136; Shul'gin, "Podrobnosti," *Otrechenie*, 232; Voeikov, *S tsarem*, 224.

36. Martin, "For the Firm Maintenance," 389-422; Martin, "Law, Succession," 225-242.

37. Gronsky and Astrov, *War and Russian Government*, 97. The illegality of this succession was noticed by Mordvinov and Naryshkin at the time; Mordvinov, "Poslednie dni," *Otrechenie*, 156-158.

38. Miliukov, *Russian Revolution*, vol. 1, 35.

39. Guchkov's deposition, *Padenie*, vol. 6, 265.

40. Andrei Vladimirovich, "Dnevniki," *Gibel' monarkhii*, 351; Danilov, "Moi vospominaniia," 237.

41. Andrei Vladimirovich, "Iz dnevnika" (1928), 207; Shul'gin, *Dni* (1925), 270-271; Guchkov's letter to Bazili, in Basily, *Abdication*, 128-129; Danilov, "Moi vospominaniia," 237; Danilov, "Na puti," 395-396; Shul'gin, "Podrobnosti," 231-232; Shul'gin, "Dni," *Otrechenie*, 250-251.

42. Naryshkin's note does not state that there was a break or intermission during the negotiations. See No. 25, Steinberg and Khrustalev, *Fall of the Romanovs*, 97-98.

43. Storozhev, "Fevral'skaia revoliutsiia," 141-142; Mel'gunov, *Martovskie dni*, 194; No. 97, Shashkova, *Fevral'skaia revoliutsiia*, 226. For Guchkov and Shulgin's justification for accepting Nicholas's amendment, see Guchkov, *Guchkoiv rasskazyvaet*, 69-70; Guch-

kov, "Vospominaniia," *Poslednie novosti*, September 16, 1930; Ioffe, *Velikii Oktiabr'*, 77–78; Kulikov, "Otrechenie," 400–401. Kulikov argues that Guchkov's plot for a palace coup took the possibility of Mikhail's succession into consideration. He further argues that having Nicholas succeeded by Mikhail would be more acceptable to such "republicans" as Tereshchenko and Nekrasov in the plot. Kulikov, "Otrechenie," 403–405.

44. No. 25, Steinberg and Khrustalev, *Fall of the Romanovs*, 98–99; Storozhev, "Fevral'skaia revoliutsiia," 141; No. 97, Shashkova, *Fevral'skaia revoliutsiia*, 226.

45. Kulikov, "Otrechenie," 403. Guchkov later claimed that he did not believe that Mikhail would refuse to assume the throne. Guchkov, *Guchkov rasskazyvaet*, 70.

46. For Guchkov and Shulgin's justification for accepting Nicholas's amendment, see Ioffe, *Velikii Oktiabr'*, 77–78.

47. Guchkov's deposition, *Padenie*, vol. 6, 268–269.

48. Shulgin's two-sentence draft manifesto is given in Startsev, *Vnutrenniaia politika*, 73.

49. Danilov, "Moi vospominaniia," 238; Shul'gin, "Podrobnosti," *Otrechenie*, 233–234; Sworakowski, "Authorship," 282.

50. Guchkov statement in Basily, *Abdication*, 136–137. The draft copy of this "manifesto" with Nicholas's handwritten corrections has not been found.

51. "Protokol sobytii," 142–143; "Protokol zasedanii," 277, 286–287; Browder and Kerensky, *Russian Provisional Government*, 104; No. 26, Steinberg and Khrustalev, *Fall of the Romanovs*, 100–102; Nicholas to Alekseev, No. 40, Telegrammy Ruzskago, 144–145. See a facsimile copy of the abdication "manifesto" in Steinberg and Khrustalev, *Fall of the Romanovs*, 101.

52. Storozhev, "Fevral'skaia revoliutsiia," 142; "Protokol sobytii," 141–142; "Protokol zasedanii," 276; Guchkov statement in Basily, *Abdication*, 137; Danilov, "Moi vospominaniia," 238.

53. "Razkaz polkovnika V. V. Stupina," *Solntse Rosii*, No. 367 (9), April 1917, 2. A copy of *Solntse Rossii* is in Nikolai Bazili Papers, Box 27, File 8, HIA.

54. Boldyrev to Lukomskii, No. 1243/B, sent 0:28, received 0:40, 3/III, *KA* (2), 15; Nos. 41–42, Telegrammy Ruzskago, 145; Ruzsky's remark on Nicholas's telegram to Alekseev, No. 40, Telegrammy Ruzskago, 145; Guchkov, "V tsarskom poezde," *Otrechenie*, 262–263; Mordvinov, "Poslednie dni," *Otrechenie*, 158–159. For the fate of the original copy of the "manifesto," see Safonov, "Stavka," 469–474. As will be discussed at greater length in Chapter 12, the two copies are not identical; because of this, there are numerous conspiracy theories as to the authenticity of the "manifesto," and thus Nicholas's abdication itself. See Safonov, "Stavka," 474.

55. Mordvinov, "Poslednie dni," *Otrechenie*, 159; Shul'gin, "Dni," *Otrechenie*, 254.

56. Danilov, "Na puti," 397; Danilov, "Moi vospominaniia," 239.

57. Guchkov and Shulgin to Chief of General Staff, 3/III, *KA* (2), 15–16.

58. Andrei Vladimirovich, "Dnevniki," *Gibel' monarkhii*, 351.

59. Guchkov note in Basily, *Abdication*, 138.

60. Danilov, "Moi vospominaniia," 239–240; Danilov, "Na puti," 398. The copy of the "manifesto" was kept at the northern front until May 17, 1917, when Ruzsky was relieved of the post of the commander and Danilov was transferred to command the Fifth Army. It was

sent back to Lvov of the Provisional Government. Another copy was brought by Guchkov and Shulgin to Petrograd. Which copy is kept at GARF is not known.

61. According to Thal, Voeikov summoned him, and instructed him to send a telegram from Nicholas to Mikhail: "Petrograd, to Your Highness. Hope to see you soon, Niki." Thal immediately sent the telegram and reported to Voeikov. Thal's information is questionable, however. He had no way of knowing where the grand duke was staying, and even if he sent the telegram, there was no guarantee that it reached the grand duke, and the telegraph communications were under the control of the Duma Committee. Tal', *Memuary*, 57–58.

62. Spiridovich, *Velikaia voina*, vol. 3, 314.

63. Nikolai Mikhailovich, "Zapiski," *Gibel' monarkhii*, 76–77.

64. "Dnevniki Nikolaia II," *Otrechenie*, 36; Nicholas II, *Dnevnik Imperatora*, 623; No. 98, Shashkova, *Fevral'saia revoliutsiia*, 227–228; No. 30, Steinberg and Khrustalev, *Fall of the Romanovs*, 107.

65. Nikolaev, "Lidery," 94–95. Rodzyanko consulted General Nikolai Petrovich Mikhnevich (interim chief of staff), Lieutenant General Pyotr Ivanovich Averiyanov, Generals Nikolai Stepanovich Anosov and Aleksandr Dmitrievich Nosov, and Rodzyanko's son, Nikolai Mikhailovich Rodzyanko. According to Nikolaev, his son's recommendation was a decisive factor in Kornilov's appointment.

66. Brusilov to Alekseev, No. 768, sent 21:10, received 21:32, 2/III, *KA* (2), 8; No. 239, *Stavka i revoliutsiia*, 322.

67. Alekseev to Nicholas, No. 1890, 18:55, 2/III, *KA* (2), 9–10; No. 229, *Stavka i revoliutsiia*, 315–316; No. 37, Telegrammy Ruzskago, 142–143; Alekseev to Brusilov, No. 1891, 18:59, 2/III, *KA* (2), 8; No. 230, *Stavka i revoliutsiia*, 316. Rodzianko's telegram to Alekseev was sent at 17:45, and received at the Stavka at 18:02, *KA* (2), 9. Nicholas's note is not in *KA*, but only in Telegrammy Ruzskago. The document cited in *Stavka i revoliutsiia* noted: "Sent to nowhere."

68. Danilov to Alekseev, No. 1241/B, sent 21:20, received 21:29, 2/III, *KA* (2), 10; No. 237, *Stavka i revoliutsiia*, 321.

69. Alekseev to Rodzianko, No. 1898, 22:19, 2/III, *KA* (2), 10; No. 242, *Stavka i revoliutsiia*, 325.

70. Lomonosov, *Vospominaniia* (1994), 244–249.

71. Ibid., 245.

## Chapter 12: Mikhail's Renunciation of the Throne

1. Basily, *Abdication*, 132.

2. Danilov to Alekseev, No. 1244/B, received 01:28, 3/III, *KA* (2), 16; *Stavka i revoliutsiia*, 345; Dokumenty Lukomskago, 266; No. 46, Telegrammy Ruzskago, 146.

3. Basily, *Abdication*, 132–133; Bazili's conversation with Paléologue is in Paléologue, *Ambassador's Memoirs*, vol. 3, 250–251.

4. Basily, *Abdication*, 134–135.

5. Alekseev to Rodzianko, No. 60, 2:04, 3/III, RGIA, f. 1278, op. 10, d. 5, l. 11. He sent the telegram three times, at 2, 4:04, and 7; ibid., ll. 12, 13. Where he sent them is not clear, but likely either to the war minister's residence or to the General Staff.

6. Alekseev to Nikolai Nikolaevich, No. 1907, 02:57, 3/III, *KA* (2), 17; No. 281, *Stavka i revoliutsiia*, 355; Nikolai Nikolaevich to Alekseev, No. 330, 06:28, 3/III, *KA* (2), 18; No. 288, *Stavka i revoliutsiia*, 363–364.

7. Alekseev to Evert, Brusilov, Sakharov and Rusin, No. 1908, 3/III, *KA* (2), 17–18; No. 282, *Stavka i revoliutsiia*, 356. This telegram was sent between 3:19 and 3:40 a.m.

8. Alekseev to L'vov, No. 1909, "Verkhovnoe komandovanie," 282.

9. Alekseev to L'vov and Miliukov, No. 1911, "Verkhovnoe komandovanie," 282.

10. Guchkov and Shulgin to chief of staff, *KA* (2), 15–16; "Protokol sobytii," 142; "Protokol zasedanii," 276; No. 44, Telegrammy Ruzskago, 146. The draft of this telegram was written in pencil by Guchkov in a fourfold letter paper. On the top of this paper is "Petrograd, to the Chief of the General Staff" and below is "Encoded by Lieutenant-Colonel Mediokritskii, 3/III, 1917," written in red pencil. On the left margin, General Danilov wrote, "Gen. kv [General Quartermaster], 3/3, D." The second copy of the draft, which is deposited in the Military Historical Archive, was written in the same handwriting with the same contents, except with the last sentence: "Inform immediately the situation of the family of Count Fredericks," crossed out. On the left margin, Danilov wrote; "Encrypted and given by the [telegraph] apparatus to Colonel Shikheev (Commandant of the Petrorad-Warsaw line of the Northwestern Railway Line), and signed by Commandant, Station Pskov." Footnote 2, *KA* (2), 15–16. When exactly Guchkov and Shulgin sent this telegram and when Rodzyanko received this telegram is not clear, since the time of dispatch of this telegram is not indicated either in the *KA* collection or in the northern front record (Telegrammy Ruzskago).

11. According to Genrikh Ioffe, when Guchkov and Shulgin's telegram reached Warsaw station, fifteen soldiers led by two officers came in two automobiles and arrested the telegraph operators who were attempting to transmit the telegram to Rodzyanko. Safonov considered this Kerensky's action to prevent the telegram from reaching Rodzyanko. Kerensky in his memoirs says nothing about this. This conspiracy theory should be taken with a grain of salt. Ioffe, *Revoliutsiia* (1992), 67; Ioffe, *Velikii Oktiabr'*, 79; Safonov, "Lozh' i pravda," 267; Kerensky, *Russia and History's Turning Point*, 214–215.

12. Lomonosov, *Vospominaniia* (1994), 249.

13. Safonov, "Lozh' i pravda," 262.

14. The "manifesto" was addressed to the chief of staff, Stavka. There were two copies of the original "manifesto." The first one was left with Ruzsky of the northern front, and the second was brought by Guchkov and Shulgin to Petrograd. These two copies contain some discrepancies: the copy at the northern front had Nicholas's signature in pencil, while the one brought to Petrograd had his signature in ink. In addition, the one brought by Shulgin and Guchkov had a different time (15:05), while the copy at the northern front had merely "15." The original draft on which Nicholas made corrections with pencil was never found. See Safonov, "Lozh' i pravda," 256–264. From these discrepancies, neo-monarchist historians argue that the "manifesto" was a forgery. See Mul'tatuli, *Nikolai II*, 540–567. There is also the puzzle of why one copy of Nicholas's signature was in ink, if Nicholas signed two copies in pencil.

15. Hereafter, I call this document an abdication "manifesto" for the sake of convenience rather than qualifying it as a "manifesto," in quotation marks.

16. See Safonov, "Stavka," 258–264; Mul'tatuli, *Nikolai II*, 540–567.

17. Lomonosov, *Vospominaniia* (1994), 250.

18. Rodzyanko and Lvov returned to the Tauride Palace after 8:45 a.m., more likely after 9 a.m. The discussion on the abdication continued for half an hour after Rodzyanko's return. "Protokol sobytii," 143; "Protokol zasedanii," 278.

19. Kerensky interview, in Lyandres, *Fall of Tsarism*, 234. See Kolonitskii, *"Tovarishch' Kerenskii,"* 82–102; Kolonitskii, *"Comrade Kerensky,"* 43–59; Hasegawa, "Aleksandr Fedorovich Kerenskii," 29–33, 40–41.

20. Miliukov, *Vospominaniia*, vol. 2, 316; Miliukov, *Russian Revolution*, vol. 1, 38.

21. See Wortman, *Scenarios of Power.*

22. "Protokol sobytii," 139–140.

23. Miliukov, *Istoriia vtoroi russkoi revoliutsii i*, 23; Nekrasov interview, Lyandres, *Fall of Tsarism*, 149–150.

24. Kerensky interview, Lyandres, *Fall of Tsarism*, 235; "Protokol sobytii," 143; "Protokol zasedanii," 278.

25. N. N. Ivanov, "Otrechenie," Bakhmeteff Archive, 1; Ganelin, "Velikii kniaz'," 420.

26. Rodzianko, "Gosudarstvennaia duma," 62.

27. Hasegawa, *February Revolution* (2017), 620–624.

28. Lyandres, *Fall of Tsarism*, 153–154.

29. Nekrasov, "N. V. Nekrasov v Kieve," *Poslednie Novosti* (Kiev), morning edition, May 16, 1917. I obtained this document courtesy of Nikolaev and Ekaterina Gavrirova. Earlier, Nikolaev took the view that this agreement was reached after Nicholas's double abdication (*Dumskaia revoliutsiia*, vol. 2, 222–224). But in a later article, he wrote that this agreement had been reached on the night of March 1 ("Lidery," 97); he believed that Nekrasov's date was wrong. I believe they struck a deal after Nicholas's abdication; that is more plausible than before the historic Rodzyanko-Ruzsky conversation.

30. Rodzianko to Alekseev, No. 187, to Brusilov, No. 188, to Ruzskii, No. 189, to Evert, No. 190, to Tiflis, No. 191, RGIA, f. 1278, op. 10, d. 5, l. 19; Rodzianko to Alekseev, No. 187, 4:40, 3/III, *Stavka i revoliutsiia*, 356–357.

31. Ruzskii-Rodzianko conversation, *KA* (2), 27–29; No. 284, *Stavka i revoliutsiia*, 357–359; No. 46, Telegrammy Ruzskago, 146–147; Dokumenty Lukomskago, 266–268; Browder and Kerensky, *Russian Provisional Government*, 109–110; No. 28, Steinberg and Khrustalev, *Fall of the Romanovs*, 103–105. According to the archives at the northern front, this conversation began at 5 a.m. But the *Krasnyi arkhiv* collection recorded that the conversation began at 8:45 a.m. In Hasegawa, *February Revolution* (1981), I used the time cited in the *Krasnyi arkhiv*, not from Telegrammy Ruzskago, but after seeing the *Stavka i revoliutsiia*, I changed my mind and now believe that the Rodzianko-Ruzsky conversation preceded the Rodzianko-Alekseev conversation.

32. Ruzskii-Rodzianko conversation, *KA* (2), 29; No. 284, *Stavka i revoliutsiia*, 359.

33. Ruzskii-Rodzianko conversation, *KA* (2), 28; No. 284, *Stavka i revoliutsiia*, 359; No. 46, Telegrammy Ruzskago, 149; Browder and Kerensky, *Russian Provisional Government*, 110; No. 27, Steinberg and Khrustalev, *Fall of the Romanovs*, 105.

34. *Izvestiia*, March 3, 1917; Browder and Kerensky, *Russian Provisional Government*, 133; Safonov, "Lozh' i pravda," 245.

35. Tugan-Baranovskii interview, Lyandres, *Fall of Tsarism*, 122.

36. Mezhraiontsy was a Marxist group that took a position between the Bolsheviks and the Mensheviks. Leon Trotsky, though he was still in exile, belonged to this group before he joined the Bolshevik Party later.

37. See "Protokol sobytii," 143; "Protokol zasedanii," 278.

38. Rodzianko-Alekseev conversation, 6:00–6:46, 3/III, *KA* (2), 25–27; No. 287, *Stavka i revoliutsiia*, 361–362; Browder and Kerensky, *Russian Provisional Government*, 111–112.

39. Alekseev to front commanders, No. 1913, 6:45, 3/III, *KA* (2), 19; No. 290, *Stavka i revoliutsiia*, 365–366; No. 47, Telegrammy Ruzskago, 150; Dokumenty Lukomskago, 268.

40. Conversation between Stavka and staffs of front commanders, 3/III, *KA* (2), 18–19; conversation between Colonel Tikhobrazov and staff of aviation, 7:43, 3/III; see the questionnaire on the distribution of Nicholas II's "manifesto of abdication," *KA* (2), 20; No. 289, *Stavka i revoliutsiia*, 364–365.

41. Nikolai Nikolaevich to Alekseev, No. 332, 07:58, 3/III, No. 3318, 18:22, 3/III, *KA* (2), 20; No. 293, *Stavka i revoliutsiia*, 367.

42. Lebedev to Lukomskii, No. 6219, 7:54, 3/III, *KA* (2), 21; No. 295, *Stavka i revoliutsiia*, 308; Lebedev to Lukomskii, No. 6222, 9:58, 3/III, *KA* (2), 21; No. 301, *Stavka i revoliutsiia*, 372; Lebedev to Lukomskii, No. 6224, 10:40, 3/III, *KA* (2), 21; No. 306, *Stavka i revoliutsiia*, 375–376; Kvetsinskii to Lukomskii, No. 6226, 11:42, 3/III, *KA* (2), 21; No. 307, *Stavka i revoliutsiia*, 326.

43. Alekseev to Ruzskii, Evert, Brusilov, Sakharov, No. 1918, *KA* (2), 23; No. 309, *Stavka i revoliutsiia*, 378–379; Dokumenty Lukomskago, 208–209; No. 49, Telegrammy Ruzskago, 151–153. This judgment was widely shared at the Stavka. Bazili also repeated the danger of the radical socialists' influence on the Duma Committee; Basily, *Abdication*, 142.

44. Guchkov, *Guchkov rasskazyvaet*, 109.

45. Shul'gin, *Dni* (1925), 286; Shul'gin, *Dni* (1989), 194–195.

46. Lomonosov, *Vospominaniia* (1994), 258. See Solzhenitsyn, *March 1917*, Book 3, 50–53, for a fictionalized scene of Guchkov's encounter with the railway workers.

47. Lomonosov, *Vospominaniia* (1994), 258.

48. Shul'gin, *Dni* (1925), 289–294; Tugan-Baranovskii interview, Lyandres, *Fall of Tsarism*, 123; "Protokol sobytii," 143–144; "Protokol zasedanii," 278–279. There are contradictions between Shulgin's account and Tugan-Baranovsky's. Tugan-Baranovsky states that the Military Commission dispatched its representative to rescue Guchkov from the workers who gathered near the Technological Institute. If Guchkov and Shulgin did not use the automobile dispatched either by Bublikov or by the Military Commission, then they must have been cautious to avoid using it and decided to use the automobile provided by the insurgents.

49. Nekrasov interview, Lyandres, *Fall of Tsarism*, 150.

50. Startsev omits Konovalov and Rzhevsky from the participants. Startsev, *Vnutrenniaia politika*, 106. According to Matveev, Rodzyanko asked Matveev not to start the meeting until Guchkov and Shulgin had arrived. Matveev, *Memoirs*, 13, Bakhmeteff Archive.

51. Nekrasov interview, Lyandres, *Fall of Tsarism*, 150.

52. "Otkaz Velikago Kniazia Mikhaila Aleksandrovicha ot prestola: Razkaz A. I. Guchkova," 1, Box 22, File 1, Bazili Papers, HIA.

53. Shul'gin, *Dni* (1925), 299–300. According to Startsev, Kerensky was the second to speak after Rodzyanko. Startsev, *Vnutrenniaia politika*, 106.

54. Guchkov, "Kak Velikago Kniazia," 1, Box 22, File 1, Bazili Papers, HIA.

55. Deposition of Guchkov, *Padenie*, vol. 6, 267; Basily, *Memoirs*, 144; Paléologue, *Ambassador's Memoirs*, vol. 3, 240.

56. Shul'gin, *Dni* (1925), 310.

57. Mel'gunov, *Martovskie dni*, 227; Shul'gin, *Dni* (1925), 297; Startsev, *Vnutrenniaia politika*, 109.

58. Paléologue, *Ambassador's Memoirs*, vol. 3, 240–241; Basily, *Memoirs*, 144; Nekrasov interview, Lyandres, *Fall of Tsarism*, 151.

59. Nikolai Nikolaevich Johnson was born in St. Petersburg as a son of Captain of Grenadier Brigade Nikolai Aleksandrovich Johnson and Liza Aleksandrovna Johnson. He was raised Russian Orthodox, attended the Mikhailovskii artillery school, and served as the artillerist in the army. After Grand Duke Mikhail fired Anatoly Mordvinov, who was hostile to his mistress Natalia Wulfert (his future wife, Natasha Brasova), he appointed Johnson as his secretary. He established a close relationship with Johnson, who became not only his trusted aide but also a good friend. Johnson followed Mikhail to Gatchina after the February Revolution. When Mikhail was arrested, British ambassador Buchanan suggested that Johnson emigrate to England, but he refused to part with the grand duke. When Mikhail was executed in Perm on the night of June 12–13, 1918, Johnson was also murdered by the Bolshevik executioners, together with his longtime friend.

60. Nekrasov interview, Lyandres, *Fall of Tsarism*, 151.

61. Basily, *Memoirs*, 144–145; Nekrasov interview, Lyandres, *Fall of Tsarism*, 150–151, 154; Guchkov, *Guchkov rasskazyvaet*, 109–110.

62. Rodzianko, "Gosudarstvennaia duma," 62; Khrustalev, *Permskaia Golgofa*, 70.

63. Quoted in Shul'gin, *Dni* (1989), 279.

64. GARF f. 6501, op. 1. d. 203, ll. 21ob–22, quoted in Khrustalev, *Permskaia Golgofa*, 68.

65. Paley, *Memories*, 57.

66. According to Mordvinov, who served as Mikhail's aide-de-camp until 1912, Mikhail told him that he knew that he was unfit and unprepared to be the tsar, and never wished to be the tsar. Mordvinov, "Poslednie dni," *Otrechenie*, 179.

67. Shul'gin, *Dni* (1989), 206. But this account is not corroborated by other witnesses' memories.

68. Shul'gin, *Dni* (1989), 279.

69. Khrustalev, *Velikii kniaz' Mikhail Aleksandrovich*, 397.

70. Kerensky, *Catastrophe*, 70.

71. Nekrasov interview, Lyandres, *Fall of Tsarism*, 151.

72. Altfater-Goncharov conversation, 10:25, 3/III, *KA* (2), 32; No. 305, *Stavka i revoliutsiia*, 375.

73. Alekseev to commanders, No. 1913, 6:45, 3/III, *KA* (2), 19; No. 290, *Stavka i revoliutsiia*, 365–366.

74. Bazili's note on chronology about abdication is in Bazili Papers, Box 23, File 15, HIA.

75. Alekseev to Ruzskii, Evert, Brusilov, Sakharov, No. 1918 (sent to Ruzskii 13:27, to Evert 13:30, to Brusilov 13:13, and to Sakharov 13:40), 3/III, *KA* (2), 22–24; No. 309, *Stavka i revoliutsiia*, 378–379; Dokumenty Lukomskago, 208–209; No. 49, Telegrammy Ruzskago, 151–153. For the insurrection of the sailors in the Baltic Fleet at Helsingfors (Helsinki), see Saul, *Sailors in Revolt*; Mawdsley, *Russian Revolution and the Baltic Fleet*, 1–21. The revolt of the Baltic Fleet is beyond the scope of this book.

76. Alekseev to commanders, No. 1918, 3/III, *KA* (2), 24; No. 309, *Stavka i revoliutsiia*, 380.

77. Alekseev to commanders, No. 1918, 3/III, *KA* (2), 24; No. 309, *Stavka i revoliutsiia*, 380.

78. No. 49, Telegrammy Ruzskago. The quote is from Lukomskii, "Iz vospominanii," *ARR* 2, 269.

79. Baranovskii to Rodzianko, No. 60/1, 15:00, 3/III, RGIA, f. 1278, op. 10, d. 5, l. 21.

80. No. 48, Ruzskii to 1, 5, 12 army commanders, 42 army corps, commander of Baltic Fleet, 8:15, 3/III; Telegrammy Ruzskago, 150.

81. Ruzskii to Alekseev, No. 1254/b, received 16:20, 3/III, *KA* (2), 24; No. 324, *Stavka i revoliutsiia*, 392; No. 50, Telegrammy Ruzskago, 153.

82. Sakharov to Alekseev, No. 03411, received 14:55, 3/III, *KA* (2), 25: No. 320, *Stavka i revoliutsiia*, 388–389.

83. Evert to Alekseev, No. 6245, received 19:53, 3/III, *KA* (2), 42–44; No. 333, *Stavka i revoliutsiia*, 401–402.

84. Alekseev to L'vov and Guchkov, No. 78, 8/III, RGIA, f. 1278, op. 10, d. 5, l. 25; No. 503, *Stavka i revoliutsiia*, 546.

85. Brusilov to Alekseev, 17:15, 3/III, *KA* (2), 24; No. 329, *Stavka i revoliutsiia*, 395–396.

86. Nikolai Nikolaevich to Alekseev, No. 332, received 7:58, 3/III, *KA* (2), 20; No. 292, *Stavka i revoliutsiia*, 367.

87. Alekseev-Guchkov conversation, 18:07–18:35, 3/III, *KA* (2), 36–37; No. 331, *Stavka i revoliutsiia*, 397–399.

88. Alekseev-Guchkov conversation, 18:07–18:35, 3/III, *KA* (2), 38; No. 331, *Stavka i revoliutsiia*, 398–399.

89. Immediately after this conversation, he talked to Engel'gardt, who told him that Guchkov had resigned as war minister. It turned out to be a miscommunication, and Guchkov remained as war minister. Alekseev-Engel'gardt conversation, 3/III, *KA* (2), 39; No. 334, *Stavka i revoliutsiia*, 404.

90. Nikolai Nikolaevich to Alekseev, No. 3318, received 18:22, 3/III, *KA* (2), 25; No. 332, *Stavka i revoliutsiia*, 400. This telegram was followed by another, which was sent at 9 p.m. on March 3, and reached the Stavka at 6:35 a.m. on March 4. He repeated the same argument. See Nikolai Nikolaevich to Alekseev, 21:00, March 3, "Verkhovnoe komandovanie," 280.

91. No. 337, rescript of Nikolai Nikolaevich, 19:45, 3/III, *Stavka i revoliutsiia*, 405. This is not included in the *Krasnyi arkhiv* collection. Also see Robinson, *Grand Duke*, 298.

92. No. 341, Alekseev to front commanders, 20:25, 3/III, *Stavka i revoliutsiia*, 408. This document is not included in the *Krasnyi arkhiv* collection.

93. Alekseev to Rodzianko, No. 60/4, 21:16, 3/III, RGIA, f. 1278, op. 10, d. 5, l. 24.

94. No. 356, Alekseev to Nikolai Nikolaevich, No. 1941, 2:20, 4/III, *Stavka i revoliutsiia*, 422–423. This document is not included in the *Krasnyi arkhiv* collection.

95. Bazili's revision of Mikhail's "manifesto" is in Bazili Papers, Box 27, File 4, HIA. According to Matveev, Lvov and Rodzyanko also took part in drafting the "manifesto." Matveev, *Memoirs*, 15, Bakhmeteff Archive.

96. Shul'gin, *Dni* (1989), 208. For the full text of the manifesto, see "Otrechenie Velikogo Kniazia Mikhaila Aleksandrovicha," *Izvestiia Komiteta Petrogradskikh zhurnalistov*, No. 9, March 4, 1917, 1; "Protokol sobytii," 144; "Protokol zasedanii," 279, 287. Matveev was consulted regarding the revisions to the "manifesto"; Matveev, *Memoirs*, 15, Bakhmeteff Archive.

97. Nabokov, "Vremennoe pravitel'stvo," 21; Lomonosov, *Vospominaniia* (1921), 70.

98. Lomonosov, *Vospominaniia* (1994), 260.

99. Ibid. It is most likely Yury Mikhailovich Steklov who leaked the information to *Izvestiya*, for which he was the chief editor.

100. The following members attended the meeting: G. E. Lvov, Milyukov, Tereshchenko, Kerensky, Shingarev, Godnev, V. M. Lvov, Nekrasov; Nikolaev, *Revoliutsiia i vlast'*, 562. Guchkov and Konovalov must have been absent, although Milyukov remembered that Guchkov was present at this meeting; Miliukov, *Vospominaniia*, 318. In addition to this list, Yakov Vasilievich Glinka, Baron Nolde, and Nabokov were present as secretariat and legal advisers to the Provisional Government.

101. GARF, f. 601, op. 1, d. 2103, ll. 1ob–2, quoted in No. 28, *Permskaia Golgofa*, 103–104; Storozhev, "Fevral'skaia revoliutsiia," 143; No. 55, Shashkova, *Fevral'skaia revoliutsiia*, 161–162.

102. See Nikolaev, *Dumskaia revoliutsiia*, vol. 2, 225–241.

103. Dehn, *Real Tsaritsa*, 164.

104. Paley, *Memories of Russia*, 60–61; Benckendorff, *Last Days*, 16–17.

105. Dehn, *Real Tsaritsa*, 167.

106. Buxhoeveden, *Life and Tragedy*, 263; Benckendorff, *Last Days*, 17.

107. Buxhoeveden, *Life and Tragedy*, 265.

108. Ibid., 255–256, 267–268.

### Chapter 13: Arrests and Reunion

1. "Dnevniki Nikolaia II," *Otrechenie*, 36; Nicholas II, *Dnevnik Imperatora*, 625.

2. Nicholas to Mikhail, sent 14:56, 3/III, No. 29, *Permskaia Golgofa*, 105; Voeikov, *S tsarem*, 229.

3. The telegram reached Petrograd at 15:10, March 3, but where in Petrograd it was dispatched is not indicated. We do not know if Nicholas was aware that Mikhail was staying in Countess Putyatina's house. It is likely that it reached Bublikov, of the Ministry of Transport, who controlled the network of railway telegraph communications.

4. Voeikov, *S tsarem*, 229.

5. Basily, *Abdication*, 143.

6. Ibid., 143–144. According to Nicholas's diary, he arrived at Mogilev at 8:20 p. m., but according to Thal, he arrived at 10:40 p.m. Tal', *Memuary*, 77.

7. Voeikov believes that Alekseev sent Bazili as a spy to see how the entourage was reacting to the abdication. Voeikov, *S tsarem*, 233.

8. Basily, *Abdication*, 143; Voeikov, *S tsarem*, 233.

9. Basily, *Abdication*, 144.

10. Denikin, *Ocherki russkoi smuty*, vol. 1, part 1, 54.

11. According to Solzhenitsyn, Alekseev told him about Mikhail's refusal to take the throne, and it was the first time that Nicholas learned about Mikhail's decision. But as I noted above, Bazili had informed the tsar of Mikhail's refusal. Solzhenitsyn, *March 1917*, Book 3, 166.

12. See Appendix 1 in Pronin, *Poslednie dni*, 78. Two "manifestos" were also distributed in Mogilev, but officers confiscated these flyers. Tal', *Memuary*, 63–64.

13. Denikin, *Ocherki russkoi smuty*, vol. 1, pt. 1, 54. Nicholas's handwritten note, however, has not been discovered by historians.

14. Basily, *Abdication*, 148; also see Pronin, *Poslednie dni*, 48–49.

15. Voeikov, *S tsarem*, 234; Dubenskii, "Kak proizoshel perevorot," 70–71.

16. Nicholas II, *Dnevnik Imperatora*, 625; No. 101, Shashkova, *Fevral'skaia revoliutsiia*, 232.

17. Rodzianko-Alekseev conversation, *KA* (2), 41; No. 344, *Stavka i revoliutsiia*, 413; No. 100, Shashkova, *Fevral'skaia revoliutsiia*, 230–232.

18. Rodzianko-Alekseev conversation, *KA* (2), 41–42; No. 344, *Stavka i revoliutsiia*, 413.

19. Rodzianko-Alekseev conversation, *KA* (2), 42; No. 344, *Stavka i revoliutsiia*, 413–414.

20. Rodzianko-Alekseev conversation, *KA* (2), 42; No. 344, *Stavka i revoliutsiia*, 414.

21. No. 21, *Petrogradskii Sovet*, 81–82; No. 40, "Iz protokola zasedaniia ispolkoma Petrosoveta ob areste chlenov Dinastii Romanovykh," *Permskaia Golgofa*, 116.

22. Paraphrased from Schama, *Citizens*, 651.

23. GARF, f. 601, op. 1, d. 2103, l. 2, quoted in *Permskaia Golgofa*, 104. Based on this archival document, Khrustalev dates this meeting to March 2, but it could not possibly be on March 2, when Mikhail's "abdication" was not even raised. Mel'gunov dates this meeting to March 4—that is, after the resolution of the Soviet Executive Committee. Mel'gunov, *Sud'ba*, 14.

24. Mel'gunov, *Sud'ba*, 16–17.

25. Pronin, *Poslednie dni*, 50–51.

26. Quoted in Massie, *Nicholas and Alexandra*, 425–426.

27. Tikhmenev, "Poslednii priezd," in *Otrechenie*, 284.

28. Dubenskii, "Kak proizoshel perevorot," 70–71.

29. Kudrina, *Imperatritsa*, 162–163; Voeikov, *S tsarem*, 242; Dubenskii, "Kak proizoshel perevorot," 71–72; Massie, *Nicholas and Alexandra*, 426. According to Massie, they talked in Maria Fyodorovna's railcar, but this is inaccurate.

30. Kudrina, *Imperatritsa*, 164.

31. Alexander Mikhailovich, *Once a Grand Duke*, 288.

32. Quoted in Khrustalev, *Permskaia Golgofa*, 74.

33. Alexander Mikhailovich, *Once a Grand Duke*, 288.

34. Dubenskii, "Kak proizoshel perevorot," 67.

35. Alekseev to the front commanders, No. 1943, between 1:45 and 3:40, 4/III, *KA* (2), 44; No. 354, *Stavka i revoliutsiia*, 329. Strangely, the text of Mikhail's "manifesto" was not included, merely stating: "The content of Grand Duke Mikhail Aleksandrovich's Manifesto was as follows: ( . . . )" with the parentheses left blank.

36. No. 361, Kvetsinskii-Lukomskii conversation, 4:37, 4/III, *Stavka i revoliutsiia*, 426–427: Lukomskii-Danilov conversation, 4/III, *KA* (2), 45–46; No. 53, Lukomskii-Danilov conversation, Telegrammy Ruzskago, 155–156; No. 326, *Stavka i revoliutsiia*, 429–430. No. 361 of *Stavka i revoliutsiia* is not included in the *KA* collection.

37. No. 383 (Finland), No. 387 (northern front), No. 393 (Smolensk), *Stavka i revoliutsiia*, 445, 447–448, 452.

38. Ruzskii to Alekseev, 14:25, 4/III, *KA* (2), 50–51; No. 382, *Stavka i revoliutsiia*, 444.

39. Nikolai Nikolaevich, No. 4138, in Alekseev to front commanders, No. 1947, 4/III, *KA* (2), 45; Alekseev to L'vov and Guchkov, sent at 13:40, 4/III, "Verkhovnoe komandovanie," 284.

40. "Prikaz nachal'nika shtaba verkhovnago glanokomanduiushchago, 4 marta 1917 goda, No. 343," Alekseev Papers, Box 1, File 9, HIA; also see Alekseev to front commanders, No. 1947, between 4:34 and 5:55, 4/III, *KA* (2), 45; No. 360, *Stavka i revoliutsiia*, 425–426.

41. Alekseev to Guchkov, No. 1953, 12:15, 4/III, *KA* (2): 48–49; No. 374, *Stavka i revoliutsiia*, 438.

42. Alekseev to Guchkov, No. 1990, 5/III, *KA* (2), 54–55; No. 426, *Stavka i revoliutsiia*, 480; Dubenskii, "Kak proizoshel perevorot," 71; Tal', *Memuary*, 69–70; Mordvinov, "Poslednie dni," *Otrechenie*, 172–173, 175–176.

43. No. 348, dispatch from Stavka to Guchkov, 3/III–10/III, *Stavka i revoliutsiia*, 417.

44. Bubnov, "V tsarskoi Stavke," 154. On the way back to his estate in Penza, Voeikov was arrested, and sent to Petrograd to be imprisoned.

45. Klembovskii to Ivanov, No. 1940, 1:25, 4/III, *KA* (2), 44; Voeikov, *S tsarem*, 248.

46. Nicholas's note, *KA* (2), 53–54. This note was written on an octavo sheet in pencil and included in Lukomsky's papers.

47. Bazili's interview with Lukomskii, 24 February 1933, 2, Bazili Papers, Box 22, File 11, HIA.

48. L'vov to Alekseev, No. 938, 6/III, *KA* (2), 55; No. 435, *Stavka i revoliutsiia*, 487–488.

49. Alekseev to L'vov and Rodzianko, No. 55, 5/III, No. 422, *Stavka i revoliutsiia*, 476.

50. Fredericks went to see British diplomat John Hanbury-Williams and told him that he had nothing to live for anymore and did not care what happened to him; the only reason he did not commit suicide was that he did not want to cause any trouble for the deposed tsar. Hanbury-Williams, *Emperor Nicholas II*, 164. Fredericks was arrested in Gomel and sent back to the Tauride Palace in Petrograd. The Provisional Government's Investigating Commission sent him to a psychiatric hospital; later he was released and lived in Petrograd.

51. Nicholson, *Michael Romanov*, 55–56; Benckendorff, *Last Days*, 18–19; Mel'gunov, *Martovskie dni*, 241; Matveev, *Memoirs*, 15, Bakhmeteff Archive.

52. Buranov and Khrustalev, *Gibel' imperatorskogo doma*, 60, citing TsGAOR (now GARF), f. 1779, op. 2, d. 1, ch. 1, l. 5ob.

53. Dubenskii, "Kak proizoshel perevorot," 79–80; Mordvinov, "Poslednie dni," *Otrechenie*, 179–180.

54. Paléologue, *Ambassador's Memoirs*, vol. 3, 247; "Dnevniki Nikolaia II," *Otrechenie*, 37; Nicholas II, *Dnevnik Imperatora*, 626.

55. Perry and Pleshakov, *Flight of the Romanovs*, 162.

56. Hanbury-Williams, *Emperor Nicholas II*, 159–164.

57. Ibid., 168–170.

58. Alekseev to L'vov and Rodzianko, No. 54, 5/III, *KA* (2), 54; No. 395, *Stavka i revoliutsiia*, 453.

59. Bazili's interview with Lukomskii, 24 February 1933, 2–3, Bazili Papers, Box 22, File 11, HIA.

60. Alexander Mikhailovich, *Once a Grand Duke*, 291.

61. Benckendorff, *Last Days*, 20–21.

62. Solzhenitsyn, *March 1917*, Book 3, 340–345.

63. Dehn, *Real Tsaritsa*, 174.

64. Massie, *Nicholas and Alexandra*, 435; Buxhoeveden, *Life and Tragedy*, 266.

65. Dehn, *Real Tsaritsa*, 174–175.

66. "Dnevniki Nikolaia II," *Otrechenie*, 38; Nicholas II, *Dnevnik Imperatora*, 626.

67. Nikolai Nikolaevich to Alekseev, 1:40, 6/III, "Verkhovnoe komandovanie," 281; No. 437, Alekseev to L'vov, Guchkov, and Rodzianko, 12:02, 6/III, *Stavka i revoliutsiia*, 490.

68. For the grand duke's popularity, see No. 473, Alekseev to L'vov and Guchkov, 1103, 7/III, *Stavka i revoliutsiia*, 521–522; No. 555, Alekseev's report on congratulatory telegrams he received on Nikolai Nikolaevich's appointment, 10/III, *Stavka i revoliutsiia*, 588–590; Robinson, *Grand Duke*, 295–296, 299–300.

69. Alekseev and L'vov-Guchkov conversation, 6/III, *KA* (2), 59–64; No. 445, *Stavka i revoliutsiia*, 496–501.

70. Kolonitskii, *Tragicheskaia erotika*, 508–510; Kolonitskii, "*Comrade Kerensky*," 6–7, 72–74.

71. Andrei Vladimirovich, "Dnevniki," 334.

72. Dubenskii, "Kak proizoshel perevorot," 107.

73. "Zhurnal zasedanii Vremennogo pravitel'stva," vol. 1, 49. The following members were present at the meeting: G. E. Lvov, Guchkov, Milyukov, Nekrasov, Tereshchenko, V. N. Lvov, I. V. Godnev, and the deputy minister of international affairs, D. M. Shchepkin. Kerensky was absent.

74. Order of the Chief of Staff of Supreme Commandership, March 8, 1917, No. 371, quoted in Dubenskii, "Kak proizoshel perevorot," 96–97; Tal', *Memuary*, 74–76; Pronin, *Poslednie dni*, 72–73; No. 514, *Stavka i revoliutsiia*, 556.

75. Dubenskii, "Kak proizoshel perevorot," 97–98; Pronin, *Poslednie dni*, 73.

76. Tikhmenev, "Poslednii priezd," *Otrechenie*, 286–287. According to Colonel Sergeevsky, Alekseev immediately told Nicholas about the Provisional Government's arrest

order. The deposed emperor told Alekseev that he would have to obey the order but that no one should know about this order until his departure. Sergeevskii, *Otrechenie*, 75. But judging from Nicholas's behavior before his arrest, Sergeevsky's account is questionable.

77. For Alekseev's order, see Borel', "Stavka v miatezhnye dni," Alekseev Papers, Box 1, File 20, 12, HIA.

78. Hanbury-Williams, *Emperor Nicholas II*, 171.

79. Pronin, *Poslednie dni*, 68.

80. My account for the farewell meeting is based on Tikhmenev, "Poslednii priezd," *Otrechenie*, 286–299; Pronin, *Poslednie dni*, 68–71; and Mikhail Borel', "Stavka v miatezhnye dni," Alekseev Papers, Box 1, File 20, 12–14, HIA. Solzhenitsyn also describes the scene, presumably based on Tikhmenev's memoirs but he adds certain details using his artistic liberty. Solzhenitsyn, *March 1917*, Book 3, 516–520.

81. Massie, *Nicholas and Alexandra*, 424.

82. Sergeevskii, *Otrechenie*, 78–79.

83. Mordvinov, *Otrechenie*, 184.

84. "Dnevniki Nikolaia II," *Otrechenie*, 38; Nicholas II, *Dnevnik Imperatora*, 626.

85. "Dnevniki Nikolaia II," *Otrechenie*, 38; Nicholas II, *Dnevnik Imperatora*, 626.

86. Bublikov, *Russkaia revoliutsiia* (1918), 52; Mel'gunov, *Sud'ba*, 31.

87. Dubenskii, "Kak proizoshel perevorot," 101.

88. Bukblikov, *Russkaia revoliutsiia* (1918), 52.

89. Dubenskii, "Kak proizoshel perevorot," 100–101.

90. Bublikov, *Russkaia revoliutsiia* (2016), 89–90; Dubenskii, "Kak proizoshel perevorot," 101.

91. Bublikov, *Russkaia revoliutsiia* (2016), 88.

92. Dubenskii, "Kak proizoshel perevorot," 101.

93. "Dnevniki Nikolaia II," *Otrechenie*, 38; Nicholas II, *Dnevnik Imperatora*, 626.

94. Alexander Mikhailovich, *Once a Grand Duke*, 292.

95. Massie, *Nicholas and Alexandra*, 426–427; Alexander Mikhailovich, *Once a Grand Duke*, 292; Solzhenitsyn, *March 1917*, Book 3, 558–561.

96. Benckendorff, *Last Days*, 30–34; Buxhoeveden, *Life and Tragedy*, 269; Mel'gunov, *Sud'ba*, 32–33.

97. Benckendorff, *Last Days*, 29–35; Solzhenitsyn, *March 1917*, Book 3, 522–524; Bulygin, *Murder*, 190; Massie, *Nicholas and Alexandra*, 436–437.

98. Benckendorff, *Last Days*, 37–38; Mel'gunov, *Sud'ba*, 35.

99. Gilliard, *Thirteen Years*, 214–215; Massie, *Nicholas and Alexandra*, 438.

100. Bublikov, *Russkaia revoliutsiia* (2016), 93.

101. Benckendorff, *Last Days*, 43.

102. Ibid. According to Massie, "Alexandra sprang to her feet and ran to meet her husband" at the entrance. This apparently was not what happened, according to Benckendorff.

103. Massie, *Nicholas and Alexandra*, 439–440.

104. Alekseev and L'vov-Guchkov conversation, 6/III, *KA* (2), 64; No. 445, *Stavka i revoliutsiia*, 495.

105. Alekseev to L'vov and Guchkov, No. 2044, 11:03, 7/III, *KA* (2), 65; No. 493, *Stavka i revoliutsiia*, 521–522.

106. No. 536, L'vov to Nikolai Nikolaevich, 9/III, *Stavka i revoliutsiia*, 576–577.

107. No. 565, Nikolai Nikolaevich to Alekseev, No. 2, 14:40, 11/III, *Stavka i revoliutsiia*, 597; No. 569, *Stavka i revoliutsiia*, 598 (Klembovskii's appointment); No. 569, Nikolai Niko-laevich to L'vov, 14:50, 3/11, *Stavka i revoliutsiia*, 601–602 (Nikolai Nikolaevich's resignation letter); No. 574, Nikolai Nikolaevich's oath, 19:25, 11/III, *Stavka i revoliutsiia*, 606.

108. Alekseev conversation with L'vov and Guchkov, 14:40 to 15:50, 11/III, *KA* (2), 68–70; No. 567, *Stavka i revoliutsiia*, 598–601.

### Epilogue

1. Raeff, "The Well-Ordered Police State," 1221–1243; Raeff, *Well-Ordered Police State*; Raeff, *Understanding Imperial Russia*.

2. Pipes, *Russia Under the Old Regime*, 54, 315.

3. Wortman, *Scenarios of Power*, 334–360, 370–396.

4. See Rosenberg, *States of Anxiety*.

5. See Kolonitskii, *Tragicheskaia erotika*.

6. Brinton, *Anatomy of Revolution*.

7. For instance, Mul'tatuli, *Nikolai II*.

8. See Mul'tatuli, *Nikolai II*, as the most glaring example.

9. See Service, *Last of the Tsars*; Perry and Pleshakov, *Flight of the Romanovs*; Steinberg and Khrustalev, *Fall of the Romanovs*; Rappaport, *Race to Save the Romanovs*.

### Acknowledgments

1. A single exception is Semion Lyandres, who published a valuable translation of the Polievktov Commission interviews with the leading figures of the February Revolution, and introduced new research in his co-edited journal, *Journal of Modern Russian History and Historiography*.

# INDEX

Bloody Sunday (1905), 27, 35, 93,
    196–197
Bloody Sunday (1917), 170, 172, 179
Bobrinsky, Aleksei
    Aleksandrovich, 134
Bogdanov, Aleksandr Nikolaevich, 129
Boisman, Vladimir Vasilievich, 164
Boldyrev, Vasily Georgievich, 241, 266,
    282, 315
Bologoe, 225, 227, 233–234
Bolsheviks, 1, 52, 141, 155, 437
Bonapartism, 401
Boris Vladimirovich (grand duke), 30,
    87, 126, 128, 129, 145, 406
Borodin Company, 265–266
Borodino, Battle of, 41, 418
Bosnia-Herzegovina, 41–42
Bosnian Crisis, 41–42, 45
Botkin, Evgeny Sergeevich, 379
Brasova, Natalia (Natasha, Wulfert),
    23, 26, 110, 169, 214, 309, 322,
    396, 432
Brest-Litovsk, 64
Brinton, Crane, 421
Brusilov, Aleksei Alekseevich, 119,
    169, 181, 272, 276, 338–339, 424
    abdication support, 298, 302,
    305, 306
    as Eighth Army commander, 58
    meeting with grand duke Mikhail,
    130–131
    notification of abdication, 342
    opposition to military conference,
    370–371
    palace coup support, 145, 153
    as southwestern front commander,
    96–98, 176, 191

support for Nikolai Nikolaevich,
    81–82
troops dispatched to
    Petrograd, 208
urged Nicholas to recognize Duma
    Committee, 267
Brusilov Offensive, 97–98
Bublikov, Aleksandr Aleksandrovich
    chose Lomonosov as assistant,
    219–220
    Nicholas's arrest order, 403, 405,
    408–411
    manipulation of imperial trains'
    movement, 231–232, 235,
    237–239, 423–424
    obstruction of military trains, 248,
    255, 261, 339–340
    occupation of Ministry of
    Transport, 215–216
    orders to restore rail service, 261
    telegram announcing Duma
    Committee takeover of capital,
    216–219, 223–225
Bubnov, Aleksandr Dmitrievich, 94,
    182, 192, 300, 395
Buchanan, George, 143, 257
Buchanan, Meriel, 16–17
Budget Commission, 104, 105
Burdukov, Nikolai Fyodorovich, 171
Burdzhalov, Edvard, 243
bureaucracy, 11, 37, 78
Buxhoeveden, Sofia Karlovna, 220,
    222, 254, 379

Cantacuzene, Julia Grant, 51, 127
Carpathian campaign, 62–63
Catherine Palace, 69

Index

Freemasons, 281, 346, 428
imperial train, 226–227
pressure on Mikhail to refuse
 throne, 346–347, 348, 361–365
Petrograd Soviet Executive
 Committee on abdication, 244
treatment of deposed tsar, 389,
 398, 410
opposition to Nikolai Nikolaevich
 as supreme commander, 402
Kern, Ivan F., 232–234
Khabalov, Sergei Semyonovich
complaints about Ruzsky,
 139–140
forbids use of arms on
 demonstrators, 163
as head of Petrograd Military
 District, 136–140, 189, 190,
 271–272
knowledge of coup possibility, 153
orders to shoot demonstrators,
 166–169
replaced by Ivanov, 191
reports on Petrograd unrest,
 165–167, 171–172, 184–185, 198,
 205–207, 259–260
warning to potential
 demonstrators, 155
Khatisov, Aleksandr Ivanovich, 147
Khodynka Field tragedy, 18, 29
Khvostov, Aleksandr Alekseevich, 83,
 90, 98–99, 103
Khvostov, Aleksei Nikolaevich, 89,
 90–91, 95, 99
Khvostov Memorandum, 91
Kiev, 69, 108
King, Greg, 12

Kirill Vladimirovich (grand duke,
 Nicholas's cousin), 26, 27–28, 30,
 87, 126, 128, 129, 145
grand dukes' manifesto, 212–215,
 253–255, 289
Kirpichnikov, Timofei Ivanovich,
 179–180
Kiselev, Pavel Dmitrievich, 37
Kishkin, Nikolai Mikhailovich, 147
Kislyakov, Vladimir Nikolaevich,
 216–217, 220, 405
Klembovsky, Vladislav
 Napoleonovich, 269–270, 276,
 301, 312, 414
Klopov, Anatoly Alekseevich, 169
Kobylinsky, Evgeny Stepanovich, 411
Kokovtsov, Vladimir Nikolaevich,
 40, 72
Kolchak, Aleksandr Vasilievich,
 298, 308
Kolonitskii, Boris, 39, 67, 68, 88, 147, 421
Komarov, Vladimir
 Aleksandrovich, 211
Konovalov, Aleksandr Ivanovich, 39,
 76, 148, 153, 155, 281, 346, 360
Konstantin Konstantinovich (KR,
 grand duke), 79
Kornilov, Lavr Georgievich, 316,
 338–339, 399, 411–412, 436
Kossikovskaya, Aleksandra, 23, 149
Kossikovsky, Dmitry Vladimirovich,
 149–150
Kotsebu, Pavel Pavlovich, 411
Kremlin, 17
Kresty prison, 180
Kriger-Voinovsky, Edvard
 Bronislavovich, 204, 216

533